Fromme

# POSTCARDS

FROM

# ARIZONA

*Marble Canyon and the Colorado River, viewed from the less explored North Rim of the Grand Canyon. See chapter 6. © David Muench/Tony Stone Images.*

*The Desert Botanical Garden in Phoenix is exclusively devoted to cacti and other desert plants. See chapter 4. © John Elk III Photography.*

*Horseback riding in the Superstition Mountains, which, according to legend, harbor a lost gold mine. See chapter 4. © John Elk III Photography.*

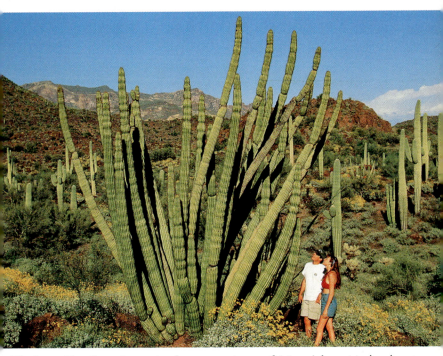

*The Organ Pipe Cactus is a national monument in one of Arizona's least visited and most remote areas. See chapter 10. © Tom Bean/Tony Stone Images.*

*Arizona draws countless visitors for its golfing alone. See chapter 1 for our favorite courses.*
*© Richard Maack/Adstock Photos.*

*Biking in Oak Creek Canyon, near Sedona. Sedona offers some of the best outdoor access of any city in the Southwest. See chapter 5. © Michael Shedlock/New England Stock.*

*A mile deep, 277 miles long, and up to 18 miles wide, the Grand Canyon is Arizona's number one attraction—and it never fails to inspire. See chapter 6. Opposite: Mule riders descend to the bottom. © Tom Bean/Tony Stone Images. Top: Whitewater rafting on the Colorado River. © Dewitt Jones Productions. Bottom: A magnificent view of the canyon from Cape Solitude on the South Rim. © Chuck Lawsen/Adstock Photos.*

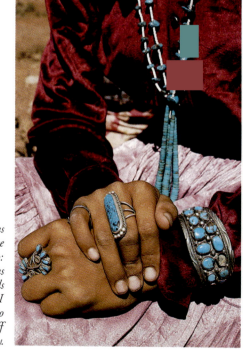

*Native American crafts are ubiquitous in the Four Corners region. See chapter 7 for a primer. Top photo: Navajo rugs, like these at the famous Hubbell Trading Post, take hundreds of hours to make. © John Elk III Photography. Bottom photo: Navajo turquoise jewelry. © Dave Bartruff Photography.*

*A Hopi Kachina doll, used to bring rain and ensure health, happiness, long life, and harmony in the universe. See chapter 7. © John Elk III Photography.*

*The dramatic landscape of Monument Valley is a favorite backdrop for Hollywood and television directors. See chapter 7. © John Elk III Photography.*

*The 37-mile-long Paria Canyon trailhead follows the meandering route of a narrow slot canyon for much of its length. See chapter 7. © James Kay/Adstock Photos.*

*Betatakin, an Anasazi cliff dwelling, is part of the Navajo National Monument. See chapter 7.*
*© Dewitt Jones Productions.*

*The popular Lake Powell, created by the damming of the Colorado River at Glen Canyon, is a strange oasis in the middle of hundreds of miles of parched desert land. See chapter 7.*
*© Nik Wheeler Photography.*

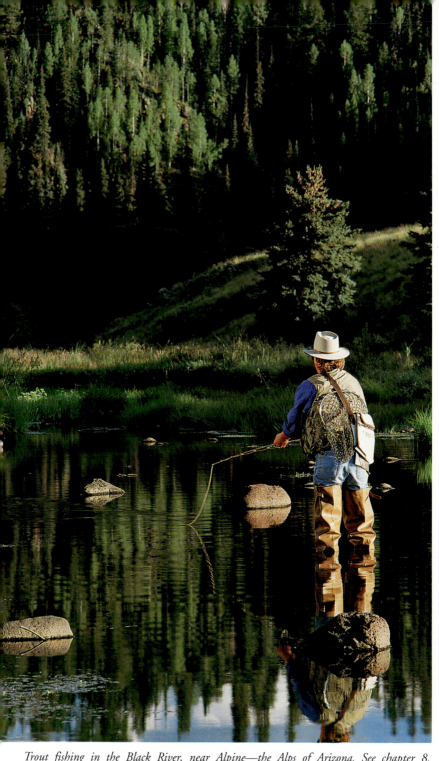

*Trout fishing in the Black River, near Alpine—the Alps of Arizona. See chapter 8.*
© *Richard Maack/Adstock Photos.*

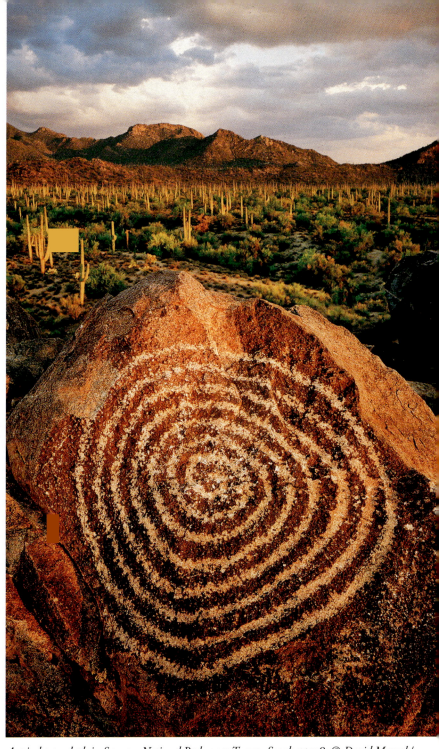

*A spiral petroglyph in Saguaro National Park, near Tucson. See chapter 9. © David Muench/ Tony Stone Images.*

*The desert provides the perfect environment for hot-air ballooning—cool, still air and wide-open spaces. See chapters 4, 5, and 9 for ballooning companies in Phoenix, Sedona, and Tucson. © Michael R. Stoklos/Adstock Photos.*

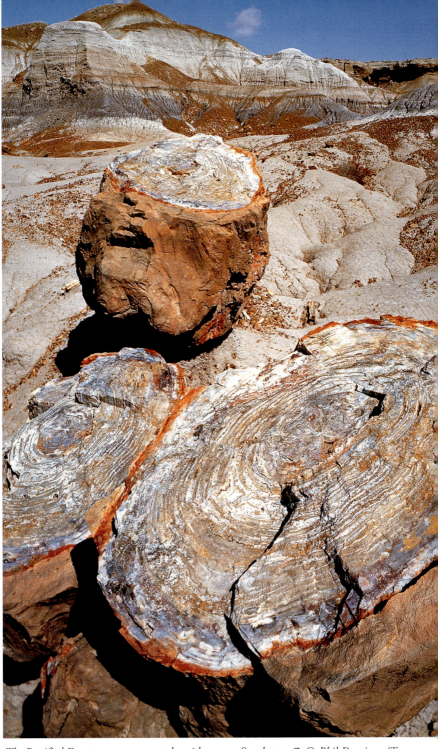

*The Petrified Forest was once a vast, humid swamp. See chapter 7. © Phil Degginger/Tony Stone Images.*

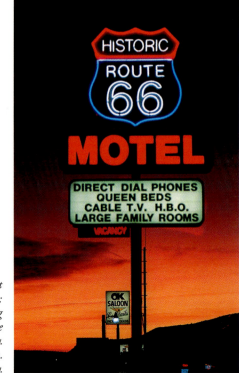

*Legendary Route 66 symbolizes a lost America. See chapters 7 and 11. Above: The Wigwam Motel has been causing double takes along Route 66 since the 1940s. © John Elk III Photography. Right: A self-conscious motel sign. © Nik Wheeler Photography.*

# Frommer's® 2000

# Arizona

**by Karl Samson**
**with Jane Aukshunas**

Online Directory by Michael Shapiro

MACMILLAN • USA

## ABOUT THE AUTHORS

**Karl Samson** and **Jane Aukshunas,** husband-and-wife travel-writing team, find that the sunny winter skies of the Arizona desert are the perfect antidote to the dreary winters of their Pacific Northwest home. Each winter they flee the rain to explore Arizona's deserts, mountains, cities, and small towns. It is the state's unique regional style, Native American cultures, abundance of contemporary art, and, of course, the boundless landscapes that keep the duo fascinated by Arizona. Summers find the team researching their other books, including *Frommer's Washington, Frommer's Oregon,* and *Frommer's Seattle & Portland.*

# MACMILLAN TRAVEL

Macmillan General Reference USA, Inc.
1633 Broadway
New York, NY 10019

Find us online at **www.frommers.com**.

ISBN 0-02-862961-2
ISSN 1053-2471

Editor: David Gibbs
Production Editor: Tammy Ahrens
Photo Editor: Richard Fox
Design by Michele Laseau
Staff Cartographers: John Decamillis, Roberta Stockwell
Page Creation: Melissa Auciello-Brogan, Judith McMullen, Sean Monkhouse, and Linda Quigley
Front cover photo: Monument Valley

## SPECIAL SALES

Bulk purchases (10+ copies) of Frommer's and selected Macmillan travel guides are available to corporations, organizations, mail-order catalogs, institutions, and charities at special discounts, and can be customized to suit individual needs. For more information write to Special Sales, Macmillan General Reference, 1633 Broadway, New York, NY 10019.

Manufactured in the United States of America

5  4  3  2  1

# Contents

# List of Maps

## AN INVITATION TO THE READER

In researching this book, we discovered many wonderful places—hotels, restaurants, shops, and more. We're sure you'll find others. Please tell us about them, so we can share the information with your fellow travelers in upcoming editions. If you were disappointed with a recommendation, we'd love to know that, too. Please write to:

*Frommer's Arizona 2000*
Macmillan Travel
1633 Broadway
New York, NY 10019

## AN ADDITIONAL NOTE

Please be advised that travel information is subject to change at any time—and this is especially true of prices. We therefore suggest that you write or call ahead for confirmation when making your travel plans. The authors, editors, and publisher cannot be held responsible for the experiences of readers while traveling. Your safety is important to us, however, so we encourage you to stay alert and be aware of your surroundings. Keep a close eye on cameras, purses, and wallets, all favorite targets of thieves and pickpockets.

## WHAT THE SYMBOLS MEAN

### ✪ Frommer's Favorites

Our favorite places and experiences—outstanding for quality, value, or both.

The following abbreviations are used for credit cards:

| | | | |
|---|---|---|---|
| AE | American Express | EURO | Eurocard |
| CB | Carte Blanche | JCB | Japan Credit Bank |
| DC | Diners Club | MC | MasterCard |
| DISC | Discover | V | Visa |
| ER | enRoute | | |

## FIND FROMMER'S ONLINE

**Arthur Frommer's Budget Travel Online** (**www.frommers.com**) offers more than 6,000 pages of up-to-the-minute travel information—including the latest bargains and candid, personal articles updated daily by Arthur Frommer himself. No other Web site offers such comprehensive and timely coverage of the world of travel.

# The Best of Arizona 1

Planning a trip to a state as large and diverse as Arizona involves
making lots of decisions (other than which resort to stay at or which
golf clubs to take), so in this chapter we've tried to give you some direction. Below we've chosen what we feel is the very best the state has to
offer—the places and experiences you won't want to miss. Most are
written up in more detail elsewhere in this book; this chapter should
give you an overview of Arizona's highlights and get you started planning your trip.

## 1 The Best Scenic Drives

- **Apache Trail** (east of Phoenix): Much of this winding road,
  which passes just north of the Superstition Mountains, is
  unpaved and follows a rugged route once ridden by Apaches.
  This is some of the most remote country you'll find in the
  Phoenix area, with far-reaching desert vistas and lots to see and
  do along the way. See chapter 4.
- **Oak Creek Canyon** (Sedona): Slicing down from the pine
  country outside Flagstaff to the red rocks of Sedona, Oak Creek
  Canyon is a cool oasis. From the scenic overlook at the top of the
  canyon to the swimming holes and hiking trails at the bottom,
  this canyon road provides a rapid change in climate and landscape. See chapter 5.
- **Through Monument Valley** (north of Kayenta): This valley of
  sandstone buttes and mesas is one of the most photographed
  spots in America and is familiar to people all over the world from
  the countless movies, TV shows, and commercials that have been
  shot here. A 17-mile dirt road winds through the park, giving visitors close-ups of such landmarks as Elephant Butte, the Mittens,
  and Totem Pole. See chapter 7.
- **Up Mount Lemmon** (Tucson): Sure the views of Tucson are
  great from the foothills to the north of the city, but the views
  from Mount Lemmon are even better. With a ski area at its
  summit, Mount Lemmon rises up from the desert like an island
  rising from the sea. Along the way the road climbs from cactus
  country to cool pine forests. See chapter 9.
- **Canyon de Chelly National Monument** (Chinle): This fascinating complex of canyons on the Navajo Indian Reservation has
  only limited public access because it is still home to numerous

# Arizona

COLORADO

NEW MEXICO

Canyon de Chelly National Monument

Chinle

Ganado

Window Rock

191

St. Johns

191

191

191

Petrified Forest National Park

180

180

160

Navajo National Monument

Reservation

264

87

377

Holbrook

77

61

Kayenta

DESERT

377

Apache-Sitgreaves National Forest

180

260

Indian

Hopi Indian Reservation

PAINTED

Winslow

Lake Powell

Monument Valley Navajo Tribal Park

Page

98

Navajo

Wupatki National Monument

40

89

Flagstaff

87

Glen Canyon National Recreation Area

89

Cameron

San Francisco Peaks

Humphreys Peak

Sedona

Coconino

Camp Verde

UTAH

Grand Canyon Village

89

The Grand Canyon

Ariz. 64

89

17

Oak Creek Canyon

National Forest

87

15

89

ALT 89

Kaibab National Forest

Grand Canyon North Rim

Kaibab National Forest

180

64

Williams

Jerome

Ariz. 179

Ariz. 89

279

Ariz. 260

67

Seligman

Kaibab National Forest

Prescott National Forest

Ariz. 89

89

Kaibab National Park

Grand Canyon National Park

Havasupai Indian Reservation

66

Prescott National Forest

69

Lake Mead National Recreation Area

Hualapai Indian Reservation

Colorado River

40

Prescott

NEVADA

The Grand Canyon

Grand Canyon West

93

Kingman

Lake Havasu City

Temple Bar

Lake Mead National Recreation Area

68

Bullhead City

40

Las Vegas

Hoover Dam

Lake Mead

93

Lake Mohave

Laughlin

95

Lake Havasu

NEVADA

CALIFORNIA

93

Needles

60 Miles

0

60 Kilometers

0

NA-0248

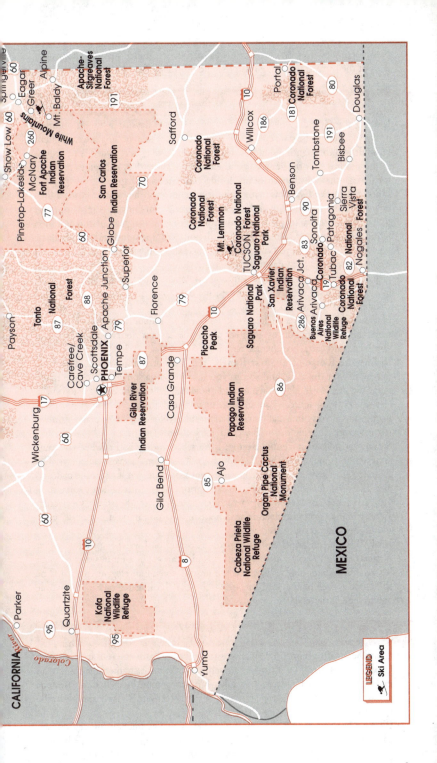

3

Navajo families. However, there are two roads that parallel the north and south rims of the canyon providing lots of scenic overlooks. See chapter 7.

## 2 The Best Active Vacations

- **Rafting the Grand Canyon:** Whether you go for 3 days or 2 weeks, no other active vacation in the state comes even remotely close to matching the excitement of a raft trip through the Grand Canyon. Sure the river is crowded with groups in the summer, but the grandeur of the canyon is more than enough to make up for seeing other adventurous souls during your trip. See chapter 6.
- **Hiking Into the Grand Canyon:** Not for the unfit or the faint of heart, a hike down into the Grand Canyon is a journey through millions of years of time set in stone. This trip takes plenty of advance planning just to get a permit and then requires some very strenuous hiking. With both a campground and a lodge at the bottom of the canyon, you can choose to make this trip with either a fully loaded backpack or just a light daypack. See chapter 6.
- **Hiking Into Havasu Canyon:** Turquoise waters at the foot of cascading water-falls, strange terraces formed by limestone deposits, and a cottonwood-shaded stream—that's what lures backpackers the 11 miles down to the campground in Havasu Canyon. This is the heart of the Havasupai Indian Reservation and, aside from the narrow ribbon of greenery along the canyon floor, is a landscape of sandstone and cacti. See chapter 6.
- **Riding the Range at a Guest Ranch:** Yes, there are still cowboys. They ride ranges all over the state, and so can you if you book a stay at one of the many guest ranches (formerly known as dude ranches). You might even get to do the city slicker thing and drive some cattle down the trail. After a long or short day in the saddle, you can usually soak in a hot tub, go for a swim, or play a game of tennis before chowing down. See chapters 5, 9, and 10.
- **Staying at a Golf or Tennis Resort:** If horseback riding and cowboy cookouts aren't your thing, how about as much golf or tennis as you can play? The Phoenix/Scottsdale area has the greatest concentration of resorts in the country, and Tucson and Sedona add even more options to the mix. There's something very satisfying about swinging a racquet or club with the state's spectacular scenery in the background, and the climate means you can do it practically year-round. See chapters 4, 5, and 9.
- **Bird Watching in Southeastern Arizona:** As avid bird watchers, we know that this isn't the most active of sports, but a birder can get in a bit of walking when it's necessary (like, maybe to get to the nesting tree of an elegant trogon). The southeast corner of the state is one of the best birding regions in the whole country. See chapter 10.

## 3 The Best Day Hikes & Nature Walks

- **Camelback Mountain** (Phoenix): For many Phoenicians the trail to the top of Camelback Mountain is a ritual, a Phoenix institution. Sure there are those who make this a casual but strenuous hike, but many more turn it into a serious workout by jogging to the top and back. We prefer a more leisurely approach, the better to enjoy the views. See chapter 4.
- **Picacho Peak State Park** (south of Casa Grande): The hike up this central Arizona landmark is short but strenuous, and from the top there are superb views out over the desert. The best time of year to make the hike is in spring, when the

peak comes alive with wildflowers. Picacho Peak is between Casa Grande and Tucson just off I-10. See chapter 4.

- **The West Fork Oak Creek Trail** (outside Sedona): The West Fork of Oak Creek is a tiny stream that meanders for miles in a narrow steep-walled canyon. This is classic canyon country, and the hardest part of a hike here is deciding not to see what's around that next bend up ahead. See chapter 5.

- **Bright Angel Trail** (Grand Canyon South Rim): It's a human highway near the top, but this most popular trail into the Grand Canyon offers everyone the chance to say that they've hiked the Grand Canyon. Despite its popularity, Bright Angel Trail is a strenuous hike even if you go only a mile or so down the trail. Remember, the trip back is all uphill. See chapter 6.

- **The Keet Seel Trail** (Navajo National Monument): There is something magical and mystical about arriving at an ancient cliff dwelling after hiking 8 miles through a desert canyon. At the end of your hike, after resting for a while, you can explore the ruins. There's a campsite nearby, so you can sleep with the ghosts of the Anasazi for a night. See chapter 7.

- **The White House Ruins Trail** (Canyon de Chelly): There's only one Canyon de Chelly hike that the general public can go on without a Navajo guide, and that's the 2½-mile trail to White House Ruins. The trail leads from the canyon rim across bare sandstone, through a tunnel, and down to the floor of the canyon. Though it seems as if you've left the modern world behind, when you finally reach the ruins, you'll likely find quite a few four-wheel-drive vehicles parked near the ancient Anasazi cliff dwelling. See chapter 7.

- **Antelope Canyon** (Page): More a slow walk of reverence than a hike, this trail lets you see the amazing beauty that can be created when water and rock battle one another in the Southwest. It leads through a sandstone canyon only a few feet wide in places. See chapter 7.

- **Seven Falls** (Tucson): There is something irresistible about waterfalls in the desert, and on this trail you get more than enough falls to satisfy any craving to cool off on a hot desert day. This trail is in the popular Sabino Canyon Recreation Area in the northeast corner of Tucson at the foot of the Santa Catalina Mountains. See chapter 9.

- **Heart of Rocks Trail** (Cochise County): While the big national parks and monuments in northern Arizona get all the publicity, Chiricahua National Monument, down in the southeast corner of the state, quietly lays claim to some of the most spectacular scenery in Arizona. On this trail you'll hike through a wonderland of rocks. See chapter 10.

# 4  The Best Places to Commune with Cacti

- **Desert Botanical Garden** (Phoenix): There's no better place in the state to learn about the plants of Arizona's Sonoran Desert and the many other deserts of the world. Displays at this Phoenix botanical garden explain plant adaptations and how indigenous tribes once used many of the wild plants of this region. The gardens stay open until after dark so you can see how the desert changes as it cools off. See chapter 4.

- **Boyce Thompson Southwestern Arboretum** (east of Phoenix): Located just outside the town of Superior, this was the nation's first botanical garden established in a desert environment. It's set in a small canyon framed by cliffs, with desert plantings from all over the world—a fascinating place for an educational stroll in the desert. See chapter 4.

- **Arizona–Sonora Desert Museum** (Tucson): The name is misleading—this is actually more of a zoo and botanical garden than a "museum." Naturalistic settings house dozens of species of desert animals, including a number of critters you wouldn't want to meet in the wild (rattlesnakes, tarantulas, scorpions, black widows, and Gila monsters). See chapter 9.
- **Saguaro National Park** (Tucson): Lying both east and west of Tucson, this preserve is a forest of saguaro cacti. It's the very essence of the desert as so many people imagine it. You can hike it, bike it, or drive it. See chapter 9.
- **Tohono Chul Park** (Tucson): Although this park is not all that large, it packs a lot of desert scenery into its modest space. Impressive plantings of cacti are the star attractions here, but there are also good wildflower displays in the spring. See chapter 9.
- **Organ Pipe Cactus National Monument** (west of Tucson): The organ pipe cactus is a smaller, multitrunked relative of the giant saguaro and lives only along the Mexican border about 100 miles west of Tucson. This remote national monument has hiking trails, scenic drives, even a large natural spring. All that's missing are the crowds you may encounter at Saguaro National Park. See chapter 10.

## 5 The Best Golf Courses

- **The Boulders South Course** (Carefree, near Phoenix; ☎ 800/553-1717 or 480/488-9009): If you've ever seen a photo of someone teeing off beside a massive balancing rock and longed to play that same hole, then you've dreamed about playing The Boulders South Course. That tee of dreams is number 7, which is the most photographed tee box in the state. The South Course, a desert-style design by Jay Morrish, plays around and through the jumble of massive boulders for which the resort is named. Now you may not think rocks on fairways are such a good idea, but here at The Boulders, they're not just a challenge to your swing, but to your powers of concentration as well. See chapter 4.
- **The Wigwam Gold Course** (Litchfield Park, near Phoenix; ☎ 623/935-3811): If you're a traditionalist who eschews those cactus- and rattlesnake-filled desert target courses, you'll want to beg, borrow, or steal a tee time on the Wigwam Resort's Gold Course. This 7,100-yard resort course way out on the west side of the Valley of the Sun has long been an Arizona legend. You might want to work your way up to the Gold Course on the Blue and Red courses. See chapter 4.
- **Gold Canyon Golf Resort** (at Gold Canyon Ranch, Apache Junction, near Phoenix; ☎ 480/982-9449): Although it's out of the mainstream of Valley of the Sun resorts, the Gold Canyon Ranch offers superb golfing at the foot of the Superstition Mountains, where knocking wood takes on a whole new meaning. The second, third, and fourth holes on the Dinosaur Mountain Course are the truly memorable ones. They play across the foot of Dinosaur Mountain and are rated among the tops in the state. With the Superstitions staring you straight in the face, no matter how great your concentration, you'll be distracted when you tee off here. Try for a late-afternoon starting time. See chapter 4.
- **Troon North Golf Club** (Scottsdale; ☎ 480/585-5300): Designed by Tom Weiskopf and Jay Morrish, this semiprivate desert-style course in north Scottsdale is named for the famous Scottish links that overlook both the Firth of Forth and the Firth of Clyde—but that's where the similarities end. Troon North has two 18-hole courses, but the original, known as the Monument Course, is still the favorite. See chapter 4.

- **The Tournament Players Club (TPC) of Scottsdale** (Scottsdale; ☎ 480/585-3600 or 480/585-3939): If you've always dreamed of playing where the pros play, then you may want to schedule a visit to the Scottsdale Princess and book a tee time on the Stadium Course, which is the site of the PGA Tour's Phoenix Open. Alternatively, you could play the resort's Desert Course. See chapter 4.
- **Sedona Golf Resort** (Sedona; ☎ 520/284-9355): It's easy to think that all of Arizona's best courses are in the Phoenix and Tucson areas, but it just isn't so. Up in the red-rock country, at the mouth of Oak Creek Canyon, lies the Sedona Golf Resort, a traditional course that is among the best in the state. If you can keep your eye on the ball when facing all that gorgeous scenery, you're a pretty good golfer. See chapter 5.
- **Ventana Canyon Golf and Racquet Club** (Tucson; ☎ 520/577-1400): Two Tom Fazio–designed courses, one a canyon course and the other a mountain course, are shared by two of the city's finest resorts. Both desert-style courses play through some of the most stunning scenery anywhere in the state. If we had to choose between the two, we'd go for the Canyon Course; even on an off day, you can enjoy the surroundings. See chapter 9.
- **Starr Pass Golf Club** (Tucson; ☎ 520/670-0400): Where once stagecoaches rumbled through the desert, golfers now swing their clubs on a course designed by Robert Cupp and Craig Stadler. Built along an old stagecoach route just west of downtown, the Starr Pass course seduces players with its deceptively difficult 15th hole, which plays right through a narrow pass. See chapter 9.
- **Omni Tucson National Golf Resort and Spa** (Tucson; ☎ 520/575-7540): With its wide expanses of grass, this traditional course, site of the PGA Tour's Tucson Open, is both challenging and forgiving. The 18th hole of the Orange and Gold courses is considered one of the toughest finishing holes on the tour. See chapter 9.
- **Emerald Canyon Golf Course** (Parker; ☎ 520/667-3366): Canyons, cliffs, and ravines are the hazards you'll be avoiding on this very interesting municipal course way out on the bank of the Colorado River. While it may not be the best in the state, it plays through some astounding scenery and is a good value. See chapter 11.

## 6  The Best Bird Watching

- **Madera Canyon:** The mountain canyons of southern Arizona tend to attract a variety of bird life, from species common in the lowland deserts to those that prefer thick forest settings. Madera is a good place to experience this variety. See chapter 9.
- **Buenos Aires National Wildlife Refuge:** Gray hawks and masked bobwhite quails are among the refuge's rarer birds, but a wetland (cienaga), lake, and stream attract plenty of others. See chapter 10.
- **Patagonia:** With a year-round stream and a Nature Conservancy preserve on the edge of town, Patagonia is one of the best spots in the state for sighting various flycatcher species. See chapter 10.
- **Ramsey Canyon:** Nearly 200 species of birds, including 14 species of hummingbirds, frequent this canyon, making it one of the top birding spots in the country. See chapter 10.
- **San Pedro Riparian National Conservation Area:** Water is a scarce commodity in the desert, so it isn't surprising that the San Pedro River attracts a lot of animal life, including more than 300 bird species. This is a life-list bonanza spot. See chapter 10.

- **Cave Creek Canyon:** Though there are other rare birds to be seen in this remote canyon, most people come in hopes of spotting the elegant trogon, which reaches the northernmost limit of its range here. See chapter 10.
- **Willcox Ponds:** Wading birds in the middle of the desert? You'll find them at the Willcox sewage-treatment ponds south of town. Avocets, sandhill cranes, and a variety of waterfowl all frequent these shallow bodies of water. See chapter 10.

## 7 The Best Offbeat Travel Experiences

- **Taking a Vortex Tour in Sedona:** Crystals and pyramids are nothing compared to the power of the Sedona vortexes, which just happen to be in the middle of some very beautiful scenery. Organized tours shuttle believers from one vortex to the next. If you offer it, they will come. See chapter 5.
- **Touring Walpi Village:** Of the Hopi villages that stand atop the mesas of northeastern Arizona, only Walpi, one of the oldest, offers guided tours. The Hopi guides share information on the history of the village and the Hopi culture. See chapter 7.
- **Sleeping in a Wigwam:** Back in the heyday of Route 66, the Wigwam Motel in Holbrook lured passing motorists with its unusual architecture: concrete wigwam-shaped cabins. Today this little motel is still a great place for anyone who appreciates retro style. See chapter 7.
- **Gazing at the Stars:** Insomniacs and stargazers will find plenty to keep them sleepless in the desert as they peer at the stars through telescopes at Lowell Observatory in Flagstaff or Kitt Peak National Observatory near Tucson. In the town of Benson, you can even stay at a B&B that doubles as an astronomical observatory. See chapters 6 and 9.
- **Digging for Artifacts at Raven Site Ruin:** Looking at Anasazi ruins is all well and good, but how would you like to get your hands dirty digging for ancient artifacts? At the White Mountain Archaeological Center near St. Johns, you can (for a fee) participate in an ongoing archaeological dig. See chapter 8.
- **A Visit to Biosphere 2:** This giant terrarium, in which humans were the residents, is a research center for understanding how the earth's ecosystems operate. The giant greenhouses in the middle of the desert are straight out of postapocalyptic sci-fi. See chapter 9.
- **Walking Across the London Bridge:** The famous bridge was falling down until a far-sighted (and perhaps slightly daft) developer transported it to the middle of the Arizona desert. You'll find the bridge in Lake Havasu City, and if it's not too blazingly hot, you can stroll across it and admire all the surrounding pseudo-Tudor architecture. See chapter 11.

## 8 The Best Family Experiences

- **Pioneer Arizona Living History Museum** (north of Phoenix): This museum features old buildings and costumed interpreters who show and tell what life was like for Arizona pioneers 100 years ago. See chapter 4.
- **Wild West Restaurants:** No family should visit Arizona without spending an evening at a "genuine" cowboy steak house. With gunslingers and gimmicks (one place cuts off your necktie, another has a slide from the bar to the dining room), cowboy bands, and false-fronted buildings, these Arizona eateries are all entertainment and loads of fun. See chapters 4 and 9.
- **Riding the Grand Canyon Railway:** Not only is this train excursion a fun way to get to the Grand Canyon, but it also lets you avoid the parking problems and

congestion that can prove so wearisome. Shoot-outs and train robberies are to be expected in this corner of the Wild West. See chapter 6.

- **A Week on a Houseboat:** Renting a floating vacation home on lakes Powell, Mead, Mohave, or Havasu is a summer tradition for many Arizona families. With a houseboat, you aren't tied to one spot and can cruise from one scenic beach to the next. See chapters 6 and 11.
- **Arizona–Sonora Desert Museum** (Tucson): This is actually a zoo featuring the animals of the Sonoran Desert. There are rooms full of snakes, a prairie dog town, mountain goats, mountain lions, and an aviary full of hummingbirds. Kids and adults love this place. See chapter 9.
- **Shoot-Outs at the O.K. Corral:** Tombstone may be "the town too tough to die," but poor Ike Clanton and his buddies the McLaury boys have to die over and over again at the frequent reenactments of the famous gunfight. See chapter 10.

## 9  The Best Museums

- **Heard Museum** (Phoenix): This is one of the nation's premier museums and is devoted to Native American cultures. In addition to historical exhibits, a huge kachina collection, and an excellent museum store, there are annual exhibits of contemporary Native American art as well as dance performances and demonstrations of traditional skills. See chapter 4.
- **Phoenix Art Museum** (Phoenix): This large art museum has acres of wall space and houses an outstanding collection of contemporary art as well as a fascinating exhibit of miniature rooms. See chapter 4.
- **Scottsdale Museum of Contemporary Art** (Scottsdale): This is the Phoenix area's newest museum and is noteworthy as much for its bold contemporary architecture as for its wide variety of exhibits. Unlike the majority of area art galleries, this museum eschews cowboy art. See chapter 4.
- **Museum of Northern Arizona** (Flagstaff): The geology, ethnography, and archaeology of this region are all explored in fascinating detail at this Flagstaff museum. Throughout the year there are excellent special exhibits and festivals focusing on the region's different tribes. See chapter 6.
- **University of Arizona Museum of Art** (Tucson): This collection ranges from the Renaissance to the present, with a set of 15th-century Spanish religious panels the focus of the collection. Georgia O'Keeffe and Pablo Picasso are among the artists whose works are on display here. See chapter 9.
- **Amerind Foundation Museum** (west of Willcox): Though located in the remote southeastern corner of the state near Willcox, this museum and research center houses a superb collection of Native American artifacts. Displays focus on tribes of the Southwest, but other tribes are also represented. See chapter 10.

## 10  The Best Places to Discover the Old West

- **Rodeos:** Any rodeo, and this state has plenty, will give you a glimpse of the Old West, but Arizona has two that claim title to being the oldest in the country. Whether you head for the rodeo in Prescott or the one in Payson, you'll see plenty of bronco busting, bull riding, and beer drinking. See chapters 5 and 8.
- **Monument Valley** (north of Kayenta): John Ford made it the hallmark of his Western movies, and today the starkly beautiful and fantastically shaped buttes and mesas of this valley are the quintessential Western landscape. You'll recognize it the moment you see it. See chapter 7.

- **Old Tucson Studios** (Tucson): Though many of the original movie sets burned in a 1995 fire, this combination back lot and amusement park provides visitors with a glimpse of the most familiar Old West—the Hollywood West. Sure the shoot-outs and cancan reviews are silly, but it's all in good fun, and everyone gets a thrill out of seeing the occasional film crew in action. See chapter 9.
- **Tombstone:** This is the real Old West—Tombstone is a real town, unlike Old Tucson. However, "the town too tough to die" was reincarnated long ago as a major tourist attraction with gunslingers in the streets, stagecoach rides, and shoot-outs at the O.K. Corral. See chapter 10.
- **Guest Ranches:** The Old West lives on at guest ranches all over the state, where rugged wranglers lead city slickers on horseback rides through desert scrub and mountain meadows. Campfires, cookouts, and cattle are all part of the experience. See "The Best Guest Ranches," below.

## 11  The Most Intriguing Native American Ruins

- **Tonto National Monument** (east of Phoenix): Located east of Phoenix on the Apache Trail, this is one of the only easily accessible cliff dwellings in Arizona that you can still visit; you don't have to just observe from a distance. See chapter 4.
- **Besh-Ba-Gowah Archaeological Park** (Globe): These reconstructed ruins have been set up to look the way they might have appeared 700 years ago, providing a bit more cultural context than other ruins in the state. See chapter 4.
- **Casa Grande Ruins National Monument** (west of Florence): Unlike most of the other ruins in the state, this large and unusual structure is built of packed desert soil. Inscrutable and perplexing, Casa Grande seems to rise from nowhere. See chapter 4.
- **Montezuma Castle, Camp Verde:** Located just off I-17, this is the most easily accessible cliff dwelling in Arizona, though it cannot be entered. Nearby Montezuma's Well also has some small ruins. See chapter 5.
- **Wupatki** (north of Flagstaff): Not nearly as well known as the region's Anasazi cliff dwellings, these ruins are set on a wide plain. A ball court similar to those found in Central America hints at cultural ties with the Aztecs. See chapter 6.
- **Canyon de Chelly:** Small cliff dwellings up and down the length of Canyon de Chelly can be seen from overlooks. A trip into the canyon itself offers a chance to see some of these ruins close up. See chapter 7.
- **Keet Seel/Betatakin** (west of Kayenta): Although both of these ruins, located in Navajo National Monument, are at the end of long hikes, their size and state of preservation make them among the finest examples of Anasazi cliff dwellings. See chapter 7.

## 12  The Best Guest Ranches

- **Kay El Bar Guest Ranch** (Wickenburg; ☎ 800/684-7583 or 520/684-7593): What this guest ranch lacks in size it more than makes up in old West character. With its historic buildings and classic 1950s dude ranch styling, the inn captures the essence of a small desert ranch. See chapter 5.
- **Merv Griffin's Wickenburg Inn and Dude Ranch** (Wickenburg; ☎ 800/942-5362): So maybe you like to ride horses, but your spouse prefers tennis, your daughter lives for ponies, and your son wants to see rattlesnakes. No problem. The Wickenburg Inn, a combination guest ranch and tennis resort that doubles as a nature preserve, should keep the whole family happy. See chapter 5.

- **Tanque Verde Ranch** (Tucson; ☎ **800/234-DUDE** or 520/296-6275): One of the state's most luxurious guest ranches, the Tanque Verde Ranch combines a superb setting, authentic ranch feel, creature comforts, and excellent food. See chapter 9.
- **Rancho de la Osa** (Sasabe; ☎ **800/872-6240** or 520/823-4257): Set on a historic 200-year-old ranch in a remote stretch of grasslands near the Mexican border, this guest ranch still has a feel of the Old West in its adobe buildings and remote location. An artistic flare sets this ranch apart from others. See chapter 10.
- **Circle Z Ranch** (Patagonia; ☎ **888/854-2525** or 520/394-2525): In business since 1925 and the oldest working cattle ranch in the state, the Circle Z is set on the banks of Sonoita Creek and is surrounded by national forest and a Nature Conservancy preserve. This all adds up to lots of places to ride. See chapter 10.

## 13  The Best Luxury Hotels & Resorts

- **Arizona Biltmore Resort & Spa** (Phoenix; ☎ **800/950-0086** or 602/955-6600): Combining discreet service and the architectural styling of Frank Lloyd Wright, the Arizona Biltmore has long been one of the most popular resorts in the state. Recent renovations have done much to improve the quality of the rooms, and a new pool is a big hit with families. See chapter 4.
- **The Boulders** (Carefree; ☎ **800/553-1717** or 480/488-9009): Taking its name from the massive blocks of eroded granite that are scattered about the grounds of this resort, the Boulders is among the most exclusive and expensive resorts in the state. Pueblo architecture fits seamlessly with the landscape, and the golf course is the most breathtaking in Arizona. See chapter 4.
- **Hyatt Regency Scottsdale** (Scottsdale; ☎ **800/233-1234** or 480/991-3388): Contemporary desert architecture, dramatic landscaping, a water playground with its own beach, a staff that's always at the ready to assist you, several good restaurants that aren't overpriced, and even gondola rides—it all adds up to a lot of fun at one of the most smoothly run resorts in Arizona. See chapter 4.
- **Marriott's Camelback Inn** (Scottsdale; ☎ **800/24-CAMEL** or 480/948-1700): This is one of the few Scottsdale resorts that retains an old Arizona atmosphere without sacrificing comfort or modern conveniences. A full-service spa caters to those who crave pampering, while two golf courses provide plenty of challenging fairways and greens. See chapter 4.
- **The Phoenician** (Scottsdale; ☎ **800/888-8234** or 480/941-8200): This Xanadu of the resort world is brimming with marble, crystal, and works of art. With staff seemingly around every corner, the hotel offers its guests impeccable service. Two of the resort's dining rooms are among the finest restaurants in the city, and the views are hard to beat. See chapter 4.
- **Royal Palms Hotel and Casitas** (Phoenix; ☎ **800/672-6011** or 602/840-3610): With its Mediterranean styling and towering royal palms, this resort seems far removed from the glitz that prevails at most area resorts. This resort is a classic, perfect for romantic getaways. The 14 designer showcase rooms are among the most dramatically styled rooms in the valley. See chapter 4.
- **Scottsdale Princess** (Scottsdale; ☎ **800/441-1414** or 480/585-4848): The Moorish styling and numerous fountains and waterfalls of this Scottsdale resort create a setting made for romance. Two superb restaurants—one serving Spanish cuisine and one serving gourmet Mexican fare—top it off. See chapter 4.
- **Enchantment Resort** (Sedona; ☎ **800/826-4180** or 520/282-2900): A dramatic setting in a red-rock canyon outside Sedona makes this the most stunningly

situated resort in the state. Guest rooms are for the most part quite large and are constructed in a pueblo architectural style. If you want to feel as if you're vacationing in the desert, this place fills the bill. See chapter 5.

- **Loews Ventana Canyon Resort** (Tucson; ☎ **800/234-5117** or 520/299-2020): With the Santa Catalina Mountains rising up in the backyard of this resort and an almost-natural waterfall only steps away from the lobby, this is Tucson's most dramatic resort. Contemporary styling throughout makes constant reference to the desert setting. See chapter 9.
- **Sheraton El Conquistador Resort & Country Club** (Tucson; ☎ **800/325-7832** or 520/544-5000): The craggy ramparts of Pusch Ridge rising to the east and some of the best sunsets in the state are two of the outstanding features of this resort. Add to that three golf courses, several good restaurants, riding stables, and plenty of other exercise facilities, and you have the makings of a thoroughly enjoyable resort stay. See chapter 9.

## 14  The Best Moderately Priced Hotels

- **Hotel San Carlos** (Phoenix; ☎ **800/528-5446** or 602/253-4121): Arizona doesn't have many historic hotels, and downtown Phoenix doesn't have many hotels, period. So this restored Phoenix hotel is a welcome choice for anyone looking for character, economical rates, and a downtown location. See chapter 4.
- **Fiesta Inn** (Tempe; ☎ **800/528-6481** or 480/967-1441): With all the amenities of a big, expensive resort, this economical Tempe resort has managed to keep its rates well below those of other comparable resort hotels in the Valley of the Sun. Don't expect the height of chic, but the shady grounds, pool, and other recreational facilities will certainly keep you busy. See chapter 4.
- **Sky Ranch Lodge** (Sedona; ☎ **888/708-6400** or 520/282-6400): Accommodations in Sedona tend to be pricey, but at this motel you get your money's worth in the form of spectacular mesa-top views of the red rocks and the city far below. See chapter 5.
- **Bright Angel Lodge & Cabins** (Grand Canyon Village; ☎ **303/297-2757**): Located right on the rim of the Grand Canyon, this hotel offers a wide variety of room types and a wide range of rates. If you can get a reservation here, you'll get to experience the best hotel deal in the national park. See chapter 6.
- **Cameron Trading Post** (Cameron; ☎ **800/338-7385** or 520/679-2231): It's tough finding accommodations anywhere near the Grand Canyon during the summer, so if you're turned away at the park and don't mind a bit of a drive, this motel affiliated with a historic trading post offers attractively furnished rooms and a scenic location. See chapter 6.
- **Goulding's Lodge** (Monument Valley; ☎ **435/727-3231**): Anyone planning on staying the night near Monument Valley should try to get a reservation here first. From your balcony, you'll be able to see the buttes and mesas of the valley. See chapter 7.
- **Best Western Ghost Ranch Lodge** (Tucson; ☎ **800/456-7565** or 520/791-7565): This older motel isn't in a very attractive neighborhood, but a sign designed by Georgia O'Keeffe, a superb cactus garden, and a guest-ranch feel make this a good economical choice in Tucson. See chapter 9.
- **The Lodge on the Desert** (Tucson; ☎ **800/456-5634** or 520/325-3366): Sort of a poor-man's version of the Arizona Inn, this classic old desert lodge has Santa Fe–style adobe buildings, old gardens, and a sense of being removed from the

modern Tucson that now surrounds it. The hotel was recently renovated and is still undergoing expansion. See chapter 9.

- **Sunstone Guest Ranch** (Tucson; ☎ **520/749-1928**): With its huge old mesquite trees and beautiful green lawns, this place isn't exactly a guest ranch, but offers a ranch-like setting in a pocket of grassland surrounded by desert and suburbs. Basically, its best of both worlds—a little bit country and a little bit city. See chapter 9.
- **High Desert Inn** (Bisbee; ☎ **800/281-0510** or 520/432-1442): This small hotel is Bisbee's most luxurious lodging and is housed in the former Cochise County Jail (ca. 1901). On the first floor is an excellent little restaurant. See chapter 10.

## 15 The Best Historic Inns & Hotels

- **Hassayampa Inn** (Prescott; ☎ **800/322-1927** or 520/778-9434): Built as a luxury hotel in 1927, the Hassayampa is Prescott's premier historic inn and sits only a block off Courthouse Plaza. Many of the rooms, which vary considerably in size, have original furnishings, and one is said to be haunted. See chapter 5.
- **El Tovar Hotel** (Grand Canyon Village; ☎ **303/297-2757**): This classic log-and-stone mountain lodge stands in Grand Canyon Village only feet from the south rim of the Grand Canyon. Although the lobby is small, it's decorated with the requisite trophy animal heads and has a stone fireplace. See chapter 6.
- **Grand Canyon Lodge** (Grand Canyon North Rim; ☎ **303/297-2757**): This, the Grand Canyon's other grand lodge, sits right on the north rim of the canyon. Rooms are primarily in cabins, which aren't quite as impressive as the main lodge building, but guests tend to spend a lot of time sitting on the lodge's two viewing terraces or in the sunroom. See chapter 6.
- **La Posada** (Winslow; ☎ **520/289-4366**): Designed by Mary Elizabeth Jane Colter, who also designed many of the buildings on the South Rim of the Grand Canyon, La Posada opened in 1930 and was the last of the great railroad hotels. Today the hotel is in the process of being restored to its former glory. See chapter 7.
- **Arizona Inn** (Tucson; ☎ **800/933-1093** or 520/325-1541): With its pink stucco walls and colorful, fragrant gardens, this small Tucson resort epitomizes slower times and dates from Arizona's earliest days as a vacation destination, when guests came for the entire winter, not for a quick weekend away. See chapter 9.

## 16 The Best B&Bs

- **Rocamadour Bed & Breakfast for (Rock) Lovers** (Prescott; ☎ **888/771-1933** or 520/771-1933): Set amid the rounded boulders of the Granite Dells just north of Prescott, this inn combines a spectacular setting with French antiques and very luxurious accommodations. You won't find a more memorable setting anywhere in the state. See chapter 5.
- **Briar Patch Inn** (Sedona; ☎ **888/809-3030** or 520/282-2342): Oak Creek Canyon, near Sedona, where this collection of luxurious cottages is located, is an oasis in the desert. Few experiences are more restorative than breakfast on the shady banks of the creek. See chapter 5.
- **The Graham Bed & Breakfast Inn & Adobe Village** (Sedona; ☎ **800/ 228-1425** or 520/284-1425): With its little "village" of luxury suites, this B&B is

among the most elegant in the state. Everything about the inn's casita suites is calculated to pamper and put you in a mood for a romantic getaway. Forget about
the red rocks, these rooms are reason enough for a visit to Sedona. See chapter 5.

- **The Inn on Oak Creek** (Sedona; ☎ 800/499-7896 or 520/282-7896): Built
right out over Sedona's Oak Creek, with shade trees all around and the Tlaquepaque Shopping Plaza only a block away, this inn offers a wide array of luxurious
and interestingly decorated rooms, most of which have creek or red-rock views.
See chapter 5.

- **Saddle Rock Ranch** (Sedona; ☎ 520/282-7640): With some of the best
views in Sedona, this stone-and-adobe home dates from 1926 and has its own
little swimming pool. Of the three available rooms, the little cottage, with
its peeled-log bed and flagstone floors, has the most Western character. See
chapter 5.

- **The Inn at 410** (Flagstaff, ☎ 800/774-2008 or 520/774-0088): This restored
1907 bungalow offers a convenient location in downtown Flagstaff, pleasant surroundings, comfortable rooms, and delicious breakfasts. Rooms all feature different, distinctive themes, and seven of them have their own fireplaces. See
chapter 6.

- **Red Setter Bed & Breakfast Inn** (Greer; ☎ 888/99-GREER or 520/735-
7441): This large, new log home in the quaint mountain village of Greer is one
of Arizona's most enjoyable and romantic B&Bs. It's set on the bank of the Little
Colorado River in the shade of large ponderosa pine trees. The inn is also a great
place for ski vacations. See chapter 8.

- **Paisley Corner Bed & Breakfast** (Eagar; ☎ 520/333-4665): Although this inn
is not nearly as luxurious as others on this list, it is noteworthy for its authenticity of interior design. Victorian antiques fill the house, including the kitchen.
There's even a vintage soda fountain in one of the parlors. See chapter 8.

- **Casa Tierra** (Tucson; ☎ 520/578-3058): This modern adobe home is located
near Saguaro National Park west of downtown Tucson and is an ideal choice for
those who really want to feel as if they're staying in the desert. See chapter 9.

- **"Across The Creek" at Aravaipa Farms** (☎ 520/357-6901): If you're looking
for the quintessential desert B&B experience, this is it, though it isn't exactly for
everyone. To reach this inn, you have to drive *through* Aravaipa Creek (or have
the innkeeper shuttle you across). Exploring the nearby wilderness area is the
main activity in this remote area. See chapter 9.

## 17 The Best Swimming Pools

- **Arizona Biltmore** (Phoenix; ☎ 800/950-0086 or 602/955-6600): The main
pool here, which was added a few years back, mixes old and new with its private
cabanas (available for a fee) and its Frank Lloyd Wright–inspired water-slide
tower. See chapter 4.

- **Wyndham Buttes Resort** (Tempe; ☎ 800/WYNDHAM or 602/225-9000): A
lush stream cascading over desert rocks seems to feed this free-form pool; it's a
desert oasis fantasy world unmatched in the state. A narrow canal connects the
two halves of the pool, and tucked in among the rocks are several whirlpools. See
chapter 4.

- **Hyatt Regency Scottsdale** (Scottsdale; ☎ 800/233-1234 or 480/991-3388):
This Scottsdale resort boasts a 10-pool, 2½-acre water playground complete with
sand beach, waterfalls, sports pool, lap pool, adult pool, three-story water slide,
massive whirlpool, and lots of waterfalls. See chapter 4.

- **The Phoenician** (Scottsdale; ☎ **800/888-8234** or 480/941-8200): This system of seven pools is as impressive as the Hyatt's but has a much more sophisticated air about it. Waterfalls, a water slide, play pools, a lap pool, and the crown jewel, a mother-of-pearl pool (actually opalescent tile) all add up to plenty of aquatic fun. See chapter 4.
- **Pointe Hilton Squaw Peak Resort** (Phoenix; ☎ **800/876-4683** or 602/997-2626): They don't just have a pool here, they have a River Ranch, with an artificial tubing river, water slide, and a waterfall pouring into the large, free-form main pool. See chapter 4.
- **Pointe Hilton Tapatio Cliffs Resort** (Phoenix; ☎ **800/876-4683** or 602/866-7500): The Falls, a slightly more adult-oriented pool complex than that at sister property Pointe Hilton Squaw Peak Resort, includes two lagoon pools, a 40-foot waterfall, a 130-foot water slide, and rental cabanas. See chapter 4.
- **Arizona Inn** (Tucson; ☎ **800/933-1093** or 520/325-1541): Although the pool at this historic lodge isn't very large, it more than makes up for its size with its pleasant setting in a garden filled with fragrant flowering vines and citrus trees. See chapter 9.
- **Westin La Paloma** (Tucson; ☎ **800/WESTIN-1** or 520/742-6000): With a 170-foot water slide and enough poolside lounge chairs to put a cruise ship to shame, the pool at this Tucson foothills resort is a fabulous place to while away an afternoon. There's an adults-only pool too. See chapter 9.

## 18  The Best Restaurants

- **Vincent Guerithault on Camelback** (Phoenix; ☎ **602/224-0225**): The bold flavors of the Southwest are the focus of this ever-popular Phoenix restaurant, where presentation is every bit as important as taste. Even if you aren't a fan of chilies, you'll find plenty of unusual flavor combinations to tempt your palate. See chapter 4.
- **T. Cook's** (Phoenix; ☎ **602/808-0766**): Located within the Mediterranean cloisters of the Royal Palms Resort, T. Cook's is the most romantic restaurant in Phoenix. No other restaurant (with the possible exception of Marquesa) so thoroughly transports you to another place with both its decor and its cuisine. The restaurant's lounge is equally memorable and not to be missed. See chapter 4.
- **Marquesa** (Scottsdale; ☎ **480/585-4848**): Located amid the Moorish architecture of the Scottsdale Princess resort, this Spanish restaurant specializes in Catalonian dishes. To dine here is to be totally immersed in a Mediterranean experience. See chapter 4.
- **Mary Elaine's** (Scottsdale; ☎ **480/423-2530**): Located in Scottsdale's posh Phoenician resort, Mary Elaine's is where the elite dine in the Valley of the Sun. The menu focuses primarily on modern French flavors, though the chef doesn't limit himself. See chapter 4.
- **The Heartline Cafe** (Sedona; ☎ **520/282-0785**): Combining the zesty flavors of the Southwest with the best of the rest of the world, Sedona's Heartline Cafe frequently comes up with surefire winners guaranteed to please jaded palates. See chapter 5.
- **El Tovar Dining Room** (Grand Canyon Village; ☎ **520/638-2631,** ext. 6432): It would be hard for the food to match the setting, a historic mountain lodge on the rim of the Grand Canyon, but this restaurant does its best. The menu features a mix of continental and Southwestern flavors, though the latter are the better choices. See chapter 6.

- **Café Poca Cosa** (Tucson; ☎ **520/622-6400**): It's small, it's hip, and it's very reasonably priced. Located in the Clarion Hotel & Suites Santa Rita, the Cafe Poca Cosa serves some of the most creative and complex Mexican food since *Like Water for Chocolate.* See chapter 9.
- **Janos** (Tucson; ☎ **520/615-6100**): Serving a combination of regional and Southwestern dishes, Janos has for many years been one of Tucson's premiere restaurants. Located just outside the front door of the Westin La Paloma resort, this restaurant is as formal a place as you'll find in Tucson. See chapter 9.
- **The Tack Room** (Tucson; ☎ **520/722-2800**): Superb service, creative Southwestern dishes, and an authentic Arizona atmosphere make Tucson's Tack Room one of the finest restaurants in the West. Though the steaks are the traditional favorite, other dishes are well worth consideration. See chapter 9.
- **Cose Buone** (Patagonia; ☎ **520/394-2366**): Fine dining and a Laundromat side by side? Yes its true. Very reasonably priced four-course Italian dinners are served in this casual spot in eclectic Patagonia. See chapter 10.

# Planning a Trip to Arizona

## 2

**W**hether you're headed to Arizona to raft the Grand Canyon or to play golf in Phoenix, you'll find all the advance-planning answers you need at your fingertips in this chapter—everything from when to go to how to get there.

## 1 The Regions in Brief

**The Valley of the Sun**   This name refers to the sprawling metropolitan Phoenix area, which covers more than 400 square miles and includes more than 20 cities and communities surrounded by several distinct mountain ranges. It's the economic and population center of the state.

**The Sonoran Desert**   Extending from the state of Sonora, Mexico, in the south to central Arizona in the north, the Sonoran Desert is surprisingly green and characterized by the massive saguaro cactus. It's in the Sonoran Desert that most of Arizona's cities are found.

**The Four Corners**   The point where Arizona, Utah, Colorado, and New Mexico come together is the only place in the United States where four states share a common boundary. The Four Corners region of Arizona is almost entirely Hopi and Navajo reservation land. This high-plateau region of spectacular canyons and towering mesas and buttes includes Canyon de Chelly, the Painted Desert, the Petrified Forest, and Monument Valley.

**The White Mountains**   Located in eastern Arizona, the White Mountains are laced with trout streams, covered by a huge pine forest, and home to far more wildlife than people. Arizona's largest and most popular ski area is located here on the White Mountain Apache Indian Reservation near the town of McNary. Cooler temperatures make this region a very popular summer-vacation destination.

**Arizona's West Coast**   Though Arizona is a landlocked state, its western region is referred to as the West Coast because of the hundreds of miles of lakeshore that were created by the damming of the Colorado River. The low-lying stretches of the Colorado River are the hottest places in Arizona.

**Canyon Country**   From the Grand Canyon in the north to Oak Creek Canyon in the south, the rugged north-central part of the state alternates high, forested mountains with deep canyons. The 2,000-foot-high Mogollon Rim cuts through this region.

For a map of these regions of Arizona, see chapter 1.

**The Arizona Strip**    Located north of the Grand Canyon and bordering on southern Utah, this is one of the most remote and untraveled sections of Arizona. The Grand Canyon acts as a natural boundary between this region and the rest of the state.

**Southeastern Arizona**    Mile-high elevations give this region one of the most temperate climates in the world. Tucson is at the northern edge of this region (and not so temperate), but otherwise there are few towns of any size. Mountain "islands" that rise out of the desert are home to more than 200 species of birds, and the wide grassy valleys make this a ranching region.

# 2  Visitor Information & Money

## VISITOR INFORMATION

If you have more questions than we can answer in this book, there are a number of places that may have the answers for you. For statewide travel information, contact the **Arizona Office of Tourism,** 2702 N. Third St., Suite 4015, Phoenix, AZ 85004 (☎ **800/842-8257** or 602/230-7733). And keep in mind that every city and town in Arizona has either a tourism office or a chamber of commerce that can give you information. See the individual chapters for addresses of these sources.

If you're a member of the **American Automobile Association (AAA),** remember that you can get a map and guidebook covering Arizona and New Mexico. You can also request the club's free *Southwestern CampBook,* which includes campgrounds in Arizona, Utah, Colorado, and New Mexico, by calling your local AAA chapter.

## MONEY

What will a vacation in Arizona cost? That depends on your comfort needs. If you drive an RV or carry a tent, you can get by very inexpensively and find a place to stay almost anywhere in the state. If you don't mind staying in motels that date from the Great Depression and can sleep on a sagging mattress, you can stay for less money in Arizona than almost anyplace else in the United States (under $30 a night for a double). On the other hand, you can easily spend several hundred dollars a day on a room at one of the state's world-class resorts. If you're looking to stay in clean, modern motels at interstate highway off-ramps, expect to pay $45 to $65 a night for a double room in most places.

It's never a problem to find an ATM machine when you're on the road. Throughout the state, the Star, Cirrus, and Plus networks are widely available, so you can get cash through these networks as well as with a major credit card as you travel. If you should have trouble finding an ATM, you can call ☎ **800/424-7787** for Cirrus locations or ☎ **800/843-7587** for Plus locations. Expect to pay $1.50 service fee at most ATMs in the state.

But some people still prefer the security of traveler's checks, which are accepted at hotels, motels, restaurants, and most stores. Call American Express (☎ **800/ 221-7282**) for more information.

# 3  When to Go

Arizona is a year-round destination, though people head to different parts of the state at different times of year. In Phoenix, Tucson, and other parts of the desert, the high season runs from October to mid-May, with the highest hotel rates in effect during

# Money-Saving Tips

- You can save a substantial amount on hotel rates by joining the American Automobile Association (AAA). The savings on just a few nights' lodging can cover the cost of the annual AAA membership.
- To avoid ATM fees, use your card as a debit card at a grocery store and get cash back from your purchase.
- Have lunch at an expensive restaurant, and you'll be able savor the ambience at a fraction of the cost of dinner. Often the lunch menu includes some items from the dinner menu at much lower prices.
- Ask when hotel room rates drop for the summer and schedule your trip for right after the rates go down (or just before they go back up in the fall). Many resorts also have a short discounted season just before Christmas. Travel then and you can save hundreds of dollars over a visit in January.
- Pick up rental cars somewhere other than the Phoenix or Tucson airports. Rental car companies operating inside the airport charge 20% or more in taxes and service fees. Taxes and service charges outside the airport are about half as much.

January and February. However, up at the Grand Canyon the busy season is during the summer; that's when hotel rates are the highest and crowds are the largest.

The all-around best times to visit are in spring and autumn, when temperatures are cool in the mountains and warm in the desert, but without extremes (although you shouldn't be surprised to get a bit of snow as late as Memorial Day in the mountains and thunderstorms in the desert in August and September). These are also good times to save money because summer rates are in effect at the desert resorts and the crowds aren't as dense at the Grand Canyon. This time period sometimes also coincides with the spring wildflower season, which begins in midspring and extends until April and May, when the tops of saguaro cacti become covered with waxy white blooms.

If for some reason you happen to be visiting the desert in August, be prepared for sudden thunderstorms. These storms often cause flash floods that make many roads in the state briefly impassable. Road signs warning motorists not to enter low areas when flooded are meant to be taken very seriously.

Also, don't even think about venturing into narrow slot canyons, such as Antelope Canyon near Page or the West Fork of Oak Creek Canyon, if there's any chance of a storm anywhere in the region. Rain falling miles away can send flash floods roaring down narrow canyons with no warning. In 1997, several hikers died when they were caught in a flash flood in Antelope Canyon.

## CLIMATE

The first thing you should know is that the desert can be cold as well as hot. Although winter is the prime tourist season in Phoenix and Tucson, night temperatures can be below freezing and days can even be too cold for sunning or swimming. However, on the whole, winters in Arizona are positively delightful.

In the winter, sunseekers flock to the deserts, where temperatures average in the high 60s by day. In the summer, when desert temperatures top 110°F, the mountains of eastern and northern Arizona are pleasantly warm, with daytime averages in the low 80s. Yuma is one of the desert communities where winter temperatures are the highest in the state, and Prescott and Sierra Vista, in the 4,000- to 6,000-foot elevation range, claim two of the most temperate climates in the world.

The accompanying climate charts will give you an idea of the state's climatic diversity.

### Phoenix's Average Temperatures (°F) & Days of Rain

|  | Jan | Feb | Mar | Apr | May | June | July | Aug | Sept | Oct | Nov | Dec |
|---|---|---|---|---|---|---|---|---|---|---|---|---|
| Avg. High | 65 | 69 | 75 | 84 | 93 | 102 | 105 | 102 | 98 | 88 | 75 | 66 |
| Avg. Low | 38 | 41 | 45 | 52 | 60 | 68 | 78 | 76 | 69 | 57 | 45 | 39 |
| Days of Rain | 4 | 4 | 3 | 2 | 1 | 1 | 4 | 5 | 3 | 3 | 2 | 4 |

### Flagstaff's Average Temperatures (°F) & Days of Rain

|  | Jan | Feb | Mar | Apr | May | June | July | Aug | Sept | Oct | Nov | Dec |
|---|---|---|---|---|---|---|---|---|---|---|---|---|
| Avg. High | 41 | 44 | 48 | 57 | 67 | 76 | 81 | 78 | 74 | 63 | 51 | 43 |
| Avg. Low | 14 | 17 | 20 | 27 | 34 | 40 | 50 | 49 | 41 | 31 | 22 | 16 |
| Days of Rain | 7 | 6 | 8 | 6 | 3 | 3 | 12 | 11 | 6 | 5 | 5 | 6 |

# Arizona Calendar of Events

## January

- **Fiesta Bowl Game,** Sun Devil Stadium, Tempe. College football classic. For information, call ☎ **800/635-5748** or 480/350-0900. January 1 or 2.
- **Phoenix Open Golf Tournament,** Scottsdale. Prestigious PGA golf tournament at the Tournament Players Club. Phone ☎ **602/870-0163** for details. Mid- to late January.
- **Wings Over Willcox,** Willcox. Birding tours, workshops, and, of course, watching the sandhill cranes at the Willcox sewage recycling ponds. Call ☎ **520/ 384-2272** for details. Third weekend in January.

## February

- **Parada del Sol Parade and Rodeo,** Scottsdale. The state's longest horse-drawn parade, plus a street dance and rodeo. For more information, call ☎ **480/ 502-1880.** Early February.
- **Tubac Festival of the Arts,** Tubac. Exhibits by North American artists and craftspeople. For more information, call ☎ **520/398-2371.** Early to mid-February.
- **Arizona Renaissance Festival,** Apache Junction. This 16th-century English country fair has costumed participants and includes tournament jousting. Phone ☎ **602/463-2700** for details. Weekends from early February to March.
- **Tucson Gem and Mineral Show.** This huge show at the Tucson Convention Center offers seminars, museum displays from around the world, and dealers selling just about any kind of rock you can imagine. For details, call ☎ **520/ 322-5773.** Mid-February.
- **O'odham Tash,** Casa Grande. One of the largest annual Native American festivals in the country, attracting dozens of tribes who participate in rodeos, arts-and-crafts exhibits, and dance performances. Call ☎ **520/836-4723.** Mid-February.
- **Tucson Open.** A major stop on the golf tour, held at the Omni Tucson National Golf Resort and Spa. Call ☎ **800/882-7660** or 520/571-0400 for information. Mid- to late February.
- **La Fiesta de los Vaqueros,** Tucson. Cowboy festival and rodeo at the Tucson Rodeo Grounds, including the Tucson Rodeo Parade, the world's largest non-motorized parade. Call ☎ **520/741-2233** for details. Late February.

- **Flagstaff Winterfest.** Sled-dog races, sleigh rides, music and family snow games. For details, call ☎ **800/842-7293** or 520/774-4505. Month of February.

## March

- **Heard Museum Guild Indian Fair,** Phoenix. Indian cultural and dance presentations and one of the greatest selections of Native American crafts in the Southwest make this a fascinating festival. Plus, with the festival entrance fee you get admission to the Heard Museum. Go early to avoid the crowds. Call ☎ **602/252-8840** for details. First weekend in March.
- **Franklin Templeton Tennis Classic,** Scottsdale. Top names in men's professional tennis such as Andre Agassi and Pete Sampras compete in this tournament at the Scottsdale Princess hotel. For information, call ☎ **602/514-8800.** Early March.
- **Wiener Dog Nationals,** Phoenix. How about those dachshunds? Watch this great low-ridin' action at the Phoenix Greyhound Park. You'll see the greyhounds run, too. Call ☎ **602/273-7181.** Early March.
- **Chandler Ostrich Festival,** Chandler. Live music, a carnival, and, of course, ostrich races. For more details, call ☎ **480/963-4571.** Early to mid-March.
- **Scottsdale Arts Festival,** Scottsdale Mall. This visual and performing arts festival has free concerts, an art show, and children's events. For more information, phone ☎ **480/994-2787.** Second weekend in March.
- **Wak Pow Wow,** Tucson. Tohono O'odham celebration at Mission San Xavier del Bac, featuring many Southwestern Native American groups. Call ☎ **520/ 294-5727** for more information. Mid-March.
- **Northern Arizona Book Festival,** Flagstaff. Noted authors gather for a series of talks and presentations. Last year's guests included Michael Ondaatje, author of *The English Patient,* and Nobel prize–winning author Czeslaw Milosz. For more details, call ☎ **800/842-7293** or 520/556-0313. Mid-March.
- **Yaqui Easter Lenten Ceremony,** Tucson. Religious ceremonies at Old Pasqua Village blending Christian and Yaqui Native American beliefs. For further information, phone ☎ **520/791-4609.** Holy Week.
- **Territorial Days,** Tombstone. Tombstone's birthday celebration. For more information, call ☎ **800/457-3423.** Late March.
- **World Championship Hoop Dance,** Phoenix. Native American dancers from around the nation take part in this colorful competition held at the Heard Museum. Call ☎ **602/252-8840** for details. Late March.
- **Welcome Back Buzzards,** Superior. A flock of turkey buzzards arrives annually at the Boyce Thompson Arboretum to roost in the eucalyptus trees, and this festival celebrates their arrival. For details, call ☎ **520/689-2811** or 520/689-2723. Late March.
- **The Tradition,** Scottsdale. This Senior PGA tournament at Cochise Course at Desert Mountain hosts the big names. Call ☎ **480/595-4070** for more information. Late March to early April.

## April

- **Tucson International Mariachi Conference.** Mariachi bands from all over the world come to compete before standing-room only crowds. Call ☎ **520/884-9920,** ext. 243, for more information. Mid- to late April.
- **Allstate Golf & Celebrity Tennis Tournament,** Tucson. One of the largest celebrity tennis events in the United States, held at the Randolph Tennis Center. Phone ☎ **520/623-6165** for more information. Mid- to late April.

- **Waila Festival,** Tucson. A festival celebrating the social dances of the Tohono O'odham nation, featuring "chicken scratch" music—a kind of polka—and native foods. Call ☎ 520/628-5774 for more information. Late April.
- **All-Arabian Horse Show,** Scottsdale's Westworld. A celebration of the Arabian horse. For additional information, call ☎ **480/483-8800.** Late April.
- **Maricopa County Fair,** Phoenix. The Arizona State Fairgrounds hosts a midway, agricultural and livestock exhibits, and entertainment. For details, phone ☎ **602/252-0717.** Late April to early May.

## May

- **Cinco de Mayo,** Tucson, Phoenix, and other cities. Celebration of the Mexican victory over the French in a famous 1862 battle, complete with food, music, and dancing. Call ☎ **602/262-4627** for details on the festivities in Phoenix; call ☎ **520/623-8344** for more information on the celebration in Tucson's Kennedy Park. Around May 5.
- **Phippen Western Art Show and Sale,** Prescott. This is the premier Western art sale. For more information, call ☎ **520/778-1385.** Memorial Day weekend.
- **Wyatt Earp Days,** Tombstone. Gunfight reenactments in memory of the shoot-out at the O.K. Corral. Call ☎ **800/457-3423** for further details. Late May.
- **Sedona Chamber Music Festival,** Sedona. Chamber music is performed by companies from around the world at various venues. Phone ☎ **520/526-2256** for details. Late May.
- **Enduring Creations: Masterworks of Native American Art,** Flagstaff. The finest Hopi, Zuni, Navajo, and Pai art and craft work is offered for sale in changing exhibits at the Museum of Northern Arizona. For details, phone ☎ **520/774-5213.** Ongoing event from late May to September.

## June

- **Juneteenth Festival,** Tucson. Festival in Kennedy Park celebrating African American Independence Day, including food, a fashion show, and a craft marketplace. Call ☎ **520/791-4355.** Third weekend in June.

## July

- **Independence Day.** For information about fireworks displays in Phoenix, call ☎ **602/495-5490;** in Tucson, phone ☎ **520/791-4860.** July 4.
- **Annual Hopi Artists Exhibition,** Flagstaff. Exhibition and sale at the Museum of Northern Arizona, including cultural events. Call ☎ **520/774-5213** for more details. Fourth of July weekend.
- **Prescott Frontier Days,** Prescott. This is the oldest rodeo in the United States. Phone ☎ **800/266-7534** or 520/445-3103 for details. First week of July.
- **Annual Navajo Artists Exhibition,** Flagstaff. Exhibition and sale at the Museum of Northern Arizona, including cultural events. For details, call ☎ **520/774-5213.** Last weekend in July or first weekend in August.

## August

- **Payson Rodeo,** Payson. The second of Arizona's rodeos claiming to be the world's oldest. For details, call ☎ **800/672-9766** or 520/474-4515. Mid-August.
- **Southwest Wings Birding Festival,** Sierra Vista. Spotting hummingbirds and looking for owls and bats keep participants busy. Includes lectures and field trips. For more information, phone ☎ **800/288-3861** or 520/459-EVNT. Mid-August.

- **Arizona Cowboy Poets' Gathering,** Prescott. Not just traditional and contemporary poetry, but yodeling and storytelling that focuses on the cowboy lifestyle. For more information, call ☎ **520/445-3122.** Third weekend in August.
- **La Fiesta de San Agustín,** Tucson. Celebration to honor the patron saint of Tucson, with a Mexican fiesta theme. For more information, phone ☎ **520/762-5806.** Late August.

## September

- **Plaza Suite,** Tucson. Open-air jazz concerts at St. Philip's Plaza. For details, call the Tucson Jazz Society at ☎ **520/743-3399.** Sundays in September and October.
- **Navajo Nation Fair,** Window Rock. A very large fair featuring traditional music and dancing by North American tribes. Call ☎ **520/871-6478** for more information. Early September.
- **State Championship Old Time Fiddler's Contest,** Payson. Fiddlers from around Arizona try their best to out-fiddle each other, along with clogging and buck dancing. For details, call ☎ **520/474-5242.** Late September.
- **Scottsdale Center for the Arts Annual Gala.** Jazz, ballet, music, art exhibits, and special events. Phone ☎ **480/994-2787** for further information. Late September.
- **Jazz on the Rocks,** Sedona. Open-air jazz festival held in the red rocks. For details, call ☎ **520/282-1985.** Late September.

## October

- **Coors Rodeo Showdown,** Phoenix. Top rodeo stars compete in this world finals rodeo at the America West Arena. For details, call ☎ **800/638-4253** or 602/678-2222. Early to mid-October.
- **Sedona Arts Festival,** Sedona. One of the best arts festivals in the state. For additional information, phone ☎ **800/288-7336** or 520/204-9456. Mid-October.
- **Fiesta de los Chiles,** Tucson. Lots of hot chiles, served in dishes from around the world, along with crafts and music. For more information, call ☎ **520/326-9686.** Mid-to late October.
- **Helldorado Days,** Tombstone. Fashion show of 1880s clothing, tribal dancers, and street entertainment. Call ☎ **800/457-3423** for details. Third weekend of October.
- **Arizona State Fair,** Phoenix. This shindig at the Arizona State Fairgrounds features rodeos, top-name entertainment, and ethnic food. Phone ☎ **602/252-6771** for more information. Late October-early November.
- **Annual Cowboy Artists of America Exhibition,** Phoenix. The Phoenix Art Museum hosts the most prestigious and best-known Western art show in the region. For details, call ☎ **602/257-1222.** Late October to late November.

## November

- **Thunderbird Balloon Classic,** Scottsdale. More than 150 hot-air balloons fill the Arizona sky. Call ☎ **602/978-7208** or 602/978-7330 for details. Early November.
- **Western Music Festival,** Tucson. Concerts and workshops by Western music performers. Phone ☎ **520/743-9794** for details. Mid-November.
- **Festival of Lights**, Sedona. Thousands of luminárias are lit at dusk at the Tlaquepaque Arts and Crafts Village on Thanksgiving eve, and stay up until mid-January. For details, call ☎ **800/288-7336.** Thanksgiving to mid-January.

## December

- **Old Town Fall Festival of the Arts,** Tempe. Hundreds of artists and artisans, featuring free entertainment and plenty of food, set up along Mill Avenue. For additional information, call ☎ **480/967-4877.** Early December.
- **Luminária Nights,** Tucson. A glowing display of holiday lights at the Botanical Gardens. For details, call ☎ **520/326-9255.** Early December.
- **Fourth Avenue Street Fair,** Tucson. Outdoor arts-and-crafts festival. Phone ☎ **520/624-5004** for more information. Mid-December.
- **Fiesta de Guadalupe,** Tucson. Celebration of Mexico's patron saint. For further information, call ☎ **520/299-9192.** Early December.
- **Fiesta Bowl Parade,** Phoenix area. Huge parade, featuring floats and marching bands, which is nationally televised. Phone ☎ **800/635-5748** or 480/350-0900 for more information. December 31.

## 4 The Active Vacation Planner

Arizona is known the world over for active, adventure-oriented vacations for the sole reason that the state is home to the Grand Canyon—the most widely known white-water-rafting spot in the world. For others, Arizona is synonymous with winter golf and tennis. Whichever category of active vacationer you fall into, you'll find information below to help you arrange your trip to Arizona.

**BIKING** With its wide range of climates, Arizona offers good biking somewhere in the state every month of the year. In the winter there's good road biking around Phoenix and Tucson, while from spring through fall, the southeastern corner of the state offers some good routes. In the summer the White Mountains in the eastern part of the state and Kaibab National Forest between Flagstaff and Grand Canyon National Park offer good mountain biking. There is also excellent mountain biking at several Phoenix parks, and Tucson is one of the most bicycle-friendly cities in the country. **Backroads,** 801 Cedar St., Berkeley, CA 94710-1800 (☎ **800/462-2848** or 510/527-1555), offers a 6-day, inn-to-inn mountain-bike trip through the red-rock country of central Arizona.

**BIRD WATCHING** Arizona is a birder's bonanza. Down in the southeastern corner of the state, many species found primarily south of the border reach the northern limits of their territories. Combine this with several mountains that rise like islands from the desert and provide an appropriate habitat for hundreds of species, and you have some of the best bird watching in the country. Birding hot spots include Ramsey Canyon Preserve (known for its many species of hummingbirds), Cave Creek Canyon (nesting site for elegant trogons), Patagonia-Sonoita Creek Sanctuary (home to 22 species of flycatchers, kingbirds, and phoebes, as well as Montezuma quails), Madera Canyon (another "mountain island" that attracts many of the same species seen at Ramsey Canyon and Sonoita Creek), Buenos Aires National Wildlife Refuge (home to masked bobwhite quail and gray hawks), and the sewage ponds outside the town of Willcox (known for its avocets and sandhill cranes). To find out which rare birds have been spotted lately, call the **Tucson Audubon Society's Rare Bird Hotline** (☎ **520/ 789-1005**).

Serious birders who want to be sure of adding lots of rare birds to their life lists may want to visit southeastern Arizona on a guided tour. These are available through **High Lonesome Ecotours** (☎ **520/458-9446;** www.hilonesome.com), which charges about $1,500 to $1,850 for a week-long birding trip.

**CANOEING/KAYAKING** OK, so maybe these sports don't jump to mind when you think of the desert, but yes there are rivers in the desert (and they happen to be some of the best places to see wildlife). Contact **Permagrin River Adventures,** 6331 S. College St., Tempe, AZ 85283 (☎ **480/755-1924**); Permagrin also offers various canoeing and kayaking courses.

There are also a couple of companies that rent canoes on the Colorado River south of Lake Mead. See chapter 11 for details.

**FISHING**    The fishing scene in Arizona is as diverse as the landscape. Large and small lakes around the state offer excellent fishing for warm-water game fish such as largemouth, smallmouth, and striped bass. Good trout fishing can be found up on the Mogollon Rim and in the White Mountains there, as well as in the Grand Canyon, and the more easily accessible sections of the free-running Colorado River between Glen Canyon Dam and Lees Ferry.

Fishing licenses for nonresidents are available for 1 day, 5 days, 4 months, and 1 year. Various special stamps and licenses may also apply. Nonresident fishing-license prices range from $8 for a 1-day license to $38 for a 1-year license. Also keep in mind that if you're heading for an Indian reservation, you'll have to get a special permit for that reservation. For more information, contact the **Arizona Game and Fish Department,** 2221 W. Greenway Rd., Phoenix, AZ 85021 (☎ **602/942-3000**).

**GOLF**    For many of Arizona's winter visitors, golf is the main reason to visit the state. The state's hundreds of golf courses range from easy public courses to PGA championship links that have challenged the best.

In Phoenix and Tucson, greens fees, like room rates, are seasonal. In the popular winter months, fees at resort courses range from $70 to $185 for 18 holes, though this usually includes a mandatory golf-cart rental. In the summer months, fees often drop to less than half this amount. Almost all resorts also offer special golf packages as well.

For information on some of the state's top courses, see "Hot Links," the special golf feature in this chapter. For more information on golfing in Arizona, contact the **Arizona Golf Association,** 7226 N. 16th St., Suite 200, Phoenix, AZ 85020 (☎ **800/458-8484** within Arizona or 602/944-3035), which publishes a directory ($5) listing all the courses in the state. You can also contact *Golf Arizona,* 16446 Tombstone Dr., Fountain Hills, AZ 85268 (☎ **800/942-5444**), which publishes a guide to where to play golf in Arizona. You can also pick up a copy of the *Greater Phoenix Golf Guide* at the Visitors Bureau, golf courses, and many hotels and resorts.

**HIKING/BACKPACKING**    Despite its reputation as a desert state, a large percentage of Arizona is forestland and within these forests are wilderness areas and countless miles of hiking trails. In northern Arizona, there are good day hikes in Grand Canyon National Park, in the San Francisco Peaks north of Flagstaff, outside Page (near Lake Powell), and in Navajo National Monument. In the Phoenix area, popular day hikes include the trails up Camelback Mountain and Squaw Peak and the many trails in South Mountain Park. In the Tucson area, there are good hikes on Mount Lemmon and in Saguaro National Park, Sabino Canyon, and Catalina State Park. In the southern part of the state, there are good day hikes in Chiricahua National Monument, Coronado National Forest, in the Nature Conservancy's Ramsey Canyon Preserve and Patagonia-Sonoita Creek Sanctuary, in Cochise Stronghold, and in Organ Pipe National Monument. See the individual chapters for details on these areas.

The state's two most popular overnight backpack trips are the hike down to Phantom Ranch and the hike into Havasu Canyon, a side canyon of the Grand Canyon. Another popular multiday backpack trip is through Paria Canyon, beginning in Utah and ending in Arizona at Lees Ferry. There are also backpacking opportunities in the San Francisco Peaks north of Flagstaff and in the White Mountains of eastern Arizona.

# Hot Links

You don't have to be a hotshot golfer to get all heated up over the prospect of a few rounds of golf in Arizona. Combine near-perfect golf weather with great views and some very unique challenges, and you've got all the makings of a great game. Phoenix and Tucson are well known as winter golf destinations, but the state also offers golf throughout the year at higher-altitude courses in such places as Prescott, Flagstaff, and the White Mountains.

State legislation aimed at conserving water now limits golf courses in Arizona to no more than 90 acres of irrigated land, far less than is found on most traditional golf courses. This legislation has not only conserved both water and the desert, but also has given the state some of the most distinctive and difficult courses in the country. These desert or "target" courses are characterized by minimal fairways surrounded by natural desert landscapes. You might find yourself teeing off over the tops of cacti and searching for your ball amid boulders and mesquite (actual encounters with rattlesnakes are rare). If your ball comes to rest in the desert, you can play the ball where it lies or drop it to within two club lengths of the nearest point of grass, but no nearer the hole, with a one-stroke penalty.

Keep in mind that resort courses are not cheap. For most of the year, greens fees, which include golf-cart rentals, range from around $90 to $150 or more. Greens fees at daily fee public courses are often about the same as at resort courses. Municipal courses, on the other hand, offer very reasonable greens fees of less than $30 for 18 holes, with golf-cart rental costing extra (usually less than $20).

It may not seem so initially, but summer is really a good time to visit many of Arizona's golf resorts. No, they don't have air-conditioned golf carts or indoor courses, but in summer greens fees can be less than half what they are in winter. How does $38 for a round on the famous Gold Course at the Wigwam Golf and Country Club sound? Plus, most resorts charge next to nothing for rooms in the summer (and those rooms *do* have air-conditioning).

With more golf courses per capita than any other state—more than 250 in all—the only problem is choosing where you'd like to play.

The Phoenix/Scottsdale area, known as the Valley of the Sun, has the greatest concentration of golf courses in the state. Whether you're looking to play one of the area's challenging top-rated resort courses or an economical-but-fun municipal course, you'll find plenty of choices.

For spectacular scenery at a resort course, it's just plain impossible to beat **The Boulders** (☎ 480/488-9009), located north of Scottsdale in the town of Carefree. Elevated tee boxes beside giant balanced boulders are enough to distract anyone's concentration. Way over on the east side of the valley in Apache Junction, the **Gold Canyon Golf Resort** (☎ 480/982-9449) has what have been rated as three of the best holes in the state: the second, third, and fourth holes on the Dinosaur Mountain course. Jumping over to Litchfield Park, on the far west side of the valley, you'll find the **Wigwam Golf and Country Club** (☎ 623/935-3811) and its three 18-hole courses; the Gold Course here is legendary. Other noteworthy resort courses in the area include the links at **The Phoenician** (☎ 480/423-2449), which mix traditional and desert-style holes. The **Gainey**

**Ranch Golf Club,** at the Hyatt Regency Scottsdale Resort at Gainey Ranch (☎ **480/951-0022**) offers three decidedly different 9-hole courses: the Dunes, the Arroyo, and the Lakes courses, each with its own set of challenges.

The area's favorite public course is the **Papago Golf Course** (☎ **602/275-8428**), which has a killer 17th hole. The semiprivate **Troon North Golf Club** (☎ **480/585-5300**), a course that seems only barely carved out of raw desert, garners the most local accolades. If you want to swing where the pros do, beg, borrow, or steal a tee time on the Stadium Course at the **Tournament Players Club of Scottsdale** (☎ **480/585-3600**). **The Superstition Springs Golf Club** (☎ **480/962-GOLF**) is another popular course and also a PGA Tour qualifying site.

With nearly 40 courses, Tucson has been giving the Valley of the Sun some golf competition in recent years. Among the city's resort courses, the Mountain Course at the **Ventana Canyon Golf and Racquet Club** (☎ **520/577-1400**) is legendary and has been ranked among Arizona's top 10 by *Golf Digest*. A spectacular 107-yard par-3 hole here is the most talked-about hole in the city. If you want to play where the pros play, book a room at the **Omni Tucson National Golf Resort and Spa** (☎ **520/575-7540**), home of the Tucson Open. The eighth hole at the Sunrise Course of the **El Conquistador Country Club** (☎ **520/544-1800**) has been rated the toughest par 3 in Tucson.

Of Tucson's public courses, **Randolph North** (☎ **520/325-2811**) gets the nod for best municipal course and is the site of an annual LPGA tournament. The **Silverbell Municipal Course** (☎ **520/743-7284**) boasts a bear of a par-5 17th hole. For a little history with your fairways, try the **Starr Pass Golf Club** (☎ **520/670-0400**). The 15th hole here plays through a narrow pass once used by stagecoaches.

Courses worth trying in other parts of the state include the 18-hole course at **Rancho de los Caballeros** (☎ **520/684-2704**), a luxury ranch resort outside Wickenburg. *Golf Digest* has rated its course one of Arizona's top 10. For concentration-taxing scenery, there are few courses that compare with the **Sedona Golf Resort** (☎ **520/284-9355**), which is surrounded by red-rock cliffs; try it at sunset. In mile-high Prescott, the **Antelope Hills Golf Club** (☎ **520/776-7888**) offers two 18-hole courses that provide a respite from the summer heat in the lowlands. Even higher and cooler in summer, the **Alpine Country Club** (☎ **520/339-4944**) offers golfing among the pine trees of the White Mountains. South of Tucson near Nogales, the **Rio Rico Resort and Country Club** (☎ **520/281-8567**) offers a challenging back nine as well as cooler temperatures and lower greens fees than you'll find in Tucson. Over along the Colorado River, there are a couple of memorable courses. Lake Havasu City's **London Bridge Golf Club** (☎ **520/855-2719**) offers a view of, you guessed it, the London Bridge. For more dramatic, though far less famous, views check out the **Emerald Canyon Golf Course** (☎ **520/667-3366**), a municipal course that plays up and down small canyons and offers the sort of scenery usually only associated with the most expensive desert resort courses.

*One last tip:* If your ball should happen to land in the coils of a rattlesnake, consider it lost and take your penalty. Rattlesnakes make lousy tees.

Guided backpack trips of various durations and levels of difficulty are offered by the **Grand Canyon Field Institute,** P.O. Box 399, Grand Canyon, AZ 86023 (☎ 520/638-2485; www.thecanyon.com/fieldinstitute). **Backroads,** 801 Cedar St., Berkeley, CA 94710-1800 (☎ **800/462-2848** or 510/527-1555), better known for its bike trips, also offers a 6-day walking/hiking trip in Arizona. **Wilderness Adventures,** 4211 E. Elwood St., Suite 1, Phoenix, AZ 85040 (☎ **602/438-1800;** www.wildernessadventures.com), which specializes in team building and rock climbing, has a variety of guided backpacking trips including trips along various sections of the Arizona Trail and a trip down into Havasu Canyon. This company also offers trips exploring some little-known Arizona canyons. These trips combine hiking and rock climbing.

**HORSEBACK RIDING/WESTERN ADVENTURES**    All over Arizona there are stables where you can saddle up for short rides. Among the more scenic spots for riding are the Grand Canyon, Monument Valley Navajo Tribal Park, Canyon de Chelly National Monument, the red-rock country around Sedona, Phoenix's South Mountain Park, at the foot of the Superstition Mountains east of Phoenix, and at the foot of the Santa Catalina Mountains outside Tucson. See the individual chapters for listings of riding stables; see below for information on overnight guided horseback rides.

Among the most popular guided adventures in Arizona are the mule rides down into the Grand Canyon. These trips vary in length from 1 to 3 days; for reservations and more information, call **Amfac Parks & Resorts** (☎ **303/297-2757**). Be advised, however, that you'll need to make mule ride reservations many months in advance. If at the last minute (5 days or less from the day you want to ride) you decide you want to go on a mule trip into the Grand Canyon, contact **Grand Canyon National Park Lodges** (☎ **520/638-2631**), on the off chance that there may be space available.

It's also possible to do overnight horseback rides and cattle drives. For more information, contact **Don Donnelly Stables,** 6010 Kings Ranch Rd., Gold Canyon (☎ **800/346-4403** or 480/982-7822), which does overnight horseback trips in Monument Valley, the White Mountains, and the Superstition Mountains, among other places; **Arizona Trail Tours** (☎ **520/394-2701**), which offers a 4-day trip through Coronado National Forest in southern Arizona; or **Rocky Mountain Cattle Moovers** (☎ **800/826-9666**), which does day-long cattle drives.

**HOT-AIR BALLOONING**    For much of the year the desert provides the perfect environment for hot-air ballooning—cool, still air and wide-open spaces. Consequently, there are dozens of hot-air balloon companies operating across the state. Most are found in the Phoenix and Tucson areas, but several others operate near Sedona, which is by far the most picturesque spot in the state for a balloon ride. See the individual chapters for specific information.

**HOUSEBOATING**    With the Colorado River turned into a long string of lakes, houseboat vacations are a natural in Arizona. Though this doesn't have to be an active vacation, fishing, hiking, and swimming are usually part of a houseboat stay. Rentals are available on Lake Powell, Lake Mead, Lake Mohave, and Lake Havasu. However, the canyon lands scenery of Lake Powell makes it the hands-down best spot for a houseboat vacation—reserve well in advance for a summer trip. No prior experience (or license) is necessary, and plenty of hands-on instruction is provided before you leave the marina. See chapters 7 and 11 for more information on houseboat rentals.

**SKIING**    Although Arizona is better known as a desert state, it does have plenty of mountains and even a few ski areas. The two biggest and most popular ski areas are **Arizona Snowbowl** (☎ **520/779-1951**) outside Flagstaff and **Sunrise Park** (☎ **520/735-7518** or 520/735-7600) on the Apache Reservation outside the town of McNary

# The Arizona Trail

While it sounds as though it could have been a movie starring John Wayne, the Arizona Trail is actually an ambitious plan to build a border-to-border trail across the state of Arizona from Utah to Mexico. The trail, which will be 790 miles long and link many existing trails, will be open for nonmotorized travel only. Hikers, mountain bikers, horseback riders, and cross-country skiers will all be able to enjoy various sections of the trail, which will at times cross through designated wilderness areas (closed to mountain bikes).

Connecting alpine meadows and desert arroyos, free-flowing rivers and man-made reservoirs, ponderosa pine forests and stands of saguaros, the 750-mile-long trail will cross through the seven life zones and many landscapes that comprise Arizona. As it meanders across the state, the trail will take in some of the most spectacular scenery in the Southwest, including the Grand Canyon, the San Francisco Peaks, the Mogollon Rim, and the Santa Catalina Mountains. The Arizona Trail Association's goal is to complete the Trail by the year 2000; for more information, contact the **Arizona Trail Association,** P.O. Box 36736, Phoenix, AZ 85067 (☎ **602/252-4794;** www.primenet.com/~aztrail).

in the White Mountains. Snowbowl is the more popular because of the ease of the drive from Phoenix and its proximity to good lodging and dining options in Flagstaff. Although Arizona Snowbowl has more vertical feet of skiing, Sunrise offers almost twice as many runs and the same snow conditions. Both of these ski areas offer ski rentals and lessons. When it's a good snow year, Tucsonians head up to **Mount Lemmon Ski Valley** (☎ **520/576-1321**), the southernmost ski area in the United States. Snows here aren't as reliable as they are farther north.

Cross-country skiers will find plenty of snow-covered forest roads to ski around Flagstaff (there's a Nordic center at Arizona Snowbowl), Sunrise Park outside the town of McNary, at the South Rim of the Grand Canyon, in the White Mountains around Greer and Alpine, outside Payson on the Mogollon Rim, and on Mount Lemmon outside Flagstaff.

**TENNIS**   Resorts all over Arizona have tennis courts; after golf, this is the most popular winter sport in the desert. Many resorts require you to wear traditional tennis attire and don't include court time in the room rates. Although there may be better courts in the state, none can match the views you'll have from the courts at Enchantment Resort outside Sedona. Just don't let the scenery ruin your game.

**WHITE-WATER RAFTING**   The desert doesn't support a lot of roaring rivers, but with the white water in the Grand Canyon you don't need too many other choices. Rafting the Grand Canyon is the dream of nearly every white-water enthusiast, and if rafting the canyon is one of your dreams, plan ahead. Companies and trips are limited, and they tend to fill up early. For a discussion and list of companies that run trips down the canyon, see chapter 6.

For 1- and 2-day trips on the Colorado below the Grand Canyon, contact **Hualapai River Runners,** P.O. Box 246, Peach Springs, AZ 86434 (☎ **800/622-4409** or 520/769-2210). These trips actually cover the same distance; you just take it slower on the overnight trip and spend the night camped by the river. For a half- or full-day float on the Colorado above the Grand Canyon, contact **Wilderness River Adventures,** P.O. Box 717, Page, AZ 86040 (☎ **800/992-8022** or 520/645-3279), which runs trips from the Glen Canyon Dam to Lees Ferry.

Daylong and multiday rafting trips are also available on the upper Salt River east of Phoenix. **Sun Country Rafting** (☎ **800/2-PADDLE** or 602/493-9011), **Far Flung Adventures** (☎ **800/231-7238** or 520/425-7272), and **Mild to Wild Rafting** (☎ **800/567-6745**) all run trips of varying lengths down this river (conditions permitting).

## 5 Educational & Volunteer Vacations

A number of opportunities exist in Arizona for those wishing to combine a vacation with an educational or volunteer experience.

If you'd like to turn a trip to the Grand Canyon into an educational vacation, contact the **Grand Canyon Field Institute,** P.O. Box 399, Grand Canyon, AZ 86023 (☎ **520/638-2485**), which offers a variety of programs from rim-based day hikes to backpacking to indoor classes. Programs are offered from early spring to late fall and include photography and drawing classes, backpacking trips for women, a llama trek, birding trips, and plenty of guided hikes and backpacking trips with a natural history or ecological slant.

Learning Expeditions, a program run by the **Arizona State Museum,** offers scholar-led archaeological tours, including a trip to Navajo and Hopi country, a tour to the Sonoran Desert (including northern Mexico), and a tour which retraces the footsteps of the Spanish explorers. For more information, call the marketing department at Arizona State Museum (☎ **520/626-8381;** w3.arizona.edu/~asm), P.O. Box 210026, Tucson, AZ 85721. The **Museum of Northern Arizona** offers educational backpacking, river rafting, and van tours primarily in the Colorado Plateau in Northern Arizona in a program called Ventures. Trips range in length from several days to more than a week. For details, contact the Museum of Northern Arizona, 3101 N. Fort Valley Rd., Flagstaff, AZ 86001 (☎ **520/774-5213;** www.musnaz.org).

**The Nature Conservancy,** 300 E. University Blvd., Suite 230, Tucson, AZ 85705 (☎ **520/622-3861;** www.tnc.org), is a nonprofit organization dedicated to the global preservation of natural diversity. The Conservancy accomplishes this goal by identifying and purchasing land that is home to rare plants, animals, and natural communities. The organization has several preserves in Arizona, seven of which are open to the public for hiking, bird watching, and nature study and to which they operate educational field trips of 1 to 4 days. Trips are listed in the Conservancy's Arizona chapter newsletter; information about overnight accommodations, trips, and membership ($25 annually) is also available by phone.

If you enjoy the wilderness and want to get more involved in its preservation, consider a Sierra Club Service Trip. These trips are for the purpose of building, restoring, and maintaining hiking trails in wilderness areas. It's a lot of work, but a lot of fun as well. For more information on Sierra Club trips, contact the **Sierra Club Outing Department,** 85 Second St., Second Floor, San Francisco, CA 94105 (☎ **415/977-5630**). The Sierra Club also offers hiking, camping, and other sorts of adventure trips to various destinations in Arizona.

You can also join a work crew organized by the **Arizona Trail Association** (☎ **602/252-4794;** www.primenet.com/~aztrail). These crews spend 1 to 2 days building and maintaining various stretches of the Arizona Trail, which will eventually stretch from the Utah state line to the Mexico border.

Another sort of service trip is being offered by the National Park Service. It accepts volunteers to pick up garbage left by thoughtless visitors to Glen Canyon National Recreation Area. In exchange for picking up trash, you'll get to spend 5 days on a houseboat called the Trash Tracker, cruising through the gorgeous canyon lands of Lake Powell. Volunteers must be at least 18 years old and must provide their own food, sleeping bag, and transportation to the marina. For more information, contact **Glen Canyon National Recreation Area,** P.O. Box 1507, Page, AZ 86040 (☎ **520/608-6404**).

If you'd like to lend a hand at an archaeological dig, contact the **White Mountain Archaeological Center and Raven Site Ruin,** H.C. 30, Box 30, St. Johns, AZ 85936 (☎ **520/333-5857**), which is located near Springerville on the edge of the White Mountains.

Finally, if you are interested in architecture or the ecology of urban design, you may be interested in helping out on the continued construction of **Arcosanti,** the slow realization of architect Paolo Soleri's dream of a city that merges architecture and ecology. Located 70 miles north of Phoenix, Arcosanti offers 5-week learning-by-doing workshops. For an application, contact the Cosanti Foundation, Arcosanti, HC 74, Box 4136, Mayer, AZ 86333 (☎ **520/632-7135;** www.arcosanti.org).

## 6 Health & Insurance

**STAYING HEALTHY**   If you've never been to the desert before, you should be sure to prepare yourself for this harsh environment. No matter what time of year it is, the desert sun is strong and bright. Use sunscreen when you're outdoors—particularly if you're up in the mountains, where the altitude makes sunburn more likely. The bright sun also makes sunglasses a necessity.

Even if you don't feel hot in the desert, the dry air steals moisture from your body, so drink plenty of fluids. You may want to use a body lotion as well. Skin dries out quickly in the desert air.

It's not only the sun that makes the desert a harsh environment. There are poisonous creatures out there, too, but with a little common sense and some precautions you can avoid them. Rattlesnakes are very common in the desert, but your chances of meeting one are slight (except during the mating season in April and May) because they tend not to come out in the heat of the day. However, never stick your hand into holes among the rocks in the desert and look to see where you're going to step before putting your foot down.

Arizona also has a large poisonous lizard called the Gila monster. These black-and-orange lizards are far less common than rattlesnakes, and your chances of meeting one are slight.

Although the tarantula has developed a nasty reputation, the tiny black widow is more likely to cause illness. Scorpions are another insect danger of the desert. Be extra careful whenever turning over rocks or logs that might harbor either black widows or scorpions.

**INSURANCE**   Before going out and spending money on various sorts of travel insurance, check your existing policies to see if they'll cover you while you're traveling. Make sure your health insurance will cover you when you're away from home. Some credit and charge cards offer automatic flight insurance when you purchase an airline ticket with that card. These policies insure against death or dismemberment in the case of an airplane crash. Also, check your cards to see if any of them pick up the loss-damage waiver (LDW) when you rent a car. The LDW can run as much as $17 a day and can add 50% or more to the cost of renting a car. Check your automobile insurance policy; it, too, may cover the LDW. If you own a home or have renter's insurance, see if that policy covers off-premises theft and loss wherever it occurs. If you're traveling on a tour or have prepaid a large chunk of your travel expenses, you might want to ask your travel agent about trip-cancellation insurance.

If, after checking all your existing insurance policies, you decide that you need additional insurance, reputable issuers of travel insurance include **Travel Guard International,** 1145 Clark St., Stevens Point, WI 54481 (☎ **800/826-1300**) and **Travelex**

**Insurance Services,** P.O. Box 9408, Garden City, NY 11530-9408 (☎ **800/228-9792**). Both companies offer medical, baggage, trip cancellation or interruption insurance, and flight insurance against death or dismemberment.

## 7 Tips for Travelers with Special Needs

**FOR TRAVELERS WITH DISABILITIES**    When making airline reservations, always mention your disability. Airline policies differ regarding wheelchairs and Seeing Eye dogs. Most hotels now offer wheelchair-accessible accommodations, and some of the larger and more expensive resorts also offer TDD telephones and other amenities for the hearing and sight impaired.

*A World of Options,* a 658-page book of resources for disabled travelers, covers everything from biking trips to scuba outfitters. It costs $35 ($30 for members) and is available from **Mobility International USA,** P.O. Box 10767, Eugene, OR, 97440 (☎ **541/343-1284,** voice and TDD; www.miusa.org). Annual membership for Mobility International is $35, which includes their quarterly newsletter, *Over the Rainbow.*

Rick Crowder of the **Travelin' Talk Network,** P.O. Box 3534, Clarksville, TN 37043-3534 (☎ **931/552-6670** Monday through Friday between 1 and 5pm central time), organizes a network for travelers with disabilities. A directory listing a global electronic network of people and organizations that provide firsthand information about a chosen destination to travelers with disabilities is available for about $35.

Vision-impaired travelers should contact the **American Foundation for the Blind,** 11 Penn Plaza, Suite 300, New York, NY 10001 (☎ **800/232-5463**), for information on traveling with Seeing Eye dogs.

Many of the major car-rental companies now offer hand-controlled cars for drivers with disabilities. Avis can provide such a vehicle at any of its locations in the United States with 48-hour advance notice; Hertz requires between 24 and 72 hours of advance reservation at most of its locations. **Wheelchair Getaways** (☎ **888/824-7413** or 480/348-9219; www.blvd.com/wg.htm) rents specialized vans with wheelchair lifts and other features for travelers with disabilities in more than 100 cities across the United States.

Travelers with disabilities may also want to consider joining a tour that caters specifically to them. Both **Accessible Journeys** (☎ **800/TINGLES** or 610/521-0339), for slow walkers and wheelchair travelers, and **The Guided Tour** (☎ **215/782-1370**) offer excursions to the Tucson and the Phoenix areas. **Wilderness Inquiry** (☎ **800/728-0719** or 612/379-3858) offers trips to the Grand Canyon for persons of all abilities.

If you plan to visit many of Arizona's national parks or monuments, you can avail yourself of the **Golden Access Passport.** This lifetime pass is issued free to any U.S. citizen or permanent resident who has been medically certified as disabled or blind. The pass permits free entry into national parks and monuments.

**FOR GAY MEN & LESBIANS**    To get in touch with the Phoenix gay community, you can contact the **Gay and Lesbian Community Center,** 24 W. Camelback Rd., Suite C (☎ **602/265-7283**). At the community center and at gay bars around Phoenix, you can pick up various community publications, including *Echo* and *Heat Stroke.* **Wingspan,** Tucson's lesbian, gay, and bisexual community center, is at 300 E. Sixth St. (☎ **520/624-1779**). *Observer* (☎ **520/622-7176**) is a local Tucson gay newspaper available at Wingspan and Antigone Bookstore, located at 411 N. Fourth Ave. (☎ **520/792-3715**).

**FOR SENIORS**    When making airline reservations, always mention that you're a senior citizen—many airlines offer discounts. You should also carry some sort of photo

> **❷ Did You Know?**
>
> • Arizona has more mountainous regions than Switzerland (nearly 20,000 square miles) and more forestland than Minnesota (nearly 20,000,000 acres).
> • Arizona was the last territory in the continental United States to become a state.
> • The Grand Canyon is one of the seven natural wonders of the world.
> • The Hopi village of Oraibi is one of the two oldest continuously inhabited settlements in the United States (Acoma, New Mexico, is the other).
> • The Spanish were in Arizona a quarter century before St. Augustine, Florida, was founded and 70 years before the British founded Jamestown, Virginia.
> • The bolo tie is the official state neckwear of Arizona.
> • Arizonan Sandra Day O'Connor was the first woman appointed to the United States Supreme Court.

ID card (driver's license, passport, and so on) to avail yourself of senior-citizen discounts on attractions, hotels, motels, and public transportation, as well as one of the best deals in Arizona for senior citizens: the **Golden Age Passport,** which is available for $10 to U.S. citizens and permanent residents age 62 and older. This federal government pass allows lifetime entrance privileges at national parks and monuments. You can apply in person for this passport at a national park, national forest, or other location where it's honored, and you must show reasonable proof of age.

If you aren't a member of the **American Association of Retired Persons (AARP),** 601 E. St. NW, Washington, DC 20049 (☎ **800/424-3410** or 202/434-2277), you should consider joining. This association provides discounts for many lodgings, car rentals, airfares, and attractions throughout Arizona, although you can sometimes get a similar discount simply by showing your ID.

*The Mature Traveler,* a monthly 12-page newsletter on senior citizen travel is a valuable resource. It is available by subscription ($32 a year) from GEM Publishing Group, Box 50400, Reno, NV 89513-0400. GEM also publishes *The Book of Deals,* a collection of more than 1,000 senior discounts on airlines, lodging, tours, and attractions around the country; it's available for $9.95 by calling ☎ **800/ 460-6676.**

**Grand Circle Travel** is another of the literally hundreds of travel agencies specializing in vacations for seniors (347 Congress St., Suite 3A, Boston, MA 02210 (☎ **800/221-2610** or 617/350-7500). *But beware:* Many of them are of the tour-bus variety, with free trips thrown in for those who organize groups of 20 or more. Seniors seeking more independent travel should probably consult a regular travel agent. **SAGA International Holidays,** 222 Berkeley St., Boston, MA 02116 (☎ **800/343-0273**), offers inclusive tours and cruises for those 50 and older. SAGA also sponsors the more substantial "Road Scholar Tours" (☎ 800/621-2151), which are fun-loving but with an educational bent.

If you'd like to do a bit of studying on vacation in the company of like-minded older travelers, consider looking into **Elderhostel,** 75 Federal St., Boston, MA 02110-1941 (☎ **877/426-8056;** www.elderhostel.org).

Phoenix and the Valley of the Sun have long been popular with retirees. Over the years entire cities (such as Sun City) have developed for senior citizens. *Arizona Senior World Newspaper* (☎ **602/438-1566**) is a monthly newspaper with information relevant to senior citizens. You can find it in public libraries, restaurants, and Wal-Mart stores.

# 8  Getting There

## BY PLANE

Arizona is served by many airlines flying to both Phoenix and Tucson from around the United States. Dozens of car-rental companies are located both at Sky Harbor International Airport in Phoenix and at Tucson International Airport.

Phoenix and Tucson are both served by the following airlines: **America West** (☎ 800/235-9292), **American** (☎ 800/433-7300), **Continental** (☎ 800/525-0280), **Delta** (☎ 800/221-1212), **Northwest/KLM** (☎ 800/225-2525), **Southwest** (☎ 800/435-9792), and **United** (☎ 800/241-6522). The following airlines serve Phoenix but not Tucson: **Aero México** (☎ 800/237-6639), **Alaska Airlines** (☎ 800/426-0333), **Frontier Airlines** (☎ 800/432-1359), **TWA** (☎ 800/221-2000), and **US Airways** (☎ 800/428-4322).

**Consolidators,** also known as bucket shops, are a good place to find low fares. Consolidators buy seats in bulk from the airlines and then sell them back to the public at prices below even the airlines' discounted rates. Their small boxed ads usually run in the Sunday travel section of newspapers at the bottom of the page. Before you pay, however, ask for a confirmation number from the consolidator and then call the airline itself to confirm your seat. Be prepared to book your ticket with a different consolidator—there are many to choose from—if the airline can't confirm your reservation. Also be aware that bucket shop tickets are usually nonrefundable or rigged with stiff cancellation penalties, often as high as 50% to 75% of the ticket price. And when an airline runs a special deal, you won't always do better with a consolidator.

For discount and last-minute bookings, contact **McCord Consumer Direct** (☎ **800/FLY-ASAP** or 800/454-7700), which can often get you tickets at significantly less than full fare. **1-800-airfare** (www.1800airfare.com) was formerly owned by TWA but now offers the deepest discounts on many other airlines, and can sometimes provide a next-day ticket. There are also "rebators" such as **Travel Avenue** (☎ **800/333-3335** or 312/876-1116) and the **Smart Traveller** (☎ **800/448-3338** in the U.S., or 305/448-3338), which rebate part of their commissions to you.

## BY CAR

The distance to Phoenix from Los Angeles is approximately 369 miles; from San Francisco, 778 miles; from Albuquerque, 455 miles; from Salt Lake City, 660 miles; from Las Vegas, 287 miles; and from Santa Fe, 516 miles.

If you're planning to travel through northern Arizona anytime in the winter, carry chains.

## BY TRAIN

Flagstaff and Phoenix have **Amtrak** (☎ **800/872-7245** in the United States and Canada for information and reservations; www.amtrak.com) service from Los Angeles to the west and Albuquerque, Santa Fe, Kansas City, and Chicago to the east aboard the Southwest Chief. The Sunset Limited connects Orlando, New Orleans, Houston, San Antonio, El Paso, and Los Angeles with Tucson and Phoenix. The train stops in Flagstaff or Tucson, and passengers must take a shuttle bus to Phoenix. At press time, the fare from Los Angeles to Phoenix was $68 one-way and $136 round-trip. This trip, including shuttle bus, can take between 12 and 19 hours, depending on the schedule. Earlier bookings secure lower fares.

## PACKAGE TOURS

If you prefer to let someone else do all your travel preparations, then a package tour might be for you—whether you just want to lie by the pool at a resort for a week or see the whole state in 2 weeks. The best way to find out about package tours to Arizona is to visit a travel agent, who will likely have several booklets about different tours and airfare/hotel-room packages offered by different airlines.

**Gray Line of Phoenix,** P.O. Box 21126, Phoenix, AZ 85036 (☎ **800/732-0327** or 602/495-9100), offers Arizona excursions lasting from 1 to 3 days. Tours include the Grand Canyon by way of Sedona and Oak Creek Canyon.

**Maupintour,** 1421 Research Park Dr., Suite 300, Lawrence, KS 66049-3858 (☎ **800/255-4266** or 785/843-1211), one of the largest tour operators in the world, offers several Arizona itineraries that cover the Grand Canyon, the Four Corners region, Phoenix, and Scottsdale.

Smaller companies with similar tours include **Open Road Tours** (☎ **800/766-7117** or 602/997-6474), and **Silver Coach Tours** (☎ **800/607-3466** or 602/439-0337).

**SPECIALTY TOURS**  If you have an interest in the Native American cultures of Arizona, you may want to consider doing a tour with **Discovery Passages,** 1161 Elk Trail, Box 630, Prescott, AZ 86303 (☎ **520/717-0519**), which has tours that visit the Hopi, Navajo, Apache, Tohono O'odham, Hualapai, Yavapai, and Havasupai reservations. **Crossing Worlds,** P.O. Box 623, Sedona, AZ 86339 (☎ **800/350-2693** or 520/649-3060), also offers 1-day and multiday tours throughout the Four Corners region. Tours go to the Hopi mesas, as well as to backcountry ruins on the Navajo Reservation to view cliff dwellings and rock art.

**Canyon Calling Tours,** 215 Disney Lane, Sedona, AZ 86336 (☎ **800/664-8922** or 520/282-0916; www.canyoncalling.com), offers weeklong tours of the Four Corners region for women only. These tours visit Canyon de Chelly, Lake Powell, the Grand Canyon, and Havasu Canyon. The cost is $1,495 per person. They have recently added a 5-day southern Arizona tour and a Grand Canyon rafting trip.

If you'd like to add a tour into Mexico to your Arizona visit, contact **Ajo Stage Line,** 1041 Solana Rd., Ajo, AZ 85321 (☎ **800/942-1981** or 520/387-6467). Owner Will Nelson leads 1-day and multiday trips to the Gulf of California at Puerto Peñasco, to 17th-century missions in northern Mexico, and to the rugged El Pinacate region of the Sonoran Desert. Prices range from $60 to $395.

If you're an experienced motorcycle rider looking for a new way to tour Arizona and the Southwest, consider a guided motorcycle tour with **Ride-Away World Adventures** (☎ **480/488-0080;** www.rideaway.com), which offers tours of 1 to 10 days and can arrange motorcycle rentals as well. Some tours use the Phoenix/Scottsdale area as a base for extended day trips, while other tours head out across the state. Shorter tours are around $185 per day; prices vary on the 10-day tours from about $2,300 to $3,950. Motorcycle rentals run $65 to $175 per day.

## 9  Getting Around

### BY CAR

Because Phoenix and Tucson are major resort destinations, they both have dozens of **car-rental agencies.** Prices at rental agencies elsewhere in the state tend to be higher, so if at all possible, try to rent your car in either Phoenix or Tucson. Major rental-car companies with offices in Arizona include **Alamo** (☎ 800/327-9633), **Avis** (☎ 800/331-1212), **Budget** (☎ 800/527-0700), **Dollar** (☎ 800/800-4000), **Enterprise** (☎ 800/736-8222), **Hertz** (☎ 800/654-3131), **National** (☎ 800/227-7368), and **Thrifty** (☎ 800/367-2277).

Rates for rental cars vary considerably between companies and with the model you wish to rent, the dates you rent, and your pickup and drop-off points. If you call the same company three times and ask about renting the same model car, you may get three different quotes, depending on current availability of vehicles. It pays to start shopping early and ask lots of questions—rental agents don't always volunteer information about how to save, so you have to experiment with all the parameters. At press time, Budget was charging $194 per week for a compact car with unlimited mileage in Phoenix.

If you're a member of a frequent-flyer program, check to see which rental-car companies participate in your program. Also, when making a reservation, be sure to mention any discount you might be eligible for, such as corporate, military, or AAA, or any specials offered. Beware of coupons offering discounts on rental-car rates— these often discount the highest rates only. It's always cheaper to rent by the week, so even if you don't need a car for 7 days, you might find that it's still cheaper than renting for 4 days only.

Taxes on car rentals vary between 10% and 24% or more and are always at the high end at both the Phoenix and Tucson airports. You can save up to 10% (the airport concession fee recoupment charge) by renting your car at an office outside the airport. Be sure to ask about the tax and the loss-damage waiver (LDW) if you want to know what your total rental cost will be before making a reservation.

A right turn on a red light is permitted after a complete stop. Seat belts are required for the driver and for all passengers; children 4 years and younger, or who weigh 40 pounds or less, must be in a children's car seat. General speed limits are 25 to 35 m.p.h. in towns and cities, 15 m.p.h. in school zones, and 55 m.p.h. on two-lane highways, except rural interstate highways, where the speed limit ranges from 65 to 75 m.p.h.

Always be sure to keep your gas tank topped off. It's not unusual to drive 60 miles without seeing a gas station in many parts of Arizona.

A breakdown in the desert can be more than just an inconvenience—it can be dangerous. Always carry drinking water with you while driving through the desert, and if you plan to head off on back roads, it's a good idea to carry extra water for the car as well.

The best road maps of Arizona are produced by the American Automobile Association (you have to be a member to get these) and by *Arizona Highways* (☎ **800/ 543-5432**), a local magazine. Other maps are available from tourist information offices in Phoenix and Tucson. You can also pick up state road maps at almost any gas station.

## BY PLANE

Arizona is a big state (the sixth largest), so if your time is short, you might want to consider flying between cities. Several small commuter airlines offer service within the state. These include **America West Airlines** and **America West Express** (☎ 800/ 235-9292), **Mesa Airlines** (☎ 800/637-2247), **Sunrise Airlines** (☎ 800/347-3962 or 888/394-1851), **Skywest** (☎ 800/ 453-9417), and **United Express** (☎ 800/ 241-6522). Cities and towns served by these airlines include Phoenix, Tucson, Flagstaff, the Grand Canyon, Kingman, Prescott, Sedona, Show Low, Sierra Vista, Bullhead City, Lake Havasu City, Yuma, and Page.

## BY TRAIN

The train is not really a viable way of getting around much of Arizona because there is no north-south Amtrak train service between Grand Canyon/Flagstaff and Phoenix or Tucson and Phoenix. However, Amtrak will sell you a ticket to Phoenix, which includes a shuttle-bus ride from Flagstaff or Tucson. There's also an excursion train that runs from Williams (30 miles west of Flagstaff) to Grand Canyon Village at the South Rim of the Grand Canyon (see chapter 6 for details).

# Fast Facts: Arizona

**American Express**    There are offices or representatives in Phoenix, Tucson, Green Valley, Flagstaff, Sun City, Mesa, and Scottsdale. For more information, call American Express at ☎ **800/528-4800.**

**Banks & ATM Networks**    ATMs in Arizona generally use the following systems: Star, Cirrus, Plus, American Express, MasterCard, and Visa.

**Advance Reservations    Inn Arizona/Mi Casa-Su Casa Bed & Breakfast Reservation Service,** P.O. Box 950, Tempe, AZ 85280-0950 (☎ **800/456-0682** or 480/990-0682), is a reservation service that can book accommodations at more than 65 homes in the Valley of the Sun (as well as elsewhere in the state), as can **Arizona Trails Bed & Breakfast Reservation Service,** P.O. Box 18998, Fountain Hills, AZ 85269-8998 (☎ **888/799-4284** or 480/837-4284; fax 480/816-4224; www.arizonatrails.com), which also books tour and hotel reservations. The **Arizona Association of Bed and Breakfast Inns,** P.O. Box 22086, Flagstaff, AZ 86002 (☎ **800/284-2589;** www.bbonline.com/az/aabbi/index. html), is another organization representing B&Bs across the state. Contact it for a list of members.

**Business Hours**    The following are general open hours; specific establishments may vary. **Banks:** Monday through Friday from 9am to 5pm (some are also open on Saturday from 9am to noon). **Stores:** Monday through Saturday from 10am to 6pm and on Sunday from noon to 5pm (malls usually stay open until 9pm Monday through Saturday). **Bars:** Although they generally open around 11am, bars in Arizona are legally allowed to be open Monday through Saturday from 6am to 1am and on Sunday from 10am to 1am.

**Camera/Film**    Because the sun is almost always shining in Arizona, you can use a slower film—that is, one with a lower ASA number. This will give you sharper pictures. If your camera accepts different filters, and especially if you plan to travel in the higher altitudes of the northern part of the state, you'd do well to invest in a polarizer, which reduces contrast, deepens colors, and eliminates glare. Also, be sure to protect your camera and film from heat. Never leave your camera or film in a car parked in the sun—temperatures inside the car can climb to more than 130°F, which is hot enough to damage sensitive film.

**Car Rentals**    See "Getting Around," earlier in this chapter.

**Climate**    See "When to Go," earlier in this chapter.

**Driving Rules**    See "Getting Around," earlier in this chapter.

**Emergencies**    In most places in Arizona, ☎ **911** is the number to call in case of a fire, police, or medical emergency. A few small towns have not adopted this emergency phone number, so if 911 doesn't work, dial 0 (zero) for the operator and state the type of emergency.

**Information**    See "Visitor Information," in section 1 of this chapter, and individual city chapters and sections for local information offices.

**Legal Aid**    If you're in need of legal aid, first look in the White Pages of the local telephone book under Legal Aid. You may also want to contact the Travelers Aid Society. In Phoenix the phone number for Community Legal Services is ☎ **602/258-3434.** In Tucson the number for Southern Arizona Legal Aid is ☎ **800/234-7252** or 520/623-9465, and for Travelers Aid of Tucson it's ☎ **520/ 622-8900.**

**Liquor Laws**   The legal age for buying or consuming alcoholic beverages is 21. You cannot purchase any alcoholic drinks from 1 to 6am Monday through Saturday and from 1 to 10am on Sunday.

**Pets**   Many hotels and motels in Arizona accept pets, though sometimes a small fee is charged to allow the pet to stay in your room. Others don't allow pets at all, especially bed-and-breakfast inns. If you plan to travel with a pet, it's always best to check when making hotel reservations. At Grand Canyon Village, there's a kennel where you can board your pet while you hike down into the canyon.

**Police**   In most places in Arizona, phone ☎ **911.** A few small towns have not adopted this emergency phone number, so if 911 doesn't work, dial 0 (zero) for the operator and state the type of emergency.

**Safety**   When driving long distances, always carry plenty of drinking water, and if you're heading off onto dirt roads, extra water for your car's radiator is also a good idea. When hiking or walking in the desert, keep an eye out for rattlesnakes; these poisonous snakes are not normally aggressive unless provoked, so give them a wide berth and they'll leave you alone. Black widow spiders and scorpions are also desert denizens that can be dangerous, though the better-known tarantula is actually much less of a threat. If you go turning over rocks or logs, you're likely to encounter one of Arizona's poisonous residents.

**Taxes**   There's a state sales tax of 5.5% (local communities levy additional taxes), car-rental taxes ranging from around 10% to more than 20%, and hotel room taxes ranging from around 6% to around 14%.

**Time Zone**   Arizona is in the mountain time zone. However, the state does not observe daylight saving time, so time differences between Arizona and the rest of the country vary with the time of year. From the last Sunday in October until the first Sunday in April, Arizona is 1 hour later than the West Coast and 2 hours earlier than the East Coast. The rest of the year Arizona is on the same time as the West Coast and is 3 hours earlier than the East Coast. There is an exception, however—the Navajo Reservation observes daylight saving time. However, the Hopi Reservation, which is completely surrounded by the Navajo Reservation, does not.

**Weather**   For current weather information, call ☎ **602/265-5550.**

# For Foreign Visitors 3

The American West is well known and well loved in many countries. Arizona's images are familiar from Western novels, movies, television shows, and advertisements. And of course, the Grand Canyon is one of the wonders of the world. However, despite Arizona being the Wild West, you are likely to encounter typically American situations in Arizona, and this chapter should help you prepare for your trip.

## 1 Preparing for Your Trip

### ENTRY REQUIREMENTS

Immigration laws are a hot political issue in the United States these days, and the following requirements may have changed somewhat by the time you plan your trip. Check at any U.S. embassy or consulate for current information and requirements. You can also plug into the **U.S. State Department's** Internet site at **http://www.state.gov**.

**VISAS**  The U.S. State Department has a **Visa Waiver Pilot Program** allowing citizens of certain countries to enter the United States without a visa for stays of up to 90 days. At press time these included Andorra, Argentina, Australia, Austria, Belgium, Brunei, Denmark, Finland, France, Germany, Iceland, Ireland, Italy, Japan, Liechtenstein, Luxembourg, Monaco, the Netherlands, New Zealand, Norway, San Marino, Slovenia, Spain, Sweden, Switzerland, and the United Kingdom. Citizens of these countries need only a valid passport and a round-trip air or cruise ticket in their possession upon arrival. If they first enter the United States, they may also visit Mexico, Canada, Bermuda, and/or the Caribbean islands and return to the United States without a visa. Further information is available from any U.S. embassy or consulate. Canadian citizens may enter the United States without visas; they need only proof of residence.

Citizens of all other countries must have (1) a valid passport that expires at least 6 months later than the scheduled end of their visit to the United States, and (2) a tourist visa, which may be obtained without charge from any U.S. consulate.

**OBTAINING A VISA**  To obtain a visa, the traveler must submit a completed application form (either in person or by mail) with a 1½-inch-square photo, and must demonstrate binding ties to a residence abroad. Usually you can obtain a visa at once or within 24 hours, but it may take longer during the summer rush from June through August. If you cannot go in person, contact the nearest U.S. embassy or consulate for directions on applying by mail. Your travel agent or airline office may also be able to provide you with visa applications and instructions. The U.S. consulate or embassy that issues your visa will determine whether you will be issued a multiple- or single-entry visa and any restrictions regarding the length of your stay.

British subjects can obtain up-to-date passport and visa information by calling the **U.S. Embassy Visa Information Line** (☎ **0891/200-290**) or the **London Passport Office** (☎ **0990/210-410** for recorded information).

**MEDICAL REQUIREMENTS**  Unless you're arriving from an area known to be suffering from an epidemic (particularly cholera or yellow fever), inoculations or vaccinations are not required for entry into the United States. If you have a disease that requires treatment with narcotics or syringe-administered medications, carry a valid signed prescription from your physician to allay any suspicions that you may be smuggling narcotics (a serious offense that carries severe penalties in the U.S.).

For HIV-positive visitors, requirements for entering the United States are somewhat vague and change frequently. INS officials may keep out people whom they suspect are HIV-positive. For up-to-the-minute information concerning HIV-positive travelers, contact the Center for Disease Control's **National Center for HIV** (☎ **404/332-4559;** www.hivatis.org) or the **Gay Men's Health Crisis** (☎ **212/367-1000;** www.gmhc.org).

**DRIVER'S LICENSES**  Foreign driver's licenses are mostly recognized in the U.S., although you may want to get an international driver's license if your home license is not written in English.

**CUSTOMS REQUIREMENTS**  Every visitor over 21 years of age may bring in, free of duty, the following: (1) 1 liter of wine or hard liquor; (2) 200 cigarettes, 100 cigars (but not from Cuba), or 3 pounds of smoking tobacco; and (3) $100 worth of gifts. These exemptions are offered to travelers who spend at least 72 hours in the United States and who have not claimed them within the preceding 6 months. It is altogether forbidden to bring into the country foodstuffs (particularly fruit, cooked meats, and canned goods) and plants (vegetables, seeds, tropical plants, and the like). Foreign tourists may bring in or take out up to $10,000 in U.S. or foreign currency with no formalities; larger sums must be declared to U.S. Customs on entering or leaving, which includes filing form CM 4790. For more specific information regarding U.S. Customs, call your nearest U.S. embassy or consulate, or the **U.S. Customs** office at ☎ **202/927-1770** or www.customs.gov/travel/travel.htm.

## INSURANCE

Although it's not required of travelers, health insurance is highly recommended. Unlike many European countries, the United States does not usually offer free or low-cost medical care to its citizens or visitors. Doctors and hospitals are expensive, and in most cases will require advance payment or proof of coverage before they render their services. Other policies can cover everything from the loss or theft of your baggage and trip cancellation to the guarantee of bail in case you're arrested. Good policies will also cover the costs of an accident, repatriation, or death. See "Health & Insurance" in chapter 2 for more information. Packages such as **Europ Assistance** in Europe are sold by automobile clubs and travel agencies at attractive rates. **Worldwide Assistance Services** (☎ **800/821-2828**) is the agent for Europ Assistance in the United States.

Though lack of health insurance may prevent you from being admitted to a hospital in nonemergencies, don't worry about being left on a street corner to die: The American way is to fix you now and bill the living daylights out of you later.

# MONEY

**CURRENCY**   The U.S. monetary system has a decimal base: one American **dollar** ($1) = 100 **cents** (100¢).

Dollar bills commonly come in $1 (a "buck"), $5, $10, $20, $50, and $100 denominations (the last two are not welcome when paying for small purchases and are not accepted in taxis). There are also $2 bills (seldom encountered). Note that a newly redesigned $100 and $50 bill were introduced in 1996, and a redesigned $20 bill in 1998. Expect to see redesigned $10 and $5 notes in the year 2000. Despite rumors to the contrary, the old-style bills are still legal tender.

There are six denominations of coins: 1¢ (1 cent, or a "penny"), 5¢ (5 cents, or a "nickel"), 10¢ (10 cents, or a "dime"), 25¢ (25 cents, or a "quarter"), 50¢ (50 cents, or a "half dollar"), and, prized by collectors, the rare $1 piece (the older, large silver dollar and the newer, small Susan B. Anthony coin). A new gold $1 piece will be introduced by the year 2000. Note that U.S. coins are not stamped with their numeric value.

The foreign-exchange bureaus so common in Europe are rare even at airports in the United States, and nonexistent outside major cities. Try to avoid having to change foreign money or traveler's checks not denominated in U.S. dollars at a small-town bank, or even a branch bank in a big city. In fact, leave any currency other than U.S. dollars at home—it may prove more nuisance to you than it's worth.

**TRAVELER'S CHECKS**   Traveler's checks *denominated in U.S. dollars* are readily accepted at most hotels, motels, restaurants, and large stores, but may not be accepted at small stores or for small purchases. The best place to change traveler's checks is at a bank. Do not bring traveler's checks denominated in other currencies. The three traveler's checks that are most widely recognized are **Visa, American Express,** and **Thomas Cook.**

**CREDIT CARDS & ATMs**   Credit cards are the most widely used form of payment in the United States: **Visa** (BarclayCard in Britain), **MasterCard** (Eurocard in Europe, Access in Britain, Chargex in Canada), **American Express, Diners Club, Discover,** and **Carte Blanche.** You must have a credit or charge card to rent a car. There are, however, a handful of stores and restaurants that do not take credit cards, so be sure to ask in advance. Most businesses display a sticker near their entrance to let you know which cards they accept. (Note: Often businesses require a minimum purchase price, usually around $10, to use a credit card.)

It is strongly recommended that you bring at least one major credit card. Hotels, car-rental companies, and airlines usually require a credit-card imprint as a deposit against expenses, and in an emergency a credit card can be priceless.

You'll find automated-teller machines (ATMs) on just about every block in larger cities. Some ATMs will allow you to draw U.S. currency against your bank and credit cards. Check with your bank before leaving home, and remember that you will need your personal identification number (PIN) to do so. Most accept Visa, MasterCard, and American Express, as well as ATM cards from other U.S. banks. Expect to be charged up to $3 per transaction, however. One way around these fees is to ask for cash back at grocery stores that accept ATM cards and don't charge usage fees. Of course, you'll have to purchase something first.

**Travel Tip**

Be sure to keep a copy of all your travel papers separate from your wallet or purse, and leave a copy with someone at home should you need it faxed in an emergency.

# SAFETY

**GENERAL SAFETY SUGGESTIONS**   While tourist areas are generally safe, crime is on the increase everywhere, and U.S. urban areas tend to be less safe than those in Europe or Japan. You should always stay alert. This is particularly true of large U.S. cities. It is wise to ask your hotel front desk staff or the city or area's tourist office if you're in doubt about which neighborhoods are safe.

Avoid deserted areas, especially at night, and don't go into public parks at night unless there's a concert or similar occasion that will attract a crowd.

Avoid carrying valuables with you on the street, and don't display expensive cameras or electronic equipment. If you are using a map, consult it inconspicuously—or better yet, try to study it before you leave your room. Hold onto your pocketbook, and place your billfold in an inside pocket. In theaters, restaurants, and other public places, keep your possessions in sight.

Remember also that hotels are open to the public, and in a large hotel, security may not be able to screen everyone entering. Always lock your room door—don't assume that once inside your hotel you are automatically safe and no longer need to be aware of your surroundings.

**DRIVING**   Safety while driving is particularly important. Ask your rental agency about personal safety or request a brochure of traveler safety tips when you pick up your car. Obtain written directions, or a map with the route marked in red from the agency, to show you how to get to your destination. If possible, arrive and depart during daylight hours.

Recently more and more crime has involved cars and drivers. If you drive off a highway into a doubtful-looking neighborhood, leave the area as quickly as possible. If you have an accident, even on the highway, stay in your car with the doors locked until you assess the situation or until the police arrive. If you are bumped from behind on the street or are involved in a minor accident with no injuries, and the situation appears to be suspicious, motion to the other driver to follow you to the nearest police precinct, gas station, or open store. *Never* get out of your car in such situations.

Park in well-lit, well-traveled areas if possible. Always keep your car doors locked, whether the vehicle is attended or unattended. Look around you before you get out of your car and never leave any packages or valuables in sight. If someone attempts to rob you or steal your car, do *not* try to resist the thief/carjacker—report the incident to the police department immediately by calling ☎ **911.**

Also, make sure that you have enough gasoline in your tank to reach your intended destination, so that you're not forced to look for a service station in an unfamiliar and possibly unsafe neighborhood—especially at night.

## 2  Getting to the U.S.

Airlines with direct or connecting service from London to Phoenix (along with their phone numbers in Great Britain) include **American** (☎ 0345/567-567; www. americanair.com), **British Airways** (☎ 0345/222-111; www.british-airways.com), **Continental** (☎ 0800/776-464; www.flycontinental.com), **Delta** (☎ 0800/414-767; www.delta-air.com), **Northwest/KLM** (☎ 0990/56-1000; www.nwa.com), **TWA** (☎ 0181/814-0707 in London, or 0800/221-2000; www.twa.com), **United** (☎ 0181/990-9900 in London, or 0800/888-555 outside London; www.ual.com), and **US Airways** (☎ 0800/783-5556; www.usairways.com). All of these airlines except British Airways, TWA, and US Airways also fly into Tucson.

From Canada there are flights to Phoenix from Toronto on **Air Canada** (☎ 800/ AIR-CANADA; www.aircanada.ca), **American** (☎ 800/433-7300; www.americanair. com), **Delta** (☎ 800/221-1212; www.delta-air.com), **Northwest** (☎ 800/225-2525; www.nwa.com), **United** (☎ 800/241-6522; www.ual.com), and **US Airways** (☎ 800/ 428-4322; usairways.com) and from Vancouver on **Alaska Airlines** (☎ 800/426-0333; www.alaskaair.com), **America West** (☎ 800/235-9292; www.americawest.com) and **Northwest.**

There are flights to Tucson from Toronto on **American, Continental** (☎ 800/ 231-0856; www.flycontinental.com), **Delta, Northwest,** and **United,** and from Vancouver on **American, America West,** and **Delta.**

From New Zealand and Australia, there are flights to Los Angeles on **Qantas** (☎ 13 13 13; www.qantas.com.au) and **Air New Zealand** (☎ 0800/737-000 in Auckland; www.airnewzealand.co.nz). Continue on to Phoenix or Tucson on a regional airline such as **America West** (☎ 800/235-9292; www.americawest.com) or **Southwest** (☎ 800/435-9792; www.southwest.com). If you're heading to the Grand Canyon, it's easier to take a flight from Los Angeles to Las Vegas.

**AIRLINE DISCOUNTS** Travelers from overseas can take advantage of the **advance-purchase excursion (APEX)** fares offered by the major U.S. and European carriers. For more money-saving airline advice, see "Getting There," in chapter 2.

**IMMIGRATION & CUSTOMS CLEARANCE** The visitor arriving by air, no matter what the port of entry, should cultivate patience before setting foot on U.S. soil. Getting through Immigration Control may take as long as 2 hours on some days, especially summer weekends. Add the time it takes to clear Customs, and you'll see that you should make a very generous allowance for delay in planning connections between international and domestic flights—an average of 2 to 3 hours at least.

In contrast, travelers arriving by car or by rail from Canada will find border-crossing formalities streamlined practically to the vanishing point. And air travelers from Canada, Bermuda, and some places in the Caribbean can sometimes go through Customs and Immigration at the point of departure, which is much quicker.

## 3 Getting Around the U.S.

For specific information on traveling to and around Arizona, see "Getting There" and "Getting Around" in chapter 2.

**BY PLANE** Some large airlines (for example, Northwest and Delta) offer travelers on their transatlantic or transpacific flights special discount tickets under the name **Visit USA,** allowing mostly one-way travel from one U.S. destination to another at very low prices. These discount tickets are not on sale in the United States and must be purchased abroad in conjunction with your international ticket. This system is the best, easiest, and fastest way to see the United States at low cost. You should obtain information well in advance from your travel agent or the office of the airline concerned, since the conditions attached to these discount tickets can be changed without advance notice.

**BY CAR** The United States is a car culture through and through. Driving is the most cost-effective, convenient, and comfortable way to travel through the West. The interstate highway system connects cities and towns all over the country, and in addition to these high-speed, limited-access roadways, there's an extensive network of federal, state, and local highways and roads. Driving will give you a lot of flexibility in making, and altering, your itinerary and in allowing you to see some off-the-beaten-path destinations that cannot be reached easily by public transportation. You'll also have easy access to inexpensive motels at interstate highway off-ramps.

**BY TRAIN**   International visitors can also buy a **USA Railpass,** good for 15 or 30 days of unlimited travel on **Amtrak** (☎ **800/USA-RAIL**). The pass is available through many foreign travel agents. Prices in 1999 for a 15-day pass are $285 off-peak, $425 peak; a 30-day pass costs $375 off-peak, $535 peak. (With a foreign passport, you can also buy passes at some Amtrak offices in the United States, including locations in San Francisco, Los Angeles, Chicago, New York, Miami, Boston, and Washington, D.C.) Reservations are generally required and should be made for each part of your trip as early as possible. Amtrak also offers an **Air/Rail Travel Plan** that allows you to travel both by train and plane; for information call ☎ **800/440-8202.**

**BY BUS**   Although bus travel is often the most economical form of public transit for short hops between U.S. cities, it can also be slow and uncomfortable—certainly not an option for everyone (particularly when Amtrak, which is far more luxurious, offers similar rates). **Greyhound/Trailways** (☎ **800/231-2222**), the sole nationwide bus line, offers an **Ameripass** for unlimited travel for 7 days at $199, 15 days at $299, 30 days at $409, and 60 days at $599. Passes must be purchased at a Greyhound terminal. Special rates are available for senior citizens and students.

## Fast Facts: For the Foreign Traveler

**Automobile Organizations**   Auto clubs will supply maps, suggested routes, guidebooks, accident and bail-bond insurance, and emergency road service. The **American Automobile Association (AAA)** is the major auto club in the United States. If you belong to an auto club in your home country, inquire about AAA reciprocity before you leave. You may be able to join AAA even if you're not a member of a reciprocal club; to inquire, call **AAA** (☎ **800/222-4357**). AAA is actually an organization of regional auto clubs; so look under "AAA Automobile Club" in the White Pages of the telephone directory. AAA has a nationwide **emergency road service** telephone number (☎ **800/AAA-HELP**).

**Business Hours**   The following are general open hours; specific establishments may vary. **Banks:** Monday through Friday from 9am to 5pm (some are also open on Saturday from 9am to noon); there's usually 24-hour access to ATMs at most banks and other outlets. **Stores:** Monday through Saturday from 10am to 6pm and on Sunday from noon to 5pm (malls usually stay open until 9pm Monday through Saturday). **Bars:** Although they generally open around 11am, bars in Arizona are legally allowed to be open Monday through Saturday from 6am to 1am and on Sunday from 10am to 1am.

**Climate**   See "When to Go" in chapter 2.

**Currency**   See "Money" under "Preparing for Your Trip," earlier in this chapter.

**Currency Exchange**   You'll find currency-exchange services in major international airports. There's a **Thomas Cook** office (☎ **800/287-7362**) at Sky Harbor Airport in Phoenix, but not at Tucson International Airport. Elsewhere, they may be quite difficult to come by. In Phoenix the following banks exchange money: **Norwest Bank,** 3717 Third Ave. (☎ **602/248-1251**), or **Bank of America,** 101 N. First Ave. (☎ **602/597-5000**).

**Drinking Laws**   The legal age for purchase and consumption of alcoholic beverages is 21; proof of age is required and often requested at bars, nightclubs, and restaurants, so it's always a good idea to bring ID when you go out. Beer and wine can often be purchased in supermarkets, but liquor laws vary from state to state.

Do not carry open containers of alcohol in your car or any public area that isn't zoned for alcohol consumption. The police can, and probably will, fine you on the spot. And nothing will ruin your trip faster than getting a citation for DUI ("driving under the influence"), so don't even think about driving while intoxicated.

**Electricity**    Like Canada, the United States uses 110 to 120 volts AC (60 cycles), compared to 220 to 240 volts AC (50 cycles) in most of Europe, Australia, and New Zealand. If your small appliances use 220 to 240 volts, you'll need a 110-volt transformer and a plug adapter with two flat parallel pins to operate them here. Downward converters that change 220 to 240 volts to 110 to 120 volts are difficult to find in the United States, so bring one with you.

**Embassies & Consulates**    All embassies are located in the nation's capital, Washington, D.C. Some consulates are located in major U.S. cities, and most nations have a mission to the United Nations in New York City. If your country isn't listed below, call for **directory information** in Washington, D.C. (☎ **202/555-1212**) for the number of your national embassy.

The embassy of **Australia** is at 1601 Massachusetts Ave. NW, Washington, DC 20036 (☎ **202/797-3000;** www.austemb.org). There is no consulate in Arizona; the nearest is at Century Plaza Towers, 19th Floor, 2049 Century Park East, Los Angeles, CA 90067 (☎ **310/229-4800**). There are also consulates in New York, Honolulu, Houston, and San Francisco.

The embassy of **Canada** is at 501 Pennsylvania Ave. NW, Washington, DC 20001 (☎ **202/682-1740;** www.cdnemb-washdc.org). There is no consulate in Arizona; the nearest is at 550 S. Hope St., 9th Floor, Los Angeles, CA 90071 (☎ **213/346-2700**). Other Canadian consulates are in Buffalo (NY), Detroit, New York, and Seattle.

The embassy of **Ireland** is at 2234 Massachusetts Ave. NW, Washington, DC 20008 (☎ **202/462-3939**). There is no consulate in Arizona; the nearest is at 44 Montgomery St., Suite 3830, San Francisco, CA 94104 (☎ **415/392-4214**). Other Irish consulates are in Boston, Chicago, and New York.

The embassy of **New Zealand** is at 37 Observatory Circle NW, Washington, DC 20008 (☎ **202/328-4800;** www.nzemb.org). There is no consulate in Arizona; the nearest is in Los Angeles at 12400 Wilshire Blvd., Suite 1150, Los Angeles, CA 90025 (☎ **310/207-1605**). Other New Zealand consulates are in Salt Lake City, San Francisco, and Seattle.

The embassy of the **United Kingdom** is at 3100 Massachusetts Ave. NW, Washington, DC 20008 (☎ **202/462-1340**). There is no consulate in Arizona; the nearest is in Los Angeles at 11766 Wilshire Blvd., Suite 400, Los Angeles, CA 90025 (☎ **310/477-3322**). Other British consulates are in Atlanta, Boston, Chicago, Cleveland, Houston, New York, San Francisco, and Seattle.

**Emergencies**    Call ☎ **911** to report a fire, call the police, or get an ambulance. This is a toll-free call (no coins are required at a public telephone).

If you encounter problems, check the local telephone directory to find an office of the **Traveler's Aid Society,** a nationwide nonprofit social-service organization geared to helping travelers in difficult straits. The society's services might include reuniting families separated while traveling, providing food and/or shelter to people stranded without cash, or even emotional counseling. If you're in trouble, seek it out.

**Gasoline (Petrol)**    Petrol is known as gasoline (or simply "gas") in the United States, and petrol stations are known as both gas stations and service stations.

Gasoline costs less here than it does in Europe, and taxes are already included in the printed price. One U.S. gallon equals 3.8 liters or .85 Imperial gallons.

**Holidays**　Banks, government offices, post offices, and many stores, restaurants, and museums are closed on the following legal national holidays: January 1 (New Year's Day), the third Monday in January (Martin Luther King, Jr. Day), the third Monday in February (Presidents' Day, Washington's Birthday), the last Monday in May (Memorial Day), July 4 (Independence Day), the first Monday in September (Labor Day), the second Monday in October (Columbus Day), November 11 (Veterans' Day/Armistice Day), the fourth Thursday in November (Thanksgiving Day), and December 25 (Christmas). Also, the Tuesday following the first Monday in November is Election Day and is a federal government holiday in presidential-election years (held every four years, and next in 2000).

**Legal Aid**　The foreign tourist will probably never become involved with the American legal system. If you are "pulled over" for a minor infraction (for example, of the highway code, such as speeding), never attempt to pay the fine directly to a police officer; this could be construed as attempted bribery, a much more serious crime. Pay fines by mail, or directly into the hands of the clerk of the court. If accused of a more serious offense, say and do nothing before consulting a lawyer. Here the burden is on the state to prove a person's guilt beyond a reasonable doubt, and everyone has the right to remain silent, whether he or she is suspected of a crime or actually arrested. Once arrested, a person can make one telephone call to a party of his or her choice. Call your embassy or consulate.

**Mail**　If you aren't sure what your address will be in the United States, mail can be sent to you, in your name, c/o General Delivery at the main post office of the city or region where you expect to be (call ☎ **800/275-8777** for information on the nearest post office). The addressee must pick mail up in person and must produce proof of identity (driver's license, passport, etc.). Most post offices will hold your mail for up to 1 month, and many post offices are open Monday to Friday from 8am to 5pm, and Saturday from 9am to 3pm.

Generally found at intersections, mailboxes are blue with a red-and-white stripe and carry the inscription U.S. MAIL. If your mail is addressed to a U.S. destination, don't forget to add the five-digit postal code (or ZIP code), after the two-letter abbreviation of the state to which the mail is addressed.

At press time domestic postage rates were 20¢ for a postcard and 33¢ for a letter. For international mail, a first-class letter of up to one-half ounce costs 60¢ (46¢ to Canada and 40¢ to Mexico); a first-class postcard costs 50¢ (40¢ to Canada and 35¢ Mexico); and a preprinted postal aerogramme costs 50¢.

**Medical Emergencies**　To call an ambulance, dial ☎ **911** from any phone. No coins are needed.

**Newspapers/Magazines**　National newspapers include *The New York Times, USA Today,* and the *Wall Street Journal.* National news weeklies include *Newsweek, Time,* and *U.S. News & World Report.* In large cities most newsstands offer a small selection of the most popular foreign periodicals and newspapers, such as *The Economist, Le Monde,* and *Der Spiegel.* For information on local publications, see the "Fast Facts" sections for Phoenix and Tucson (chapters 4 and 9).

**Safety**　See "Safety" in "Preparing for Your Trip," earlier in this chapter.

**Taxes**　The United States does not have a value-added tax (VAT) or other indirect tax at a national level. Every state, and each county and city in it, is allowed to levy its own local tax on purchases (including hotel and restaurant checks, airline tickets, and so on) and services. Taxes are already included in the price of certain services, such as public transportation, cab fares, telephone calls, and gasoline. The amount of sales tax varies from about 4% to 12%, depending on the state and city, so when you're making major purchases, such as photographic equipment, clothing, or stereo components, it can be a significant part of the cost.

In Arizona the state sales tax is 5.5%, but communities can add local sales tax on top of this. Expect to pay around 20% tax on car rentals at either the Tucson or Phoenix airport (considerably less if you rent outside these airports). Hotel room taxes range from around 6% to 14%. Travelers on a budget should keep both car-rental and hotel-room taxes in mind when planning a trip.

**Telephone, Telegraph, Telex & Fax**   The telephone system in the United States is run by private corporations, so rates, especially for long-distance service and operator-assisted calls, can vary widely. Generally, hotel surcharges on long-distance and local calls are astronomical, so you're usually better off using a **public pay telephone,** which you'll find clearly marked in most public buildings and private establishments as well as on the street. Convenience grocery stores and gas stations always have them. Many convenience groceries and packaging services sell **prepaid calling cards** in denominations up to $50; these can be the least expensive way to call home. Many public phones at airports now accept American Express, MasterCard, and Visa credit cards. **Local calls** made from public pay phones in most locales cost either 25¢ or 35¢. Pay phones do not accept pennies, and few will take anything larger than a quarter

Most long-distance and international calls can be dialed directly from any phone. **For calls within the United States and to Canada**, dial 1 followed by the area code and the seven-digit number. **For other international calls,** dial 011 followed by the country code, city code, and the telephone number of the person you are calling.

Calls to area codes **800, 888,** and **877** are toll-free. However, calls to numbers in area codes **700** and **900** (chat lines, bulletin boards, "dating" services, and so on) can be very expensive—usually a charge of 95¢ to $3 or more per minute, and they sometimes have minimum charges that can run as high as $15 or more.

For **reversed-charge or collect calls,** and for **person-to-person calls,** dial 0 (zero, not the letter O) followed by the area code and number you want; an operator will then come on the line, and you should specify that you are calling collect, or person-to-person, or both. If your operator-assisted call is international, ask for the overseas operator.

For **local directory assistance** ("information"), dial 411; for long-distance information, dial 1, then the appropriate area code and 555-1212.

**Telegraph and telex services** are provided primarily by Western Union. You can bring your telegram into the nearest **Western Union** office (there are hundreds across the country) or dictate it over the phone (☎ **800/325-6000**). You can also telegraph money or have it telegraphed to you, very quickly over the Western Union system, but this service can cost as much as 15% to 20% of the amount sent.

Most hotels have **fax machines** available for guest use (be sure to ask about the charge to use it), and many hotel rooms are even wired for guests' fax machines. A less expensive way to send and receive faxes may be at stores such as Mail Boxes

Etc., a national chain of packing service shops (look in the Yellow Pages directory under "Packing Services").

There are two kinds of telephone directories in the United States. The **White Pages** list private households and business subscribers in alphabetical order. The inside front cover lists emergency numbers for police, fire, ambulance, the Coast Guard, poison-control center, crime-victims hotline, and so on. The first few pages will tell you how to make long-distance and international calls, complete with country codes and area codes. Government numbers are usually printed on blue paper within the White Pages. Printed on yellow paper, the **Yellow Pages** list all local services, businesses, industries, and houses of worship according to activity with an index at the front or back. (Drugstores/pharmacies and restaurants are also listed by geographic location.) The Yellow Pages also include city plans or detailed area maps, postal ZIP codes, and public transportation routes.

**Time**    The United States is divided into six time zones. From east to west, these are eastern standard time (EST), central standard time (CST), mountain standard time (MST), Pacific standard time (PST), Alaska standard time (AST), and Hawaii standard time (HST). Always keep the changing time zones in mind if you are traveling (or even telephoning) long distances in the United States. For example, noon in New York City (EST) is 11am in Chicago (CST), 10am in Phoenix (MST), 9am in Los Angeles (PST), 8am in Anchorage (AST), and 7am in Honolulu (HST).

Arizona is in the mountain time zone, but it does *not* observe daylight saving time (summertime). Consequently, from the first Sunday in April until the last Sunday in October, there is no time difference between Arizona and California and other states on the West Coast. However, there is a 2-hour difference to Chicago and 3 hours to New York.

**Tipping**    Tipping is so ingrained in the American way of life that the annual income tax of tip-earning service personnel is based on how much they should have received in light of their employers' gross revenues. Accordingly, they may have to pay tax on a tip you didn't actually give them.

Here are some rules of thumb:

In hotels, tip **bellhops** at least $1 per bag ($2 to $3 if you have a lot of luggage) and tip the **chamber staff** $1 to $2 per day (more if you've left a disaster area to clean up, or if you're traveling with kids and/or pets). Tip the **doorman** or **concierge** only if he or she has provided you with some specific service (for example, calling a cab for you or obtaining difficult-to-get theater tickets). Tip the **valet parking attendant** $1 every time you get your car.

In restaurants, bars, and nightclubs, tip **service staff** 15% to 20% of the check, tip **bartenders** 10% to 15%, tip **checkroom attendants** $1 per garment, and tip **valet parking attendants** $1 per vehicle. Tip the **doorman** only if he has provided you with some specific service (such as calling a cab for you). Tipping is not expected in cafeterias and fast-food restaurants.

Tip **cab drivers** 15% of the fare.

As for other service personnel, tip **skycaps** (luggage carriers) at airports at least $1 per bag ($2 to $3 if you have a lot of luggage) and tip **hairdressers** and **barbers** 15% to 20%.

Tipping ushers at movies and theaters, and gas-station attendants, is not expected.

**Toilets**    You won't find public toilets or "rest rooms" on the streets in most U.S. cities, but they can be found in hotel lobbies, bars, restaurants, museums, department stores, railway and bus stations, or service stations. Note, however, that restaurants and bars in resorts or heavily visited areas may reserve their rest rooms for the use of their patrons. Some establishments display a notice that toilets are for the use of patrons only. You can ignore this sign or, better yet, avoid arguments by paying for a cup of coffee or a soft drink, which will qualify you as a patron. Large hotels and fast-food restaurants are probably the best bet for good, clean facilities. If possible, avoid the toilets at parks and beaches, which tend to be dirty.

# 4

# Phoenix, Scottsdale & the Valley of the Sun

Like the phoenix of ancient mythology, Arizona's capital city of Phoenix rose from its own ashes—in this case, the ruins of an ancient Indian village. The name Phoenix, given to the city by an early settler from Britain, has proven apt. Rising from the dust of the desert, this city has become one of the largest metropolitan areas in the country.

Though the city has had its economic ups and downs, the Phoenix metropolitan area, often referred to as the Valley of the Sun, is currently booming. The Camelback Corridor, which leads through north-central Phoenix, has become the corporate heartland of the city and shiny glass office towers keep pushing up toward the desert sky. This burgeoning stretch of road has also become a corridor of upscale restaurants and shopping plazas, anchored by the Biltmore Fashion Park, the city's temple of high-end consumerism. Today Phoenicians are flocking to this area both for work and play.

Even downtown Phoenix, long abandoned as simply a place to work, is taking on a radically new look of late. Two new museums—the Phoenix Museum of History and the Arizona Science Center—have been built adjacent to historic Heritage Square, and the Phoenix Museum of Art has undergone a major renovation and expansion. However, the biggest project in downtown Phoenix in recent years was the construction of the Bank One Ballpark, a covered baseball stadium with a retractable roof. This stadium is now the home of the Arizona Diamondbacks baseball team.

Throughout the metropolitan area the population is growing at such a rapid pace that an alarm has been raised: Slow down before we become another Los Angeles! Why the phenomenal growth? In large part it's due to the climate. More than 300 days of sunshine a year is a powerful attraction. Sure, summers are hot, but the mountains—and cooler air—are only 2 hours away. And it's in the winter that the Valley of the Sun truly shines. While most of the country is frozen solid, the valley is sunny and warm. This great winter climate has helped make this area the resort capital of the United States. However, with stiff competition from resorts in the Caribbean, Mexico, and Hawaii, Valley of the Sun resorts have had to do a lot of keeping up with the Joneses in recent years. Bigger and splashier pools have been added, and now seemingly every resort in the valley is rushing to build a full-service health spa.

Golf, tennis, and lounging by the pool are only the tip of the iceberg (so to speak). With the cooler winter weather comes the cultural season, and between Phoenix and the neighboring cities of Scottsdale,

Tempe, and Mesa, there's an impressive array of music, dance, and theater to be enjoyed. Scottsdale is also well known as a center of the visual arts, ranking only behind New York and Santa Fe in its concentration of art galleries.

Over the years, Phoenix has both enjoyed the benefits and suffered the problems of rapid urban growth. It has gone from tiny agricultural village to sprawling cosmopolitan metropolis in little more than a century. Along the way it has lost its past amid urban sprawl and unchecked development; at the same time, it has forged a city that's quintessentially 20th-century American. Shopping malls, the gathering places of America, are raised to an art form in Phoenix. Luxurious resorts create fantasy worlds of waterfalls and swimming pools. Wide boulevards stretch for miles across land that was once desert but has been made green through irrigation. Perhaps it's this willingness to create a new world on top of an old one that attracts people to Phoenix. Then again, maybe it's just all that sunshine.

## 1  Orientation

### ARRIVING

**BY PLANE**    Centrally located 3 miles from downtown Phoenix, **Sky Harbor Airport** has three terminals—two, three, and four—and in these three terminals you'll find car-rental desks, information desks, hotel-reservation centers with direct lines to various valley hotels, and a food court. There's a free 24-hour shuttle bus operating every 5 to 10 minutes between the three terminals (less frequently during the night). For general airport information, call ☎ **602/273-3300;** for airport paging, call **602/273-3456;** for lost and found, call **602/273-3307.**

**Getting to & from the Airport**    There are two entrances to the airport. The west entrance can be accessed from either the Squaw Peak Parkway (Ariz. 51) or 24th Street, and the east entrance can be accessed from the Hohokam Expressway (Ariz. 143) which is an extension of 44th Street. If you're headed to downtown Phoenix, leave by way of the 24th Street exit and continue west on Washington Street. If you're headed to Scottsdale, take the 24th Street exit, go north on the Squaw Peak Parkway to the Indian School Road or Lincoln Drive exit, and then drive east; or alternatively, get on the 202 east loop to 101 north. For Tempe or Mesa, take the 44th Street exit.

If you want to come and go in style, you can arrange to have a stretch limo pick you up and take you back to the airport (or anywhere else in town for that matter). **Transtyle** (☎ **800/410-5479** or 480/948-6131) charges a flat fee of $100 between the airport and most Phoenix and Scottsdale resorts.

**SuperShuttle** (☎ **800/BLUE-VAN** or 602/244-9000) offers 24-hour door-to-door van service between Sky Harbor Airport and resorts, hotels, and homes throughout the valley. Fares average about $7 to $10 to the downtown and Tempe area ($6 for each additional person), and about $14 to $28 per person to Scottsdale and the northern area of the city. When heading back to the airport for a departure, call in advance ☎ **602/244-9000.**

Taxis can also be found waiting outside all three airport terminals, or you can call **Yellow Cab** (☎ **602/252-5252**) or **Checker Cab** (☎ **602/257-1818**).

Valley Metro provides **public bus service** throughout the valley with the Red Line (R) operating between the airport and downtown Phoenix, Tempe, and Mesa. The Red Line operates daily between about 5am and 10pm. You can pick up a copy of *The Bus Book,* a guide and route map for the Valley Metro bus system, at Central Station, at the corner of Central Avenue and Van Buren Street.

**BY CAR**    Phoenix is connected to Los Angeles and Tucson by I-10 and to Flagstaff via I-17. If you're headed to Scottsdale, the easiest route is to take the Red Mountain

# Phoenix, Scottsdale & the Valley of the Sun

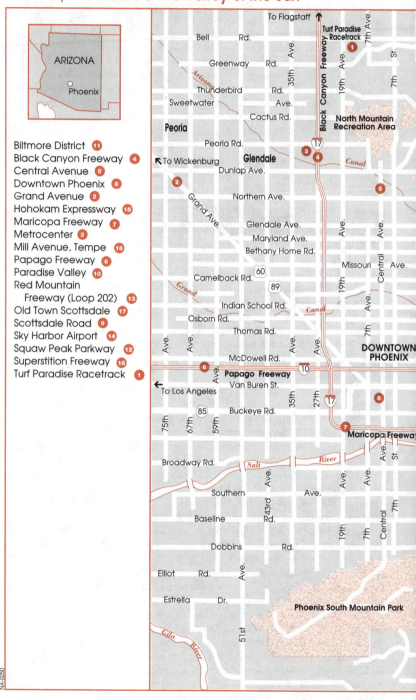

Biltmore District **11**
Black Canyon Freeway **4**
Central Avenue **5**
Downtown Phoenix **8**
Grand Avenue **2**
Hohokam Expressway **15**
Maricopa Freeway **7**
Metrocenter **3**
Mill Avenue, Tempe **16**
Papago Freeway **6**
Paradise Valley **10**
Red Mountain
   Freeway (Loop 202) **13**
Old Town Scottsdale **17**
Scottsdale Road **9**
Sky Harbor Airport **14**
Squaw Peak Parkway **12**
Superstition Freeway **18**
Turf Paradise Racetrack **1**

ARIZONA

Phoenix

To Flagstaff

Turf Paradise Racetrack **1**

Bell Rd.

Greenway Rd.

Thunderbird Rd.

Sweetwater Ave.

Cactus Rd.

North Mountain Recreation Area

Peoria

Peoria Rd.

To Wickenburg

Glendale

Dunlap Ave.

Canal

Northern Ave.

Glendale Ave.

Maryland Ave.

Bethany Home Rd.

Missouri Ave.

Camelback Rd.  60

Grand  89

Indian School Rd.

Canal

Osborn Rd.

Thomas Rd.

McDowell Rd.

DOWNTOWN PHOENIX

Papago Freeway  10

To Los Angeles

Van Buren St.

Buckeye Rd.  85

Broadway Rd.

Salt River

Maricopa Freeway **7**

Southern Ave.

Baseline Rd.

Dobbins Rd.

Elliot Rd.

Estrella Dr.

Phoenix South Mountain Park

Gila River

NA-0250

52

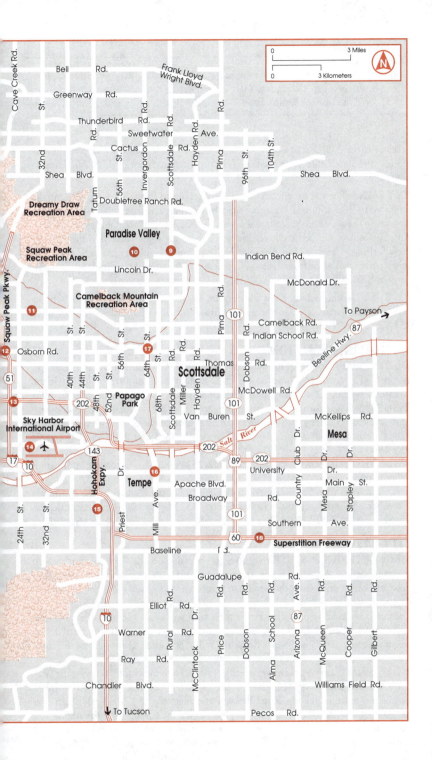

Cave Creek Rd.

Bell Rd.

Greenway Rd.

Frank Lloyd Wright Blvd.

St.

32nd

Thunderbird Rd.

Rd.

Sweetwater

Ave.

Cactus

St.

Rd.

Scottsdale Rd.

Hayden Rd.

Pima

96th St.

104th St.

Shea Blvd.

Invergordon

Tatum

56th

Shea Blvd.

**Dreamy Draw Recreation Area**

Doubletree Ranch Rd.

**Paradise Valley**

**10**

**9**

Lincoln Dr.

Indian Bend Rd.

McDonald Dr.

**Squaw Peak Recreation Area**

**Camelback Mountain Recreation Area**

Pima Rd.

**101**

Camelback Rd.

To Payson

**87**

**11**

St. St.

St.

St.

Rd.

Rd.

Rd.

Indian School Rd.

Beeline Hwy.

Squaw Peak Pkwy.

**12**

Osborn Rd.

56th St.

64th St.

Thomas

Dobson Rd.

**51**

40th St.

44th St.

68th

**Scottsdale**

McDowell Rd.

**13**

202

48th

52nd

**Papago Park**

Scottsdale Rd.

Miller Rd.

Hayden Rd.

**101**

**Sky Harbor International Airport**

Van Buren St.

McKellips Rd.

**Mesa**

**14**

**143**

202

Salt River

Country Club Dr.

**17**

**10**

Hohokam Expy.

**16**

**Tempe**

Apache Blvd.

89

202

University

Dr.

Main St.

Mesa Dr.

Stapley Dr.

Dr.

Broadway

Rd.

**101**

Southern Ave.

Priest

Mill Ave.

24th St.

32nd St.

**15**

60

**18**

**Superstition Freeway**

Baseline Rd.

Guadalupe Rd.

Rd.

Rd.

Ave.

Rd.

Rd.

Rd.

Elliot Rd.

Dr.

School

Arizona

**87**

**10**

Warner Rd.

Rural Rd.

McClintock Dr.

Price

Dobson

Alma

McQueen

Cooper

Gilbert

Ray Rd.

Chandler Blvd.

Williams Field Rd.

To Tucson

Pecos Rd.

53

*As the mythical phoenix rose reborn from its ashes, so shall a great civilization rise here on the ashes of a past civilization. I name thee Phoenix.*
—"Lord" Bryan Philip Darrel Duppa, the British settler who named Phoenix

Freeway (Ariz. 202) east to U.S. 101 north. U.S. 101 will eventually loop all the way around the north side of the valley. The Superstition Freeway (U.S. 60) leads to Tempe, Mesa, and Chandler.

**BY TRAIN**    There is no direct passenger rail service to Phoenix. However, Amtrak's Southwest Chief connects Phoenix (via a bus connection from Flagstaff) with Los Angeles to the west and Albuquerque, Santa Fe, Kansas City, and Chicago to the east. Amtrak's Sunset Limited connects Phoenix (via a bus from Tucson) with Orlando, New Orleans, Houston, San Antonio, El Paso, and Los Angeles. Amtrak connector buses arrive and depart from the old Phoenix **Amtrak railroad terminal,** 401 W. Harrison St. (☎ **800/872-7245** or 602/253-0121; www.amtrak.com).

**BY BUS**    Greyhound connects Phoenix to the rest of the United States with its extensive bus system. The **Greyhound terminal** is at 2115 E. Buckeye Rd. (☎ **800/231-2222** or 602/389-4202).

## VISITOR INFORMATION

You'll find **tourist information desks** in the baggage claim areas of all three terminals at Sky Harbor Airport. However, the city's main visitor information center is the **Greater Phoenix Convention and Visitors Bureau,** 50 N. Second St. (☎ **602/254-6500;** www.arizonaguide.com/phoenix), on the corner of Adams Street in downtown Phoenix. The city also operates a small visitor center at the Biltmore Fashion Park shopping center at the corner of Camelback Road and 24th Street (☎ **602/955-1963**).

The **Visitor Information Line** (☎ **602/252-5588**) has recorded information about current events in Phoenix.

If you're staying in Scottsdale, you may want to contact or drop by the **Scottsdale Chamber of Commerce and Visitors Center,** 7343 Scottsdale Mall, Scottsdale, AZ 85251-4498 (☎ **800/877-1117** or 480/945-8481; www.arizonaguide.com/scottsdale).

## CITY LAYOUT

**MAIN ARTERIES & STREETS**    Over the past decade, the Phoenix area has seen the construction of numerous new freeways, and the construction is continuing. It is now possible to drive from the airport to Scottsdale by freeway rather than having to deal with stoplights and local traffic. U.S. 101, which currently exists only in two unconnected sections (one between Tempe and Scottsdale and the other between north Phoenix and Peoria on the east side of the valley) will eventually form a loop around the east, north, and west sides of the valley, providing freeway access to Scottsdale from I-17 on the north side of Phoenix and from U.S. 60 in Tempe.

**I-17 (Black Canyon Freeway),** which connects Phoenix with Flagstaff, is the city's main north-south artery. This freeway curves to the east just south of downtown (where it is renamed the **Maricopa Freeway** and merges with I-10). **I-10,** which connects Phoenix with Los Angeles and Tucson, is called the **Papago Freeway** on the west side of the valley and as it passes north of downtown; as it curves around to pass south of the airport, it merges with I-17 and is renamed the Maricopa Freeway. At Tempe, this freeway curves around to the south and heads out of the valley.

North of the airport, **Ariz. 202 (Red Mountain Freeway)** heads east from I-10 and passes along the north side of Tempe, providing access to downtown Tempe, Arizona State University, Mesa, and Scottsdale (via U.S. 101). On the east side of the airport, **Ariz. 143 (Hohokam Expressway)** connects Ariz. 202 with I-10.

At the interchange of I-10 and Ariz. 202, northwest of Sky Harbor Airport, **Ariz. 51 (Squaw Peak Freeway)** heads north through the center of Phoenix and is the best north-south route in the city. This freeway is currently being extended north to Bell Road and will eventually link up with the U.S. 101 loop.

Just south of the airport, **U.S. 60 (Superstition Freeway)** heads east to Tempe, Chandler, Mesa, and Gilbert. **U.S. 101** leads north from U.S. 60 (and Ariz. 202) toward Scottsdale. This freeway is currently being extended north from McDonald Road to Shea Boulevard. This highway now provides the best route from the airport to the Scottsdale resorts.

Secondary highways in the valley include the **Beeline Highway (Ariz. 87),** which starts out as Country Club Drive in Mesa and leads to Payson, and **Grand Avenue (U.S. 60 and U.S. 89),** which starts downtown and leads to Sun City and Wickenburg.

Phoenix and the surrounding cities of Mesa, Tempe, Scottsdale, and Chandler, and even those cities farther out in the valley, are laid out in a grid pattern with major avenues and roads about every mile. For traveling east to west across Phoenix, your best choices are Camelback Road, Indian School Road, and McDowell Road. For traveling north and south, 44th Street, 24th Street, and Central Avenue are good choices. Hayden Road is a north-south alternative to Scottsdale Road, which gets jammed at rush hours.

**FINDING AN ADDRESS**     **Central Avenue,** which runs north to south through downtown Phoenix, is the starting point for all east and west street numbering. **Washington Street** is the starting point for north and south numbering. North-to-south numbered *streets* are to be found on the east side of the city, while north-to-south numbered *avenues* will be found on the west. For the most part, street numbers change by 100 with each block. Odd-numbered addresses are on the south and east sides of streets, while even-numbered addresses are on north and west sides of streets.

For example, if you're looking for 4454 East Camelback Rd., you'll find it 44 blocks east of Central Avenue between 44th and 45th streets on the north side of the street. If you're looking for 2905 North 35th Ave., you'll find it 35 blocks west of Central Avenue and 29 blocks north of Washington Street on the east side of the street. Just for general reference, Camelback marks the 5,000 block north.

**STREET MAPS**     The street maps handed out by rental-car companies are almost useless for finding anything in Phoenix, so, as soon as you can, stop in at a minimart and buy a Phoenix map. Unfortunately, you'll probably also have to buy a separate Scottsdale map. You can also get a simple map at either the airport tourist information desks or at the downtown visitor information center.

# Neighborhoods in Brief

Because of urban sprawl, Phoenix has yielded its importance to the Valley of the Sun, an area encompassing Phoenix and its metropolitan area of more than 20 cities. Consequently, neighborhoods, per se, have lost much of their significance as outlying cities have taken on regional importance. However, this said, there are some neighborhoods worth noting.

**Downtown Phoenix**     Roughly bordered by Thomas Road on the north, Buckeye Road on the south, 19th Avenue on the west, and Seventh Street on the east, downtown is primarily a business, financial, and government district, where both the city hall and state capitol are located. However, in the past few years, downtown Phoenix has been rising from the ashes of neglect and positioning itself as the valley's prime sports, entertainment, and museum district. The Arizona Diamondbacks play big-league baseball in the **Bank-One Ballpark,** while the Phoenix Suns pound the planks of the basketball court at the **America West Arena.** Not surprisingly, there are several sports bars and a brew pub in the area. There are also three major performing arts venues—the historic **Orpheum Theatre, Phoenix Symphony Hall,** and the **Herberger Theater Center.** At the Arizona Center shopping and entertainment plaza, there is a huge multiplex movie theater. Downtown museums include the **Phoenix Museum of History** and the **Arizona Science Center,** both of which are located in Heritage and Science Park. Other attractions in the downtown area include **Heritage Square** (historic homes), the **Arizona State Capitol Museum,** and **the Arizona Mining & Mineral Museum.** On the northern edge of downtown are the **Heard Museum,** the **Phoenix Central Library** (an architectural gem), and the **Phoenix Art Museum.**

**Biltmore District**   The Biltmore District, also known as the **Camelback Corridor,** centers along Camelback Road between 24th Street and 44th Street and is Phoenix's upscale shopping, residential, and business district. The area is characterized by modern office buildings and is anchored by the Arizona Biltmore Hotel and Biltmore Fashion Park shopping mall. It's here you'll find such cultural icons as Planet Hollywood and the Hard Rock Cafe.

**Scottsdale**   A separate city of nearly 200,000 people, Scottsdale extends from Tempe in the south to Carefree in the north, a distance of more than 20 miles. **"Resort Row"** is the name given to Scottsdale Road between Indian School Road and Shea Boulevard, as along this section of road are more than a dozen major resorts. **Old Scottsdale** capitalizes on its cowboy heritage and has become the valley's main shopping district, with boutiques, jewelers, Native American crafts stores, souvenir shops, and numerous restaurants.

**Tempe**   Tempe is the home of Arizona State University and has all the trappings of a university town. Nightclubs and bars abound here. The center of activity, both day and night, is **Mill Avenue,** which has dozens of interesting shops along a stretch of about 4 blocks. This is one of the few areas in the valley where locals actually walk the streets and hang out at sidewalk cafes (Old Town Scottsdale often has people on its streets, but few are locals).

**Paradise Valley**   If Scottsdale is Phoenix's Beverly Hills, then Paradise Valley is its Bel-Air. The most exclusive neighborhood in the valley is almost entirely residential, but you won't see too many of the more lavish homes because they're set on large tracts of land.

**Mesa**   This eastern suburb of Phoenix has in recent years become something of a high-tech area. Large shopping malls, several inexpensive motels, and a museum attract both locals and visitors to Mesa.

**Glendale**   Located west of Phoenix proper, Glendale has numerous historic buildings in its downtown and has, with its dozens of antiques stores, become the antiques capital of the valley.

**Carefree & Cave Creek**   Located about 20 miles north of Old Scottsdale, these two communities represent the Old West and the New West. Carefree is a planned community and is home to the prestigious Boulders resort and El Pedregal shopping center. Cave Creek plays up its Western heritage in its architecture and preponderance of bars, steakhouses, and shops selling Western crafts and other gifts.

# 2  Getting Around

## BY CAR

Phoenix and the surrounding cities that together make up the Valley of the Sun sprawl over some 420 square miles, so if you want to make the best use of your time, it's essential to have a car. Outside downtown Phoenix, there's almost always plenty of free parking wherever you go.

**RENTALS**    All the major rental-car companies have offices in Phoenix, with desks inside the airline terminals at Sky Harbor Airport, and because this is a major tourist destination, there are often excellent rates. However, taxes on car rentals at Sky Harbor airport run about 24%. The best rates are those reserved at least a week in advance, but car-rental companies change rates frequently as demand goes up and down. If you book far enough in advance, you might get a compact car for less than $160 per week. See also chapter 3 for general tips on car rentals.

All the major rental-car companies have offices at Sky Harbor Airport as well as other locations in the Phoenix area. Among them are the following: **Alamo** (☎ 800/ 327-9633, 602/273-9690 or 602/244-0897); **Avis** (☎ 800/331-1212 or 602/ 273-3222); **Budget** (☎ 800/527-0700 or 602/267-4000); **Dollar** (☎ 800/ 800-4000 or 602/224-2382); **Enterprise** (☎ 800/325-8007 or 602/225-0588); **Hertz** (☎ 800/ 654-3131 or 602/267-8822); **National** (☎ 800/227-7368 or 602/ 275-4771); and **Thrifty** (☎ 800/367-2277 or 602/244-0311).

If you'd like a bit more style while you cruise from resort to golf course to nightclub to wherever, how about a Corvette? **Rent-a-Vette,** 1215 N. Scottsdale Rd., Tempe (☎ **480/941-3001**), can put you behind the wheel of a car that will get you a bit more respect from valet parking attendants at area restaurants. A Corvette will run you $129 to $249 a day. Rent-a-Vette also rents Porsche Boxters, Mustang GTs, Jaguars XKAs, and Plymouth Prowlers, with rates topping out at $399 a day for a Prowler.

At the rugged end of the car-rental spectrum is **Great Escapes,** 7677 N. 16th St., Phoenix (☎ **602/674-8469**), which rents Jeep Wranglers for $99.95 a half day or $129.95 for a full day. Rates go down the more days you rent, and special lower rates are sometimes available. Along with your rental, you can get a trail book and directions for various trails into the desert. For two or more people, this is an economical alternative to doing a Jeep tour.

If a Jeep still doesn't offer enough excitement and wind in your hair, how about a motorcycle? **Western States Motorcycle Tours,** 9401 N. Seventh Ave. (☎ **602/ 943-9030**), rents Harley-Davidson, BMW, and Suzuki motorcycles for between $75 and $175 per day ($450 to $750 per week). You must have a valid motorcycle driver's license to rent one of these bikes. In Arizona you don't have to wear a helmet, so you really can ride with the wind in your hair.

## BY PUBLIC TRANSPORTATION

Unfortunately **Valley Metro** (☎ **602/253-5000**), the Phoenix public bus system, is not very useful to tourists. It's primarily meant to be used by commuters, and most routes stop running before 9pm. There's no bus service on Sunday (except in Tempe), and some buses don't run on Saturday either. But if you decide you want to take the bus, pick up a copy of *The Bus Book* at one of the tourist information desks in the airport (where it's sometimes available), at Central Station at the corner of Central Avenue and Van Buren Street, or any Frys or Safeway supermarkets. There are both local and express buses. Local bus fare is $1.25, and express bus fare is $1.75. A 10-ride ticket book, all-day passes, and monthly passes are available.

Of slightly more value to visitors is the **Downtown Area Shuttle (DASH),** which provides bus service for 30¢ a ride within the downtown area. These purple buses with orange racing stripes operate Monday through Friday between 6:30am and 6pm. The buses stop at regular bus stops every 6 to 12 minutes. This shuttle is primarily for downtown workers, but attractions along the route include the state capitol, Heritage Square, and the Arizona Center shopping mall. In Tempe, **Free Local Area Shuttle (FLASH)** buses provide a similar service on a loop around Arizona State University. The route includes Mill Avenue and Sun Devil Stadium, and as the name implies, these buses are free. For information on both DASH and FLASH, phone ☎ **602/ 253-5000.**

In Scottsdale you can ride **Ollie the Trolley** (☎ **480/970-8130**) buses between many area resorts and shopping areas. An all-day pass is $5.

## BY TAXI

Because distances in Phoenix are so great, the price of an average taxi ride can be quite high. However, if you don't have your own wheels and the bus isn't running because it's late at night or the weekend, you won't have any choice but to call a cab. **Yellow Cab** (☎ **602/252-5252**) charges $3 for the first mile and $1.50 per mile after that. **Scottsdale Cab** (☎ **480/994-1616**) charges $2 per mile, with a $5 minimum.

# Fast Facts: Phoenix

**American Express**    There are American Express offices at 2508 E. Camelback Rd. (☎ **602/468-1199**), open Monday through Saturday from 10am to 6pm; and at 6900 E. Camelback Rd., Scottsdale (☎ **480/949-7000**), open Monday through Friday from 10am to 6pm and Saturday from 10am to 3:30pm.

**Airport**    See "Orientation," earlier in this chapter.

**Baby-sitters**    If your hotel can't recommend or provide a sitter, contact the **Granny Company** (☎ **602/956-4040**).

**Car Rentals**    See "Getting Around," earlier in this chapter.

**Climate**    See "When to Go," in chapter 2.

**Dentist**    Call the **Central Arizona Dental Society** at ☎ **602/957-4864** for a referral.

**Doctor**    Call the **Maricopa County Medical Society** (☎ **602/252-2844**) or the **Physician Referral and Resource Line** (☎ **602/230-2273**) for doctor referrals.

**Emergencies**    For police, fire, or medical emergency, phone ☎ **911.**

**Eyeglass Repair**    The **Nationwide Vision Center** has more than 10 locations around the valley, including 5130 N. 19th Ave. (☎ **602/242-5293**); 3202 E. Greenway, Paradise Valley (☎ **602/788-8413**); 4615 E. Thomas Rd. (☎ **602/ 952-8667**); and 933 E. University Dr., Tempe (☎ **480/966-4992**).

**Hospitals**    The **Good Samaritan Regional Medical Center,** 1111 E. McDowell Rd. (☎ **602/239-2000**), is one of the largest hospitals in the valley.

**Hotlines**    The Visitor **Information Line** (☎ **602/252-5588**) provides recorded tourist information on Phoenix and the Valley of the Sun. **Pressline**

(☎ **602/271-5656**) provides access to daily news, the correct time, weather, and other topics.

**Information**    See "Visitor Information" under "Orientation," earlier in this chapter.

**Internet Access**    If your hotel doesn't provide Internet access, your next best bet is to visit one of the Kinkos in the area. There are Kinkos locations in downtown Phoenix at 259 N. First Ave. (☎ **602/252-4055**), off the Camelback corridor at 4801 N. Central Ave. (☎ **602/241-9440**), and in Scottsdale at 4000 N. Scottsdale Rd. (☎ **480/946-0500**), and at a couple of other locations.

**Lost Property**    If you lose something in the airport, call ☎ **602/273-3307;** on a bus, call ☎ **602/253-5000.**

**Maps**    See "City Layout" under "Orientation," earlier in this chapter.

**Newspapers/Magazines**    *The Arizona Republic* (called "The Rep") is Phoenix's daily newspaper. The Thursday paper has a special section with schedules of the upcoming week's movie, music, and cultural performances. *New Times* is a free weekly news and arts journal with comprehensive listings of cultural events, film, and rock-music club and concert schedules. The best place to find *New Times* is at corner newspaper dispensers in downtown Phoenix, Scottsdale, or Tempe.

**Pharmacies**    Call ☎ **800/WALGREENS** for the Walgreens pharmacy that's nearest you; some are open 24 hours a day.

**Police**    For police emergencies, phone ☎ **911.**

**Post Office**    The **Phoenix Main Post Office** is at 4949 E. Van Buren St. (☎ **800/275-8777**), open Monday through Friday from 8am to 5pm .

**Safety**    Don't leave valuables in view in your car, especially when parking in downtown Phoenix. Put anything of value in the trunk, or under the seat if you're driving a hatchback. Take extra precautions after dark in the south-central Phoenix area and downtown. Violent acts of road rage are all too common in Phoenix, so it's a good idea to be polite when driving. Aggressive drivers should be given plenty of room.

Many hotels now provide in-room safes, for which there's sometimes a daily charge. Others will be glad to store your valuables in a safety-deposit box at the front office.

**Taxes**    State sales tax is 5% (plus variable local taxes). Hotel room taxes vary by city but are mostly between 10.25% and 10.625%. However, it is in renting a car that you really get pounded. Expect to pay taxes in excess of 20% when renting a car at Sky Harbor Airport. Add to this an additional $2.50 Cactus League charge, and you end up with a considerable amount on top of the rental fee. You can save up to 10% (the airport concession fee recoupment charge) by renting your car at an office outside the airport.

**Taxis**    See "Getting Around," earlier in this chapter.

**Television**    Valley of the Sun stations are channels 3 (Warner), 5 (CBS), 8 (PBS), 10 (Fox), 12 (NBC), 15 (ABC), and 45 (United Paramount Network).

**Transit Information**    For **Phoenix Transit System** public bus information, call ☎ **602/253-5000.**

**Weather**    The phone number for weather information is ☎ **602/271-5656,** ext. 1010.

## 3  Where to Stay

Because the Phoenix area has long been popular as a winter refuge from cold and snow, it now has the greatest concentration of resorts in the continental United States. However, even with all the hotel rooms here, sunshine and spring training make it hard to find a room on short notice between February and April (the busiest time of year in the valley), so if you're planning to visit at this time, make your reservations as many months in advance as possible. During the winter, the Phoenix metro area has some of the highest room rates in the country. Sure, the city has plenty of moderately priced motels, but even these places tend to jack up their prices in winter. Hotels are increasingly turning to the airline model: Rates go up and down with demand, so you never know what they might be charging on a given date. It's often possible to get a lower room rate simply by asking. If a hotel isn't full and isn't expected to be, you should be able to get a lower rate. Unfortunately, the reverse also holds true.

With the exception of valet parking services and parking garages at downtown convention hotels, parking is free at most Phoenix hotels. If there is a parking charge, we have noted it. You'll find that all hotels have no-smoking and all but the cheapest have wheelchair-accessible rooms.

Also, keep in mind that most resorts offer a variety of weekend, golf, and tennis packages, as well as special off-season discounts and corporate rates (which you can often get just by asking). We've given only the official "rack rates," or walk-in rates, below, but it always pays to ask if there's any kind of special discount or package available. Don't forget your AAA or AARP discounts if you belong to these organizations. (If you aren't already a member, it's worth joining just to get the discounts.) Also keep in mind that business hotels downtown and near the airport often lower their rates on weekends.

Consider traveling during the shoulder seasons of late spring and late summer. Temperatures are not at their midsummer peak nor are room rates at their midwinter highs. (And if you can stand the heat of summer, you can often save more than 50% on room rates.) If you'll be traveling with children, always ask whether your child will be able to stay for free in your room, and whether there's a limit to the number of children who can stay for free.

Request a room with a view of the mountains whenever possible. You can overlook a swimming pool anywhere, but some of the main selling points of Phoenix and Scottsdale hotels are the views of Mummy Mountain, Camelback Mountain, and Squaw Peak.

**BED & BREAKFAST INNS**    While most people dreaming of an Arizona winter vacation have visions of luxury resorts dancing in their heads, there are also plenty of bed-and-breakfast inns around the valley. **Advance Reservations Inn Arizona/ Mi Casa-Su Casa Bed & Breakfast Reservation Service,** P.O. Box 950, Tempe, AZ 85280-0950 (☎ **800/456-0682** or 480/990-0682), can book you into more than 65 homes in the Valley of the Sun (or elsewhere in the state), as can **Arizona Trails Bed & Breakfast Reservation Service,** P.O. Box 18998, Fountain Hills, AZ 85269-8998 (☎ **888/799-4284** or 480/837-4284; fax 480/816-4224; www.arizonatrails.com), which also books tour and hotel reservations.

**PRICE CATEGORIES**    Because it is such a popular winter resort destination, the Valley of the Sun is one of the more expensive places in the United States for a vacation. If you've been thinking of saving money by skipping the Caribbean or Hawaii this year, think again. When a standard room at a top resort goes for well over $250 and a Super 8 Motel charges close to $100, price categories become very subjective.

Consequently, we have categorized accommodations based on their relative cost when compared with other Valley of the Sun accommodations.

# SCOTTSDALE
## VERY EXPENSIVE

**Gardiner's Resort on Camelback.** 5700 E. McDonald Dr., Phoenix, AZ 85253-5268. ☎ **800/245-2051** or 480/948-2100. Fax 480/483-7314. 100 units. Jan–May $295 double, $425–$665 suite; June to mid-Sept $189 double, $245–$325 suite; mid-Sept to Dec $245 double, $355–$565 suite. Rates include continental breakfast. Tennis packages available. AE, DC, DISC, MC, V.

If your idea of the perfect vacation is a week in the sun playing as much tennis as your elbow can stand, this is the place for you. Located on the north slope of Camelback Mountain, Gardiner's is set on a lushly landscaped hillside and has a long history of helping tennis players improve their games. The resort is small and, with its gated entry, has the feel of a private country club. There are 20 tennis courts, so getting court time usually isn't a problem, and with eight pools, there are also plenty of places to cool off.

Guest rooms are individually decorated condos, and some have large balconies or sunrooms. Each morning, you'll find fresh-squeezed orange juice and a newspaper at your door, and all rooms have coffeemakers and hair dryers. The resort also has houses for rent, all of which have private pools and some of which have a private tennis court.

**Dining/Diversions:** There's a great view of Mummy Mountain from the bar and dining room, which features new American dishes.

**Amenities:** In addition to the tennis courts and pools, you'll find whirlpools, a sauna, a fitness center, a business center, and a full-service spa offering various massages and body treatments. Room service, valet/laundry service, tennis lessons, children's programs, and baby-sitting are available.

✪ **Hyatt Regency Scottsdale.** 7500 E. Doubletree Ranch Rd., Scottsdale, AZ 85258. ☎ **800/233-1234** or 480/991-3388. Fax 480/483-5550. 493 units. A/C MINIBAR TV TEL. Jan to late May $335–$490 double, from $800 suites and casitas; late May to early Sept $145–$295 double, from $240 suites and casitas; early Sept to Dec $320–$450 double, from $450 suites and casitas. AE, DC, DISC, EURO, MC, V.

From the colonnades of palm trees to the lobby walls that slide away, this luxurious resort is designed to astonish. Future archaeologists excavating the site would probably think it was a temple. Surrounded by a lake, gardens, fountains, and fishponds, the 2½-acre water playground is the resort's focal point. This extravagant complex of 10 swimming pools includes a water slide, a sand beach, a water-volleyball pool, waterfalls, and a huge whirlpool spa. (You'd never know this was the desert.) The resort's Hopi Learning Center, staffed by Hopi interpreters, provides a glimpse into Native American culture.

The grounds are planted with hundreds of tall palm trees that frame the gorgeous views of the distant McDowell Mountains; closer at hand, original works of art have been placed throughout the resort. Guest rooms are luxurious and very comfortable and reflect the desert location. Robes, hair dryers, and scales are all standard.

**Dining/Diversions:** The Golden Swan, serving Southwestern cuisine, includes a popular waterside terrace dining area (see "Where to Dine," below). There's also a casual Southwestern restaurant and an Italian cafe that offers after-dinner gondola rides. A lobby bar features live music nightly. There are also two bars and a grill near the pool.

**Amenities:** Twenty-seven outstanding holes of golf (with lots of water hazards), 10 pools, 8 tennis courts, a croquet court, jogging and bicycling trails, and a full-service health spa with exercise equipment, aerobics classes, saunas, and body and

# Phoenix, Scottsdale & the Valley of the Sun Accommodations

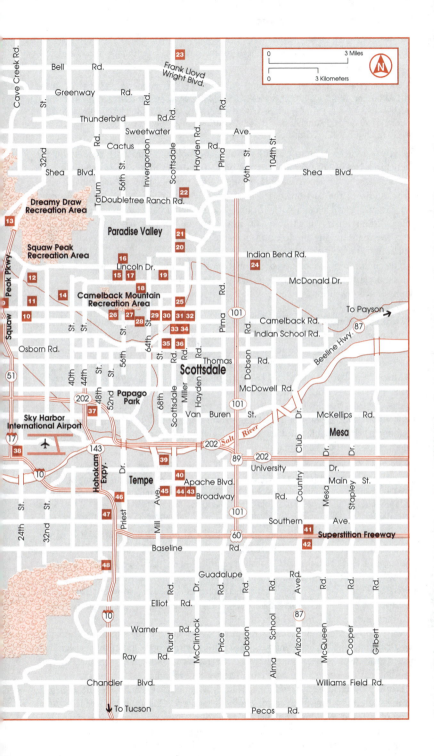

beauty treatments. A concierge, 24-hour room service, valet/laundry service, and children's programs are available.

✪ **Marriott's Camelback Inn.** 5402 E. Lincoln Dr., Scottsdale, AZ 85253. ☎ **800/ 24-CAMEL** or 480/948-1700. Fax 480/951-8469. www.camelbackinn.com. 453 units. A/C MINIBAR TV TEL. Jan–May $329–$389 double, $495–$2,025 suite; June–Aug $119–$275 double, $150–$1,500 suite; Sept–Dec $255–$295 double, $380–$1,520 suite. AE, CB, DC, DISC, EURO, JCB, MC, V. Small pets accepted.

Set at the foot of Mummy Mountain and overlooking Camelback Mountain, the Camelback Inn offers a tranquil setting only 10 minutes from downtown Scottsdale. The resort, which opened in 1936, is one of the grande dames of the Phoenix hotel scene, and over the past few years it's undergone $35 million worth of renovations. But the resort still retains its traditional Southwestern character and solid sense of place. Although the two 18-hole golf courses are the main attraction for many guests here, the spa is among the finest in the state and there is an extensive pool complex that appeals to families.

The guest rooms, which are spread out over the sloping grounds, are decorated with contemporary Southwestern furnishings and art, and all have balconies or patios. The bathrooms are well lit and come with hair dryers, a large basket of toiletries, and a shaving mirror.

**Dining/Diversions:** The Chaparral, the last part of the resort to be renovated, now serves new American cuisine in a relaxed atmosphere. The Navajo Room is more casual, and the spa also has a restaurant (serving healthful meals, of course). There are also two snack bars, a lounge for cocktails, and a cafe for espresso and pastries.

**Amenities:** Two outstanding 18-hole golf courses, a pitch-and-putt course, six tennis courts, three pools, three whirlpools, a playground, basketball and volleyball courts, a full-service health spa (offering numerous body and beauty treatments, a lap pool, aerobics room and classes, saunas, steam rooms, whirlpools, and lots of exercise equipment), bike rentals, concierge, room service, baby-sitting, children's programs, valet/laundry service, car-rental desk.

✪ **The Phoenician.** 6000 E. Camelback Rd., Scottsdale, AZ 85251. ☎ **800/888-8234** or 480/941-8200. Fax 480/947-4311. www.thephoenician.com. 654 units. A/C MINIBAR TV TEL. Late Dec to mid-June $450–$625 double, $1,075–$5,300 suite; mid-June to mid-Sept $185– $225 double, $500–$5,300 suite; mid-Sept to late Dec $415–$465 double, $1,075–$5,300 suite. AE, CB, DC, DISC, JCB, MC, V. Valet parking $15. Pets under 25 lbs. accepted.

Situated on 250 acres at the foot of Camelback Mountain, The Phoenician consistently ranks among the finest resorts in the world. No expense was spared in the construction of this palatial resort. Polished marble and sparkling crystal abound in the lobby, but the view of the valley through a long wall of glass is what commands most guests' attention. Service here is second to none, and the pool complex is one of the finest in the state. The resort's spa offers all the pampering anyone could ever need, and there are 27 challenging holes of golf.

Guest rooms are as elaborate as the public areas and include sunken bathtubs for two, Berber carpets, three phones, large patios, terry robes, bathroom scales, hair dryers, and wall safes. And that's just the *standard* room. The separate Canyon Building has its own private pool complete with rental cabanas.

**Dining/Diversions:** Mary Elaine's, featuring modern French cuisine, offers elegant dining and great views. The Terrace Dining Room serves Italian dishes in a less formal atmosphere, and Windows on the Green features Southwestern cuisine with a golf course view. There are also poolside snack bars and an ice cream parlor. Afternoon tea is served in the lobby, off of which there is also a lounge with a valley view.

**Amenities:** In addition to the golf course and full-service spa, there are nine pools (including one lined with opalescent tiles), a water slide, a putting green, 12 tennis courts, a whirlpool, lawn games, a volleyball court, rental bikes, and a shopping arcade. Also available are a car-rental desk, business center, concierge, 24-hour room service, valet/laundry service, baby-sitting, and children's programs.

**Renaissance Cottonwoods Resort.** 6160 N. Scottsdale Rd., Scottsdale, AZ 85253. ☎ **800/HOTELS-1** or 480/991-1414. Fax 480/951-3350. www.renaissancehotels.com. 171 units. A/C MINIBAR TV TEL. Jan–May $180–$349 double, $248–$349 suite; June–Aug $79–$129 double, $99–$129 suite; Sept–Dec $149–$299 double, $199–$299 suite. Rates include continental breakfast. AE, DC, DISC, MC, V. Pets under 25 lb. accepted ($50 deposit).

Located behind the Borgata, Scottsdale's upscale shopping plaza that's designed to resemble an Italian village, the Cottonwoods Resort is an unpretentious-yet-upscale boutique resort. Set amid shady lawns in a sort of apartment-complex layout, the resort consists of spacious suites that are designed for those who need plenty of room and comfort. More than 100 of the suites have their own private hot tubs on private patios, and all the suites are done in Southwestern style. Several excellent restaurants are within walking distance, which makes this a good choice for gourmands who don't want to spend their vacation fighting rush-hour traffic on Scottsdale Road.

**Dining/Diversions:** A lounge and the resort's restaurant are in a separate building (in front of the Borgata) a bit removed from the rest of the resort. There's also a pool-side bar.

**Amenities:** Around the resort's spacious grounds you'll find two swimming pools, two hot tubs, four tennis courts, a jogging trail, putting green, and a croquet lawn. There are also bicycles for guests and access to a nearby health club. A concierge, room service, and valet/laundry service are all available.

**Scottsdale Princess.** 7575 E. Princess Dr., Scottsdale, AZ 85255. ☎ **800/441-1414** or 480/585-4848. Fax 480/585-0086. www.cphotels.com. 650 units. A/C MINIBAR TV TEL. $119–$519 double; $239–$3,519 suite. AE, CB, DC, DISC, MC, V.

Located a 20-minute drive north of downtown Scottsdale, this resort will delight anyone in search of a romantic hideaway. With its royal palms, tiled fountains, water-falls, and classical art and antiques, the Princess is a modern rendition of a Moorish palace and offers a truly exotic atmosphere unmatched by any other valley resort. It's also home to the Phoenix Open golf tournament, as well as a tennis tournament, which means the two golf courses here are superb and the courts are top-notch. For those not tempted by golf or tennis, there's a full-service spa and fitness center.

The guest rooms all have distinct living and work areas, wet bars, refrigerators, and private balconies. The decor is elegant Southwestern, and the roomy bathrooms include two sinks, a separate shower and tub, a vanity, and a telephone. For more space, there's a wide variety of suites available.

**Dining/Diversions:** The Marquesa is a highly acclaimed, and high-priced, Spanish restaurant. For gourmet Mexican and strolling mariachis, there's La Hacienda. See "Where to Dine," below for more information on these two restaurants. There are a couple of casual restaurants as well as a quiet lounge and a rowdy Wild West saloon, and at the golf course, there's a steakhouse.

**Amenities:** In addition to the two 18-hole golf courses, there are seven tennis courts; three pools; whirlpools; racquetball, squash, and basketball courts; a fitness trail; a complete spa and fitness center; boutiques; tennis and golf pro shops; and a business center. There's even a fishing pond here (which kids love). A concierge, 24-hour room service, valet/laundry service, baby-sitting, and shopping shuttle are also available.

## EXPENSIVE

**Doubletree La Posada Resort.** 4949 E. Lincoln Dr., Scottsdale, AZ 85253. ☎ **800/733-5466** or 602/952-0420. Fax 602/840-8576. 262 units. A/C MINIBAR TV TEL. Mid-Jan to mid-May $215–$225 double, $325–$550 suite; mid-May to mid-Sept $99–$115 double, $225–$425 suite; mid-Sept to early Nov $195–$215 double, $275–$550 suite; early Nov to mid-Jan $175–$185; $275–$550 suite. AE, CB, DC, DISC, MC, V. Pets under 20 lbs. accepted.

If you prefer to spend your time by the pool rather than on the fairways, consider La Posada, which is located on the northern flanks of Camelback Mountain with great poolside views. The pool here covers half an acre and features its own two-story water-fall that cascades over artificial boulders. Connecting the two halves of the pool is a swim-through grotto complete with bar/cafe.

Mission-revival architecture prevails here, though the interior of the lobby is more Vegas glitz than Spanish colonial. The somewhat nondescript guest rooms are larger than average and have coffeemakers and hair dryers. The tiled bathrooms feature two sinks and plenty of counter space.

**Dining/Diversions:** The Garden Terrace restaurant has a nice view of Camelback Mountain and offers Southwestern cuisine at high prices. The adjacent lounge is a large, flashy place with occasional live music. There's also a poolside grill.

**Amenities:** In addition to facilities mentioned above, there are tennis and racquet-ball courts, two putting greens, four whirlpools, a fitness room and sauna (under the pool waterfall), volleyball court, horseshoe pits, pro shop, beauty salon, car-rental desk, concierge, room service, and laundry/valet service.

✪ **Doubletree Paradise Valley Resort.** 5401 N. Scottsdale Rd., Scottsdale, AZ 85250. ☎ **800/222-TREE** or 480/947-5400. Fax 480/481-0209. 387 units. A/C MINIBAR TV TEL. Jan–May $215–$259 double, $560–$2,000 suite; May to early Sept $95–$189 double, $230–$480 suite; early Sept to Dec $159–$199 double, $480–$2,000 suite. AE, CB, DC, DISC, MC, V.

This resort gives a bow to the pioneering architectural style of Frank Lloyd Wright, and thus stands out from other comparable Scottsdale resorts. Built around several courtyards containing swimming pools, bubbling fountains, and desert gardens, the resort has much the look and feel of Hyatt's nearby Gainey Ranch megaresort but on a less grandiose scale. Mature palm trees lend a sort of Moorish feel to the grounds and cast fanciful shadows in the gardens.

Guest rooms were all completely renovated in 1998 and now have a very contem-porary feel, with lots of blond wood, and, in some cases, high ceilings that make the rooms feel particularly spacious. Large closets, separate dressing rooms and bath-rooms, and coffeemakers, hair dryers, and irons and ironing board, make these rooms very convenient.

**Dining/Diversions:** Off to one side of the lobby is a skylit dining room serving Southwestern dishes. A lobby lounge serves drinks and light meals to the accompa-niment of live music many evenings. There's also a patio bar adjacent to the main pool.

**Amenities:** Two outdoor pools (set in palm-shaded courtyards and with small waterfalls), two lighted tennis courts, a fitness center, two racquetball courts, saunas, steam room, whirlpools, beauty salon, business center, gift shop, car-rental desk, concierge, room service, valet/laundry service, baby-sitting.

**Holiday Inn Hotel & Conference Center.** 7353 E. Indian School Rd., Scottsdale, AZ 85251. ☎ **800/695-6995** or 480/994-9203. Fax 480/941-2567. 206 units. A/C TV TEL. Late Dec to late Apr $145 double, $275–$375 suite; late Apr to May $120 double, $225–$350 suite; June to early Sept $90 double, $175–$250 suite; early Sept to Dec $120 double, $225–$350 suite. AE, CB, DC, DISC, JCB, MC, V.

While the guest rooms at this low-rise hotel in Old Town Scottsdale have been recently redone, they're still fairly small (as are the bathrooms), but the location right on the beautifully landscaped Scottsdale Civic Center Mall (a park, not a shopping center) is very appealing. You're also only a block off Scottsdale's famous shopping and gallery neighborhood and the Scottsdale Center for the Arts is just across the mall. All the rooms now have hair dryers and coffeemakers, but the best rooms are those opening onto the mall—be sure to request one.

**Dining/Diversions:** The hotel's dining room is a steakhouse overlooking the park. There's also a lively lounge.

**Amenities:** A small outdoor pool, a tennis court, a whirlpool, and a putting green provide recreational activities. Room service and a shopping shuttle are also available.

**Marriott's Mountain Shadows Resort & Golf Club.** 5641 E. Lincoln Dr., Scottsdale, AZ 85253. ☎ **800/228-9290** or 480/948-7111. Fax 480/951-5430. 337 units. A/C MINIBAR TV TEL. Jan–May $179–$239 double, $275–$750 suite; June–Aug $99–$199 double, $110–$630 suite; Sept–Dec $159–$199 double, $230–$630 suite. AE, CB, DC, DISC, MC, V. Small pets accepted.

Located across the road from the Camelback Inn, Mountain Shadows offers better views of Camelback Mountain but an entirely different ambience. Mountain Shadows was built in the late 1950s and, though architecturally dated, is well maintained and appeals to families and younger travelers looking for a more informal atmosphere than is found at the Camelback Inn. An 18-hole executive course (with economical greens fees for this area) keeps most guests happy, but for the more serious golfer, there is access to the Camelback Inn's two outstanding courses. Guests here can also use the Camelback Inn's superb spa facilities. This resort is scheduled to begin a $35 million renovation in the summer of 2000 and should be a very different place when all the work is done.

Standard rooms are large and have high ceilings, wet bars, king-size beds, and balconies. The rooms around the main pool, though large, can be a bit noisy. Those rooms in the Palm section offer the best views of the mountain. Some suites have whirlpool tubs.

**Dining/Diversions:** There's a seafood restaurant and a more casual Southwest-style cafe, as well as a bar and grill, a country club dining room, and a poolside snack bar.

**Amenities:** In addition to the golf course, there are eight tennis courts, three pools (one of which is quite large), two whirlpools, saunas, a fitness center (and access to the Camelback Inn's spa), a volleyball court, pro shops, and a business center. A concierge, room service, valet/laundry service, a car-rental desk, baby-sitting, children's programs, and guided mountain hikes are available.

**Radisson Resort Scottsdale.** 7171 N. Scottsdale Rd., Scottsdale, AZ 85253. ☎ **800/333-3333** or 480/991-3800. Fax 480/948-1381. 318 units. A/C TV TEL. Mid-Jan to late May $255–$275 double, $375–$1,500 suite; late May to late June $175–$199 double, $295–$1,500 suite; late June to mid-Sept $125–$149 double, $199–$1,500 suite; mid-Sept to mid-Jan $220–$245 double, $325–$1,500 suite. AE, CB, DC, DISC, EURO, JCB, MC, V.

Although not nearly as lavish as the area's other top resorts, this well-maintained place opts for a formal and traditional atmosphere that seems to appeal to an older clientele, many of whom come to play tennis on the resort's 21 tennis courts or golf on the two 18-hole golf courses. However, the recent addition of a large Japanese-style health spa seems aimed at helping this resort keep up with the times. For the most part, the resort eschews Southwestern styling both in its landscaping and in its rooms, and what with all the green lawns and big trees here, you'd never know you were in the desert. Most rooms are large and have comfortable chairs, private patios, and marble bathrooms with two sinks. Bilevel suites feature kitchenettes, sleeping lofts, second-floor decks, and two bathrooms. The golf-course rooms are our favorites simply because of the views of the greens and the McDowell Mountains.

**Dining/Diversions:** There's a rather formal dining room serving Southwestern fare, a spa restaurant, a pub with pool tables and backgammon boards, a poolside snack bar, and even a tiny patisserie.

**Amenities:** In addition to the extensive golf and tennis facilities, you'll find a pro shop, three pools, whirlpool, volleyball court, a health club, and a beauty salon. A concierge, 24-hour room service, valet/laundry service, a car-rental desk, massages and other body and skin treatments, and tennis lessons are also available.

**Regal McCormick Ranch Resort & Villas.** 7401 N. Scottsdale Rd., Scottsdale, AZ 85253-3548. ☎ **800/222-8888** or 480/948-5050. Fax 480/991-5572. www.regal-hotels.com. 179 units. A/C MINIBAR TV TEL. Jan 1–May 31 $195–$295 double, $285–$370 suite, from $305 villa; June 1 to mid-Sept $129–$165 double, $180 suite, from $205 villa; mid-Sept to Dec 31 $205–$285 double, $305 suite, from $305 villa. AE, MC, V.

If you like the heat but not the desert, this resort, with its lakefront setting, is a good bet. Surrounded by green lawns and a golf course (and with bellmen wearing knickers and argyle socks), Regal McCormick Ranch does what it can to make you think you're not in the desert, and because it's smaller than many resorts in the area, it has a more personal feel. The focal point is, of course, the lake, where you can rent small sailboats if you like. More traditional resort activities are available at the two 18-hole golf courses and on the three tennis courts. The guest rooms all have their own private balconies or patios, and more than half the rooms overlook the lake. If you're here with your family, consider the spacious villas.

**Dining/Diversions:** One restaurant here serves Southwestern fare while the other serves new American. Both have views of the lake.

**Amenities:** Two 18-hole golf courses, outdoor pool overlooking lake, three lighted tennis courts, tennis pro shop, tennis lessons and clinics, whirlpool, complimentary boats, walking and jogging paths, sand volleyball court, concierge, room service, valet/laundry service.

**Scottsdale Marriott Suites.** 7325 E. 3rd Ave., Scottsdale, AZ 85251. ☎ **800/228-9290** or 480/945-1550. Fax 480/945-2005. 251 units. A/C TV TEL. Jan–May $150–$238 double; June–Aug $78–$199 double; Sept–Dec $159–$199 double. AE, DISC, MC, V.

Although primarily a business hotel, this also makes an excellent base if shopping is one of your reasons for coming to Scottsdale. The hotel is located only 2 blocks from the famous Fifth Avenue Shops, and Scottsdale Fashion Square is only slightly farther. All the rooms here are suites and have two telephones and two TVs, as well as refrigerators, wet bars, coffeemakers, and irons and ironing boards. In the marble bathrooms you'll find hair dryers and separate showers and tubs. This all adds up to spaciousness and luxury that even leisure travelers will appreciate.

**Dining:** There's a casual restaurant serving moderately priced meals.

**Amenities:** Outdoor pool, whirlpool, exercise room, saunas, concierge, business center, room service, and valet/laundry service.

✪ **The Sunburst.** 4925 N. Scottsdale Rd., Scottsdale, AZ 85251-7692. ☎ **800/528-7867** or 480/945-7666. Fax 480/946-4056. www.sunburstresort.com. 210 units. A/C MINIBAR TV TEL. Jan to mid-Apr $235–$285 double, $635–$1,000 suite; mid-Apr to late May $215–$255 double; $575–$900 suite; late May to mid-Sept $95–$135 double, $300–$475 suite; mid-Sept to Dec $185–$225 double, $500–$800 suite. AE, CB, DC, DISC, JCB, MC, V.

An exceptional location in the heart of the Scottsdale shopping district and a dramatic Southwestern styling are the primary appeals of this resort. The focal point of the lobby is a massive sandstone fireplace surrounded by lounging chairs evocative of the

Southwest. The resort's courtyard is lushly planted and features a small lagoon-style pool complete with sand beach, short water slide, and flame-topped columnar waterfalls. An artificial stream, waterfalls, and fake sandstone ruins all add up to a fun desert fantasy landscape (although not on the grand scale to be found at some area resorts).

Guest rooms are comfortable and decorated in new "Old West" styling, with cowhide-print stools and peeled log furnishings. Bathrooms have two sinks, and French doors open onto patios.

**Dining/Diversions:** The same Southwestern styling seen in the lobby prevails in the restaurant as well, and the menu features a mix of Mediterranean and Southwestern flavors. In addition, there's a lobby bar.

**Amenities:** A whirlpool and fitness room add to the recreational facilities here. Although there is no golf course, tee times can be arranged at nearby courses. A concierge, room service, and valet/laundry service are also available.

## MODERATE/INEXPENSIVE

In addition to the hotels listed below, Scottsdale has a few inexpensive and moderately priced chain motel options, although during the winter season prices are higher than you might expect. The rates given here are for the high season; see the appendix for toll-free telephone numbers. Try the **Days Inn—Scottsdale/Fashion Square Resort,** 4710 N. Scottsdale Rd. (☎ **480/947-5411**), charging $79 to $122 double; **Motel 6—Scottsdale,** 6848 E. Camelback Rd. (☎ **480/946-2280**), charging $64 double; and **Rodeway Inn—Phoenix/Scottsdale,** 7110 E. Indian School Rd. (☎ **480/946-3456**), charging $99 to $109 double.

✪ **Holiday Inn SunSpree Resort.** 7601 E. Indian Bend Rd., Scottsdale, AZ 85250. ☎ **800/ 852-5205** or 480/991-2400. Fax 480/998-2261. 200 units. A/C TV TEL. Jan to late Apr $129–$199 double; late Apr to May $99–$129 double; June–Sept $49–$109 double; Oct–Dec $99–$129 double. AE, CB, DC, DISC, EURO, JCB, MC, V.

During the winter and spring, it's almost impossible to find a reasonably priced resort in Scottsdale, but this attractive and economical hotel fits the bill. Situated on 16 acres amid wide expanses of lawn with both a small (though none too attractive) lake and a golf course adjacent, the SunSpree Resort certainly is not as luxurious as most other area resorts, but with its relatively low rates and policy of allowing kids under 12 to eat free in the resort's main restaurants, this is a good choice for families. Guest rooms have been recently renovated and now have a plush feel that belies the economical rates here. Ask for a mountain view room or a lakeside room with a patio. There's a restaurant overlooking the lake, as well as a lobby lounge and poolside bar, and room service is available. In addition to a swimming pool and whirlpool, the resort has a fitness room, tennis, volleyball, croquet, and horseshoes.

**La Hacienda Resort.** 7320 E. Camelback Rd., Scottsdale, AZ 85251. ☎ **480/994-4170.** 22 units. Mid-Nov to late May $99–$149 double, $159–$279 suite; mid-May to Dec 31 $79–$89 double, $99–$179 suite. AE, MC, V. Pets accepted.

Don't be taken in by the name, this little place is hardly a resort, but it is a well-placed and well-priced getaway spot with the look and feel of an updated 1960s apartment court. Funky and hip are the watchwords here, although the hipness is mostly in the tiny lobby, which has decoupaged walls and faux-painted floors. Just outside the lobby is an equally diminutive sidewalk cafe area. The inn's grassy little courtyard, which has a small pool and a hot tub, is set off from busy Camelback Road by a brick wall that gives the complex a private, residential feel. Rooms, which are a bit worn and a bit tacky, range from big to huge and most have full kitchens, though the bathrooms are small. Within just a few blocks are lots of nightclubs, great restaurants, and excellent shopping.

**Scottsdale's Fifth Avenue Inn.** 6935 Fifth Ave., Scottsdale, AZ 85251. ☎ **800/528-7396** or 480/994-9461. Fax 480/947-1695. 92 units. A/C TV TEL. Early Jan to mid-Apr $79–$99 double; mid-Apr to May 31 $64–$69 double; June 1–Sept 30 $54–$59 double; Oct 1 to early Jan $69–$74 double. Rates include continental breakfast. AE, DISC, MC, V.

For convenience and price, this motel can't be beat (at least not in Scottsdale). Located at the west end of the Fifth Avenue shopping district, this motel is within walking distance of some of the best shopping and dining in Scottsdale. The guest rooms are large and have held up well since their last renovation. The three-story building is arranged around a central courtyard where you'll find the pool and a whirlpool.

# CENTRAL PHOENIX & THE CAMELBACK CORRIDOR
## VERY EXPENSIVE

✪ **Arizona Biltmore Resort & Spa.** 24th St. and Missouri Ave., Phoenix, AZ 85016. ☎ **800/950-0086** or 602/955-6600. Fax 602/381-7600. www.arizonabiltmore.com. 750 units. A/C TV TEL. Early Sept to Dec $310–$430 double, from $530 suite; Jan 1 to early May $370–$520 double, from $650 suite; early May to mid-June $265–$340 double, from $495 suite; mid-June to early Sept, $165–$245 double, from $340 suite. Additional $12 incidentals fee also charged. AE, CB, DC, DISC, EURO, JCB, MC, V. Pets under 15 lb. accepted in cottage rooms with $250 deposit, $50 nonrefundable.

For tasteful elegance, superb service, prime location (near the foot of Squaw Peak and not far from Biltmore Fashion Park), and historic character (Frank Lloyd Wright helped in the design), no other resort in the valley can touch the Arizona Biltmore. What this all means is that the Biltmore is *the* Phoenix address for those who can afford to stay anywhere they want (including plenty of celebs and politicos). While the two superb golf courses are the main draw for many guests, the children's activities center has made this a popular choice for families as well.

Of the several different styles of accommodations, the "resort rooms" are the largest and most comfortable and have balconies or patios. Some also offer views of Squaw Peak. The rooms in the main building are the smallest and have neither balconies nor patios. The villa suites are the Biltmore's most spacious and luxurious accommodations.

**Dining/Diversions:** Wright's offers a formal setting (jackets preferred but not required) and serves excellent new American cuisine amid the handiwork of Frank Lloyd Wright. The Biltmore Grill serves meals with a touch of the Southwest both in flavors and decor. There's a quiet lobby/terrace bar and a poolside bar/restaurant. Afternoon tea, a Phoenix institution, is served in the lobby.

**Amenities:** Two 18-hole golf courses, 18-hole putting course, a full-service spa offering all manner of body and beauty treatments, five swimming pools (including one with a water slide and one with rental cabanas), two whirlpool spas, six lighted tennis courts, fitness center, sauna, steam room, jogging paths, rental bicycles, lawn games, business center, shops, concierge, room service, courtesy car, valet/laundry service, car-rental service.

**Hermosa Inn.** 5532 N. Palo Cristi Rd., Paradise Valley, AZ 85253. ☎ **800/241-1210** or 602/955-8614. Fax 602/955-8299. www.hermosainn.com. 35 units. A/C TV TEL. Early Jan to mid-April $245–$315 double, $415–$595 suite; mid-April to mid-May $160–$200 double, $320–$495 suite; mid-May to early Sept $95–$140 double, $275–$395 suite; early Sept to early Jan $195–$245 double, $345–$475 suite. Rates include continental breakfast. AE, CB, DC, DISC, MC, V. Pets under 20 lb. accepted with $250 deposit, $50 nonrefundable. Take 32nd St. north from Camelback Rd., turn right on Stanford Rd. and then turn left on N. Palo Cristi Rd. From Lincoln Dr., turn south on N. Palo Christi Rd. (east of 32nd St.).

Once a guest ranch, this luxurious boutique hotel is now one of the only hotels in the Phoenix area to offer a bit of Old Arizona atmosphere. Originally built as the home of Western artist Lon Megargee in 1930, the inn is situated in a quiet residential neighborhood on more than 6 acres of neatly landscaped gardens. If you don't like the crowds of big resorts, but do enjoy the luxury, this is the spot for you.

Rooms here vary from cozy to spacious and are all individually decorated in tastefully contemporary Western and Southwestern decor that would look at home on the pages of any interior design magazine. The largest suites incorporate a mixture of contemporary and antique Southwestern furnishings and accent pieces; these have more Southwestern flavor than just about any other rooms in the area.

**Dining:** Lon's, the hotel's dining room, is named for former owner and cowboy artist Lon Megargee and is located in Megargee's original adobe home. Excellent new American and Southwestern cuisine is served in the rustic, upscale setting. See "Where to Dine," below for more information.

**Amenities:** Situated around the grounds are a small outdoor pool (kept steaming hot in winter), a couple of whirlpools (one in a shady garden setting), and three tennis courts. Concierge available.

**The Ritz-Carlton Phoenix.** 2401 E. Camelback Rd., Phoenix, AZ 85016. ☎ **800/241-3333** or 602/468-0700. Fax 602/468-0793. 281 units. A/C MINIBAR TV TEL. Early Sept to late May $305–$365 double, $450–$550 suite; late May to early Sept $159–$199 double, $239–$279 suite. AE, CB, DC, DISC, EURO, JCB, MC, V. Valet parking $18. Dogs under 10 lb. accepted.

Located directly across the street from the Biltmore Fashion Park shopping center in the heart of the Camelback Corridor business and shopping district, the Ritz-Carlton is the city's finest nonresort hotel and is known for providing impeccable service. The public areas are filled with European antiques, and though this decor may seem a bit out of place in Phoenix, it's still utterly sophisticated. In the guest rooms, you'll find reproductions of antique furniture and marble bathrooms with ornate fixtures. For additional pampering, opt for the club level (breakfast and other snacks and drinks included in the rates). Although there's no golf course here, the Arizona Biltmore's courses are quite close.

**Dining/Diversions:** In Bistro 24, a casual and lively French bistro atmosphere prevails, with a menu to match. The elegant lobby lounge serves afternoon tea as well as cocktails, while in The Club, fine cigars and premium spirits are the order of the day. There's also a bar and grill by the pool.

**Amenities:** A small outdoor pool (with bar and grill), fitness center, and saunas provide some recreational possibilities. Also available are a concierge, 24-hour room service, valet/laundry service, baby-sitting, massages, and a complimentary golf shuttle.

✪ **Royal Palms Hotel and Casitas.** 5200 E. Camelback Rd., Phoenix, AZ 85018. ☎ **800/672-6011** or 602/840-3610. Fax 602/840-6927. 116 units. A/C TV TEL. Jan–May $335–$495 double, $385–$3,500 suite; May to early Sept $175–$295 double, $200–$2,500 suite; early Sept to Dec $285–$415 double, $325–$3,500 suite. AE, CB, DC, DISC, MC, V.

The Royal Palms, located midway between Scottsdale and Biltmore Fashion Park, reopened in 1997 after a complete renovation and is now one of the finest and most romantic resorts in the valley. The main building, which was constructed more than 50 years ago, was built by Cunard Steamship executive Delos Cooke in the Spanish mission style and is filled with European antiques that once belonged to Cooke. Antique water fountains and lush walled gardens give the property the tranquil feel of a Mediterranean monastery cloister.

The most memorable rooms at the resort are the individually designed deluxe casitas. Each of these rooms has a very distinctive decor (ranging from opulent contemporary to classic European). These rooms also have completely private back patios and front patios that can be enclosed by heavy curtains. Other rooms are luxuriously appointed, though not quite so opulent.

**Dining/Diversions:** T. Cook's, the resort's main dining room, serves Mediterranean cuisine amid European antiques and is one of the best restaurants in the area (see "Where to Dine," below). An adjacent bar/lounge conjures up a romantic Spanish villa setting. There's also a poolside bar and grill.

**Amenities:** Swimming pool surrounded by cabanas, one tennis court, a large exercise room. Concierge, room service, car-rental service, valet/laundry service.

## EXPENSIVE

**Embassy Suites Biltmore.** 2630 E. Camelback Rd., Phoenix, AZ 85016. ☎ **800/EMBASSY** or 602/955-3992. Fax 602/955-6479. 232 units. A/C TV TEL. Early Jan to late May $215–$235 double; late May to early Sept $125–$145 double; early Sept to early Jan $179–$199 double. Rates include full breakfast. AE, CB, DC, DISC, EURO, MC, V. Valet parking $5.

Located across the parking lot from the Biltmore Fashion Park (Phoenix's most upscale shopping center), this atrium hotel makes a great base if you want to be within walking distance of such places as Planet Hollywood, the Hard Rock Cafe, and half a dozen other good restaurants. The huge atrium is filled with interesting tile work (including colorful lizards) and other artistic Southwestern touches, as well as tropical greenery, waterfalls, and ponds filled with koi (Japanese carp). The curved wall of glass that forms the atrium looks out on a fairly large oval pool.

The rooms, all suites, are a bit of a let-down after passing through the atrium greenhouse, but they're certainly large enough to spread out in. Every suite has a microwave, refrigerator, wet bar, coffeemaker, two TVs, two dual-line phones, iron and ironing board, and hair dryer.

**Dining/Diversions:** The hotel's atrium houses the breakfast area and a romantic lounge with huge banquettes shaded by palm trees. Just off the atrium is a steakhouse with a contemporary decor. There's a complimentary evening cocktail hour.

**Amenities:** Large outdoor pool, whirlpool, fitness room, concierge, room service, valet/laundry, courtesy car. Preferred tee times available at Arizona Biltmore's two golf courses.

## MODERATE

**Hacienda Alta.** 5750 E. Camelback Rd., Phoenix, AZ 85018. ☎ and fax **480/945-8525.** 3 units. A/C TV. $100–$110 double; $150 suite. Rates include full breakfast. No credit cards.

Located adjacent to The Phoenician, yet very much in its own separate world surrounded by a desert landscape, this home offers a very convenient location, reasonable rates, and a chance to feel away from it all in the middle of the city. Don't expect the fussiness of most other B&Bs; owners Margaret and Ed Newhall make this casual, eclectic place a fun home away from home. The inn is housed in a 1920s territorial-style adobe home, and in the old gardens you'll find orange and grapefruit trees, which often provide juice for breakfast. A new addition offers a large suite with a sleeping loft, whirlpool tub, fireplace, and balcony overlooking the Phoenician's golf course.

**Maricopa Manor.** 15 W. Pasadena Ave. (P.O. Box 7186), Phoenix, AZ 85013-2001. ☎ **800/ 292-6403** or 602/274-6302. Fax 602/266-3904. www.maricopamanor.com. 6 suites. A/C TV TEL. Sept–May $129–$229 double; June–Aug $89–$129 double. Rates include continental breakfast. AE, DC, DISC, MC, V.

Centrally located between downtown Phoenix and Scottsdale and particularly popular with business travelers, this elegant B&B is just a block off busy Camelback Road. However, the orange trees, palms, and large yard all lend a country air. The inn's main home was built in 1928 and is designed to resemble a Spanish manor house. All the guest rooms are large suites, two of which are located in a separate guest house. One suite has a sunroom and kitchen, while another has two separate sleeping areas. Breakfast is delivered to your door each morning in a basket and can be eaten in the room

## ⓘ Family-Friendly Hotels

**Hyatt Regency Scottsdale** *(see p. 61)*  Not only is there a totally awesome water playground complete with sand beach and water slide, but the Kamp Hyatt Kachina program provides supervised structured activities.

**The Phoenician** *(see p. 64)*  Kids absolutely love the water slide here; it's the fastest resort slide in the valley. Kids and parents both appreciate the Funicians Club, a supervised activities program for children ages 5 to 12. Kids get to play games, make crafts, and burn up lots of excess energy. A putting green and croquet court offer further diversions.

**Doubletree La Posada Resort** *(see p. 66)*  If you're a kid, it's hard to imagine a cooler pool than the one here. It's got a two-story waterfall, a swim-through cave, and big artificial boulders all around. There are also horseshoe pits, a volleyball court, and a pitch-and-putt green.

**Pointe Hilton Squaw Peak Resort** *(see below)*  A water slide, tubing river, waterfall, water volleyball, a miniature golf course, a video games room, and a kids' program guarantee that your kids will be exhausted by the end of the day. This is the best resort in the valley for families.

or at one of the tables in the garden. The inn has a pool and hot tub, and guests also have access to a nearby health club.

**Sierra Suites.** 5235 N. 16th St., Phoenix, AZ 85016. ☎ **800/4-SIERRA** or 602/265-6800. Fax 602/265-1114. 113 units. A/C TV TEL. Oct–Apr $99–$139; May–Sept $59–$79. AE, DISC, MC, V.

Billing itself as a temporary residence and offering discounts for stays of 7 days or more, this hotel consists of studio-style apartments and is located just north of Camelback Road and not far from Biltmore Fashion Park. Though designed primarily for corporate business travelers on temporary assignment in the area, this hotel makes a good choice for families as well. All rooms have full kitchens, big closets and bathrooms, irons and ironing boards, and separate sitting areas. Facilities include an exercise room, a pool, and a whirlpool. Local phone calls are free.

## NORTH PHOENIX
### VERY EXPENSIVE

✪ **Pointe Hilton Squaw Peak Resort.** 7677 N. 16th St., Phoenix, AZ 85020-9832. ☎ **800/876-4683** or 602/997-2626. Fax 602/997-2391. 564 units. A/C MINIBAR TV TEL. Late Dec to early May $279–$339 double, $879 grande suite; early May to late May and mid-Sept to mid-Dec $189–$269 double, $729 grande suite; late May to mid-Sept and mid-Dec to late Dec $99–$129 double, $489 grande suite. AE, CB, DC, DISC, EURO, EURO, JCB, MC, V.

Located at the foot of Squaw Peak, this lushly landscaped resort in north Phoenix makes a big splash with its Hole-in-the-Wall River Ranch, an impressive 9-acre aquatic playground that features a tubing "river," water slide, waterfall, sports pool, and lagoon pool. An 18-hole putting course, game room, and children's activity center together make this a great family vacation spot. The resort is done in the Spanish villa style, and all the guest rooms are suites, studios, or two-story casitas furnished with a mixture of contemporary and Spanish colonial–style furnishings.

**Dining:** There's a fun Mexican restaurant housed in an 1880 adobe building and a Western-theme restaurant in a building that dates from the 1930s. There's also a more upscale dining room that serves contemporary American and Southwestern dishes.

**Amenities:** In addition to the River Ranch pools, there are four other pools, as well as several whirlpool spas. An 18-hole golf course (4 miles away), four tennis courts, jogging trails, rental bikes, shops, and a business center round out the adult facilities. The full-service spa offers various body and beauty treatments and has racquetball courts, free weights, exercise machines, a lap pool, sauna, steam room, and aerobics classes. A concierge, room service, valet/laundry service, rental-car desk, complimentary afternoon cocktails, baby-sitting, and children's programs are also available.

**Pointe Hilton Tapatio Cliffs Resort.** 11111 N. Seventh St., Phoenix, AZ 85020. ☎ **800/ 876-4683** or 602/866-7500. Fax 602/993-0276. 584 suites. A/C MINIBAR TV TEL. Late Dec to early May $279–$339 double, $879 grande suite; early May to late May and mid-Sept to mid-Dec $189–$269 double, $729 grande suite; late May to mid-Sept and mid-Dec to late Dec $99–$129 double, $489 grande suite. AE, CB, DC, DISC, EURO, JCB, MC, V.

Situated on the shoulder of North Mountain, Tapatio Cliffs offers the steepest and lushest grounds of the three Pointe resorts (get your heart and brakes checked before staying here). The Falls, a 3-acre water playground, includes two lagoon pools, a 138-foot water slide, and impressive 40-foot-high cascades that tumble over real and artificial boulders and through terraced pools. Poolside rental cabanas provide an extra dash of luxury for those who can afford it. Hikers will enjoy the easy access to trails in the adjacent North Mountain Recreation Area, while golfers can avail themselves of the resort's golf course. A small spa offers a variety of body and beauty treatments. All rooms are spacious suites with Southwest furnishings. Corner rooms, with their extra windows, are particularly bright.

**Dining/Diversions:** The hilltop Different Pointe of View offers stupendous views, an international menu, and an extensive wine cellar (see "Where to Dine," below). At the Waterin' Hole there are steaks on the grill and sawdust on the floor, while at Pointe in Tyme, marble floors and mahogany paneling lend a classic clublike atmosphere. There are also two poolside snack bars.

**Amenities:** Other facilities include 11 lighted tennis courts, five other pools, whirlpool spas, a fitness center with steam room and sauna, a small health spa, a game room, rental bikes, a gift shop, tennis shop, golf shop, and a business center. You'll also find a concierge, room service, complimentary afternoon cocktails, massages, a rental-car desk, a free shuttle between Pointe Hilton properties, horseback riding, and baby-sitting.

**Sheraton Crescent Hotel.** 2620 W. Dunlap Ave., Phoenix, AZ 85021. ☎ **800/423-4126** or 602/943-8200. Fax 602/371-2856. www.arizonaguide.com/sheratoncrescent. 342 units. A/C TV TEL. Jan 1 to late May $159–$275 double; late May to mid-Sept $89–$150 double, from $100 suite; mid-Sept to Dec 31 $149–$215 double, from $280 suite. AE, CB, DC, DISC, EURO, JCB, MC, V. Small pets accepted ($100 deposit, $25 nonrefundable).

Located in the north-central high-tech business district and across I-17 from the Metrocenter mall, this business hotel is a sister property to The Phoenician and displays much the same decorative style, albeit on a more subdued level. Although situated away from downtown and the Camelback Corridor business districts, this is still one of the city's better choices for business travelers, especially for those who like to exercise when they aren't working (lots of athletic facilities). Marble abounds in the lobby and also shows up in guest room bathrooms. Guest rooms are designed with business travelers in mind, and provide plenty of space, comfort, and convenience. The king rooms with balconies are worth asking for.

**Dining/Diversions:** The hotel's big, casual restaurant serves new American cuisine. The adjacent lounge is small and subdued.

**Amenities:** The hotel's small main pool is in a lush garden setting and a has a long waterslide that's a hit with kids. Other facilities include a large fitness center, whirlpool spa, sauna, two tennis courts, two squash courts, and volleyball and basketball courts. Concierge, room service, and valet/laundry service are available.

## EXPENSIVE

**Embassy Suites—Phoenix North.** 2577 W. Greenway Rd., Phoenix, AZ 85023-4222. ☎ **800/EMBASSY** or 602/375-1777. Fax 602/375-4012. 314 units. A/C TV TEL. Jan–May $189–$209 double; June–Aug $109–$119 double; Sept–Dec $149–$159 double. Rates include full breakfast. AE, CB, DC, DISC, MC, V.

This resortlike hotel in north Phoenix, is right off I-17 and is well away from the rest of the valley's resorts (and good restaurants), but if you happen to have relatives in Sun City or are planning a trip north to Sedona or the Grand Canyon, it's a good choice. The lobby of this Mission-style, all-suite hotel has the feel of a Spanish church interior, but instead of a cloister off the lobby, there is a garden courtyard with a huge swimming pool and lots of palm trees. The guest rooms are all suites with two TVs, wet bars, refrigerators, coffeemakers, safes, and irons and ironing boards, though furnishings are budget-motel basic. The bathrooms are small, but they do have hair dryers.

**Dining/Diversions:** The casual restaurant in the lobby serves moderately priced meals. There's a piano lounge in the lobby and poolside bar. Complimentary cocktails are served each evening.

**Amenities:** In addition to the large pool, there are two tennis courts, an exercise room, a whirlpool, a sauna, a sand volleyball court, and two racquetball courts. Room service and valet/laundry service are available.

## MODERATE/INEXPENSIVE

Among the better moderately priced chain motels in north Phoenix are the **Best Western InnSuites Hotel Phoenix,** 1615 E. Northern Ave. at 16th Street (☎ **602/997-6285**), charging $99 to $129 double; and the **Best Western Bell Motel,** 17211 N. Black Canyon Hwy. (☎ **602/993-8300**), charging $89 to $109 double. Rates are for the high season; for toll-free phone numbers, see the appendix.

Among the better budget chain motels in the north Phoenix area are the **Motel 6—Sweetwater,** 2735 W. Sweetwater Ave. (☎ **602/942-5030**), charging $52 double; and **Super 8—Phoenix Metro/Central,** 4021 N. 27th Ave. (☎ **602/248-8880**), charging $50 to $56 double. Rates are for the high season; for toll-free phone numbers, see appendix B.

# DOWNTOWN PHOENIX
## EXPENSIVE

**Crowne Plaza—Phoenix Downtown.** 100 N. First St., Phoenix, AZ 85004. ☎ **800/2CROWNE** or 602/333-0000. Fax 602/333-5181. 532 units. A/C TV TEL. Oct–Apr $189–$255 double; May–Sept $89–$129 double. AE, DC, DISC, MC, V. Valet parking $10.

This business and convention hotel is currently your best choice in downtown, though with the crowds of conventioneers, individual travelers are likely to feel overlooked. A Mediterranean villa theme has been adopted throughout the public areas with slate flooring and walls painted to resemble cracked stucco. Guest rooms continue the Mediterranean feel and are designed with the business traveler in mind. Hair dryers, safes, irons and ironing boards, and coffeemakers all add up to a high level of convenience.

**Dining/Diversions:** There's a cafe for breakfast and a bar and grill with a bit of character (but very standard fare). There's also a Starbucks.

**Amenities:** Fitness room, swimming pool, whirlpool spa, room service, concierge, massages, valet/laundry service, gift shop, business center.

**Hyatt Regency Phoenix.** 122 N. 2nd St., Phoenix, AZ 85004. ☎ **800/233-1234** or 602/252-1234. Fax 602/254-9472. 712 units. A/C TV TEL. $214–$255 double; $450–$1,500 suite. AE, CB, DC, DISC, JCB, MC, V. Valet parking $15; self-parking $10.

Located directly across the street from the Phoenix Civic Plaza, this high-rise Hyatt is almost always packed with conventioneers and consequently does not offer the sort of seasonal price breaks of other area hotels. Whether full or empty, the hotel always seems understaffed, so don't expect top-notch service if you're stuck here on a convention. However, the recently remodeled lobby certainly provides plenty of space for lounging. The rooms are fairly standard, though comfortably furnished. Ask for a room above the eighth floor to take advantage of the views from the glass elevators.

**Dining/Diversions:** The Compass Room is Arizona's only rotating rooftop restaurant and serves Southwestern dishes. The food is usually decent, and the views are fascinating. There's also the more casual and inexpensive Terrace Café in the hotel's atrium and a contemporary restaurant/bar at street level.

**Amenities:** Small outdoor pool, exercise room, whirlpool, tennis courts, shopping arcade, concierge, room service, and valet/laundry service.

## MODERATE

✪ **Hotel San Carlos.** 202 N. Central Ave., Phoenix, AZ 85004. ☎ **800/528-5446** or 602/253-4121. Fax 602/253-6668. 132 units. A/C TV TEL. Jan–Apr $139 double, $185 suite; May–Sept $89 double, $125 suite; Oct–Dec $105 double, $169 suite. AE, CB, DC, DISC, MC, V. Valet parking $10; self-parking $6. Pets allowed, $25.

If you don't mind staying in downtown Phoenix with the convention crowds, you'll get a great value at this historic hotel. Built in 1928 and listed on the National Register of Historic Places, the San Carlos is a small European-style hotel that provides that touch of elegance and charm missing from the other standardized high-rise hotels downtown. Crystal chandeliers, a travertine check-in desk, and comfortable couches give the small lobby a touch of sophistication. The rooms, though small by today's standards, feature wingback chairs, ceiling fans, and coffeemakers. There's an Italian restaurant in the lobby, an adjacent espresso bar, and an Irish pub. The hotel also features valet/laundry service, a rooftop pool, and an exercise room.

# TEMPE, MESA, SOUTH PHOENIX & THE AIRPORT AREA
## VERY EXPENSIVE

✪ **Wyndham Buttes Resort.** 2000 Westcourt Way, Tempe, AZ 85282. ☎ **800/WYNDHAM** or 602/225-9000. Fax 602/438-8622. 353 units. A/C MINIBAR TV TEL. Jan 1 to late May $249–$344 double, $575–$1,500 suite; late May to early Sept $99–$209 double, $475–$1,500 suite; early Sept to Dec 31 $175–$294 double, $575–$1,500 suite. AE, DC, DISC, MC, V.

Located only 3 miles from Sky Harbor Airport, this spectacular resort makes the utmost of its craggy hilltop location, and although some people complain that the freeway in the foreground ruins the view, we disagree. From its circular restaurant to its free-form swimming pool and desert landscaping, every inch of this resort is calculated to take your breath away. Behind the reception desk is a cactus garden through which flows a stream that cascades over a precipice into a fish pond in the restaurant on the lower level. The rocky setting firmly plants this resort in the desert (if you want green and lush, try somewhere else).

Despite the contemporary architecture here, a recent room renovation opted for a classic feel. Most rooms have good views across the valley (marred slightly by the adjacent freeway). Unfortunately for fans of long soaks, most bathrooms have only ¾-size tubs.

**Dining/Diversions:** The Top of the Rock restaurant snags the best view around, and sunset dinners are always packed (see "Where to Dine," below). An informal dining room, complete with waterfall and fish pond, is located below the lobby. There are bars below Top of the Rock (with only a partial view), in the lobby, and by the pool.

**Amenities:** Two free-form pools with waterfalls and a connecting swim-through canal are the best reason to stay here, and among the resort's four whirlpools is the most romantic whirlpool in the valley. Other amenities include four tennis courts, a fitness center, concierge, room service, valet/laundry service, and a business center.

**The Pointe Hilton South Mountain Resort.** 7777 S. Pointe Pkwy., Phoenix, AZ 85044. ☎ **800/876-4683** or 602/438-9000. Fax 602/431-6528. 638 units. A/C MINIBAR TV TEL. Late Dec to early May $279–$339 double, $879 grande suite; early May to late May and mid-Sept to mid-Dec $189–$269 double, $729 grande suite; late May to mid-Sept and mid-Dec to late Dec $99–$129 double, $489 grande suite. AE, CB, DC, DISC, EURO, EURO, JCB, MC, V.

Located on the south side of the valley, this Pointe Hilton resort abuts the 17,000-acre South Mountain Park, though the resort's manicured grounds keep nature at a distance. While the grand scale of this resort seems designed primarily to accommodate convention crowds, individual travelers, especially active ones, will find plenty to keep them busy here. Golfers get great views from the greens, urban cowboys can ride right into the sunset on South Mountain, and if it's abs and pecs that you want to work on, the 40,000-square-foot fitness center should keep you pumped up.

All the guest rooms here are suites and feature contemporary Southwestern furnishings; even the smallest are quite roomy. Mountainside suites offer the best views of the golf course and South Mountain.

**Dining:** Rustler's Rooste is a Western-themed restaurant featuring cowboy bands and rattlesnake appetizers (see "Where to Dine," below). Another Pointe in Tyme features a more sedate atmosphere and continental cuisine. There's also a casual Mexican restaurant and a place for healthful meals at the fitness center.

**Amenities:** Two 18-hole golf courses, 10 tennis courts, five racquetball courts, six swimming pools, two volleyball courts, riding stables, a beauty salon, gift shop, pro shop, health club (which offers aerobics classes), concierge, room service, valet/laundry service, massages, a rental-car desk, complimentary afternoon cocktails, and baby-sitting.

## EXPENSIVE

**Tempe Mission Palms Hotel.** 60 E. 5th St., Tempe, AZ 85281. ☎ **800/547-8705** or 480/894-1400. Fax 480/968-7677. www.missionpalms.com. 303 units. A/C TV TEL. Jan–May $189–$259 double, $409 suite; June–Aug $99–$139 double, $269 suite; Sept–Dec $169–$239 double, $389 suite. AE, DC, DISC, JCB, MC, V.

College students, their families, and anyone else who wants to be close to Tempe's nightlife will find this an ideal, though overpriced, location. Situated right in the heart of the Mill Avenue shopping, restaurant, and nightlife district, this hotel has recently undergone a face-lift and now plays up its mission-style design. When you've had enough of the hustle and bustle on Mill Avenue, you can retreat to the hotel's rooftop pool. Guest rooms benefited greatly from the recent remodeling and now boast lots of wood, marble, and granite. For the most part, they're quite comfortable.

**Dining/Diversions:** The restaurant serves Southwestern meals at reasonable prices, and there's also a Mediterranean-influenced lounge.

**Amenities:** Medium-size outdoor pool, tennis court, fitness center, whirlpool, sauna, business center, room service, complimentary airport shuttle, valet/laundry service.

**Twin Palms Hotel.** 225 E. Apache Blvd., Tempe, AZ 85281. ☎ **800/367-0835** or 480/967-9431. Fax 480/968-1877. www.twinpalmshotel.com. 140 units. A/C TV TEL. Jan–Apr $159 double; May–Sept $79 double; Oct–Dec $129 double. Suite $170–$350 year-round. AE, CB, DC, DISC, MC, V.

Although the rooms at this midrise hotel just off the ASU campus are just standard rooms (with coffeemakers), the Twin Palms is a great choice for fitness fanatics. Hotel guests have full access to the nearby ASU Student Recreation Complex, which covers 135,000 square feet and includes a huge weight-training room; Olympic pool; and racquetball, tennis, and basketball courts. When you stay here, you're also close to Sun Devil Stadium, the ASU-Karsten Golf Course, and busy Mill Avenue.

**Diversions:** There's a small bar off the lobby.

**Amenities:** In addition to fitness center access, there's a complimentary airport shuttle, and local phone calls are free.

## MODERATE/INEXPENSIVE

Apache Boulevard in Tempe becomes Main Street in Mesa, and along this stretch of road there are numerous old motels charging some of the lowest rates in the valley. However, these motels are very hit-or-miss. If you're used to staying at nonchain motels, you might want to cruise this strip and check out a few places. Otherwise, try the chain motels mentioned below (which tend to charge $20 to $40 more per night than nonchain motels).

Chain motel options in the Tempe area include the **Days Inn—Tempe,** 1221 E. Apache Blvd. (☎ **480/968-7793**), charging $69 to $124 double; **Super 8—Tempe/Scottsdale,** 1020 E. Apache Blvd. (☎ **480/967-8891**), charging $77 to $80 double; and **Travelodge—Tempe,** 1005 E. Apache Blvd. (☎ **480/968-7871**), charging $80 double. See the appendix for toll-free phone numbers.

Chain motel options in the Mesa area include the **Days Inn—Mesa,** 333 W. Juanita Ave. (☎ **480/844-8900**), charging $86 to $101 double; **Motel 6—Mesa North,** 336 W. Hampton Ave. (☎ **480/844-8899**), charging $54 double; and **Super 8—Mesa,** 6733 E. Main St. (☎ **480/981-6181**), charging $65 to $69 double. See the appendix for toll-free numbers.

Chain motels in the airport area include the **Best Western Airport Inn,** 2425 S. 24th St. (☎ **602/273-7251**), charging $90 to $119 double; and **Rodeway Inn Airport East,** 1550 S. 52nd St. (☎ **480/967-3000**), charging $70 to $120 double. Rates are for the high season; for toll-free phone numbers, see appendix B.

✪ **Fiesta Inn.** 2100 S. Priest Dr., Tempe, AZ 85282. ☎ **800/528-6481** or 480/967-1441. Fax 480/967-0224. 270 units. A/C TV TEL. Jan 1–May 31 $139–$165 double, $225–$275 suite; June 1–Sept 30 $79–$85 double, $100–$135 suite; Oct 1–Dec 31 $122–$142 double, $150–$195 suite. AE, CB, DC, DISC, MC, V.

Reasonable rates, shady grounds, extensive recreational facilities (three tennis courts, putting green, driving range, pool, and fitness room), and a location close to ASU and Tempe's Mill Avenue make this older, casual resort hotel one of the best deals in the valley. You're also only a few minutes from the airport. OK, so it isn't as fancy as the resorts in Scottsdale, but who can argue with the rates? Guest rooms are large, with refrigerators, coffeemakers, and hair dryers, and local phone calls are free. The restaurant serves reliable American fare, and there's a lounge with a big-screen TV. Services include concierge, room service, complimentary airport shuttle, and valet/laundry service.

**Wyndham Garden Hotel—Phoenix Airport.** 427 N. 44th St., Phoenix, AZ 85008. ☎ **800/WYNDHAM** or 602/220-4400. Fax 602/231-8703. 210 units. A/C TV TEL. Jan–Apr $109–$179 double, $119–$199 suite; May $89–$149 double, $99–$169 suite; June–Sept

$59–$94 double, $69–$114 suite; Oct–Dec $89–$149 double, $99–$169 suite. AE, CB, DC, DISC, MC, V.

If you're in town for just a day or two or are getting in late, this business hotel is conveniently located only a mile from the east airport exit and is comfortable, modern, and convenient. The "king" rooms are particularly well designed, each with a comfortable chair, a work desk, and a bureau that separates the sleeping area from the sitting/working area. Other room amenities include hair dryers, coffeemakers, and two telephones. There's a clublike lounge to one side of the lobby and an inexpensive casual restaurant as well. Amenities include an outdoor pool (but jet noises will prevent you from doing much relaxing out here), complimentary airport shuttle, room service, and valet/laundry service.

## OUTLYING VALLEY OF THE SUN RESORTS

At press time, several new resorts, including a Westin, a Mariott, and a Four Seasons were under construction or in planning for north Scottsdale.

✪ **The Boulders.** 34631 N. Tom Darlington Dr. (P.O. Box 2090), Carefree, AZ 85377. ☎ **800/553-1717** or 480/488-9009. Fax 480/488-4118. 160 casitas. A/C MINIBAR TV TEL. Mid-Dec to late May $425–$545 double; late May to Sept $175–$295 double; Oct to early Dec $425 double; early Dec to mid-Dec $250 double. 1-, 2-, and 3-bedroom villas also available. AE, CB, DC, MC, V. Pets accepted ($50 nonrefundable deposit).

Set amid a jumble of giant boulders 45 minutes north of Scottsdale, this resort epitomizes the Southwest aesthetic and is the state's premier golf resort. Adobe buildings blend unobtrusively into the desert, as do the two noted golf courses, which feature the most breathtaking tee boxes in Arizona. If you can tear yourself away from the fairways, you can relax around either of two pools, play tennis (no boulders on the courts), or take advantage of the full-service spa. The distance from Scottsdale is this resort's only real shortcoming.

The lobby is an organic adobe structure with tree-trunk pillars, a flagstone floor, and a collection of Native American artifacts on display. The guest rooms continue the adobe styling with stucco walls, beehive fireplaces, and beamed ceilings. The bathrooms are large and luxuriously appointed with tubs for two, separate showers, double sinks, and hair dryers. The best views are from second-floor rooms.

**Dining/Diversions:** The Latilla Room, the resort's premier restaurant, serves innovative American cuisine. The Palo Verde Room is a more casual spot serving Southwestern dishes. There's also a country club dining room, and, in the resort's El Pedregal shopping center, a bakery and a Mexican/Southwestern restaurant. A comfortable lounge features live jazz in the evenings.

**Amenities:** Two 18-hole golf courses, full-service spa, fitness center (with a lap pool, sauna, and state-of-the-art exercise machines), six tennis courts, two pools, jogging and hiking trails, pro shop, rental bikes, concierge, room service, valet/laundry service, airport shuttle, baby-sitting, children's programs, rock climbing program, night-vision guided hikes.

**Gold Canyon Golf Resort.** 6100 S. Kings Ranch Rd., Gold Canyon, AZ 85219. ☎ **800/624-6445** or 480/982-9090. Fax 480/983-9554. www.goldcanyongolfresort.com. 101 units. A/C TV TEL. Late Dec to mid-May $150–$230 double; mid-May to Sept $125–$155 double; Oct to late Dec $175–$205 double. AE, DC, DISC, MC, V.

Although Gold Canyon Ranch is way out on the east side of the valley near Apache Junction, it's still very popular with golfers who come to play some of the most scenic holes in the state. The Superstition Mountains provide the backdrop, and even non-golfers will appreciate the scenery. However, the small pool here is more a place to cool off after a round of golf than a place to lounge away the day. The guest rooms are large and are housed in blindingly white pueblo-inspired buildings. Some rooms have fireplaces, others whirlpools; all have hair dryers and coffeemakers.

**Dining/Diversions:** The main dining room serves Southwestern and new American fare, and there's a bar and grill, with simple meals as well.

**Amenities:** Two gorgeous 18-hole golf courses should both be open by the time you read this. There are also two lighted tennis courts, a pool, whirlpool, horseback riding, rental bikes, and room service.

**The Wigwam Resort.** 300 Wigwam Blvd., Litchfield Park, AZ 85340. ☎ **800/327-0396** or 623/935-3811. Fax 623/935-3737. www.wigwamresort.com. 331 units. A/C MINIBAR TV TEL. Early Jan to early May $330–$390 double, $390–$475 suite; early May to late June $245–$295 double, $295–$380 suite; late June to early Sept $145–$185 double, $185–$225 suite; early Sept to early Jan $245–$295 double, $295–$380 suite. AE, CB, DC, DISC, MC, V. Pets under 20 lb. accepted ($50 deposit, $25 nonrefundable).

Located 20 minutes west of downtown Phoenix and twice as far from Scottsdale, this resort opened its doors to the public in 1929 and remains one of the nation's premier golf resorts. Three challenging golf courses and superb service are the reasons most people choose this resort, which, though elegant, is set amid flat lands that lack the stunning desert scenery of the Scottsdale area.

Most of the guest rooms are in Santa Fe–style buildings and are surrounded by green lawns and colorful gardens. All rooms are spacious and feature contemporary Southwestern furniture. Some rooms have fireplaces, but the most popular rooms are those along the golf course.

**Dining/Diversions:** The resort's Terrace Dining Room serves continental cuisine indoors or on the terrace beside the pool. The equally elegant Arizona Kitchen serves acclaimed Southwestern cuisine and features an exhibition grill. Golfers have their own conveniently located restaurant in the clubhouse. Afternoon tea and evening cocktails are served in a lobby lounge, and sports fans can retreat to the Arizona Bar to catch the games on big-screen TVs.

**Amenities:** Three golf courses, putting green, golf lessons, nine tennis courts, tennis lessons, pro shop, two pools, bicycles, volleyball, croquet, trap and skeet shooting range, exercise room, sauna, holiday and summer children's programs, concierge, room service, valet/laundry service, massages.

## 4  Where to Dine

Just as the Valley of the Sun boasts some terrific resorts, it is also full of excellent restaurants, and Scottsdale and the Biltmore Corridor are home to most of the city's best dining establishments. If you have only one expensive meal while you're here, I'd suggest a resort restaurant that offers a view of the city lights. Other meals not to be missed are the cowboy dinners served amid Wild West decor at such places as Pinnacle Peak and Rustler's Rooste.

Phoenix also has plenty of those big and familiar chains that you've heard so much about. There's a **Hard Rock Cafe,** 2621 E. Camelback Rd. (☎ 602/956-3669), and a **Planet Hollywood,** 2402 E. Camelback Rd. (☎ 602/954-7827), where you toss down a burger and then buy that all-important T-shirt to prove you've been here. As Phoenix has become more and more Arizona's version of Los Angeles, it has also acquired all the important California chains such as **California Pizza Kitchen,** 2400 E. Camelback Rd. (☎ 602/553-8382), located in the Biltmore Fashion Park (along with Planet Hollywood).

The big chain steakhouses are also duking it out here in Phoenix. You'll find two **Ruth's Chris** steakhouses: in the Scottsdale Seville shopping plaza, 7001 N. Scottsdale Rd., Scottsdale (☎ 480/991-5988), and in the Biltmore district at the corner of 22nd

Street and Camelback Road (☎ **602/957-9600**); and, in north Scottsdale across from the Scottsdale airport, there's a **Morton's Steakhouse,** 15233 N. Kierland Blvd. (☎ **480/951-4440**).

Good places to go trolling for a place to eat include the trendy Biltmore Fashion Park and Old Town Scottsdale. At the former, which by the way is a shopping mall, not a park, you'll find the above mentioned chain restaurants—Planet Hollywood and California Pizza Kitchen—as well as nearly a dozen other excellent restaurants. In Old Town Scottsdale, within an area of roughly 4 square blocks, you'll also find about a dozen good restaurants. A few of our favorites in both places are listed here.

# SCOTTSDALE
## EXPENSIVE

**The Chaparral.** At Marriott's Camelback Inn, 5402 E. Lincoln Dr. ☎ **480/948-1700,** ext. 7888. Reservations highly recommended. Main courses $24–$34. AE, CB, DC, DISC, MC, V. Daily 6–10pm. NEW AMERICAN.

They've changed the decor and the menu, but rest assured that Camelback Mountain is still the view out the window. No longer does the menu feature the timeless continental classics it once did. These days you'll start off with herb-laced focaccia, potato rolls, and salted rosemary lavosh—all incredibly tempting. The rich lobster bisque—covered with puff pastry and served with a spoonful of caviar crème fraîche—is a holdover from the old menu; it's an elegant dining experience not to be missed. Some dishes are more successful than others. Hits include a moist and flavorful sea bass crusted with tomato and parsley, and, for garlic lovers, a lavender-spiced pork tenderloin served with garlic jam. Service is as attentive as you would expect, and some wines are even fairly moderately priced. Not as formal an environment as it once was, you can now get away with dressing "comfortably casual" here.

**El Chorro Lodge.** 5550 E. Lincoln Dr. ☎ **480/948-5170.** Reservations recommended. Lunch $8–$17; full dinner $11–$63. AE, CB, DC, DISC, MC, V. Mon–Fri 11am–3pm and 5:30–11pm, Sat–Sun 5:30–11pm. CONTINENTAL.

Built in 1934 as a school for girls and converted to a lodge and restaurant 3 years later, El Chorro Lodge is a valley landmark set on its own 22 acres of desert. It's one of the area's last old traditional restaurants. At night, spotlights shine on the palo verdes and cacti, and the restaurant takes on a timeless tranquillity, even if the interior is a little dowdy. The adobe building houses several dining rooms, but the patio is the place to sit, either in the daytime or on a chilly night near the crackling fireplace. The traditional decor and the menu that features such classic dishes as chateaubriand and rack of lamb are popular with both old-timers and families. In addition to the favorites, there are several dishes that are low in salt and fat, as well as seafood dishes. Save room for the legendary sticky buns.

**Golden Swan.** At the Hyatt Regency Scottsdale Resort at Gainey Ranch, 7500 E. Doubletree Ranch Rd. ☎ **480/991-3388.** Reservations recommended. Main courses $26–$35; Sun brunch $34. AE, DC, DISC, MC, V. Daily 6–10pm, Sun brunch 9:30am–2pm. SOUTHWESTERN.

At this restaurant within the Hyatt Regency Scottsdale Resort, a combination of cuisine and setting make for very special meals. Dramatically spotlit royal palms, geometric architecture, and the sound of fountains and waterfalls set the tone, while the food is just as pleasurable, beautifully presented with plenty of attention to details. You might start your meal with olive bread for dipping in a sort of olive oil fondue (a concoction of basil, tomatoes, and olives in olive oil). Artistically presented entrees generally offer several distinctive flavors—some subtle, some bold. For example, tequila and lime marinated shrimp and scallops on a cheese quesadilla with avocado salsa or

# Phoenix, Scottsdale & the Valley of the Sun Dining

NA-0252

82

0            3 Miles

0            3 Kilometers

N

Cave Creek Rd.

Bell    Rd.    23    Frank Lloyd Wright Blvd.

Greenway    Rd.    St.

Thunderbird    Rd.    24    Rd.

Sweetwater    Ave.

Cactus    St.    Invergordon    Scottsdale    Hayden Rd.    Pima    96th    St.    104th St.

32nd    Tatum    56th

Shea    Blvd.    25    Shea    Blvd.

26

Dreamy Draw Recreation Area    Doubletree Ranch Rd.    27

28

Paradise Valley

Squaw Peak Recreation Area    33

22    Lincoln Dr.    29   30    Indian Bend Rd.

Peak Pkwy.    31    McDonald Dr.

32   34

17    Camelback Mountain Recreation Area

10   13    14    16    20    21    19    42    40    101    To Payson

2   11    15    18    44   37    35    Camelback Rd.    87

Dobson Rd.    Indian School Rd.    Beeline Hwy.

Osborn Rd.    38   36    43

39    Thomas    Rd.

41

40th   44th    St.    56th    64th    St.    Scottsdale    Miller   Rd.    Hayden   Rd.    Pima    Scottsdale

51    St.    McDowell    Rd.

202    48th   52nd    Papago Park    68th    101

Sky Harbor International Airport    45    Van Buren    St.    McKellips    Rd.

Salt   River    Mesa

202    Country   Club    Dr.

17    143    46   47    89    202

10    Hohokam   Expy.    Tempe    University    Mesa    Stapley

Dr.    Apache Blvd.    Main    St.

24th   St.    Ave.    Broadway    Rd.    Dr.

48    101

32nd   St.    50    Priest    Mill    Southern    Ave.    51

60    Superstition Freeway

Baseline    Rd.

49    Guadalupe    Rd.

Ave.

Elliot    Rd.    Dr.    Rd.    Rd.    School    Arizona    Rd.    Rd.    Rd.

10    87

Warner    Rd.    Rural    McClintock    Price    Dobson    Alma    McQueen    Cooper    Gilbert

Ray    Rd.

Chandler    Blvd.    Williams   Field   Rd.

To Tucson    Pecos    Rd.

roasted garlic marinated pork tenderloin with chili mashed potatoes in a potato tower. Save room for one of the Golden Swan's decadent desserts—perhaps a silky chocolate mousse cake with fresh berries soaked in zinfandel sauce accented by bright green crushed pistachios. Before or after dinner, the open-air lounge at the resort is a romantic place to have a drink and listen to live music.

✪ **La Hacienda.** At the Scottsdale Princess resort, 7575 E. Princess Dr. (about 12 miles north of downtown Scottsdale). ☎ **480/585-4848.** Reservations recommended. Main courses $20–$27.50. AE, CB, DC, DISC, MC, V. Sun–Thurs 6–10pm, Fri–Sat 6–11pm. GOURMET MEXICAN.

As you might have guessed by the price range above, this is not your average taco stand. La Hacienda serves gourmet Mexican cuisine in an upscale, glamorous-but-rustic setting reminiscent of an early 1900s Mexican ranch house (stone tiled floor, Mexican glassware and crockery, a beehive fireplace). Gourmet Mexican means such dishes as roast stuffed quail with three bean salad and prickly pear sauce, or rack of lamb unlike any you may have had before—with a pumpkin seed crust and chili plum sauce. For dessert, you might consider orange flan or chocolate jalapeño ice cream.

**Mancuso's.** At the Borgata, 6166 N. Scottsdale Rd. ☎ **480/948-9988.** Reservations recommended. Main courses $18–$27, pastas $16–$19. AE, CB, DC, DISC, MC, V. Daily 5–10pm. ITALIAN/FRENCH/CONTINENTAL.

With its ramparts, towers, stone walls, and narrow, uneven alleyways leading through the complex, the Borgata is built in the style of a medieval Italian village, so it seems only fitting that Mancuso's would affect the look of an elaborate baronial banquet hall. A cathedral ceiling, stone walls, arched windows, and huge roof beams set the stage for the gourmet continental cuisine; and a pianist playing soft jazz sets the mood. If you lack the means to start your meal with the beluga caviar, perhaps *carpaccio di manzo*—sliced raw beef with mustard sauce and capers—will do. Veal is a specialty, but it is always difficult just to get past the pasta offerings. Lately, more fish and daily seafood specials have been added to the menu. The professional service will have you feeling like royalty by the time you finish your dessert and coffee.

✪ **Marquesa.** At the Scottsdale Princess resort, 7575 E. Princess Dr. (about 12 miles north of downtown Scottsdale). ☎ **480/585-4848.** Reservations recommended. Main courses $28–$38; tapas $8.95; champagne brunch $42. AE, DC, DISC, MC, V. Tues–Thurs 6–10pm, Fri–Sat 6–11pm; Sun brunch 10:30am–2:30pm. SPANISH/CATALAN.

The Marquesa is as romantic a restaurant as you're likely to find in the valley: High-backed chairs, chandeliers, muted lighting, and large classical Spanish paintings create an ambience reminiscent of an 18th-century Spanish villa. The menu is a contemporary interpretation of Catalonian (regional Spanish) cuisine. Crabmeat and fontina cheese in baked sweet red peppers with almond sauce or sautéed shrimp with saffron potatoes and truffles make for robustly flavored starters. *Paella Valenciana* is the restaurant's signature dish and should not be missed. Some dishes are low in fat and sodium, but not the desserts. Among the caloric works of art you might find a saffron crème fraîche flan with roasted pears. There's a separate tapas bar outside the main dining area (a great way to sample a few Marquesa dishes without going over a tight dinner budget), and a Sunday brunch that is one of the best in the valley.

✪ **Mary Elaine's.** At The Phoenician, 6000 E. Camelback Rd., Scottsdale. ☎ **480/423-2530.** Reservations highly recommended. Jacket required for men (except during summer). Main courses $30–$43; 6-course seasonal tasting menu $110 (matched wines are an additional $55). AE, CB, DC, DISC, MC, V. Mon–Thurs 6–9:30pm, Fri–Sat 6–10pm (closed Sun–Mon in summer). MODERN AMERICAN/FRENCH.

Located on the top floor of The Phoenician's main building, Mary Elaine's is one of the finest restaurants in the valley and boasts one of the best views as well. The restaurant is the height of elegance and sophistication (German crystal, Reed and Barton silver, and Wedgewood china), though those seeking a more casual, al fresco setting can dine on the patio most of the year.

The chef focuses on the flavors of the modern French kitchen, which are usually dictated by the changing seasons. A recent menu included pan-seared foie gras with caramelized kumquats, black sea bass with a lobster sauce, and garlic and herb crusted rack of lamb with goat cheese risotto. For the health conscious, some dishes are particularly low in fat and cholesterol, and Mary Elaine's will go out of its way to accommodate a vegetarian. Call beforehand to make a request. The extensive wine list has won numerous awards.

**Windows on the Green.** At The Phoenician, 6000 E. Camelback Rd., Scottsdale. ☎ **480/ 423-2530.** Reservations recommended. Main courses $19–$36; regional tasting menu $50. AE, CB, DC, DISC, MC, V. Wed–Mon 6–10pm. SOUTHWESTERN.

Slightly more casual than The Phoenician's premier restaurant, Mary Elaine's, but no less elegant, Windows on the Green has a sweeping view of the resort's golf course. Chef Michael Snoke turns the familiar into the extraordinary when serving up such dishes as quail stuffed with jalapeño cheddar grits, rattlesnake *posole,* and prickly pear sorbet. While the flavors on the menu here are predominantly Southwestern, not every dish is doused with chili peppers. Diners with sensitive palates will find plenty to choose from. The wine list is chosen to complement these regional flavors. All in all a good but somewhat pricey introduction to Southwestern cuisine.

## MODERATE

Another area restaurant worth trying is **Sam's Cafe,** North Scottsdale Road and Shea Boulevard (☎ **480/368-2800**), which has other branches around the valley. For more information on Sam's Cafe, see the "Downtown Phoenix" section of this chapter.

✪ **Café Terra Cotta.** At the Borgata, 6166 N. Scottsdale Rd., Suite 100. ☎ **480/ 948-8100.** Reservations recommended for dinner. Main courses $12–$22. AE, DISC, MC, V. Sun–Thurs 11am–10pm, Fri–Sat 11am–11pm. SOUTHWESTERN.

Café Terra Cotta started out in Tucson, where it invented the concept of trendy foods, and they haven't stopped cookin' since. The list of Southwestern choices at this casually sophisticated and low-key restaurant is long, including wood-oven pizzas, sandwiches, and smaller meals as well as full-size main courses. Imaginative combinations are the rule, so you'll want to take your time with the menu before ordering. For example, roll this over your imaginary taste buds: chili-roasted duck breast with chipotle sauce on a potato-horseradish pancake and carrot-jicama salad.

**Cowboy Ciao Wine Bar & Grill.** 7133 E. Stetson Dr. (corner 6th Ave.). ☎ **480/ WINE-111.** Reservations recommended. Main courses $6–$10 at lunch, $15–$23 at dinner. AE, DC, DISC, MC, V. Tues–Thurs 11:30–2:30 and 5–10pm, Fri–Sat 11:30–2:30 and 5–10:30pm, Sun 5–10pm. NEW AMERICAN.

Delicious food, low prices, and a fun and trendy atmosphere furnished in "cowboy chic"—that sums up what makes Cowboy Ciao a great place for a meal. Located in fashionable downtown Scottsdale, this place attracts a diverse group of people who like to dive into the likes of crab cakes with roasted corn sauce or honey bourbon pork tenderloin with quinoa (a toasty-tasting grain). Large, fresh salads get two thumbs up. Cowboy Ciao is also notable for its wine list and bar, where customers can order a flight (tasting assortment) of wines. We wouldn't miss the chocolate lottery dessert, consisting of a double chocolate and espresso torte plus an Arizona State lottery ticket.

✪ **Franco's Trattoria.** 8120 N. Hayden Rd. ☎ **480/948-6655.** Reservations recommended. Main courses $13–$25, pastas $10–$16. AE, MC, V. May–Oct Tues–Sat 5:15–10pm; Oct–May Mon–Sat 5:15–10pm. Closed from 2nd week in July to 2nd week in Aug. TUSCAN ITALIAN.

Dining at Franco's Trattoria is like taking a trip to Tuscany. Franco bustles around shaving hard cheeses, which arrive on the table accompanied by bread and olive oil, and chats with his regulars in an atmosphere that's both congenial and romantic. For starters, the *insalata capricciosa,* a salad of fennel, goat cheese, sun-dried tomatoes, beans, arugula, radicchio, and red onion, fairly bursts with flavor, as do the homemade raviolis and risottos. If you want something spicy (you are in the Southwest), try the *spezzatino di vitello dolce forte,* veal with tomato, rosemary, raisins, vinegar and hot pepper. Lot's of places claim to make the world's best tiramisu, but Franco's, made from his grandmother's recipe, truly takes the cake. It's the best you'll ever have, and it packs a wallop with it's brandy, amaretto, and espresso–infused lady fingers. Wines are very reasonably priced, and the service is knowledgeable and personable.

**L'Ecole.** At the Scottsdale Culinary Institute, 8100 E. Camelback Rd. (just east of Hayden Rd.). ☎ **480/990-7639.** Reservations highly recommended several days in advance. 3 courses $9–$11 at lunch, $22–$28 at dinner. DISC, MC, V. Mon–Fri 11:30am–1pm and 6:30–8:30pm. CONTINENTAL/INTERNATIONAL.

This culinary opportunity is a well-kept local secret—there aren't many places where you can get a three-course lunch for under $10, or dinner for under $22. The cooking and serving is all done by students, and the decor is somewhat sedate and elegant. For an appetizer, you might try the duck confit salad; for an entree, grilled salmon with mustard dill sauce is nice, followed by cherries jubilee flamed tableside with house-made ice cream. There is a respectable selection of wines and liquors to accompany the meal. This is such a good deal that people drive from all over the valley to eat here.

**Pepin.** 7363 Scottsdale Mall. ☎ **480/990-9026.** Reservations recommended. Main courses $13–$25; tapas $5–$9. AE, CB, DC, DISC, MC, V. Tues–Fri 11:30am–2pm and 4:30–11pm, Sat 11:30am–11pm, Sun 5–11pm. Happy hour, Tues–Fri 4:30–6pm. SPANISH.

For traditional Spanish fare and plenty of lively entertainment, you won't do better than Pepin. Located on the Scottsdale Mall, this small Spanish restaurant offers such a wide selection of tapas that you can easily have dinner without ever glancing at the main-course list. However, there are also several styles of paella, most of which are seafood extravaganzas. Thursday through Saturday evenings, there are live flamenco performances, and from 10pm on Friday and Saturday, there's Latino dancing.

**Rancho Pinot Grill.** 6208 N. Scottsdale Rd. (south of Lincoln Dr.). ☎ **480/468-9463.** Reservations recommended. Main courses $17–$26. DISC, MC, V. Tues–Sat 5:30–10pm. Summer hours subject to change. NEW AMERICAN.

Rancho Pinot, which is located in a shopping center adjacent to the Borgata, combines a "homey" Southwestern decor with nonthreatening contemporary American cuisine and has long been a favorite with Scottsdale and Phoenix residents. The menu here changes regularly, and tends to emphasize well-cooked meats served with vegetables that are allowed to express their own distinctiveness rather than wallowing in heavy sauces. Look elsewhere if you're craving wildly creative flavor combinations, but if you like simple, well-prepared food, Rancho Pinot may be the place. You might start with grilled squid salad with preserved lemon and then move on to a house specialty, Nonni's chicken, braised with white wine, mushrooms, and herbs; or a handmade pasta. There's a short but well-chosen list of beers and wines by the glass, and for dessert, delectably rich homemade ice cream. The staff is friendly and tends to treat you as if you were a regular even if it's your first visit.

**Razz's Restaurant and Bar.** 10321 N. Scottsdale Rd. ☎ **480/905-1308.** Reservations recommended. Main courses $15–$23. AE, DC, MC, V. Tues–Sat 5–10pm. INTERNATIONAL.

Razz Kamnitzer, a native Venezuelan, is one in a line of seven chefs in his family. No wonder his restaurant is such a hit. Located in a nondescript shopping mall on the southeast corner of Shea Boulevard and Scottsdale Road, the restaurant is chic, but not stuffy, crowded, and lively. Razz has been on the Phoenix restaurant scene for some years and is known for his cuisine, which includes edible flowers, herbs, and exotic vegetable and fruits. On a recent night, the menu included such wide-ranging dishes as twice-roasted duck breast with lingonberry-orange sauce; an Indonesian-style noodle dish with chicken, shrimp, pork, and vegetables; and grilled rack of lamb with tamarind and garlic marinade.

✪ **Restaurant Hapa.** 6204 N. Scottsdale Rd. (behind Trader Joes). ☎ **480/998-8220.** Reservations recommended. Main courses $14–$26, small plates $6–$9. MC, V. Mon–Sat 5:30–10pm. ASIAN AMERICAN.

Brought to you by the owners of Rancho Pinot (see above), Restaurant Hapa has a similar formula that seems to work. This small and somewhat intimate space is popular with all ages and features a Zen decor, with huge mirrors covering one wall. They have a way with a grill here that really brings out the flavor of shrimp and fish and also turns out some excellent grilled vegetables. From the depths of the wood-burning oven come such dishes as game hen and deftly prepared fish with roasted vegetables. We like the small plates a lot: mussels with Thai coconut sauce; shrimp, duck, and chicken satay with three sauces; and chilled shrimp rolls with citrus dipping sauce. To round out this Asian American eating experience, try a delicious dessert such as warm chocolate mango cake with lemongrass ice cream and mango fruit sauce, a melting melange of contrasting flavors.

**Roaring Fork.** 7243 E. Camelback Rd. ☎ **480/947-0795.** Reservations highly recommended. Main courses $14–$25. AE, MC, V. Mon–Thurs 6–10pm, Fri–Sat 5:30–11pm. SOUTHWESTERN.

This trendy and very Southwestern restaurant, near the intersection of Camelback and Scottsdale roads, is the creation of chef Robert McGrath, formerly of The Phoenician's Windows on the Green. With its stone walls, melange of Mexican hacienda and Italian villa architectural styles, and impeccably upscale Southwestern interior, Roaring Fork is a much more casual space than Windows on the Green and yet the cuisine is just as creative. Just be sure you try the pinto bean ravioli with dried ham and Monterey Jack cheese. Equally memorable is the sugar-chile glazed duck breast with green chile macaroni (a house specialty). Filled with herb-infused rolls and cranberry corn muffins accompanied by honey-chile butter, the bread basket alone is enough to make you weep with joy. There may not be any chilies in the desserts, but they're still worth saving room for. Before you leave, be sure to check out the rebar lariats in the bar; they hold bowls of bar munchies, including pieces of spicy jerky.

**6th Avenue Bistrot.** 7150 E. 6th Ave. ☎ **480/947-6022.** Reservations recommended. Main courses $7–$12 at lunch, $14–$20 at dinner. AE, MC, V. Tues–Thurs 11am–2pm and 5–9pm, Fri 11am–2pm and 5–10pm, Sat 5–10pm. CLASSIC FRENCH.

Who says French has to be fussy? This little French-operated bistro less than a block off Scottsdale Road is as casual as a French restaurant gets. The draw here is a simple menu of reliable dishes at fairly reasonable prices: a bit of country pâté, tenderloin of pork with port-wine sauce, a hearty Beaujolais, all topped off with *mousse au chocolat*, and you have a perfect French dinner. Lunch here is a great deal, and wines by the glass are reasonably priced.

✪ **Veneto Trattoria Italiana.** 6137 N. Scottsdale Rd. (in Hilton Village). ☎ **480/948-9928.** Reservations recommended. Main courses $8–$22. AE, DC, DISC, MC, V. Mon–Sat 11:30am–2:30pm and 5–10pm. VENETIAN ITALIAN.

This casual and pleasantly low-key bistro, specializing in the cuisine of Venice, serves simple and satisfying "peasant food" (surprising, since the owner formerly ran the restaurant at the Giorgio Armani boutique in Beverly Hills). Mozzarella, tomato, and basil salad or tender calamari rings served over spinach and savoy cabbage make great starters, followed by *uganega con verzette e polenta*, a lightly spiced sausage with perfectly prepared polenta. *Baccala mantecato* (creamy fish mousse on grilled polenta, made with dried salt cod soaked in milk overnight) may sound unusual, but it's heavenly—for this alone we would recommend the restaurant. For a finale, the *semifreddo con frutta secca*, a partially frozen meringue with dry fruits in a pool of raspberry sauce, has an intoxicating texture. There's outdoor seating on the patio (you can almost forget that you're in a shopping mall) and a welcoming bistro ambience inside.

## INEXPENSIVE

✪ **Bandera.** 3821 N. Scottsdale Rd., Scottsdale. ☎ **480/994-3524.** Reservations not accepted. Main courses $10–$20. AE, MC, V. Sun–Thurs 4:30–10pm, Fri–Sat 4:30–11pm. AMERICAN.

If you just spent all day wandering in and out of Scottsdale galleries without buying a single bronze statue, you just might be a frugal traveler. If so, you'll want to know about Bandera. Actually, if you've been craving barbecue or grilled chicken for a few hours, chances are it's because you've been smelling the wood-roasted chickens turning on the rotisseries in Bandera's back-of-the-building, open-air stone oven. What an aroma! The succulent spit-roasted chicken is served with the ultimate comfort food, a mountain of creamy mashed potatoes flecked with green onion and black pepper. Sure, you could order prime rib, jambalaya, or leg of lamb, but you'd be a fool if you did. Stick with the chicken or maybe the honey-barbecued ribs, and you won't go wrong. This place may be a California chain, but, hey, Californians know good food.

**Carlsbad Tavern.** 3313 N. Hayden Rd., Scottsdale (south of Osborn). ☎ **480/970-8164.** Reservations recommended at dinner. Main courses $7–$19. AE, DC, DISC, MC, V. Mon–Thurs 11am–10pm, Fri–Sat 11am–11pm, Sun 1–10pm; limited menu available until 1am. NEW MEXICAN.

Carlsbad Tavern blends the fiery tastes of New Mexican cuisine with a hip and humorous atmosphere featuring bats (a reference to Carlsbad Caverns). On the menu you'll find traditional New Mexican dishes, such as lamb *pierna* and *carne adovada*, simmered in a fiery red chili sauce. Nouvelle Southwestern specialties include a spicy peppercorn cream sauced pasta with grilled chicken, andoullie sausage and pine nuts, and a robust chorizo meat loaf sandwich. Cool off your taste buds with a margarita made with fresh-squeezed juice. A lagoon makes this place feel like a beach bar, and a big patio fireplace is really cozy on a cold night.

✪ **El Guapo's Taco Shop & Salsa Bar.** 3015 N. Scottsdale Rd., Scottsdale ☎ **480/423-8385.** Main dishes $2–$8. No credit cards. Mon–Sat 10:30am–8pm. MEXICAN.

*El Guapo* means "handsome," which certainly doesn't refer to this little hole-in-the-wall taco shop, but might be referring to Danny, the proprietor. The tacos—among them mahimahi, *carne asada,* or marinated pork—are prepared without the standard lettuce and tomatoes so that you can build your own by liberally dousing your order with salsa and vegetable toppings from the salsa cart. It takes two or three tacos to make a meal, so you can try a few different types. El Guapo has homemade-style cheese crisps, burritos, and nachos, too. Try the armadillo eggs—jalapeño peppers stuffed with cheese and deep fried. There are only half a dozen tables here, and the salsa bar takes up a good part of the shop.

**Oregano's Pizza Bistro.** 3622 N. Scottsdale Rd. (south of Indian School Rd.). ☎ **480/ 970-1860.** Reservations not accepted. Main courses $6–$17. AE, DC, DISC, MC, V. Mon–Thurs 11am–10pm, Fri–Sat 11am–11pm, Sun noon–10pm. PIZZA/PASTA.

With very reasonable prices and a location convenient to the many shops and galleries of Old Scottsdale, this sprawling pizza joint (two buildings and the courtyard/parking lot between) is a big hit with the area's young crowd. Both the thin-crust pizzas—topped with barbecue chicken and feta cheese (and, by the way, too much for one person)—and the Chicago stuffed pizza are all the good things pizza should be. But pizza isn't all they have here—there's artichoke lasagna, barbecue wings, a variety of salads, and even a pizza cookie for dessert. Because this is such a popular spot, expect a wait at dinner.

Other locations are in Phoenix at 130 E. Washington St. (☎ **602/253-9577**) and in Tempe at 523 W. University Dr. (☎ **480/858-0501**).

**P. F. Chang's China Bistro.** 7014 E. Camelback Rd. (in Scottsdale Fashion Square), Scottsdale. ☎ **480/949-2610.** Reservations not accepted, but call ahead to get onto wait list. Main courses $6–$13. AE, DISC, MC, V. Sun–Thurs 11am–11pm, Fri–Sat 11am–midnight. CHINESE.

Located inside the valley's most fashionable shopping mall, this restaurant has long been a favorite upscale, low-price Chinese spot for the young and financially challenged of the Scottsdale area. Year in and year out, it remains so popular that you can expect a 2-hour wait for a table. However, if you come early or ask to sit at the bar, you can usually get a seat fairly quickly. The straightforward Chinese food is usually well prepared, but not really worth such a long wait. What sets this restaurant apart from so many other Chinese restaurants around the city is the very upscale decor. This is as much a place to be seen as a place to be fed.

## CENTRAL PHOENIX & THE CAMELBACK CORRIDOR
### EXPENSIVE

**Christopher's Fermier Brasserie and Paola's Wine Bar.** 2584 E. Camelback Rd. (in Biltmore Fashion Park). ☎ **602/522-2344.** Reservations recommended. Main courses $9–$11 at lunch, $17–$28 at dinner. AE, DISC, MC, V. Sun–Thurs 11am–10pm, Fri 11am–11pm, Sat noon–11pm, Sun noon–10pm. RUSTIC FRENCH.

Christopher Gross's new venue in Biltmore Fashion Park covers many bases. There's a wine bar, a brewery, a cigar room, and a restaurant. Unfortunately, our experience here was one of style, not substance, but you might want to give it a try since Gross has such a good reputation and it may have just been an off night. Tasty standouts include a velvety roasted red bell pepper soup with truffle essence and the house-smoked salmon, both holdovers from Gross's previous restaurant. Duck cassoulet with Merguez sausage was remarkably uninteresting. The brewery produces a wide range of beer styles; to give them all a try, order a flight. We prefer the darker ones. A wine bar menu is served from 3 to 5pm and 10pm to midnight, when you can nibble on such things as smoked chicken pizza, French and New York State cheeses with wine, or Gross's signature dessert, a chocolate mousse tower.

**Eddie Matney's Epicurean Trio.** 2398 E. Camelback Rd. ☎ **602/957-3214.** Reservations recommended. Bistro main courses $17–$30, main dining room main courses $32–$35; tasting menu $70 or $120 with wine. AE, DISC, MC, V. Bistro Sun–Thurs 5–10:30pm, Fri–Sat 5–11pm. Main dining room Tues–Sat 6–10pm. NEW AMERICAN/CONTINENTAL.

Located in the same space that formerly housed Christopher Gross's eponymously named restaurant, this gourmand's paradise duplicates much of the Christopher's formula. The restaurant is named for its chef, and there are two separate dining areas (plus a members-only cigar-and-wine bar). The bistro is, of course, less formal and less expensive. Expect the likes of Eddie's famous meatloaf, pan-seared turkey tenderloin, grilled veal chops with spaghetti squash, and cambazola hash with cranberry-chipotle jus. The main dining room, on the other hand, is one of the most expensive restaurants in Phoenix, the sort of place where you're tempted to start your dinner with beluga caviar and a glass of Veuve Clicquot Ponsardin for $85. It is here that Eddie Matney is making his bid to become Phoenix's preeminent chef. Offerings such as foie gras with caramelized pineapple and citrus sauce with toasted mushroom brioche; wild game consommé with spicy seared loin of rabbit; and roasted pheasant with poblano chile stuffed with artichokes, pancetta, shiitake mushrooms, and goat cheese make it clear that this restaurant is only for serious epicures.

**Harris'.** 3101 E. Camelback Rd. ☎ **602/508-8888.** Reservations highly recommended. Main courses $8–$19 at lunch, $13–$31 at dinner. AE, DC, DISC, MC, V. Mon–Fri 11:30am–2pm and 5:30–10pm, Sat 5:30–11pm. STEAKS.

If you haven't noticed yet, beef is back in a big way. Enormous slabs of steak, perfectly cooked and allowed to express their inner beefiness unsullied by silly sauces are de rigueur from Manhattan to Marin County these days, and no longer is it necessary to visit some steakhouse that has aged longer than the meat it serves. Today steaks are being served in settings once reserved for various incarnations of nouvelle cuisine. Harris, smack in the middle of the bustling big-money Camelback Corridor, is Phoenix's newest and biggest contemporary steakhouse. With a Southwestern pueblo-modern styling, valet parking attendants, and prime rib a specialty of the house, this impressive restaurant leaves no doubt that this is where you'll find your beef. Make sure you've got plenty of space left on your credit card—a meal here will definitely set you back some bucks,

✪ **Lon's.** At the Hermosa Inn, 5532 N. Palo Cristi Rd. ☎ **602/955-7878.** Reservations recommended late in the week. Main courses $7.50–$12 at lunch, $18–$25 at dinner. AE, CB, DISC, MC, V. Mon–Fri 11:30am–2pm and 6–10pm, Sat 6–10pm, Sun 10am–2pm (brunch) and 6–10pm. AMERICAN REGIONAL.

What we like most about this place is the setting. It's one of the most "Arizonan" places in the Phoenix area—a Mexican-style hacienda with tile roof and gardens all around. The hacienda once belonged to Lon Megargee, a cowboy artist whose paintings decorate the interior of the restaurant. At midday this place is popular with both retirees and the power-lunching set, and at dinner the place really bustles with a wide mix of people, including smart young things. Begin with rosemary-infused sourdough rolls and a large platter of fried sweet potatoes and red onion rings, which are delicious—salty-sweet and crispy. Dinner entrees are beautifully presented works of art, blending subtle flavors such as grilled loin of pork with apple-fig compote and tiger prawns on sun-dried tomato risotto with a watercress sauce. There's a great selection of wines by the glass, a little on the pricey side, and an emphasis on after-dinner drinks. The little bar is cozy and romantic, and the patio offers beautiful views of Camelback Mountain.

**Roxsand.** 2594 E. Camelback Rd. ☎ **602/381-0444.** Reservations recommended. Main courses $9–$12 at lunch, $17–$26 at dinner. AE, DC, DISC, MC, V. Mon–Thurs 11am–4pm and 5–10pm, Fri–Sat 11am–4pm and 5–10:30pm, Sun noon–4pm and 5–9:30pm. NEW AMERICAN/FUSION.

Located on the second floor of the exclusive Biltmore Fashion Park shopping mall, Roxsand is a place of urban sophistication, a restaurant to see and be seen at. Here you'll find fusion cuisine, a creative combination of international influences. We attempted to choose among Moroccan *b'stilla* (braised chicken in phyllo with roasted-eggplant puree), African spicy shrimp salad, and curried lamb tamale. And those were just the appetizers. Perhaps because of the diversity of the menu, some of the dishes can be hit or miss. Sauces sometimes lack complexity, but we can recommend the air-dried duck with pistachio onion marmalade, buckwheat crepes, and three sauces: Szechuan black-bean sauce, evil jungle prince sauce, and plum sauce. After dinner, get some exercise and amble over to the dessert case; your choice will be served to you on a dinner plate adorned with additional cookies and perhaps a dollop of sorbet.

✪ **T. Cook's.** In the Royal Palms Resort, 5200 E. Camelback Rd. ☎ **602/808-0766.** Reservations highly recommended. Main courses $17–$29. AE, DC, DISC, MC, V. Daily 6–10am, 11am–2pm, and 6–10pm, with Sun brunch 10am–2pm. MEDITERRANEAN.

Simply put, there is no restaurant in the Valley of the Sun more romantic than T. Cook's. Located within the walls of the Mediterranean-inspired Royal Palms resort, this restaurant is surrounded by decades-old gardens and even has palm trees growing right through the roof of the dining room. The focal point of T. Cook's open kitchen is a wood-fired oven that produces dishes such as rosemary pork loin with fig-apple chutney and garlic mashed potatoes, and spit-roasted chicken. However, dishes that don't originate in the wood oven, such as the sautéed lobster with fresh tortellini and asparagus are also worth considering. T. Cook's continues to make big impressions right through to the dessert course. If you happen to be a chocoholic, you'll find nirvana in the chocolate sampler, a collection of confectionery sculptures guaranteed to dazzle the eye as well as satisfy the primordial need for chocolate. Though this is one of the most popular upper-end restaurants in Phoenix these days, it luckily manages to avoid pretentiousness.

✪ **Vincent Guerithault on Camelback.** 3930 E. Camelback Rd. ☎ **602/224-0225.** Reservations highly recommended. Main courses $7–$10 at lunch, $14.50–$25 at dinner. AE, DC, MC, V. Mon–Fri 11:30am–2:30pm and 6–10:30pm, Sat 5:30–10:30pm, Sun 6–10:30pm. Closed on Sun from mid-May to mid-Oct. SOUTHWESTERN.

Vincent Guerithault has long been a local restaurant celebrity, and his restaurant has an intimate, unpretentious French country atmosphere. Despite the continental decor, the cuisine is solidly Southwestern, with chilies appearing in numerous guises. For a starter, it's hard to beat the aggressive flavors of a smoked-salmon quesadilla with dill and horseradish cream. Moving on to the main course, grilled meats and seafood are the specialty here and might come accompanied by a cilantro salsa or by habañero pasta. The extensive wine list has both Californian and French wines. There's a parking attendant at the door, and the number of luxury cars here should tip you off that this is one of Phoenix's top restaurants. At lunch, the menu is basically the same as at dinner (only with smaller portions). With nearly all items under $10, lunchtime is a great opportunity to taste the food if you're on a budget.

## MODERATE

**Altos.** 5029 N. 44th St. (at the NE corner of 44th St. and Camelback). ☎ **602/808-0890.** Reservations recommended. Main courses $7–$13 at lunch, $16–$22 at dinner. AE, MC, V. Mon–Thurs 5:30–10pm, Fri–Sat 5:30–11pm. CONTEMPORARY SPANISH.

Located in the back of a shopping plaza, Altos is a little difficult to find, but it's worth searching out. It's a chic and mellow out-of-the-way place to enjoy some tapas and a glass of fruit-filled sangria from the large jar on the bar, but the entrees are also quite good. What you'll find here is a contemporary treatment of Spanish food, including tapas of artichoke hearts stuffed with serano ham and Spanish goat cheese, dipped in saffron batter and fried. Paella with seafood, chicken Basque sausage, and saffron rice is a complex melding of flavors, while some dishes are more straightforward, such as the *pinchos* (kebabs). A dish of flan, brandy bread pudding, or mocha crème brûlée rounds out the experience, along with live flamenco guitar on weekends.

**Richardson's.** 1582 E. Bethany Home Rd. ☎ **602/265-5886** or 602/230-8718. Reservations accepted only for parties of 4 or more. Main courses $9–$21. AE, CB, DC, MC, V. Mon–Fri 11am–midnight, Sat–Sun 10am–midnight. NEW MEXICAN.

Tucked into an older corner shopping center with far too few parking spaces, Richardson's is almost invisible amid the glaring lights and flashing neon of this otherwise unmemorable neighborhood. This place is generally a mob scene at dinner; however, if you enjoy creative, spicy cooking at good prices, it's worth the wait. Have a margarita while you're at it. If you're in the mood for a light meal, try Stone's skewers—chicken, beef, shrimp, and sausage grilled over pecan wood. A more substantial appetite may be assuaged by a New Mexican platter containing a tamale, a chile relleno, a burrito, rice and beans, and green chile. The pecan-wood pizza oven is always fired up to cook delicious pizzas, and for dessert, prickly pear–syrup flan is as creamy as a good crème brûlée. Richardson's also serves Southwestern-style breakfasts daily from 10 or 11am until 4pm.

## INEXPENSIVE

**Blue Burrito Grille.** In the Biltmore Plaza, 3118 E. Camelback Rd. ☎ **602/955-9596.** Reservations not accepted. Main courses $5–$6.50. AE, MC, V. Daily 11am–11pm.

Located in a shopping plaza that also houses the most exclusive and expensive jewelry store in the valley, this is obviously not your usual greasy-tortilla Mexican joint. Catering to a health-conscious affluent community, the Blue Burrito specializes in healthful Mexican food (with no lard and plenty of vegetarian offerings). OK, so the deep-fried chimichanga isn't good for you, but the chicken fajita burritos, fish tacos, enchiladas rancheras, and tamales Mexicanos certainly are. If you want to blow the healthfulness of your meal, have it with a mango margarita. This is a great place for fast, cheap, healthy food smack in the middle of the Camelback Corridor shopping district. Also at 7318 E. Shea Blvd. in Scottsdale (☎ **480/951-3151**) and 420 S. Mill St., Tempe (☎ **480/921-1332**).

**Ed Debevic's Short Orders Deluxe.** 2102 E. Highland Ave. ☎ **602/956-2760.** Reservations not accepted. Sandwiches and blue-plate specials $4–$8. AE, DC, DISC, MC, V. Sun–Thurs 11am–9pm, Fri–Sat 11am–10pm. AMERICAN.

Hidden away behind the Smitty's supermarket in the Town and Country Shopping Center, Ed's is a classic 1950s diner right down to the little jukeboxes in the booths. Not only does it make its own burgers, chili, and bread, but Ed Debevic's serves the best malteds in Phoenix. The sign in the front window that reads WAITRESSES WANTED, PEOPLE SKILLS NOT NECESSARY should give you a clue that service here is unique. This place stays busy, and the waitresses are overworked (though they do break into song now and again), so don't be surprised if your waitress sits down in the booth with you to wait for your order. That's just the kind of place Ed runs, and as Ed says, "If you don't like the way I do things—buy me out."

**5 & Diner.** 5220 N. 16th St. ☎ **602/264-5220.** Sandwiches/plates $5–11. AE, MC, V. Daily 24 hours. AMERICAN.

If it's 2am and you just have to have a big burger and a side of fries after a night of dancing, head for the 24-hour 5 & Diner. You can't miss it; it's the classic streamlined diner that looks as if it just materialized from New Jersey.

> ### ⓘ Family-Friendly Restaurants
>
> **Ed Debevic's Short Orders Deluxe** *(see p. 92)*   This classic 1950s diner is full of cool stuff, including little jukeboxes in the booths. You can tell your kids about hanging out in places like this when you were a teenager.
>
> **Pinnacle Peak Patio** *(see p. 96)*   Way out in north Scottsdale, this restaurant is a Wild West steakhouse complete with cowboys, shoot-outs, hayrides, and live Western music nightly.
>
> **Rawhide Western Town & Steakhouse** *(see p. 97)*   Kids love dancing to the country music and pretending they're in a real Old West town, which isn't difficult, since Rawhide, with its big wide street, looks pretty authentic. Did you know that they cook up 50 *tons* of beans here annually?
>
> **Rustler's Rooste** *(see p. 97)*   Similar to Pinnacle Peak, but closer to the city center, Rustler's Rooste has a slide from the lounge to the main dining room, a big patio, and live cowboy bands nightly. See if you can get your kids to try the rattlesnake appetizer—it tastes like chicken.

There's another location in Phoenix at 12802 N. Tatum Blvd. (☎ **602/996-0033**) and one in Scottsdale at Scottsdale Pavilions, 9069 E. Indian Bend Rd. (☎ **480/949-1957**).

✪ **Vintage Market.** 24th St. and Camelback Rd. (Biltmore Fashion Park). ☎ **602/955-4444.** Reservations not necessary. Salads/sandwiches $7–$11. AE, DC, MC, V. Mon–Wed 10am–7:30pm, Thurs–Sat 10am–10pm, Sun 11am–6pm. UPSCALE DELI.

This is a prime people-watching spot and a great place for European-style sandwiches, accompanied by strong coffee in demitasse cups or a glass of wine chosen from a long list that which even contains some local Arizonan wines. There's also a wine bar. Prices here are lower than at practically any other place in Biltmore Fashion Park, and you can get the likes of a Mediterranean panini or Asian vegetable and shrimp salad.

## DOWNTOWN PHOENIX
### MODERATE

✪ **Sam's Cafe.** In the Arizona Center, 455 N. 3rd St. ☎ **602/252-3545.** Reservations recommended. Main courses $8–$19. AE, CB, DISC, MC, V. Mon–Thurs 11am–10pm, Fri–Sat 11am–11pm, Sun 11am–9pm. SOUTHWESTERN.

Sam's Cafe, one of only a handful of decent downtown restaurants, serves food that's every bit as imaginative, but not nearly as expensive, as that served at other (often overrated) Southwestern restaurants in Phoenix. Breadsticks served with picante-flavored cream cheese, grilled vegetable tacos, and angle-hair pasta in a spicy jalapeño sauce with shrimp and mushrooms all have a nice balance of flavors and are just spicy enough. Salads and dipping sauces are complex and interesting. The downtown Sam's has a large patio that stays packed with the lunchtime, after-work, and convention crowd and overlooks a fountain and palm garden.

Other Sam's restaurants are located in the Biltmore Fashion Park at 2566 E. Camelback Rd. (☎ **602/954-7100**) and in Scottsdale at North Scottsdale Road and Shea Boulevard (☎ **480/368-2800**).

### INEXPENSIVE

**Alice Cooper'stown.** 101 E. Jackson St. ☎ **602/253-7337.** Reservations not accepted. Sandwiches/barbecue $6–$16. AE, MC, V. Daily 11am–11pm. BARBECUE.

Another venue comes to the realm of eat-o-tainment with the opening of Alice Cooper's sports-and-rock theme restaurant located between the Bank One Ballpark and America West Arena. Sixteen video screens are the centerpiece of the restaurant (and most likely they'll be showing sports), but there is also an abundance of memorabilia on the walls, from Alice Cooper's platinum records to guitars from Fleetwood Mac and Eric Clapton to plenty of celebrity photographs. Barbecue occurs in various permutations, from a huge and pretty tasty sandwich to "Welcome to My Nightmare" chili. There are plenty of other choices too, such as a 2-foot-long hot dog, ribs, and "Mega Death" meatloaf. The wait staff even wears Alice Cooper makeup.

**Honey Bear's BBQ.** 2824 N. Central Ave. ☎ **602/279-7911**. Sandwiches and dinners $3.65–$13.50. AE, MC, V. Mon–Sat 10am–10pm, Sun 10am–9:30pm. BARBECUE.

We can definitely say that Honey Bear's has a dud-free menu, and it couldn't be simpler—pork barbecue, beef barbecue, or chicken barbecue. Accompanied maybe by some coleslaw to stick on top of a sandwich, or sweet potato pie for dessert. This fast food joint has another location at 5012 E. Van Buren St. (☎ **602/273-9148**).

**✪ MacAlpine's Nostalgic Soda Fountain & Coffee Shoppe.** 2303 N. 7th St. ☎ **602/252-7282.** Sandwiches/specials $3.25–$5.50. AE, MC, V. Mon–Thurs 6am–6pm, Fri–Sat 6am–midnight, Sun 11am–6pm. AMERICAN.

This very authentic place hasn't changed much since its beginnings in 1928—in fact, it's the oldest operating soda fountain in the Southwest. The atmosphere is laid back, helped along by a jukebox that plays favorite oldies. They'll be glad to fix you up a breakfast egg on a bagel, or a big hamburger or tuna sandwich on good bread. To wash it down, order a chocolate phosphate or raspberry iced tea.

**✪ Pizzeria Bianco.** In Heritage Square, 623 E. Adams St. ☎ **602/258-8300.** Reservations accepted for 6 or more. Pizzas $8–$11. MC, V. Tues–Fri 11:30am–2pm and 5:30–10pm, Sat 5:30–10pm, Sun 5:30–9pm. ITALIAN.

Even though this historic brick building is located smack dab in the center of downtown Phoenix, the atmosphere is so friendly and cozy it feels like your neighborhood local. The wood-burning oven turns out deliciously rustic, chewy-crusted pizzas, such as one with red onion, Parmesan, rosemary, and crushed pistachio. Pizzeria Bianco makes its own fresh mozzarella cheese, which can be ordered as an appetizer or on a pizza. We also liked the roasted vegetables and the salad with fennel, radicchio, parsley, and orange, drizzled with olive oil.

## TEMPE, MESA, SOUTH PHOENIX & THE AIRPORT AREA
### MODERATE

**✪ House of Tricks.** 114 E. 7th St., Tempe. ☎ **480/968-1114.** Reservations recommended. Main courses $13–$18. AE, CB, DC, DISC, MC, V. Mon–Sat 11am–10pm. Closed first 2 weeks of Aug. NEW AMERICAN.

Because this restaurant is housed in a pair of Craftsman bungalows surrounded by an attractive garden of shady trees, it has a completely different feel from Mill Avenue, Tempe's main drag, which is only 2 blocks away. This is where Arizona State University students take their parents when they come to visit, but it's also a nice spot for a romantic evening and a good place to try innovative cuisine without blowing your vacation budget. The grape arbor–covered patio, where there's also a shady bar, is the preferred seating area. The menu changes regularly and consists of a single page of tempting salads, appetizers, and main dishes. The garlic-inspired Caesar salad and the house-smoked salmon with avocado, capers, and lemon cream are good bets for starters. Among the entrees, look for the pork rack with jalapeño marmalade.

**Monti's La Casa Vieja.** 3 W. 1st St. (at the corner of Mill Ave.), Tempe. ☎ **480/967-7594.**
Reservations recommended for dinner. Main courses $8–$27. AE, CB, DC, DISC, MC, V.
Sun–Thurs 11am–10pm, Fri–Sat 11am–midnight. AMERICAN.

If you're tired of the glitz and glamour of the Valley of the Sun and are looking for Old
Arizona, head down to Tempe to Monti's La Casa Vieja. The adobe building was constructed in 1873 (*casa vieja* means "old house" in Spanish) on the site of the Salt River
ferry in the days when the Salt River flowed year-round and Tempe was nothing more
than a ferry crossing. Today local families who have been in Phoenix for generations
know Monti's well and rely on the restaurant for solid meals and low prices—you can
get a filet mignon for under $11. The dining rooms are dark and filled with memora-
bilia of the Old West.

**San Carlos Bay Seafood Restaurant.** 1901 E. McDowell Rd., just west of the Squaw Peak
Pkwy. (Ariz. 51). ☎ **602/340-0892.** Reservations recommended on weekends. Main courses
$9–$21. No credit cards. Daily 10am–9pm. MEXICAN.

If you've ever spent time in a Mexican beach town, you probably have fond memories
of great fish dinners. But unfortunately you rarely get great Mexican seafood dishes
north of the border. This basic little place remedies that problem. From whole fried
fish to octopus in garlic to shrimp stew, San Carlos Bay does seafood and does it right.
This restaurant is very popular with the local Hispanic population, so you might want
to practice your Spanish before visiting.

**The Stockyards Restaurant.** 5001 E. Washington St. ☎ **602/273-7378.** Reservations
recommended. Main courses $7–$14 at lunch, $10–$30 at dinner. AE, CB, DC, DISC, MC, V.
Mon–Fri 11am–2pm and 5–10pm, Sat 5–10pm, Sun 4:30–9pm. STEAK/SEAFOOD.

Once surrounded by 200 acres of feedlots and frequented almost exclusively by
cattlemen, this steakhouse knows its business. It's an institution that today attracts
the Arizona gentry, who come to enjoy perfectly cooked steaks and cowboy beans
in a traditional 1889 decor. There are several dining rooms, two of which have walls
decorated with murals.

### INEXPENSIVE

✪ **The Farm at South Mountain.** 6106 S. 32nd St. ☎ **602/276-6360.** Sandwiches and
salads $7.95. AE, DC, MC, V. Tues–Sun 8am–3pm. Take Exit 151A off I-10 and go south on
32nd St. SANDWICHES & SALADS.

If being in the desert has you dreaming of shady trees and green grass, you'll enjoy this
little oasis reminiscent of a New England orchard or Midwestern farm. A rustic out-
building surrounded by potted flowers has been converted to a stand-in-line restaurant where you can order a mesquite grilled eggplant sandwich or have a choice of
fresh salads such as a pecan turkey Waldorf with sour cream and dried apricot dressing.
Breakfast choices are baked goods such as muffins and scones, teas, and juices. The
grassy lawn is ideal for a picnic on a blanket under the pecan trees.

Friday and Saturday nights, seven-course gourmet dinners using garden produce are
served at the old farm house. Dinners are $55 per person and reservations are a neces-
sity; call **Quiescence** at ☎ **602/305-8192** for more information.

**Organ Stop Pizza.** 1149 E. Southern Ave., Mesa (southwest corner of Southern Ave. and Stapley Dr.). ☎ **480/813-5700.** Pizza and pastas $4–$14. Credit cards not accepted. Sun–Thurs
5–9pm, Fri–Sat 5–10pm. PIZZA.

The pizza here may not be the best in town, but the Würlitzer theater organ, the
largest in the world, sure is memorable. The massive instrument contains over 5,500
pipes, and four turbine blowers provide the wind to create the sound. Forty-foot ceilings make for great acoustics. Performances begin at 5:30 and continue throughout

the evening. As you marvel at the music, you can enjoy simple pizzas, pastas, or snack foods such as jalapeño poppers (jalapeño peppers filled with cream cheese and covered with batter) or fried zucchini.

## DINING WITH A VIEW

**Different Pointe of View.** At the Pointe Hilton Tapatio Cliffs Resort, 11111 N. 7th St. ☎ **602/863-0912.** Reservations highly recommended. Main courses $26–$36. AE, CB, DC, DISC, MC, V. Mon–Thurs 5:30–9:30pm, Fri–Sat 5:30–10pm (lounge open later), Sun 10am–1:30pm (brunch) and 5:30–9:30pm. REGIONAL AMERICAN.

Built right into a mountaintop, this restaurant takes in dramatic, sweeping vistas of the city, mountains, and desert through its curving walls of glass. Come early, and you can enjoy views to the north from the lounge before heading into the south-facing dining room. The menu changes regularly but is always dependable (herb crusted rack of lamb with sweet potato fries; sautéed shrimp and sea scallops with lobster sherry sauce). However, despite the excellent food, award-winning wine list, and live jazz Wednesday through Saturday, the view steals the show.

✪ **Top of the Rock.** At The Buttes, 2000 Westcourt Way, Tempe. ☎ **602/225-9000.** Reservations recommended. Main courses $19–$29 at dinner; Sun brunch $29. AE, CB, DC, DISC, MC, V. Sun–Thurs 5–10pm, Fri–Sat 5–11pm, Sun 10am–2pm (brunch) and 5–10pm. NEW AMERICAN/SOUTHWESTERN.

All the best views in Phoenix are from resorts and their restaurants, so if you want to dine with a view of the valley, you're going to have to pay the price. Luckily, quality accompanies the high prices here at the Top of the Rock, which is built into a rocky hillside and has a dramatic desert setting above Tempe. And in addition to the stunning, romantic setting, you can enjoy some very creative cuisine. On the appetizer list, the lobster Napoleon (lobster layered with wonton and Boursin cheese in a white-wine chervil butter sauce) should not be missed. Sauces on the entree menu offer a good range of flavors from mellow to bold. The ambience is a little on the formal side, so dress up for this dining experience. You won't go wrong ordering any desert made with chocolate.

## COWBOY STEAKHOUSES

Though Arizona doesn't claim to have invented the steakhouse or cow towns, the state certainly has cornered the market on combining the two. Wild West theme restaurants abound here in the Phoenix area. These family restaurants generally provide big portions of grilled steaks and barbecued ribs, outdoor and "saloon" dining, live country music, and various sorts of entertainment, including stagecoach rides and shoot-outs in the street.

**Pinnacle Peak Patio.** 10426 E. Jomax Rd., Scottsdale. ☎ **480/585-1599.** Reservations recommended on weekends. Main courses $5–$26. DISC, MC, V. Mon–Thurs 4–10pm, Fri–Sat 4–11pm, Sun noon–10pm. Take Scottsdale Rd. north to Pinnacle Peak Rd., turn right, and continue to Pima Rd., where you turn left; at this point just follow the signs. STEAK.

Businessmen beware! Wear a tie into this restaurant, and you'll have it cut off and hung from the rafters. The casual dress code is strictly enforced at this Wild West restaurant about 20 minutes north of downtown Scottsdale up in the hills overlooking the valley. A meal at the Pinnacle Peak Patio is more an event than an opportunity to satisfy your hunger. Though you can indulge in mesquite-broiled steaks (they even have a 2-lb. porterhouse monster) with all the traditional trimmings, the real draw here is all the free Wild West entertainment—gunfights, cowboy bands, two-stepping, and cookouts.

**✪ Rawhide Western Town & Steakhouse.** 23023 N. Scottsdale Rd. (4 miles north of Bell Rd.), Scottsdale. ☎ **480/502-5600.** Reservations accepted for parties of 9 or more. Main courses $12–$26. AE, DISC, MC, V. Oct–May Mon–Thurs 5–10pm, Fri–Sun 11am–10pm; June–Sept daily 5–10pm. STEAKS.

Sure its a tourist trap, but Rawhide is so much fun and such a quintessentially Phoenician experience that it's one of our favorite valley restaurants. There's plenty of entertainment, including country-music bands, shoot-outs, stagecoach rides, a petting zoo, and a resident magician. Kids love pretending they're in a real old Western town, which isn't difficult, since Rawhide, with its big wide street, looks pretty authentic. Along with mesquite-broiled steaks, including not only beef but also buffalo and elk, you'll find a few barbecue items and fruit pie à la mode. They get a lot of visitors here, as evidenced by the fact that the kitchen cooks up about 200,000 pounds of steak and 50 tons of beans annually.

**✪ Rustler's Rooste.** At the Pointe Hilton on South Mountain, 7777 S. Pointe Hwy., Phoenix. ☎ **602/431-6474.** Reservations recommended. Main courses $9–$24. AE, CB, DC, DISC, MC, V. Sun–Thurs 5–10pm, Fri–Sat 5–11pm. STEAKS.

This location doesn't exactly seem like cowboy country. However, up at the top of the hill you'll find a fun Western-theme restaurant where you can slide from the bar down to the main dining room. The view north across Phoenix is entertainment enough for most people, but there are also Western bands playing for those who like to kick up their heels. If you've ever been bitten by a snake, you can exact your revenge here by ordering the rattlesnake appetizer. Follow that (if you've got the appetite of a hard-working cowpoke) with the enormous cowboy "stuff" platter consisting of, among other things, broiled sirloin, barbecued pork ribs, cowboy beans, beer-batter shrimp, barbecued chicken, and swordfish kebabs.

## CAFES & COFFEEHOUSES

**Coffee Plantation** is the Phoenix area's most popular coffeehouse chain and has several locations, but two of the largest are at the corner of 680 S. Mill Ave., Tempe (☎ **480/829-7878**), and at Biltmore Fashion Park, East Camelback Road and 24th Street (☎ **602/553-0203**). Both of these espresso bars are popular student hangouts. **Dos Baristas,** at the Town and Country Shopping Center, 4743 N. 20th St. (☎ **602/957-2236**), also sells imported crafts. **Jamaican Blue,** tucked into a small mall at 4017 N. Scottsdale Rd., Scottsdale (☎ **480/947-2160**), is a cool respite with couches that has live performances in the evening.

## BREAKFAST, BRUNCH & QUICK BITES

Most of Phoenix's best **Sunday brunches** are to be had at restaurants in major hotels and resorts. Among the finest are those served at ✪ **Marquesa** (in the Scottsdale Princess), at the Golden Swan (in the Hyatt Regency Scottsdale Resort at Gainey Ranch), at Wright's (in the Arizona Biltmore Resort & Spa), and at the Terrace Dining Room (in The Phoenician). For information on the two former restaurants, see the "Scottsdale" section of "Where to Dine," above. For information on the latter two restaurants, see "Where to Stay," above. The Desert Botanical Garden, 1201 N. Galvin Pkwy. (☎ **480/941-1225**), in Papago Park, serves brunch in conjunction with its Music in the Garden concerts held on Sundays between September and March. Tickets are $13.50 and include admission to the gardens. Sunday brunch is served for an additional charge.

If your idea of the perfect breakfast is a French pastry and a good cup of coffee, try **Pierre's Pastry Café,** 7119 E. Shea Blvd., Scottsdale (☎ **480/443-2510**), where the croissants and brioche have a luxurious, buttery texture (desserts here are also irresistible). Along Camelback Road, in the Biltmore Plaza shopping center, try **La Madeleine,** 3102 E. Camelback Rd. (☎ **602/952-0349**), which is *the* place for a luscious and leisurely French breakfast amid old French farm implements. The bakery here also does great breads, if you happen to be thinking about a picnic. There's another La Madeleine at Fashion Square Mall, 7014 E. Camelback Rd. (☎ **480/945-1663**) in Scottsdale.

For fruit smoothies and muffins and healthy things, try **Wild Oats Community Market,** which has stores at 3933 E. Camelback Rd. (☎ **602/954-0584**) and, in Scottsdale, at 7129 E. Shea Blvd. (☎ **480/905-1441**) at the corner of Scottsdale Road. Almost three dozen different kinds of bagels, plus large, inexpensive delicatessen-style breakfasts can be had at **Chompie's,** 3202 E. Greenway Rd. (☎ **602/971-8010**), 9301 E. Shea Blvd. (☎ **480/860-0475**) and the newest one at 1160 E. University Dr., Tempe (☎ **480/557-0700**).

For a quick bite when in downtown Phoenix, the **Gardenside Food Court** at the Arizona Center offers several options.

## 5 Seeing the Sights

### DISCOVERING THE DESERT & ITS NATIVE CULTURES

✪ **Heard Museum.** 2301 N. Central Ave. ☎ **602/252-8840.** Admission $7 adults, $6 seniors, $3 children 4–12. Daily 9:30am–5pm. Closed some holidays. Bus: Blue (B), Red (R), O.

One of the nation's finest museums dealing exclusively with Native American cultures, the Heard Museum makes a very informative first stop before you head out to discover the indigenous cultures of Arizona. In early 1999, the Heard unveiled its $18 million expansion that added new galleries and educational facilities.

*Native Peoples of the Southwest* is an extensive exhibit that examines the culture of each of the major tribes of the region. Included in the exhibit are a Navajo hogan, an Apache wickiup, and a Hopi corn-grinding display. A large kachina doll gallery will give you an idea of the number of different kachina spirits that populate the Hopi and Zuni religions. *Our Voices, Our Land* is an audiovisual presentation in which Indians express their thoughts on their heritage. *Old Ways, New Ways* is an unusual interactive exhibit that's aimed at children, but is also interesting to adults. You can join a drumming group on a video, duplicate a Northwest tribal design, or set up a miniature teepee. The museum's Crossroads Gallery offers a fascinating look at contemporary Native American art. On many weekends there are performances by Native American singers and dancers, and throughout the week artists demonstrate their work. Guided tours of the museum are offered daily.

The biggest event of the year is the annual spring **Indian Fair and Market,** which is held on the first weekend in March and includes performances of traditional dances as well as arts and crafts demonstrations and sales.

The museum also operates the **Heard Museum North,** El Pedregal Festival Marketplace, 34505 N. Scottsdale Rd. (☎ **480/488-9817**), which is adjacent to The Boulders resort in Carefree. This fairly large gallery features changing exhibits and is open Monday through Saturday from 10am to 5:30pm and Sunday from noon to 5pm. Admission is $2 for adults and $1 for children ages 4 to 12.

✪ **Desert Botanical Garden.** Papago Park, 1201 N. Galvin Pkwy. ☎ **480/941-1225.** Admission $7.50 adults, $6.50 seniors, $1.50 children 5–12, children under 5 free. Oct–Apr daily 8am–8pm; May–Sept daily 7am–8pm. Closed Dec 25. Bus: 3.

Located adjacent to the Phoenix Zoo and devoted exclusively to cacti and other desert plants, this botanic garden displays more than 20,000 plants from all over the world.

The Plants and People of the Sonoran Desert trail explains the science of ethnobotany through interactive displays that demonstrate how the inhabitants of the Sonoran Desert once used wild and cultivated plants. You can practice grinding corn and pounding mesquite beans, or make a yucca-fiber brush. The Center for Desert Living features demonstration gardens and the Desert House, an energy- and water-conservation research house. If you come late in the day, you can stay until after dark and see night-blooming flowers and dramatically lit cacti. A cafe on the grounds serves surprisingly good food. In the spring and fall, there are Sunday brunches and concerts in the garden.

**Pueblo Grande Museum & Cultural Park.** 4619 E. Washington St. (between 44th St. and 48th St.). ☎ 602/495-0901. Admission $2 adults, $1.50 seniors, $1 children 6–17; free on Sun. Mon–Sat 9am–4:45pm, Sun 1–4:45pm. Closed Thanksgiving, Christmas, Memorial Day, July 4, Labor Day. Bus: Yellow (Y).

Located near Sky Harbor Airport and downtown Phoenix, the Pueblo Grande Museum and Cultural Park houses the ruins of an ancient Hohokam village. This was one of several villages located along the Salt River between A.D. 300 and 1400. Sometime around 1450, this and other villages were mysteriously abandoned. One speculation is that drought and a buildup of salts from irrigation water reduced the fertility of the soil and forced the people to leave their homes and seek more fertile lands. Before touring the grounds to view the partially excavated ruins, you can walk through the small museum, which displays many of the artifacts that have been dug up on the site. Changing exhibits focus on different aspects of ancient and contemporary Indian cultures. The museum also sponsors interesting workshops, demonstrations, and tours throughout the year.

**Deer Valley Rock Art Center.** 3711 W. Deer Valley Rd. ☎ 623/582-8007. Admission $3 adults, $2 seniors, $1 children 6–12, free for children 5 and under. Oct–Apr Tues–Sat 9am–5pm, Sun noon–5pm; May–Sept Tues–Fri 8am–2pm, Sat 9am–5pm, Sun noon–5pm. Closed major holidays. Take Deer Valley Rd. exit off I-17 on the north side of Phoenix and go west to just past 35th Ave.

Located in the Hedgepeth Hills in the northwest corner of the Valley of the Sun, the Deer Valley Rock Art Center preserves an amazing concentration of Native American petroglyphs, some of which date back 5,000 years. Although these petroglyphs may not at first seem as impressive as more famous images that have been reproduced ad nauseam in recent years, the sheer numbers make this a fascinating spot. The drawings, which range from simple spirals to much more complex renderings of herds of deer, are on volcanic boulders along a ¼-mile trail. An interpretive center provides background information on this site and on rock art in general.

**Ho-Hoogam Ki Museum.** 10005 E. Osborn Rd., Scottsdale. ☎ 602/850-8190. Admission by donation. Mon–Fri 10am–4pm. Take Indian School Rd. east to Longmore Rd. and turn right.

If you're interested in learning more about the Native American history of the Valley of the Sun, you might want to visit this small museum in the Pima-Maricopa Indian Community on the east side of Scottsdale. There are exhibits on Pima basketry and Maricopa pottery, and occasionally you can see basket makers and potters at work. There are also exhibits on how the ancient Hohokam people farmed this area long before the arrival of white settlers.

## ART MUSEUMS

✪ **Phoenix Art Museum.** 1625 N. Central Ave. (at the northeast corner of McDowell Rd.). ☎ 602/257-1222. Admission $6 adults, $4 seniors and students, $2 children 6–18, free for children under 6; no admission charge on Thurs. Tues–Wed and Sat–Sun 10am–5pm, Thurs–Fri 10am–9pm. Closed major holidays. Bus: Blue (B), Red (R), O.

# Phoenix, Scottsdale & The Valley of the Sun Attractions

Arizona Biltmore 11
Arizona Doll & Toy Museum 8
Arizona Historical Society Museum 25
Arizona Mining & Mineral Museum 6
Arizona Museum for Youth 28
Arizona Science Center 8
Arizona State Capitol Museum 5
Arizona State University Art Museum 27
Buffalo Museum of America 15
Castles & Coasters 1
City Hall 7
Cosanti 14
CrackerJax Family Fun & Sports Park 16
Desert Botanical Garden 23
Fleischer Museum 17
Hall of Flame Firefighting Museum 26
Heard Museum 2
Heritage Square 8
Ho-Hoogam Ki Museum 19
McCormick-Stillman Railroad Park 13
Mesa Southwest Museum 29
Mystery Castle 9
Orpheum Theatre 7
Phoenix Art Museum 3
Phoenix Central Library 4
Phoenix Museum of History 8
Phoenix Zoo 24
Pueblo Grande Museum & Cultural Park 21
Scottsdale Museum of Contemporary Art 20
Scottsdale Center for the Arts 20
Shemer Art Center 12
Taliesin West 18
Tovrea Castle 22
Wrigley Mansion 10

NA-0263

This is the largest art museum in the Southwest and acres of wall space enable it to display canvases of a size rarely seen in museums. Little exhibit halls tucked into out-of-the-way corners, dead-end hallways hung with art, and the museum's two buildings (connected by an enclosed stainless-steel pedestrian bridge) make this a place to spend plenty of time exploring. If you're the linear type, it's easy to completely miss entire exhibit areas here.

Housed within this labyrinth, you'll find a very respectable collection that spans the major artistic movements from the Renaissance to the present. The collection of modern and contemporary art is particularly good, with works by Diego Rivera, Frida Kahlo, Pablo Picasso, Karel Appel, Mark Rothko, Alexander Calder, Henry Moore, Georgia O'Keeffe, Henri Rousseau, and Auguste Rodin.

The large first-floor gallery is used for special exhibits including major touring retrospectives. The Thorne Miniature Collection is one of the museum's most popular exhibits and consists of tiny rooms on a scale of 1 inch to 1 foot. The rooms are exquisitely detailed, right down to the leaded-glass windows of an English lodge kitchen. Other exhibits include decorative arts, historic fashions, Asian art, Spanish colonial furnishings and religious art, and, of course, a Western American exhibit featuring works by members of the Cowboy Artists of America. One-hour tours of the museum are offered Tuesday through Sunday.

⭐ **Scottsdale Museum of Contemporary Art.** 7380 E. Second St., Scottsdale. ☎ **480/994-ARTS.** Admission $5 adults, $3 students, free for children under 15; no admission charge on Tues. Tues–Wed 10am–5pm, Thurs–Fri 10am–9pm, Sat 10am–5pm, Sun noon–5pm. Bus: 41, 50, 72. Also accessible on Ollie the Trolley.

Scottsdale may seem at times to be obsessed with paintings of lonesome cowboys and solemn Indians, but with the 1999 opening of this boldly designed museum, the city has made it clear that patrons of contemporary art are also welcome here. Exhibits during the museum's first months of operation included art glass from around the world; a retrospective of the work of Will Bruder (the architect of the museum); tongue-in-cheek installations by The Art Guys; a mixed media exhibit that included videos by William Wegman; and an exhibit of the abstract landscapes of Jim Waid.

In addition to the galleries in the main museum building, there are several more galleries in the adjacent Scottsdale Center for the Arts, which also has a pair of Dale Chihuly art-glass installations. These galleries host changing exhibits of everything from Native American artifacts to contemporary art, and art by emerging artists and children. In the center's main hall, you'll find two installations by famed glass artist Dale Chihuly.

Docent-led tours are offered Sunday at 1:30pm and Tuesday at 2pm.

**Arizona State University Art Museum.** In the Nelson Fine Arts Center, 10th St. and Mill Ave., Tempe. ☎ **480/965-2787.** Free admission. Tues 10am–9pm, Wed–Sat 10am–5pm, Sun 1–5pm. Closed major holidays. Bus: Red (R), Yellow (Y), 66, or 72.

Though it isn't very large, the Arizona State University Art Museum is memorable for its innovative architecture and excellent temporary exhibitions. The building, stark and angular, captures the colors of sunset on desert mountains with its purplish gray stucco facade and pyramidal shape. The museum entrance is down a flight of stairs that lead to a cool underground garden area. Inside are galleries for crafts, prints, contemporary art, Latin American art, a temporary exhibition gallery, and two outdoor sculpture courts. The museum's collection of American art includes works by Georgia O'Keeffe, Edward Hopper, and Frederic Remington.

**Fleischer Museum.** Perimeter Center, 17207 N. Perimeter Dr., Scottsdale. ☎ **480/585-3108.** Free admission. Daily 10am–4pm. Closed major holidays. Take Pima Rd. north to just north of the intersection with Frank Lloyd Wright Blvd.

Located in a modern office park in north Scottsdale, this museum was the country's first gallery dedicated to the California School of American Impressionism, which drew extensively on French Impressionist styles and holds a quiet place in American art history.

**Shemer Art Center.** 5005 E. Camelback Rd. ☎ **602/262-4727.** Free admission. Tues 10am–9pm, Wed–Fri 10am–5pm, Sat 9am–1pm. Bus: 50.

Housed in a historic Santa Fe mission–style home built in the 1920s, the Shemer Art Center stages changing exhibits of traditional and contemporary art. The center also offers classes, concerts, sales, and lectures. Though it's small, this gallery usually stages very interesting exhibitions.

## HISTORY MUSEUMS & HISTORIC LANDMARKS

**Phoenix Museum of History.** 105 N. 5th St. ☎ **602/253-2734.** Admission $5 adults, $3.50 seniors, AAA, and students, $2.50 children 6–12, free for children under 6. Mon–Sat 10am–5pm, Sun noon–5pm. Closed major holidays. Bus: Red (R) or Yellow (Y).

Located adjacent to Heritage Square in downtown Phoenix, this state-of-the-art museum is one of the anchors of the city's downtown revitalization plan. It presents an interesting look at the history of a city that, to the casual visitor, might not seem to *have* any history. Interactive exhibits get visitors involved in the displays, while unusual exhibits make this place much more interesting than your average local history museum. Aroma barrels offer a sniff of how Phoenix once smelled. A beer-bottle sidewalk shows how one saloon keeper solved the problem of the muddy streets that once plagued the city. Yet another exhibit shows how "lungers" (tuberculosis sufferers) inadvertently helped originate the tourism industry in Arizona.

**Arizona Historical Society Museum—Marley Center.** Papago Park, 1300 N. College Ave. (just off Curry Rd.), Tempe. ☎ **480/929-0292.** Free admission. Mon–Sat 10am–4pm, Sun noon–4pm. Bus: 66.

This museum, at the headquarters of the Arizona Historical Society, focuses its modern, well-designed exhibits on the history of central Arizona over the past century. In particular, there are frequently changing exhibits on the lives and works of the people who helped shape this region. One of the more interesting exhibits features life-size statues of everyday people from Arizona's past (a Mexican miner, a Chinese laborer, and so on). Quotes relate their individual stories, and props reveal what items they might have traveled with during their days in the desert.

**Heritage Square.** 115 N. 6th St., at Monroe. ☎ **602/262-5029** or 602/262-5071. Rosson House tours, $3 adults, $2 seniors, $1 children 6–12, free for children under 6. Wed–Sat 10am–3:30pm, Sun noon–3:30pm (call for summer hours). Bus: Red (R), Yellow (Y), 0.

Though the city of Phoenix was founded as recently as 1870, much of its history has been obliterated. Heritage Square is a collection of some of the few remaining houses in Phoenix that date from the last century and the original Phoenix town site. All the buildings are listed on the National Register of Historic Places, and most display Victorian architectural styles popular just before the turn of the century. Today they house museums, restaurants, and gift shops. The Eastlake Victorian Rosson House is furnished with period antiques and is open for tours. The Silva House, a neoclassical revival-style home, houses historical exhibits on turn-of-the-century life in the Valley of the Sun. In the Stevens-Haustgen House, you'll find a gift shop, and in the Stevens House you'll find the Arizona Doll and Toy Museum. The Burgess Carriage House contains a gift shop and ticket window for the Rosson House tours. The Teeter House, an 1899 bungalow, is a Victorian tearoom, and an 1897 mule barn houses a cafe. The old Baird Machine Shop contains Pizzeria Bianco.

✪ **Arizona State Capitol Museum.** 1700 W. Washington St. ☎ **602/542-4581.** Free admission. Mon–Fri 8am–5pm, Sat 10am–3pm. Closed state holidays. Bus: Yellow (Y).

In the years before Arizona became a state, the territorial capital moved from Prescott to Tucson, then back to Prescott, and finally settled in Phoenix. In 1898, a stately territorial capitol building was erected (with a copper roof to remind the local citizenry of the importance of that metal in the Arizona economy). Atop this copper roof was placed the statue *Winged Victory,* which still graces the old capitol building today. This building no longer serves as the actual state capitol, but has been restored to the way it appeared in 1912, the year Arizona became a state. Among the rooms on view are the senate and house chambers, as well as the governor's office. Excellent historical exhibits provide interesting perspectives on early Arizona events and lifestyles.

**Scottsdale Historical Museum.** 7333 E. Scottsdale Mall, Scottsdale. ☎ **480/945-4499.** Free admission. Wed–Sat 10am–5pm, Sun noon–4pm. Closed July–Aug.

If you're not convinced that Scottsdale really is an old town, drop by the Little Red Schoolhouse on the Scottsdale Mall. Here you'll find a one-room schoolhouse display, artifacts that belonged to the town's founder, vintage furnishings, and other displays on the town's history.

## SCIENCE & INDUSTRY MUSEUMS

✪ **Arizona Science Center.** 600 E. Washington St. ☎ **602/716-2000.** Admission $8 adults, $6 seniors and children 4–12, free for children under 4. Planetarium and film combination tickets also available. Daily 10am–5pm. Closed Thanksgiving and Christmas. Bus: Red (R), Yellow (Y), 0.

Aimed primarily at children but also loads of fun for adults, the Arizona Science Center, a hands-on facility, is one of the anchors of Phoenix's ongoing renewal of the city's downtown. In this large facility you'll find state-of-the-art interactive exhibits covering a variety of topics from the human body to coping with living in the desert. However, it is not the topics so much as the individual displays that make this museum fun. There's a huge ant farm, a virtual reality game that puts you inside a video game, a massive truck tire weighing almost 4 tons, a flight simulator, and a cloud maker. The ever-popular soap-bubble play area is housed on a terrace on the museum's roof, as is a star-gazing area. In addition to the many exhibits, the science center includes a planetarium (night sky and laser shows) and a large-screen theater, both of which carry additional charges. You could easily spend all day here. Temporary exhibits change every 4 months.

**Mesa Southwest Museum.** 53 N. MacDonald St. (at the corner of 1st St.), Mesa. ☎ **480/644-2230.** Admission $4 adults, $3.50 seniors, $2 children 3–12, free for children under 3. Tues–Sat 10am–5pm, Sun 1–5pm. Closed major holidays. Bus: Red (R).

Located in downtown Mesa, this museum appeals mostly to children, but its exhibits on prehistoric indigenous cultures in the region will likely interest adults as well. Exhibits cover Mesoamerican art and Spanish mission life. Kids will love the fossils (including a complete mammoth skeleton) and animated dinosaurs, and they can even pan for gold. The mine and jail (this really was the old jail) displays are also a lot of fun for kids. There are usually a couple of different temporary exhibits at any given time that may include displays of contemporary art or regional history. The museum is currently in the process of expanding and by 2000 will have doubled its display space.

The museum also operates the nearby **Sirrine House Historic Home Museum,** 160 N. Center St., which is filled with period antiques from the late 19th and early 20th centuries. This historic home is open on weekends only.

## ❷ Did You Know?

- Phoenix is the sixth-largest metropolitan area in the United States.
- The Phoenix area has more than 180 golf courses and more than 1,000 tennis courts.
- Some of the canals that water the Valley of the Sun were dug by hand by Native Americans hundreds of years ago.
- The city of Peoria, west of Phoenix, boasts the largest baseball spring training center in the country.
- Every president since Herbert Hoover has stayed at the Arizona Biltmore Hotel.
- Each year Phoenix enjoys sunshine during 86% of all daylight hours, for a total of 300 to 315 sunny days.
- The tallest water fountain in the world (560 feet) is in the community of Fountain Hills east of Scottsdale.

## A MUSEUM MISCELLANY: PLANES, FLAMES & MORE

**Champlin Fighter Aircraft Museum.** 4636 Fighter Aces Dr., Mesa (at Falcon Field Airport off McKellips Rd.). ☎ **480/830-4540.** Admission $6.50 adults, $3 children 5–12, free for children under 5. Sept 16–Apr 14 daily 10am–5pm; Apr 15–Sept 15 daily 8:30am–3:30pm. From U.S. 60, take the Greenfield exit, go north to McKellips Blvd. and follow the green signs.

This aeronautical museum, dedicated exclusively to fighter planes and the fighter aces who flew them, houses aircraft from World Wars I and II, the Korean War, and the Vietnam War, with a strong emphasis on the wood-and-fabric biplanes and triplanes of World War I (several Sopwiths and Fokkers). From World War II, there's a Spitfire, a Messerschmitt, and a Goodyear Corsair. Jet fighters from more recent battles include a MiG-15, a MiG-17, and an F4 Phantom. In total, there are 33 flyable fighters here.

**Buffalo Museum of America.** 10261 N. Scottsdale Rd. (at the southeast corner of Shea Blvd.), Scottsdale. ☎ **480/951-1022.** Admission $3 adults, $2.50 seniors, $2 children 6–17, free for children under 6. Mon–Fri 9am–5pm. Closed major holidays. Bus: 72 or 106.

Scottsdale may not be the home where the buffalo roam, but it does have a fascination with the Old West, so it seems appropriate to find here a museum dedicated to these fabled behemoths of the plains. This small museum is the culmination of one man's infatuation with the American bison, which is commonly known as the buffalo. The museum houses stuffed buffaloes, bronze buffaloes, buffalo paintings, and all manner of buffalo memorabilia, including a rifle that once belonged to Buffalo Bill Cody.

**Hall of Flame Firefighting Museum.** Papago Park, 6101 E. Van Buren St. ☎ **602/ 275-3473.** Admission $5 adults, $4 seniors, $3 students 6–17, $1.50 children 3–5, free for children under 3. Mon–Sat 9am–5pm, Sun noon–4pm. Closed Jan 1, Thanksgiving, and Dec 25. Bus: 3.

The world's largest firefighting museum houses a fascinating collection of vintage fire trucks. The displays date from a 1725 English hand pumper to several classic fire engines from this century. All are beautifully restored and, of course, fire-engine red (mostly). In all, there are more than 100 vehicles on display.

**Arizona Mining & Mineral Museum.** 1502 W. Washington St. ☎ **602/255-3795.** Free admission. Mon–Fri 8am–5pm, Sat 11am–4pm. Closed state holidays. Bus: Yellow (Y).

Arizonans have been romancing the stones for more than a century at colorfully named mines such as the Copper Queen, the Sleeping Beauty, the No-Name Creek,

---

### ✪ Frommer's Favorite Phoenix Experiences

**Hiking up Camelback Mountain or Squaw Peak.** Hiking the trails up these two mountains is a favorite activity among the city's more active residents. Both trails are steep climbs, but the views from up top are superb. Bring water and start early in the morning if it's going to be a hot day.

**Having Dinner with a View.** There's something bewitching about gazing down at the twinkling lights of the city while enjoying a delicious meal at one of the area's few hillside restaurants.

**Lounging by the Pool.** Nothing is more relaxing than lounging by one of the spectacular pools and gazing up at the desert mountains from a world-class Valley of the Sun resort.

**Taking the Scottsdale Art Walk.** Thursday evenings from October to May both dilettantes and connoisseurs turn out to visit the nearly 60 art galleries in downtown Scottsdale, many of which have artists on hand and provide complimentary refreshments.

**Attending a Spring Training Baseball Game.** Get a head start on all your fellow baseball fans by going to a spring-training game while you're in Phoenix. Just be sure to book your hotel well in advance; these games are the biggest thing going in the valley each spring.

**Mountain Biking in South Mountain or Papago Park.** The trails of these two desert parks are ideal for mountain biking, and whether you're a novice making your first foray onto the dirt or a budding downhill racer, you'll find miles of riding that are just your speed.

**Spending the Day at a Spa.** When it comes to stress relief, there's nothing like a massage or an herbal wrap. The chance to lie back and do nothing at all is something few of us take the time for anymore, so a day at the spa just might be the best thing you can do for yourself on an Arizona vacation.

---

the Lucky Boy, and the Bluebird. Out of such mines have come countless tons of copper, silver, and gold, as well as beautiful minerals with tongue-twisting names. Azurite, chalcanthite, chalcoaluminate, malachite, and chrysocolla are just some of the richly colored and fascinatingly textured minerals on display at this small downtown museum, which is dedicated to the state's mining industry. Rather than playing up the historical or profit-making side of the industry, exhibits focus on the amazing variety and beauty of Arizona minerals.

## ARCHITECTURAL HIGHLIGHTS

In addition to the architectural landmarks listed below, there are a couple of other buildings of which Phoenix is justly proud.

The **Arizona Biltmore,** 24th Street and Missouri Avenue (☎ **602/955-6600**), though not designed by Frank Lloyd Wright, shows the famed architect's hand in its distinctive cast-cement blocks and also displays sculptures, furniture, and stained glass designed by Wright. The best way to soak up the ambience of this exclusive resort (if you aren't staying here) is over dinner, a cocktail, or tea. If you'd like to spend the day by the pool, you can even rent a cabana.

On a hilltop adjacent to the Arizona Biltmore, you can see the famed **Wrigley Mansion,** 2501 E. Telawa Trail. (☎ **602/955-4079**), a classically elegant mansion that was built by chewing-gum magnate William Wrigley Jr. between 1929 and 1931 as a present for his wife, Ada. Built with Italianate styling, the many levels and red-tile roofs make it seem like an entire village. Today the mansion is a National Historic Landmark with the interior restored to its original elegance. Tours are offered Tuesday and Thursday at 10am and 3pm and cost $10. Although this is currently a private club, lunch is open to the public.

**Tovrea Castle,** 5041 E. Van Buren St. (☎ **602/262-6412**), another architectural confection of the Phoenix landscape, has been likened to a giant wedding cake and is currently under renovation. However, it is scheduled to open to the public some time in 2000 or 2001. Call for information.

Among the more recent buildings to garner architectural praise in Phoenix are the **new City Hall,** and restored **Orpheum Theatre,** which sit back to back on Third Avenue between Washington and Adams streets. The new City Hall is a bold contemporary construction as intriguing as the main library, while the Orpheum is a classically elegant historic building. The two styles clash in a manner that typifies old and new Phoenix.

**Burton Barr Central Library.** 1221 N. Central Ave. ☎ **602/262-4636.** Free admission. Mon–Thurs 9am–9pm, Fri–Sat 9am–6pm, Sun 1–5pm. Closed major holidays. Bus: Red (R) or 0.

Opened in 1995, the Phoenix Central Library is among the most daring pieces of public architecture in the city. No fan of futurist art or science fiction should miss a visit. The entrance, with all its steel and glass, and elevators rising above, makes you feel as though you've just stepped inside a gargantuan computer or 21st-century space station.

The five-story cube is partially clad in ribbed copper sheeting, enough copper to produce roughly 17,500,000 pennies (it took a lot of overdue books to pay for that feature). The building's design makes use of the desert's plentiful sunshine to provide plenty of light for reading, but also incorporates computer-controlled louvers and shade sails to reduce heat and glare. The fifth-floor reading room, which covers more than an acre and is the largest library reading room in the United States, is topped by a "floating" ceiling that is suspended from cables. Either you'll love it or you'll hate it, but don't miss it.

✪ **Taliesin West.** 12621 Frank Lloyd Wright Blvd. (at 114th St.), Scottsdale. ☎ **480/860-2700.** Basic tours, Oct 1–May 31 $14 adults, $11 seniors and students, $3 children 4–12, free for children 3 and under; June 1–Sept 30 $10 adults, $8 students and seniors, $3 children 4–12, free for children 3 and under. Oct 1–May 31 daily 10am–4pm; June 1–Sept 30 daily 8am–3pm. Closed Easter, Thanksgiving, Christmas, New Year's Day, and occasional special events. From Scottsdale Rd., go east on Shea Blvd. to 114th St., then north 1 mile to the entrance road.

Architect Frank Lloyd Wright fell in love with the Arizona desert and in 1937 opened a winter camp here that served as his office and school. Today Taliesin West is the headquarters of the Frank Lloyd Wright Foundation and School of Architecture.

Tours explain the buildings of this campus and also include a general background introduction to Wright and his theories of architecture. Wright believed in using local materials in his designs, and this shows up at Taliesin West where local stone was used for building foundations. He developed a number of innovative methods for dealing with the extremes of the desert climate, such as sliding wall panels to let in varying amounts of air and light.

Architecture students, and anyone interested in the work of Wright, will enjoy browsing through the excellent books in the gift shop. Expanded basic tours called Insight Tours ($20 adults, $16 seniors, students, and children), behind-the-scenes tours ($35 per person), and guided desert hikes ($20 per person) are also available at certain times of year and at specific times of day. Call ahead and check the schedule to be sure you can get the tour you want at the time you want.

**Cosanti.** 6433 Doubletree Ranch Rd., Scottsdale. ☎ **480/948-6145.** Admission by dona-tion; guided tours: minimum 5 people, $5 per person. Daily 9am–5pm. Closed major holi-days. Drive 1 mile west of Scottsdale Rd. on Doubletree Ranch Rd.

This complex of cast-concrete structures served as a prototype and learning project for architect Paolo Soleri's much grander Arcosanti project currently under construction north of Phoenix (see chapter 5 for details). It's here at Cosanti that Soleri's famous bells are cast, and you can see the foundry in action on most weekday mornings.

**Mystery Castle.** 800 E. Mineral Rd. ☎ **602/268-1581.** Admission $5 adults, $4 seniors, $2 children 6–15. Thurs–Sun 11am–4pm. Closed July–Sept. Take Central Ave. south to Mineral Rd. (2 miles south of Baseline Rd.) and turn east.

Built for a daughter who longed for a castle more permanent than those built in sand at the beach, Mystery Castle is a wondrous work of folk-art architecture. Boyce Luther Gulley, who had come to Arizona in hopes of curing his tuberculosis, constructed the castle during the 1930s and early 1940s using stones from the property. The resulting 18-room fantasy has 13 fireplaces, a wedding chapel, parapets, and many other unusual touches. This castle is a must for fans of folk-art constructions, and tours are usually led by the daughter for whom the castle was built.

## ZOOS & PARKS

Among the city's most popular parks are its natural areas and preserves. These include South Mountain Park, Papago Park, Phoenix Mountains Preserve (site of Squaw Peak), North Mountain Preserve, North Mountain Recreation Area, and Camelback Mountain-Echo Canyon Recreation Area. For more information on these parks, see "Hiking," "Bicycling," and "Horseback Riding" under "Outdoor Pursuits," later in this chapter.

**The Phoenix Zoo.** Papago Park, 455 N. Galvin Pkwy. ☎ **602/273-1341.** Admission $8.50 adults, $7.50 seniors, $4.25 children 3–12, free for children under 3. Labor Day–Apr daily 9am–5pm; May 1–Labor Day daily 7:30am–4pm. Closed Dec 25. Bus: 3.

"Wow! Look at all the turtles." That's almost always the first reaction when visitors approach this zoo on a bridge over a very primordial-looking pond. Home to more than 1,300 animals, the Phoenix Zoo is known for its mixed-species, 4-acre African veldt exhibit and its baboon colony. The Southwestern animal exhibits are also of par-ticular interest, as are the giant Galápagos tortoises. All the animals in the zoo are kept in naturalistic enclosures and what with all the palm trees and tropical vegetation, it's easy to forget that this is the desert, especially when you wander through the rain-forest exhibit. For an additional charge, you can take a narrated tram tour of the grounds.

   Kids will enjoy the Harmony Farm exhibit, an interactive farm that teaches about the interconnectedness of people, plants, and animals.

**Out of Africa Wildlife Park.** Fort McDowell Rd., Fountain Springs. ☎ **480/837-7779.** Admission $13.95 adults, $12.95 seniors, $4.95 children ages 4–12, free for children under 4. Oct 1–Memorial Day Tues–Sun 9:30am–5pm; Memorial Day–Sept Wed–Sun 9:30am–5pm. Take Ariz. 87 northeast from Mesa and 2 miles past Shea Blvd., turn right on Fort McDowell Rd.

Lions and tigers and bears, oh my! That's what you'll see at this small wildlife park northeast of Scottsdale, and all these animals will be putting on shows for you rather than just lazing in the shade as they do at most zoos. The most popular perfor-mances are those in the park's swimming pool. You've probably never seen tigers, wolves, and bears having so much fun in the water. There are also exotic bird and reptile shows.

## ESPECIALLY FOR KIDS

In addition to the children's activities suggested below, kids are also likely to enjoy the Arizona Science Center, the Mesa Southwest Museum, Mystery Castle, the Hall of Flame Firefighting Museum, the Phoenix Zoo, and Out of Africa Wildlife Park—all described in detail above.

**Arizona Doll & Toy Museum.** In Heritage Square, 602 E. Adams St. ☎ **602/253-9337.** Admission $2.50 adults, $1 children. Tues–Sat 10am–4pm, Sun noon–4pm. Closed Aug. Bus: Red (R), Yellow (Y), 0.

Located in the Stevens House on Heritage Square in downtown Phoenix, the Arizona Doll and Toy Museum is as interesting to adults as it is to kids. There's a 1912 schoolroom display in which the children are all antique dolls.

**Arizona Museum for Youth.** 35 N. Robson St. (between Main and 1st sts.), Mesa. ☎ **480/644-2467.** Admission $2, free for children under 2. Fall–spring Sun and Tues–Fri 1–5pm, Sat 10am–5pm; summer Tues–Fri 9am–5pm, Sat 10am–5pm, Sun 1–5pm. Closed for 2 weeks between exhibits. Bus: R.

Using both traditional displays and participatory activities, this museum allows children to explore the fine arts and their own creativity. The museum is housed in a refurbished grocery store, which has for past exhibits been transformed into a zoo, a farm, and a foreign country. Exhibits are geared mainly to toddlers through 12-year-olds, but all ages can work together to make an object or experience the activities.

**McCormick-Stillman Railroad Park.** 7301 E. Indian Bend Rd., Scottsdale. ☎ **480/312-2312.** Train and carousel rides $1. Hours vary with the season, call for schedule. Bus: 72.

If you or your kids happen to like trains, then you won't want to miss this Scottsdale park dedicated to railroading. Within the park are a 5/12-scale model railroad that takes visitors around the park, restored cars and engines, two old railway depots, and model railroad layouts operated by a local club. There's also a 1929 carousel. In June and July there are concerts in the park. You'll find the park on the corner of Scottsdale Road and Indian Bend Road.

**Castles & Coasters.** 9445 N. Metro Pkwy. E. ☎ **602/997-7575.** Ride and game prices vary (all-day passes available). Daily (hours change seasonally; call ahead). Bus: Red (R) or 27.

Located adjacent to Metrocenter, one of Arizona's largest shopping malls, this small amusement park boasts a very impressive roller coaster and plenty of tamer rides. There are also four 18-hole miniature-golf courses and a huge pavilion full of video games.

**CrackerJax Family Fun & Sports Park.** 16001 N. Scottsdale Rd. (1/4 mile south of Bell Rd.), Scottsdale. ☎ **480/998-2800.** Activity prices vary. Daily (hours change seasonally; call ahead). Bus: 72.

Three miniature-golf courses are the main attraction here, but you'll also find a bilevel driving range, batting cages, go-cart tracks, sand volleyball courts, and a video-game arcade.

## 6  Organized Tours

The Valley of the Sun is a sprawling, often congested, place, and if you are unfamiliar with the area, you may be surprised at how great the distances are. If map reading and urban navigation are not your strong points, you may want to consider taking a guided tour. There are numerous companies offering tours of both the Valley of the Sun and the rest of Arizona. However, tours of the valley tend to include only brief stops at highlights.

**BUS TOURS    Gray Line of Phoenix** (☎ 800/732-0327 or 602/495-9100) is one of the largest tour companies in the valley. It offers a 3½-hour tour of Phoenix and the Valley of the Sun for $30 per adult. The tour points out such local landmarks as the state capitol, Heritage Square, Arizona State University, and Old Town Scottsdale.

**GLIDER RIDES    The thermals that form above the mountains in the Phoenix area are ideal for sailplane (glider) soaring. On the south side of the valley, **Arizona Soaring** (☎ 800/861-2318 in Arizona or 520/568-2318; 480/821-2903 for information), in the community of Maricopa, offers sailplane rides as well as instruction. A basic 20-minute flight is $69.95, and for $99.95 you can take an aerobatic flight with loops, rolls, and inverted flying. To reach the airstrip, take I-10 east to exit 164 (Maricopa Road), go 15 miles, turn west on Ariz. 238 and continue for 6½ miles more. On the north side of the valley, there's **Turf Soaring School,** 8700 W. Carefree Hwy., Peoria (☎ 602/439-3621), which charges $75 for a basic flight and $110 for an aerobatic flight. This outfit also offers flights for two people, though your combined weight can't exceed 300 pounds. These flights run $125 to $155.

**HOT-AIR BALLOON RIDES    The still morning air of the Valley of the Sun is perfect for hot-air ballooning, and because of the stiff competition, prices are among the lowest in the country—between $110 and $135 per person for a 1 to 1½ hour ride. Companies to try include **A Aerozona Adventure** (☎ 888/991-4260 or 480/991-4260; e-mail: boothballoon@earthlink.net), **Adventures Out West** (☎ 800/755-0935 or 602/996-6100), and **Unicorn Balloon Company** (☎ 800/468-2478 or 480/991-3666; www.unicornballoon.com).

**JEEP TOURS    Want to get off the pavement and do a little four-wheeling? Jeep tours through the desert are offered by a dozen or more companies around the valley. Most hotels and resorts have particular companies that they work with, so if you want to do a Jeep tour, try contacting the concierge at your hotel. Alternatively, you can contact one of the following companies. Most will pick you up at your hotel, take you off through the desert, give you lots of information on this corner of the West, and maybe even let you try shooting a six-gun while you're out in the desert. Tour prices are around $60 to $90 for a 4-hour tour. Companies to try include **Western Events** (☎ 800/567-3619 or 480/860-1777), **Arizona Bound Tours** (☎ 480/994-0580), and **Rawhide Land & Cattle** (☎ 800/294-JEEP or 480/488-0023). The last company operates out of the popular Rawhide Wild West town/restaurant. For slightly more unique tours, try **Desert Storm Hummer Tours** (☎ 480/922-0020), which uses those ultimate sport utility vehicles, or **Arizona Unique Buggy Adventures** (☎ 480/982-7661), which uses unusual open-sided off-road buggies for its tours.

Some Jeep tour companies also offer the chance to do some gold panning. If this interests you, contact **Western Events** (☎ 800/567-3619 or 480/860-1777), which also does ghost-town excursions, or **Arrowhead Desert Tours** (☎ 800/514-9063 or 602/942-3361). Expect to pay $50 to $82 per person.

**SCENIC FLIGHTS    If you're short on time but still want to at least see the Grand Canyon, you can book an air tour in a small plane. **Sunrise Airlines** (☎ 800/445-8738 or 480/991-8252), which operates out of the Scottsdale Airport, will fly you up to the canyon (though not over it) and give you a ground or helicopter tour for between $262 and $345. **Westwind Tours** (☎ 888/869-0866 or 480/991-5557) charges $220 to $275 for its Grand Canyon tours and also offers a trip for $395 that takes in Monument Valley as well. This company flies out of the Deer Valley Airport in the northwest part of the valley.

# 7   Outdoor Pursuits

**BICYCLING**   Though the Valley of the Sun is a sprawling place, it's mostly flat, which makes bicycling a breeze as long as it isn't windy or in the heat of summer. **Wheels 'n Gear,** 7607 E. McDowell Rd., Scottsdale (☎ **480/945-2881**), rents mountain bikes for between $18 and $40 per day and has off-road trail maps available. Among the best mountain-biking spots in the city are South Mountain Park (use the entrance off 48th Street), Papago Park (at Van Buren Street and Galvin Parkway), and North Mountain Recreation Area (off Seventh Street between Dunlap Avenue and Thunderbird Road).

If you'd rather have someone show you some of the desert's best mountain biking, contact **Desert Biking Adventures** (☎ **888/249-BIKE** or 602/320-4602), which leads 2-, 3-, and 4-hour mountain-bike tours through the desert (and specializes in downhill rides). Tour prices range from $50 to $80.

If you'd rather confine your cycling to a paved surface, there's no better route than Scottsdale's **Indian Bend Wash greenbelt,** a paved multiuse path that extends for more than 12 miles along Hayden Road (from Indian Bend Road to Washington Street). This trail also connects north all the way to Frank Lloyd Wright Boulevard and south to Tempe's Mill Avenue. The Indian Bend Wash pathway can be accessed at many points along Hayden Road.

**GOLF**   With nearly 200 courses in the Valley of the Sun, golf is just about the most popular sport in Phoenix and one of the main reasons people flock here during the winter months. Sunshine, spectacular views, and coyotes, quail, and doves for company make playing a round of golf in the valley a truly memorable experience.

However, despite the number of courses, it can still be difficult to get a tee time on any of the more famous and popular courses (especially during the busy months of February through April). If you are staying at a resort with a golf course, be sure to make your tee-time reservations at the same time you make your room reservations. If you aren't staying at a resort, you may still be able to play a round on a resort course if you can get a last-minute tee time. Try one of the tee-time reservation services below.

The only thing harder than getting a winter or spring tee time in the Valley of the Sun is facing the bill at the end of your 18 holes. Greens fees at most public and resort courses range from around $90 to $125, with the top courses at the most expensive resorts often charging around $150 (or even more). Municipal courses, on the other hand, charge less than $30. You can save money on many courses by opting for twilight play, which usually begins at 1, 2, or 3pm. We've listed high- and low-season greens fees below; you'll find that spring and fall fees fall somewhere in-between.

You can get more information on Valley of the Sun golf courses from the **Greater Phoenix Convention & Visitors Bureau,** 50 N. Second St., Phoenix, AZ 85004 (☎ **602/254-6500**). You can also pick up a copy of the *Greater Phoenix Golf Guide* at the Visitors Bureau, golf courses, and many hotels and resorts.

To assure that you get to play those courses you've been dreaming about, it's a good idea to make reservations well in advance. Many companies around the valley will save you the hassle of booking tee times by making reservations for you. One of these companies, **Golf Xpress** (☎ **800/878-8580** or 602/404-GOLF), can make reservations farther in advance than you could if you called the golf course direct. This company also makes hotel reservations, rents golf clubs, and provides other assistance to golfers visiting the Valley. **Par-Tee-Time Golf** (☎ **800/827-2223** or 602/230-7223) is another company that makes advance reservations. For last-minute reservations, call **Stand-by Golf** (☎ 480/874-3133).

The valley's many resort courses are, of course, the favored fairways of valley visitors. For spectacular scenery, the two Jay Morrish–designed 18-hole courses at ✪ **The Boulders,** 34631 N. Tom Darlington Dr., Carefree (☎ **800/553-1717** or 480/488-9009), just can't be beat. Given the option, play the South Course and watch out as you approach the tee box on the seventh hole—it's a real heart stopper. Tee times for nonresort guests are very limited in the winter and spring, and you'll pay $165 for a round. However, in summer you can play here for only $75 (just be sure you get the earliest possible tee time and bring plenty of water).

Jumping over to Litchfield Park, on the far west side of the valley, you'll find **The Wigwam Golf and Country Club,** 300 Wigwam Blvd. (☎ **623/935-3811**), and, count 'em, three championship 18-hole courses. ✪ **The Gold Course** here is legendary, but even the Blue and Red courses are worth playing. These are traditional courses, for purists who want vast expanses of green instead of cactus and boulders. In the high season, greens fees are $125 for the Gold Course and $95 for the Blue and Red courses (in summer, $34 Monday to Thursday and $38 Friday to Sunday). High-season reservations for non-guests can be made no more than 5 days in advance.

Way over on the east side of the valley at the foot of the Superstition Mountains is the ✪ **Gold Canyon Golf Resort,** 6100 S. Kings Ranch Rd., Gold Canyon (☎ **480/982-9449**), which has been rated one of the best public courses in the state and also has what have been rated as three of the best holes in the state—the second, third, and fourth holes on the Dinosaur Mountain course, a visually breathtaking desert-style course. Greens fees on this course range from $75 to 125 in winter and from $36 to $70 in summer. The resort's second course, the Sidewinder, is a more traditional course and is less dramatic, but is also much more economical. Greens fees in winter range from $39 to $65 and from $25 to $45 in summer. Make reservations a week in advance. Well worth the drive.

If you want to swing where the pros do, beg, borrow, or steal a tee time on the Tom Weiskopf and Jay Morrish–designed Stadium Course at the ✪ **Tournament Players Club (TPC) of Scottsdale,** 17020 N. Hayden Rd. (☎ **480/585-3600** or 480/585-3939), which annually hosts the Phoenix Open. The 18th hole here has standing room for 40,000 spectators, but it is hoped there won't be that many around (or any TV cameras) the day you double bogey on this hole. The TPC's second 18, the Desert Course, is actually a municipal course thanks to an agreement with the landowner, the Bureau of Land Management. Stadium course greens fees are $170 in the winter/spring and $45 in the summer. Desert Course greens fees range from $38 to $45.

At the **Gainey Ranch Golf Club,** at the Hyatt Regency Scottsdale Resort at Gainey Ranch, 7600 E. Gainey Club Dr. (☎ **480/951-0022**), you'll find three decidedly different 9-hole courses (the Dunes, the Arroyo, and the Lakes courses), each with its own set of challenges. However, these courses are open only to guests of the resort.

If a traditional course that has challenged presidents and celebrities alike interests you, then try to get a tee time at one of the two 18-hole courses at the **Arizona Biltmore Country Club,** 24th Street and Missouri Avenue (☎ **602/955-9655**). The two courses here are more relaxing than challenging; good to play if you're not yet up to par. Greens fees are $75 to $130 in the winter/spring and $30 to $45 in summer. Reservations can be made 30 days in advance. There's also a championship 18-hole putting course at the hotel.

The two courses at the **Camelback Golf Club,** 7847 N. Mockingbird Lane (☎ **480/596-7050**), offer distinctly different experiences. However, in 1999, the Padre course underwent a complete redesign (which still might not be completed by the time you read this), with new water features being added, among other changes. A new clubhouse was also scheduled to be built. The Indian Bend course is a links-style course with great mountain views and lots of water hazards. Greens fees are $160 to $185 in winter/spring and $35 to $50 in summer. Make reservations up to 30 days in advance.

Set at the base of Camelback Mountain, **The Phoenician Golf Club,** 6000 E. Camelback Rd. (☎ **800/888-8234** or 480/423-2449), at the valley's most glamorous resort, has 27 holes that mix traditional and desert styles. Greens fees if you aren't staying at the resort are $140 to $160 in winter/spring and $85 to $90 in summer.

Of the valley's many daily-fee courses, it is the two 18-hole courses at ✪ **Troon North Golf Club,** 10320 E. Dynamite Blvd., Scottsdale (☎ **480/585-5300**), seemingly just barely carved out of raw desert, that garner the most local accolades. Greens fees are $180 in February and March and $75 to $90 through the summer. Reservations are taken up to 30 days in advance (and fill up quickly in winter).

However, the Pete Dye–designed **ASU-Karsten Golf Course,** 1125 E. Rio Salado Pkwy., Tempe (☎ **480/921-8070**), part of Arizona State University, is also highly praised and is a very challenging training ground for top collegiate golfers. Greens fees are $62 to $87 in the winter and $20 to $30 in the summer. Make reservations at least 5 days in advance in the winter.

If you haven't yet gotten your handicap down, but want to try a desert-style course, then head to **Tatum Ranch Golf Club,** 29888 N. Tatum Ranch Dr., Cave Creek (☎ **480/585-2399**), which is regarded as a forgiving course with a desert sensibility. However, this course is in the process of going private and may no longer be accepting outside play by the time you read this. Greens fees are $70 to $110 in the winter and $30 to $50 in the summer.

Other worthwhile daily-fee courses include **Kokopelli Golf Resort,** 1800 W. Guadalupe Rd., Gilbert (☎ **480/926-3589** or 480/962-GOLF), with greens fees of $85 to $95 in winter and $45 to $50 in summer, and **The Legend at Arrowhead,** 21027 N. 67th Ave., Glendale (☎ **623/561-1902** or 480/962-GOLF), with greens fees of $105 to $130 in winter and $35 to $50 in summer. The **Kierland Golf Club,** 15636 Clubgate Dr., Scottsdale (☎ **480/922-9283**), which was designed by Scott Miller and consists of three 9-hole courses that can be played in combination, is another much-talked-about local daily-fee course. Greens fees are $120 to $140 in winter and $50 to $60 in summer.

Of the municipal courses in Phoenix, **Papago Golf Course,** 5595 E. Moreland St. (☎ **602/275-8428**), at the foot of the red sandstone Papago Buttes, offers fine views and economical rates ($18 to $28 in high season) and has a killer 17th hole. **Encanto Golf Course,** 2775 N. 15th Ave. (☎ **602/253-3963**), is equally inexpensive for a round of golf ($18 to $28 in the high season). Keep in mind that these rates don't include a golf cart, which is another $20 to $22.

**HIKING**    Several mountains around Phoenix, including Camelback Mountain and Squaw Peak, have been set aside as parks and nature preserves, and these natural areas are among the city's most popular hiking spots. The city's largest nature preserve, **Phoenix South Mountain Park,** said to be the largest city park in the world, contains miles of nature, hiking, mountain-biking, and horseback-riding trails. The views of Phoenix from here are spectacular, especially at sunset. To reach the park, simply drive south on Central Avenue or 48th Street.

Perhaps the most popular hiking trail in the city is the trail to the top of ✪ **Camelback Mountain,** which is near the boundary between Phoenix and Scottsdale. This is the highest mountain in Phoenix, and the 1.2-mile trail to the summit is very steep. Don't attempt this one in the heat of the day, and take at least a quart of water with you. The reward for your effort is the city's finest view. To reach the trailhead for Camelback Mountain, drive up 44th Street until it becomes McDonald Drive, then turn right on East Echo Canyon Drive, and continue up the hill until the road ends at a large parking lot.

At the east end of Camelback Mountain you'll find the Cholla Trail, which is longer than the trail at the west end and sees far fewer hikers. The only parking for this trail is along Invergordon Road at Chapparal Road, just north of Camelback Road and along the east boundary of The Phoenician resort (be sure to park in a legal parking space and watch the hours that parking is allowed). This trail starts out fairly easy and then toward the top gets steep, rocky, and more difficult. However, there are great views down onto the fairways of The Phoenician's golf course.

Squaw Peak in the Phoenix Mountains Preserve offers another aerobic workout of a hike and has views that are almost as spectacular as those from Camelback Mountain. Squaw Peak is reached from Squaw Peak Drive off Lincoln Drive between 22nd Street and 23rd Street.

For much less vigorous hiking, try the North Mountain Recreation Area in North Mountain Preserve. This natural area, which is located on either side of Seventh Street between Dunlap Avenue and Thunderbird Road, has more flat hiking than Camelback Mountain or Squaw Peak.

Farther afield there are numerous hiking opportunities in the Superstition Mountains to the east and the McDowell Mountains to the north.

**HORSEBACK RIDING** Even in the urban confines of the Phoenix metro area, people like to play at being cowboys, and if you get the urge to saddle up, there are plenty of places around the valley to rent a horse. On the south side of the city, try **Ponderosa Stables,** 10215 S. Central Ave. (☎ **602/268-1261**), or **South Mountain Stables,** 10005 S. Central Ave. (☎ **602/276-8131**), both of which lead rides into South Mountain Park and charge $16 per hour. In the Scottsdale area, try **MacDonald's Ranch,** 26540 N. Scottsdale Rd. (☎ **480/585-0239**), which charges $20 for a 1-hour ride and $30 for a 2-hour ride (1-hour free ride on your birthday).

If you're a city slicker looking to move some cattle, then contact **Rocky Mt. Cattle Moo-vers** (☎ **800/826-9666** or 623/875-9676). They'll put you in the saddle and let you round up some doggies and move 'em on down the trail. They've got all-day cattle drives as well as breakfast, lunch, and sunset drives ($80–$210). Combination Jeep tours and cattle drives or basic horseback rides are also available.

There are also several riding stables out near the Superstition Mountains on the east side of the valley. See the "The Apache Trail" in the "Side Trips from Phoenix" section of this chapter for details. Keep in mind that most stables require reservations.

**IN-LINE SKATING** In the Scottsdale area, you can rent in-line skates, including all protective equipment, at **Scottsdale Bladez,** 14692 Frank Lloyd Wright Blvd. (☎ **480/391-1139**), for $4 per hour or $12 per day. You can also rent equipment at **Wheels 'n Gear,** 7607 E. McDowell Rd. (☎ **480/945-2881**), which is in the Plaza Del Rio Shopping Center (adjacent to the popular Indian Bend Wash greenbelt trail) and charges $6 for 2 hours or $12 per day.

The folks at these shops can point you toward nearby spots that are good for skating. One of the best places to skate is the **Indian Bend Wash greenbelt,** a paved multiuse path that extends for more than 12 miles. It runs parallel to Hayden Road in Scottsdale from Indian Bend Road to Washington Street, with connections north all the way to Frank Lloyd Wright Boulevard and south to Tempe's Mill Avenue (this last stretch of trail follows the Salt River, which in the future will be turned into a lake on the north side of the ASU campus). The Indian Bend Wash pathway can be accessed at many points along Hayden Road.

**TENNIS**   Most major hotels in the area have one or more tennis courts, and there are several tennis resorts around the valley. If you're staying someplace without a tennis court, try the **Scottsdale Ranch Park,** 10400 E. Via Linda, Scottsdale (☎ **480/ 312-7774**). Court fees range from $3 to $6 for 1½ hours of singles play.

**WATER PARKS**   At **Waterworld Safari Water Park,** 4243 W. Pinnacle Peak Rd., Glendale (☎ **623/581-1947**), you can free-fall 6½ stories down the Avalanche speed water slide or catch a gnarly wave in the wave pool. Other water slides offer tamer times. **Mesa Golfland-Sunsplash,** 155 W. Hampton, Mesa (☎ **480/834-8319**), has a wave pool and a tunnel called "the Black Hole." **Big Surf,** 1500 N. McClintock Rd. (☎ **480/947-7873**), has a wave pool, underground tube slides, and more.

All three of these parks charge about $15 for adults and $12.50 for children 4 to 11 (prices tend to go down after 3 or 4pm). All are open from approximately Memorial Day to Labor Day, Monday to Saturday from 10am to about 8 or 9pm (Big Surf until 6pm only) and Sunday from 11am to 7pm.

**WHITE-WATER RAFTING & TUBING ON THE SALT RIVER**   The desert may not seem like the place for white-water rafting, but up in the mountains to the northeast of Phoenix, the ✪ **Upper Salt River** still flows wild and free and offers some exciting rafting. Most years from about late February to late May, snowmelt from the White Mountains turns the river into a class III and IV river filled with exciting rapids (however, some years there just isn't enough water). Companies operating full-day, overnight, and multiday rafting trips on the upper Salt River (conditions permitting) include **Far Flung Adventures** (☎ **800/231-7238** or 520/425-7272; www.farflung. com), **Sun Country Rafting** (☎ **800/272-3353** or 602/493-9011), and **Mild to Wild Rafting** (☎ **800/567-6745**). Prices range from around $75 to $97 for a day trip up to around $650 for a multiday trip. Mild to Wild also offers 2- and 4-day float trips on the Verde River.

Tamer river trips can be had from **Salt River Recreation** (☎ **480/984-3305**), which has its headquarters 20 miles northeast of Phoenix on the Bush Highway (Power Road) at the intersection of Usery Pass Road in the Tonto National Forest. For $9 the company will rent you a large inner tube and shuttle you by bus upriver for the float down. The inner-tubing season runs from May through September.

## 8  Spectator Sports

Phoenix has gone nuts over pro sports and is now one of the few cities in the country with all four of the major sports teams (baseball, basketball, football, and hockey). Add to this baseball's spring training; a second ice hockey team; professional women's basketball; three major golf tournaments; the annual Fiesta Bowl college football classic; and ASU football, basketball, and baseball, and you have enough action to keep even the most rabid sports fans happily cheering on a local team no matter what month of the year. However, the all-around best month to visit is probably March when you could feasibly catch spring baseball training, the Suns, the Coyotes, and ASU basketball and baseball, as well as the Franklin Templeton Tennis Classic, The Tradition, and the Standard Register PING LPGA Tournament.

Call **Dillard's Box Office** (☎ **800/638-4253** or 480/503-5555) or **Ticketmaster** (☎ **480/784-4444**) for tickets to most of the events below. For tickets to sold-out events, try **Tickets Unlimited** (☎ **800/289-8497** or 602/840-2340) or **Ticket Exchange** (☎ **800/800-9811** or 602/254-4444).

**AUTO RACING**   At the **Firebird International Raceway Park,** at 20000 Maricopa Rd. (at Exit 162A off I-10), Chandler (☎ **480/268-0200**), you can see NHRA races and amateur drag racing. Ticket prices range from $19 to $35. At the **Phoenix**

**International Raceway,** 7602 S. 115th Ave. (at Baseline Road), Avondale (☎ **602/252-2227**), there is NASCAR and Indy car racing on the world's fastest 1-mile oval. Tickets range from $20 to $45.

**BASEBALL**    The **Arizona Diamondbacks** (☎ **602/514-8400**) play in downtown Phoenix at the Bank One Ballpark, a state-of-the-art stadium with a retractable roof that allows for comfortable play during Phoenix's blistering summer temperatures. The retractable roof makes this the only enclosed baseball stadium with natural grass. Tickets ($4–$55) are available at the Bank One Ballpark ticket office and through Dillard's Box Office outlets (☎ **480/503-3111**).

For decades, however, it has been spring training that has given Phoenix its annual shot of baseball, and don't think that the Cactus League's preseason exhibition games will be any less popular just because the Diamondbacks are in town. Spring-training games may rank second only to golf in popularity with winter visitors to the valley. Seven major league baseball teams have spring-training camps around the valley during March and April, and exhibition games are scheduled at six different stadiums. Ticket prices range from $3 to $18. Tickets for the A's and the Cubs are sold through Dillard's Box Office outlets (☎ **800/638-4253** or 480/503-5555) and tickets for the Padres, Mariners, Brewers, Giants, and Angels are sold through Ticketmaster (☎ **480/784-4444**). Get a schedule of games from the convention and visitors bureau, a Dillard's Box Office outlet, or check the *Arizona Republic* while you're in town. Games often sell out, especially on weekends, so be sure to order tickets in advance if you're a serious fan.

Teams training in the valley include the **San Francisco Giants,** Scottsdale Stadium, 7408 E. Osborn Rd., Scottsdale (☎ 480/312-2580); the **Oakland A's,** Phoenix Municipal Stadium, 5999 E. Van Buren St., Phoenix (☎ 602/495-7239); the **Anaheim Angels,** Tempe Diablo Stadium, 2200 W. Alameda Dr., Tempe (☎ 480/438-9300); the **Chicago Cubs,** Hohokam Park Stadium, 1235 N. Center St., Mesa (☎ 480/503-5555 or 480/964-4467), the **San Diego Padres,** Peoria Sports Complex, 16101 N. 83rd Ave., Peoria (☎ 800/409-1511 or 623/878-4337), the **Seattle Mariners,** Peoria Sports Complex, 16101 N. 83rd Ave., Peoria (☎ 800/409-1511 or 623/878-4337), and the **Milwaukee Brewers,** Maryvale Baseball Park, 3600 W. 51st Ave., Phoenix (☎ 623/245-5500).

For those who just can't get enough baseball, there is also the **Arizona Fall Baseball League** (☎ **480/496-6700**) with games from late September through November. The six teams in this league are made up of the top rookies from throughout the major leagues. Games are held at the same stadiums used for spring training, and tickets ($4 for adults, $3 seniors and students) are sold at the stadiums where games are held.

**BASKETBALL**    The NBA's **Phoenix Suns** play at the America West Arena, 201 E. Jefferson St. (☎ **602/379-7900**). Tickets are $11 to $75 and are available at the America West Arena box office and through Dillard's Box Office outlets (see above). Suns tickets are hard to come by. If you want good seats, you really have to buy your tickets on the day they go on sale in mid-September. If you forget to plan ahead, try contacting the box office the day before or the day of a game to see if tickets have been returned. Otherwise, you'll have to try a ticket agency and pay the premium.

Phoenix also has a Women's National Basketball Association (WNBA) team, the **Phoenix Mercury** (☎ **602/252-WNBA** or 602/379-7800), which plays at the America West Arena, 201 E. Jefferson St., between mid-June and mid-August. Ticket prices range from $8 to $34.

**FOOTBALL**    The **Arizona Cardinals** (☎ **800/999-1402** or 602/379-0102) play at Arizona State University's Sun Devil Stadium, which is also home to the Fiesta Bowl

Football Classic. Tickets are $30 to $125. Except for a few specific games each season, it is generally possible to get Cardinals tickets.

While the Cardinals get to use Sun Devil Stadium, this field really belongs to Arizona State University's **Sun Devils** (☎ 480/965-2381). Tickets run $20 to $35 and are sold through Dillard's Box Office outlets (see above).

Despite the desert heat and presence of a baseball team, Phoenicians don't give up football just because it's summer. The **Arizona Rattlers** arena football team (☎ 602/514-8383) plays 50-yard indoor football at the America West Arena, 201 E. Jefferson St. Tickets are $9 to $41 and are available at the America West Arena box office.

**GOLF TOURNAMENTS**   It's not surprising that, with nearly 200 golf courses and ideal golfing weather throughout the winter and spring, the Valley of the Sun hosts three major PGA tournaments each year. Tickets for all three tournaments are available through Dillard's Box Office outlets (see above).

The **Phoenix Open Golf Tournament** (☎ 602/870-0163; www.phoenixopen. com) in January is the largest. Held at the Tournament Players Club (TPC) of Scottsdale, this tournament attracts more spectators than any other golf tournament in the world (nearly 400,000 each year). The 18th hole of the TPC has standing room for 40,000. Tickets usually go on sale in June with prices starting around $20.

Each March, the **Standard Register PING LPGA Tournament** (☎ 602/495-4653), held each year at the Moon Valley Country Club, lures the top 100 women golfers from around the world. Daily ticket prices range from around $10 to $15, and weekly tickets are around $75.

**The Tradition** (☎ 480/595-4070), a Senior PGA Tour event held each late March or early April at the Desert Mountain golf course, has a loyal following of fans who would rather watch the likes of Jack Nicklaus and Lee Trevino than see Tiger Woods win yet another tournament. Only weekly tickets ($100 to $250) are sold, and these usually go on sale in January.

Now even amateurs can get in on some tournament action at the **Phoenix Amateur Golf Championship** (☎ 877/988-GOLF), which is held in mid-July (partly to prove that it's possible to play golf in the summer in Phoenix).

**HOCKEY**   Ice hockey in the desert? It may not make sense, but even Phoenicians are crazy about ice hockey (maybe it's all those northern transplants). The NHL's **Phoenix Coyotes** (☎ 888/255-PUCK or 480/563-PUCK) play at America West Arena, 201 E. Jefferson St. Tickets range from $18.50 to $200 (up against the glass). Tickets are sold through Dillard's Box Office outlets (see above).

**HORSE/GREYHOUND RACING**   The **Phoenix Greyhound Park,** 3801 E. Washington St. (☎ 602/273-7181), is one of the nation's premier greyhound tracks. The large, fully enclosed, and air-conditioned facility offers seating in various grandstands, lounges, and restaurants. There's racing nightly throughout the year, and tickets are $1.50 to $3.

**Turf Paradise,** 1501 W. Bell Rd. (☎ 602/942-1101), is Phoenix's horse-racing track. The season runs from October to May, with post time at 12:30pm Friday through Tuesday. Admission ranges from $1 to $5.

**RODEOS, POLO & HORSE SHOWS**   Cowboys, cowgirls, and other horsey types will find plenty of the four-legged critters going through their paces most weeks at **Westworld Equestrian Center,** 16601 N. Pima Rd., Scottsdale (☎ 480/312-6802). With its 500 stables, 11 equestrian arenas, and a polo field, this 400-acre complex provides an amazing variety of entertainment and sporting events. There are rodeos, polo matches, an Arabian horse show, horse rentals, and horseback-riding instruction. Ticket prices vary with the event.

**TENNIS TOURNAMENTS**   Each March, top international men's tennis players compete at the **Franklin Templeton Tennis Classic** (☎ **480/922-0222**), which is held at the Scottsdale Princess Resort, 7575 E. Princess Dr., Scottsdale. Tickets run $10 to $55 and are available through Dillard's Box Office outlets (see above).

## 9 Day Spas

Ever since the first "lungers" showed up in the Phoenix area hoping to cure their tuberculosis, the desert has been a magnet for those looking to get healthy. In the first half of the 20th century, health spas were all the rage in Phoenix, and with the health-and-fitness trend continuing to gather steam, it comes as no surprise that health spas are now immensely popular in the Valley of the Sun. In the past few years, several of the area's top resorts have added new full-service health spas or expanded existing ones to cater to guest's increasing requests for services such as massages, body wraps, mud masks, and salt glows.

If you can't or don't want to spend the money to stay at a top resort and avail yourself of the spa, you may still be able to indulge. Most of the valley's resorts open the doors of their spas to the public, and, for the cost of a body treatment or massage, you can spend the day at the spa, taking classes, working out in a fitness room, lounging by the pool, and otherwise living the life of the rich and famous. Barring this indulgence, you can slip into a day spa, of which there are many scattered around the valley, and take a stress-reduction break the way other people take a latte break.

Located high on the flanks of Mummy Mountain with a nice view over the valley, **The Spa at Camelback Inn**, 5402 E. Lincoln Dr., Scottsdale (☎ **480/596-7020**), is a great place to spend the day being pampered. For the cost of a single 1-hour treatment—between $90 and $105—you can use all the facilities. Among the treatments available are a para-joba body moisturizer that will leave your skin feeling like silk. Multiple-treatment packages range in price from $140 to $230.

The **Centre for Well Being,** at The Phoenician, 6000 E. Camelback Rd., Scottsdale (☎ **800/843-2392** or 480/423-2452), is the valley's most prestigious day spa, the place to head if you want to be pampered with the rich and famous. For anywhere from $90 to $335, you can spend the day at the spa receiving several treatments and utilizing the spa's many facilities. A single treatment (say a thermal moor mud wrap or a Turkish body scrub) entitles you to use the facilities for the rest of the day.

If you want a truly spectacular setting for your day at the spa, head north to Carefree and the **Sonoran Spa at The Boulders,** 34631 N. Tom Darlington Dr. (☎ **480/488-9009**). Here individual treatments cost $99 to $135, and day-packages run $185 to $285. Included with any treatment is use of the extensive facilities and lap pool. At press time, there were plans to build a Golden Door health spa in 2001. When completed, this should become one of the valley's top spas.

The historic setting and convenient location of the **Arizona Biltmore Spa,** 24th Street and Missouri Avenue (☎ **800/950-0086** or 602/955-6600), make this 20,000-square-foot facility an excellent choice if you're spending time along the Camelback Corridor. The spa menu is extensive and includes the likes of balneotherapy, water goddess Sedona mud purification treatment, lymphatic massages, and bindi herbal body treatments. If you aren't staying at the resort, you can use the facilities for $25; body and beauty treatments range from $50 to $145.

**The Mist Spa,** at the Radisson Resort & Spa Scottsdale, 7171 N. Scottsdale Rd., Scottsdale (☎ **877/MIST-SPA** or 480/905-2882) was the valley's newest resort spa at press time. The 20,000-square-foot spa has a Japanese design, complete with

Japanese-style massage rooms and a tranquil rock garden in a central covered court-yard. Spa treatments, which include the likes of collagen facials, honey steam wraps, Dead Sea mud wraps, and green tea detoxifying wraps, cost between $55 and $115.

Nonresort day spas can also be found around the valley. The **Elizabeth Arden Red Door Salon,** 2472 E. Camelback Rd. (☎ **602/553-8800**), which bears the name of one of Arizona's health spa pioneers, is conveniently located in Biltmore Fashion Park. In Old Town Scottsdale, you'll find **Spa du Soleil,** 7040 E. Third Ave., Scottsdale (☎ **480/994-5400**).

## 10  Shopping

For the most part, shopping in the valley means malls. They're everywhere, and they're air-conditioned, which, we're sure you'll agree, makes shopping in the desert far more enjoyable when it's 110°F outside.

Scottsdale and the Biltmore District of Phoenix (along Camelback Road) are the valley's main upscale shopping areas, while Old Scottsdale (one of the few outdoor shopping areas) plays host to hundreds of boutiques, galleries, jewelry stores, and Native American crafts stores. The Western atmosphere of Old Scottsdale is partly real and partly a figment of the local merchants' imaginations, but nevertheless it's the most popular tourist shopping area in the valley. It also happens to be the heart of the valley's art market, with dozens of art galleries along Main Street.

Shopping hours are usually Monday through Saturday from 10am to 6pm and on Sunday from noon to 5pm, and malls usually stay open until 9pm Monday through Saturday.

### ANTIQUES

Downtown Glendale (located west of Phoenix) is the valley's main antiques district. Here, you'll find more than three dozen stores specializing in everything from auto-mobilia to 1950s kitsch to vintage sports equipment.

Ten months of the year, the Phoenix Antique Market (☎ **800/678-9987** or 602/943-1766) stages Arizona's largest collectors' shows at the Arizona State Fair-grounds, 19th Avenue and McDowell Road. Call for dates.

**The Antique Gallery/Central Antiques.** In Uptown Plaza, 5037 N. Central Ave. (at Camelback Rd.). ☎ **602/241-1174** or 602/241-1636.

These two antiques malls are some of the more upscale in the area and together house about 130 antiques dealers. Offerings include porcelain, silver, crystal, and European furniture.

**Antiques Super-Mall.** 1900 N. Scottsdale Rd., Scottsdale. ☎ **480/874-2900.**

If you make only one antiques stop, make it here. This is one of the biggest antiques malls in the valley and within a block there are two others: the **Antique Centre,** 2012 N. Scottsdale Rd. (☎ **480/675-9500**) and the **Antique Trove,** 2020 N. Scotts-dale Rd. (☎ **480/947-6074**).

**Arizona West Galleries.** 7149 E. Main St., Scottsdale. ☎ **480/994-3752.**

Nowhere else in Scottsdale will you find such an amazing collection of cowboy collectibles and Western antiques. There are antique saddles and chaps, old rifles and six-shooters, sheriff's badges, spurs, and the like.

**Bishop Gallery for Art & Antiques.** 7164 Main St., Scottsdale. ☎ **480/949-9062.**

This cramped shop is wonderfully eclectic, featuring everything from Asian antiques to unusual original art. Definitely worth a browse.

✪ **Bo's Funky Stuff.** 5605 W. Glendale Ave., Glendale. ☎ **623/842-0220.**

Billing itself the "wildest shop north of the border," Bo's is a repository of midcentury modern collectibles, including Beatles memorabilia, 1950s furniture, neon signs, old advertisements, bakelite jewelry, Western collectibles, and generally odd and unusual stuff. Note that this store doesn't open until noon.

# ART

Only Santa Fe is a more important art market than Scottsdale, and along the streets of Old Scottsdale you'll find dozens of ✪ **art galleries** selling everything from monumental bronzes to contemporary art created from found objects. All the galleries mentioned below are within walking distance of each other. On Main Street, you'll find primarily cowboy art, both traditional and contemporary, while on North Marshall Way, you'll find much more imaginative and daring contemporary art.

**Art One.** 4120 N. Marshall Way, Scottsdale. ☎ **480/946-5076.**

If you want to see the possible directions that area artists will be heading in the next few years, stop in at this Marshall Way gallery that specializes in works by art students and other area cutting-edge artists. The works here can be surprisingly good, and the prices are very reasonable.

**materia/The Hand & The Spirit.** 4222 N. Marshall Way, Scottsdale. ☎ **480/949-1262.**

This gallery is currently one of our favorite places to visit in downtown Scottsdale. Work displayed is at the cutting edge of new crafts, using new materials or traditional materials in innovative ways; even the jaded art viewer will be impressed. Between the two galleries is a sculpture courtyard.

✪ **Lisa Sette Gallery.** 4142 N. Marshall Way, Scottsdale. ☎ **480/990-7342.**

If you aren't a fan of cowboy or Native American art, you may think that Phoenix has little serious contemporary art to offer. Don't jump to that conclusion before you stop here. Lisa Sette represents premier glass-artist William Morris as well as many others. International, national, and local artists share wall space here, with a wide mix of media represented.

**Meyer Gallery.** 7173 E. Main St., Scottsdale. ☎ **480/947-6372.**

This gallery is most notable for its selection of Old West, landscape, and mood paintings by living impressionists. The proprietor also has a cute Jack Russell terrier that likes to chase tennis balls.

**Overland Gallery.** 7155 Main St., Scottsdale. ☎ **480/947-1934.**

Traditional Western paintings and a collection of Russian Impressionist paintings form the backbone of this gallery's fine collection. These are museum-quality works (prices sometimes approach $100,000) and definitely worth a look.

**Roberts Gallery.** In El Pedregal Festival Marketplace, 34505 N. Scottsdale Rd., Carefree. ☎ **480/488-1088.**

The feathered masks and sculptures of Virgil Walker are the highlights at this gallery, and if you have an appreciation for fine detail work, you'll likely be fascinated by these pieces. Walker creates fantasy figures, every inch of which are covered with feathers.

**Riva Yares.** 3625 Bishop Lane, Scottsdale. ☎ **480/947-3251.**

You can't miss this gallery. The front patio is full of huge metal sculptures (yes, they're for sale), and inside you'll find contemporary and modern painting and sculpture. The Riva Yares gallery has been around for 30 years.

# In case you want to see the world.

At American Express, we're here to make your journey a smooth one. So we have over 1,700 travel service locations in over 130 countries ready to help. What else would you expect from the world's largest travel agency?

do more    AMERICAN EXPRESS

Travel

Call 1 800 AXP-3429 or visit
www.americanexpress.com/travel

# In case you want to be welcomed there.

We're here to see that you're always welcomed at establishments everywhere. That's why millions of people carry the American Express® Card — for peace of mind, confidence, and security, around the world or just around the corner.

do more  **Cards**

# In case you're running low.

We're here to help with more than 190,000 Express Cash locations around the world. In order to enroll, just call American Express at 1 800 CASH-NOW before you start your vacation.

do more **AMERICAN EXPRESS**

**Express Cash**

# And in case you'd rather be safe than sorry.

We're here with American Express® Travelers Cheques. They're the safe way to carry money on your vacation, because if they're ever lost or stolen you can get a refund, practically anywhere or anytime. To find the nearest place to buy Travelers Cheques, call 1 800 495-1153. Another way we help you do more.

do more  **AMERICAN EXPRESS**

**Travelers Cheques**

## BOOKS

Major chain bookstores in the Phoenix and Scottsdale area include **Borders Books Music & Café** at 2402 E. Camelback Rd., Phoenix (☎ **602/957-6660**) and **Barnes & Noble Booksellers** at 10235 N. Metro Parkway East, Phoenix (☎ **602/678-0088**), 4847 E. Ray Rd., Phoenix (☎ **480/940-7136**), and 10500 N. 90th St., Scottsdale (☎ **480/391-0048**).

**Changing Hands Bookstore.** 414 Mill Ave., Tempe. ☎ **480/966-0203.**

Located in the heart of Mill Avenue, adjacent to Arizona State University, this bookstore satisfies cravings for an intellectual collegiate atmosphere. It's not big—only three small floors—but there are books both new and used on all kinds of topics and easy chairs in which to relax. A second store is located at 6430 S. McClintock Dr., Tempe (☎ **480/730-0205**).

**T. A. Swinford.** 7134 W. Main St., Scottsdale. ☎ **480/946-0022.**

Rare and out-of-print books about the American West are the specialty here. If you're looking for *The Cegiha Language* (1890), *Triggernometry, A Gallery of Gunfighters* (1934), or *Range Murder: How the Red-Sash Gang Dry-Gulched Deputy United States Marshal George Wellman* (1955), you'll find it here.

## A CHOCOLATERIE

✪ **Chocolaterie Bernard C.** In Hilton Village, 6137 N. Scottsdale Rd. ☎ **480/483-3139.**

If you have *ever* had a genuine Belgian praline (chocolate, not one of those puffy cookies), then you will not want to leave Scottsdale without paying a visit to this chocolate shop. If you have *never* had a Belgian chocolate, you won't want to miss this shop either. The exquisite chocolate confections here will make you forget all about Godiva.

## CRAFTS

✪ **Mind's Eye Gallery.** 4200 N. Marshall Way, Scottsdale. ☎ **602/941-2494.**

At this Scottsdale gallery, you'll find jewelry, ceramics, wood, clothing, paper, and glass by many of the nation's finest contemporary craftspeople. The wildly imaginative kaleidoscopes are fascinating, and the contemporary handcrafted furniture is timelessly beautiful.

## FASHION

See also "Western Wear," below.

### WOMEN'S WEAR

In addition to the shops mentioned below, there are also many excellent shops in malls all over the city. Favorite spots for upscale fashions include Biltmore Fashion Park, the Borgata of Scottsdale, El Pedregal Festival Marketplace, and Scottsdale Fashion Square. See "Malls & Shopping Centers," below, for details on these malls and shopping plazas.

**Carol Dolighan.** At the Borgata, 6166 N. Scottsdale Rd., Scottsdale. ☎ **480/922-0616.**

The hand-painted, hand-woven, and handmade dresses, skirts, and blouses here abound in rich colors. Each is unique. There's another Carol Dolighan store in El Pedregal Festival Marketplace, 34505 N. Scottsdale Rd. (☎ **480/488-4505**) in Carefree.

**Paris Paris.** In Biltmore Fashion Park, 2438 E. Camelback Rd. ☎ **602/955-9663.**

Up-to-the-minute fashion separates are pulled together on the racks of this upscale boutique so that you can visualize the effect before heading to the dressing room. There's very pricey lingerie in the loft and men's fashions in the basement.

## Ten Fun Ways to Blow 100 Bucks (More or Less) in the Valley of the Sun

With greens fees for 18 holes of golf as high as $150, it is obvious that the Valley of the Sun is not exactly a cheap place for a vacation. Still, if you've budgeted plenty of money for your vacation or simply want to splurge on a memorable experience, there are quite a few great ways to blow 100 bucks while in town. Here are some of our favorites.

1. **Spend a day at the Spa at Camelback Inn** (☎ **480/596-7020**). It's not often you can blow 100 bucks and come away feeling good about it, but for between $90 and $105, you can spend the day at this luxurious spa getting pampered and de-stressed. You can also spend quite a bit more than $100 in a day here.

2. **Rent a Vette** (☎ **480/941-3001**). Sometimes you just have to go over budget. For $149 a day, you can rent a new Corvette from Rent-a-Vette and head out for a high-speed spin in the desert or just cruise around Scottsdale looking like you belong.

3. **Hire a stretch limo for a couple of hours.** For $110 (plus a mandatory 20% gratuity for the driver) you can rent a six-passenger stretch limo from Arizona Limousines (☎ **800/678-0033** or 602/267-7097) for 2 hours. Just ride around, or maybe have the limo take you to a resort for a cocktail.

4. **Play a round of golf on an Arizona legend.** If you can get a tee time, $125 will get you on the Gold Course at the Wigwam Resort (☎ **623/935-3811**) out west in Litchfield Park. This is one of the oldest and most famous courses in the valley.

5. **Rent a cabana at the Pointe Hilton Tapatio Cliffs Resort** (☎ **602/866-7500**). If you've got a Motel 6 vacation budget but long for the resort life, why not rent a poolside cabana at this north Phoenix resort? The cabanas go

**Uh Oh.** In Hilton Village, 6137 N. Scottsdale Rd., Scottsdale. ☎ **480/991-1618.**

You'll find simple, tasteful, and oh-so-elegant fashions, footwear, jewelry, and accessories. The Southwestern contemporary styling makes this a great place to pick up something to be seen in. A second store is in La Mirada shopping plaza, 8900 E. Pinnacle Peak Rd., Scottsdale (☎ **480/515-0203**).

### MEN'S WEAR

✪ **The Clotherie Ltd.** In Biltmore Fashion Park, 2552 E. Camelback Rd. ☎ **602/956-8600.**

This is considered the best men's shop in the valley, with friendly wardrobe consultants and in-store tailoring. You'll find the best quality domestic and European menswear, from casual to suits, including accessories and footwear. They also carry special collections of extralong sizes for tall men.

### CHILDREN'S WEAR

**The Children's Collection.** 7001 N. Scottsdale Rd., Suite 185, Scottsdale. ☎ **480/998-1401.**

If you happen to be staying at a Scottsdale resort, then you'll probably be able to afford to buy your grandkids some of the outfits in this store. If you're staying at the Motel 6, for $95 a day and are located in the resort's aquatic playground known as The Falls. Sure it would be cheaper to go to Big Surf, but the experience just wouldn't be the same.

6. **Take a hot-air balloon ride.** There is no better way to see the desert than drifting above it at dawn in a hot-air balloon, and there's just about no cheaper way in the country to take to the air than in the oldest form of flying machine. For $110 to $135 you can get airborne. See "Organized Tours," above.

7. **Take a hummer of a back-roads tour.** Why ride in a Jeep when you can ride in a Hummer, the ultimate off-road vehicle? For about $90, Desert Storm Hummer Tours (☎ 480/922-0020) will give you a ride to remember, and you'll get an up-close and personal look at the Arizona desert.

8. **Order the seasonal tasting menu at Mary Elaine's (☎ 480/423-2530).** If you've never had a $100 dinner, maybe now is the time to indulge. How else will you ever be able to call yourself a true gourmand? This six-course dinner will set you back $110 (not including tax, tip, wine, or the cost of proper dining attire).

9. **Do the city slicker thing and drive some cattle down the trail.** For $90 you can do a breakfast cattle drive with Rocky Mt. Cattle Moo-vers (☎ 800/826-9666) and get a taste of the cowboyin' life. If you've got more money to blow, you can ride herd at lunch, sunset, or all day long.

10. **Go on a C-note shopping spree at Biltmore Fashion Park.** Maybe $100 won't buy much at this boutique-filled upscale shopping plaza, but the fun of it can be trying to find the best $100 buy in the mall. Now there's a challenge to keep a shopaholic busy for the afternoon.

don't even think about coming here. Linen separates, velvet T-shirts, and the like fill the racks.

**Lil' People.** At the Arizona Center, 3rd and Van Buren sts. in downtown Phoenix. ☎ 602/252-2241.

"Oh, isn't that cute!" Exclamations like that keep this shop doing a brisk business in gifts for the little ones. Cute and bright cotton playwear for children newborn to 8 years old are the mainstays. There's a second shop at Scottsdale Fashion Square, Scottsdale and Camelback roads (☎ 480/423-2021).

## GIFTS & SOUVENIRS

One of the best places to shop for souvenirs is the Arizona Center mall in downtown Phoenix. See "Malls/Shopping Centers," below for details.

**Arizona Highways Gift Shop.** In Arizona Center, 455 N. 3rd St. ☎ 602/257-0381.

If you're familiar with the magazine *Arizona Highways*, then you'll know what to expect from this store—beautiful photographs everywhere and interesting Arizona-themed gifts.

**Arizona State University Art Museum Store.** In the Arizona State University Art Museum, Nelson Fine Arts Center, 10th St. and Mill Ave., Tempe. ☎ 480/965-2787.

A good selection of interesting and reasonably priced gifts, including Mexican folk-art, pottery, children's toys, jewelry, books, T-shirts, and greeting cards, can be found here.

✪ **Bischoff's Shades of the West.** 7247 Main St., Scottsdale. ☎ **480/945-3289.**

This is one-stop shopping for all things Southwestern. From T-shirts to regional food-stuffs, this sprawling store has it all. It's got a good selection of candles, chile garlands (*ristras*), and wrought-iron cabinet hardware that can give your kitchen a Western look, and Mexican crafts that all fit in with a Southwest interior decor.

**Phoenix Art Museum Store.** In the Phoenix Art Museum, 1625 N. Central Ave. (at the northeast corner of McDowell Rd.). ☎ **602/257-1880.**

Crafts, greeting cards, unique photo frames and other decorative items, and a wide selection of art-related books make up a large portion of the items available here.

✪ **Scottsdale Center for the Arts Museum Store.** On the Scottsdale Mall, 7380 E. 2nd St. ☎ **480/874-4644.**

With creative T-shirts, music CDs, arty knickknacks, whimsical children's toys, cards, and books, this shop is a great place for gifts that go beyond the standard Southwest souvenirs to be found in most Scottsdale gift shops.

## A GOLF SHOP

✪ **In Celebration of Golf.** 7001 N. Scottsdale Rd., Suite 172, Scottsdale. ☎ **480/951-4444.**

Sort of a supermarket for golfers (with a touch of Disneyland thrown in), this amazing store sells everything from clubs and golf shoes to golf art (including a huge bronze golf club for $28,000) and golf antiques. There are even unique golf cars on display in case you want to take to the greens in a custom car. A golf simulation room allows you to test out new clubs and get in a bit of video golfing at the same time. An old club-maker's workbench, complete with talking mannequin, makes a visit to this shop educational as well as a lot of fun.

## JEWELRY

**Jewelry by Gauthier.** 4211 N. Marshall Way, Scottsdale. ☎ **888/411-3232** or 602/941-1707.

This store sells the designs of the phenomenally talented jewelry designer Scott Gauthier. Very stylish, modern designs using precious stones make every piece of jewelry in this shop a miniature work of art. This is the only place you'll see Gauthier's work for sale in the United States. The elegant shop features a lit-from-below green onyx floor. Limo service to the store is provided.

✪ **materia/The Hand & The Spirit.** 4222 N. Marshall Way, Scottsdale. ☎ **480/949-1262.**

Each piece of jewelry here is an individual work of art—ornate, contemporary, one-of-a-kind pieces that share a talisman-like quality. The work of many different jewelry artists are displayed, and unique and stylish artist-created garments take up the rest of the shop/gallery.

**Molina Fine Jewelers.** 3134 E. Camelback Rd. ☎ **602/955-2055.**

While you don't have to have an appointment to shop at this very exclusive jewelry store, it's highly recommended. With an appointment, you'll get personalized service as you peruse the Tiffany exclusives and high-end European jewelry. If you can spend as much on a necklace as you can on a Mercedes, this is where to shop for your baubles.

# MALLS & SHOPPING CENTERS

**Arizona Center.** Van Buren St. between 3rd and 5th sts. ☎ **480/949-4-FUN.**

With its gardens and fountains, this modern downtown shopping center near the convention center is both a peaceful oasis amid downtown's asphalt and a great place to shop for Arizona souvenirs (check out the Arizona Highways Gift Shop). Arizona Center is also home to several nightclubs and some of downtown's best restaurants.

**Biltmore Fashion Park.** E. Camelback Rd. and 24th St. ☎ **602/955-1963.**

With its garden courtyards, this open-air shopping plaza is *the* place to be if shopping is your obsession and you keep your wallet full of platinum cards. Shops bear the names of international designers and exclusive boutiques such as Polo, Gucci, Laura Ashley, Ann Taylor, Nicole Miller, and Cole Haan. Saks Fifth Avenue and Macy's are the two anchors. There are also more than a dozen moderately priced restaurants here, and valet parking is available.

✪ **The Borgata of Scottsdale.** 6166 N. Scottsdale Rd. ☎ **480/998-1822.**

Designed to resemble a medieval Italian village complete with turrets, stone walls, and ramparts, the Borgata is far and away the most architecturally interesting shopping mall in the valley. There are about 50 upscale boutiques, art galleries, and restaurants here, and on Friday afternoons from October to April there's a Farmers Market.

✪ **El Pedregal Festival Marketplace.** Scottsdale Rd. and Carefree Hwy., Carefree. ☎ **480/488-1072.**

Located adjacent to The Boulders resort north of downtown Scottsdale, El Pedregal is the most self-consciously Southwestern shopping center in the valley. It's worth the long drive out here just to see the neo–Santa Fe architecture and colorful accents. The shops offer high-end merchandise, fashions, and art. Among our favorites are Imagine Gallery and Conrad Leather Boutique, which carry upscale Southwestern fashions. The Heard Museum also has a branch here.

**Metrocenter.** 9617 Metro Pkwy. W. ☎ **602/997-2641** or 602/678-0017.

One of the largest shopping centers in the Southwest, the Metrocenter has more than 200 specialty shops, five major department stores (Dillard's, Macy's, Robinsons-May, JCPenney, and Sears), and about 40 eating establishments.

**Scottsdale Fashion Square.** 7014–590 E. Camelback Rd. (at Scottsdale Rd.), Scottsdale. ☎ **602/941-2140.**

Scottsdale has long been the valley's shopping mecca, and for years this huge mall has been the reason why. It now houses five major department stores—Nordstrom, Dillard's, Neiman Marcus, Robinsons-May, and Sears—and smaller stores such as the Nature Company, Bally, Eddie Bauer, J. Crew, Bang & Olufsen, and Louis Vuitton. This is *the* hangout for wealthy teenage mall rats.

**Town & Country.** 20th St. and Camelback Rd. ☎ **602/955-6850.**

Sort of a Western anchor for the Camelback Corridor (Phoenix's main shopping, business, dining, and nightlife district), this open-air shopping plaza offers a much more affordable alternative to the nearby Biltmore Fashion Park. You'll find high fashion as well as bargains, kitsch gifts, the UNICEF Shop, a discount bookstore, and many other small shops.

# NATIVE AMERICAN ARTS, CRAFTS & JEWELRY

**✪ Bischoff's Shades of the West.** 3925 N. Brown St., Scottsdale. ☎ **480/946-6155.**

This museum-like store and gallery is affiliated with Bischoff's at 7247 Main St. (see above under "Gifts & Souvenirs"), which, compared to this shop, is more like the general store. Here you'll find higher-end jewelry, including old pawn, Western-style home furnishings and clothing, ceramics, books and music with a regional theme, and contemporary paintings.

**Chief Dodge Indian Jewelry & Fine Arts.** 1332 N. Scottsdale Rd., Scottsdale (in Papago Plaza). ☎ **800/553-5604** or 480/970-1133.

You can watch Indian craftspeople create beautiful silver jewelry, sand paintings, rugs, and other crafts right in the store and then peruse the cases searching for a kachina, bowl, or basket to take home.

**Faust Gallery.** 7103 E. Main St., Scottsdale. ☎ **480/946-6345.**

Here you'll find old Native American baskets and pottery, as well as a large selection of old and new Navajo rugs. The gallery also sells Native American and Southwest art, including ceramics, colorful paintings, bronzes, home furnishings, and unusual sculptures.

**Gilbert Ortega Museum Gallery.** 3925 N. Scottsdale Rd. ☎ **480/990-1808.**

You'll find Gilbert Ortega shops all over the valley (including several in Old Scottsdale), but this is the biggest and best. As the name implies, there are museum displays throughout the store. Cases full of jewelry are the main attraction here, but there are also baskets, sculptures, pottery, rugs, paintings, and kachinas. Other branches are located at 7237 E. Main St., Scottsdale (☎ **480/481-0788**); 7252 E. First Ave., Scottsdale (☎ **480/945-1819**); at Koshari I in the Borgata, 6166 N. Scottsdale Rd., Scottsdale (☎ **480/998-9699**); and at the Hyatt Regency Hotel, 122 N. Second St., Phoenix (☎ **602/265-9923**).

**Grey Wolf, Native American Gallery.** 7239 E. 1st Ave., Scottsdale. ☎ **480/423-0004.**

You'll find the valley's largest selection of Indian artifacts—everything from shields to war bonnets—plus hand-crafted kachina dolls, music, rugs, and pottery here. A specialty is contemporary Native American jewelry, and there are Northwest and Plains Indians artifacts as well.

**✪ Heard Museum Gift Shop.** In the Heard Museum, 2301 N. Central Ave. ☎ **602/252-8344.**

The Heard Museum (see "Seeing the Sights," above) has an awesome collection of very aesthetic, extremely well-crafted, and very expensive Native American jewelry, art, and crafts of all kinds. Fortunately, because the store doesn't have to charge sales tax, you'll save a bit of money. This is the best place in the valley to shop for Native American arts and crafts; you can be absolutely assured of the quality. And with the remodeling of the Heard, the shop is even bigger than before.

**✪ John C. Hill Antique Indian Art.** 6962 E. 1st Ave., Suite 104, Scottsdale. ☎ **480/946-2910.**

This store is for collectors and has one of the finest selections of Navajo rugs in the valley, including quite a few older ones. There are also kachinas, superb Navajo and Zuni silver-and-turquoise jewelry, baskets, and pottery. This shop sells only the highest quality items, so you can familiarize yourself with what the best looks like.

**Old Territorial Shop.** 7220 E. Main St., Scottsdale. ☎ **480/945-5432.** Closed Mon July–Aug.

This is the oldest Indian arts-and-crafts store on Main Street; it offers good values on a large selection of jewelry, sand paintings, concha belts, kachinas, fetishes, pottery, and Navajo rugs.

## OUTLET MALLS & DISCOUNT SHOPPING

**My Sister's Closet.** 6206 N. Scottsdale Rd., Scottsdale (near Trader Joes). ☎ **480/443-4575.**

This is where the crème de la crème of Scottsdale's used clothing comes to be resold. You'll find such labels as Armani, Donna Karan, and Calvin Klein. Prices are pretty reasonable, too. Also at **Town & Country** shopping plaza at 20th Street and Camelback Road, Phoenix (☎ **602/954-6080**).

**Prime Outlets at New River.** 4250 W. Honda Bow Rd. ☎ **623/465-9500.** Take Exit 229 (Desert Hills Rd.) off I-17.

If your idea of a great afternoon is searching out deals at factory outlet stores, then you'll be in heaven at this large outlet mall. Among the stores here are Barneys, Ann Taylor, Bugle Boy, Gap, Geoffrey Beene, and Levi's. It's a 30-minute drive from downtown Phoenix and is a popular stop en route to or from Sedona or Flagstaff.

**Arizona Mills.** 5000 Arizona Mills Circle, Tempe. ☎ **480/491-9700.** From I-10, take the Baseline Rd. east exit. From AZ 60, exit Priest Dr. south.

This huge new shopping mall in Tempe is on the cutting edge when it comes to shop-o-tainment. Not only will you find Gap, Guess?, Ann Taylor Loft, and bebe outlets, but you'll also find a GameWorks video arcade, an IMAX theater, and a Virgin Megastore. With nearly ¾ mile of sensory bombardment, it might be a good idea to bring earplugs and walking shoes.

**Last Chance.** 1919 E. Camelback Rd. ☎ **602/248-2843.**

This is it, the last chance for men's and women's clothes and shoes. If it doesn't sell here, it's headed south of the border where they sell clothes by the pound. If ever there were such a thing as combat shopping, you'd find it here. The clothes are unbelievably cheap, but are often damaged goods (returns and such), so be sure to inspect every article closely before committing.

**Wigwam Outlet Stores.** 1400 N. Litchfield Rd. ☎ **623/935-9733.** Take the Litchfield Rd. exit off I-10.

If you're headed west from Phoenix and need a shopping break, you'll likely find some good deals at this outlet mall near the famous Wigwam resort. Bass, Bugle Boy, Harry & David, Mikasa, and Levi's are just some of the many stores.

## WESTERN WEAR

**Az-Tex Hat Company.** 3903 N. Scottsdale Rd., Scottsdale. ☎ **800/972-2116** or 480/481-9900.

If you're looking to bring home a cowboy hat from your trip to Arizona, this is a good place to pick one up. This small shop in Old Scottsdale offers custom shaping and fitting of woven hats and felt hats, which vary in quality from 7x to 100x. The highest numbers are the softest because they contain the most beaver fur. A salesperson will help you select a hat that complements your body type and face. There's a second store at 15044 N. Cave Creek Rd., Phoenix (☎ **602/971-9090**).

**Heritage Hats.** 13602 N. Cave Creek Rd. ☎ **602/867-3323.**

If it ain't for your head, they ain't got it. A huge selection of hats (the largest in the United States) in countless styles makes this one of the best place in the valley to shop for a cowboy hat. Heritage has all the styles you've seen on your favorite country music stars. Prices range from $15 to $400, and custom hats can be ordered.

**Out West.** In El Pedregal Festival Marketplace, 34505 N. Scottsdale Rd., Carefree. ☎ **888/ 454-WEST** or 480/488-0180.

If the revival of 1950s cowboy fashions and interior decor has hit your nostalgia button, then you'll want to hightail it up to this eclectic shop. All things Western are available, and the fashions are both beautiful and fun (though fancy and pricey). They've even got home furnishings.

**Saba's Western Stores.** 7254 Main St., Scottsdale. ☎ **480/949-7404.**

Since 1927, this store has been outfitting Scottsdale's cowboys and cowgirls, visiting dude ranchers, and anyone else who wants to adopt the look of the Wild West. Call for other locations around Phoenix.

✪ **Sheplers Western Wear.** 9201 N. 29th Ave. ☎ **602/870-8085.**

Though it isn't the largest Western-wear store in the valley, Sheplers is still sort of a department store of cowboy duds. If you can't find it here, it just ain't available in these parts. Other locations include 8979 E. Indian Bend Rd., Scottsdale (☎ **480/ 948-1933**); 2643 E. Broadway Rd., Mesa (☎ **480/827-8244**); and 2700 W. Baseline Rd., Tempe (☎ **602/438-7400**).

**Stockman's Cowboy & Southwestern Wear.** 23587 N. Scottsdale Rd. (at the corner of Pinnacle Peak Rd.), Scottsdale. ☎ **480/585-6142.**

This is one of the oldest Western-wear businesses in the valley, though the store is now housed in a modern shopping plaza. You'll find swirly skirts for cowboy dancing, denim jackets, suede coats, and flashy cowboy shirts. Prices are reasonable and quality is high.

# 11 Phoenix After Dark

If you're looking for nightlife in the Valley of the Sun, you won't have to look hard, but you may have to drive quite a ways. Though much of the valley's nightlife scene is centered around Old Scottsdale, Tempe's Mill Avenue, and downtown Phoenix, you'll find things going on all over.

The best place to look for nightlife listings is in the *Phoenix New Times,* a weekly newspaper that tends to have the most comprehensive listings. This is also the publication to check for club listings and schedules of rock concerts at various concert halls. *The Rep Entertainment Guide,* published by *The Arizona Republic,* is another good place to look for listings of upcoming events and performances, though you won't find as many club listings as in the *New Times. The Rep* is included in the Thursday edition of the paper but is also distributed free of charge from designated newspaper boxes on sidewalks around the Valley. Other publications to check for abbreviated listings are *Valley Guide Quarterly* and *Quick Guide Arizona,* which are free and can usually be found at hotels and resorts.

Tickets to many concerts, theater performances, and sporting events are available through **Ticketmaster** (☎ **480/784-4444**), which has outlets at Wherehouse Records, Tower Records, and Robinsons-May department stores. Tickets are also available at all **Dillard's** department store box offices (☎ **800/638-4253** or 480/503-5555).

## THE CLUB & MUSIC SCENE
The Valley of the Sun has a very diverse club and music scene that's spread out across the length and breadth of the valley. However, there are a few concentrations of clubs and bars.

With at least three sports bars, as many regular bars, a massive multiplex movie theater, and half a dozen restaurants, downtown Phoenix's **Arizona Center** is a veritable entertainment mecca. Within a few blocks of this megaentertainment complex, you'll also find Phoenix Symphony Hall, the Herberger Theater Center, and Majerle's Sports Grill. With all this going on, downtown Phoenix has become a magnet for barhoppers. However, much of the action revolves around games and concerts at the America West Arena and the Bank One Ballpark. On game nights, downtown bars stay packed. Convention attendees and the after-show crowds leaving the Herberger Theater Center and Phoenix Symphony Hall further add to the crowds filling these bars.

Another place to wander around until you hear your favorite type of music is **Mill Avenue** in Tempe. Because Tempe is a college town, there are plenty of clubs and bars on this short stretch of road.

In **Scottsdale,** you'll find an eclectic array of clubs in the neighborhoods surrounding the corner of Camelback Road and Scottsdale Road (especially along Stetson Drive, which is divided into two sections east and west of Scottsdale Road). The Scottsdale club scene has gotten pretty sophisticated in the past couple of years, and some regulars have even begun comparing it favorably to the L.A. club scene.

As we're sure you know if you're a denizen of any urban club scene, nightclubs come and go. If you're interested in finding the club of the moment, check the *New Times* for ads of places that play your kind of music. Many dance clubs in the Phoenix area are open only on weekends, so be sure to check what night the doors will be open. Bars and clubs are allowed to serve alcohol until 1am.

### COUNTRY
✪ **Handlebar-J.** 7116 E. Becker Lane, Scottsdale. ☎ **480/948-0110.** No cover Sun–Thurs, $3 Fri–Sat.

We're not saying that this Scottsdale landmark is a genuine cowboy bar, but cowpokes do make this one of their stops when they come in from the ranch. You'll hear live git-down two-steppin' music and can even get free dance lessons on Wednesday, Thursday, and Sunday.

**The Rockin' Horse Saloon Steakhouse and Dancehall.** 7316 E. Stetson Dr., Scottsdale. ☎ **480/949-0992.** Cover varies from $5 to $25.

Located in the heart of Scottsdale, the Rockin' Horse is an ever-popular bar that has diverged from its solid country roots to showcase an eclectic blend of country, blues, jazz, swing, and world music. Tickets for the bigger acts are available from Ticketmaster.

**Rusty Spur Saloon.** 7245 E. Main St. (Old Scottsdale). ☎ **480/941-2628.**

A small, rowdy, drinkin' and dancin' place frequented by tourists, this bar is a lot of fun, with peanut shells all over the floor, dollar bills stapled to the ceiling, and the occasional live act in the afternoon or evening.

**Toolie's Country Saloon & Dance Hall.** 4231 W. Thomas Rd. (at SE 43rd Ave.). ☎ **602/272-3100.** Cover $5.

Once a Safeway supermarket, Toolie's is now the best country-and-western bar in the valley (and some say in the whole country). A false-front cow-town facade beckons enthusiasts of all ages to come on in and git down. Nationally known acts make this their Phoenix stop, and when the famous aren't on stage, Toolie's books the best of the local C&W bands.

## ROCK & R&B

**Balboa Café.** 404 S. Mill Ave., Tempe. ☎ **480/966-1300.** No cover–$4.

Located in downtown Tempe, Balboa's is a restaurant with a college-bar atmosphere serving sandwiches. Local bands play several times a week, but it's really the drink specials and happy hour buffets that draw in the crowds.

**The Bash on Ash.** 230 W. 5th St., Tempe. ☎ **480/966-8200.** Cover $4–$7.

Also located in downtown Tempe, this small club specializes in swing and rock music. On Tuesday, Thursday, and Saturday, you'll find people taking swing lessons and doing the Lindy Hop to either a DJ or a live band (sometimes a national act). Friday is rock night, with a local rock showcase.

✪ **Cajun House.** 7117 E. 3rd Ave., Scottsdale. ☎ **480/945-5150.** Cover $5–$12.

You know you're in the middle of Arizona, but when you step through the front door of this cavernous theme nightclub, you'll swear you're in the French Quarter. The interior is done up as a New Orleans street scene with doors opening into various bars, dining rooms, and lounges. At the end of the street, there's a stage where live bands play most nights of the week. Lots of fun and well worth checking out.

**Long Wong's.** 701 S. Mill Ave. ☎ **480/966-3147.** Cover $1–$3.

This scruffy club is tiny and stays packed most nights with college students who come to hear the best of the local rock bands and nosh on great buffalo wings.

## BLUES

**The Blue Note Cool Cafe.** 8040 E. McDowell Rd., Scottsdale. ☎ **480/946-6227.** Cover $5 weekends.

If you're looking to hear some blues not far from the resorts of Scottsdale, check out this club. There's live music 7 nights a week, and a full menu is served.

**Char's Has the Blues.** 4631 N. 7th Ave. ☎ **602/230-0205.** Cover $3–$5 weekends.

Yes, indeed, Char's does have those mean-and-dirty, lowdown blues, and if you want them too, this is where you head in Phoenix. All the best blues brothers and sisters from around the city and around the country make the scene here to the enjoyment of hard-drinkin' crowds. You'll find this club 4 blocks south of Camelback Road.

**The Rhythm Room.** 1019 E. Indian School Rd. ☎ **602/265-4842.** No cover–$15 (mostly $4–$6). Closed Mon.

This acoustically oriented blues club, long the valley's most popular, books quite a few national acts as well as the best of the local scene, and has a dance floor if you want to move to the beat.

## JAZZ

Call the **Jazz in AZ Hotline** (☎ 602/254-4545) for a schedule of jazz performances all over the state.

✪ **Axis/Radius Nightclubs.** 7340 E. Indian Plaza, Scottsdale. ☎ **480/970-1112.** $7 women, $10 men on weekend.

Adopting a speakeasy-for-the-nineties attitude, though with walls of glass that put the two-floor bar's scene on display to anyone passing by, Axis is currently Scottsdale's most boldly contemporary watering hole and music venue. There's a lively singles scene here, with high energy dance music and a restaurant. You'll find this bar 2 blocks east of Scottsdale Road and 1 block south of Camelback.

**Beeloe's Cafe & Underground Bar.** 501 S. Mill Ave. ☎ **480/894-1230.** Cover $3.

Yes, this place really is underground, and though the crowd is mostly college students from ASU, the setting is reminiscent of old Greenwich Village basement jazz clubs. A lot of the people who perform here are faculty members in the ASU jazz program, so you know they know their stuff.

**Orbit Restaurant & Jazz Club.** In Uptown Plaza, Central Ave. and Camelback Rd. ☎ **602/265-2354.** No cover or specific minimum, but you're expected to have a meal and/or drinks.

Big and trendy, this space has a very urban feel to it, which is surprising considering its shopping plaza location. Originally just a coffeehouse, Orbit has become one of the most popular jazz clubs in the valley. The music actually includes jazz, blues, and Motown, so if you're looking for strictly jazz, you might want to check the schedule.

✪ **Timothy's.** 6335 N. 16th St. ☎ **602/277-7634.** No cover.

This is the valley's top upscale jazz spot, and with entrees in the $10 to $30 range, it attracts a well-off crowd. There's live jazz nightly, performed by either the house band or touring combos. If you can afford it, Timothy's is hard to beat when you're looking for an elegant, romantic evening of dining and listening to lively jazz.

## COMEDY & CABARET

**The Tempe Improv.** 930 E. University Dr., Tempe. ☎ **480/921-9877.** Cover $12–$15 plus 2-item minimum.

With the best of the national comedy circuit harassing the crowds and rattling off one-liners, the Improv is the valley's most popular comedy club. Weekend lines are long, but your reward is a chance to see the same folks that appear on TV stand-up comedy shows. Dinner is served and reservations are advised.

**Yesterday's.** 8041 N. Black Canyon Hwy. ☎ **602/433-1000.** No cover; $15 minimum.

Singing waiters and waitresses perform Broadway show tunes and other songs from the 1920s to the 1990s, while host David Lindsay plays Hammond organ and makes comic observations on life in Phoenix. Meals are around $20, and reservations are required. In the winter you should book at least a week in advance.

## DANCE CLUBS & DISCOS

**Anderson's Fifth Estate.** 6820 5th Ave., Scottsdale. ☎ **480/994-4168.** No cover–$4.

Phoenix has a thriving scene for alternative music, and this is where a lot of it gets played. Most nights there's a DJ spinning the dance music (alternative, eighties retro, seventies disco), but there are also occasional live shows featuring the likes of Blur and Warren Zevon. One side of this place doubles as a sports bar with pool tables and big-screen TVs.

**Buzz Original Funbar.** Southeast corner of Scottsdale Rd. and Shea Blvd. ☎ **480/991-FUNN.** No cover–$7.

In Scottsdale, folks like to think big. The resorts are big, the houses are big, the cars are big, the restaurants are big, and the nightclubs are big. Buzz boasts five different theme areas under one roof (including a bit of tropical fantasy for that Polynesian cocktail scene), plus a patio up on the roof.

**Club Rio.** 430 N. Scottsdale Rd., Tempe. ☎ **480/894-0533.** Cover $5.

This cavernous club has a dance floor big enough for football practice. From barely legal ASU students to the Porsche-and-pony set from Scottsdale, everyone agrees that Club Rio is *the* place to dance to the latest Top 40, alternative, and retro music. Plenty of live shows, too.

**Pepin.** 7363 Scottsdale Mall, Scottsdale. ☎ **480/990-9026.** Cover $7.

A DJ plays Latin dance music from 10pm on Friday and Saturday at this small Spanish restaurant located on the Scottsdale Mall. Thursday through Saturday evenings, there are live flamenco performances.

**Studebakers.** 1290 N. Scottsdale Rd., Tempe. ☎ **480/829-8617.** No cover–$5.

With an old Studebaker coupe parked in the middle of the club, there's no question that it's nostalgia music that's played here. Disc jockeys play music from the 1950s to 1980s, and Wednesdays are ballroom dancing nights (very popular with the over-50 crowd). There are free happy-hour buffets Wednesday through Friday night.

# THE BAR, LOUNGE & PUB SCENE
## BARS

**AZ88.** 7353 Scottsdale Mall, Scottsdale. ☎ **480/994-5576.**

Located across the park from the Scottsdale Center for the Arts, this sophisticated bar has a cool ambience that's just right for a martini before or after a performance.

**The Famous Door.** 7419 Indian Plaza, Scottsdale. ☎ **480/970-1945.**

Scottsdale's ultimate cigar bar, the Famous Door, fairly new on the scene, affects a Rat Pack aesthetic and treats cigars with reverence. Plenty of different martinis are available for accompaniment.

**Moondoggie's.** In Arizona Center, 455 N. 3rd St. ☎ **602/253-5200.**

This is the latest watering hole to take up residence in the popular Arizona Center shopping plaza in downtown Phoenix. Sporting a beach theme, it bills itself as a retro dance club.

**Phoenix Live! at Arizona Center.** 455 N. 3rd St. ☎ **602/252-2502.**

With three different clubs and a restaurant side-by-side in a modern shopping mall, this sprawling bar complex is the fulcrum of downtown after-hours activity and offers Phoenix barhoppers a chance to do all their hopping under one roof. Included here are Ltl Ditty's, a piano bar; Decades, a dance club playing seventies, eighties, and nineties music; and America's Original Sports Bar.

## LOUNGES

**Another Pointe in Tyme.** In the Pointe Hilton South Mountain Resort, 7777 S. Pointe Pkwy. ☎ **602/431-6472.**

If you feel most comfortable when surrounded by walls of mahogany and sitting on brocade or velvet, or if a little light jazz or piano music is your idea of the perfect music to drink by, then you'll be content here.

✪ **Hyatt Regency Scottsdale Lobby Bar.** 7500 E. Doubletree Ranch Rd., Scottsdale. ☎ **480/991-3388.**

The open-air lounge just below the main lobby of this posh Scottsdale resort sets a romantic stage for nightly live music (often by Spanish guitarist Estéban). Wood fires burn in patio fire pits, and royal palms are dramatically uplit. The terraced gardens offer plenty of dark spots for a bit of romance, and off in the distance the pools glow an ethereal turquoise color.

**The Squaw Peak Bar.** In the Arizona Biltmore Resort & Spa, 24th St. and Missouri Ave. ☎ **602/955-6600.**

Even if you can't afford the lap of luxury, at least you can pull up a comfortable chair in the lounge of the luxurious Arizona Biltmore. Sink into a seat next to the one you love and watch the sunset test its color palate on Camelback Mountain. Alternatively, you can slide into a seat near the piano and let the waves of mellow jazz wash over you. For the mere cost of a drink, you can have a Biltmore experience.

**T. Cook's.** 5200 E. Camelback Rd. ☎ **602/808-0766.**

Even if you aren't planning on having dinner at this opulent Mediterranean restaurant, you'll certainly enjoy lounging in the bar. With its mix of Spanish colonial and fifties tropical rattan furnishings, this is as romantic a lounge as you'll find anywhere in the valley. For even more romance, snuggle up out on the patio by the fireplace. The cigar room here has the feel of an ancient wine cellar.

## PUBS

**Bandersnatch Brew Pub.** 125 E. 5th St., Tempe. ☎ **480/966-4438.**

With good house brews and a big patio in back, Bandersnatch is a favorite of those unusual ASU students who prefer quality to quantity when it's beer-drinking time. There's live music on Wednesday (with a focus on Celtic music), Friday, and Saturday nights.

✪ **Coyote Springs Brewing Company.** In the Town and Country Shopping Plaza, 4883 N. 20th St. ☎ **602/468-0403.**

This brew pub is a casual, friendly place, and on any given night has a half dozen or more of its own brews on tap. A second pub is located in downtown Phoenix at 122 E. Washington St. (☎ **602/256-6645**). This latter pub has a sports theme in keeping with its location near the America West Arena and Bank One Ballpark.

**Hops! Bistro & Brewery.** Scottsdale Fashion Square, 7014 E. Camelback Rd. ☎ **480/946-1272.**

Take a down-home idea—brewing your own beer—and mix it up with a bit of Phoenix chic (by way of San Diego) and you get Hops!, a huge, upscale brew pub with a boldly contemporary dining room that serves creative American cuisine.

**Timber Wolf.** 740 E. Apache Blvd., Tempe. ☎ **480/517-9383.**

While this is not a brew pub, it does have an astounding 400-plus brews from all over the world, and about 150 of these are on tap! You can't miss this place as you drive east from Mill Avenue on Apache Boulevard. It's the huge log cabin that looks as if it's pining for some snow.

## COCKTAILS WITH A VIEW

The Valley of the Sun has more than its fair share of spectacular views. Unfortunately, most of them are from expensive restaurants. All these restaurants have lounges, though, where for the price of a drink (and perhaps valet parking) you can sit back and ogle a crimson sunset and the purple mountains' majesty.

Your choices include **Different Pointe of View** at the Pointe Hilton Tapatio Cliffs Resort, **Rustler's Rooste** at the Pointe Hilton on South Mountain, and **Top of the Rock** at The Buttes. All these restaurants can be found in the restaurant section of this chapter. One other choice is **The Thirsty Camel** at The Phoenician resort. You may never drink in more ostentatious surroundings than here at Charles Keating's Xanadu.

## SPORTS BARS

**America's Original Sports Bar.** 455 N. 3rd St. ☎ **602/252-2502.** Cover $5 Fri–Sat.

Located in the Arizona Center, this huge sports bar (nearly an acre) is a sort of fun center for grown-ups. There's a huge back deck, innumerable TVs, a dozen of which are giant-screen, and a small video-games arcade. There's even a Phoenix Sports Hall of Fame.

**Majerle's Sports Grill.** 24 N. 2nd St. ☎ **602/253-9004.**

If you're a Phoenix Suns fan, you won't want to miss this sports bar only a couple of blocks from the America West Arena where the Suns play. Suns memorabilia covers the walls, and the players often drop in.

✪ **Max's.** 6727 N. 47th Ave., Glendale. ☎ **623/937-1671.**

These days it seems that sports bars are as common as knee injuries on the football field. Most are little more than a bar with a big-screen TV, but Max's is the real thing. In fact, it's a sports museum filled with NFL football helmets, restaurant, dinner theater, and off-track betting parlor all wrapped up in one.

**McDuffy's.** 230 W. 5th St., Tempe. ☎ **480/966-5600.**

Voted the best sports bar in America by an industry magazine, this bar is a favorite of Sun Devils fans. There are more than 60 TVs and nearly two dozen beers on tap.

## GAY & LESBIAN BARS

✪ **Ain't Nobody's Business.** 3031 E. Indian School Rd. ☎ **602/224-9977.**

Located in a small shopping plaza, this is the city's most popular lesbian bar, with pool tables and a no-smoking lounge. Sometimes there's live music by local musicians. Weekends the dance floor is usually packed.

**Amsterdam.** 718 N. Central Ave. ☎ **602/258-6112.**

Just a few doors away from Crowbar, Amsterdam draws a crowd that prefers sipping martinis to tossing down beers. There's no sign outside—you just have to look carefully for the number.

**Charlie's.** 727 W. Camelback Rd. ☎ **602/265-0224.**

This nondescript bar just a dozen or so blocks off I-17 is a good bet if you're staying in the Camelback Corridor area. Country music dominates the airwaves here, and the boys like to do the urban cowboy thing. Dance lessons are Thursday and Saturday at about 7pm.

**Crowbar.** 702 N. Central Ave. ☎ **602/258-8343.**

Created by the same people who made The Works the most popular gay dance club in Scottsdale, this downtown Phoenix club stays packed with sweaty bodies on weekends. The decor is sort of industrial Gothic, with lots of big candles dripping wax down faux stone pillars. The after-hours scene pulls in the underagers and goes on until 4am.

**Nu Towne Saloon.** 5002 E. Van Buren St. ☎ **602/267-9959.**

After more than a quarter of a century in business, this nondescript and virtually unmarked bar continues to be a favorite of the valley's leather-and-Levi's set. The atmosphere is friendly and funky, and the Tuesday night beer bust is a favorite.

**307 Lounge.** 222 E. Roosevelt St. ☎ **602/252-0001.**

Female impersonator shows and talent contests keep this gay (and straight-friendly) bar lively Thursday through Saturday and make it one of the most fun scenes in the valley.

## THE PERFORMING ARTS

The performing-arts scene in the Valley of the Sun grows more robust with each passing year. Major performing-arts venues are scattered across the valley, so no matter where you happen to be staying, you're likely to find performances being held somewhere nearby. Downtown Phoenix claims the valley's greatest concentration of performance halls, including the Phoenix Symphony Hall, the Orpheum Theatre, and the Herberger Theater Center. You'll also find large performance halls in Scottsdale, Mesa, Tempe, Chandler, and Sun City.

Calling these venues home are the valley's major performance companies—the Phoenix Symphony, Scottsdale Symphony Orchestra, the Arizona Opera Company, Ballet Arizona, Center Dance Ensemble, Actors Theatre Company, and Arizona Theatre Company. Adding to the performances held by these companies are the wide variety of touring companies that make stops in the valley throughout the year. These national and international acts give the valley just the diversity of performers you would expect to find in a city of this size.

While you'll find box office phone numbers listed below, you can also purchase most performing-arts tickets through **Ticketmaster** (☎ **480/784-4444**) or **Dillard's Box Office** outlets (☎ **800/638-4253** or 480/503-5555), found in Dillard's department stores around the city. For tickets to sold-out shows, check with your hotel concierge if you are staying at a hotel that has a concierge. Or, try **Western States Ticket Service** (☎ **602/254-3300**) or **Tickets Unlimited** (☎ **800/289-8497** or 602/840-2340).

### MAJOR PERFORMING-ARTS CENTERS

Phoenix's premier performance venue is the **Phoenix Symphony Hall,** 225 E. Adams St. (☎ **800/AT-CIVIC** or 602/262-7272), which is home to the Phoenix Symphony and the Arizona Opera Company and also hosts other classical music performances, Broadway touring shows, and various other concerts and theatrical productions. The box office, which is at the entrance to the Phoenix Convention Center, Lobby 2, Plaza South, is open Monday through Friday from 9:30am to 5pm and sells tickets (with a service charge) for the symphony, ballet, and Orpheum Theatre, as well as other venues.

The **Orpheum Theatre,** Adams Street and Second Avenue (☎ **602/262-7272**), a historic Spanish colonial baroque theater, was built in 1929 and at the time was considered the most luxurious theater west of the Mississippi. Today its ornately carved sandstone facade stands in striking contrast to the glass-and-steel City Hall building with which the theater shares a common wall (step inside the lobby of City Hall to see the exposed brick wall of the theater). Today, the Orpheum is once again the most elegant performance hall in the valley, and if you have time for only one show while in town, try to make it here.

In Scottsdale, the **Scottsdale Center for the Arts,** 7380 E. Second St., Scottsdale (☎ **480/994-ARTS;** www.ScottsdaleArts.org), on the Scottsdale Mall, hosts a wide variety of performances and series ranging from alternative dance to classical music. It may be the wealth of the local population, but for whatever reason, this center seems to get the best of the touring performers who come through the valley. The box office is open Monday through Saturday from 10am to 5pm (to 9pm on Thursday and Friday) and on Sunday from noon to 5pm. Ticket prices range from $10 to $40.

The Frank Lloyd Wright–designed **Grady Gammage Memorial Auditorium,** Mill Avenue and Apache Boulevard, Tempe (☎ **480/965-3434**), on the Arizona State University campus, is at once massive and graceful. This 3,000-seat hall hosts everything from barbershop quartets to touring Broadway shows. The box office is open Monday through Friday from 10am to 6pm and on Saturday from 10am to 4pm.

Several other halls around the valley also schedule interesting performances throughout the year. **ASU's Kerr Cultural Center,** 6110 N. Scottsdale Rd., Scottsdale (☎ **480/965-5377**), offers up an eclectic season that includes music from around the world. The **Chandler Center for the Arts,** 250 N. Arizona Ave., Chandler (☎ **480/ 786-2680**), books a few name entertainers each year and fills out its season with a variety of other acts. The **Sundome Center for the Performing Arts,** 19403 R. H. Johnson Blvd., Sun City West (☎ **623/975-1900**), seats more than 7,000 people and stages shows that appeal to the many retirees who call Sun City home.

## OUTDOOR VENUES

Given the weather, it should come as no surprise that Phoenicians like to go to performances under the stars.

The city's top outdoor venue is the **Blockbuster Desert Sky Pavilion** (☎ **602/ 254-7200**), located ½ mile north of I-10 between 79th and 83rd avenues. This 20,000-seat amphitheater is open year-round and hosts everything from Broadway musicals to rock concerts; tickets run $12.50 to $70.

The **Mesa Amphitheater,** at the corner of University Drive and Center Road in Mesa (☎ **480/644-2567**), is a much smaller amphitheater that holds rock concerts throughout the summer and occasionally other times.

The **Scottsdale Center for the Arts** (☎ **480/994-ARTS**) heads outdoors for many of its summer concerts, which are held in the Scottsdale Amphitheater on the Scottsdale Civic Center Mall.

Outdoor concerts are also held at various parks and plazas around the valley during the warmer months of the year. Check local papers for listings of such events.

Two perennial favorites of valley residents take place in particularly attractive surroundings. The Music in the Garden concerts at the **Desert Botanical Garden,** 1201 N. Galvin Pkwy. (☎ **480/941-1225**), in Papago Park, are held on Sundays between September and March. The season always includes an eclectic array of musical styles. Tickets are $13.50 and include admission to the gardens. Sunday brunch is served for an additional charge. Way up in Carefree, the **El Pedregal Festival Marketplace** (☎ **480/488-1072**) stages jazz, blues, and rock concerts on Thursday evenings (7 to 9:30pm) from April through June and the month of September. Tickets are $5 to $10.

## OTHER VENUES

When big-name music stars come to town, they often perform at the **America West Arena,** 201 E. Jefferson St. (☎ **602/379-7800**), known locally as the Purple Palace. This arena is also home to the Phoenix Suns, the NHL's Phoenix Coyotes hockey team, the Arizona Rattlers arena football team, the WNBA's Phoenix Mercury, and many other sporting and entertainment events. The **Celebrity Theatre,** 440 N. 32nd St., Phoenix (☎ **602/267-1600**), is a theater-in-the-round, with a revolving stage so everyone gets a good view. Acts are mostly musical but there are also occasional stage productions. Tickets range from $7.50 to $75. The **Red River Music Hall,** 730 N.

Mill Ave., Tempe (☎ **480/829-6779**), just across the Salt River from ASU, presents jazz, gospel, and rock music concerts; tickets are generally $26 to $46.

## CLASSICAL MUSIC, OPERA & DANCE

The **Phoenix Symphony** (☎ **800/776-9080** or 602/495-1999), the Southwest's leading symphony orchestra, performs at the Phoenix Symphony Hall (tickets run $15 to $39), while the **Scottsdale Symphony Orchestra** (☎ **480/945-8071** or 480/994-2787) performs at the Scottsdale Center for the Arts (tickets go for about $12 to $20). The **Mesa Symphony** (☎ **480/897-2121**) stages a limited number of concerts each season at the Chandler Center for the Arts and other venues (tickets range from $8 to $22).

Opera buffs may want to see what the **Arizona Opera Company** (☎ **602/266-7464**) has scheduled. This company stages up to five operas, both familiar and more obscure, each year and splits its time between Phoenix and Tucson (tickets cost $17 to $69). Performances are held in Phoenix Symphony Hall.

**Ballet Arizona** (☎ **602/381-1096**) performs at the Phoenix Symphony Hall, the Orpheum, and the Herberger Theater Center and stages both classical and contemporary ballets (tickets run $16 to $48). The **Center Dance Ensemble** (☎ **602/252-8497**), the city's contemporary dance ensemble, stages several productions a year (one during the Christmas holidays) at the Herberger Theater Center (tickets go for $7 to $18). Between September and March each year **Southwest Dance** (☎ **602/482-6410**) brings acclaimed dance companies from around the world to Phoenix, with performances staged at various area venues (tickets range from about $10 to $75).

## THEATER

In the past few years, Phoenix has been expanding the range of its theater productions. With nearly a dozen professional companies and the same number of nonprofessional companies taking to the boards throughout the year, there is always some play being staged somewhere in the valley. So, if you're a fan of live theater, check around. You're likely to find something to pique your interest.

The city's main hall for live theater is the **Herberger Theater Center,** 222 E. Monroe St. (☎ **602/252-8497**), which is located downtown and vaguely resembles a Spanish colonial church. Its two Broadway-style theaters together host more than 600 performances each year, including productions by the **Actors Theatre of Phoenix (ATP)** and the **Arizona Theatre Company (ATC).** ATP has, in the past decade, become one of Phoenix's premier acting companies. Plays tend to be smaller, lesser-known off-Broadway–type works, with musicals, dramas, and comedies equally represented; tickets go for $19 to $33. ATC is the State Theatre of Arizona and splits its performances between Phoenix and Tucson. Founded in 1967, the ATC has grown into a major force in the Arizona thespian scene. Productions tend towards classics and well-known contemporary works. Tickets run $24 to $34. Also performing at the Herberger is the **Arizona Jewish Theatre Co.,** which stages plays by Jewish playwrights and with Jewish themes. Tickets range from $18 to $24.

The **Phoenix Theatre,** 100 E. McDowell Rd. (☎ **602/258-1974** or 602/254-2151), has been around for more than 70 years and stages a wide variety of productions; tickets are $23 to $25. If your interest lies in Broadway plays, see what the **Valley Broadway Series** (☎ **480/965-3434**) has scheduled. The series, focusing mostly on comedies and musicals, is held at the Gammage Auditorium in Tempe; tickets cost about $35 to $70. The **Theater League** (☎ **602/952-2881**) is another series that brings in Broadway musicals. Performances are held in the Orpheum

Theatre, and tickets cost about $28 to $37. Scottsdale's small **Stagebrush Theatre,** 7020 E. Second St. (☎ **480/990-7405**), is a community theater that stages tried-and-true comedies and musicals, with the occasional drama thrown in. Tickets are $12 to $17. For more daring new works and children's theater, check the schedule at **PlayWright's Theatre,** 1121 N. First St. (☎ **602/253-5151**). Tickets are no more than $12.

## FILM

In addition to the IMAX theater listed here, there is a similar large-screen theater at the Arizona Science Center (see "Seeing the Sights," above).

**IMAX Theatre Scottsdale.** 5th Ave. and Civic Center Blvd. ☎ **480/945-4629.** Tickets $7–$9.75 adults, $6–$8.50 seniors, $5–$7.50 children 12 and under.

The massive IMAX screen puts you in the midst of the action. There are usually two or three different films showing here on any given day. The higher-priced tickets are for a double feature.

## CASINOS

**Fort McDowell Casino.** On Fort McDowell Rd. off Ariz. 87, 2 miles northeast of Shea Blvd., Fountain Hills. ☎ **800/THE-FORT.**

Phoenicians, once among the mainstay clientele of casinos in Nevada, now need not even leave the valley to throw their hard-earned dollars at the slot and video-poker machines. This casino's open 24 hours a day, and there's even free transportation from Phoenix.

**Gila River Casino.** Exit 162 off I-10 south of Phoenix. ☎ **800/WIN-GILA.**

With two separate casino buildings at the same exit off I-10, the Gila River Casino wants to make sure it snags some business from passing motorists. Keno, bingo, and slots machines are available.

**Harrah's Phoenix Ak-Chin Casino.** 15406 Maricopa Rd., Maricopa. ☎ **800/HARRAHS.**

Located 25 miles south of Phoenix and just south of the town of Maricopa, this glitzy casino on the Ak-Chin Indian Reservation brings Las Vegas–caliber gambling to the Phoenix area. Lots of slot machines, video poker, a card room, keno, and bingo. To reach the casino, take Exit 164 (Queen Creek Road) off I-10, turn right and drive 17 miles to Maricopa.

# 12  Side Trips from Phoenix

## THE APACHE TRAIL

There isn't a whole lot of desert or history left in Phoenix, but only an hour's drive to the east you'll find quite a bit of both. ✪ **The Apache Trail,** a winding, partially gravel road that snakes its way around the north side of the Superstition Mountains, offers some of the most scenic desert driving in central Arizona. Along the way there are ghost towns and legends, saguaros and century plants, ancient ruins and artificial lakes.

This tour includes a lot of driving on a narrow, winding gravel road, and if you'd rather leave the driving to someone else, you can take a tour of the area with **Apache Trail Tours** (☎ **480/982-7661**), which offers four-wheel-drive tours of different lengths ($50 to $115 per person), as well as hiking trips ($10 per person per hour) into the Superstition Mountains.

To start this drive, head east on U.S. 60 to the town of Apache Junction and then head north on Ariz. 88. Just 3½ miles north of Apache Junction, you'll come to

**Goldfield Ghost Town** (☎ 480/983-0333), a reconstructed 1890s gold-mining town. Though it's a bit of a tourist trap—gift shops, an ice-cream parlor, and the like—it's also home to the **Superstition Mountain/Lost Dutchman Museum** (☎ 480/983-4888), with interesting exhibits about the history of the area. Of particular note is the exhibit on the Lost Dutchman gold mine, perhaps the most famous mine in the country despite the fact that its location is unknown. Admission to the museum is $3 for adults, $2.50 for seniors, and $1 for children. **Goldfield Ghost Town and Mine Tours** (☎ 480/983-0333) provides guided tours of the gold mine beneath the town ($4 for adults, $2 for children ages 6 to 12). The company also operates a narrow-gauge railroad train, which circles the town (rides are $4 for adults, $2 for children ages 5 to 12). If it's lunchtime already, you can get a meal at the steakhouse/saloon.

Not far from Goldfield is **Lost Dutchman State Park** (☎ 480/982-4485), where you can hike into the rugged Superstition Mountains and see what the region's gold seekers have been up against. Park admission is $5 per vehicle, and there is a campground that charges $10 per site.

If you're game to see the Superstitions from horseback, contact **Trail Horse Adventures,** 2151 N. Warner Rd., Apache Junction (☎ 800/SADDLEUP or 480/982-6353), which offers rides ranging in length from 1 hour to all day ($20 to $80) or longer. The company arranges riding lessons, overnight pack trips, picnics, and hayrides. You can also try **OK Corral Horse Rentals** (☎ 480/982-4040), which is close to Goldfield ghost town and charges $18 for a 1-hour ride.

You can get a bird's-eye view on a helicopter tour with **Heliservices** (☎ 480/ 830-9410), which operates out of Goldfield Ghost Town. Per person fares range from $39 for a 12-minute flight to $159 for a 3-hour flight.

Continuing northeast, you'll next come to **Canyon Lake,** the first of three reservoirs you'll pass on this drive. The three lakes provide much of Phoenix's drinking water, without which the city would never have been able to grow as large as it is today. Here at Canyon Lake you can go for a swim or take a cruise on the *Dolly* steamboat (☎ 480/827-9144). A 90-minute cruise on this reproduction paddle wheeler costs $14 for adults and $8 for children 6 to 12. Lunch and dinner cruises are also available, and you can rent powerboats at the Canyon Lake Marina. If you're hungry, grab a bite at the Lakeside Restaurant, which overlooks the marina. Or, for a taste of the Old West, hold out for **Tortilla Flat** (☎ 480/984-1776), an old stagecoach stop that has a restaurant, saloon, and general store, all of which are papered with business cards and more than $50,000 worth of dollar bills left by travelers who have stopped here. The prickly pear ice cream served here is worth a try (guaranteed spineless).

A few miles past Tortilla Flat, the pavement ends and the truly spectacular desert scenery begins. Among the rocky ridges, arroyos, and canyons of this stretch of road, you'll see saguaro cacti and century plants (a type of agave that sends up a 15-foot-tall flower stalk after years or even decades of slow growth and then dies). Next you'll come to **Apache Lake,** which is in a deep canyon flanked by colorful cliffs and rugged rock formations. This lake also has a marina, as well as a campground, motel, restaurant, and general store.

Shortly before reaching pavement again, you'll reach **Theodore Roosevelt Dam.** This dam, which forms Roosevelt Lake, is the largest masonry dam in the world and was built in 1911. A recent renovation has given it a face-lift and increased the holding capacity of Roosevelt Lake.

Continuing on Ariz. 88, you'll next come to ✪ **Tonto National Monument** (☎ 520/467-2241), which preserves the southernmost cliff dwellings in Arizona.

# The Lost Dutchman of the Superstitions

The Superstition Mountains rise up to the east of Phoenix, dark and ominous, jagged and hot. Cacti bristle across the mountains' flanks, and water is almost nonexistent. Yet for more than a century, gold-crazed prospectors have been scouring these forbidding mountains for a gold mine that may not even exist. The power of a legend is strong, and few legends are as well documented as the legend of the Lost Dutchman gold mine.

The year was 1870 when two German miners, Jacob Waltz and Jacob Weiser, set off into the Arizona wilderness east of Phoenix in hopes of striking it rich. When these two "Dutchmen" (an appellation derived from the German word *Deutsch*) returned to civilization, they carried with them pouches filled with gold nuggets. Though unsavory prospectors tried to track them to their mother lode in hopes of claim jumping, none was successful. Through visits to saloons and brothels, the two Jacobs remained tight-lipped about their mine's where-abouts.

Jacob Weiser eventually disappeared from the scene amid speculation that his partner did him in so as to keep all the gold to himself. Waltz eventually gave up prospecting in the Superstitions in 1889 at the age of 80. On his deathbed in 1891, he gave detailed directions to a Phoenix woman he had befriended. She and her foster son and the foster son's father and brother spent the next 40 years searching fruitlessly for Waltz's Lost Dutchman mine. Waltz's dying directions just weren't good enough to lead the searchers through these rugged, uncharted mountains.

Clues to the mine's location abound, and hopeful prospectors and treasure hunters have followed every possible lead in their quest for the mine. However, gold fever has led more than a few to their deaths in this harsh wilderness. While skeptics say that there's no proof there ever was a Lost Dutchman mine, others see in the mine's continued elusiveness hope that they might one day be the prospector to find this fabled mother lode.

These pueblos were built between 1100 and 1400 by the Salado people, and are some of the few remaining traces of this people who once cultivated lands now flooded by Roosevelt Lake. The lower ruins are ½ mile up a steep trail from the visitor center, and the upper ruins are a 3-mile round-trip hike from the visitor center. The lower ruins are open daily year-round except Christmas, and the upper ruins are open November through April by reservation (reserve at least a couple of weeks in advance). The park is open daily from 8am to 5pm (you must begin the lower ruin trail by 4pm), and admission is $4 per car.

Continuing on Ariz. 88 will bring you to the copper-mining town of **Globe.** The mines here are open pits, and though you can't see the mines themselves, the tailings (remains of rock removed from the copper ore) can be seen piled high all around the town. In Globe, be sure to visit ✪ **Besh-Ba-Gowah Archaeological Park** (☎ **520/425-0320**), which is on the eastern outskirts of town (open daily from 9am to 5pm; admission $3). This Salado Indian pueblo site has been partially reconstructed, and several rooms are set up to reflect the way they might have looked when they were first occupied about 700 years ago. These are among the most fascinating ruins in the state. To reach Besh-Ba-Gowah, head out of Globe on South Broad Street to Jesse Hayes Road.

From Globe, head west on U.S. 60. On the west side of Superior, you'll come to ✪ **Boyce Thompson Southwestern Arboretum,** 37615 U.S. 60 (☎ **520/689-2811**), which is dedicated to researching and propagating desert plants and instilling in the public an appreciation for desert plants (open daily, except Christmas, from 8am to 5pm; admission $5 adults and $2 children 5 to 12, free for children 4 and under). This was the nation's first botanical garden established in the desert, and the cactus gardens here are impressive. The setting in Queen Creek and Anett canyons is quite dramatic with cliffs for a backdrop and a stream running through the gardens. As you hike the miles of nature trails, watch for the two bizarre boojum trees. It doesn't matter where you live; you can learn a lot here about landscaping in the desert.

If it's not too late and you didn't go riding in the morning, you can finish your day with a horseback ride at **Don Donnelly Stables,** 6010 Kings Ranch Rd., Gold Canyon (☎ **800/346-4403** or 480/982-7822). A 2-hour sunset ride costs $32 per person. These stables also do overnight rides, cookouts, and hayrides.

If after a long day on the road you're looking for a good place to eat, stop in at **Gold Canyon Golf Resort,** 6100 S. Kings Ranch Rd., Gold Canyon (☎ **480/982-9090**), which has a good, though expensive, dining room. There's also a bar and grill serving basic burgers and sandwiches.

## CAVE CREEK & THE OLD WEST

A drive north from Phoenix can give you glimpses into how the pioneers once lived—and how Hollywood imagines Western towns should look.

Head north out of Phoenix on I-17 for about 20 miles and take the Pioneer Road exit. Here you'll find the ✪ **Pioneer Arizona Living History Museum,** 3901 W. Pioneer Rd. (☎ **623/465-1052**). This museum includes 28 original and reconstructed buildings, and inside (or nearby) you'll find costumed interpreters practicing traditional frontier activities. There are also melodramas and gunfights staged daily. Among the buildings are a carpentry shop, a blacksmith shop, a miner's cabin, a stagecoach station, a one-room schoolhouse, an opera house, a church, farmhouses, and a Victorian mansion. The museum is open October through May, Wednesday through Sunday from 9am to 5pm, June through September Friday through Sunday from 5 to 9pm. Admission is $5.75 adults, $5.25 seniors and students, $4 children 4–12, and free for children under 4. Wear sturdy shoes.

Heading back south on I-17, take Exit 223 and head east to **Cave Creek** and **Carefree.** Cave Creek, founded as a mining camp in the 1870s, clings to its Wild West image and looks something like the fake cow towns that are all over the Arizona desert. Carefree, on the other hand, is all New West retirees, mansions, and golf courses. To learn more about the history of this area, stop in at the **Cave Creek Museum** at the corner of Skyline Drive and Basin Road (☎ **480/488-2764**). The museum is open October through May Wednesday through Sunday from 1 to 4:30pm, and admission is by donation.

Cave Creek is home to several Western steakhouses, saloons, and shops selling Western and Native American crafts and antiques; you can easily spend several hours wandering through the shops here. When you've worked up a thirst or a hunger, wander over to **Crazy Ed's Satisfied Frog Saloon,** 6245 E. Cave Creek Rd. (☎ **480/488-3317**), where you can get some hearty Western fare and sample Cave Creek chile beer, each bottle of which has a chile pepper in it. For dining with a little more finesse, consider the **Tonto Bar & Grill,** 5734 E. Rancho Mañana Blvd. (☎ **480/488-0698**), which overlooks the Rancho Mañana golf course. Patio dining and a contemporary American menu make this place an inviting spot for a meal. Rancho Mañana Boulevard is at the west end of town just off of Cave Creek Road; if you can, call for a reservation.

**Carefree** is a much more subdued place, a planned community established in the 1950s and popular with retirees. Ho and Hum roads and Easy Street are just a couple of local street names that reflect the sedate nature of the town, which is home to the exclusive Boulders resort. Boasting one of the most spectacular settings of any resort in Arizona, The Boulders also has a couple of excellent restaurants.

On Easy Street, in what passes for downtown in Carefree, you'll find one of the world's largest sundials. The dial is 90 feet across, and the gnomon (the part that casts the shadow) is 35 feet tall. From the gnomon hangs a colored-glass star, and in the middle of the dial, there's a pool of water and a fountain. This elaborate timepiece shows the correct time on vernal and autumnal equinoxes, but on other days of the year, you have to consult a chart next to the sundial to figure out what time to set your watch to.

In downtown Carefree, you'll also find a sort of reproduction Spanish village shopping area, and just south of town, adjacent to The Boulders resort, you'll find the upscale El Pedregal Festival Marketplace shopping center, where there are lots of interesting shops, art galleries, and a few restaurants.

If you'd like to do a bit of horseback riding while you're in the area, contact **Cave Creek Outfitters** (☎ **480/471-4635**), located just off Dynamite Boulevard on 144th Street. They charge $55 for a 2-hour ride. There's also plenty of good mountain biking in the area, and if you'd like do a bit of fat-tire riding, you can rent a bike from **Cave Creek Bikes,** 6149 Cave Creek Rd. (☎ **480/488-5261**), which charges $25 to $40 a day for mountain bikes.

## CASA GRANDE & FLORENCE

Driving southeast from Phoenix on I-10 for about 60 miles will bring you to the Florence and Casa Grande area, where you can learn about Indian cultures both past and present and view the greatest concentration of historic buildings in Arizona.

At Exit 175 (Casa Blanca Road), you'll find the **Gila River Arts and Crafts Center,** which is located on the Gila River Indian Reservation. The center has a museum with historical photos and artifacts, including beautiful Pima baskets.

To reach Florence, continue south on I-10 to Exit 185 (Ariz. 387) and head east. Before reaching Florence, near the town of Coolidge, you'll come to ✪ **Casa Grande Ruins National Monument** (☎ **520/723-3172**). In Spanish, the name means "Big House," and that's exactly what you'll find. In this instance, the big house is the ruin of an earth-walled structure that was built 650 years ago by the Hohokam people. Although it's still not known what purpose this unusual structure served, the building provides a glimpse of a style of ancient architecture rarely seen. Instead of using adobe bricks or stones, the people who built this structure used layers of hard-packed soil that have survived the ravages of the weather. The Hohokam people who once occupied this site began farming the valleys of the Gila and Salt rivers about 1,500 years ago, and eventually built an extensive network of irrigation canals for watering their fields. By the middle of the 15th century, however, the Hohokam had abandoned both their canals and their villages and disappeared without a trace. The monument is open daily from 8am to 5pm (closed Christmas), and admission is $2 for adults.

Continuing east, you'll soon come to the farming community of **Florence.** Though at first glance this town may seem like any other small town, closer inspection turns up more than 150 buildings on the National Register of Historic Places. The majority of these buildings are constructed of adobe and were originally built in the Sonoran style, a style that was influenced by Spanish architectural ideas. Most buildings were altered over the years and now display aspects of various architectural styles popular during territorial days in Arizona.

# To-Die-For Pies

Lying at the northern edge of the Valley of the Sun, about 30 minutes north of Phoenix, the town of Rock Springs is barely a wide spot in the road and is easily missed by drivers roaring up and down I-17. However, if you are a fan of pies, then *do not* miss Exit 242 off the Interstate. Here you'll find the **Rock Springs Cafe** (☎ **623/374-5794,** or 602/258-9065 in Phoenix), which has been in business since 1910. Though this aging and nondescript building looks like the sort of place that would best be avoided, the packed parking lot says different. Why so popular? No its not the coffee or the "hogs in heat" barbecue or even the Bradshaw Mountain oysters. No, what keeps this placed packed are Penny's pies, the most famous pies in Arizona (31,328 sold in 1998). The bakery here keeps turning out the pies all day long, and no matter what your favorite type might be, you'll likely find it in the pie case. If one slice isn't enough, order a whole pie to go; you can enjoy it when your day's driving is over. As the menu says, this place is "worth the drive from anywhere."

Before touring the town, stop in at the **Pinal County Historical Society Museum,** 715 S. Main St. (☎ **520/868-4382**), to learn more about the history of the area. It's open Wednesday to Saturday 11am to 4pm and Sunday noon to 4pm (closed from mid-July through August). Admission is by donation.

At the corner of Main Street and Ruggles Street, you'll find the **McFarland State Historic Park** (☎ **520/868-5216**), which is housed in a former Pinal County Courthouse that was built in 1878. It's open Thursday to Monday from 8am to 5pm; admission is $2 adults, $1 children ages 12 to 18. The current county courthouse, built in 1891, rises above the center of town and displays an unusual combination of different architectural styles.

To find out more about the buildings of Florence, stop in at the **Pinal County Visitors Center,** at Butte Avenue and Florence Street (☎ **520/868-4331**), or the **Florence Visitors Center,** 291 N. Bailey St. (☎ **800/437-9433** or 520/868-9433), which is housed in a historic 1891 bakery in the center of town. Each year on the first Saturday in February there's a tour of historic buildings. Contact the visitors centers for more information.

If you're interested in shopping deals, there are a couple of **factory-outlet shopping malls** in the town of Casa Grande at exits 194 and 198 off I-10. These are only a short distance out of your way to the south if you are headed back to Phoenix.

If you are continuing south toward Tucson from Florence, we suggest taking the scenic **Pinal Pioneer Parkway** (Ariz. 79), which was the old highway between Phoenix and Tucson. Along the way you'll see signs identifying desert plants and a memorial to silent-film star Tom Mix, who died in a car crash here in October 1940.

Alternatively, if you're heading to Tucson by way of I-10, and it isn't too hot out, consider a stop at ✪ **Picacho Peak State Park** (☎ **520/466-3183**), which is 20 miles south of Casa Grande at Exit 219. Picacho Peak, a wizard's cap of rock rising 1,500 feet above the desert, is a visual landmark for miles around. Hiking trails lead around the lower slopes of the peak and up to the summit, and these trails are especially popular in spring, when the wildflowers bloom (the park is well known as one of the best places in Arizona to see wildflowers, in fact). In addition to its natural beauty, Picacho Peak was the site of the only Civil War battle to take place in Arizona. Park admission is $5 per car and campsites are $10, or $15 with electricity and water.

# 5

# Central Arizona

**E**ncompassing the Mogollon Rim, the fertile Verde River valley, Oak Creek Canyon, the red rocks of Sedona, the pine-forested mountains around Prescott, and the desert in the Wickenburg area, central Arizona packs an amazing amount of variety within its boundaries and has played an important role in Arizona history for more than 1,500 years.

Ancient Hohokam and Sinagua peoples, as well as early settlers, were drawn to the fertile valley of the Verde River. Though the early tribes had disappeared by the time the first white settlers arrived in the area in the 1860s, hostile Apache and Yavapai tribes inhabited the area. It was in order to protect settlers that the U.S. Army established Fort Verde in 1871.

When Arizona became a U.S. territory in 1863, Prescott, due to its central location, was chosen as its capital. Though the town would eventually lose that title to Tucson and then to Phoenix, it was the most important city in Arizona for part of the late 19th century. Wealthy merchants and legislators rapidly transformed this pioneer outpost into a beautiful town filled with stately Victorian homes surrounding an imposing county courthouse.

Settlers were lured to this region not only by fertile land but also by the mineral wealth that lay hidden in the ground. Miners founded a number of communities in central Arizona, among them Jerome. When the mines shut down, Jerome was almost completely abandoned, but now artists and craftspeople have moved in to reclaim and revitalize the old mining town.

Artists also found their way to Sedona, but only after the movie industry had hit upon its red rock country as a striking backdrop for Westerns. Situated at the mouth of Oak Creek Canyon, one of Arizona's major recreational areas, Sedona attracts artists, retirees, and New Agers (who come to visit Sedona's mystical vortexes).

Once called the dude ranch capital of the world, Wickenburg clings to its Western roots and has restored much of its downtown to its 1880s appearance. There are even a few dude ranches—now called "guest ranches"—still in business.

## 1 Wickenburg

53 miles NW of Phoenix; 61 miles S of Prescott; 128 miles SE of Kingman

Once the Dude Ranch Capital of the World, Wickenburg attracted celebrities and families from all over the country. Those were the days when the West had just stopped being wild, and spending the winter

# Central Arizona

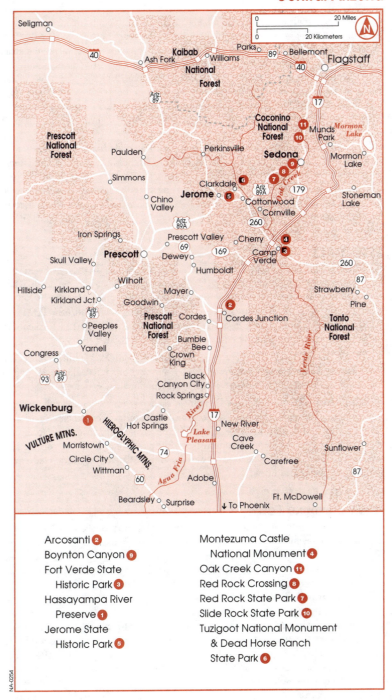

20 Miles
20 Kilometers

Seligman

Kaibab
National
Forest

Ash Fork
Williams
Parks
Bellemont
Flagstaff

Prescott
National
Forest

Paulden
Perkinsville

Coconino
National
Forest

Munds
Park

Mormon
Lake

Sedona

Mormon
Lake

Simmons

Clarkdale
Jerome
Chino
Valley
Cottonwood
Cornville

Oak Creek

Stoneman
Lake

Iron Springs
Prescott Valley
Cherry
Camp
Verde

Skull Valley
Prescott
Dewey

Humboldt

Wilhoit
Mayer
Strawberry
Pine

Hillside
Kirkland
Goodwin
Cordes
Cordes Junction

Kirkland Jct.

Tonto
National
Forest

Peeples
Valley
Prescott
National
Forest

Yarnell

Bumble
Bee
Crown
King

Congress

Black
Canyon City
Rock Springs

Wickenburg

Castle
Hot Springs

VULTURE MTNS.

HIEROGLYPHIC MTNS.

Morristown

Circle City

Wittman

Lake
Pleasant

New River

Cave
Creek

Sunflower

Beardsley
Surprise

Adobe

Carefree

Ft. McDowell

↓ To Phoenix

Verde River

Agua Fria

River

Arcosanti **2**

Boynton Canyon **9**

Fort Verde State
Historic Park **3**

Hassayampa River
Preserve **1**

Jerome State
Historic Park **5**

Montezuma Castle
National Monument **4**

Oak Creek Canyon **11**

Red Rock Crossing **8**

Red Rock State Park **7**

Slide Rock State Park **10**

Tuzigoot National Monument
& Dead Horse Ranch
State Park **6**

NA-0264

in Arizona was both a blessing and an adventure. Today, though the area has only a handful of dude (or guest) ranches still in business, Wickenburg clings to its Wild West image. A chance to ride the range (and maybe play some golf or tennis) is the area's main attraction, and the dude ranches that remain range from rustic to luxurious.

Wickenburg lies at the northern edge of the Sonoran Desert on the banks of the Hassayampa River, one of the last free-flowing rivers in the Arizona desert. The town was founded in 1863 by Prussian gold prospector Henry Wickenburg, who discovered what would eventually become the most profitable gold and silver mine in Arizona: the Vulture Mine.

When the dude ranches flourished back in the 1920s and 1930s, Wickenburg realized that visitors wanted a taste of the Wild West, so the town gave the tenderfoots what they wanted—trail rides, hayrides, cookouts, the works. To play up its Western heritage, Wickenburg has preserved one of its downtown streets much as it may have looked in 1900. If you've come to Arizona searching for the West the way it used to be, Wickenburg is a good place to look. Just don't expect staged shoot-outs in the streets; this ain't Tombstone.

## ESSENTIALS

**GETTING THERE**  From Phoenix, take U.S. 60, which heads northwest and becomes Ariz. 93/U.S. 89. U.S. 89 also comes down from Prescott in the north, while U.S. 60 comes in from I-10 in western Arizona. U.S. 93 comes down from I-40 in northwestern Arizona. **Airport Express of Wickenburg** (☎ **888/684-TOMS** or 520/684-0925) offers a shuttle from the Phoenix Sky Harbor Airport to Wickenburg for $65 for two people (with 24 hours' notice) or $75 without a reservation.

**VISITOR INFORMATION**  For more information about Wickenburg, contact the **Wickenburg Chamber of Commerce,** 216 N. Frontier St., Wickenburg, AZ 85390 (☎ **800/942-5242** or 520/684-5479; www.wickenburgchamber.com).

**SPECIAL EVENTS**  **Gold Rush Days,** held each year on the second full weekend in February, is the biggest festival of the year in Wickenburg. Events include gold panning, a rodeo, and shoot-outs in the streets. On the second full weekend in November, the **Bluegrass Festival** features contests for fiddle and banjo. Each year on the first weekend in December, Wickenburg holds its annual **Cowboy Poetry Gathering,** with lots of poetry and music.

## WHAT TO SEE & DO
### A WALK AROUND TOWN

While Wickenburg's main attraction remains the several guest ranches outside of town, a stroll around downtown Wickenburg provides a glimpse of the Old West. Most of the buildings were built between 1890 and the 1920s (although a few are older), and though not all of these old buildings look their age, there is just enough Western character to make a walk around on foot worthwhile (if the heat isn't too bad).

The old **Santa Fe train station** is now the Wickenburg Chamber of Commerce, which should be your first stop in town. You can pick up a map that tells a bit about the history of the town's older buildings. The brick **post office** building, almost across the street from the train station, once had a ride-up window providing service to people on horseback. **Frontier Street** is preserved as it looked in the early 1900s. The covered sidewalks and false fronts are characteristic of frontier architecture; the false fronts often disguised older adobe buildings that were considered "uncivilized" by settlers from back east. The oldest building in town is the **Etter General Store,** adjacent to the Gold Nugget Restaurant. The old adobe-walled store was built in 1864 and has long since been disguised with a false wooden front.

Two of the town's most unusual attractions aren't buildings at all. The **Jail Tree,** behind the Circle K store at the corner of Wickenburg Way and Tegner Street, is an old mesquite tree that served as the local hoosegow. Outlaws were simply chained to the tree. Their families would often come to visit and have a picnic in the shade of the tree. The second, equally curious, town attraction is the **Wishing Well,** which stands beside the bridge over the Hassayampa. Legend has it that anyone who drinks from the Hassayampa River will never tell the truth again. How it became a wishing well is unclear.

## MUSEUMS & MINES

**Desert Caballeros Western Museum.** 21 N. Frontier St. ☎ **520/684-2272.** Admission $5 adults, $4 senior citizens, $1 children 6–16, free for children under 6. Mon–Sat 10am–5pm, Sun noon–4pm. Closed major holidays.

Wickenburg thrives on its Western heritage, and inside this museum you'll find Western art depicting life on the range in the days of "cowboys and Indians." Though it's not too large, the museum manages to convey a great deal about the history of this part of Arizona. There's an excellent display of colorful minerals and a small collection of Indian artifacts. On the main floor, dioramas depict important scenes from the history of the Wickenburg region. Downstairs, a 1900 street scene from a Western town is re-created, complete with saloon and general store. There are also regularly scheduled special exhibits and an art collection containing work by Remington, Russell, and members of the Cowboy Artists of America.

**Robson's Arizona Mining World.** Ariz. 71, 26 miles west of Wickenburg. ☎ **520/685-2609.** Admission $5 adults, $4.50 seniors, free for children 10 and under. Mon–Fri 10am–4pm, Sat–Sun 8am–6pm. Closed May 1–Oct 1. Head west out of Wickenburg on U.S. 60 and, after 22 miles, turn north on Ariz. 71.

Boasting the world's largest collection of antique mining equipment, this private museum is a must for anyone who is fascinated by Arizona's rich mining history. Located on the site of an old mining camp, the museum consists of 26 buildings filled with antiques. More like a ghost town than a museum, Robson's buildings contain displays pertaining to life in a mining camp. In addition to touring the museum, you can pan for gold or hike to see Native American petroglyphs. A hotel and restaurant are also on the premises.

**The Vulture Mine.** Vulture Mine Rd. ☎ **602/859-2743.** Admission $5 adults, $4 children 6–12, free for children under 6. Oct–Mar daily 8am–4pm; Apr–June closed Tues and Wed; July–Sept closed Mon–Fri. Take U.S. 60 west out of town, turn left on Vulture Mine Rd. and drive 12 miles south.

Lying at the base of Vulture Peak (the most visible landmark in the Wickenburg area), the Vulture Mine was first staked by Henry Wickenburg in 1863. It was this mine that fueled the small gold rush that helped populate this section of the Arizona desert. Today, the Vulture Mine has the feel of a ghost town and can be explored by self-guided tour, or guided tour with prior arrangements.

## A BIRDER'S PARADISE

✪ **Hassayampa River Preserve.** 49614 U.S. 60 (3 miles south of Wickenburg on U.S. 60). ☎ **520/684-2772.** Admission $5 suggested donation (free for Nature Conservancy members). Mid-Sept to mid-May Wed–Sun 8am–5pm; mid-May to mid-Sept Wed–Sun 6am–noon. Closed major holidays.

At one time the Arizona desert was laced with rivers that flowed for most, if not all, of the year. In the past 100 years, however, these rivers, and the riparian (waterside) habitats they once supported, have disappeared at an alarming rate due to the damming of rivers and the lowering water tables caused by the large number of wells drilled throughout the state. Riparian areas support trees and plants that require more water than is usually available in the desert, and this lush growth provides food and shelter for hundreds of species of birds, mammals, and reptiles. Thus the rapidly disappearing riparian areas of the state play an ever more important role in supporting wild plants and animals in the desert. Today, the riparian cottonwood-willow forests of the desert Southwest are considered the country's most endangered forest type.

The Nature Conservancy, a nonprofit organization dedicated to purchasing and preserving threatened and endangered habitats, owns and manages the Hassayampa River Preserve, which is now one of the state's most important bird-watching sites (more than 230 species of birds have been spotted within the preserve). Nature trails lead along the river beneath cottonwoods and willows and past the spring-fed Palm Lake. There is a visitor center and book shop, and naturalist-guided walks are offered. Though the guided walks are free, reservations are required (call the preserve for the current schedule).

## OUTDOOR PURSUITS

Even if you aren't staying at a guest ranch, you can go horseback riding in the Wickenburg area. **No Fences on Moonlight Mesa** (☎ 520/684-3308) is run by Dianna Tangen, who offers guided horseback rides on well-trained quarter horses. Two-hour rides cost $35 per person, and a 6-hour ride in Box Canyon costs $60.

Jeep tours of the area are available through **Wickenburg Jeep Tours,** 295 E. Wickenburg Way (☎ 800/596-5337 or 520/684-0438). Tour prices range from $50 to $70 for adults, and from $25 to $35 for children ages 12 and under.

If you want to play a round of golf, try **Los Caballeros Golf Club,** 1551 S. Vulture Mine Rd. (☎ 520/684-2704), which has been rated one of the best courses in the state. Greens fees are about $105 in peak season and $40 in the summer.

If you'd rather do some hiking, there are a couple of interesting options. Southwest of town at the end of Vulture Mine Road (off U.S. 60), you can climb **Vulture Peak,** which is a steep climb best done in the cooler months. However, the views from up top are well worth the effort. For an easier hike, stop by the Wickenburg Chamber of Commerce information center and get its map of **Box Canyon,** a scenic stretch of the Hassayampa River.

# WHERE TO STAY
## GUEST RANCHES

**Flying E Ranch.** 2801 W. Wickenburg Way, Wickenburg, AZ 85390. ☎ **520/684-2690.** Fax 520/684-5304. www.flyingeranch.com. 17 units. A/C TV. $210–$275 double. Rates include all meals. Minimum stay is 2–4 nights. No credit cards. Closed May–Oct. Drive 4 miles west of town on U.S. 60.

Of the handful of guest ranches still operating in Wickenburg, this is the only real working cattle ranch, and there are 20,000 high, wide, and handsome acres for you and the cattle to roam. Family owned since 1952, this ranch attracts plenty of repeat business, with families finding it a particularly appealing and down-home kind of place. The main lodge features a spacious lounge where guests like to gather by the fireplace. The guest rooms vary in size, but all have Western-style furnishings. There are either twin or king-size beds in the rooms.

**Dining/Diversions:** Three family style meals are served in the wood-paneled dining room, but there's no bar, so you'll need to bring your own liquor. There are also breakfast cookouts, lunch rides, and evening chuck-wagon dinners.

**Amenities:** Horseback riding ($20 to $30 per day additional), small outdoor pool, whirlpool, sauna, exercise room, tennis court, shuffleboard, table tennis, horseshoes, hayrides, guest rodeos, square dances in the barn.

✪ **Kay El Bar Guest Ranch.** Rincon Rd. (off U.S. 93; P.O. Box 2480), Wickenburg, AZ 85358. ☎ **800/684-7583** or 520/684-7593. Fax 520/684-4497. www.kayelbar.com. 10 units, 1 cottage. $275 double; $300 cottage for 2. Rates include all meals. MC, V. Closed May 1 to mid-Oct.

This is the smallest and oldest of the Wickenburg guest ranches, and its old adobe buildings, built between 1914 and 1925, are listed in the National Register of Historic Places. New owners John and Nancy Loftis, who took over in 1997, have added two new rooms. The rest of the ranch, which has been in business for more than 70 years, remains unchanged. However, it is well maintained and quintessentially Wild West in style and decor (telegraph poles hold up the ceiling of the main lodge, where there is a large stone fireplace). The setting, on the bank of the (usually dry) Hassayampa River bed lends the ranch a surprisingly lush feel compared with the arid surrounding landscape. While the cottage and the new Casa Grande room are the most spacious here, the smaller lodge rooms, in the adobe main lodge, have the original Monterey-style furnishings and other classic 1950s dude ranch decor. The ranch has only 60 acres, but it abuts thousands of acres of public lands where guests can ride or hike.

**Dining/Diversions:** A tile floor and beehive fireplace in the dining room provide an authentic Southwestern feel. The meals vary from Chinese to prime rib, and are served in heaping portions. There's also a fully stocked bar.

**Amenities:** Horseback riding (included in rates), small outdoor pool.

✪ **Merv Griffin's Wickenburg Inn and Dude Ranch.** 34801 N. Hwy. 89, Wickenburg, AZ 85390. ☎ **800/942-5362.** Fax 520/684-2981. 63 units. A/C TV TEL. Mid-Feb to May $315–$365 double, $415–$730 casita; June–Sept $198–$215 double, $225–$420 casita; Oct to mid-Feb $278–$320 double, $368–$685 casita. Rates include all meals and horseback riding. 16% gratuity added to all bills. AE, DC, DISC, MC, V.

Located 8 miles north of Wickenburg and 2 miles down a gravel road, the Wickenburg Inn is big country, just the sort of place people dream about when they think of an Arizona ranch vacation. As you enter the ranch down its long driveway, the view takes in nothing but miles of open desert. However, don't expect cowboy accommodations; this place is also as luxurious as most resorts, just without the glitz. With its nature center and educational programs for kids, this is also a good place to bring the family.

The casitas here are cottages built to resemble old Spanish colonial adobes, with red-tile roofs and porches made from rough-hewn logs. Inside are kitchenettes with tile counters, fireplaces, high-beamed ceilings, and wet bars. Deluxe suites have sundecks, and studios have similar styling to suites. Lodge rooms are fairly small, but they offer the most economical choice.

**Dining/Diversions:** Meals are a combination of Southwestern fare and steaks, and a couple of nights each week there are campfire cookouts in the desert.

**Amenities:** Horseback riding and lessons (all-day rides and cattle drives are an additional charge), two pools (one, with sand beach, for kids), whirlpool, tennis courts, self-service laundry, arts-and-crafts center, nature center, jogging trail, tennis lessons, children's programs, baby-sitting, guided nature hikes.

**Rancho de los Caballeros.** 1551 S. Vulture Mine Rd. (off U.S. 60 west of town), Wickenburg, AZ 85390. ☎ **800/684-5030** or 520/684-5484. Fax 520/684-2267. 79 units. A/C TV TEL. Oct–Jan and May $279–$329 double, $399 suite; Feb–Apr $329–$389 double, $499 suite. Rates include all meals (riding and golf packages also available). 14% gratuity added to all bills. No credit cards. Closed mid-May to mid-Oct.

Located on 20,000 acres 2 miles west of Wickenburg, Rancho de los Caballeros is part of an exclusive country club–resort community and as such has more the feel of an exclusive resort than of a guest ranch. Peace and quiet are the keynotes of a visit here, and most guests focus on golfing (the golf course is one of the best in the state) and horseback riding (an additional charge). The classically Southwestern lobby has sand-stone floors, brick walls, open ceiling beams, a large copper fireplace, and a painting by Frederic Remington. The guest rooms have either tile floors or carpeting and hand-crafted Southwestern-style furnishings. Exposed-beam ceilings and Indian rugs complete the Southwestern motif. Some rooms have their own fireplaces. The 12 luxury suites are definitely the best rooms on the ranch.

**Dining:** The dining room features homemade fare prepared from local ingredients, and the dinner menu includes a choice of five main dishes. Proper attire is required in the dining room. Lunch is served buffet style.

**Amenities:** Horseback riding ($30 to $45 per ride), small outdoor pool, four tennis courts, 18-hole golf course ($90 greens fee with cart), pro shop, trap and skeet shooting ($28 per round), laundry service, in-room massages, children's programs, baby-sitting.

## OTHER ACCOMMODATIONS

**Best Western Rancho Grande.** 293 E. Wickenburg Way, Wickenburg, AZ 85390. ☎ **800/854-7235** or 520/684-5445. Fax 520/684-7380. 80 units. A/C TV TEL. $65–$110 double or suite. AE, CB, DC, DISC, MC, V. Pets accepted.

Located right in the heart of downtown Wickenburg, this Best Western is built in Spanish colonial style, with tile roofs, stucco walls, arched colonnades, and tile murals. There's a wide range of room types and prices. At the higher end you get a larger room, a larger bathroom (with a phone), large towels, and a coffeemaker. The motel's "Gay Nineties" theme restaurant and lounge are across the street. The hotel also offers an outdoor pool, a whirlpool, and a tennis court.

**Historic Sombrero Ranch Bed & Breakfast.** 31910 W. Brralliar Rd., Wickenburg, AZ 85390. ☎ **520/684-0222.** www.wick-web.com/sombrero. 5 units. $75–$85 double. MC, V. Located 1 mile north of town off U.S. 89.

If you aren't up for doing the dude ranch thing but want to spend some time out Wickenburg way, consider this comfortable B&B. Set atop a steep hill on 49 acres of desert land, the lodge has a commanding view of the town and its surroundings. The lodge itself dates from 1937 and was built in mission revival style. Rooms are simply furnished, though spacious. For relaxing, there's a swimming pool in the garden.

## WHERE TO DINE

✪ **Griff's at the Wickenburg Inn.** Ariz. 89 (Prescott Hwy.). ☎ **520/684-7811.** Reservations recommended. Lunch items $6–$8; main courses $8–$23 at dinner; barbecue cookouts $25 adults, $15 children 11 and under. AE, DC, DISC, MC, V. Daily 7–10am, 11:30–2:30pm, and Sun–Mon and Wed–Fri 5:30–9pm. 8 miles north of town on Ariz. 89. AMERICAN.

While most of the people eating here are usually guests of the ranch, the restaurant is open to the public by advance reservation and is one of the best places in the area for a meal if you aren't already staying at another guest ranch. The remote setting amid rolling desert hills and the old-fashioned Southwestern feel of the lodge make a meal here a very Arizona experience. Stone and raw wood give the dining room a rugged feeling, but creature comforts are not overlooked. Main courses are typically ranch fare (meatloaf, turkey and T-bone steak). The restaurant is closed on Tuesday and Saturday nights, when cookouts are offered. Call for cookout reservations and starting time.

**House Berlin.** 169 E. Wickenburg Way. ☎ **520/684-5044.** Main courses $9–$15. MC, V. Tues–Sun 11:30am–2:30pm and 5–9pm. GERMAN/CONTINENTAL.

For some strange reason, Germans seem to love the desert, so it shouldn't really come as a surprise that good German food is available in Wickenburg. The restaurant is small and casual and serves a mix of German and other continental dishes. Because of bad visibility when exiting from the restaurant's parking lot, it's a good idea to park on the street.

**Rancho de los Caballeros.** 1551 S. Vulture Mine Rd. ☎ **520/684-5484.** Reservations required. Jackets required for men. Lunch $11–$14, complete dinner $23. No credit cards. Mon–Sat 12:30–1:30pm and 6:30–8:30pm, Sun noon–2pm (buffet lunch) and 6:30–8:30pm. Closed mid-May to mid-Oct. CONTINENTAL/SOUTHWESTERN.

Wickenburg's most exclusive guest ranch also opens its restaurant to the public. The menu is fairly conservative, and although it changes daily, you always have a choice of two soups, two salads, five main courses, and six or seven desserts. You might start your meal with onion soup followed by a smoked-salmon salad and then move on to a choice of roast New York sirloin, chicken Caesar salad, Southwest halibut, wild mushroom chicken, or penne pasta with Italian sausage. For dessert, you might choose Mexican flan, pecan pie, or a peach-berry crisp. Men are required to wear a jacket, and women must also dress appropriately.

## EN ROUTE TO PRESCOTT

Between Wickenburg and Prescott, Ariz. 89 climbs up out of the desert at the town of **Yarnell,** which lies at the top of a steep stretch of road. The landscape around Yarnell is a jumble of weather-worn granite boulders that give the town a unique appearance. Several little craft and antiques shops here are worth a stop, but the town's main claim to fame is the **Shrine of St. Joseph of the Mountains,** which is known for its carved stone stations of the cross.

## 2  Prescott

100 miles N of Phoenix; 60 miles SW of Sedona; 87 miles SW of Flagstaff

A stately courthouse on a tree-shaded square, a well-preserved historic downtown business district, and quite a few old Victorian homes give Prescott a timeless American hometown atmosphere. However, the main charm of Prescott is that it has just about everything a small town should have: a soda fountain (Deja Vu), a burger shop (Kendall's), an 1890s saloon (The Palace), an old cattlemen's hotel (Hassayampa Inn), a brew pub (Prescott Brewing Company); a French creperie (Provence), and a European-style cafe (Café St. Michaels). Several small museums, a couple of historic hotels, and the nearby Prescott National Forest all ensure that visitors with a diverse range of interests spend time here.

The town's Anglo history dates from 1863, when the Walker party discovered gold in the mountains of central Arizona. Soon miners were flocking to the area to seek their own fortunes. A year later, in 1864, Arizona became a U.S. territory, and the new town of Prescott, located right in the center of Arizona, was made the territorial capital. Prescott later lost its statewide influence when the capital moved to Phoenix, but because of the importance of ranching and mining in central Arizona, Prescott continued to be a very important regional town. Today, Prescott has become an upscale retirement community, as retirees (primarily from California) rediscover Arizona's once-bustling territorial capital and the mild year-round climate here. In summer, Prescott is also a popular weekend getaway for Phoenicians, since it is usually 20° cooler here than it is in Phoenix.

## ESSENTIALS

**GETTING THERE**    Prescott is at the junction of U.S. 89, U.S. 89A, and Ariz. 69. If you're coming from Phoenix, take the Cordes Junction exit (Exit 262) from I-17. If you're coming from Flagstaff, the most direct route is I-17 to Ariz. 169 to Ariz. 69. From Sedona, just take U.S. 89A all the way.

There is regularly scheduled service between Prescott's Ernest A. Love Airport, on U.S. 89, and the Phoenix Sky Harbor Airport on **America West** airlines (☎ **800/ 235-9292** for schedule information).

Shuttle "U" provides shuttle service between Prescott and the Phoenix Sky Harbor Airport. The fare is $22 one way and $39 round-trip. Phone ☎ **800/304-6114** (out of the Prescott area) or 520/772-6114 for schedule information.

**ORIENTATION**    U.S. 89 comes into Prescott on the northeast side of town, where it joins with Ariz. 69 coming in from the east. Five miles north of town, Ariz. 89A from Sedona also merges with U.S. 89. The main street into town is **Gurley Street,** which forms the north side of the Courthouse Plaza. **Montezuma Street,** also known as Whiskey Row, forms the west side of the plaza. If you continue south on Montezuma Street, you'll be on U.S. 89 heading toward Wickenburg.

**VISITOR INFORMATION**    For more information on Prescott, contact the **Prescott Chamber of Commerce,** 115 W. Goodwin St. (P.O. Box 1147), Prescott, AZ 86302 (☎ **800/266-7534** or 520/445-2000).

**GETTING AROUND**    If you need to rent a car, contact **Budget** (☎ **800/ 527-0700** or 520/778-3806) or **Enterprise Rent-A-Car** (☎ **800/RENT-A-CAR** or 520/778-6506). If you need a taxi, call **Ace City Cab** (☎ **520/445-1616**).

**SPECIAL EVENTS**    The ✪ **World's Oldest Rodeo** is held each year in early July as part of the city's Prescott Frontier Days celebration. Also included in this celebration is a Western art show, a golf tournament, a carnival, and a parade. Territorial Days, held in early to mid-June, is another big annual festival with special art exhibits, performances, tournaments, races, and lots of food and free entertainment. In mid-July, the Sharlot Hall Museum hosts the **Prescott Indian Art Market,** and on the third weekend in August the **Arizona Cowboy Poets Gathering** takes place there as well. Prescott is also officially recognized as Arizona's Christmas City. During December, the city is decked out with lights, and there are numerous holiday events.

## EXPLORING THE TOWN

A walk around the **Courthouse Plaza** should be your introduction to Prescott. The stately old courthouse in the middle of the tree-shaded plaza sets the tone for the whole town. The building, far too large for a small regional town such as this, dates from the days when Prescott was the capital of the Arizona Territory. Under the big shade trees of this plaza, you'll find several large bronze statues of cowboys and soldiers.

Surrounding the courthouse and extending north for a block is Prescott's **historic business district.** Stroll around admiring the brick buildings, and you'll realize that Prescott was once a very important place. Duck into an old saloon or the lobby of one of the town's two historic hotels, and you'll understand that the town was also part of the Wild West. After you've gotten a taste of Prescott, there are several museums, listed below, you might like to visit.

To learn more about the history of Prescott, contact **Prescott Historical Tours,** 815 Bertrand Ave. (☎ **520/445-4567**), which charges a $7 per person rate for an informative tour of the city. Call for a reservation.

✪ **Sharlot Hall Museum. 415 W. Gurley St.** ☎ **520/445-3122.** Admission by suggested donation, $4 adult, $3 senior citizens, $5 family. Apr 1–Oct 31 Mon–Sat 10am–5pm, Sun 1–5pm; Nov 1–Mar 31 Mon–Sat 10am–4pm, Sun 1–5pm. Closed Thanksgiving, Christmas, and New Year's Day.

In 1882, at the age of 12, Sharlot Hall traveled to the Arizona territory with her parents. From an early age she was fascinated by frontier life. As an adult, she became a writer and historian and began collecting artifacts from Arizona's pioneer days. From 1909 to 1911 she was the territorial historian, an official government position. In 1928 she opened this museum in Prescott's **Old Governor's Mansion,** a log home that was built in 1864. Eventually, through the donations of others and the activities of the local historical society, the museum grew into the present complex of historic buildings and gardens.

In addition to the Old Governor's Mansion, which is furnished much as it might have been when it was built, there are several other interesting buildings that can be toured. The **Frémont House** was built in 1875 for the fifth territorial governor. Its traditional wood-frame construction shows how quickly Prescott grew from a remote logging and mining camp into a civilized little town. The 1877 **Bashford House** reflects the Victorian architecture that was popular throughout the country around the turn of the century. The **Sharlot Hall Building** was built of stone and pine logs in 1934 and now houses museum exhibits on prehistoric and historic Native American cultures and territorial Arizona. Other buildings of interest include a blacksmith's shop, a schoolhouse, a gazebo, a ranch house built by Sharlot Hall, and an old windmill.

The museum's rose garden honors famous women of Arizona. Every year in early summer, artisans, craftspeople, and costumed exhibitors participate in the **Folk Arts Fair.**

**Phippen Museum.** 4701 U.S. 89N. ☎ **520/778-1385.** Admission $3 adults, $2 seniors and students, children 12 and under free. Mon and Wed–Sat 10am–4pm, Sun 1–4pm.

If you're a fan of classic Western art, you won't want to miss this small museum. Located on a hill a few miles north of town, the Phippen Museum exhibits works by both established Western artists and newcomers and is named after the first president of the prestigious Cowboy Artists of America organization. The museum also displays historical artifacts and photos that help place the artwork in the context of the history of the region. Each year on Memorial Day weekend the museum sponsors the **Phippen Western Art Show.** In the museum store, more than 100 Arizona artists are represented.

**The Smoki Museum.** 147 N. Arizona St. ☎ **520/445-1230.** Admission $2. May–Sept Mon–Tues and Thurs–Sat 10am–4pm, Sun 1–4pm; Oct Fri–Sun 10am–4pm. Closed Nov–Apr.

This interesting little museum, which houses a collection of Native American artifacts in a historic stone building, is named for the fictitious Smoki tribe. The tribe was dreamed up in 1921 by a group of non-Indians who wanted to inject some new life into Prescott's July 4th celebrations. Despite its phony origins, the museum contains genuine artifacts and basketry from many different tribes, mainly Southwestern.

## ENJOYING THE OUTDOORS

Prescott's most readily recognizable natural landmark is **Thumb Butte,** a rocky outcropping that towers over the forest just west of town. A trail leads nearly to the top of this butte, and from the saddle near the top of the butte there is a panoramic vista of the entire region. To hike up Thumb Butte, head west out of town on Gurley Street, which becomes Thumb Butte Road. Follow the road until you see the National Forest signs, after which there's a parking lot and picnic area and a trailhead for the trail that leads up the butte. Parking costs $2. The trail itself is very steep but is paved much of the way. The very summit of the butte is a popular rock-climbing spot. An alternative return trail makes a loop hike possible.

A few miles north of town is an unusual and very scenic area known as the **Granite Dells.** Here, jumbled hills of rounded granite suddenly jut up from the landscape, creating a maze of huge boulders and smooth rock. Set in this strange geological feature is an artificial lake that makes the scene even more picturesque. This is a great place to go for a walk or to shoot some photos. The best access to the Granite Dells area is at Watson Lake Park just a few miles north of Prescott on Ariz. 89.

Prescott is situated on the edge of a wide expanse of high plains with the pine forests of **Prescott National Forest** at its back. There are hiking trails, several lakes, and campgrounds within the national forest. Of particular note is the Granite Mountain Wilderness northwest of town. Here you'll find excellent hiking opportunities. For maps and information, stop by the Prescott National Forest Office, 344 S. Cortez St. (☎ **520/771-4700**).

If you want to explore the area on horseback, there are several options. **Trail Horse Adventures** (☎ **800/SADDLE-UP** or 520/771-8303), offers half-day rides ($83.50 per person), as well as shorter and longer rides, including overnight rides in Prescott National Forest. **Rafter 6 Outdoor Adventures,** P.O. Box 618, Chino Valley, AZ 86323 (☎ **520/636-5007**), does everything from 1½-hour rides ($28) to overnight cowboy campouts to the Upper Verde River ($150 per day) to chuck wagon rides ($60 to $85). On the way, you stop at an Indian ruin. **Prescott Ranch** (☎ **800/684-7433** or 520/636-9737), located about 25 minutes north of Prescott off Ariz. 89 near the town of Paulden, also offers guided trail rides in the Prescott National Forest. A 1-hour trail ride is $15. Also in the Paulden area, the **Double D Ranch** (☎ **520/636-0418**), which also operates a B&B, leads all-day rides into the Prescott National Forest. These rides visit ancient Indian ruins and even include a bit of six-gun and Winchester practice. Rides run $65 to $150 per person depending on the number of people in the group.

Reasonably priced golfing is available at the **Antelope Hills Golf Courses,** 1 Perkins Dr. (☎ **800/972-6818** in Arizona, or 520/776-7888).

## SHOPPING

Downtown Prescott is filled with antiques stores, especially along North Cortez Street. In the Hotel St. Michael's shopping arcade, check out **Hotel Trading,** 110 S. Montezuma St. (☎ **520/778-7276**), an Indian arts shop that carries some genuine antique Native American artifacts at reasonable prices. Also in this same block of Montezuma Street, is the **Arts Prescott Cooperative Gallery,** 134 S. Montezuma St. (☎ **520/776-7717**), a cooperative of local artists. Prices here are very reasonable.

## WHERE TO STAY
### EXPENSIVE

**Double D Ranch Bed and Breakfast.** P.O. Box 334, Paulden, AZ 86334. ☎ **520/636-0418.** www.virtualcities.com. 2 units. $150 double ($135 if 2 or more nights). Rates include full breakfast. MC, V.

Located out in the ranch country north of Prescott, this B&B is something of a miniature guest ranch—there are lots of horses, chickens, and other ranch animals, and guests tend to spend their days horseback riding. At the end of a day in the saddle, you can soak your sore muscles in the inn's unique "cowboy hot tub," which is made from a horse watering trough! Innkeepers Doug and Denise Dipietro (the Double Ds of the name) take only one group of guests at a time, so when you show up, you'll have the unusual rammed-earth ranch house all to yourself. With its flagstone floors and contemporary decor, the house is much more 1990s than 1890s. All-day rides into the adjacent national forest run $65 to $150 per person, including lunch, depending on the size of the group. For $40 per person, Denise, a certified chef, can prepare gourmet dinners. Family style dinners are available for $15 per person.

✪ **Hassayampa Inn.** 122 E. Gurley St., Prescott, AZ 86301. ☎ **800/322-1927** or 520/778-9434. Fax 520/445-8590. E-mail: inn@primenet.com. 68 units. A/C TV TEL. Apr–Oct $109–$130 double, $150–$185 suite; Nov–Mar $99–$120 double, $140–$170 suite. Rates include full breakfast. AE, DC, DISC, MC, V.

The Hassayampa Inn, which is listed on the National Register of Historic Places, was built as a luxury hotel in 1927 and evokes the time when Prescott was the bustling capital of the Arizona Territory. In the lobby, stenciled exposed ceiling beams, wrought-iron chandeliers, and arched doorways all reflect a Southwestern heritage. Each guest room is unique and features either original furnishings or antiques. One room is even said to be haunted, and any hotel employee will be happy to tell you the story of the ill-fated honeymooners whose ghosts are said to reside here.

**Dining/Diversions:** The Peacock Room exudes the same classic elegance as the rest of the hotel. A small lounge with art nouveau styling provides a quiet place to have a drink in the evening.

**Amenities:** Room service, laundry service, access to nearby health club.

**Prescott Resort, Conference Center and Casino.** 1500 Hwy. 69, Prescott, AZ 86301. ☎ **800/96-PINES** or 520/776-1666. Fax 520/776-8544. www.prescottresort.com. 160 units. A/C TV TEL. $129–$229 double; $149–$229 suite. AE, CB, DC, DISC, JCB, MC, V.

This is Prescott's only full-service resort hotel; and though its focus is on conferences, its small casino is aimed at siphoning off some of the business that once went to Laughlin or Las Vegas. Built high on a hill overlooking the city and the surrounding valley and mountains, the resort has the best view of any lodging in Prescott. However, with the red fluorescent lights and the "win this car" car parked in the middle of the lobby, it's more Vegas glitz than Prescott history. The town's Western heritage is played up only in the overabundance of Western art that covers the walls leading out from the lobby. Public rooms aside, the guest rooms are spacious and comfortable, and each has its own balcony overlooking the valley.

**Dining/Diversions:** The dining room here offers a stunning panorama to accompany the fine meals. For a drink and conversation, there's a lobby lounge. The 24-hour casino is the resort's biggest draw for many guests.

**Amenities:** Outdoor pool, tennis courts, racquetball courts, exercise room, art gallery, beauty salon, room service, valet/laundry service.

## MODERATE

**Hotel Vendome—Clarion Carriage House Inn.** 230 S. Cortez St., Prescott, AZ 86303. ☎ **888/468-3583** or 520/776-0900. Fax 520/771-0395. www.vendomehotel.com. 21 units. TV TEL. $69–$149 double; $99–$169 suite. Rates include continental breakfast. AE, DC, DISC, MC, V.

Built in 1917 as a lodging house, this restored two-story brick building is only 2 blocks from the action of Whiskey Row but far enough away from the noise that you can get a good night's sleep. The guest rooms are outfitted with new furnishings, but some still have original claw-foot tubs in the bathrooms. Others have modern oval tubs, and all have built-in water filters, air filters, and overhead fans. Of course, this hotel has its own resident ghost as well. Not quite as luxurious as the Hassayampa, yet not as basic as the St. Michael, this hotel offers a good middle-price choice for anyone who wants to stay in a historic hotel but doesn't want to do the standard B&B thing.

**The Marks House Victorian Bed & Breakfast.** 203 E. Union St., Prescott, AZ 86303. ☎ **800/370-6275** or 520/778-4632. www.virtualcities.com/ons/az/r/azr2602.htm. 4 units. $75–$120 double. Rates include full breakfast. DISC, MC, V.

Located high on a hill only a block from the courthouse, this large Victorian inn has the best views of any B&B in town. While not as immaculate as some of the others, The Marks House has the most authentic atmosphere and some of the most interesting rooms. The Princess Victoria room features an unusual copper bath house–style tub, while in the Queen Anne room, you'll find a claw-foot tub in one corner of the room and a small turret sitting area in another. The evening social hour is a good time to get to know the innkeepers. While so many B&Bs claim to be just like Grandma's house, this one really is.

⚙ **Rocamadour Bed & Breakfast for (Rock) Lovers.** 3386 N. Hwy. 89, Prescott, AZ 86301. ☎ **888/771-1933** or 520/771-1933. 4 units. A/C TV TEL. $95–$135 double (discounts for stays of 2 or more nights); $195 suite. Rates include full breakfast. No credit cards.

The Granite Dells, just north of Prescott, are the area's most amazing feature, and should you wish to stay amid these jumbled boulders, there is no better choice than Rocamadour. At this inn you'll enjoy luxurious surroundings in the midst of a fantastic landscape. Owners Mike and Twila Coffey honed their innkeeping skills as owners of a 40-room château in France before moving to Prescott, and pieces of antique furniture from the château can now be found throughout this inn. The most elegant pieces are in the Chambre Trucy, which also has an amazing underlit whirlpool tub. For those who really want to be in the midst of the rocks, there is a cottage built into the boulders with a large whirlpool tub on its deck. The unique setting, engaging innkeepers, and thoughtful details everywhere you turn make this one of the state's must-stay inns. If you need more room and your own kitchen, there is the Suite Amérique, which is filled with Americana.

### INEXPENSIVE

In addition to the following hotel, Prescott has several budget chain motels. See appendix B for toll-free phone numbers. Try the **Super 8 Motel,** 1105 E. Sheldon St. (☎ **520/776-1282**), charging $47 to $58 double; and **Motel 6,** 1111 E. Sheldon St. (☎ **520/776-0160**), charging $42 to $52 double.

**Hotel St. Michael.** 205 W. Gurley St., Prescott, AZ 86301. ☎ **800/678-3757** or 520/776-1999. Fax 520/776-7318. 75 units. A/C TV TEL. $50–$80 double; $75–$95 suite. Rates include continental breakfast. AE, DISC, MC, V.

Located right on Whiskey Row, this restored hotel complete with resident ghost and the oldest elevator in Prescott, offers a historic setting at budget prices (don't expect the best of mattresses or most stylish furnishings). All rooms are different; and some have bathtubs but no showers. Among the St. Michael's past guests are Teddy Roosevelt and Barry Goldwater. The casual Café St. Michael, where the complimentary breakfast is served, has brick walls and a pressed-tin ceiling and overlooks Courthouse Square.

## WHERE TO DINE

The best place in town to savor a mocha and pastry while watching the world go by is at the **Café St. Michael,** 205 W. Gurley St. (☎ **520/776-1999**), on the ground floor of the historic hotel of the same name. With its high ceiling, brick walls, and battered wood floor, this place has the feel of an old saloon and offers a view of the city's 19th-century courthouse. Light meals are also available. For an authentic and tasty crepe, try **Provence** (☎ **520/445-2325**), a little espresso bar at 108 W. Gurley St. For a milk shake, an ice cream soda, or an espresso, don't miss **Déjà Vu,** 134 N. Cortez St. (☎ **520/445-6732**), which is inside an old saloon that now houses an antiques store.

## MODERATE

**Murphy's.** 201 N. Cortez St. (a block from Courthouse Plaza). ☎ **520/445-4044.** Reservations recommended for parties of 5 or more. Main courses $15–$25. AE, DISC, MC, V. Sun–Thurs 11am–10pm, Fri–Sat 11am–11pm. AMERICAN.

Murphy's, housed in the oldest mercantile building in the Southwest, has long been Prescott's favorite special-occasion restaurant and is best known for its mesquite-broiled prime rib and excellent, traditional seafood dishes. The building, which is on the National Register of Historic Places, was built in 1890, and many of the shop's original shelves can be seen in the restaurant's lounge area. Sparkling leaded-glass doors usher diners into a high-ceilinged room with fans revolving slowly overhead. In keeping with the historical nature of the building, antiques are on display throughout the restaurant.

✪ **The Palace.** 120 S. Montezuma St. ☎ **520/541-1996.** Reservations suggested on weekends. Main courses $6–$10 at lunch, $11.50–$19 at dinner. AE, MC, V. Sun–Thurs 10am–3pm and 4:30–9:30pm, Fri–Sat 10am–3pm and 4:30–10:30pm. SOUTHWEST/STEAK/SEAFOOD.

The Palace is the oldest frontier bar in Arizona (in business for more than 120 years) and in 1996 was beautifully renovated and returned to the way it might have looked around the turn of the century. This grand hall tends to be noisy and bustling and is a good place for people watching. The menu includes choices such as a tasty appetizer of grilled tiger prawns wrapped in basil and prosciutto; citrus salmon; corn chowder; and generous portions of steak, pork chops, and seafood. The bar area in front is an alternative to waiting for a table, but it can be smoky. If you're in town for only one meal, have it here.

✪ **The Rose Restaurant.** 234 S. Cortez St. ☎ **520/777-8308.** Reservations recommended. Main courses $13–$26. AE, DISC, MC, V. Wed–Sun 5–9:30pm. CONTINENTAL.

Chef Linda Rose worked for nearly a decade at the Hassayampa Hotel's Peacock Room, and now she brings her creative flair to her own restaurant. The manicotti and double-cut lamb chops are house specialties well worth trying. The dining rooms here are small, and tables are close together, but that doesn't dissuade both locals and visitors from enjoying the excellent food and reasonably priced wines. Dishes are attractively presented (often with a rose of whipped yam on the plate), and there is usually a wide selection of desserts.

## INEXPENSIVE

**Gurley St. Grill.** 230 W. Gurley St. ☎ **520/445-3388.** Reservations only for parties of 5 or more at dinnertime. Main courses $6–$14. AE, DISC, MC, V. Daily 11am–10pm; late-night menu daily 10am–midnight. ITALIAN/AMERICAN.

The Gurley Street Grill is located a block off Courthouse Plaza and is run by the same people who operate Murphy's. Brick walls, ceiling fans, and beveled glass reflect the building's historic heritage. You'll see lots of families who have come for the pastas, pizzas, steaks, burgers, and rotisserie chicken. At lunch, the Sonoran black-bean turkey chili is a good bet, while at dinner, the roast chicken with Asiago cheese and pasta is not only delicious but plentiful. The restaurant's bar has many microbrews on tap and attracts a lively, professional crowd. Service here can be unpredictable.

**Kendall's Famous Burgers & Ice Cream.** 113 S. Cortez St. ☎ **520/778-3658.** Burgers $4–$6. No credit cards. Mon–Sat 11am–8pm, Sun 11am–6pm. BURGERS.

Ask anyone in town where to get the best burger in Prescott and you'll be sent to Kendall's on Courthouse Plaza. This bright and noisy luncheonette serves juicy burgers with a choice of 14 condiments. A basket of fries is a mandatory accompaniment.

**Prescott Brewing Company.** 130 W. Gurley St. ☎ **520/771-2795.** Main courses $5.75–$12. AE, DISC, MC, V. Sun–Thurs 11am–10pm, Fri–Sat 11am–11pm. AMERICAN/PUB FOOD.

Popular primarily with a younger crowd, this brew pub keeps a good selection of its own beers and ales on tap, but is just as popular for its cheap and filling meals. Fajita fondue is a specialty, and of course, there are such pub standards as fish-and-chips, bangers and mash, and not-so-standard spent-grain beer-dough pizzas and vegetarian dishes. The Caesar salad with chipotle dressing packs a wallop. And what better accompaniment to a good wheat beer than a slice of rich, heavy chocolate ale cake?

## PRESCOTT AFTER DARK

Back in the days when Prescott was the territorial capital and a booming mining town, it supported dozens of rowdy saloons, most of which were concentrated along Montezuma Street on the west side of Courthouse Plaza. This section of town was known as **Whiskey Row,** and legend has it that there was a tunnel from the courthouse to one of the saloons so lawmakers wouldn't have to be seen ducking into the saloons during regular business hours. On July 14, 1900, a fire consumed most of Whiskey Row, including 25 saloons and bawdy houses. However, concerned cowboys and miners managed to drag the tremendously heavy bar of the Palace Saloon across the street before it was damaged by the fire. (The saloon continued to do business in its new open-air location.)

Today Whiskey Row is no longer the sort of place where respectable women shouldn't be seen, although it does still have a few noisy saloons with genuine Wild West flavor. Most of these feature live country music on weekends and are the dark, dank sorts of places that cowboys tend to gravitate to. If, however, you'd rather see what this street's saloons looked like back in the old days, drop by **The Palace,** 120 S. Montezuma St. (☎ **520/541-1996**), which though now primarily a restaurant, still has a classic bar area up front. Just push through the swinging doors and say howdy to the fellow with the six-guns or shotgun; he's the owner. A couple of times a month, The Palace presents dinner theatre performances; call to find out if anything is happening while you are in town. Just around the corner, you'll find the **Prescott Brewing Company,** 130 W. Gurley St. (☎ **520/771-2795**), which is today's answer to the saloons of yore, brewing and serving its own microbrews. Good pub fare is also served.

If you're feeling lucky, head up to **Bucky's Casino,** 1500 Hwy. 69 (☎ **800/ SLOTS-44**), which is located at the Prescott Resort. In addition to 300 slot machines, the casino has a poker room and keno. Across the street from the entrance to the Prescott Resort, you'll find the **Yavapai Casino,** which is under the same management and offers slot machines and bingo.

The **Prescott Fine Arts Association,** 208 N. Marina St. (☎ **520/445-3286**), sponsors plays, music performances, children's theater, and art exhibits (tickets $9 to $12). The association's main building is a former church that was built in 1899 and is on the National Register of Historic Places.

## EN ROUTE TO OR FROM PHOENIX: INNOVATIVE ARCHITECTURE & FRESH PRODUCE

If you have an interest in innovative architecture, you may want to continue another 25 miles south from Camp Verde on I-17 to Cordes Junction and Italian architect Paolo Soleri's vision of the future. ✪ **Arcosanti** (☎ **520/632-7135**) is the slow realization of Soleri's dream of a city that merges architecture and ecology.

Soleri, who came to Arizona to study with Frank Lloyd Wright at Taliesin West, envisions a compact, energy-efficient city that disturbs the natural landscape as little as possible—and that's just what's rising out of the Arizona desert here at Arcosanti. The organic design of this city built of cast concrete will fascinate both students of architecture and those with only a passing interest in the discipline. Arcosanti has been built primarily with the help of students and volunteers who come and live here for various lengths of time.

To help finance the construction, Soleri designs and sells **wind-bells** that are cast in bronze or made of ceramic. These distinctive bells are available at the gift shop here.

If you'd like to stay overnight, there are basic accommodations ($25 to $75 double per night) available by reservation, but you must arrive before 5pm. You'll also find a bakery and cafe on the premises. Arcosanti is open daily from 9am to 5pm, and **tours** are held hourly from 10am to 4pm ($5 suggested donation).

If you crave a taste of the country life, stop by **Young's Farm** (☎ **520/632-7272**), a country store at the intersection of Ariz. 69 and 169 between I-17 and Prescott. This country farm stand in the middle of the desert sells a wide variety of produce as well as gourmet and unusual foods. You might find any of a number of various seasonal festivals going on here, such as a Pumpkin Festival during the month of October.

## 3 Jerome

35 miles NE of Prescott; 28 miles W of Sedona; 130 miles N of Phoenix

Clinging to the slopes of Cleopatra Hill high on Mingus Mountain, the former copper-mining town of Jerome beckons to today's travelers just as it once beckoned to miners. It was never easy mining the copper ore beneath Jerome. The high elevation made shipping ore an expensive proposition that eventually prompted mining interests to build a smelter at the base of the mountain. For many years the mountain's copper ore was mined using an 88-mile-long network of underground railroads. However, in 1918, a fire broke out in the mine tunnels, and mining companies were forced to abandon the tunnels in favor of open-pit mining. One unforeseen hazard of this type of mining was the effect dynamiting would have on a town built on a 30° slope. Buildings in downtown Jerome began sliding downhill, and eventually the town jail broke loose and slid 225 feet down (now that's a jailbreak).

Between 1883 and 1953, Jerome experienced an economic roller-coaster ride as the price of copper rose and fell. In the early 1950s, when it was no longer profitable to mine the copper ore of Cleopatra Hill, the last mining company shut down its operations and almost everyone left town. By the early 1960s Jerome looked as if it were on its way to becoming just another ghost town, but then artists, who had discovered the phenomenal views and dirt-cheap rents, began moving in and slowly the would-be ghost town developed a reputation as an artists' community. Soon tourists began visiting to see, and buy, the artwork that was being created in Jerome, and old store fronts turned into galleries.

Today Jerome is far from a ghost town, and on summer weekends the streets are packed with visitors shopping at galleries and crafts shops. The same remote and rugged setting that once made it difficult and expensive to mine copper here has now become one of the town's main attractions.

Jerome is divided into two sections by an elevation of 1,500 vertical feet, with the upper part of town 2,000 feet above the Verde Valley. On a clear day (of which there are quite a few), the view from up here is stupendous—it's possible to see for more than 50 miles, with the red rocks of Sedona, the Mogollon Rim, and the San Francisco Peaks all visible in the distance.

Because Jerome is built on a 30° slope, streets through town switchback from one level of houses to the next. Old brick and wood-frame buildings built into the side of the mountain have windows gazing out into the distance. Narrow streets, alleys, and stairways connect the different levels of town.

In recent years the newly arrived artists began to restore and renovate the old houses. Residences, studios, shops, and galleries stand side by side looking (externally, anyway) much as they did when Jerome was an active mining town. The entire town has been designated a National Historic Landmark.

## ESSENTIALS

**GETTING THERE**    Jerome is on Ariz. 89A roughly halfway between Sedona and Prescott. Coming from Phoenix, take Ariz. 279 from Camp Verde.

**VISITOR INFORMATION**    For information on Jerome, contact the **Jerome Chamber of Commerce,** 50 Main Ave. (P.O. Drawer K), Jerome, AZ 86331 (☎ 520/634-2900).

## EXPLORING THE TOWN

Wandering the streets, soaking up the atmosphere, and shopping are the main pastimes in Jerome. However, before you launch yourself on a shopping tour, you can learn about the town's past at the **Jerome State Historic Park,** off U.S. 89A on Douglas Road in the lower section of town (☎ 520/634-5381). Located in a mansion that was built in 1916 as a home for mine owner "Rawhide Jimmy" Douglas and as a hotel for visiting mining executives, the Jerome State Historic Park contains both exhibits on mining and a few of the mansion's original furnishings. Built on a hill above Douglas's Little Daisy Mine, the mansion overlooks Jerome and, dizzyingly far below, the Verde Valley. Constructed of adobe bricks made on the site, the mansion contained a wine cellar, billiard room, marble shower, steam heat, and a central vacuum system. The mansion's library has been restored as a period room, while other rooms contain exhibits on copper mining and the history of Jerome. Various types of colorful ores are on display, along with the tools that were once used to extract the ore from the mountain. Admission is $2.50 for adults, $1 for children 7 to 13, and free for children 6 and under. It's open daily from 8am to 5pm, except Christmas Day.

To learn even more about Jerome's history, you can take a guided tour of town with Nancy Rayne Smith, who operates **NRSmith Enterprises** (☎ 520/634-8654). Tours are $10 per person with a $25 minimum for a 1½- to 2-hour tour. To get a wider perspective on both the mining history and Native American history of this area, try a four-wheel-drive tour with **Copper Canyon Tours** (☎ 520/634-3497), which is operated by Clay Miller (who also works as a guide on the nearby Verde Canyon Railroad and is a fount of information on this region). Clay also offers hiking explorations and shamanistic counseling. For that classic mining town tourist trap experience, follow the signs up the hill from downtown Jerome to the **Gold King Mine and Ghost Town,** where you can see lots of old, rusting, metal mining equipment.

However, most visitors come to Jerome for the shopping. The shops offer an eclectic blend of urban art, chic jewelry, one-of-a-kind handmade fashions, unusual imports and gifts, and the inevitable tacky souvenirs and ice cream (alas, no place stays undiscovered for long anymore; at least there's no McDonald's). To see what local artists are creating, stop in at the **Jerome Artists Cooperative** (☎ 520/639-4276), which is on the west side of the street where Hull Avenue and Main Street fork as you come up the hill into town. The **Raku Gallery,** 250 Hull Ave. (☎ 520/639-0239), has gallery space on two floors and walls of glass across the back of both floors. If you can tear your eyes from the view out the back (yes, those are the red rocks of Sedona in the distance), you'll find lots of interesting art by artists from around the country. The **Jerome Gallery,** 240 Hull Ave. (☎ 520/634-7033), also has good quality raku ware and ceramics. **Sky Fire,** 140 Main St. (☎ **520/634-8081**), has a fascinating collection of Southwestern and ethnic gifts and furnishings. On this same block, you'll also find ✪ **Nellie Bly,** 136 Main St. (☎ **520/634-0255**), with a room full of colorful, handmade kaleidoscopes (ask to see the kaleidoscopes in the back room) and **Nellie Bly II,** 130 Main St. (☎ **520/634-7825**), which specializes in jewelry made from semiprecious stones.

## WHERE TO STAY

**Ghost City Inn.** 541 N. Main St. (P.O. Box 382), Jerome, AZ 86331. ☎ **888/63-GHOST** or 520/63-GHOST. Fax 520/63-GHOST. 5 units, 1 with bathroom. TV. $75–$95 double. Rates include full breakfast. AE, DISC, MC, V.

With its long verandas on both floors, this restored old house is hard to miss as you drive into Jerome from Clarkdale. Most of the rooms, though rather plain and small, have great views across the Verde River Valley. There's a hot tub for guests in the terraced back yard.

**The Inn at Jerome.** 309 Main St. (P.O. Box 901), Jerome, AZ 86331. ☎ **800/634-5094** or 520/634-5094. 8 units, 2 with bathroom. TV. $55–$85 double. AE, DISC, MC, V.

This B&B has similar styling to the Ghost City Inn, but its antique-filled rooms lend quite a bit more character. One room has a rustic log bed so tall that you have to climb up into it. Other beds are equally attractive, including a wrought-iron bed, a spool bed, and a sleigh bed. All the rooms have terry robes, ceiling fans, and evaporative coolers (almost as good as air-conditioning), though only two rooms have valley views. Reception is at the restaurant downstairs. Note that breakfast is not included in the room rate.

✪ **The Surgeon's House.** 101 Hill St. (P.O. Box 998), Jerome, AZ 86331. ☎ **800/639-1452** or 520/639-1452. www.virtualcities.com. E-mail: surgehouse1@wildapache.net. 3 units. A/C TV. $100–$150 suite. Rates include full breakfast. MC, V.

Built in 1917 as the home of Jerome's resident surgeon, this Mediterranean-style home has a jaw-dropping view of the Verde Valley and is surrounded by beautiful gardens. All three units are suites; but the old chauffeur's quarters ($150), located in a separate cottage across the inn's garden, is the one to request. This unconventionally designed room has a wall of glass opposite the bed so you can soak in the view from under the covers, an old tub in one corner, and a wall of glass blocks around the toilet. The two rooms in the main house are much more traditional and are filled with antiques that conjure up Jerome's heyday. However one of these rooms has a unique private bathroom that's so tiny everything gets wet when you shower; it's designed as a combination shower stall and toilet (strange but fun). The inn is on a narrow side lane toward the top of town.

## WHERE TO DINE

**Flatiron Café.** In the Flatiron Building, at the corner of Main St. and Hull Ave. ☎ **520/634-2733**. Breakfast and sandwiches $4–$8. No credit cards. Daily 7:30am–5pm in summer; closes at 3pm weekdays during off-season. BREAKFAST/LIGHT MEALS.

The tiny Flatiron Café is Jerome's outpost of urban flavors and serves breakfast and light meals such as black-bean hummus, grilled prosciutto panini, smoked-salmon quesadillas, fresh juices, and espresso drinks. It looks as though you could hardly squeeze in here, but there's more seating across the street. Definitely not your usual ghost town lunch counter.

**House of Joy.** Hull Ave. ☎ **520/634-5339**. Reservations required. 3-course meal $22–$35. No credit cards. Sat 3–9pm, Sun 3–8pm. CONTINENTAL.

If you know exactly when you'll be in town, and it happens to be a Saturday or Sunday, you might want to make a dinner reservation at the House of Joy. This continental restaurant is housed in a building that was once a bordello, and the interior decor is reminiscent of its colorful history (albeit with dozens of costumed teddy bears all over the dining room). Reservations are an absolute necessity and must be made several weeks in advance as there are only a handful of tables in the restaurant. Lamb, veal, Cornish hen, and seafood are served in various permutations, but you won't find any steak or vegetarian options here.

**Apizza Heaven.** Near the corner of Main St. and Hull Ave. ☎ **520/649-1834.** Pizzas, pastas, sandwiches $6–$19. No credit cards. Daily 11am–8pm, sometimes later on Fri–Sat. PIZZA/SOUTHERN ITALIAN.

These folks specialize in East Coast–style pizza, which seems to taste good just about anywhere. We like to get it to go (this place isn't very big) and then grab a seat with a view at the nearby public park. You can also dig into such things as a hearty eggplant parmigiana dinner or a sausage and pepper sandwich.

## 4  The Verde Valley

Camp Verde: 30 miles S of Sedona; 95 miles N of Phoenix; 20 miles E of Jerome

The Verde Valley, named for its green lushness by early Spanish explorers passing through an otherwise brown desert landscape, has long been a magnet for both wildlife and people. With its headwaters in the Juniper Mountains of the Prescott National Forest, the Verde River flows down through a rugged canyon before meandering slowly across the plains of the Verde Valley. Today these plains are among Arizona's richest agricultural and ranching regions (and are quickly gaining popularity with retirees).

However, long before the first European explorers entered the Verde Valley, the Sinagua people were living by the river and irrigating their fields with its waters. Sinagua ruins can still be seen at Tuzigoot and Montezuma national monuments, and there are even primitive cave dwellings along the banks of the river. By the time the first pioneers began settling in this region, the Sinaguas had long since disappeared, but Apaches had claimed the river valley as part of their territory. Inevitably, there were clashes with the Apaches, and the U.S. Army established Fort Verde to protect the settlers. Today, hundreds of years of Verde Valley history can be viewed at sites such as Fort Verde State Park and Tuzigoot and Montezuma Castle national monuments. This valley is also the site of the most scenic railroad excursion in the state.

## ESSENTIALS

**GETTING THERE**    Camp Verde is just off I-17 at the junction with Ariz. 260. This latter highway leads northwest through the Verde Valley for 12 miles to Cottonwood.

**VISITOR INFORMATION**    For more information on the Verde Valley, contact the **Cottonwood/Verde Valley Chamber of Commerce,** 1010 S. Main St., Cottonwood, AZ 86326 (☎ **520/634-7593**).

## EXPLORING THE VERDE VALLEY
### A RAILWAY EXCURSION

✪ **Verde Canyon Railroad.** 300 N. Broadway, Clarkdale. ☎ **800/293-7245** or 520/639-0010. Admission is $35.95 for adults, $32.95 for seniors, $20.95 for children 12 and under; a first-class ticket is $54.95. The schedule is different every month, but, in general: Trains leave at 1pm and return at 5pm Wed–Mon Oct–May; June–Sept trains run only Wed, Thurs, Sat, and Sun. Call for exact schedule and reservations.

When the town of Jerome was busily mining copper, a railway was built to link the booming town with the territorial capital at nearby Prescott. Because of the rugged mountains between Jerome and Prescott, the railroad was forced to take a longer but less difficult route north along the Verde River before turning back south toward Prescott. Today you can ride these same tracks aboard the Verde Canyon Railroad. The route through the Verde River Canyon traverses both the remains of a copper smelter and unspoiled desert that's inaccessible by car and is part of the Prescott National Forest. The views of the rocky canyon walls and green waters of the Verde River are quite dramatic, and if you look closely along the way, you'll see ancient Sinagua cliff dwellings. In the late winter and early spring, nesting bald eagles can also be spotted. Of the three excursion train rides in Arizona, this is by far the most scenic (though the Grand Canyon Railway certainly has a more impressive destination). Live music and a very informative narration make the ride entertaining as well.

## INDIAN RUINS & AN ARMY FORT

**Tuzigoot National Monument.** Just outside Clarkdale off U.S. 89A. ☎ **520/634-5564.** Admission is $2 for adults, free for children 16 and under. Late May to early Sept daily 8am–7pm; mid-Sept to mid-May daily 8am–5pm.

Perched atop a hill overlooking the Verde River, this small, stone-walled pueblo was built by the Sinagua people, contemporaries of northern Arizona's Anasazi people, and was inhabited between 1125 and 1400. The *Sinagua* people, whose name is Spanish for "without water," were traditionally dry-land farmers relying entirely on rainfall to water their crops. When the Hohokam, who had been living in the Verde Valley since A.D. 600, moved on to more fertile land around 1100, the Sinagua moved into this valley. Their buildings progressed from individual homes called pit houses to communal pueblos.

An interpretive trail leads through the Tuzigoot ruins, explaining different aspects of Sinaguan life, and inside the visitor center is a small museum displaying many of the artifacts unearthed here. Desert plants, many of which were utilized by the Sinagua, are also identified along the trail.

✪ **Montezuma Castle National Monument.** Exit 289 off I-17. ☎ **520/567-3322.** Admission $2 adults, free for children 16 and under; there's no charge to see Montezuma Well. Late May to early Sept daily 8am–7pm; mid-Sept to mid-May daily 8am–5pm.

Despite the name, the ruins within this monument are neither castle nor Aztec dwelling—as the reference to Aztec ruler Moctezuma (traditionally Montezuma) implies. Rather, the Sinagua cliff dwelling, among the best preserved in Arizona, consists of two impressive stone pueblos. The more intriguing of the two is set in a shallow cave 100 feet up in a cliff overlooking Beaver Creek. Construction on this five-story, 20-room village began sometime in the early 12th century. Because Montezuma Castle has been protected from the elements by the overhanging roof of the cave in which it was built, the original adobe mud that was used to plaster over the stone walls of the dwelling is still intact. Another structure, containing 45 rooms on a total of six levels, stands at the base of the cliff. This latter dwelling which has been subjected to rains and floods over the years is not nearly as well preserved as the cliff dwelling.

For some as-yet-unknown reason, these buildings were abandoned by the Sinagua people, who disappeared without a trace in the early 14th century. The visitor center displays artifacts that have been unearthed at the ruins.

Located 11 miles north of Montezuma Castle (and part of the national monument), **Montezuma Well** is a water-filled sinkhole that has for centuries served as an oasis in the desert. Occupied first by the Hohokam and later by the Sinagua, this sunken pond was formed when a cavern in the porous limestone bedrock here collapsed. Underground springs quickly filled the sinkhole, which today contains a pond measuring 368 feet across and 65 feet deep. Over the centuries, the presence of year-round water attracted both the Hohokam and the Sinagua peoples, who built irrigation canals to utilize the water for growing crops. Some of these irrigation channels can still be seen. An excavated Hohokam pit house, built around 1100, and Sinagua houses and pueblos stand around the sinkhole.

**Fort Verde State Historic Park.** 125 Holloman St. ☎ **520/567-3275**. Admission $2 adults, $1 children 7 to 13, free for children under 7. Daily from 8am–5pm.

Just south of Montezuma Castle and Montezuma's Well, in the town of Camp Verde, you'll find Fort Verde State Historic Park. Established in 1871, Fort Verde was the third military post in the Verde Valley and was occupied until 1891, by which time tensions with the Indian population had subsided and made the fort unnecessary. The military had first come to the Verde Valley in 1865 at the request of settlers who wanted protection from the local Tonto Apache and Yavapai. The tribes, traditionally hunters and gatherers, had been forced to raid the settlers' fields for food after their normal economy was disrupted by the sudden influx of whites and Mexicans into the area. Between 1873 and 1875 most of the Indians in the area were rounded up and forced to live on various reservations. An uprising in 1882 led to the last clash between local tribes and Fort Verde's soldiers.

Today the state park, which covers 10 acres, preserves three officers' quarters, an administration building, and some ruins. The buildings that have been fully restored house exhibits on the history of the fort and what life was like here in the 19th century. With their white lattices and picket fences, gables, and shake-shingle roofs, the buildings of Fort Verde suggest that life at this remote post was not so bad, at least for officers.

There are costumed military reenactments here on the third Saturday in May and the second Saturday in October.

## OTHER VERDE VALLEY ATTRACTIONS & ACTIVITIES
### IN & AROUND CAMP VERDE

If you have an interest in 19th-century reenactments or antique cowboy and military gear, stop in at **Kicking Mule Outfitters,** 545 S. Main St., Camp Verde (☎ **520/ 567-2501**). This store specializes in reproduction Western leather holsters, gun belts, saddles, and the like. It also sells Western antiques and rents equipment to movie companies. Another place worth a look is **White Hills Indian Arts,** 567 S. Main St. (☎ **520/567-3490**), which is housed in an 1883 stagecoach stop and specializes in Native American arts and crafts.

**Horseback Adventures** (☎ **520/567-5502**), offers horseback rides ranging from 1 hour ($23.50) to all day ($95). The 1- and 2-hour rides along Beaver Creek are probably the most enjoyable if you haven't spent much time in the saddle.

For a completely different sort of entertainment in Camp Verde, drop by the **Cliff Castle Casino,** 353 Middle Verde Rd. (☎ **520/567-6956**), at exit 289 off of I-17.

If you want to do some wine tasting while you're in the area, drop by the **San Dominique Winery** (☎ **480/945-8583**), 11 miles south of Camp Verde. To get to the winery, take exit 169 off I-17 (the Cherry Road exit), go east, then turn right on the dirt road that leads to the winery. You may have to look hard to see the winery's small sign. There are always plenty of wines available for tasting at a quarter a taste. The winery also sells lots of garlic-flavored foods, as well as different types of pickles. Sandwiches and light meals are also available.

## In & Around Cottonwood & Clarkdale

Cottonwood, located 6 miles from Jerome, isn't nearly as atmospheric as the old copper town, but there are a few blocks of historic buildings that are slowly filling up with interesting shops that seem to be spillovers from the old hippie days in Jerome. **Old Town Cottonwood's Main Street,** one side of which has a covered sidewalk, contains several shops, galleries, and cafes and is a pleasant place to stroll. Also here in town, you'll find the **Clemenceau Heritage Museum,** 1 N. Willard St. (☎ 520/634-2868), which is housed in an old school building. The museum's most interesting display is a model railroad layout of the region's old system of mining railroads. The museum is open Wednesday from 9am to noon, and Friday through Sun 11am to 3pm. Admission is free.

On the outskirts of Cottonwood, not far from Tuzigoot National Monument, you'll find **Dead Horse Ranch State Park** (☎ 520/634-5283), which is set on the banks of the Verde River and offers picnicking, fishing, swimming, hiking, and camping. Trails beginning here lead into the adjacent national forest, so you can actually get in many miles of scenic hiking. Park admission is $4 per vehicle per day.

## WHERE TO STAY

**Best Western Cliff Castle Lodge & Casino.** 333 Middle Verde Rd., Camp Verde, AZ 86322. ☎ **800/524-6343** or 520/567-6611. Fax 520/567-9455. 80 units. A/C TV TEL. $42–$78 double. AE, CB, DC, DISC, MC, V.

Although most people staying at this motel just off I-17 at Exit 289 are here to do a little gambling in the adjacent casino, the motel also makes a good base for exploring the Verde Valley. Rooms are standard motel issue, and there is a pool in summer and a whirlpool year-round.

## WHERE TO DINE

**Blazin' M Ranch Chuckwagon Suppers.** Off 10th St., Cottonwood. ☎ **800/WEST-643** or 520/634-0334. Reservations recommended. $18.95 adults, $8.95 children age 10 and under. AE, DISC, MC, V. Wed–Sat 5–8:30pm. Closed Jan and Aug. AMERICAN.

Located adjacent to the Dead Horse State Park, the Blazin' M Ranch is more a slice of the Old West than just a place to have dinner. The chuck wagon suppers include not only a belly-fillin' heap o' food but also a Western variety show. Lots of fun for kids (pony rides, farm animals, a little cow town).

**Gas Works Mexican Restaurant.** 1033 N. Main St., Cottonwood. ☎ **520/634-7426.** Meals $2–$7. No credit cards. Sun–Fri noon–7pm. MEXICAN.

If you happen to be hungry and can't hold out for Jerome (or couldn't handle the crowds up at the top of the hill), check out this eclectic hole in the wall in old town Cottonwood. Not only can you get good burritos and enchiladas, you can also check out the very expensive hand-embroidered denim jackets. Occasionally there's live music.

✪ **Main Street Cafe.** 315 S. Main St., Cottonwood. ☎ **520/639-4443.** Reservations recommended. Main courses $7–$22. MC, V. Mon 11am–3pm, Tues–Sat 11am–3pm and 5–9pm, Sun 11am–2pm and 5–9pm. SOUTHWESTERN.

Though set amid the strip malls in the newer section of Cottonwood, this restaurant is surprisingly sophisticated (Debussy on the stereo) yet casual and very reasonably priced. The menu is a mix of both the familiar (fajitas and lemon pepper fettuccini) and more creative dishes. It is in the latter realm that the restaurant usually shines. The green corn tamale in chipotle cream sauce makes a savory starter, or try the Southwest corn chowder. Steak fans shouldn't miss the Southwest blackened sirloin with fresh salsa. Although many of the dishes here are pretty fiery, there are plenty of mild dishes as well. The wine list contains more than 100 wines.

## 5 Sedona & Oak Creek Canyon

106 miles S of the Grand Canyon; 116 miles N of Phoenix; 56 miles NE of Prescott

Although in recent years housing developments and strip malls have sprawled across the hills at the mouth of Oak Creek Canyon, the town of Sedona can still claim the most beautiful setting in the Southwest. Red rock buttes, eroded canyon walls, and mesas rise into blue skies. Off in the distance, the Mogollon Rim looms, its forests of juniper and ponderosa pine dark against the red rocks. Imagine Monument Valley with a wealthy southern California suburb, and you have a pretty good idea of Sedona today.

However, with national forest surrounding the city (and even extending fingers of forest into what would otherwise be the city limits), Sedona has some of the best outdoor access of any city in the Southwest. All over the city, alongside highways, and down side streets in suburban neighborhoods, there are trailheads. Head down any one of these trails, and you leave the city behind and enter the world of the red rocks. Just don't be too surprised if you come around a bend in the trail and find yourself in the middle of a wedding ceremony or a group of 30 people doing tai chi.

Located at the mouth of Oak Creek Canyon, Sedona was first settled by pioneers in 1877, but the word of Sedona's beauty did not begin to spread until Hollywood filmmakers began using the region's red rock as backdrop to their Western films. Next came artists, lured by the landscapes and desert light (it was here in Sedona that the Cowboy Artists of America organization was formed). However, though still much touted as an artists' community, Sedona's art scene these days is geared more toward tourists than toward collectors of fine art.

More recently, the spectacular views and mild climate were discovered by retirees. Today Sedona's hills are alive with the sound of construction as ostentatious retirement mansions sprout from the dust like desert toads after an August rainstorm. When a New Age channeler discovered the "Sedona vortexes," yet another group discovered that Sedona was where their cosmic energy fields converged. Most recently, mountain bikers have begun to ride the red rock, and the word is slowly spreading that the biking here is almost as good as up north in Moab, Utah.

The waters of Oak Creek were what first attracted settlers and native peoples to this area, and today this stream still lures visitors to Sedona—especially in the summer months, when the cool shade and even cooler creek waters are a glorious respite from the heat of the desert. Two of Arizona's finest swimming holes are located on Oak Creek, only a few miles from Sedona, and one of these, Slide Rock, has been made into a state park.

With its drop-dead scenery, dozens of motels and resorts, and plethora of good restaurants, Sedona makes an excellent base for exploring central Arizona. Several ancient Indian ruins (including an impressive cliff dwelling), the "ghost town" of Jerome, and the scenic Verde Canyon Railroad are within easy driving distance, and even the Grand Canyon is but a long day trip away.

## ESSENTIALS

**GETTING THERE**    Sedona is on Ariz. 179 at the mouth of scenic Oak Creek Canyon. From Phoenix, take I-17 to Ariz. 179 north. From Flagstaff, head south on I-17 until you see the turnoff for Ariz. 89A and Sedona. Ariz. 89A also connects Sedona with Prescott.

**Sedona Phoenix Shuttle** (☎ **800/448-7988** in Arizona, or 520/282-2066) operates several trips daily between the Phoenix Sky Harbor Airport and Sedona. The one-way fare is $35 and the round-trip fare is $60. Call for schedule information.

**VISITOR INFORMATION** Contact the **Sedona–Oak Creek Chamber of Commerce,** P.O. Box 478, Sedona, AZ 86339 (☎ **800/288-7336** or 520/282-7722; www.arizonaguide.com/sedona), which also operates a visitor center on the corner of Ariz. 89A and Forest Road near uptown Sedona.

**GETTING AROUND** Whether traveling in a car or on foot, you'll need to cultivate patience when trying to cross major roads in Sedona. Traffic here, especially on weekends, is some of the worst in the state. Also be prepared for slow traffic on roads that have good views; drivers are often distracted by the red rocks. You may hear or see references to the **"Y"** while you're in Sedona. The term refers to the intersection of Ariz. 179 and Ariz. 89A between the Tlaquepaque shopping plaza and uptown Sedona.

Rental cars are available in Sedona through **Enterprise Rent-a-Car** (☎ **800/325-8007** or 520/282-2052), **Practical Rent-a-Car** (☎ **800/464-8697** or 520/282-6702), and **Sedona Car Rentals** (☎ **520/282-2227**). For between $100 and $130 a day, you can also rent a Jeep from **Canyon Jeep Rentals** (☎ **800/224-2229** or 520/282-6061), **Desert Jeep Rentals** (☎ **888/GO-4-JEEP** or 520/284-1099), or **Arizona Jeep Rentals** (☎ **800/879-JEEP** or 520/282-2227).

For a taxi, call Bob's Sedona Taxi (☎ **520/282-1234**).

**SPECIAL EVENTS** The **Sedona International Film Festival** (☎ **520/ 282-0747**), held in early March, has been getting good publicity across the state and has been booking quite a few interesting films.

One of the year's biggest events is the world-class **Sedona Chamber Music Festival,** held each year in late May; contact the Sedona Chamber Music Society, P.O. Box 153, Sedona, AZ 86339-0153 (☎ **520/526-2256**), for details.

The **Jazz on the Rocks Benefit Festival** is held each year on the fourth Saturday in September in an outdoor amphitheater with a superb view of the red rocks. For more information, contact Sedona Jazz on the Rocks, P.O. Box 889, Sedona, AZ 86339 (☎ **520/282-1985**).

In early October (usually a week after the jazz festival), an annual benefit for the Native American Scholarship Project called the **Verde Valley Music Festival** is staged by Jackson Browne. This concert always includes musical friends of Browne's such as Bruce Cockburn, Crosby, Stills & Nash, and Marc Cohn. In the past the concert has been held at the Verde Valley School's Warren Amphitheater, but the venue may change when the Sedona Cultural Center is completed. Tickets are around $30 and are sold through Dillard's department store ticket outlets. For information, contact the Sedona Chamber of Commerce.

In mid-December each year, Sedona celebrates the **Festival of Lights** at Tlaquepaque (☎ **520/282-4838**) by the lighting of thousands of luminárias (paper bags partially filled with sand and containing a single candle) beginning at sunset.

## EXPLORING RED ROCK COUNTRY

Rugged cliffs, needlelike pinnacles, and isolated buttes rise up from the green forest floor at the mouth of Oak Creek Canyon in Sedona. Layers of different-colored stone deposited during various prehistoric ages form bands through the cliffs above, the most prominent of these bands being the layer of red sandstone called the Schnebly Hill Formation. Because this rosy sandstone predominates around Sedona, the region has come to be known as the red rock country. Each evening at sunset the red rocks put on a light show that alone is reason enough for visiting Sedona.

Days can be spent exploring the red rock country in any of half a dozen different modes of transport. There are Jeep tours, hot-air-balloon flights, horseback rides, mountain-bike trails, hiking trails, and scenic drives suitable for standard cars. (See the following sections, "Organized Tours" and "Sports & Outdoor Pursuits.")

Although in the past it has been possible for passenger cars to drive **Schnebly Hill Road** for superb views of Sedona, storm runoff left the road almost impassable in the winter of 1998. As of press time the road had not been repaired. However, it is worth checking at the Sedona Visitor Center (see "Visitor Information," above) to see if it is once again driveable. If so, head south out of Sedona on Ariz. 179, turn left after you cross the bridge over Oak Creek, and head up the unpaved road. The road climbs up into the hills above town, every turn yielding a new and breathtaking view, and eventually reaching the top of the Mogollon Rim. At the rim is the Schnebly Hill overlook, offering the very best view in the area.

Just south of Sedona, on Ariz. 179, you'll see the aptly named **Bell Rock** on the east side of the road. There's a parking area at the foot of Bell Rock and trails leading up to the top. From Bell Rock, you can see **Cathedral Rock** to the west. This rock is the most photographed formation in Sedona. Adjacent to Bell Rock is **Courthouse Rock,** and not far from Bell Rock and visible from Chapel Road, are **Eagle Head Rock**

# Vortex Power

In recent years Sedona has been one of the world's centers for the New Age movement; large numbers of people come to experience the "power vortexes" of the surrounding red rock country. You'll see local bulletin boards and publications advertising such diverse New Age services as past-life regressions, crystal healing, angelic healing, tarot readings, reiki, axiatonal therapy, electromagnetic field balancing, soul recovery, channeling, aromatherapy, myofacial release, and aura photos and videos.

According to believers, a *vortex* is a site where the earth's unseen lines of power intersect to form a particularly powerful energy field. Page Bryant, an adherent of New Age beliefs, determined through channeling that there were four vortexes around Sedona. Scientists may scoff, but Sedona's vortexes have become so well known that the chamber of commerce visitor center has several handouts to explain them and a map to guide you to them. (Many of the most spectacular geological features of the Sedona landscape also happen to be vortexes.)

The four main vortexes include Bell Rock, Cathedral Rock, Airport Mesa, and Boynton Canyon. **Bell Rock** and **Airport Mesa** are both said to contain masculine or electric energy that boosts emotional, spiritual, and physical energy. **Cathedral Rock** is said to contain feminine or magnetic energy, good for facilitating relaxation. The **Boynton Canyon** vortex is considered an electromagnetic energy site, which means it has a balance of both masculine and feminine energy.

If you're not familiar with vortexes and want to learn more about the ones here in Sedona, consider a ✪ **vortex tour.** These are offered by several companies around town including **Earth Wisdom Tours** (☎ **520/282-4714**), **Spirit Steps** (☎ **800/728-4562** or 520/282-4562), **Vortex Tours** (☎ **520/282-2733**), and **Crystal Light Center** (☎ **520/282-2733**). All four of these companies offer vortex tours that combine aspects of Native American and New Age beliefs. Tours last about 3 hours and cost between $50 and $60 per person.

You can also stock up on books, crystals, and other spiritual supplies at stores such as **Crystal Magic,** 2978 W. Hwy. 89A (☎ **520/282-1622**); **Center for the New Age,** 341 Hwy. 179 (☎ **520/282-2085**); and **The Eye of the Vortex Book Center,** 1405 W. Hwy. 89A (☎ **520/282-5614**).

(from the front door of the Chapel of the Holy Cross—see "Attractions & Activities Around Town," below—look three-quarters of the way up the mountain to see the eagle's head), the **Twin Nuns** (two pinnacles standing side by side), and **Mother and Child Rock** to the left of the Twin Nuns.

If you head west out of Sedona on U.S. 89A and turn left onto Airport Road, you'll drive up onto **Airport Mesa,** which consists of three small hills commanding an unobstructed panorama of Sedona and the red rocks. About halfway up the mesa is a small parking area from which trails radiate out. The views from here are among the best in the region and the trails are very easy.

One of the most beautiful areas around Sedona is **Boynton Canyon.** To reach this spectacular canyon, drive west out of Sedona on U.S. 89A, turn right on Dry Creek Road, take a left at the T intersection, and at the next T intersection take a right. On the way to Boynton Canyon, look north from U.S. 89A, and you'll see **Coffee Pot Rock,** which is also known as Rooster Rock, rising 1,800 feet above Sedona. Three pinnacles, known as the **Three Golden Chiefs** by the Yavapai tribe, stand beside Coffee

Pot Rock. As you drive up Dry Creek Road, on your right you'll see **Capitol Butte,** which resembles the U.S. Capitol building. Just outside the gates of Enchantment Resort is a parking area for the ✪ **Boynton Canyon Trail.** From the parking area the trail leads 3 miles up into the canyon. The ancient Sinagua people once lived in Boynton Canyon, and the ruins of their homes can still be seen.

In this same area, you can visit the well-preserved Sinagua cliff dwellings at **Palatki Ruins.** To reach the ruins follow the directions to Boynton Canyon, but instead of turning right at the second T intersection, turn left onto unpaved Boynton Pass Road (FR 152). Follow this road to another T intersection and go right onto FR 125, then veer right onto FR 795, which dead ends at the ruins. Admission to the ruins is $5 per person. Don't try this if the roads are at all muddy.

South of Ariz. 89A and a bit west of the turnoff for Boynton Canyon is Upper Red Rock Loop Road, which leads to Red Rock Crossing, a National Forest Service recreation area that has become a must-see spot for almost everyone who visits Sedona these days. Its popularity stems from a beautiful photograph of Oak Creek, with **Cathedral Rock** in the background—an image that has been reproduced countless times in Sedona promotional literature and on postcards. Hiking trails beginning here lead up to Cathedral Rock. Park admission is $3.

If you continue on Upper Red Rock Loop Road, it becomes gravel for a while before turning into Lower Red Rock Loop Road and reaching **Red Rock State Park** (☎ 520/282-6907), which flanks Oak Creek. The views here take in many of the rocks listed above, and you have the additional bonus of being right on the creek (though no swimming or wading is allowed). Park admission is $5 per vehicle.

South of Sedona, near the junction of I-17 and Ariz. 179, you can visit an ancient petroglyph site at the **V Bar V Ranch.** To reach this site, head east several miles on the marked dirt road that leads to the Beaver Creek Campground. The entrance to the petroglyph site is just past the campground. From the parking area, it's about a ½-mile walk to the petroglyphs. The site is open Friday through Monday from 9:30am to 4pm.

## OAK CREEK CANYON

The **Mogollon Rim** is a 2,000-foot escarpment cutting diagonally across central Arizona and on into New Mexico. At the top of the Mogollon Rim are the ponderosa pine forests of the high mountains, while at the bottom the lowland deserts begin. Of the many canyons cutting down from the rim, Oak Creek Canyon is the best known.

Ariz. 89A runs down through the canyon from Flagstaff to Sedona, winding its way down from the rim and paralleling Oak Creek. Along the way there are overlooks, parks, picnic areas, campgrounds, cabin resorts, and small inns.

If you have a choice of how first to view Oak Creek Canyon, come at it from the north. Your first stop after traveling south from Flagstaff will be the **Oak Creek Canyon overlook,** which provides a view far down the valley to Sedona and beyond. The overlook is at the edge of the Mogollon Rim, and the road suddenly drops in tight switchbacks just south of here. You may notice that one rim of the canyon is lower than the other. This is because Oak Creek Canyon is on a geologic fault line; one side of the canyon is moving in a different direction from the other.

Though the top of the Mogollon Rim is a ponderosa pine forest and the bottom a desert, Oak Creek Canyon supports a forest of sycamores and other deciduous trees. There is no better time to drive scenic Ariz. 89A than between late September and mid-October when the canyon is ablaze with red and yellow leaves.

At the **Cave Spring Campground** there is a self-guided nature walk that describes the riparian environment of Oak Creek. (A riparian area is one along a body of water.)

Different plants live in this moist environment, and the plants and water attract a wide variety of animals. Riparian habitats are especially crucial in deserts.

The most popular spot in all of Oak Creek Canyon is ✪ **Slide Rock State Park** (☎ 520/282-3034). Located 7 miles north of Sedona on the site of an old homestead, this park preserves a natural water slide. On hot summer days the park is jammed with people splashing in the water and sliding over the algae-covered sandstone bottom of Oak Creek. Sunbathing and fishing are other popular pastimes here. The park is open daily, and admission is $5 per vehicle. There's another popular swimming area at **Grasshopper Point,** several miles closer to Sedona. Parking here is $3 per vehicle.

Within Oak Creek Canyon several hikes of different lengths are possible. By far the most spectacular and popular is the 6-mile round-trip hike up the ✪ **West Fork of Oak Creek.** This is a classic canyon-country hike with steep canyon walls rising up from the creek. At some points the canyon is no more than 20 feet wide with walls rising up more than 200 feet. You can actually hike many more miles up the canyon, which is popular for overnight backpacking trips. There is a parking fee of $3 charged at the trailhead. Stop by the Sedona–Oak Creek Chamber of Commerce to pick up a free map listing hikes in the area. The **Coconino National Forest** ranger station (☎ 520/282-4119) on Brewer Road, just west of the intersection of Ariz. 89A and Ariz. 179, is also a good source of hiking information.

If you get thirsty while driving through the canyon, hold out for **Garlands General Store** in Indian Gardens, which is about 4 miles north of Sedona. Here you can get delicious organic apple juice made from apples grown in the canyon. For one last view down the canyon, stop at **Midgely Bridge** (just watch for the parked cars and small parking area at the north end of the bridge).

## ATTRACTIONS & ACTIVITIES AROUND TOWN

Sedona's most notable architectural landmark is the ✪ **Chapel of the Holy Cross** (☎ 520/282-4069), a small church built right into the red rock on the south side of town. If you're driving up from Phoenix, you can't miss the chapel. It sits high above the road just off Ariz. 179. With its very contemporary styling, the chapel is one of the most architecturally important modern churches in the country. Marguerite Brunswig Staude, a devout Catholic painter, sculptor, and designer, had the inspiration for the chapel in 1932, but it wasn't until 1957 that her dream was finally realized. The chapel's design is dominated by a simple cross forming the wall that faces the street. The cross and the starkly beautiful chapel seem to grow directly from the rock, allowing the natural beauty of the red rock to speak for itself. The chapel is open daily from 9am to 5pm.

The **Sedona Arts Center,** Ariz. 89A at Art Barn Road (☎ 520/282-3865 or 520/282-3809), near the north end of town, serves both as a gallery for artwork by local and regional artists and as a theater for plays and music performances. Art classes are also held here.

To learn a bit about the history of Sedona, stop by the **Sedona Heritage Museum,** 735 Jordan Rd. (☎ 520/282-7038), in Jordan Historical Park. The museum, which is housed in a historic home, is furnished with antiques and also contains exhibits on the many movies that have been filmed in the area over the years. The farm was once an apple orchard and there is still apple processing equipment in the barn. The museum is open Thursday through Monday from 10am to 4pm, for a suggested donation of $3.

Out on the west side of town a new **Sedona Cultural Park** is in the works. When completed (with luck in the spring of 2000), it will contain an amphitheater and buildings for classes, workshops, and exhibitions, as well as nature trails and picnic areas. Call ☎ **800/780-2787** or 520/282-0747 for details.

If seeing the red rocks just isn't enough for you, there's always the **Supermax Theater** (☎ **520/284-3214**), which is located just off Ariz. 179 behind the factory outlet stores in the Village of Oak Creek. This big screen theater is similar to an IMAX theater.

While Sedona isn't yet a resort destination on par with Phoenix or Tucson, it does have a few **spas** and treatment centers that might add just the right bit of relaxation and pampering to your Sedona vacation. **Therapy on the Rocks,** 676 N. Hwy. 89A (☎ **520/282-3002**), with its creek-side setting, is a long-time local favorite that offers myofascial release and great views of the red rocks. At Los Abrigados resort, you'll find the more traditional **Sedona Health Spa,** 160 Portal Lane (☎ **520/282-5108**), with a wide selection of body and beauty treatments including body polishes, seaweed facials, and mineral wraps.

## ORGANIZED TOURS

If you'd like to get an overview of Sedona, you can take a tour on the **Sedona Trolley** (☎ **520/282-5400** or 520/282-6826), which leaves several times each day on two separate tours. One tour visits Tlaquepaque, the Chapel of the Holy Cross, and several art galleries, while the other goes out through west Sedona to Boynton Canyon and Enchantment Resort. Tours are $7 for adults and $2 for children 12 and under. Call for the trolley stop nearest you.

The red rock country surrounding Sedona is the city's greatest natural attraction, and there's no better way to explore the red rock country than in a four-wheel-drive vehicle. For more than 35 years, **Pink Jeep Tours,** 204 N. Hwy. 89A (☎ **800/873-3662** or 520/282-5000), has been heading deep into the Coconino National Forest. It offers nearly a dozen different tours ranging in length from 1½ hours ($30) to 4 hours ($75). You can travel the Sedona backcountry or simply visit the best views in the area.

**Sedona Red Rock Jeep Tours,** 270 N. Hwy 89A (☎ **800/848-7728** or 520/282-6826), offers similar tours for $32 to $52. This latter company also does helicopter-Jeep tours, horseback rides, and even a seasonal canoe tour to cave dwellings on the Verde River. If you want some photographic tips while you tour the red rock country, try **Sedona Photo Tours,** 252 N. Hwy 89A (☎ **800/973-3662** or 520/282-4320), which charges comparable prices.

If you're interested in getting an aerial view of the area, you have several options. **Arizona Helicopter Adventures** (☎ **800/282-5141** or 520/282-0904) and **Skydance Helicopters** (☎ **800/882-1651** or 520/282-1651) both offer short flights to different parts of this colorful region. Prices start around $36 for a 10-minute flight. **AeroVista** (☎ **520/282-7768**) and **West Wind Air Tours** (☎ **888/282-2037** or 520/282-2037) offer a variety of tours in small planes. These flights start at around $55 for a 25-minute flight. Flights as far afield as the Grand Canyon and Canyon de Chelly can be arranged.

However, our favorite tours are those of **Red Rock Biplane Tours** (☎ **888/TOO-RIDE** or 520/204-5939), which operates two modern Waco open-cockpit biplanes. With the wind in your hair, you'll feel as though you've entered the world of *The English Patient.* A 20-minute tour is about $59 per person.

If something a bit slower is more your speed, **Red Rock Balloon Adventures** (☎ **800/258-3754** or 520/284-0040), **Northern Lights Balloon Expeditions** (☎ **800/230-6222** or 520/282-2274), and **Sky High Balloon Adventures** (☎ **800/**

551-SKYS or 520/204-1395) offer peaceful hot-air-balloon rides over the canyons and sculpted buttes. Expect to pay around $145 for a 1- to 1½-hour ride.

## SPORTS & OUTDOOR PURSUITS

Hiking is by far the most popular outdoor sport in the Sedona area, and with dozens of trails leading off into the red rocks, it's easy to understand why. Among the more popular and scenic hiking trails are those starting alongside Ariz. 179 just north of the Village of Oak Creek and leading up to Bell Rock. To explore the Cathedral Rock area, turn off Ariz. 179 at the sign for the Back o' Beyond housing development and watch for the trailhead at the end of the paved road. Another access to Cathedral Rock is from the National Forest Service's Red Rock Crossing recreation area off Upper Red Rock Loop Road on the west side of Sedona. Perhaps the most popular trails in the Sedona area are those that lead into Boynton Canyon (site of Enchantment Resort). Here you'll glimpse ancient Native American ruins built into the red rock cliffs. Also in this area are a pair of easy, though scenic, trails—the Fay Canyon Arch Trail and the Vultee Arch Trail. You'll also find easy trails with great views about half way to the top of Airport Mesa on Airport Road. For more information on hiking in Oak Creek Canyon (site of the famous West Fork Trail), see "Oak Creek Canyon," above. For more information on all of these hikes, contact the **Coconino National Forest ranger station** (☎ **520/282-4119**) on Brewer Road, just west of the intersection of Ariz. 89A and Ariz. 179.

Sedona is rapidly becoming one of the **mountain-biking** meccas of the Southwest. The red rock here is every bit as challenging and scenic as the famed slick-rock country of Moab, Utah, and much less crowded. Using Sedona as a base, mountain bikers can ride year-round by heading up to Flagstaff in summer and down to the desert lowlands in winter. You can rent a mountain bike from **Sedona Sports,** Creekside Plaza below the "Y" (☎ **520/282-1317**) or **Mountain Bike Heaven,** 1695 W. Hwy. 89A (☎ **520/282-1312**). Rates start around $7 per hour, or $25 to $35 per day. **Sedona Bike & Bean Shop,** 376 Jordan Rd. in Uptown Sedona (☎ **520/282-3515**), rents bikes, has a coffee bar, and does group rides. Any of these stores can sell you a map or guide to area rides.

**Trail Horse Adventures at Kachina Stables,** Lower Red Rock Loop Road (☎ **800/SADDLE-UP** or 520/282-7252), offers guided horseback trail rides. Prices range from $28.50 for a 1-hour ride to $128 for an all-day ride (includes lunch). There are also breakfast, full-moon, lunch, sunset, and multiday pack trips. Lower Red Rock Loop Road is west of Sedona on Ariz. 89A. **Sedona Red Rock Jeep Tours** (☎ **800/848-7728** or 520/282-6826) offers horseback riding ($42 for 1 hour, $55 for 2 hours). These rides include transportation by Jeep to the ranch where the rides are held.

Oak Creek is well known in Arizona as an excellent trout stream and **fly-fishing** is quite popular here. The creek is stocked with trout during the summer. If you're looking for a fly fishing guide, call Jim McInnis of **Gon' Fishen** at ☎ **520/282-0788.** If you want to take the family fishing, try the **Rainbow Trout Farm** (☎ **520/282-3379**), 4 miles north of Sedona on Ariz. 89A.

Surprisingly, Sedona has not yet been ringed with **golf** courses. However, what few courses there are offer superb views to distract you from your game. The **Oak Creek Country Club,** 690 Bell Rock Blvd. (☎ **520/284-1660**), south of town off Ariz. 179, has stunning views from the course (greens fees $70). The ✪ **Sedona Golf Resort** (☎ **520/284-9355**), also located south of town on Ariz. 179, offers similar magnificent views of the red rocks (greens fees $79 to $105).

The **tennis courts** at Poco Diablo Resort, on the south side of Sedona, are open to the public for $12 per hour. To make reservations, call the resort at ☎ **520/282-7333.**

# SHOPPING

Ever since the famous Cowboy Artists of America organization was founded in Sedona back in 1965 (at what is now the Cowboy Club restaurant), this town has had a reputation as an artists' community. Today, with dozens of galleries around town, it is obvious that art is one of the driving forces behind the local economy. Most of Sedona's galleries specialize in traditional Western, contemporary Southwestern, and Native American art, and in some of the galleries around town, you'll see works by members of the Cowboy Artists of America. You'll find the greatest concentration of galleries and shops in the uptown area of Sedona (along Ariz. 89A just north of the "Y") and in the Tlaquepaque Arts and Crafts Village.

With more than 40 stores and restaurants, **Tlaquepaque Arts & Crafts Village** on Ariz. 179 (at the bridge over Oak Creek on the south side of Sedona), is designed to resemble a Mexican village and is named after a famous arts-and-crafts neighborhood in the suburbs of Guadalajara, Mexico. The maze of narrow alleys, connecting courtyards, fountains, and even a chapel and a bell tower, are worth a visit even if you aren't in a buying mood.

Unfortunately, many of Sedona's shops now specialize in cheap Southwestern gifts that have little to do with art, and weeding through the tacky gift shops to find the real galleries can be difficult. One place to start is at **Hozho,** a collection of several of Sedona's best galleries, on Ariz. 179 just before you cross over the Oak Creek bridge in Sedona.

**Compass Rose Gallery.** Hillside Courtyard, 671 Ariz. 179. ☎ **520/282-7904.**

Oddly out of place, but certainly welcome on the overly souvenir-oriented Sedona shopping scene, this store sells old maps (up to $3,000), old prints, and Edward S. Curtis sepia-toned photos.

**Cowboy Corral.** 219 N. Hwy. 89A. ☎ **800/457-2279** or 520/282-2040.

If you've decided you want to adopt the Wyatt Earp or Annie Oakley look, this shop can outfit you. Definitely not your standard urban cowboy Western wear shop, Cowboy Corral goes for the vintage look. Classic firearms are available to accessorize your ensemble.

**Garland's Indian Jewelry.** At Indian Gardens, 4 miles north on Ariz. 89A. ☎ **520/282-6632.**

A great location in the shade of scenic Oak Creek Canyon and a phenomenal collection of concho belts, squash blossom necklaces, and bracelets make this a worthwhile stop.

✪ **Garland's Navajo Rugs.** 411 Hwy. 179. ☎ **520/282-4070.**

With a very large collection of both contemporary and antique Navajo rugs (claimed to be the biggest in the world), Garland's is the premier Navajo rug shop in Sedona. It also carries a line of Native American baskets and pottery, Hopi kachina dolls, and Navajo sandpaintings.

**Hillside Courtyard.** 671 Hwy. 179. ☎ **520/282-4500.**

This is a shopping center dedicated to art galleries, retail shops, and a couple of restaurants. Here you'll find the Clay Pigeon, with some nice ceramics and glass, and

Exposures Gallery of the West, featuring Jack Acrey's large-format photographs of red rock landscapes.

✪ **Hoel's Indian Shop.** 9440 N. Hwy. 89A. ☎ **520/282-3925.**

Located 10 miles north of Sedona in a private residence in Oak Creek Canyon (just past Hoel's Cabins), this Native American arts-and-crafts gallery is one of the finest in the region and sells pieces of the highest quality. Most customers are serious collectors. It's a good idea to call before coming out here to make sure that the store will be open.

**Prime Outlets.** Hwy. 179, Village of Oak Creek. ☎ **888/545-7227** or 520/284-2150.

Yes, even Sedona (or more correctly the near community of the Village of Oak Creek) has an outlet mall. If you aren't in the market for art, but do need some cut-rate fashions, this is the place.

**Sedona Arts Center Gallery Shop.** Ariz. 89A and Art Barn Rd. ☎ **520/282-3865.**

Located at the north end of uptown Sedona, this shop features works by area artists. You'll find everything from jewelry to fiber arts to photography to ceramics. This is the best place in town to see the work of Sedona artists.

**Scherer Gallery.** Hillside Courtyard, 671 Hwy. 179. ☎ **520/203-9000.**

What makes this gallery unique is its collection of kaleidoscopes, which may be the largest in the country. More than a hundred kaleidoscope artists from around the world create the colorful concoctions here. You'll even find sculptural kaleidoscopes that are driven by running water.

✪ **Son Silver West.** 1476 Hwy. 179 (on the south side of town). ☎ **520/282-3580.**

For those who love everything Southwestern, this shop is a treasure trove of all kinds of interesting stuff, from Native American and Hispanic arts and crafts to antique *santo* (saint) carvings and rifles to big imported pots, chili garlands (*ristras*), and garden art.

**Touchstone.** 25 Schnebly Hill Rd. (at Ariz. 179). ☎ **520/282-2380.**

Western designers provide the drapey Sedona look for women with handwovens, hand-dyed silk, rayon, cotton, and linen done up in dresses and matching separates. Colors and textures are beautiful. They also sell estate jewelry and toddler's clothing.

# WHERE TO STAY
## EXPENSIVE

✪ **Briar Patch Inn.** 3190 N. Hwy. 89A, Sedona, AZ 86336. ☎ **888/809-3030** or 520/282-2342. Fax 520/282-2399. www.bbhost.com/briarpatch. 17 units. $149–$295 double. Rates include full breakfast. AE, MC, V.

If you're searching for tranquillity or a romantic retreat amid the cool shade of Oak Creek Canyon, this is the place. Located 3 miles north of Sedona on the banks of Oak Creek (there are even swimming holes here), this inn's cottages are set amid beautiful shady grounds where bird songs and the babbling creek set the mood. The cottages date from the 1930s but have all been very attractively renovated and updated (some with flagstone floors). A Western style predominates, and some rooms have a fireplace and kitchenette. Breakfast is often served on a terrace above the creek. All in all, the Briar Patch offers a delightful combination of solitude and sophistication—the quintessential romantic hideaway. A three-bedroom house is ideal for family reunions.

**Canyon Villa Bed & Breakfast Inn.** 125 Canyon Circle Dr., Sedona, AZ 86351. ☎ **800/453-1166** or 520/284-1226. Fax 520/284-2114. www.canyonvilla.com. 11 units. A/C TV TEL. $145–$225 double. Rates include full breakfast. AE, MC, V.

Located in the Village of Oak Creek, 6 miles south of Sedona, this big bed-and-breakfast offers luxurious accommodations and spectacular views of the red rocks. All rooms but one have views, as do the swimming pool area, living room, and dining room. If you want to just hole up at the inn, you won't be missing the best of the area; it's right out your window. Guest rooms are varied—Victorian, Santa Fe, country, rustic, Americana, wicker—but no matter what the decor, the furnishings are impeccable, and there are such amenities as terry robes, whirlpool tubs, and double sinks. All the rooms have balconies or patios, and several have fireplaces. Breakfasts are lavish affairs meant to be lingered over, and in the afternoons there is an elaborate spread of snacks.

**Doubletree Sedona Resort.** 90 Ridge Trail Dr., Sedona, AZ 86351. ☎ **800/222-TREE** or 520/284-4040. Fax 520/284-6940. 225 units. A/C TV TEL $179–$209 double. AE, CB, DC, DISC, MC, V.

Opened in late 1998, this is Sedona's newest resort; affiliated with the Sedona Golf Resort, it has one of the most breathtaking golf courses in the state. While golf is the driving force behind most stays here, anyone looking for an active vacation will find something to keep him or her busy here. All the guest rooms are suites of varying sizes and come with microwaves, minirefrigerators, coffeemakers, and fireplaces. About the only drawback to this place is that it is quite a ways outside Sedona itself (actually south of the Village of Oak Creek), so it's a bit of a drive to Sedona's restaurants and shops and the beauties of Oak Creek Canyon.

**Dining:** With its light California and Southwestern cuisine, the dining room places an emphasis on healthful cuisine and plays up its golf course and red rock views.

**Amenities:** 18-hole golf course, outdoor pool, fitness center, three racquetball and five tennis courts, full service spa with whirlpool spas, saunas, steam rooms, and various spa treatments, room service, concierge.

✪ **Enchantment Resort.** 525 Boynton Canyon Rd., Sedona, AZ 86336. ☎ **800/826-4180** or 520/282-2900. Fax 520/282-9249. www.enchantmentresort.com. 222 units. A/C MINIBAR TV TEL. $195–$325 double; $295–$425 casita parlor; $390–$650 1-bedroom suite; $655–$950 2-bedroom suite. AE, DISC, MC, V.

Located at the mouth of Boynton Canyon, this resort more than lives up to its name. The setting is breathtaking, the pueblo-style architecture of the hotel blends in with the canyon landscape, and at press time a new spa (expected to be open by December 1999) was being planned. The individual casitas of this resort can be booked as two-bedroom suites, one-bedroom suites, or as single rooms. It's worth booking a suite just so you can enjoy a casita living room that features high, beamed ceilings, beehive fireplaces, and Native American crafts. The large patios provide dramatic views of the canyon. Coffeemakers and hair dryers are standard in all the rooms. In 1998, sixty new rooms were added; try to get one of these if you can.

**Dining:** Both the resort's main restaurant, the Yavapai Dining Room (see "Where to Dine," below), and a less formal bar and grill offer terrace tables and indoor dining. Lunch on the terrace is a meal not to be missed. The menu in both restaurants features innovative American cuisine.

**Amenities:** Although you won't find an 18-hole golf course here at Enchantment, you'll find just about everything else, including 4 pools, 12 tennis courts, a croquet court, whirlpools, a fitness center, hiking trails, a six-hole putting course, and a putting green. There is a small spa just off the lobby. Aerobics classes, personal training, fitness programs, and all manner of body and beauty treatments are available.

The resort also offers a concierge, room service, tennis lessons, guided hikes, complimentary morning juice and newspaper, local airport shuttle, in-room massages, and children's programs.

✪ **The Graham Bed & Breakfast Inn & Adobe Village.** 150 Canyon Circle Dr., Sedona, AZ 86351. ☎ **800/228-1425** or 520/284-1425. Fax 520/284-0767. www.sedonasfinest. com. 10 units. A/C TV TEL. $139–$209 double; $249 suite; $269–$369 casita. Rates include full breakfast. AE, DISC, MC, V.

Located in the Village of Oak Creek, 6 miles south of Sedona, this inn lies almost at the foot of Bell Rock and features a variety of individually decorated rooms and suites. However, it is the casitas that are the most impressive—in fact, these are the most impressive rooms in the Sedona area. From the outside, the four casitas, which are approached through a huge Spanish colonial–style gateway, look like an old adobe village arranged around courtyard gardens. Inside, however, each is very different. The Purple Lizard room comes the closest to matching the exterior design and opts for a sort of colorful Taos-style interior (lots of purple, teal, and magenta) and has lots of Southwestern art. The Wilderness is a log cabin inside and has a fireplace that can be seen from both the living room and the double whirlpool tub. The Lonesome Dove is a sort of upscale cowboy cabin complete with wide plank floors, a saddle, guitar, flagstone fireplace, pot-belly stove, and swinging saloon doors leading into the bathroom, which has a round hot tub in a "barrel." The Sunset Casita features a sort of Mediterranean modern aesthetic that includes an elaborate wrought-iron four-poster bed with eight pillows and brocade bedspread, fireplaces in both the bathroom (beside the double whirlpool tub) and the living room, and a wall of glass. In addition to the whirlpool tubs, there are showers that have cascades of water rather than the usual spray you might expect. Can you say romantic?

✪ **The Inn on Oak Creek.** 556 Hwy. 179, Sedona, AZ 86336. ☎ **800/499-7896** or 520/282-7896. Fax 520/282-0696. www.sedona-inn.com. 11 units. A/C TV TEL. $155–$245 double. Rates include full breakfast. AE, DISC, MC, V.

Located right on Oak Creek and just around the corner from the Tlaquepaque shopping plaza, this luxurious modern inn offers the best of both worlds. A shady creekside setting lends it the air of a forest retreat, yet much of Sedona's shopping and many of its best restaurants are within walking distance. There is even a private little park on the bank of the creek. Guest rooms vary considerably in size, but all have interesting theme decors. Some of our personal favorites are the Garden Gate (with a picket fence headboard on the bed), Hollywood Out West (with old movie posters), the Rose Arbor (with creek views from both the tub and the bed), and the Angler's Retreat (with bentwood furniture, fly-fishing decor, and a fabulous view). Because the inn is built out over the creek, staying here is almost like staying on a cruise ship; you can look straight down into the water from your balcony. All the rooms come with VCRs and gas fireplaces, too.

**Junipine Resort.** 8351 N. Hwy. 89A, Sedona, AZ 86336. ☎ **800/742-PINE** or 520/ 282-3375. Fax 520/282-7402. 50 units. TV TEL. $170–$230 1-bedroom condo; $210–$270 2-bedroom condo. AE, DC, DISC, MC, V.

If you're coming up this way with the family and are looking for a place in the cool depths of Oak Creek Canyon (rather than amid the red rock views in Sedona proper), this condominium resort is a good bet. All the condos (here called creek houses) have loads of space (some with lofts), skylights, decks, stone fireplaces, decorative quilts on the walls, full kitchens, and contemporary styling. Some condos also have hot tubs. Best of all, the creek is right outside the door of most condos.

**Dining:** The resort's dining room serves a surprisingly sophisticated Southwestern and regional American menu at reasonable prices, so there's no need to drive all the way into Sedona for a good meal.

**Amenities:** Room service, in-room massages.

**L'Auberge de Sedona.** 301 L'Auberge Lane (P.O. Box B), Sedona, AZ 86339. ☎ **800/ 272-6777** or 520/282-1661. Fax 520/282-2885. www.lauberge.com. 100 units. A/C TV TEL. Dec–Feb (excluding holidays) $160–$210 double, $220–$250 suite, $245–$425 cottage; Mar–Nov and holidays $175–$240 double, $235–$280 suite, $315–$425 cottage. AE, CB, DC, DISC, MC, V.

Located in the heart of uptown Sedona, this romantic getaway offers a variety of room types, all of which are done in a somewhat out-of-place country French decor that is nonetheless quite attractive and luxurious. With two good restaurants and only a pool and whirlpool for activities, this lodge is more romantic getaway than desert recreational resort.

If you want spectacular views and sunsets, opt for the Orchards rooms, which face the red rocks but lack the shady setting of other rooms. If you crave a creek-side cottage set beneath shady sycamores, choose one of the cottages on the banks of Oak Creek. If the atmosphere of a French hunting lodge appeals, try a lodge room, which will have a few rustic furnishings. In all the rooms you'll find coffeemakers and hair dryers.

**Dining/Diversions:** L'Auberge, serving five-course French dinners, is one of Sedona's finest and most expensive restaurants. A more casual restaurant in the Orchards section serves simpler meals.

**Amenities:** Small outdoor pool, whirlpool, French boutique, concierge, room service, valet/laundry service, in-room massage, baby-sitting, access to nearby health club.

## MODERATE

**Best Western Arroyo Roble Hotel.** 400 N. Hwy. 89A (P.O. Box NN), Sedona, AZ 86336. ☎ **800/773-3662** or 520/282-4001. Fax 520/282-4001. 66 units. A/C TV TEL. $85–$135 double; $149–$179 suite; $169 cottage; $289 villa. AE, CB, DC, DISC, MC, V.

This five-story hotel perches above Oak Creek and provides many of the amenities of a more expensive resort, including views of the red rocks. All rooms come with king- or queen-size beds and a private balcony or patio. The villas, surrounded by Oak Creek Canyon's shady sycamores, are below the main hotel building and consist of two-bedroom condominiums with two fireplaces, 2½ bathrooms, two TVs, a stereo, a VCR, and two private patios or balconies. These latter accommodations are ideal for families. The hotel doesn't have its own restaurant, but there are plenty within walking distance.

There's an outdoor and an indoor/outdoor pool, whirlpools, two tennis courts, handball and racquetball courts, billiard room, exercise room, steam room and sauna, and video-games room.

✪ **Garland's Oak Creek Lodge.** P.O. Box 152, Sedona, AZ 86339. ☎ **520/282-3343.** 16 units. $170–$190 double (plus 15% gratuity). Rates include breakfast and dinner. 2-night minimum stay. MC, V. Closed mid-Nov to Mar 31 and Sun throughout the year.

Located 8 miles north of Sedona in the heart of Oak Creek Canyon, this lodge may be the hardest place in the area to get a reservation. People have been coming here for so many years and like it so much that they reserve a year in advance (last-minute cancellations do occur, so don't despair). What makes the lodge so special? Maybe it's that you have to drive *through* Oak Creek to get to your log cabin (don't worry, the water's shallow and the creek bottom is paved). Maybe it's the beautiful gardens overlooking the creek. Or maybe it's the slow, relaxing atmosphere of an old-time summer getaway. Cabins have all been well maintained and are rustic but comfortable. The larger cabins have their own fireplaces.

Breakfast and dinner are included in the rates and are served in a rustic dining hall. Organic fruits and vegetables grown on the property are frequently used, and each evening features a different entree accompanied by soup, salad, homemade breads, and dessert. Cocktails and wine are available.

Amenities include a tennis court and baby-sitting.

**The Lodge at Sedona.** 125 Kallof Place, Sedona, AZ 86336. ☎ **800/619-4467** or 520/204-1942. Fax 520/204-2128. www.lodgeatsedona.com. 14 units. A/C. $125–$175 double; $185–$245 suite. Rates include full breakfast. AE, DISC, MC, V.

Located in the West Sedona part of town, this large B&B is surrounded by desert landscaping that includes pine trees, rock gardens, waterfalls, sculptures, and a stone labyrinth. The rooms are all individually decorated; our personal favorites are the Lariat Room and the Master Suite (which is absolutely huge and has a stone fireplace). Upstairs rooms tend to be small and have showers only (instead of shower/tub combinations), so, if you can afford to spend a little more, opt for a downstairs room, and ask for one with a whirlpool tub. With 14 rooms and suites, this lodging may seem large for a bed-and-breakfast, but size doesn't limit the hospitality of owners Barb and Mark Dinunzio, who make all their guests feel very much at home.

**Poco Diablo.** 1752 S. Hwy. 179 (P.O. Box 1709), Sedona, AZ 86339. ☎ **800/528-4275** or 520/282-7333. Fax 520/282-9712. www.pocodiablo.com. 137 units. A/C TV TEL. Mid-Feb to mid-Nov $105–$245 double, $265 suite; late Nov to early Feb $99–$235 double, $245 suite. AE, CB, DISC, MC, V.

Although not nearly as lavish as golf resorts down in Phoenix, this older golf and tennis resort, located on the southern outskirts of Sedona, benefited from a complete renovation a couple of years ago. Oak Creek runs through the 22-acre grounds, and the green fairways of the nine-hole golf course provide a striking contrast to the red rocks and blue skies. The views here are not as good as at some other comparable properties in the area, but the staff is courteous and helpful. With its mission-style furnishings, contemporary Southwestern art, and Native American baskets and pottery, the lobby has the feel of a small inn, while the rest of the grounds all say resort. If you can afford to spend a bit more, be sure to ask for one of the rooms with a view of the golf course or the red rocks. These rooms have whirlpool tubs and fireplaces and are done in a modern rustic Southwest decor. The lower-end rooms are quite economical, but the upper-end rooms seem a bit overpriced.

The restaurant offers views of the golf course and red rocks and a Southwestern menu. The small, dark lounge is basically a sports bar. There are also two small pools, three whirlpools, four tennis courts (two lighted), racquetball courts, 9-hole golf course, concierge, room service, valet/laundry service, massages.

**Rose Tree Inn.** 376 Cedar St., Sedona, AZ 86336. ☎ **888/282-2065** or 520/282-2065. www.rosetreeinn.com. 5 units. A/C TV TEL. $85–$135 double. AE, MC, V.

This little inn is located only a block from Sedona's uptown shopping district and is tucked amid pretty gardens (yes, there are lots of roses) on a quiet street. The inn consists of an eclectic cluster of older buildings that have all been renovated. Four of the rooms have kitchenettes, which makes these good choices for families or for a longer stay. All the rooms are furnished a little bit differently—one Victorian, one Southwestern, another with a gas fireplace. There's also a whirlpool, and complimentary coffee and tea are available.

✪ **Saddle Rock Ranch.** 255 Rock Ridge Dr., Sedona, AZ 86336. ☎ **520/282-7640.** Fax 520/282-6829. www.saddlerockranch.com. 3 units. A/C TV. $125–$145 double. Rates include full breakfast. No credit cards.

The stunning views alone would make this one of Sedona's best lodging choices, but on top of the views, you get classic Western ranch styling (the house was built in 1926) in a home that once belonged to Barry Goldwater. Walls of stone and adobe, a flagstone floor in the living room, huge exposed beams, and plenty of windows to take in the scenery are enough to enchant guests even before they reach their rooms. And the rooms don't disappoint, either. In one you'll find Victorian elegance, in another an English canopy bed and stone fireplace. Dressing areas and private gardens add to the charm. The third room is a separate little Western cottage with a lodgepole-pine bed, flagstone floors, and beamed ceiling. The pool and whirlpool are surrounded by a flagstone terrace and enjoy one of the best red rock views in town.

## INEXPENSIVE

**Cedars Resort.** 20 W. Hwy. 89A (P.O. Box 292), Sedona, AZ 86339. ☎ **520/282-7010.** Fax 520/282-5372. 38 units. A/C TV TEL. $55–$88 double. AE, DISC, MC, V.

Located right at the "Y" (where it is often difficult to get out of the parking lot) and within walking distance of uptown Sedona, this economical motel is not exactly luxurious, but it has a fabulous view across Oak Creek to the towering red rocks. It also has a small pool, a hot tub, and a long stairway (77 steps) leading down to Oak Creek. Guest rooms are large, and all have refrigerators. For the best views, ask for a king-size room.

**Matterhorn Lodge.** 230 Apple Ave., Sedona, AZ 86336. ☎ **520/282-7176.** Fax 520/282-0727. www.sedona.net/hotel/matterhorn. 23 units. A/C TV TEL. Mid-Feb to Nov $74–$99 double; Dec to early Feb $49–$79 double. AE, MC, V. Small pets accepted.

Located in the heart of the uptown shopping district, the Matterhorn is convenient to restaurants and shopping, and all rooms have excellent views of the red rock canyon walls. The motel, which underwent a complete makeover a few years ago, has an adobe-style exterior and modern furnishings in the guest rooms. In-room amenities include coffeemakers, hair dryers, and refrigerators. An outdoor pool and whirlpool provide entertainment. Although the hotel overlooks busy U.S. 89A, if you lie in bed and keep your eyes on the rocks, you'll never notice the traffic below.

**Oak Creek Terrace Resort.** 4548 N. Hwy. 89A, Sedona, AZ 86336. ☎ **800/224-2229** or 520/282-3562. Fax 520/282-6061. www.sedona.net/resorts/oct. 20 units. A/C TV TEL. $72–$165 double. AE, DISC, MC, V. Small dogs accepted, $25 nonrefundable fee.

Wedged between the highway and Oak Creek about 5 miles north of Sedona on Ariz. 89A, this is sort of a romantic getaway for the financially challenged. For as little as $79 you can get a room with a fireplace and for $89 you can get a room with an in-room whirlpool. There are hammocks beside the creek, so you can stretch out in the shade, and a picnic area with barbecue grills if you want to save money on your dining budget. Rooms range from cramped to spacious, and most have a modern woodsy feel to them (though with a bit of Southwest styling thrown in). To get closer to the creek and farther from the highway, ask for a room in back. There are even on-site Jeep rentals.

**Sedona Motel.** P.O. Box 1450 (almost at the intersection of Ariz. 179 and Ariz. 89A), Sedona, AZ 86339. ☎ **520/282-7187.** 16 units. A/C TV TEL. $59–$89 double. DISC, MC, V.

Although the Sedona Motel looks like any other older motel from the outside, once you check in, you'll find a few surprises. First and foremost is the view across the parking lot to the red rocks. You can pay twice as much in Sedona and not have views this good. Despite being right on the highway, the hotel's double-paned windows help keep the rooms quiet and cool. Furnishings and bathroom fixtures are usually a cut above motel standards, which adds up to comfort and a good value.

✪ **Sky Ranch Lodge.** Airport Rd. (P.O. Box 2579), Sedona, AZ 86339. ☎ **888/708-6400** or 520/282-6400. Fax 520/282-7682. E-mail: skyranch@sedona.net. 94 units. A/C TV TEL. $75–$175 double. AE, MC, V. Pets accepted; $10 charge.

This motel is located atop Airport Mesa and has the most stupendous view in town. From here you can see the entire red rock country, with Sedona filling the valley below. Of course, the rooms with the best views are also the most expensive ($125 to $175), but if you're willing to walk a few feet for your view, you can stay here for much less. Although the rooms are fairly standard motel-style, some have such features as gas fire-places, barn-wood walls, and balconies. They all have coffeemakers.

## CAMPGROUNDS

Within the reaches of Oak Creek Canyon along U.S. 89A, there are five National Forest Service campgrounds. Of these, **Bootlegger,** 9 miles north of town, is the largest, though **Manzanita,** 6 miles north of town, is the most pleasant. Other Oak Creek Canyon campgrounds include **Pine Flat,** 13 miles north of town, and **Cave Springs,** 12 miles north of town. For more information on area campgrounds, stop by the **Coconino National Forest ranger station** (☎ 520/282-4119) on Brewer Road, just west of the intersection of U.S. 89A and Ariz. 179. Reservations can be made for Pine Flat and Cave Springs campgrounds; call ☎ 877/444-6777.

## WHERE TO DINE

For filling sandwiches and baked goodies, try **Sedona Memories,** 321 Jordan Rd. (☎ 520/282-0032), 1 block off Ariz. 89A in the uptown shopping area. Not only can you custom-design your sandwich, you can also peruse the collection of old Western movie posters and photos. **Connelly's Market,** 162 Ariz. 179, at the "Y" (☎ 520/282-4226), also makes up tasty inexpensive sandwiches to go. For breakfast, locals swear by the **Coffee Pot Restaurant,** 2050 W. Hwy. 89A (☎ 520/282-6626).

### EXPENSIVE

✪ **Cowboy Club.** 241 N. Hwy. 89A. ☎ **520/282-4200.** Reservations recommended. Main courses $6–$13 at lunch, $12–$30 at dinner. AE, MC, V. Daily 11am–4pm and 5–10pm. SOUTHWESTERN.

With its big green booths, huge steer horns over the bar, and saddles and guns adorning the walls, this place looks like a glorified cowboy steakhouse, but when you see the menu, you'll know it's more than your average meat-and-potatoes joint. This is big flavor country, and the menu isn't the sort that any real cowboy would likely have anything to do with. To start out, you can have fried cactus strips with black-bean caramel gravy or deep-fried pieces of snake with prickly pear tequila sauce. For an entree, grilled salmon with chipotle hollandaise or the baby back ribs with raspberry-plum barbecue sauce are almost too good to pass by. At lunch, burgers and sandwiches are mainstays, but you can also get a buffalo flank steak. Just don't miss the sweet

### How Sedona Got Its Name

Government bureaucracy and red tape are not new phenomena. Way back in the days when Sedona was being settled by pioneers, the new settlement needed a name. Carl Schnebly, first postmaster for this remote community, submitted two possibilities, but both were rejected by the postal service as being too long to fit on a cancellation stamp. So, at the suggestion of his brother, Schnebly named the town after his wife, Sedona (a name that fits very nicely on a cancellation stamp).

potato fries. There are usually one or two vegetarian alternatives here. Service is relaxed and friendly. By the way, it was in this building that the Cowboy Artists of America organization was formed back in 1965.

Adjacent to the Cowboy Club is an upscale version of the same restaurant, the Silver Saddle. Decor is more luxurious, with huge suede-covered booths and Western paintings, and a similar but toned-down menu with higher prices.

✪ **Dahl & DiLuca.** 2321 W. Hwy. 89A. ☎ **520/282-5219.** Reservations recommended. Main courses $10–$24. AE, DISC, MC, V. Daily 5–10pm. ROMAN ITALIAN.

In an atmosphere that is both romantic and humorous, brightly colored cherubs dance across the ceiling amid opulent decor. Maybe they're joyous because they've just eaten some *Pane roma,* which, as far as we're concerned, is the best garlic bread west of New York's Little Italy. Pasta predominates here, and portions are big. We like the linguine with calamari and mushrooms in a deep red basil sauce. The kitchen also serves up a panoply of deftly prepared seafood, chicken, and vegetarian dishes. Sautéed prawns in a garlic-parsley wine sauce are a real standout. Genial and efficient service, reasonably priced wines, and occasional live piano music make this place even more enjoyable. An amaretto crème brûlée or a deceptively light chocolate espresso mousse torte— that's the sort of difficult decision you'll have to make when it comes time for dessert.

**René at Tlaquepaque.** Tlaquepaque, Suite 118 (on Ariz. 179). ☎ **520/282-9225.** Reservations recommended. Main courses $8–$12 at lunch, $18–$29 at dinner. MC, V. Daily 11:30am–2:30pm; Mon–Thurs 5:30–8:30pm, Fri–Sat 5:30–9pm. CONTINENTAL/AMERICAN.

Slightly less expensive than the dining room at L'Auberge de Sedona resort, this elegant, traditional restaurant (lace curtains and paintings by Southwestern artists) offers the same sort of formal dining experience and traditional French fare. Located in Tlaquepaque, the city's upscale south-of-the-border-themed shopping center, René's is a great place for a special lunch or dinner. You might start off with traditional escargots or the spinach salad, followed by the house specialty rack of lamb or lamb chops with pistachio butter. More adventurous diners may want to try the excellent venison of antelope with juniper-berry sauce, or the roasted duck with sun-dried-cherry sauce. Finish with a flambéed dessert and selections from the after-dinner drink cart, then settle back to enjoy a warm glow of well-being. At lunch you could try the antelope chili or chicken marsala.

**Robert's Creekside Café.** Creekside Plaza, 251 Ariz. 179. ☎ **520/282-3671.** Reservations recommended. Main courses $6–$8 at lunch, $13–$19 at dinner. AE, DISC, MC, V. Daily 11am–9pm. SOUTHWEST.

This place bustles, and tables are small and close together, so we like to opt for a seat on the patio if it's available. At lunch, there are salads and sandwiches, such as a hearty eggplant sandwich with goat cheese and roasted red pepper. Dinner sees the likes of well-done seafoods and cracked-pepper steak. We especially like the nibble-perfect house smoked salmon pâté. There are more than the usual vegetarian choices here, especially in the realm of side dishes. If you show up on a weekend night, you just might catch some live music.

✪ **Yavapai Dining Room.** In the Enchantment Resort, 525 Boynton Canyon Rd. ☎ **520/ 204-6000.** Reservations highly recommended. Main courses $9–$16 at lunch, $19–$36 at dinner. AE, DISC, MC, V. Daily 7am–2:30pm and 5:30–9:30pm; brunch Sun 10:30am– 2:30pm. SOUTHWESTERN.

Because the view of the red rocks of Boynton Canyon are so much a part of the experience of dining here, we recommend coming for lunch or, preferably, a sunset dinner. Much of the dinner menu changes regularly, but it usually includes a few popular signature dishes. Among such dishes are the surprisingly complex black-bean soup, which gets a special touch with applewood-smoked bacon and cumin-scented tortilla strips. As for the entrees, you'll almost always find the seared tangerine pork tenderloin with an apricot chipotle glaze, which is not to be missed. The dessert tray is, of course, enchantingly decadent.

## MODERATE

**Fournos Restaurant.** 3000 W. Hwy. 89A. ☎ **520/282-3331.** Reservations highly recommended. Main courses $13–$15. No credit cards. Thurs–Sat seatings at 6 and 8pm, Sun (brunch), seating at noon. MEDITERRANEAN.

In contrast to the glitz and modern Southwest decor of so many other of Sedona's restaurants, Fournos is a refreshingly casual place run by the husband and wife team of Shirley and Demetrios Fournos. Pots and ladles hang from the kitchen ceiling in this tiny place where chef Demetrios cooks up a storm, preparing such dishes as Greek salads with homemade kalamata olives and shrimp flambéed in ouzo and baked with feta cheese. Many of the people who eat here are regulars, but even if this is your first time, Shirley will make you feel right at home. The menu is written on a chalkboard and includes specialties such as Colorado lamb Cephalonian with herbs and potatoes and poached fish Mykonos with a sauce of yogurt, onions, mayonnaise, and butter. Other specialties are rack of lamb and lamb Wellington, for a slightly higher price than the usual dinners. Greek pastries, such as a flourless semolina-honey sponge cake, come with ice cream and fruit for a delicious dessert.

✪ **The Heartline Cafe.** 1610 W. Hwy. 89A. ☎ **520/282-0785.** Reservations recommended. Main courses $6–$13 at lunch, $12–$28 at dinner. AE, DC, DISC, MC, V. Fri–Mon 11:30am–3pm; daily 5–9:15pm. SOUTHWESTERN/INTERNATIONAL.

The heart line, from Zuni mythology, is a symbol of health and longevity; it is also a symbol for the food here—healthful, and very creative. Service is good, and crusty bread appears on the table immediately (accompanied by unusual spreads made from such ingredients as butternut squash or eggplant). Attention to detail and creative flavor combinations are the order of the day, with dishes such as a watercress salad with grapes and pistachios, pecan crusted trout, or duck with dried cherry relish. Lunch fare leans toward tasty sandwiches and salads. Those searching out variety in vegetarian choices will find it here. A beautiful courtyard outside and a traditionally elegant interior are good places to savor a meal accompanied by a selection from the reasonably priced wine list, or desserts such as a fruit berry tart with warm hazelnut sauce.

**Pietro's Italian Restaurant.** 2445 W. U.S. 89A. ☎ **520/282-2525.** Reservations recommended. Main courses $16–$23; pastas $13–$17. AE, CB, DC, DISC, MC, V. Spring–fall daily 5:30–9:30pm; winter daily 5–9pm. TUSCAN.

Although in a very nondescript little building (you'd never guess from the outside that this is one of the better restaurants in town), Pietro's pushes the envelope of Italian creativity. You'll find appetizers such as calamari with smoked tomato-and-basil aioli and grilled eggplant rolled with goat cheese in a red-pepper sauce. For a pasta you might try fettuccine with duck confit, savoy cabbage, shiitake mushrooms, and figs in a port-wine sauce. Main courses are not quite as daring, but such dishes as boneless game hen with fresh rosemary, lemon, and garlic are certainly tasty. A wide range of wines, including many rare Italian reds and American boutique wines are available by the glass. From opening until 6:30pm, less expensive southern Italian dinners, such as lasagna, are served.

**Sedona Swiss Restaurant & Cafe.** 350 Jordan Rd. ☎ **520/282-7959.** Reservations recommended. Main courses $10–$24. AE, MC, V. Restaurant Mon–Sat 11am–2pm, 5:30–9:30pm. Cafe Mon–Sat 7:30am–6pm. Shorter hours in winter. SWISS/EUROPEAN.

Chef Robert Ackermann, this restaurant's founder and formerly the executive chef at the Swiss embassy in Washington, D.C., is the raison d'être for this authentically Swiss restaurant located in a quiet spot near old-town Sedona. You'll find classic Swiss and French fare such as *Rahmschnitzel* (sautéed pork scaloppini in a mushroom-cream sauce), cheese fondue, and the house specialty, *Galgenspiess*—beef tenderloin dramatically flambéed at your table. You can dine inside the cozy restaurant or outside on the patio. Visit the cafe/pastry shop for dessert and coffee.

### INEXPENSIVE

**Dara Thai.** 34 Bell Rock Plaza, in the Village of Oak Creek. ☎ **520/284-9167.** Reservations recommended Thurs–Sun for dinner. Main courses $7–$13. DISC, MC, V. Sun–Thurs 11am–3pm, 5–10pm; Fri–Sat 11am–10pm. THAI.

This is a little oasis for good Asian food in the Village of Oak Creek. *Pad Thai,* fried noodles with shrimp, chicken, bean sprouts, and topped with peanuts, is medium spicy and well flavored. The *tod mun,* patties of ground fish and curry paste, is juicy and spicy with *galangal,* a root spice, and cooled by a cucumber sauce. Although prices seemed a little on the high side for Thai food, they're probably in line with other prices in Sedona.

**The Hideaway Restaurant.** Country Square, Ariz. 179. ☎ **520/282-4204.** Reservations for 10 or more only. Main courses $5–$8 at lunch, $8.50–$11 at dinner. AE, DC, DISC, MC, V. Spring and summer daily 11am–10pm; fall and winter daily 11am–9pm. ITALIAN/DELI.

Hidden away at the back of a shopping plaza near the "Y," this casual family restaurant is as popular with locals as it is with visitors, despite the relatively high lunch prices. Pizzas, subs, sandwiches, salads, and pastas are the choices here, and though none of these dishes is particularly remarkable, the views from the deck certainly are. From the shady porch you can see the creek below and the red rocks rising up across the canyon. An early, sunset dinner is your best bet here.

## SEDONA AFTER DARK

Without a doubt, the lounge and patio at the Enchantment Resort are the best choices for a sunset cocktail. (See "Where to Stay," above, for directions.) Sedona also has its own microbrewery: **Oak Creek Brewing Co.,** 2050 Yavapai Dr. (☎ 520/204-1300), makes amber and nut brown ales as well as seasonal brews and has a small tasting room and beer garden rather than a full-scale brew pub. You'll find the brewery north of Ariz. 89A off Coffee Pot Drive.

The **Sedona Arts Center,** U.S. 89A at Art Barn Road (☎ 520/282-3865), has frequent performances of music and plays. Also check the schedule of the **Actors Repertory Theater of Sedona** (☎ 520/204-2064), a professional acting company that stages an interesting variety of plays each year. After late spring 2000, you might want to see if the **Sedona Cultural Park** (☎ 800/780-2787 or 520/282-0747) is up and running yet.

# The Grand Canyon & Northern Arizona

The Grand Canyon—the name is at once apt and inadequate. How can words sum up the grandeur of 2 billion years of the earth's history sliced open by the power of a single river? Once an impassable and forbidding barrier to explorers and settlers, the Grand Canyon is today a magnet that each year attracts millions of visitors from all over the world. Standing on the rim of what Arizonans like to call the Big Ditch, visitors gaze awestruck into the canyon's seemingly infinite depths.

Yet other parts of northern Arizona also contain worthwhile, and less crowded, attractions. Only 60 miles south of the great yawning chasm stand the San Francisco Peaks, the tallest of which, Humphreys Peak, rises 12,643 feet above sea level. These peaks, sacred to the Hopi and Navajo, are ancient volcanoes that today are popular with skiers, hikers, and mountain bikers. Smaller volcanoes in this region once made the land fertile enough to support the ancient Sinagua culture that has long since disappeared, leaving only the ruins of its ancient villages.

Amid northern Arizona's miles of windswept plains and ponderosa pine forests is the city of Flagstaff, which at 7,000 feet in elevation is one of the highest cities in the United States. It's also home to Northern Arizona University, whose students ensure that Flagstaff is a lively town. Born of the railroads and named for a flagpole, Flagstaff is best known as the jumping-off point for trips to the Grand Canyon but has also preserved its Western heritage in its restored downtown historic district.

In the name of progress and developing the desert, most of the great river canyons of Arizona have been dammed, and their sometimes quiet, sometimes angry waters have been turned into vast lakes. Among these is Lake Powell, created by the construction of the Glen Canyon Dam and now one of the biggest tourist attractions in the Southwest. The bitter fight to preserve Glen Canyon is a thing of the past, and today the lake is popular with boaters, anglers, and water-skiers, as well as sightseers who come from all over the world. This lake, with its miles of water mirroring steep canyon walls hundreds of feet high, is one of northern Arizona's curious contrasts—a vast artificial reservoir in the middle of barren desert canyons.

While it is the Grand Canyon that brings most people to northern Arizona, the region actually has much more to offer. If you only want to visit the canyon, you can do so in a group or alone, on foot or by raft, from a mule or a helicopter. Regardless of what you decide, the Grand Canyon will live up to its name.

# 1 Flagstaff

150 miles N of Phoenix; 32 miles E of Williams; 80 miles S of Grand Canyon Village

With its wide variety of accommodations and restaurants, the great outdoors at the edge of town, one of the state's finest museums, and a university that supports a lively cultural community, Flagstaff is an ideal base for exploring much of northern Arizona. However, this mountain town is best known as the jumping-off point for trips to the South Rim of the Grand Canyon.

The San Francisco Peaks, just north of the city and the site of the Arizona Snowbowl ski area, are one of Arizona's main winter playgrounds. In summer, miles of trails on these same mountains attract hikers and mountain bikers, and it's even possible to ride the ski lift at the Arizona Snowbowl for a panoramic vista that stretches 70 miles north to the Grand Canyon. Also within a short drive of the city are three national monuments, two of which preserve ancient Indian ruins and one of which preserves an otherworldly landscape of volcanic cinder cones.

Situated at 7,000 feet above sea level, Flagstaff is one of the highest cities in the country and is the county seat of Coconino County, the second-largest county in the United States. However, it was as a railroad town that Flagstaff made its fortunes. Today, after several years of renovation, the town's historic downtown now offers a glimpse of the days when the city's fortunes rode the rails. The railroad still runs right through the middle of Flagstaff, much to the dismay of many visitors, who find that most of the city's inexpensive motels are too close to the busy tracks to allow them to get a good night's sleep.

## ESSENTIALS

**GETTING THERE**    Flagstaff is on I-40, one of the main east-west interstates in the United States. I-17 also starts here and heads south to Phoenix. U.S. 89A connects Flagstaff to Sedona by way of Oak Creek Canyon. U.S. 180 connects Flagstaff with the South Rim of the Grand Canyon, and U.S. 89 connects to Page.

Flagstaff's Pulliam Airport, which is located 3 miles south of town off I-17, is served by **America West Express** (☎ **800/235-9292**) from Phoenix.

Flagstaff is also served by **Amtrak** (☎ **800/872-7245** or 520/774-8679 for schedule information) from Chicago and Los Angeles. The train station is at 1 E. Route 66.

**VISITOR INFORMATION**    For more information, contact the **Flagstaff Visitors Center,** 1 E. Route 66, Flagstaff, AZ 86001 (☎ **800/842-7293** or 520/774-9541; www.flagstaff.az.us).

**GETTING AROUND**    Car rentals are available from **Avis** (☎ **800/331-1212** or 520/774-8421), **Budget** (☎ **800/527-0700** or 520/779-5255), **Enterprise** (☎ **800/ 325-8007** or 520/526-1377), **Hertz** (☎ **800/654-3131** or 520/774-4452), and **National** (☎ **800/227-7368** or 520/774-3321).

If you need a taxi, call **Friendly Cab** (☎ **520/774-4444**).

**Pine Country Transit** (☎ **520/779-6624**), provides public bus transit around the city; the fare is 75¢ for adults.

**ORIENTATION**    Downtown Flagstaff is located just north of I-40. Milton Road, which at its southern end becomes I-17 to Phoenix, leads past Northern Arizona University on its way into downtown, where it becomes Route 66. Route 66 runs parallel to the railroad tracks. Downtown's main street is San Francisco Street, while Humphreys Street leads north out of town toward the San Francisco Peaks and the South Rim of the Grand Canyon.

# The Grand Canyon & Northern Arizona

0        15 Miles
0        15 Kilometers

**N**

**UTAH**
**ARIZONA**

Kanab        89

Fredonia        389

89A

**Pipe Spring National Monument**

Jacob Lake        89A

67

**KAIBAB PLATEAU**

Colorado River

3

**Grand Canyon National Park**

Supai

**Havasupai Indian Reservation**

**NORTH RIM**

**Hualapai Indian Reservation**

**Grand Canyon Village**

**SOUTH RIM**

Tusayan

**COCONINO PLATEAU**

18

180

64

To Grand Canyon West, Grand Canyon Caverns & Peach Springs

66

Seligman

Ash Fork

40

180

64

**Humphreys Peak**

4

Williams

**Kaibab National Forest**

5

8

Flagstaff

6

40

To Winslow & Homolovi Ruins State Park

7

89

17

89A

Glen Canyon Nat'l Rec. Area

Lake Powell        1

Lees Ferry

Marble Canyon        2        Page

**KAIBITO PLATEAU**

Echo Cliffs

98

89

**Navajo Indian Reservation**

160

Tuba City

Marble Canyon

Desert View

10        Cameron

Little Colorado River

**PAINTED DESERT**

9

**LEGEND**
✈ Airport
⛷ Ski Area

To Prescott        ↓

↙ To Sedona

Arizona Snowbowl        5
Cameron Trading Post        10
Glen Canyon Dam        2
Grand Canyon Railway        4
Havasu Canyon        3
Meteor Crater        7

Rainbow Bridge
   National Monument        1
Sunset Crater
   National Monument        8
Walnut Canyon
   National Monument        6
Wupatki National Monument        9

NA-0256

**187**

## ENJOYING THE OUTDOORS

Flagstaff is northern Arizona's center for outdoor activities. Chief among these is snow skiing at **Arizona Snowbowl** (information ☎ **520/779-1951;** snow report 520/779-4577; snow report from Phoenix 602/957-0404) on the slopes of Mount Agassiz, from which you can see all the way to the North Rim of the Grand Canyon. There are four chair lifts, 32 runs, and 2,300 vertical feet of slopes. There are also ski rentals and a children's ski program. This ski area has an excellent mix of beginner, intermediate, and advanced slopes, and consequently attracts many different types of skiers. As the ski area that's most accessible from Phoenix, Snowbowl sees a lot of weekend traffic from the snow-starved denizens of the desert. Good powder snow is not, unfortunately, as reliable as one might wish, which means that this is not the place to head for your winter vacation unless you're certain of the snow conditions. All-day lift tickets are $35 for adults, $20 for children 8 to 12, and $15 for seniors 65 to 69, free for children under 8 and seniors over 69. In the summer you can ride a chair lift almost to the summit of Mount Agassiz and enjoy the expansive views across seemingly all of northern Arizona. The round-trip lift ticket price is $9 for adults, $6.50 for seniors, $5 for children 6 to 12, free for children 5 and under.

Snowbowl also operates the **Flagstaff Nordic Center** (☎ **520/779-1951**), which is 16 miles north of Flagstaff and has 40 kilometers of groomed track. Equipment rentals and ski lessons are available. All-day trail passes are $10.

Snowmobile rentals are also available at Mormon Lake from **Mormon Lake Lodge** (☎ **520/354-2227**). If a sleigh ride is more your speed, contact **Hitchin' Post Stables,** 4848 Lake Mary Rd. (☎ **520/774-1719**), which charges $15 for a ride or $45 to $55 for a sleigh ride and dinner.

When there's no snow on the ground, there are plenty of **hiking trails** throughout the San Francisco Peaks. Many national forest trails in the area are open to mountain bikes as well as to hikers. Late September, when the aspens have turned to a brilliant golden yellow, is one of the best times of year for a hike in Flagstaff's mountains. For information on the many excellent hiking trails in the Coconino National Forest, contact the **Peaks Ranger District,** Coconino National Forest, 5075 N. Hwy. 89, Flagstaff, AZ 86004 (☎ **520/526-0866**).

If you feel like saddlin' up and hittin' the trail, contact **Hitchin' Post Stables,** 4848 Lake Mary Rd. (☎ **520/774-1719**). This horseback-riding stable offers guided trail rides, sunset steak rides, and cowboy breakfast rides. The most popular trail ride goes into Walnut Canyon, site of ancient cliff dwellings. Ride prices range from $25 for a 1-hour ride to $95 for the Walnut Canyon ride. **Flying Heart at Flagstaff** (☎ **520/526-2788**), located 3½ miles north of Flagstaff Mall on U.S. 89, leads rides up into the foothills of the San Francisco Peaks and out through the juniper and piñon forests of the lower elevations. Rides are $25 for a 1-hour ride and $40 for a 2-hour ride.

If you want to rent a mountain bike and head out on the trails around town, stop by **Mountain Sports,** 1800 S. Milton Rd. (☎ **800/286-5156** or 520/779-5156), which charges $25 (front suspension) to $45 (full suspension) a day.

Golfers can play a round at the 18-hole **Elden Hills Golf Course,** 2380 N. Oakmont Dr. (☎ **520/527-7999**).

## SEEING THE SIGHTS

Downtown Flagstaff along Route 66, San Francisco Street, Aspen Avenue, and Birch Avenue is the city's **historic district.** The old brick buildings of this neighborhood are now filled with shops selling Native American handcrafts, arts and crafts by local artisans, Route 66 souvenirs, and various other Arizona souvenirs such as rocks, minerals, and crystals. This historic area is worth a walk through even if you aren't shopping.

# Flagstaff

To Grand Canyon
and Arizona Snowbowl

Museum of
Northern
Arizona

Arizona
Historical
Society/
Pioneer
Museum

180

Buffalo Park

Fir Ave.

Juniper Ave.

Turquoise Dr.

Fort Valley Rd.

Forest Ave.

Downtown Flagstaff

Columbus Ave.

Lowell
Observatory

Elm Ave.
Dale Ave.
Cherry Ave.
Birch Ave.
Aspen Ave.

Humphreys St.
Beaver St.
Leroux St.
San Francisco St.
Agassiz St.

Switzer Canyon Dr.

Amtrak
Station
& Visitor
Center

Visitors
Center

Bus
Terminal

Milton Rd.

Humphreys St.
Beaver St.
Leroux St.
San Francisco St.

E. Route 66

To
Grand Canyon
East Entrance &
Wupatki & Sunset Crater
National Monuments

W. Route 66

Riordan Rd.

Meadows St.

Vale St.

University Ave.

Riordan
Ranch St.

Knoles Dr.

San Francisco St.

To Walnut Canyon
National Monument,
Winslow,
Meteor Crater &
Petrified Forest

Forest

Riordan
Mansion
State Park

Milton Rd.

Northern
Arizona
University

McConnell

Beulah Blvd.

40

40

17

Artz
89A

To
Phoenix

To
Mormon
Lake

0          1/2 Mile

0          1/2 Kilometer

N

NA-0257

189

During the summer, **Nava-Hopi Tours** (☎ 520/774-5003) operates a trolley tour that takes in most of the city's museums and other attractions. Tours cost $19.50 for adults and $9.50 for children ages 5 to 15.

## MUSEUMS, PARKS & CULTURAL ACTIVITIES

✪ **Museum of Northern Arizona.** 3101 N. Fort Valley Rd. (3 miles north of downtown Flagstaff on U.S. 180). ☎ **520/774-5213.** Admission $5 adults, $4 seniors, $3 students, $2 children 7–17. Daily 9am–5pm. Closed Jan 1, Thanksgiving, and Dec 25.

This small but surprisingly thorough museum is the ideal first stop on an exploration of northern Arizona. Here you'll learn, through state-of-the-art exhibits, about the archaeology, ethnology, geology, biology, and fine arts of the region. The cornerstone of the museum is an exhibit that explores life on the Colorado Plateau from 15,000 B.C. to the present. Among the other displays are a life-size kiva ceremonial room and a small but interesting collection of kachinas. The large gift shop is full of contemporary Native American arts and crafts. Throughout the summer there are special exhibits focusing on Hopi, Navajo, and Zuni arts and crafts.

The museum building itself is made of native stone and incorporates a courtyard featuring vegetation from the six life zones of northern Arizona. Outside the museum is a short self-guided nature trail that leads through a narrow canyon strewn with boulders. Kids will enjoy the dinosaur sculptures made from old car parts.

✪ **Lowell Observatory.** 1400 W. Mars Hill Rd. ☎ **520/774-2096.** Admission $3.50 adults, $3 seniors, $1.50 children 5–17. Apr–Aug daily 9am–5pm; Sept–Mar daily noon–5pm. Call for hours and days of evening telescope viewings.

Located atop aptly named Mars Hill is one of the oldest astronomical observatories in the Southwest. Founded in 1894 by Percival Lowell, the observatory has played important roles in contemporary astronomy. Among the work carried out here was Lowell's study of the planet Mars and his calculations that led him to predict the existence of the planet Pluto. It wasn't until 13 years after Lowell's death that Pluto was finally discovered, almost exactly where he had predicted it would be. Today this is still an important research facility, but most astronomical observations are now carried out at Anderson Mesa, which is 10 miles farther away from the lights of Flagstaff.

The facility consists of several observatories, a large visitor center with numerous fun and educational exhibits, and outdoor displays. Keep in mind that the telescope domes are not heated, so if you come up to observe the stars on a wintry night, be sure to dress appropriately.

**Arizona Historical Society/Pioneer Museum.** 2340 N. Fort Valley Rd. ☎ **520/ 774-6272.** Admission $1 suggested donation. Mon–Sat 9am–5pm. Closed Jan 1, Thanksgiving, and Dec 25.

This museum houses a historical collection from northern Arizona's pioneer days. The main museum building is a large stone structure that was built in 1908 as a hospital for the indigent (Poor Farm). Among the exhibits are pieces of camera equipment used by Emery Kolb at his studio on the South Rim of the Grand Canyon. Many of Kolb's photos are also on display. Several small exhibit rooms cover various aspects of life in northern Arizona during the pioneer days and later. You'll see a doctor's office filled with frightening instruments, barbed wire and brands, dolls, saddles, and trapping and timber displays.

**Riordan Mansion State Park.** 1300 Riordan Ranch St. (off Milton Rd./U.S. 89A, just north of the junction of I-40 and I-17). ☎ **520/779-4395.** Admission $4 adults, $2.50 ages 7–13, free for children 6 and under. May–Sept daily 8am–5pm; Oct–Apr daily 11am–5pm. Guided tours on the hour (advance reservations recommended). Closed Dec 25.

Built in 1904 for local timber barons Michael and Timothy Riordan, this 13,000-square-foot mansion is actually two houses connected by a large central hall. Each of the two Riordan brothers and his family occupied one half of the house, and they had the rooflines constructed differently so that visitors could tell the two sides apart. The home is built in the Craftsmen style, and though it looks like a log cabin, it's actually only faced with log slabs.

The Riordans played important roles in the early history of Flagstaff. They helped establish the first Roman Catholic church, the first library, the power company, and the phone company.

**The Arboretum at Flagstaff.** Woody Mountain Rd. ☎ **520/774-1441.** Admission May–Oct $3 adults, $1 children 6–18, free for children under 6. Mid-Mar to Apr and Nov–Dec 23 $1 adults, free for children 18 and under. May–Oct daily 9am–4pm; mid-Mar to Apr and Nov–Dec 23 Mon–Fri 9am–4pm. Guided tours at 11am and 1pm. Closed Dec 24 to mid-Mar.

Covering 200 acres, this arboretum, the highest-elevation research garden in the U.S., focuses on plants of the high desert, coniferous forests, and alpine tundra, all of which are environments found in the vicinity of Flagstaff. On the grounds, you'll also find a butterfly garden, an herb garden, a shade garden, and a passive solar greenhouse.

## NEARBY ATTRACTIONS

**Walnut Canyon National Monument.** 7 miles east of Flagstaff on Walnut Canyon Rd. (take Exit 204 off I-40). ☎ **520/526-3367.** Admission $3 adults, free for children under 17. Daily 8am–5pm (until 6pm in summer); trail closes 1 hour earlier.

The remains of hundreds of 13th-century Sinagua cliff dwellings can be seen in this dry, wooded canyon east of Flagstaff. The undercut layers of limestone in the 400-foot-deep canyon proved ideal for building dwellings well protected both from the elements and from enemies. The Sinagua were the same people who built and then abandoned the stone pueblos found in Wupatki National Monument to the north of here. It's theorized that when the land to the north lost its fertility, the Sinagua began migrating southward, and settled for 150 years in Walnut Canyon.

A self-guided trail leads from the visitor center on the canyon rim down 185 feet to a section of the canyon wall where 25 cliff dwellings can be viewed and entered. Look closely and you can still see handprints in the mud that was used to cement the dwellings' stone walls together. There's also a picnic area near the visitor center.

**Sunset Crater Volcano National Monument.** 18 miles north of Flagstaff off U.S. 89. ☎ **520/526-0502.** Admission $3 adults, free for children under 17 (admission also valid for Wupatki National Monument). Daily sunrise to sunset; visitor center daily 8am–5pm (6pm in summer). Closed Dec 25.

Dotting the landscape northeast of Flagstaff are more than 400 volcanic craters, of which Sunset Crater Volcano is the youngest. Taking its name from the sunset colors of the cinders near its summit, Sunset Crater Volcano stands 1,000 feet tall and began forming in A.D. 1064. Over a period of 100 years, the volcano erupted repeatedly, creating the red-and-yellow cinder cone we see today, and eventually covered an area of 800 square miles with ash, lava, and cinders. There's a mile-long interpretive trail that passes through a desolate landscape of lava flows, cinders, and ash as it skirts the base of this volcano. In the visitor center (at the west entrance to the national monument) you can learn more about the formation of Sunset Crater and about volcanoes in general. Near the visitor center is a small campground that's open from spring to fall.

✪ **Wupatki National Monument.** 36 miles north of Flagstaff off U.S. 89. ☎ **520/679-2365.** Admission $3 adult, free for children under 17. Daily sunrise–sunset; visitor center, daily 8am–5pm (6pm in summer). Closed Dec 25.

The landscape northeast of Flagstaff is desolate and windswept, a sparsely populated region carpeted with volcanic ash deposited in the 11th century. It comes as quite a surprise, then, to learn that this area contains hundreds of prehistoric and historic habitation sites. The most impressive ruins are those left by the *Sinagua* (the name means "without water" in Spanish) people who inhabited this area from around A.D. 1100 until shortly after 1200. The Sinagua people built small villages of stone similar to the pueblos on the nearby Hopi reservation, and today the ruins of these ancient villages can be seen, in this national monument.

The largest of the prehistoric pueblos is the Wupatki ruin in the southeastern part of the monument. Here the Sinagua built a sprawling three-story pueblo containing nearly 100 rooms. They also constructed what is believed to be a ball court, which though quite different in design from the courts of the Aztec and Maya, leaves no doubt that a similar game was played. Another circular stone structure just below the main ruins may have been an amphitheater or dance plaza.

The most unusual feature of Wupatki, however, is a natural phenomenon: a blow-hole, which may have been the reason this pueblo was constructed here. A network of small underground tunnels and chambers acts as a giant barometer, blowing air through the blowhole when the underground air is under greater pressure than the outside air. On hot days, cool air rushes out of the blowhole with amazing force.

Several other ruins within the national monument are easily accessible by car. These include Nalakihu, Citadel, and Lomaki, which are the closest to U.S. 89, and Wukoki, which is near Wupatki. Wukoki ruin is built atop a huge sandstone boulder and is particularly picturesque. The monument's visitor center is located adjacent to the Wupatki ruins. Here you'll find interesting exhibits on the Sinagua and Anasazi people who once inhabited the region.

## ORGANIZED TOURS

**Gray Line/Nava-Hopi Tours** (☎ **877/GO-SEE-AZ** or 520/774-5003) operates several day-long tours of northern Arizona. These tours include excursions to the South Rim of the Grand Canyon ($38 adults, $19 children 5 to 15); Lake Powell and Page, with a float trip on the Colorado River ($89 adults, $81 children 5 to 15); Sedona and the Verde Valley ($36 adults, $18 children 5 to 15); the Navajo Indian Reservation ($74 adults, $37 children 5 to 15); and the Petrified Forest, Painted Desert, and Meteor Crater ($58 adults, $29 children 5 to 15).

### JOINING AN ARCHAEOLOGICAL DIG

On the north side of Flagstaff on U.S. 89, there is a small archaeological site called Elden Pueblo, which is open to the public free of charge. These Sinagua ruins are not much to look at, but, if you're interested, you can help out with the excavation of the site. Each summer, the **Elden Pueblo Archaeological Project,** P.O. Box 3496, Flagstaff, AZ 86003 (☎ **520/527-3475**), hosts several public days as well as field schools for members of the Arizona Archaeological Society (AAS). Field schools cost $75 per week plus the $25 AAS membership dues.

## WHERE TO STAY
### EXPENSIVE

✪ **The Inn at 410.** 410 N. Leroux St., Flagstaff, AZ 86001. ☎ **800/774-2008** or 520/774-0088. Fax 520/774-6354. www.inn410.com. 9 units. A/C. $125–$175 double. Rates include full breakfast. MC, V.

Located only 2 blocks from downtown Flagstaff, this restored 1907 bungalow is one of the best B&Bs in Arizona and provides convenience, pleasant surroundings, comfortable rooms, and delicious breakfasts. A large front porch (complete with swing), a comfortably furnished living room and dining room, and a pleasant garden patio dining area all add up to plenty of places to lounge about. Rooms all feature different, distinctive themes, and seven of them have their own fireplaces. The Dakota Suite and the Southwest room are our personal favorites since they conjure up the inn's Western/Southwestern heritage. Some of the rooms are in a new building to one side of the old house, and one of these is wheelchair accessible. If you're lucky, you might get innkeeper Sally Krueger's award-winning curried cornbread pudding with pumpkin sauce for breakfast.

## MODERATE

**Arizona Mountain Inn.** 4200 Lake Mary Rd., Flagstaff, AZ 86001. ☎ **520/774-8959.** Fax 520/774-8837. 20 units. $90–$110 double; $80–$110 cabin. DISC, MC, V. Pets accepted, but must be supervised.

Located just a few minutes south of downtown Flagstaff, the Arizona Mountain Inn is a quiet mountain retreat set beneath shady pine trees. Though there are three bed-and-breakfast rooms in the main building, all the rest of the accommodations here are cabins that can sleep anywhere from 2 to 16 people. Many of the rustic cabins are A-frames or chalets and each is a little bit different from the others. The family oriented inn has 13 acres surrounding it, and beyond the grounds are miles of national forest. Facilities include volleyball and basketball courts, a playground, horseshoe pits, and a coin laundry.

✪ **Jeanette's Bed & Breakfast.** 3380 E. Lockett Rd., Flagstaff, AZ 86004-4043. ☎ **800/752-1912** or 520/527-1912. www.bbonline.com/az/jbb. 4 units. $95–$125 double. Rates include full breakfast. MC, V.

If you've ever wanted to step back in time and live in the early decades of the 20th century, then you might want to spend some time at this unusual B&B a few miles from downtown Flagstaff. Innkeepers Jeanette and Ray West built this new "old house" a few years ago, and their attention to details is astounding. There are vintage tubs and sinks, vintage heat grates, vintage light switches, and of course plenty of antique furniture. What you might not expect is that wardrobes and dressers and trunks are filled with vintage clothing. The house is designed as a 1912 Victorian home that has been updated to a less cluttered 1920s look. One room has a fireplace, while another has a porch with a view of nearby Mt. Elden. Mornings start with coffee in the parlor and then an elaborate Victorian breakfast.

**Little America.** 2515 E. Butler Ave., Flagstaff, AZ 86004. ☎ **800/352-4386** or 520/779-7900. Fax 520/779-7983. 248 units. A/C TV TEL. $65–$119 double; $135–$225 suite. AE, CB, DC, DISC, MC, V. Take Exit 198 off I-40.

At first it might seem as if Little Americas, of which there are several around the West, are little more than glorified truck stops, but on closer inspection you'll find that this one, a spread-out complex beneath the pines on the east side of Flagstaff, is an excellent economy hotel. The interior decor is dated but fun, with a sort of over-the-top French provincial styling, and rooms vary in size. However, all have small private balconies and huge TVs. One suite has a fireplace, and one has a sauna.

There's a casual dining room plus a more formal restaurant that serves steaks and Continental dishes. The hotel also offers room service, laundry/dry cleaning, a courtesy van, a pool, a fitness room, badminton, volleyball, croquet, and jogging/hiking trails.

**Radisson Woodlands Hotel Flagstaff.** 1175 W. Rte. 66, Flagstaff, AZ 86001. ☎ **800/333-3333** or 520/773-8888. Fax 520/773-0597. 185 units. A/C TV TEL. $89–$109 double; $99–$139 suite. AE, CB, DC, DISC, MC, V.

With its elegant marble-floored lobby, the Woodlands Hotel is easily the most upscale and luxurious hotel in Flagstaff. A white baby grand piano, crystal chandelier, traditional European furnishings, and contemporary sculpture all add to the unexpected Liberace-style luxury, as do intricately carved pieces of furniture and architectural details from different Asian countries. Traditional European styling, with Southwestern touches, is used in the guest-room decor.

One of the two restaurants here serves Japanese meals with table-side cooking and a sushi bar, while the other features traditional American fare with a few international and Southwestern dishes. The hotel also offers room service, an outdoor pool, two whirlpools, a sauna, steam room, and fitness center.

✪ **The Sled Dog Inn.** 10155 Mountainaire Rd., Flagstaff, AZ 86001. ☎ **800/754-0664** or 520/525-6212. www.sleddoginn.com. 10 units. A/C. $109–$119 double. Rates include full breakfast. AE, MC, V.

For outdoor-sports enthusiasts, this is *the* place to stay in the Flagstaff area. Located on the edge of a meadow south of the city, the Sled Dog Inn is a contemporary building that abounds in wood, much of which was salvaged from buildings that were being torn down. The inn has 15 Siberian huskies, and when there is enough snow in the winter, dog sled rides are a popular activity here. However, rock-climbing, cross-country skiing, and mountain-biking excursions are also offered. At the end of an active day, the hot tub out the back door is always welcome. There's also workout equipment in the upstairs lounge. Guest rooms are modern lodge rustic and are comfortable and uncluttered. Don't be surprised if you wake up and see elk grazing right outside your window. "Adventure du Jour" packages that include various outdoors activities are the specialty of the house here.

## INEXPENSIVE

In addition to the hotels listed below, you'll also find numerous budget chain motels in Flagstaff. These include **Motel 6,** 2440 E. Lucky Lane (☎ 520/774-8756), charging $38 to $50 for a double; and **Motel 6,** 2745 S. Woodlands Village (☎ 520/779-3757), charging $40 to $60 for a double. See appendix B for toll-free numbers. Flagstaff also has dozens of old Route 66 motels that aren't for the fussy but that usually charge under $30 for a double.

**Hotel Monte Vista.** 100 N. San Francisco St., Flagstaff, AZ 86001. ☎ **520/779-6971.** Fax 520/779-2904. 50 units, 44 with private bathroom. TV TEL. $40 double with shared bathroom, $55–$75 double with private bathroom; $90–$120 suite. AE, DISC, MC, V.

If you don't mind roughing it a bit for a chance to sleep in a hotel once frequented by the likes of Clark Gable, John Wayne, Walter Brennan, Alan Ladd, Jane Russell, Spencer Tracy, Lee Marvin, Carole Lombard, and Gary Cooper, check out the Monte Vista. Originally opened in 1927, this hotel was renovated in the mid-1980s. Today the hotel appeals mostly to a younger crowd, especially college students and young European travelers who appreciate the economical rates and the bar. In the small, dark lobby (a bit the worse for wear) are painted ceiling beams and Victorian furniture. The rooms vary in size, and many are furnished with oak furniture and ceiling fans. We like the corner rooms best because they have windows on two sides. Although the hotel has plenty of old-fashioned flair, don't expect top-notch accommodations. Check out a room first to see if this is your kind of place.

✪ **Hotel Weatherford.** 23 N. Leroux St., Flagstaff, AZ 86001. ☎ **520/779-1919.** Fax 520/773-8951. www.weatherfordhotel.com. 8 units, 5 with private bathroom; 2 dorms. $35 double with shared bathroom, $65 double with private bathroom; $16 dormitory. AE, CB, DC, DISC, MC, V.

For many years now this historic hotel has been known primarily as a youth hostel frequented by backpacking European travelers. However, as part of an ongoing 20-year restoration by owners Henry Taylor and Sam Green-Taylor, the hotel is beginning to rise above hostel level. Although only a few of the hotel's rooms have yet been renovated, for fans of historic hotels, these rooms are worth checking out. The distinctive stone-walled hotel, which was built in 1897, has a wrap-around verandah on its second floor. The second floor is also where you'll find the beautifully restored Zane Grey Ballroom, which now serves as an elegant bar. Downstairs is the ever-popular Charly's Pub & Grill, which has been booking live rock, blues, and jazz acts for two decades. There's also a diner still frequented by Flagstaff's old-timers.

## WHERE TO DINE

In addition to the restaurants mentioned below, **Oregano's Pizza Bistro,** a place for inexpensive and tasty pizzas and pastas, is located at 605 W. Riordan Rd. (☎ **520/ 773-8600**).

### MODERATE

**Chez Marc Bistro.** 503 Humphreys St. ☎ **520/774-1343.** Reservations recommended. Main courses $13–$16 at lunch, $20–$30 at dinner. AE, CB, DC, MC, V. Sun–Thurs 11:30am–3pm and 5–9:30pm, Fri–Sat 11:30am–3m and 5–10pm (closes 30 min. earlier for lunch and dinner in winter season). FRENCH.

This is the most elegant restaurant in town, and if it weren't for the busy street in front, the historic stone and half-timbered house could pass for a country inn. The renovated old house has a big front porch and inside are several small dining rooms, one of which has a cozy fireplace. Creative combinations such as pistachio duck pâté and broiled salmon with tomato onion tart may not be traditional French fare, but country French cooking is definitely the focus of the menu. The wine list is excellent.

**Cottage Place Restaurant.** 126 W. Cottage Ave. ☎ **520/774-8431.** Reservations recommended. 3-course meals $15–$23. AE, MC, V. Tues–Sun 5–9:30pm. CONTINENTAL/ NEW AMERICAN.

Located on the south side of the railroad tracks in a neighborhood mostly frequented by college students, Cottage Place is just what its name implies—an unpretentious little cottage. But despite the casual appearance, dining is a formal affair. The menu (which tends toward the rich side) is primarily continental, but there are Southwestern and Middle Eastern influences as well. The house specialties are chateaubriand and rack of lamb (both served for two), and there are always several choices for vegetarians. The appetizer sampler, with stuffed mushrooms, charbroiled shrimp, and *tiropitas* (cheese-stuffed phyllo pastries) is a winner, as is an unusual and creamy wild rice soup. There are a few wines by the glass, priced on the high side, and for dessert, a tasty nonfat yogurt mousse with berries.

✪ **Marc's Cafe Americain Brasserie & Wine Bar.** 801 S. Milton Rd. ☎ **520/556-0093.** Reservations recommended. Main courses $7–$11 at lunch, $10–$19 at dinner. AE, DC, DISC, MC, V. Daily 11am–2:30pm and 4:30–9pm. FRENCH.

This spin-off from Chez Marc (see above) is a more casual brasserie-style eatery in a strip mall along Milton Road and, despite its reasonable prices, is certainly not a college hangout. Crepes, pastas, and excellent rotisseried meats are the specialties, but you can also get bouillabaisse and a few other seafood dishes. Flavorful salad dressings, sauces, and spreads are a strong point, as are the brasserie fries, which shouldn't be missed. An open kitchen in the middle of the restaurant provides a bit of entertainment, and more than 30 wines are available by the glass. In fact, wines are emphasized here, and you'll dine surrounded by wine bottles.

## INEXPENSIVE

😊 **Beaver Street Brewery.** 11 S. Beaver St. ☎ **520/779-0079.** Main courses $7.50–$10. AE, DISC, MC, V. Sun 11am–10pm, Mon–Thurs 11am–11pm, Fri–Sat 11am–midnight. BURGERS/PIZZA.

This big microbrewery and cafe located in a former supermarket on the south side of the railroad tracks in downtown Flagstaff serves up several good brews, but it also does great pizzas and burgers. The Beaver Street pizza, which is made with roasted-garlic pesto, sun-dried tomatoes, fresh basil, and soft goat cheese is particularly tasty. There are also robust salads, such as a Mongolian beef salad with sesame-ginger dressing, and even fondue. This place stays packed with college students, but a good pint of ale helps any wait pass quickly, especially if you can grab a chair by the woodstove.

**Café Espress.** 16 N. San Francisco St. ☎ **520/774-0541.** Sandwiches/plates $5–$9. MC, V. Daily 7am–9pm. INTERNATIONAL/VEGETARIAN.

Grab a newspaper from the basket by the door, sit down at one of the tables by the front window, and ensconce yourself in college life all over again. If you happen to be a student (or one at heart), this place will become your favorite dining spot in Flagstaff. You can start the day with granola, grab a tempeh or turkey burger for lunch, and then have *spanakopita* or artichoke scampi for dinner. There are good sandwiches, a salad bar, and espresso as well.

😊 **Macy's European Coffee House & Bakery.** 14 S. Beaver St. ☎ **520/774-2243.** Meals $3–$6. No credit cards. Sun 6am–6pm, Mon–Wed 6am–8pm, Thurs–Sat 6am–9pm. COFFEE/BAKERY.

Good espresso and baked goodies draw people in here the first time, but there are also decent vegetarian pasta dishes, soups, salads, and other old college-town standbys. This is Flagstaff's counterculture hang out, and it attracts both students and professors. The opera posters on the walls add a touch of European flavor to the surroundings. For the true Macy's experience, order one of the huge lattes and a scone or other pastry.

**Pasto.** 19 E. Aspen St. ☎ **520/779-1937.** Reservations recommended. Main courses $8–$16. AE, MC, V. Sun–Thurs 5–9pm, Fri–Sat 5–9:30pm (until 10pm in summer). ITALIAN.

Operated by the same folks who run Café Espress, Pasto is a health-conscious Italian restaurant in downtown Flagstaff and is popular with the hip and young at heart. Billing itself as "Fun Italian Dining," Pasto has a flamboyant decor and casual atmosphere. The menu includes a good assortment of pastas, of course, but there are also dishes such as chicken marsala and artichoke orzo. On some weekend nights, there is a strolling violinist.

## FLAGSTAFF AFTER DARK

Check *Flare*, a free weekly arts-and-entertainment newspaper available at shops and restaurants downtown, for events taking place during your visit. The university has many musical and theatrical groups that perform throughout most of the year, and several clubs around town book a variety of live music acts.

The **Flagstaff Symphony Orchestra** (☎ 520/774-5107) provides the city with a full season of classical music. Performances are held at Ardrey Auditorium on Knoles Drive on the campus of Northern Arizona University. Ticket prices range from $12 to $35.

For professional theater, check the schedule at **Arizona TheatreWorks,** 120 N. Leroux St. (☎ 520/774-7555), which stages a surprisingly eclectic range of plays. Tickets range from about $5 to $10. The city's community theater group, **Theatrikos** (☎ 520/774-1662), performs at the Flagstaff Playhouse, 11 W. Cherry St. Tickets are $9 to $14.

For a livelier scene, check out the **Museum Club,** 3404 E. Route 66 (☎ **520/ 526-9434**), a Flagstaff institution and one of America's classic roadhouses. Built in the early 1900s and often called the Zoo Club, this cavernous log saloon is filled with deer antlers, stuffed animals, and trophy heads. There's live music, predominantly country and western, most nights.

## 2  Williams

58 miles S of the Grand Canyon; 32 miles W of Flagstaff; 220 miles E of Las Vegas

Although it's almost 60 miles south of the Grand Canyon, Williams is still the closest real town. Consequently it has dozens of motels catering to people who were unable to get a room at the park. However, Williams, founded in 1880 as a railroading and logging town, also has a bit of Western history to boast about. Old brick commercial buildings dating to the late 19th century line the main street, while modest Victorian homes sit on the tree-shaded streets that spread south from the railroad tracks.

In recent years, mid–20th-century history has taken center stage. Williams was the last town on historic Route 66 to be bypassed by I-40, and consequently, the town plays up its Route 66 heritage.

Named for famed mountain man Bill Williams, the town sits at the edge of a ponderosa pine forest atop the Mogollon Rim, and surrounding the town is the Kaibab National Forest. Within the forest and not far out of town are good fishing lakes, hiking and mountain-biking trails, and a small downhill ski area.

Most importantly, Williams is where you'll find the Grand Canyon Railway depot. The excursion train that leaves from here provides not only a fun ride on the rails but is an alternative to dealing with traffic congestion within Grand Canyon National Park. Of course, there are also the obligatory on-your-way-to-the-Grand-Canyon tourist traps nearby.

## ESSENTIALS

**GETTING THERE**   Williams is on I-40 just west of the junction with Ariz. 64, which leads north to the South Rim of the Grand Canyon.

The **Grand Canyon Railway,** Grand Canyon Railway Depot, Grand Canyon Boulevard (☎ **800/843-8724** or 520/773-1976; www.thetrain.com), operates vintage steam and diesel locomotives and 1920s coaches between Williams and Grand Canyon Village. Round-trip fares range from $49.50 to $119.50 for adults and $24.95 to $94.95 for children 16 and under (fares do not include tax or national park entrance fee). Although this is primarily a day-excursion train, it's possible to ride up one day and return on a different day—just let the reservation clerk know. If you opt to stay overnight, you'll want to be sure you have a reservation at one of the hotels right in Grand Canyon Village; otherwise, you'll end up having to take a shuttle bus or taxi out of the park to your hotel, which can be inconvenient and add a bit to your daily costs.

**Nava-Hopi Tours** (☎ **800/892-8687** or 520/774-5003) has bus service connecting Williams with the Grand Canyon ($14 round-trip), Flagstaff ($14 round-trip), and Phoenix ($58 round-trip).

**VISITOR INFORMATION**   For more information on the Williams area, including information on hiking, mountain biking, and fishing in the area, contact the **Williams–U.S. Forest Service Visitor Center,** 200 W. Railroad Ave., Williams, AZ 86046-2556 (☎ **520/635-4061**). The visitor center here is open Monday through Saturday from 8am to 5pm and Sunday from 8am to 4pm. This visitor center has books on the Grand Canyon and lots of trail maps for the adjacent national forest.

## WHAT TO SEE & DO: ROUTE 66 & BEYOND

These days, most people coming to Williams are here to board the Grand Canyon Railway (see "Getting There," above, for details).

**Route 66** fans will want to drive Williams's main street, which, not surprisingly, is named Route 66. Along this stretch of the old highway, you can check out the town's vintage buildings, many of which now house shops selling Route 66 souvenirs. There are also a few antiques stores selling collectibles from the heyday of Route 66.

Both east and west of town, there are other stretches of the "Mother Road" that you can drive. East of town, take Exit 167 off I-40 and follow the graveled Old Trails Highway (the predecessor to Route 66). A paved section of Route 66 begins at Exit 171 on the north side of the interstate and extends for 7 miles to the site of the Parks General Store. From Parks, you can continue to Brannigan Park on a graveled section of Route 66.

West of Williams, take Exit 157 and go south. If you turn east at the T intersection, you will be on a gravel section of the old highway; if you turn west, you'll be on a paved section. Another stretch can be accessed at Exit 106. If you continue another 12 miles west and take Exit 139, you will be on the longest uninterrupted stretch of Route 66 left in the country. It stretches from here through the town of Seligman, which has several interesting buildings, and all the way to Kingman.

In summer, horseback riding is an option. Contact **Mountain Ranch Stables** at the Quality Inn Mountain Ranch (☎ 520/635-0706), which is located 6 miles east of Williams at Exit 171 off I-40, or **Stable in the Pines,** 1000 Circle Pine Rd. (☎ 520/635-2626), which is 2 miles east of Williams at Exit 167 off I-40 (at the KOA campground). Both stables charge around $20 for a 1-hour ride.

In Williams, you can also play a round of golf at the **Elephant Rocks Golf Course,** 2200 Country Club Dr. (☎ 520/635-4935). Greens fees are $30 to $33 with cart.

## WHERE TO STAY
### MODERATE

**Best Western Inn of Williams.** 2600 W. Route 66, Williams, AZ 86046. ☎ **800/635-4445** or 520/635-4400. Fax 520/635-4488. 79 units. June–Aug $79–$125 double; Sept–Oct and Apr–May $69–$99 double; Nov–Mar $49–$89 double. Rates include full breakfast. AE, DC, DISC, MC, V.

Although this modern motel is not within walking distance of historic downtown Williams, the contemporary styling and location in the pines at the west end of town make it a good bet for comfortable, quiet accommodations. Guest rooms even have a couple of features you only expect in deluxe accommodations—hair dryers and bathroom phones. Plus, you'll find a whirlpool spa and an outdoor pool that's kept heated throughout the year.

✪ **Fray Marcos Hotel.** 235 N. Grand Canyon Blvd., Williams, AZ 86046. ☎ **800/843-8724** or 520/635-4010. Fax 520/773-1610. www.thetrain.com. 180 units. A/C TV TEL. Mid-Mar to mid-Oct (and holidays) $119 double; late Oct to early Mar $69 double. Railroad packages available. AE, DISC, MC, V.

Named for Fray (Father) Marcos de Niza who, some say, was the first European to set foot in what is today the state of Arizona, this hotel is affiliated with the Grand Canyon Railway and is named for a Williams hotel once run by the famous Fred Harvey Company. The railway, which runs vintage trains to the Grand Canyon, has its depot adjacent to the hotel, which makes this the ideal lodging choice if you are planning on riding the rails. The original Fray Marcos Hotel, built in 1908, now houses the Depot Cafe and a railroad museum.

The hotel combines modern comforts with the style of a classic Western railroad hotel. The high-ceilinged lobby features a large flagstone fireplace, lots of comfortable seating, and original paintings of the Grand Canyon. Guest rooms are very comfortable and feature Southwestern styling.

**Dining/Diversions:** The hotel's elegant lounge, which features a 100-year-old English bar, serves simple meals. There is also the adjacent Depot Cafe in the original hotel and a large cafeteria-style restaurant that caters primarily to large groups.

**Amenities:** Train reservations can be arranged, gift shop, adjacent railroad museum, and display trains.

**Quality Inn Mountain Ranch.** 6701 E. Mountain Ranch Rd. (at Exit 171 from I-40), Williams, AZ 86046. ☎ **800/228-5151** or 520/635-2693. www.thecanyon.com. 73 units. A/C TV TEL. Apr–Oct $55–$105 double; Nov–Mar $45–$75 double. Rates include full breakfast. AE, DC, DISC, MC, V. Supervised pets accepted.

Located 6 miles east of town, this motel is surrounded by 26 acres of forest and meadow that give it a secluded feeling. This seclusion and the hotel's recreational amenities (horseback riding, a pool, whirlpool, sauna, two tennis courts, volleyball, basketball, and a putting green) make this the best choice in the Williams area. However, the rooms, though large and usually with views of forest and mountains, are strictly motel issue. There's a restaurant on the premises, so you don't have to drive into town to eat.

**The Sheridan House Inn.** 460 E. Sheridan Ave., Williams, AZ 86046. ☎ **888/635-9345** or 520/635-9441. www.thegrandcanyon.com/sheridan. 9 units. TV. $95–$225 double. Rates include full breakfast. AE, DISC, MC, V. Closed mid-Jan to mid-Feb.

Located on a pine-shaded hillside a few blocks from downtown Williams, this B&B isn't fancy but it's plenty comfortable. Innkeepers Steve and Evelyn Gardner make people feel right at home in their little home-style resort, which includes a hot tub on the flagstone patio, a pool table and bar in the basement, a fitness room, and plenty of videotapes for watching on in-room VCRs. Guest rooms are comfortably furnished; our favorite room is the Cedar Room. Complimentary happy hour each evening includes enough hors d'oeuvres to make a meal (which somewhat offsets the relatively high rates for most of the rooms here), and the breakfast always includes an impressive array of fruits. This inn is also child friendly, so it makes a good base of operations for families.

**Terry Ranch Bed & Breakfast.** 701 Quarterhorse St., Williams, AZ 86046. ☎ **800/210-5908** or 520/635-4171. Fax 520/635-2488. www.bbonline.com/az/terryranch. 4 units. Apr–Sept $110–$130 double; Oct–Mar $100–$120 double. Rates include full breakfast. AE, DISC, MC, V.

This modern log inn on the edge of town looks as though it should be surrounded by a big cattle spread, but instead it's close to the train depot and the restaurants in downtown Williams. The guest rooms, which are furnished in Western-country style, have king beds and antiques and are named for brides who lived at the Terry Ranch in Utah back in the 1800s. Two rooms have claw-foot tubs, and two have whirlpool tubs. There are also fireplaces in two of the rooms.

## INEXPENSIVE

In addition to the motels and B&Bs listed below, there are several budget chain motels in Williams. (See the appendix for toll-free phone numbers.) There's the **Comfort Inn,** 911 Route 66 (☎ **520/635-4045**), charging $39 to $88 double; **Motel 6,** 831 Route 66 (☎ **520/635-9000**), charging $44 to $51 double; and **Super 8,** 2001 Route 66 (☎ **520/635-4700**), charging $35 to $60 double.

**Norris Motel.** 1001 W. Rte. 66 (P.O. Box 388), Williams, AZ 86046. ☎ **800/341-8000** or 520/635-2202. Fax 520/635-9202. 33 units. A/C TV TEL. Mid-May to mid-Sept $55–$107 double; Apr to early May and late Sept to Oct $44–$87; Nov–Mar $28–$59. AE, DISC, MC, V.

Run by a British family, the Norris Motel may not look like anything special from the street, but the friendliness of the welcome will immediately let you know that this is not your ordinary motel. Most of the guest units have been remodeled and have a homey feel. Many rooms also have refrigerators. There's even a whirlpool bath to soak away your aches and pains in the evening and a swimming pool for cooling off in during the hot summer months.

✪ **The Red Garter Bed & Bakery.** 137 W. Railroad Ave., Williams, AZ 86046. ☎ **800/328-1484** or 520/635-1484. www.redgarter.com. 4 units. $65–$105 double. Rates include continental breakfast. Lower rates off-season. AE, DISC, MC, V.

The Wild West lives again at this restored 1897 bordello, but these days the only tarts that come with the rooms are in the bakery downstairs. Located across the street from the Grand Canyon Railway terminal at the top of a steep flight of stairs, this B&B sports high ceilings, new carpets, attractive wood trim, and reproduction period furnishings. A couple of rooms even have graffiti written by visitors in the early part of this century.

## CAMPGROUNDS

There are several campgrounds near Williams in the Kaibab National Forest. These include Cataract Lake (2 miles northwest of Williams on Cataract Lake Road), Dogtown Lake (8 miles south of Williams off Fourth Street/County Road 73), Kaibab Lake (4 miles northeast of Williams off Ariz. 64), and Whitehorse Lake (15 miles south of Williams off Fourth Street/County Road 73). All campgrounds are first-come, first-served.

## WHERE TO DINE

**Cruiser's Café 66.** 233 W. Rte. 66. ☎ **520/635-2445.** Main courses $7–$16. AE, DISC, MC, V. Daily 3–9pm (longer hours in summer). AMERICAN.

If you're looking for a taste of old-fashioned Route 66 atmosphere, this is the place. Dig into some smoked baby back pork ribs or a platter of fajitas at Cruiser's, which is full of all manner of Route 66 memorabilia. Some tables are even flanked by a couple of old-fashioned gas pumps. The menu runs the gamut from steaks to spicy wings to pizza and calzones.

**Rod's Steak House.** 301 E. Rte. 66. ☎ **520/635-2671.** Reservations recommended. Main courses $8–$26. MC, V. Mar–Oct daily 11:30am–9:30pm; Nov–Feb Mon–Sat 11:30am–9:30pm. STEAKS/SEAFOOD.

If you're looking for a good dinner in Williams, just look for the red neon steer at the east end of town. This is the sign that beckons hungry canyon explorers to come on in and have a great steak. The menu, which is printed on a paper cutout of a steer, may be short, but the food is reliable. Prime rib au jus, the house specialty, comes in three different weights to fit your hunger. If you're not in a mood for a steak, there is trout, chicken, shrimp, and barbecued ribs.

## 3  The Grand Canyon South Rim

60 miles N of Williams; 80 miles NE of Flagstaff; 230 miles N of Phoenix; 340 miles N of Tucson

A mile deep, 277 miles long, and up to 18 miles wide, the Grand Canyon is truly one of the great wonders of the world, and it comes as no surprise to learn that the cartographers who mapped this area were deeply struck by the spiritual beauty of the canyon. Their reverence is reflected in the names of its formations: Solomon Temple, Angels Gate, the Tabernacle, Apollo Temple, Venus Temple, Thor Temple, Zoroaster Temple, Horus Temple, Buddha Temple, Vishnu Temple, Krishna Temple, Shiva Temple, and Confucius Temple.

Something of this awe infects every first time visitor to the Grand Canyon. Nothing in the slowly changing topography of the approach to the Grand Canyon prepares you for what awaits. You hardly notice the elevation gain or the gradual change from windswept scrubland to pine forest. Suddenly, it's there. No preliminaries, no warnings. Stark, quiet, a maze of colors and cathedrals sculpted by nature.

Banded layers of sandstone, limestone, shale, and schist give the canyon its colors, and the interplay of shadows and light from dawn to dusk creates an ever-changing palette of hues and textures. Written in these bands of stone are more than 2 *billion* years of history. Formed by the cutting action of the Colorado River as it flows through the Kaibab Plateau, the Grand Canyon is an open book exposing the secrets of the geologic history of this region. Geologists believe that it has taken between 3 and 6 million years for the Colorado River to carve the Grand Canyon, but the canyon's history extends much further back in time.

Millions of years ago vast seas covered this region. Sediments carried by sea water were deposited and over millions of years turned into sedimentary limestone and sandstone. When the ancient seabed was thrust upward to form the Kaibab Plateau, the Colorado River began its work of cutting through the plateau. Today 21 sedimentary layers, the oldest of which is more than a billion years old, can be seen in the canyon. However, beneath all these layers, at the very bottom, is a stratum of rock so old that it has been metamorphosed, under great pressure and heat, from soft shale to a much harder stone. Called Vishnu schist, this layer is the oldest rock in the Grand Canyon and dates from 2 billion years ago.

In the more recent past, the Grand Canyon has been home to several Native American cultures, including the Anasazi, who are best known for their cliff dwellings in the Four Corners region. About 150 years after the Anasazi and Coconino peoples abandoned the canyon in the 13th century, another tribe, the Cerbat, moved into the area. The Hualapai and Havasupai tribes, descendants of the Cerbat people, still live in and near the Grand Canyon on the south side of the Colorado River. On the North Rim lived the Southern Paiute, and in the west the Navajo.

In 1540 Spanish explorer Garcia Lopez de Cárdenas became the first European to set eyes on the Grand Canyon. However, it would be another 329 years before the first expedition would travel through the entire canyon. John Wesley Powell, a one-armed Civil War veteran, was deemed crazy when he set off to navigate the Colorado River in wooden boats. His small band of men spent 98 days traveling 1,000 miles down the Green and Colorado Rivers. Their expedition was not without mishap. When some of the expeditions boats were wrecked by the powerful rapids, part of the group abandoned the journey and set out on foot, never to be heard from again.

How wrong the early explorers were about this supposedly godforsaken landscape. Instead of being abandoned as a worthless wasteland, the Grand Canyon has become one of the most important natural wonders on the planet, a magnet for people from all over the world. By raft, by mule, on foot, and in helicopters and small planes—five million people each year come to the canyon to gaze into this great chasm.

However, there have been those in the recent past who regarded the canyon as mere wasted space, suitable for filling with water. Upstream of the Grand Canyon stands Glen Canyon Dam, which forms Lake Powell, while downstream lies Lake Mead, created by Hoover Dam. The same thing could have happened to the Grand Canyon.

Luckily, the forces for preservation have prevailed and today the Grand Canyon is the last major undammed section of the Colorado River.

The Colorado River, named by early Spanish explorers for the pinkish color of its muddy waters, once carried immense loads of silt. However, now, due to the Glen Canyon Dam, the water in the Grand Canyon is much clearer (and colder) than it once was and no longer flows murky and pink from heavy loads of eroding sandstone. The water that now rumbles through the Grand Canyon flows cold and clear from the bottom of the Glen Canyon Dam after it has had a chance to deposit its silt on the bottom of Lake Powell.

Glen Canyon Dam has had a much greater effect on the Grand Canyon than just changing the color and temperature of the Colorado. Due to changes in electricity demand, the outflow of water from Glen Canyon Dam can change dramatically over the course of a day. These frequent fluctuations have changed the natural cycle of flushing and deposition that once created beaches and backwaters within the canyon. In an attempt to reproduce the natural flooding process that once sustained the Grand Canyon's riparian environment, Glen Canyon Dam experimented in spring 1996 with larger drawdowns of water that more closely reproduced the natural cycle of spring flooding in the canyon. These drawdowns proved to be somewhat successful in restoring the banks of the Colorado River to a more natural appearance.

While the waters of the Colorado River are now clearer than before, the same can not be said for the air in the canyon. Yes, you'll find smog here, smog that has been blamed on both Las Vegas and Los Angeles to the west and a coal-fired power plant to the east near Page. Scrubbers installed on the power plant's smokestacks should help the park's air quality, though there isn't much to be done about smog drifting up from Las Vegas.

However, the most visible and frustrating negative impact on the park in recent years has been the traffic congestion at the South Rim during the busy months from spring to fall. With five million visitors each year, traffic during the summer months has become almost as bad at the South Rim as it is during rush hour in any major city, and finding a parking space can be the biggest challenge of a visit to Grand Canyon National Park. It is hoped that with the implementation of the 1995 Grand Canyon National Park General Management Plan, which calls for a new light-rail system and alternative-fuel buses, as well as a new multiuse greenway trail along the South Rim, the park's congestion problems will be alleviated over the next few years. However, these changes are still a year or two away, so expect congestion and parking problems through 2000.

Today the Canyon is at a turning point. With the implementation over the next few years of the Grand Canyon National Park General Management Plan, the park should become a far more enjoyable place to visit. However, for 2000, you can still expect parking problems and traffic congestion, but don't let these inconveniences dissuade you from visiting. Despite the crowds, the Grand Canyon still more than lives up to its name and is one of the most amazing sights on earth.

## A Grand Blunder

In May 1999, the U.S. Postal Service announced that 101 million stamps featuring the Grand Canyon had been printed with the caption "Grand Canyon, Colorado," misidentifying the canyon's home state. The costly error was caught before the stamps were made available to the public. Luckily, the postal service isn't usually so geographically challenged.

## GETTING THERE

**BY CAR**   In the past few years parking problems, traffic jams, and traffic congestion have become the norm at Grand Canyon Village during the popular summer months (and are becoming common in spring and fall as well). If at all possible, travel into the park by some means *other* than car. (Alternatives include taking the Grand Canyon Railway from Williams, flying into the Grand Canyon Airport and then taking the Tusayan-Grand Canyon Shuttle or a taxi, or taking the Nava-Hopi Tours bus service from either Williams or Flagstaff.) There are plenty of scenic overlooks, hiking trails, restaurants, and lodges in the village area, and free shuttle buses now operate along both the West Rim Drive and East Rim Drive.

If you do drive, be sure that you have plenty of gasoline in your car before setting out for the canyon; there are few service stations in this remote part of the state. The South Rim of the Grand Canyon is 60 miles north of Williams and I-40 on Ariz. 64 and U.S. 180. Flagstaff, the nearest city of any size, is 78 miles away. From Flagstaff it's possible to take U.S. 180 directly to the South Rim or U.S. 89 to Ariz. 64 and the east entrance to the park.

In 1998, Grand Canyon National Park finally announced plans to develop a combination light-rail and alternative-fuel bus system for transporting visitors to and around the South Rim and Grand Canyon Village. Plans are to have a light-rail system connect Tusayan, outside the park's south entrance, with the new Canyon View Information Plaza, which will become the South Rim's main transportation hub and the first glimpse of the canyon for most visitors. From this transit center, alternative-fuel buses will shuttle visitors to various points along the South Rim. By having day-use visitors leave their cars outside the park and take the light rail to the South Rim, much of the park's traffic congestion should be alleviated. This new transportation plan will be implemented over the next few years, with the Canyon View Information Plaza currently scheduled for completion in late 2000. Light-rail service will be added sometime after the new transit center opens, it is hoped by 2002. Funding for these projects is primarily from private donations. For information on how you can contribute to developing a new way of visiting the Grand Canyon, contact the **Grand Canyon Fund,** 3100 N. Fort Valley Rd., no. 12, Flagstaff, AZ 86001 (☎ 520/774-1760).

**BY PLANE**   The Grand Canyon Airport is 6 miles south of Grand Canyon Village in Tusayan. It's served by **Air Vegas** (☎ 800/255-7474), which charges $164 for round-trip flights. Airlines flying from Las Vegas to the Grand Canyon Airport include **Scenic Airlines** (☎ 800/446-4584), which charges $222 round-trip. Other than these two options, you'll have to fly into Flagstaff and then arrange another mode of transportation the rest of the way to the national park.

**BY TRAIN**   The **Grand Canyon Railway** operates excursion trains between Williams and the South Rim of the Grand Canyon. See the "Williams" section of this chapter for details.

For long-distance connections, **Amtrak** (☎ 800/872-7245) provides service to Flagstaff. From Flagstaff it's then possible to take a bus directly to Grand Canyon Village. Another option is to take a Greyhound bus to Williams and then take the Grand Canyon Railway excursion train from there to Grand Canyon Village.

**BY BUS**   Bus service between Phoenix, Flagstaff, Williams, and Grand Canyon Village is provided by **Nava-Hopi Tours** (☎ 800/892-8687 or 520/774-5003). Round-trip fares are as follows: $69 between Phoenix and Grand Canyon Village; $25 between Flagstaff and Grand Canyon Village; and $14 between Williams and Grand Canyon Village.

## VISITOR INFORMATION

You can get information on the Grand Canyon before leaving home by contacting the **Grand Canyon National Park,** P.O. Box 129, Grand Canyon, AZ 86023 (☎ **520/ 638-7888;** www.thecanyon.com/nps).

Once there, you should stop by the **Grand Canyon National Park Visitor Center,** located on Village Loop Drive 6 miles north of the south entrance. Here you'll find an information desk, brochures, exhibits about the canyon, and a bookshop selling maps as well as books about the canyon. The center is open daily. *The Guide,* a small newspaper crammed full of useful information about the park, is available at both South Rim entrances.

For information on service outside the park in Tusayan, contact the **Grand Canyon Chamber of Commerce,** P.O. Box 3007, Grand Canyon, AZ 86023 (☎ **520/ 638-2901;** www.thecanyon.com/chamber).

## ORIENTATION

Grand Canyon Village is built on the South Rim of the canyon and is roughly divided into two sections. At the east end of the village is the visitor center, Yavapai Lodge, Trailer Village, and Mather Campground. At the west end are El Tovar Hotel and Bright Angel, Kachina, Thunderbird, and Maswik lodges, as well as several restaurants, the train depot, and the trailhead for the Bright Angel Trail.

## GETTING AROUND

As mentioned earlier, the Grand Canyon Village area can be extremely congested, especially during the summer months. If possible you may want to use one of the transportation options below to avoid the park's traffic jams and parking problems. Just to give you an idea, in summer you can expect at least a 20- to 30-minute wait at the South Rim entrance gate just to get into the park. You can cut the waiting time here by acquiring a national park pass (Golden Eagle, Golden Age, or Golden Access) before arriving. With pass in hand, you can use the express lane for seasonal pass holders.

**BY BUS**   The **Tusayan–Grand Canyon Shuttle** (☎ 520/638-0821) operates between the Grand Canyon Airport in Tusayan, at the park's south entrance, and Grand Canyon Village, with stops in Tusayan at the Squire Inn, the Grand Canyon IMAX Theater, and the Babbitt's Store and in Grand Canyon Village at the Maswik Transportation Center. The fare is $4 each way, with service between 9:30am and 6:30pm (shorter hours outside of summer months).

Between mid-March and mid-October, free shuttle buses operate on three routes within the park. The Village Loop bus circles through Grand Canyon Village throughout the day with frequent stops at the visitor center, hotels, campgrounds, restaurants, the Yavapai Observation Center, and other facilities. The West Rim Loop bus takes visitors to eight canyon overlooks to the west of Bright Angel Lodge. The Yaki Point/South Kaibab Loop, which stops at Bright Angel Lodge, the Maswik Transportation Center (Backcountry Office), and Yavapai Lodge, provides the only access to Yaki Point, which is the trailhead for the South Kaibab Trail to the bottom of the canyon. Hikers needing transportation to or from Yaki Point when the bus is not running must use a taxi (☎ 520/638-2822).

**Trans Canyon** (☎ 520/638-2820) offers shuttle-bus service between the South Rim and the North Rim. The vans leave the South Rim at 1:30pm and arrive at the North Rim at 6:30pm. The return trip leaves the North Rim at 7am, arriving back at the South Rim at 11:30am. The fare is $60 per person one way, $100 per person round-trip.

**BY CAR**   There are **service stations** south of the park in Tusayan, outside the south entrance of the Park at Moqui Lodge, at Desert View near the east entrance (this station is seasonal), and east of the park at Cameron. Because of the long distances within the park and to towns outside the park, be sure that you have plenty of gas before setting out on a drive. Gas at the canyon is also very expensive.

**BY TAXI**    There is taxi service available to and from the airport, trailheads, and other destinations (☎ **520/638-2822**). The fare from the airport to Grand Canyon Village is $5 per person with a $10 minimum.

# Fast Facts: The Grand Canyon

**Accessibility**    *The Grand Canyon National Park Accessibility Guide* is available at the visitor center, Yavapai Observation Station, Tusayan Museum, and Desert View Information Center. The national park also provides wheelchairs for temporary use of park visitors free of charge. You can usually find one of these wheelchairs at the visitor center. You can get temporary handicapped parking permits at the visitor center or Yavapai Observation Center. There are also wheelchair accessible tours offered by prior arrangement through any lodge transportation desk or by calling Grand Canyon National Park Lodges (☎ **520/638-2631**). TDD phones are available for hotel guests who require them.

**Admission**    Admission to Grand Canyon National Park is $20 per car (or $10 per person if you happen to be coming in on a bus, by taxi, or on foot). Your admission ticket, which is good for 7 days, is nothing more than a small paper receipt similar to what you might get at a store. Don't lose it or you'll have to pay again.

**Banks & ATM Networks**    There's an ATM at the Bank One at the shopping center near Yavapai Lodge. The bank is open Monday through Thursday from 10am to 3pm and on Friday from 10am to 5pm.

**Bus Tours**    If you'd rather leave the driving to someone else and enjoy more of the scenery, you can opt for a bus or van tour of one or more sections of the park. **Grand Canyon National Park Lodges** (☎ **303/297-2757**) operates the Fred Harvey Transportation Company, which offers several different tours within the park. Tours visit the East Rim and West Rim and can be booked by calling the above phone number or by stopping at one of the transportation desks, which are located at the visitor center and at Bright Angel, Maswik, and Yavapai lodges (see "Where to Stay," below). Prices range from $10 for a 1½-hour sunset tour to $29.50 for a combination tour of both the East Rim and the West Rim.

**Climate**    The climate at the Grand Canyon is quite different from that of Phoenix, and between the rim and the canyon floor there's also a considerable difference. Because the South Rim is at 7,000 feet, it gets very cold in the winter. You can expect snow anytime between November and May, and winter temperatures can be below 0°F at night, with daytime highs in the 20s or 30s. Summer temperatures at the rim range from highs in the 80s to lows in the 50s. The North Rim of the canyon, which is slightly higher than the South Rim and stays a bit cooler throughout the year, is open to visitors only from May to October because the access road is not kept cleared of snow.

On the canyon floor temperatures are considerably higher. In summer the mercury can top 100°F with lows in the 70s, while in the winter temperatures are quite pleasant with highs in the 50s and lows in the 30s. July, August, and September are the wettest months because of frequent afternoon thunderstorms. April, May, and June are the driest months, though it might still rain or even snow. Down on the canyon floor, there is much less rain year-round.

**Drugstores**   There's a pharmacy (☎ 520/638-2460) in Grand Canyon Village on Clinic Drive, which is off Center Road (the road that runs past the National Park Service ranger office). The drugstore is open Monday through Saturday.

**Emergencies**   Dial ☎ **911.**

**Festivals**   The **Grand Canyon Music Festival** (☎ **520/638-9215**) is held each year in mid-September.

**Hospitals/Clinics**   The **Grand Canyon Clinic** (☎ **520/638-2551** or 520/ 638-2469) is located on Clinic Drive, which is off Center Road (the road that runs past the National Park Service ranger office). The clinic is open Monday through Friday from 8am to 5:30pm and on Saturday from 9am to noon. It also provides 24-hour emergency service.

**Laundry**   A coin-operated laundry is located near Mather Campground in the Camper Services building.

**Lost & Found**   Report lost items or turn in found items at the visitor center or Yavapai observation station. Call ☎ **520/638-7798** Tuesday through Friday between 8am and 5pm. For items lost or found at a hotel, restaurant, or lounge, call ☎ **520/638-2631,** ext. 6503.

**Newspapers/Magazines**   Current newspapers and magazines are available at souvenir stores and lodges in the village.

**Parking**   If you want to avoid parking headaches, try using the lot in front of the general store, which is up a side road across from the visitor center (near Yavapai Lodge). From this large parking area, a paved hiking trail leads to the historic section of the village in less than 1½ miles and most of the route is along the rim. Another alternative is to park at the Maswik Transportation Center parking lot, which is served by the Village Loop shuttle bus.

**Photographic Needs**   Film is available at all village curio shops.

**Police**   In an emergency, dial ☎ **911.** Ticketing speeders is one of the main occupations of the park's police force, so obey the posted speed limits.

**Post Office**   The post office is located in the shopping center near Yavapai Lodge.

**Radio**   KSGC, **92.1 FM,** provides news, music, the latest weather forecasts, and travel-related information for the Grand Canyon area.

**Road Conditions**   Information on road conditions in the Grand Canyon area are available by calling ☎ **520/638-7888** or 520/779-2711.

**Safety**   The most important safety tip to remember is to be careful near the edge of the canyon. Footing can be unstable and may give way. Also be sure to keep your distance from wild animals, no matter how friendly they may appear. Don't hike alone and keep in mind that the canyon rim is more than a mile above sea level (it's harder to breathe up here). Don't leave valuables in your car or tent.

## GRAND CANYON VILLAGE & VICINITY: YOUR FIRST LOOK

Grand Canyon Village is the main destination of the vast majority of the more than five million people who visit the Grand Canyon every year. Consequently it is the most crowded place in the park, but it also has the most overlooks and visitor services. Its many historic buildings, while nowhere near as impressive as the canyon itself, are also worth visiting.

For most visitors, that initial glimpse of the canyon comes at **Mather Point,** which is the first canyon overlook you reach if you enter the park through the south entrance. By the end of 2000, this viewpoint should be the site of the new Canyon View Information

# Grand Canyon Village

**Legend**
- 🅺 Trailhead
- 🅿 Parking
- 🅸 Information
- ---- Trail
- ++++ Railroad

Yaki Point

South Kaibab Trail

Mather Point

East Rim Drive

64

Yavapai Point

Park Entrance Road

Visitor Center

Center Road

Clinic Road

64

To Williams and Flagstaff →

Rim Trail

Maricopa Point

Bright Angel Trail

Powell Point

Trailview II Overlook

Trailview Overlook

West Rim Drive

Rowe Well Road

Hopi Point

Mohave Point

The Abyss

West Rim Drive

Rim Trail

Pima Point

Hermit Trailhead

Hermit's Rest

NA-0258

**Lodges and Campgrounds**
Bright Angel Lodge 4
El Tovar Hotel 7
Kachina Lodge 6
Maswik Lodge 12
Mather Campground 22
Thunderbird Lodge 5
Trailer Village 24
Yavapai Lodge 25

**Services**
Babbitt's General Store 20
Backcountry Office 18
Bank 13
Clinic and Pharmacy 14
Grand Canyon Railway Depot 10
Laundry and Showers 21
Post Office 19
Ranger Office 11
Visitor Center 17

**Attractions**
Hopi House 8
Verkamps Curios 9
Mather Amphitheater 15
Shrine of Ages 16
Sage Loop Campfire Circle 23
Kolb Studio 2
Powell Memorial 1
Lookout Studio 3
Yavapai Observation Station 26

*We are imprisoned three quarters of a mile in the depths of the earth and the great unknown river shrinks into insignificance as it dashes its angry waves against the walls and cliffs that rise to the world above.*
—Maj. John Wesley Powell, on his successful trip through the Grand Canyon

Plaza. Continuing west toward the village proper, you next come to **Yavapai Point,** which is a favorite spot for sunrise and sunset photos and is the site of the **Yavapai Observation Station.** This historic building houses a small museum and has excellent views through its large windows. Yavapai point is at the east end of a paved hiking trail that extends for almost 3 miles to the west side of Grand Canyon Village.

The next stop along Village Loop Drive is the **visitor center** (☎ **520/638-7888**), which is one of the busiest places in the park and is usually the hardest place to find a parking space. The visitor center is open daily and, in addition to providing answers to all your questions about the Grand Canyon, also houses exhibits on the canyon's natural history, human history, and exploration. Throughout the day, slide and video programs are shown. There's also an excellent little bookstore here where you can find books on all aspects of the canyon. In the center's courtyard are several boats that have navigated the canyon over the years.

In the historic district, in addition to numerous canyon viewpoints, you'll find the historic **El Tovar Hotel** and **Bright Angel Lodge,** both of which are worth brief visits.

Adjacent to El Tovar are two historic souvenir and curio shops. **Hopi House Gift Store and Art Gallery,** the first shop in the park, was built in 1905 to resemble a Hopi pueblo and to serve as a place for Hopi artisans to work and sell their crafts. Today it's full of Hopi and Navajo arts and crafts, including expensive kachinas, rugs, jewelry, and pottery. The second floor of the Hopi House is an art gallery. The nearby **Verkamps Curios** originally opened in a tent in 1898, but after John Verkamp went out of business, it was not reopened until 1905. Today it's the main place to look for souvenirs and crafts. Just inside the door is a 535-pound meteorite. Both shops are open daily; hours vary seasonally.

To the west of Bright Angel Lodge, two buildings cling precariously to the rim of the canyon. These are the **Lookout** and **Kolb studios,** both of which are listed on the National Register of Historic Places. **Kolb Studio** is named for Ellsworth and Emory Kolb, two brothers who set up a photographic studio on the rim of the Grand Canyon in 1904. The construction of this studio generated one of the Grand Canyon's first controversies—over whether buildings should be allowed on the canyon rim. Because the Kolbs had friends in high places, their sprawling studio and movie theater remained. Emory Kolb lived here until his death in 1976, by which time the building had been listed as a historic building and could not legally be torn down. Today it serves as a bookstore, and the auditorium houses special exhibits. **Lookout Studio,** built in 1914 from a design by Mary Elizabeth Jane Colter, was the Fred Harvey Company's answer to the Kolb brothers' studio. Photographs and books about the canyon were sold at the studio, which incorporates architectural styles of the Hopi and the Anasazi. The use of native limestone and an uneven roofline allows the studio to blend in with the canyon walls and gives it the look of an old ruin. Today the studio houses a souvenir store and two lookout points. Both studios are open daily; hours vary seasonally.

## THE WEST RIM DRIVE

The West Rim Drive is an 8-mile-long road leading west from Grand Canyon Village to Hermits Rest. From mid-March through mid-October, this road is closed to private automobiles, but a free shuttle operates frequently and stops at most of the overlooks. The rest of the year it's possible to drive this scenic road in your own car, stopping whenever and wherever you wish.

The first stops are **Trailview Overlook** and **Paiute Point.** From either of these points, you have a view of Grand Canyon Village to the east with the Bright Angel Trail winding down into the canyon from the village. The trail leads 3,000 feet below the rim to the Tonto Plateau, site of Indian Gardens, where there is a campground in a grove of cottonwood trees.

The next stop on the West Rim Drive is **Maricopa Point.** Here you can see the remains of the Orphan Mine, which began operation in 1893. The mine went out of business because transporting the copper to a city where it could be sold was too expensive. Uranium was discovered here in 1954, but in 1966 the mine was shut down and the land became part of Grand Canyon National Park. If you look carefully at the bottom of the canyon, you can see some of the black Vishnu schist, which is among the oldest exposed rock on earth.

The **Powell Memorial,** which is the next stop, is dedicated to John Wesley Powell, who, in 1869 with a party of nine men, became the first person to navigate the Colorado River through the Grand Canyon.

Next along the drive is **Hopi Point,** from which you can see a long section of the Colorado River. Because of the great distance, the river seems to be a tiny, quiet stream, but in reality the section you see is more than 100 yards wide and races through Granite Rapids.

**Mohave Point** is the next stop. From here you can see (and sometimes hear) Hermit Rapids, another section of white water. As with almost all rapids in the canyon, these are formed at the mouth of a side canyon where boulders loosened by storms and carried by flooded streams are deposited in the Colorado River.

The next stop is at the **Abyss,** the appropriately named 3,000-foot drop created by the Great Mojave Wall. This vertiginous view is one of the most awe-inspiring in the park. The walls of the Abyss are red sandstone that's more resistant to erosion than the softer shale in the layer below. Other layers of erosion-resistant sandstone have formed the freestanding pillars that are visible from here, the largest of which is called the Monument.

From **Pima Point** it's possible to see the remains of Hermit Camp on the Tonto Plateau. Built by the Santa Fe Railroad, Hermit Camp was a popular tourist destination between 1911 and 1930 and provided cabins and tents. Today only foundations remain.

At the end of West Rim Drive is **Hermit's Rest,** named for Louis Boucher, a prospector who came to the canyon in the 1890s and was known as the Hermit. The log-and-stone Hermit's Rest building, designed by Mary Elizabeth Jane Colter and built in 1914, is on the National Register of Historic Places.

## THE EAST RIM DRIVE

The East Rim Drive extends for 25 miles from Grand Canyon Village to Desert View. The first stop is **Yaki Point,** which is near the trailhead for the South Kaibab Trail leading to Phantom Ranch. However, from mid-March through mid-October, Yaki Point is closed to private vehicles and can only be reached by shuttle bus. The spectacular view from here encompasses a wide section of the central canyon. The large flat-topped butte to the northeast is Wotan's Throne, one of the canyon's easily recognizable features.

The next stop, **Grandview Point,** affords a view of Horseshoe Mesa, another interesting feature of the canyon landscape. The mesa was the site of the Last Chance Copper Mine in the early 1890s. Later that same decade the Grandview Hotel was built and served canyon visitors until its close in 1908.

# Shooting the Canyon: Tips for Photographers

By the time most people leave the Grand Canyon they've shot several rolls of film. This is not at all surprising considering the beauty of this rugged landscape. But it's not always easy to capture the canyon's spirit. Here are some tips to help you bring back the best possible photos from your trip:

A polarizing filter is a great investment if you have the kind of camera that will accept lens filters. A polarizing filter will reduce haze, lessen the contrast between shadowy areas and light areas, and deepen the color of the sky.

The best times to photograph the canyon are at sunrise and sunset, when filtered and sharply angled sunlight paints the canyon walls in beautiful shades of lavender and pink. At these times the shadows are also at their most dramatic. To capture these ephemeral moments, it's best to use a tripod and a long exposure. The worst time to photograph the canyon is at noon when there are almost no shadows, and thus little texture or contrast. The National Park Service includes a table with sunrise and sunset times in *The Guide,* the park's official visitor newspaper.

Something else to keep in mind is that the Grand Canyon is immense. A wide-angle lens may leave the canyon looking on paper like a distant plane of dirt. Try zooming in on narrower sections of the canyon to emphasize a single dramatic landscape element. If you're shooting with a wide-angle lens, try to include something in the foreground (people or a tree branch) to give the photo perspective and scale.

When shooting portraits against a sunrise or sunset, use a flash to illuminate your subjects; otherwise, your camera meter may expose for the bright light in the background and leave your subjects in shadow.

Next along the drive is **Moran Point,** from which you can see a bright red layer of shale in the canyon walls. This point is named for 19th-century landscape painter Thomas Moran who, through his artwork, shared the beauty of the West with the people of the eastern cities.

The **Tusayan Museum** (open daily except December 25; admission free) is the next stop along the East Rim Drive. This small museum is dedicated to the Hopi tribe and ancient Anasazi people who inhabited this region 800 years ago, and inside the museum are artfully displayed exhibits on various aspects of Anasazi life. Outside the museum is a short self-guided trail through the ruins of an Anasazi village. Free guided tours are available.

At **Lipan Point** you can see the Grand Canyon *supergroup:* several strata of rock that are tilted at an angle to the other layers of rock in the canyon. Their angle indicates that there was a period of geological mountain building prior to the deposition of layers of sandstone, limestone, and shale. The red, white, and black rocks of the supergroup are composed of sedimentary rock and layers of lava. From **Navajo Point,** the Colorado River and Escalante Butte are both visible.

**Desert View,** with its trading post, cafeteria, service station, information center, bookstore, and watchtower, is the end of this scenic drive. The road does continue east from here, but it soon leaves the park (outside the park, the Little Colorado River overlook is worth a stop). The views are breathtaking from anywhere at Desert View, but the best lookout is from atop the Desert View Watchtower (open daily, admission 25¢). Though the watchtower looks as though it had been built centuries ago, it's actually only 65 years old. Architect Mary Elizabeth Jane Colter, who is responsible for much of the park's historic architecture, designed the tower to resemble the prehistoric towers that dot the Southwestern landscape. Built as an observation tower and rest stop for tourists, the watchtower incorporates Native American designs and art. The curio shop on the ground floor is a replica of a kiva (sacred ceremonial chamber) and has lots of interesting souvenirs, Southwestern crafts, and books. The tower's second floor features artwork by Hopi artist Fred Kabotie. Covering the walls are pictographs incorporating traditional designs. On the walls and ceiling of the upper two floors are more traditional images by artist Fred Geary, this time reproductions of petroglyphs from throughout the Southwest. From the roof, which is the highest point on the South Rim (7,522 feet above sea level), it's possible to see the Colorado River, the Painted Desert to the northeast, the San Francisco Peaks to the south, and Marble Canyon to the north. Coin-operated binoculars provide close-up views of some of the noteworthy landmarks of this end of the canyon. On the roof are several black-mirror "reflectoscopes" that provide interesting darkened views of some of the most spectacular sections of the canyon. The gift shop offers a pamphlet describing the watchtower in detail.

## OTHER WAYS TO SEE THE CANYON
### MULE RIDES

After having a look at the steep drop-offs and narrow path of the Bright Angel Trail, you might decide that this isn't exactly the place to trust your life to a mule. However, the trail guides will be quick to reassure you that they haven't lost a rider yet. Mule rides into the canyon are some of the most popular activities at Grand Canyon Village and have been since the turn of the century when the Bright Angel Trail was a toll road. Trips of various lengths and to different destinations are offered. The 1-day trip descends to Plateau Point, where there's a view of the Colorado River 1,300 feet below. This grueling trip requires riders to spend 6 hours in the saddle. Those who want to spend a night down in the canyon can choose an overnight trip to Phantom Ranch, where cabins and dormitories are available at the only lodge actually in the canyon. From mid-November through March there's also a 3-day/2-night trip to Phantom Ranch. Mule trips range in price from $106.60 for a 1-day ride to Plateau Point to $294.80 for an overnight ride to Phantom Ranch to $408.45 for a 2-night ride to Phantom Ranch. Couples receive discounts on overnight rides.

There are a few rider qualifications that you should keep in mind before calling to make a reservation. You must weigh less than 200 pounds fully dressed, stand at least 4 feet 7 inches tall, and speak fluent English. Pregnant women are not allowed on mule trips.

Because these trail rides are very popular (especially in summer), reservations are taken up to 23 months in advance. You should try to make a reservation as soon as you know when you'll be visiting. For more information or to make a reservation, contact the **Grand Canyon National Park Lodges** (☎ **303/297-2757**; fax 303/ 297-3175; www.amfac.com). If at the last minute (5 days or less from the day you want to ride) you decide you want to go on a mule trip into the Grand Canyon, contact Grand Canyon National Park Lodges at its Arizona phone number (☎ **520/ 638-2631**) for the remote possibility that there may be space available. If you arrive at the canyon without a reservation and decide that you'd like to go on a mule ride, stop by the Bright Angel Transportation Desk to get your name on the next day's waiting list.

### ON HORSEBACK

Trail rides on the rim (but not into the canyon) are available from Moqui Lodge's **Apache Stables** (☎ **520/638-2891**), at the south entrance to the park. There are rides of various lengths; prices range from $25 for a 1-hour ride to $65 for a 4-hour ride. Evening wagon rides ($8.50) are also offered. The stables are usually open from March to early December (depending on the weather).

## RIDING THE RAILS

In the early part of this century, most visitors to the Grand Canyon came by train, and today it's once again possible to travel to the canyon along the steel rails. The ✪ **Grand Canyon Railway** (☎ **800/843-8724** or 520/773-1976; www.thetrain. com), which runs from Williams to the South Rim of the Grand Canyon at Grand Canyon Village, uses turn-of-the-century steam engines (during the summer) and 1950s-vintage diesel engines (other months) to pull 1920s passenger cars and a 1954 dome coach car. Trains depart from the Williams Depot, which is housed in the renovated Fray Marcos Hotel. Built in 1908, the old hotel now houses a railroad museum, gift shop, and cafe. (Grand Canyon Railway also operates a new Fray Marcos Hotel, which really is a hotel.) At Grand Canyon Village, the trains use the 1910 log railway terminal in front of El Tovar Hotel.

Passengers have the choice of five classes of service: coach, club, first class, deluxe observation class (upstairs in the dome car), and luxury parlor car. Actors posing as cowboys provide entertainment including music performances aboard the train. The round-trip takes 8 hours (including 3½ hours at the Canyon), and fares range from $49.95 to $119.95 for adults and from $24.95 to $94.95 for children 16 and under (these rates do not include tax or the national park admission).

Not only is this a fun trip that provides great scenery and a trip back in time, but by taking the train, you can avoid the traffic congestion and parking problems in Grand Canyon Village. When booking your train trip, you can also book a bus tour in the park, which will help you see more than you would on foot. The railway also operates its own hotel, the Fray Marcos Hotel in Williams, and offers different room/train packages.

## A BIRD'S-EYE VIEW

Despite controversies over noise and safety (there have been a few crashes over the years), airplane and helicopter flights over the Grand Canyon remain one of the most popular ways to see these natural wonders. Several companies operating out of the Grand Canyon Airport in Tusayan offer air tours lasting from 30 minutes to about 2 hours.

Companies offering air tours by small plane include **Air Grand Canyon** (☎ **800/247-4726** or 520/638-2686); **Airstar Airlines** (☎ **800/962-3869** or 520/638-2139); and **Grand Canyon Airlines** (☎ **800/528-2413** or 520/638-2407). Rates for 50-minute flights are between $65 and $75 for adults and from $40 to $45 for children.

Helicopter tours are available from **Airstar Helicopters** (☎ **800/962-3869** or 520/638-2622); **Kenai Helicopters** (☎ **800/541-4537** or 520/638-2764); and **Papillon Grand Canyon Helicopters** (☎ **800/528-2418** or 520/638-2419). Rates range from around $95 for a 30-minute flight to around $155 for a 45- to 55-minute flight.

## INTERPRETIVE PROGRAMS

Numerous interpretive programs are scheduled throughout the year at various South Rim locations. There are ranger-led walks that explore various aspects of the canyon, geology talks, lectures on the cultural and natural resources of the canyon, nature hikes, trips to fossil beds, and star-gazing gatherings. At Tusayan Ruin there are guided tours. Evening programs are held at either Mather Amphitheater or the Shrine of the Ages. Consult your copy of **_The Guide_** for information on times and meeting points.

---

**Impressions**

*Ours has been the first and will doubtless be the last party of whites to visit this profitless locality.*
— Lt. Joseph C. Ives, exploring the Colorado River by steamboat (1857–58)

---

## THE GRAND CANYON FIELD INSTITUTE

If you are the active type or you'd just like to turn your visit to the Grand Canyon into more of an educational experience, you may want to consider doing a trip with the **Grand Canyon Field Institute,** P.O. Box 399, Grand Canyon, AZ 86023 (☎ **520/ 638-2485;** E-mail: gcfi@grandcanyon.org). Cosponsored by the Grand Canyon National Park and the Grand Canyon Association, the field institute schedules an amazing variety of guided, educational trips, such as challenging backpacking trips through the canyon (some for women only) and programs lasting anywhere from 2 to 10 days. Subjects covered include wilderness studies, geology, natural history, human history, photography, and arts. What can you do on these trips? Maybe you'd like to observe raptors on the South Rim or study the canyon's geology. How about a 4-day photography workshop or maybe a rim-to-rim backpacking trip?

## JEEP TOURS

If you'd like to see some parts of Grand Canyon National Park that most visitors never see, try a Jeep tour with **Grand Canyon Outback Jeep Tours** (☎ 800/320-JEEP or 520/638-JEEP), which offers three different tours that visit the park as well as the adjacent Kaibab National Forest. One of the tours stops at a lookout tower where you get an elevated view of the canyon, while another tour visits an Indian ruin and site of petroglyphs and cave paintings. Tour prices range from $30 to $54 for adults and from $20 to $35 for children ages 12 and under.

## ✪ HIKING THE CANYON

There are no roads leading into the Grand Canyon, so if you want to visit the inner canyon you have to hike, ride a mule, or float. The least expensive of these options is to hike in. However, if you go very far down a trail into the canyon, you'll find out exactly why so many people content themselves with walking along the canyon's rim. Think of the Grand Canyon as an upside-down mountain. You start out by walking downhill, thus saving the harder uphill climb for the second half of your hike (when you're likely already tired out from the hike down). Don't underestimate the difficulty of hiking down into the canyon, and always carry plenty of water. However, these warnings aside, no visit to the canyon is complete without journeying below the rim. While the views don't get any better than they are from the top, they do change considerably. Gazing up at all those thousands of feet of vertical rock walls provides a very different perspective on the Grand Canyon. Should you venture far below the rim you also stand a chance of seeing fossils, old mines, petroglyphs, wildflowers, and wildlife.

The Grand Canyon offers some of the most rugged and strenuous hiking anywhere in the United States, and for this reason anyone attempting even a short walk should be well prepared. Each year people are injured or killed because they set out to hike the canyon without preparing properly. Most of these injuries and fatalities are suffered by day hikers who set out without sturdy footgear and without food or adequate amounts of water. Take precautions—don't become another Grand Canyon statistic! Unless you have proper footgear and at least 1 quart of water, you won't even be allowed on the daily ranger-led nature walk along the South Kaibab Trail. Even a short

30-minute hike in the summer can dehydrate you, and a long hike into or out of the canyon in the heat can necessitate drinking more than a gallon of water. Remember while hiking that mules have the right of way; always stay to the inside of the trail when being passed by a mule train. Don't attempt to hike from the rim to the Colorado River and back in 1 day. Many people who have tried this have died.

## DAY HIKES

Loop-trail day hikes are not possible in the Grand Canyon, but the vastly different scenery in every direction makes a return trip on the same trail a totally new experience. The easiest day hikes are those along the rim. There's a 1½-mile paved trail leading from the Yavapai Museum to the Powell Memorial. From the Powell Memorial, the trail becomes dirt and continues another 8 miles to Hermits Rest, from which, between mid-March and mid-October, you can take a free shuttle back to Grand Canyon Village.

Trails leading down into the canyon include the Bright Angel Trail, the South Kaibab Trail, Grandview Trail, and the Hermit Trail. If you plan to hike for more than 30 minutes, carry 2 quarts of water per person. If you're game to do it, hiking into the canyon even just a short distance before doubling back will allow you to escape the ever-present crowds.

The ✪ **Bright Angel Trail** starts just west of Bright Angel Lodge in Grand Canyon Village. It's the main route down to Phantom Ranch and is the most popular trail into the canyon. Day hikes on this trail include the trips to Indian Gardens or Plateau Point. Both of these trips are long and very strenuous. There are rest houses at 1½ and 3 miles (during the summer they have water), which make good turn-around points for a 3-mile or 6-mile round-trip hike.

The **South Kaibab Trail** begins near Yaki Point east of Grand Canyon Village and is the alternative route to Phantom Ranch. This trail offers the best views of any of the day hikes in the canyon. From the trailhead it's a 3-mile round-trip to Cedar Ridge. The hike is very strenuous, and there's no water available along the trail.

The **Grandview Trail** is a steep, unmaintained trail that should be attempted only by people with experience hiking in the desert. It's a very strenuous 6-mile round-trip hike to Horseshoe Mesa, and there's no water available along the trail. Allow at least 7 hours for this rugged hike.

The **Hermit Trail** begins near Hermits Rest and is also steep and unmaintained. Don't attempt this trail if you don't have some experience hiking in the desert. It's a 5-mile round-trip to Santa Maria Springs and a 6-mile round-trip to Dripping Springs. Water from these springs must be treated with either a water filter, iodine, or purification tablets or by boiling for at least 10 minutes.

## BACKPACKING

There are many miles of trails deep in the canyon and several established campgrounds for backpackers. The best times of year to backpack in the canyon are spring and autumn. During the summer, temperatures at the bottom of the canyon are regularly over 100°F, while in the winter ice and snow at higher elevations make footing on trails precarious. Be sure to carry at least 2 quarts, and preferably 1 gallon, of water whenever backpacking in the canyon.

A **Backcountry Use Permit** is required of all hikers planning to overnight in the canyon unless you'll be staying at Phantom Ranch in one of the cabins or in the dormitory.

Because a limited number of hikers are allowed into the canyon on any given day, it's important to make reservations as soon as it is possible to do so. Reservations are taken in person, by mail, by fax (but not by phone), and over the Internet. Contact the **Backcountry Reservations Office,** Grand Canyon National Park, P.O. Box 129, Grand Canyon, AZ 86023 (☎ **520/638-7875** between 1 and 5pm for information; fax 520/638-2125; www.thecanyon.com/nps). Holiday periods are the most popular. The office begins accepting reservations on the first of every month for the following 5 months. If you want to hike over the Labor Day weekend, be sure you make your reservation on May 1! If you show up without a reservation, go to the Backcountry Reservations Office (open daily from 8am to noon and from 1 to 5pm), which is at the Maswik Transportation Center, and put your name on the waiting list. When applying for a permit, you'll have to specify your exact itinerary and, once in the canyon, you must stick to this itinerary. Backpacking fees include a nonrefundable $20 backcountry permit fee and a $4 per person per night backcountry camping fee.

There are **campgrounds** at Indian Gardens, Bright Angel Campground (near Phantom Ranch), and at Cottonwood, but hikers are limited to 2 nights per trip at each of these campgrounds (except from November 15 to February 28 when 4 nights are allowed at each campground). Other nights can be spent camping at undesignated sites in certain regions of the park.

The *Backcountry Trip Planner* publication has information to help you plan your itinerary. It's available through the Backcountry Office. Maps are available through the **Grand Canyon Association,** P.O. Box 399, Grand Canyon, AZ 86023 (☎ **800/ 858-2808;** fax 520/638-2484; www.thecanyon.com/gca), and also at bookstores within the national park. These are located at the visitor center, Kolb Studio, Desert View Information Center, Yavapai Observation Station, Tusayan Museum, and, on the North Rim, in Grand Canyon Lodge.

If you are interested in guided backpacking trips, see the information on the Grand Canyon Field Institute above.

## ✪ RAFTING THE COLORADO RIVER

Rafting down the Colorado River as it roars and tumbles through the mile-deep gorge of the Grand Canyon is the adventure of a lifetime. Ever since John Wesley Powell ignored everyone who knew better and proved that it was possible to travel by boat down the tumultuous Colorado River, running the big river has become a passion and an obsession with adventurers. Today anyone from grade-schoolers to grandmothers can join the elite group who have made the run. However, be prepared for some of the most furious white water in the world.

There are 16 companies offering trips through various sections of the canyon. You can spend as few as 3 days on the river or as many as 19. You can go down the river in a huge motorized rubber raft, in a paddled- or oar-powered raft, or a wooden dory. In a motorized raft, you can travel the entire canyon from Lees Ferry to Lake Mead in only 8 days. Should you opt for an oar- or paddle-powered raft or dory, expect to spend 5 or 6 days getting from Lees Ferry to Phantom Ranch or 7 to 9 days getting from Phantom Ranch to Diamond Creek, just above Lake Mead.

Most trips start from Lees Ferry near Page and Lake Powell. However, it's also possible to start (or finish) a trip at Phantom Ranch, hiking in or out from either the North or South Rim. The main rafting season is from April to October, but some companies operate year-round. Rafting trips tend to book up well in advance, and most companies begin taking reservations in April for the following year's trips. Expect to pay around $200 per day for your white-water adventure.

The following companies are currently authorized to operate trips through the Grand Canyon: **Aramark-Wilderness River Adventures,** P.O. Box 717, Page, AZ 86040 (☎ 800/992-8022 or 520/645-3296); **Arizona Raft Adventures,** 4050-FE. Huntington Dr., Flagstaff, AZ 86004 (☎ 800/786-RAFT or 520/526-8200; www.azraft.com); **Arizona River Runners,** P.O. Box 47788, Phoenix, AZ 85068-7788

(☎ 800/477-7238 or 602/867-4866); **Canyon Explorations/Canyon Expeditions,** P.O. Box 310, Flagstaff, AZ 86002 (☎ 800/654-0723 or 520/774-4559; www. canyonx.com); **Canyoneers,** P.O. Box 2997, Flagstaff, AZ 86003 (☎ 800/525-0924 or 520/526-0924; www.thecanyon.com/canyoneers/river); **Colorado River & Trail Expeditions,** P.O. Box 57575, Salt Lake City, UT 84157-0575 (☎ 800/253-7328 or 801/261-1789); **Diamond River Adventures,** P.O. Box 1316, Page, AZ 86040 (☎ 800/343-3121 or 520/645-8866); **Grand Canyon Dories,** P.O. Box 216, Altaville, CA 95221 (☎ 800/877-3679 or 209/736-0805); **Grand Canyon Expeditions Company,** P.O. Box O, Kanab, UT 84741 (☎ 800/544-2691 or 435/644-2691; www.gcex.com); **Hatch River Expeditions,** P.O. Box 1200, Vernal, UT 84078 (☎ 800/433-8966 or 801/789-3813); **High Desert Adventures,** P.O. Box 40, St. George, UT 84771-0040 (☎ 800/673-1733 or 435/673-1733; www.funboat. com); **Moki Mac River Expeditions,** P.O. Box 21242, Salt Lake City, UT 84121 (☎ 800/284-7280 or 801/268-6667); **OARS,** P.O. Box 67, Angels Camp, CA 95222 (☎ 800/346-6277 or 209/736-2924; www.oars.com); **Outdoors Unlimited,** 6900 Townsend Winona Rd., Flagstaff, AZ 86004 (☎ 800/637-7238 or 520/526-4546); **Tour West,** P.O. Box 333, Orem, UT 84059 (☎ 800/453-9107 or 801/225-0755); and **Western River Expeditions,** 7258 Racquet Club Dr., Salt Lake City, UT 84121 (☎ 800/453-7450 or 801/942-6669; www.westernriver.com).

For information on 1- and 2-day rafting trips at the west end of the Grand Canyon, see the "South Rim Alternatives: Havasu Canyon & Grand Canyon West" section of this chapter. For information on half- and full-day trips near Page, see "Lake Powell & Page" in chapter 7.

## VIRTUAL REALITY: THE GRAND CANYON ON THE BIG SCREEN

✪ **Grand Canyon IMAX Theater.** Ariz. 64/U.S. 180, Tusayan. ☎ **520/638-2203.** Admission $8 adults, $6 children 3–11. Mar–Oct daily 8:30am–8:30pm; Nov–Feb daily 10:30am–6:30pm.

Located in the village of Tusayan at the south entrance to the park, this IMAX theater devotes its seven-story screen to a 34-minute film about the canyon. A reenactment of John Wesley Powell's first navigation of the Colorado River is the main focus, but geology, ancient history, and cultural and natural history are also included. However, the star of the show is, of course, the heart-stopping IMAX cinematography. The huge screen that fills your field of vision and the amazing high definition of the film manage to create an astoundingly realistic image of the canyon. But, you know, the real canyon is just 6 miles up the road.

## WHERE TO STAY

Keep in mind that the Grand Canyon is one of the most popular national parks in the country, and hotel rooms both within and just outside the park are in high demand. Make reservations as far in advance as possible. Don't expect to find a room if you head up here in summer without a reservation. You'll likely wind up driving back to Williams or Flagstaff to find a vacancy. There, is, however, one long-shot option. See "Inside the Park," below, for details. Who knows, you might get lucky.

### INSIDE THE PARK

All hotels inside the park are operated by Amfac Parks & Resorts. Reservations are taken up to 23 months in advance, beginning on the first of the month. If you want to stay in the economical Bright Angel Lodge, especially if you want a rim cabin, reserve at least a year in advance.

For making reservations at any of the in-park hotels listed here (as well as the Moqui Lodge, which is just outside the park), contact **Amfac Parks & Resorts,** 14001 E. Iliff

Ave., Aurora, CO 80014 (☎ **303/297-2757;** fax 303/297-3175; www.amfac.com.). It is sometimes possible, due to cancellations and no-shows, to get a same-day reservation. It's a long shot, but it happens. Same-day reservations should be made by calling **Grand Canyon National Park Lodges** (☎ **520/638-2631**), which is operated by Amfac.

For advance reservations, Amfac accepts JCB, MasterCard, and Visa credit cards. For same-day reservations, Grand Canyon National Park Lodges accepts American Express, Diners Club, Discover, JCB, MasterCard, and Visa.

## Moderate

✪ **El Tovar Hotel.** 78 units. A/C TV TEL. $114–$171 double; $194–$285 suite.

El Tovar Hotel, which first opened its doors in 1905, is the park's premier lodge. Built of local rock and Oregon pine by Hopi craftsmen, it's a rustic yet luxurious mountain lodge that perches on the edge of the canyon with awe-inspiring views (but only from some rooms). The lobby, entered from a veranda set with rustic furniture, has a small fireplace, cathedral ceiling, and log walls on which moose, deer, and antelope heads hang. The guest rooms were all recently redone and now feature modern mission-style furnishings that are in keeping with the period when the hotel was built. The standard rooms are rather small, as are the bathrooms, which were added after the hotel was built. Deluxe rooms provide more leg room. Suites, with their private terraces and stunning views, are extremely spacious and are done mostly in new Southwestern style.

The El Tovar Dining Room (see "Where to Dine," below) is the best restaurant in the village and serves excellent continental and Southwestern cuisine. Just off the lobby is a cocktail lounge with a view. Room service is also available. There's a concierge and a tour desk.

**Maswik Lodge.** 278 units, including 28 cabins. TV TEL. $73–$113 double; $60 cabin.

Set back ¼ mile or so from the rim, the Maswik Lodge offers spacious rooms and rustic cabins. If you crave modern appointments, opt for one of the Maswik North rooms. If you don't mind roughing it a bit, the rustic old cabins have lots of character and are comfortable enough. These cabins have bathtubs but not showers. There's a large cafeteria, a tour desk, and a sports lounge with a big-screen TV.

**Thunderbird & Kachina Lodges.** 104 units. A/C TV TEL. $109–$119 double.

Despite the use of native sandstone in their construction, these 1960s-vintage motel-style lodgings are far from your idea of what a national park lodge should look like, and the dated "modern" styling clashes with the traditional design of the adjacent historic lodges. However, if you want modern amenities and a fairly large room, these should be your in-park choice in this price range. The rooms in both lodges have large windows, although you'll have to request a canyon-side room on the second floor if you want a view of something more than a parking lot (the canyon-view rooms are only $10 more than those without views and are well worth the extra cost). Thunderbird Lodge registration is handled by Bright Angel Lodge, and Kachina Lodge registration is handled by El Tovar Hotel.

**Yavapai Lodge.** 358 units. TV TEL. $84–$99 double.

Located in several buildings at the east end of Grand Canyon Village (a 1-mile hike from the main section of the village), the Yavapai is the largest lodge in the park, and consequently it's where you'll likely wind up if you wait too long to make a reservation. There are no canyon views here, which is why this lodge is less expensive than the Thunderbird and Kachina lodges. The rooms in the Yavapai East section of the hotel are set under shady pines and are more attractive than the rooms in the Yavapai West section (well worth the price difference). There's a cafeteria and a tour desk.

### Inexpensive

⭐ **Bright Angel Lodge & Cabins.** 89 units (10 with sink only, 10 with sink and toilet, 14 with bathroom, 55 cabins with bathroom). $44 double with sink only, $50 double with sink and toilet, $60 double with bathroom; $70–$229 cabin.

Bright Angel Lodge, which began operation in 1896 as a collection of tents and cabins on the edge of the canyon, is the most affordable lodge in the park and offers the greatest variety of accommodations. With its flagstone-floor lobby and huge fireplace, it has a genuine, if crowded, mountain lodge atmosphere. In addition to rooms with shared bathrooms, there are also roomier cabins, including four rim cabins that have their own fireplaces. These rim cabins are the most popular and are usually booked a year in advance. The other rooms should be booked at least 6 months in advance. Most of the rooms and cabins feature rustic furnishings but have been fairly recently renovated. The Buckey Suite, the oldest structure on the canyon rim, is arguably the best room in the park, with a canyon view, fireplace, and a king-size bed. The lodge has a coffee shop, a steakhouse, and an ice cream parlor. A tour desk and museum account for the constant crowds in the lobby.

⭐ **Phantom Ranch.** Reconfirmations ☎ **520/638-3283** or 520/638-2631, ext. 6015. 11 cabins, 40 dorm beds. $65.95 double in the cabins; $22.85 dormitory bed. Mule-trip overnights (with all meals and mule ride included) $294.80 for 1 person, $523.60 for 2 people. 2-night trips are available mid-Nov to Mar.

This is the only lodge at the bottom of the Grand Canyon and as such is very popular with both hikers and mule riders. Built in 1922, Phantom Ranch has a classic ranch atmosphere. The accommodations are in rustic stone-walled cabins or 10-bedded gender-segregated dormitories. Evaporative coolers keep both the cabins and the dorms cool in the summer. Make reservations as early as possible (up to a year in advance) and don't forget to reconfirm. It's also possible to get a room on the day of departure if there are any last-minute cancellations. To attempt this, you must put your name on the waiting list at the Bright Angel Lodge transportation desk the evening before the day you wish to stay at Phantom Ranch.

Family style meals must be reserved in advance. The menu consists of beef-and-vegetable stew or vegetarian dinner for $17.60 or steak for $28.15. Breakfasts ($12.65) are hearty, and sack lunches ($7.95) are available. Between meals the dining hall becomes a canteen selling snacks, drinks, gifts, and necessities. After dinner, the dining hall becomes a beer hall. There's a public phone here, and mule-back baggage transfer between Grand Canyon Village and Phantom Ranch can be arranged ($46.15 each way).

## TUSAYAN (OUTSIDE THE SOUTH ENTRANCE)

If you can't get a reservation for a room in the park, this is the next closest place to stay. Unfortunately, this area can be very noisy because of the many helicopters and airplanes taking off from the airport and other places around town. Also, hotels outside the park are very popular with tour groups, which during the busy summer months keep many hotels full. All of the hotels listed here are lined up along U.S. 180/Ariz. 64.

There is one other motel in town, the **Seven Mile Lodge** (☎ **520/638-2291**), which is consistently the least expensive motel in town. However, this motel does not take reservations and is usually full by 2pm in the summer (it starts renting rooms at 9am).

## Expensive

✪ **Grand Canyon Suites.** P.O. Box 3251, Grand Canyon, AZ 86023. ☎ **888/538-5353** or 520/638-3100. Fax 520/638-2747. www.gcanyon.com/suites/. 32 units. A/C TV TEL. Mid-May to Sept $139–$159 double, $229 quad; Mar and Oct to early Jan $59–$79 double, $129 quad; Apr to early May $109–$119 double, $189 quad. Rates include continental breakfast. AE, MC, V.

With its spacious and interestingly decorated suites, this is one of the best lodging options in Tusayan. Each of the 32 suites is decorated in a different theme, and all have separate parlors and bedrooms. Some of the room themes of note include a Route 66 suite, Navajo and Hopi suites, a Wild Bill Hickok suite, and a Zane Grey suite. Rooms here have more character than any of the other accommodations in the area. Microwaves, coffeemakers, refrigerators, and VCRs are all standard. Unfortunately, there is no pool or whirlpool. This hotel is tucked in behind the Holiday Inn Express.

## Moderate

**Best Western Grand Canyon Squire Inn.** Ariz. 64 (P.O. Box 130), Grand Canyon, AZ 86023-0130. ☎ **800/622-6966** or 520/638-2681. Fax 520/638-2782. www.thecanyon. com/squire. 250 units. A/C TV TEL. Apr to mid-Oct $99–$175 double; mid-Oct to Mar $60–$125 double. AE, CB, DC, DISC, MC, V.

If you prefer playing tennis to riding a mule, this may be the place for you. With two tennis courts, a pool, an exercise room, whirlpool, sauna, bowling alley, pool room, video arcade, and tour desk, this hotel has the feel of a resort and seems to want to distract guests from the canyon itself. The rooms are large and have comfortable easy chairs and large windows. Many rooms have a wall of rock that lends something of a rugged mountain feel. The dining room serves continental cuisine, and there's also a less expensive coffee shop and a lounge. The inn also offers a free airport shuttle service and massages. There's even a sort of cowboy museum in the lobby.

✪ **Grand Hotel.** P. O. Box 3319, Grand Canyon, AZ 86023. ☎ **888/63-GRAND** or 520/638-3333. Fax 520/638-3131. www.canyon.com. 120 units. A/C TV TEL. May–Oct $138–$158 double; Nov–Apr $79–$109 double. AE, DISC, MC, V.

This is the newest hotel in Tusayan, and though the guest rooms have standard-issue motel styling, the hotel's lobby, with its mountain-lodge styling, is certainly quite grand. There's a flagstone fireplace, log-beam ceiling, and fake ponderosa pine tree trunks holding up the roof. Just off the lobby (past the large gift shop), there's a big dining room (with evening entertainment ranging from Native American dancers to country-music bands) and a small bar that even has a few saddles for barstools. Amenities here include an indoor pool and whirlpool spa and a fitness room. Rooms with balconies cost a bit more than those without. Try to get a room on the back side of the hotel; these face the forest rather than the parking lot.

**Holiday Inn Express—Grand Canyon.** P.O. Box 3245, Grand Canyon, AZ 86023. ☎ **800/ HOLIDAY** or 520/638-3000. Fax 520/638-0123. 166 units. A/C TV TEL. $74–$149 double; $90–$179 suite. Rates include continental breakfast. AE, DC, DISC, MC, V.

This is one of the newest lodgings in the area and has modern, well-designed, if a bit sterile and characterless, guest rooms. With no pool or restaurant, this place is really just somewhere to crash at the end of the day.

**Moqui Lodge.** Amfac Parks & Resorts, 14001 E. Iliff Ave., Aurora, CO 80014. ☎ **303/ 297-2757.** Fax 303/297-3175. www.amfac.com. 136 units. TV TEL. $94–$118 double. Rates include full breakfast. Phone reservations: JCB, MC, V; on-premises payments: AE, DC, DISC, JCB, MC, V. Closed Nov–Mar.

Managed by the same company that operates all the lodges within the park, this motel is located just outside the south entrance to the park. With its tall A-frame construction, Moqui Lodge has the feel of a ski lodge at first, but unfortunately lacks the appropriate character. The best of accommodations here are standard motel-style rooms with large windows that for the most part look out onto the parking lot, while the worst are cramped, poorly furnished, and overpriced. About the only thing this lodge has going for it is its proximity to the park entrance, its riding stables, and the fact that the shuttle bus stops here. There's a lounge and a dining room serving moderately priced Mexican and American food. There's also a tour desk.

**Quality Inn Grand Canyon.** P.O. Box 520, Grand Canyon, AZ 86023. ☎ **800/228-5151** or 520/638-2673. Fax 520/638-9537. www.thecanyon.com/gcqual. 232 units. A/C TV TEL. Apr to mid-Oct $118 double, $168 suite; late Oct to Mar $68 double, $118 suite. AE, CB, DC, DISC, MC, V.

This relatively luxurious hotel at the park's south entrance is built around two enclosed skylit courtyards, one of which houses a restaurant and the other a bar and large whirlpool spa. There's also an outdoor whirlpool, as well as an outdoor pool. The rooms are large and comfortable and have balconies or patios. Most also have mini-bars. For extra space, there are suites with separate small living rooms, microwaves, refrigerators, and coffeemakers. The hotel is located next to the IMAX Theater and is very popular with tour groups.

**Rodeway Inn Red Feather Lodge.** Ariz. 64 (P.O. Box 1460), Grand Canyon, AZ 86023. ☎ **800/228-2000** or 520/638-2414. Fax 520/638-9216. www.redfeatherlodge.com. 231 units. A/C TV TEL. Mid-Mar to to Oct $69–$119 double; Nov to mid-Mar $59–$99 double. AE, DC, DISC, MC, V. Pets accepted with $50 deposit, $45 refundable.

Try to get one of the 130 newer rooms, a bit more comfortable than the older ones. But no matter which type you get, you'll be able to avail yourself of an outdoor pool (seasonal) and whirlpool, as well as a fitness room. Kids will appreciate the game room. There is also a casual restaurant on the premises.

## OTHER AREA ACCOMMODATIONS

✪ **Cameron Trading Post Motel.** P.O. Box 339, Cameron, AZ 86020. ☎ **800/338-7385** or 520/679-2231. Fax 520/679-2350. 62 units. A/C TV TEL. Mar–Oct $74–$84 double, $145–$175 suite; Nov–Feb $59–$69 double, $145–$175 suite. AE, CB, DC, MC, V. Well-behaved pets accepted.

Located 54 miles north of Flagstaff on U.S. 89 at the junction with the road to the east entrance to the national park, this motel offers some of the most attractive rooms anywhere in the vicinity of the Grand Canyon. The motel is adjacent to the historic Cameron Trading Post and is built around the old trading post's terraced gardens, which are a shady oasis. The rooms are furnished with Southwestern-style pine furniture and are attractively decorated. Most have balconies and some have views of the canyon of the Little Colorado River. There are two restaurants here, as well as one of the best trading posts in the state.

## CAMPGROUNDS
### Inside the Park
On the South Rim, there are two campgrounds and an RV park. **Mather Campground,** in Grand Canyon Village, has 350 campsites. Reservations can be made up to 5 months in advance and are accepted for stays between March 1 and November 30 (other months reservations are not accepted). For reservations, contact the National Park Reservation Service (☎ **800/365-2267**). Between late spring and early

fall, don't even think of coming up here without a campground reservation; you'll just be setting yourself up for disappointment. However, if you don't have a reservation, your next best bet is to arrive in the morning when campsites are being vacated. Campsite fees range from $10 to $15 depending on the season.

**Desert View Campground,** with 50 sites, is located 26 miles east of Grand Canyon Village and is open only from mid-May to mid-October. No reservations are accepted for this campground. Campsites are $10 per night.

The **Trailer Village RV park,** with 192 RV sites, is located in Grand Canyon Village and charges $19 per night for full hookup sites. Reservations should be made through Amfac Parks & Resorts, 14001 E. Iliff Ave., Aurora, CO 80014 (☎ **303/297-2757;** fax 303/297-3175; www.amfac.com).

### Outside the Park

Getting a campsite inside the park is no easy feat, and if you get shut out, your next best choices lie within a few miles of the south entrance to the park. In Tusayan, you'll find **Grand Canyon Camper Village,** P.O. Box 490, Grand Canyon, AZ 86023-0490 (☎ **520/638-2887**), which is open year-round. This is primarily an RV park, but it also has sites for tents. The only drawback is that you're right in town, which is probably not what you were dreaming of when you planned your trip to the Grand Canyon. Rates here range from $15 to $23.

Three miles south of Tusayan you'll find the U.S. Forest Service's **Ten-X Campground.** The campground is open from mid-May through September and campsites are $10.

You can also camp just about anywhere within the Kaibab National Forest, which borders Grand Canyon National Park, as long as you are more than ¼ mile away from Ariz. 64/U.S. 180. Several dirt roads lead into the forest from the highway, and though you won't find designated campsites or toilets along these roads, you will find spots where others have obviously camped before. This so-called dispersed camping is usually used by campers who have been unable to find sites in campgrounds. Anyone equipped for backpacking could also just hike in a bit from any forest road rather than camping right beside the road. One of the most popular roads for this sort of camping is just north of Tusayan on the west side of the highway leading to the south park entrance. For more information, contact the **Tusayan Ranger District,** Kaibab National Forest, P.O. Box 3088, Grand Canyon, AZ 86023 (☎ **520/638-2443**).

## WHERE TO DINE

In addition to the restaurants listed below, which are all within the park, you'll find several restaurants just outside the south entrance in Tusayan. The best of these is the **Canyon Star** at the Grand Hotel and the **Coronado Dining Room** at the Best Western Grand Canyon Squire Inn. You'll also find a steak house and a pizza place, as well as familiar chains such as McDonald's, Taco Bell, Pizza Hut, and Subway.

### INSIDE THE PARK

#### Expensive

✪ **El Tovar Dining Room.** In the El Tovar Hotel. ☎ **520/638-2631,** ext. 6432. Reservations required at dinner. Main courses $7–$17 at lunch, $15–$23 at dinner. AE, DC, DISC, JCB, MC, V. Daily 6:30–11am, 11:30am–2pm, and 5–10pm. CONTINENTAL/SOUTHWESTERN.

It's easy to think that a restaurant with one of the most awe-inspiring views in the world right outside the window might get complacent and serve up mediocre food at exorbitant prices. Not so at the El Tovar. With a menu that leans heavily to the spicy flavors of the Southwest (though with plenty of milder, more familiar dishes thrown in as well), this restaurant maintains high standards and is no more expensive than a good restaurant in Phoenix. Service is excellent, and the rough-hewn ceiling beams and log walls are a surprising contrast to the fine china, crystal, and linen. Most of the ingredients used here are flown in daily to assure freshness and quality, so you don't have to worry about the quality of such dishes as crab-stuffed trout with jalapeño lobster sauce or grilled filet mignon with black truffle demiglace. Make reservations as soon as possible to get the dinner time you want.

### Moderate

**Arizona Steakhouse.** In the Bright Angel Lodge. ☎ **520/638-2631.** Reservations not accepted. Dinner $15–$21. AE, DC, DISC, JCB, MC, V. Daily 5–10pm. STEAKS.

For a moderately priced steak dinner with a view of the canyon, this is the place, and unfortunately, everyone staying in Grand Canyon Village seems to know it. There's almost always a wait for a table, so try to show up early if you can. Also keep in mind that once the sun goes down the view out the window is absolutely black (which means you could be dining anywhere). Arrive early and enjoy the sunset.

**Bright Angel Coffee Shop.** In the Bright Angel Lodge. ☎ **520/638-2631.** Reservations not accepted. Main courses $6–$18. AE, DC, DISC, JCB, MC, V. Daily 6:30–10:45am and 11:15am–10pm. AMERICAN.

As the least expensive of the three restaurants right on the rim of the canyon, this casual Southwestern-themed coffee house in the historic Bright Angel Lodge stays packed throughout the day. Meals are simple and none too memorable, but if you can get one of the tables near the windows, at least you get something of a view. Unfortunately, there just aren't that many tables with views. The menu includes everything from Southwestern favorites such as chili, tacos, and fajitas to spaghetti and meatballs (foods calculated to comfort tired and hungry hikers). Wines are available, and service is generally friendly and efficient.

### Inexpensive

If you're looking for a quick, inexpensive meal, there are plenty of options. In Grand Canyon Village, choices include **cafeterias** at the Yavapai and Maswik lodges and a **delicatessen** at Babbitt's General Store (across from the visitor center). However, the **Bright Angel Fountain,** which is at the back of the Bright Angel Lodge and serves hot dogs, sandwiches, and ice cream, seems to be the most popular food outlet in the village. **Hermits Rest Fountain** on the West Rim Drive is a snack bar. At Desert View (on the East Rim Drive) is the **Desert View Trading Post Cafeteria.** All of these places are open daily for all three meals, and all serve meals for $8 and under.

## EAST OF THE CANYON

The **Cameron Trading Post** (☎ **800/338-7385** or 520/679-2231), at the crossroads of Cameron where Ariz. 64 to Grand Canyon Village branches off U.S. 89, is the best trading post in the state and should not be missed. The original stone trading post, a historic building, now houses a gallery of old and antique Indian artifacts, clothing, and jewelry. This gallery offers museum-quality pieces, and even if you don't have $10,000 or $15,000 to drop on a rug or basket, you can still look around. The main trading post is a more modern building and is the largest trading post in northern Arizona. Don't miss the beautiful old terraced gardens in back of the original trading post.

# 4  South Rim Alternatives: Havasu Canyon & Grand Canyon West

Havasu Canyon: 200 miles W of Grand Canyon Village; 70 miles N of Ariz. 66; 155 miles NW of Flagstaff; 115 miles NE of Kingman

Grand Canyon West: 240 miles W of Grand Canyon Village; 70 miles N of Kingman; 115 miles E of Las Vegas

With five million people each year visiting the South Rim of the Grand Canyon, and traffic congestion and parking problems becoming the most memorable aspects of most people's visit to the canyon, you might want to consider an alternative to the South Rim. For most people, this means driving around to the North Rim, which, however, is open only between mid-May and late October and is already receiving a lot more visitors than it did a few years ago.

There are a couple of other lesser-known alternatives as well. A visit to Havasu Canyon, on the Havasupai Indian Reservation, entails a 20-mile round-trip hike or horseback ride similar to that from Grand Canyon Village to Phantom Ranch, though with a far more spectacular setting at the bottom of the canyon. Visiting Grand Canyon West, on the Hualapai Indian Reservation, is much less strenuous, although you will have to spend 28 miles on gravel road to get there and back.

## ESSENTIALS

**GETTING THERE   Havasu Canyon**   It isn't possible to drive all the way to Supai village or Havasu Canyon. The nearest road ends 8 miles from Supai at Hualapai Hilltop. This is the trailhead for the trail into the canyon and is at the end of Indian Route 18, which runs north from Ariz. 66. The turnoff is 6 miles east of Peach Springs and 21 miles west of Seligman. Many Arizona maps show an unpaved road between U.S. 180 and Hualapai Hilltop, but this road is not maintained on a regular basis and is passable only to four-wheel-drive vehicles *when* no fallen logs block the way.

The easiest and fastest (and by far the most expensive) way to reach Havasu Canyon is by helicopter from the Grand Canyon Airport. Flights are operated by **Papillon Grand Canyon Helicopters** (☎ **800/528-2418**). The round-trip air-and-ground day excursion is $440, and the overnight excursion is $482.

**Grand Canyon West**   If you're headed to Grand Canyon West, you've got several options, two of which entail driving nearly 50 miles of gravel roads that aren't even passable if it has rained any time recently. The best route is to head northwest out of Kingman on U.S. 93, and in 27 miles turn right onto the Pearce Ferry Road (signed for Dolan Springs and Meadview). After 28 miles on this road, turn right again onto a gravel Diamond Bar Road, which is signed for Grand Canyon West. Another 14 miles down this road brings you to the Hualapai Indian Reservation (and a bit of paved road again). A little farther along, you'll come to the Grand Canyon West Terminal (there's actually an airstrip here) where visitor permits and bus tour tickets are sold.

You can also drive to Grand Canyon West from Peach Springs via Antares Road, which adds another 32 miles of gravel to your trip (64 miles if you return this same way).

**VISITOR INFORMATION**   For information on Havasu Canyon, contact the **Havasupai Tourist Enterprises,** Supai, AZ 86435 (☎ **520/448-2121** or 520/448-2141), which handles all campground reservations. The phone system here isn't always reliable, so either keep trying to get through or write to them. For information on Grand Canyon West, contact **Hualapai Reservations,** P.O. Box 538, Peach Springs, AZ 86434 (☎ **888/255-9550** or 520/769-2230).

## HAVASU CANYON

Imagine hiking for hours through a dusty brown landscape of rocks and cacti. The sun overhead is blistering and bright. The air is hot and dry. Rock walls rise up higher and higher as you continue your descent through a mazelike canyon. Eventually the narrow canyon opens up into a wide plain shaded by cottonwood trees, a sure sign of water, and within a few minutes you hear the sound of a babbling stream. The water, when you finally reach it, is cool and crystal clear, a pleasant surprise. Following the stream, you pass through a dusty (usually cluttered and unkempt, some say dirty and depressing) Indian village of small homes. Not surprisingly in a village 8 miles beyond the last road, every yard seems to be a corral for horses. Passing through the village, you continue along the stream. As the trail descends again, you spot the first waterfall.

The previously crystal-clear water is now a brilliant turquoise blue at the foot of the waterfall. The sandstone walls look redder than before. No, you aren't having a heat-induced hallucination—the water really is turquoise, and it fills terraces of travertine that form deep pools of cool water at the base of three large ✪ **waterfalls.** Together these three waterfalls form what many claim is the most beautiful spot in the entire state.

This is Havasu Canyon, the canyon of the Havasupai tribe, whose name means "people of the blue-green waters." For centuries the Havasupai have called this idyllic desert oasis home.

The waterfalls are the main attraction here, and most people are content to go for a dip in the cool waters, sun themselves on the sand, and gaze for hours at the turquoise waters. When you tire of these pursuits, you can hike up the small side canyon to the east of Havasu Falls. Another trail leads along the west rim of Havasu Canyon and can be reached by carefully climbing up a steep rocky area near the village cemetery. There's also a trail that leads all the way down to the Colorado River, though this is an overnight hike.

In Supai village, there is a small museum dedicated to the culture of the Havasupai people. Its exhibits and old photos will give you an idea of how little the lives of these people have changed over the years.

The Havasupai entry fee is $20 per person to visit Havasu Canyon, and everyone entering the canyon is required to register at the Tourist Office across from the sports field as you enter the village of Supai. Because it's a long walk into the campground, be sure you have a confirmed reservation before setting out from Hualapai Hilltop. It's good to make reservations as far in advance as possible, especially for holiday weekends. Havasupai Tourist Enterprises operates on a cash-only basis, so be sure to bring enough money for your entire stay.

Most visitors to Havasu Canyon are backpackers who hike down from Hualapai Hilltop. Don't even think about hiking down and back in one day (it's a 21-mile round-trip). If you plan to hike down into the canyon, start early to avoid the heat of the day. The hike is beautiful, but it's 10 miles to the campground. The steepest part of the trail is the first mile or so from Hualapai Hilltop. After this section it's relatively flat.

Through the **Havasupai Tourist Enterprises** (☎ **520/448-2121** or 520/ 448-2141) you can also hire a horse to carry you or your gear down into the canyon from Hualapai Hilltop. Horses cost $55 one way and $110 round-trip. Many people who hike in decide that it's worth the money to ride out, or at least have their backpack carried out. Be sure to confirm your horse reservation a day before driving to Hualapai Hilltop. Sometimes no horses are available, and it's a long drive back to the nearest town.

## GRAND CANYON WEST

Located on the Hualapai Indian Reservation on the south side of the Colorado River, Grand Canyon West overlooks the rarely visited west end of Grand Canyon National Park. Neither as high nor as spectacular as the South Rim, Grand Canyon West nonetheless offers the chance to observe the green waters of the Colorado River as it carves its way through the multicolored cliffs of the canyon. Here at Grand Canyon West, you have several options for seeing the area, including a stop at an overlook, a hike down into the canyon, a guided bus tour along the rim, and a helicopter ride below the rim. What you won't find here, however, are crowds. In part this is because of the distance from Grand Canyon Village and the South Rim, and in part because to reach Grand Canyon West you must drive a minimum of 14 miles on a gravel road (28 miles total for the round-trip). You also won't find the sort of strip-mall development that mars Tusayan just outside the entrance to the South Rim. Instead, you'll drive through miles of wide open desert before reaching the short stretch of paved road at Grand Canyon West. If you're looking to escape the hordes and see a little-visited corner of the Grand Canyon, this is a good alternative.

If you'd just like to take in the view from this end of the canyon, head to **Quartermaster Point,** after first purchasing your sightseeing permit ($10) at the Grand Canyon West terminal. At Quartermaster Point, you'll also find a trail that leads down into the canyon.

To see more of this area, you'll have to take a **guided bus tour** that includes a barbecue lunch and time to do a bit of exploring at a canyon overlook. These bus tours stop at Eagle Point, where rock formations resemble various animals and people, and at Guano Point, where bat guano was once mined commercially. The tours, which operate daily throughout the year, cost $32.50 for adults and $22 for children 2 to 12. No reservations are accepted, so it's a good idea to arrive around 8am when Grand Canyon West opens (if you are coming from Kingman, leave yourself at least 1½ hours to get here). The barbecue lunches are served from 10am to 2:30pm.

Helicopter tours ($99) also operate here at Grand Canyon West. However, unlike South Rim helicopter flights, which stay thousands of feet above the canyon, these chopper flights actually go down into the canyon and land on the bank of the Colorado River.

## OTHER AREA ACTIVITIES

While most rafting trips in the Grand Canyon take 6 to 8 days, here at the west end of the canyon, it is possible to do 1- and 2-day trips that begin on the Hualapai Indian Reservation and are operated by **Hualapai River Runners,** P.O. Box 246, Peach Springs, AZ 86434-0246 (☎ **800/622-4409** or 520/769-2210), a tribal rafting company. Whether you opt for the 1-day trip or the 2-day trip, you'll be covering the same stretch of river; you just take it more slowly on the 2-day trip and camp out on the river bank. Expect a mix of white water and flat water (all of it very cold), and though perhaps not as exciting as longer trips in the main section of the canyon, you'll still plow through some pretty big waves. Be ready to get wet. These trips also stop at a couple of side canyons where you can get out and do some exploring. At one of these stops, there is a warm creek that flows out of a cave at the back of which is a waterfall that pours through a skylight in the top of the cave. One-day trips cost $221 per person, and 2-day trips cost $321; a discount rate on lodging at the Hualapai Lodge the night before your trip can also be arranged.

Also in this area, you can visit **Grand Canyon Caverns** (☎ **520/422-3223**), which are located just outside Peach Springs. The caverns, which are accessed via a 210-foot elevator ride, are open Memorial Day to October 15 daily 9am to 6pm; October 16 to Memorial Day daily 9am to 5pm. Admission $8.50 for adults, $5.75 for children ages 4 to 12.

# WHERE TO STAY & DINE
## In & Near Peach Springs

**Grand Canyon Caverns Inn.** P.O. Box 180, Peach Springs, AZ 86434. ☎ **520/422-3223.** 48 units. A/C TV TEL. Summer $49 double; winter $29 double. AE, DISC, MC, V. Pets accepted.

If you're planning to hike or ride into Havasu Canyon, you'll need to be at Hualapai Hilltop as early in the morning as possible. Because it's a 3- to 4-hour drive to this spot from Flagstaff, you might want to consider staying here, one of only two lodgings for miles around. As the name implies, this motel is built on the site of the Grand Canyon Caverns, which are open to the public. There's a casual restaurant and cocktail lounge. Facilities include a pool, a gift shop, and a general store with camping supplies and food. For much of the year, this motel is used by Elderhostel and stays full.

✪ **Hualapai Lodge.** 900 Rte. 66 (P.O. Box 538), Peach Springs, AZ 86434. ☎ **888/255-9550** or 520/769-2230. Fax 520/769-2372. 60 units. A/C TV TEL. $75 double. AE, DISC, MC, V.

Located in the Hualapai community of Peach Springs, this lodge opened in early 1998 and is by far the most luxurious accommodation anywhere in this region. The Hualapai Lodge was built to serve as a base for people heading out to Grand Canyon West or out rafting with Hualapai River Runners, and all around the lobby of the hotel, you'll see photos taken at Grand Canyon West and on rafting trips. Guest rooms here are spacious and modern, with a few bits of regional decor for character. The dining room is just about the only place in town to get food and serves basic American dishes and pizza.

## In Havasu Canyon

**Havasu Campground.** Havasupai Tourist Enterprise, Supai, AZ 86435. ☎ **520/448-2121** or 520/448-2141. 400 sites. $10 per person per night.

The campground is located 2 miles below Supai village, between Havasu Falls and Mooney Falls. The campsites are mostly in the shade of cottonwood trees on either side of Havasu Creek. Picnic tables are provided, but no firewood is available at the campground. Cutting any trees or shrubs is prohibited, so be sure to bring a camp stove with you. Spring water is available, and though it's considered safe to drink, we advise either treating it with a water filter, iodine, or purification tablets or boiling for at least 10 minutes.

**Havasupai Lodge.** General Delivery, Supai, AZ 86435. ☎ **520/448-2111.** 24 units. A/C. Apr–Oct $80 double; Nov–Mar $50 double. MC, V.

Located in Supai village, this lodge is, aside from the campground, the only accommodation in the canyon. The two-story building features standard motel-style rooms that are lacking only TVs and telephones, neither of which are in demand at this isolated retreat. People come to Havasu Canyon to get away from it all, and the Havasupai Lodge is happy to oblige. The only drawback of this comfortable-though-basic lodge is that it's 2 miles from Havasu Falls and 3 miles from Mooney Falls. The Havasupai Café, across from the general store, serves breakfast, lunch, and dinner. It's a very casual place, and the prices are high for what you get because all ingredients must be packed in by horse.

# 5  The Grand Canyon North Rim

42 miles S of Jacob Lake; 216 miles N of Grand Canyon Village (South Rim); 354 miles N of Phoenix; 125 miles W of Page/Lake Powell

Although the North Rim of the Grand Canyon is only 10 miles from the South Rim as the crow flies, it's 200 miles by road. It is this much greater distance from population centers such as Phoenix and Las Vegas that has helped keep this rim of the canyon much less crowded than the South Rim. Additionally, due to heavy snowfalls, the North Rim is open only from mid-May to late October or early November. There are also far fewer activities on the North Rim than there are on the South Rim (no helicopter or plane rides, no IMAX theater, no McDonald's). For these reasons, most of the millions of people who annually visit the Grand Canyon never make it to this side of the canyon. And that is exactly why quite a few people think the North Rim is a far superior place to visit. If Grand Canyon Village was more human zoo than the wilderness experience you had expected, the North Rim will probably be much more to your liking, though crowds, traffic congestion, and parking problems are not unheard of here either.

The North Rim is located on the Kaibab Plateau, which is more than 8,000 feet high on average and takes its name from the Paiute word for "mountain lying down." The higher elevation of the North Rim means that instead of the junipers and ponderosa pines of the South Rim, you'll find dense forests of ponderosa pines, Douglas firs, and aspens interspersed with large meadows. Consequently, the North Rim has a much more Alpine feel than the South Rim. The 8,000-foot elevation (1,000 feet higher than the South Rim) also means that the North Rim receives considerably more snow in the winter than the South Rim does. The highway south from Jacob Lake is not plowed in winter and consequently the Grand Canyon Lodge closes down.

The Kaibab Plateau is also home to the unique white-tailed Kaibab squirrel. Keep your eyes open for this large-eared squirrel whenever you're walking in the forest.

## ESSENTIALS

**GETTING THERE**    The North Rim is at the end of Ariz. 67 (the North Rim Parkway), which is reached from U.S. 89A.

**Trans Canyon** operates a shuttle between the North Rim and South Rim of the Grand Canyon during the months that the North Rim is open. The trip takes 5 hours, and the fare is $60 one way and $100 round-trip. Call ☎ **520/638-2820** for more information.

**VISITOR INFORMATION**    For information before leaving home, contact **Grand Canyon National Park,** P.O. Box 129, Grand Canyon, AZ 86023 (☎ **520/ 638-7888;** www.thecanyon.com/nps).

There's an **information desk** in the lobby of the Grand Canyon Lodge, open daily from 8am to 6pm. At the entrance gate you'll also be given a copy of *The Guide,* a small newspaper with information on park activities. There's a separate edition of *The Guide* for the North Rim.

**ADMISSION**    The park admission fee is $20 per car and is good for 1 week. Remember not to lose the little paper receipt that serves as your admission pass.

*Important note:* Visitor facilities at the North Rim are open only from mid-May to mid-October. From mid-October through November (or until snow closes the road to the North Rim), the park is open for day use only. The campground may be open after mid-October, weather permitting.

## EXPLORING THE AREA

While it is hard to beat the view from a rustic rocking chair on the terrace of the Grand Canyon Lodge, the best spots for viewing the canyon are Bright Angel Point, Point Imperial, and Cape Royal. **Bright Angel Point** is the closest to Grand Canyon Lodge, and from here you can see and hear Roaring Springs, which is 3,600 feet below the rim and is the North Rim's only water source. From Bright Angel Point you can also see Grand Canyon Village on the South Rim. At 8,803 feet, **Point Imperial** is the highest point on the North Rim. A short section of the Colorado River can be seen far below, and off to the east the Painted Desert is visible. However, **Cape Royal** is the most spectacular setting on the North Rim.

Along the 23-mile road to Cape Royal are several scenic overlooks. Across the road from the **Walhalla Overlook** are the ruins of an Anasazi structure, and just before reaching Cape Royal you'll come to the **Angel's Window Overlook,** which gives you a breathtaking view of the natural bridge that forms Angel's Window. Once at Cape Royal, you can follow a trail across this natural bridge to a towering promontory over-looking the valley.

After simply taking in the views, hiking along the rim is the most popular activity at the North Rim. Quite a few day hikes of varying lengths are possible here. The shortest is the ½-mile paved trail to Bright Angel Point, and the longest is the North Kaibab Trail to Roaring Springs and back, which takes 6 to 8 hours.

If you want to see the canyon from a saddle, contact **Grand Canyon Trail Rides** (☎ **435/679-8665**), which offers mule rides varying in length from 1 hour to a full day. Prices range from $15 for an hour ride up to $95 for the all-day trip.

## EN ROUTE TO OR FROM THE NORTH RIM

Between Page and the North Rim of the Grand Canyon, U.S. 89A crosses the Colorado River at **Lees Ferry** in Marble Canyon. Lees Ferry is the starting point for raft trips through the Grand Canyon and for many years was the only place to cross the Colorado River for hundreds of miles in either direction. There's also a campground here.

Lees Ferry is legendary among anglers for its trophy trout fishing, and when the North Rim closes and the rafting season comes to an end, about the only folks you'll find up here are anglers and hunters. **Lees Ferry Anglers** (☎ **800/962-9755** or 520/355-2261), located 3 miles west of the bridge at Lees Ferry, is fishing headquarters for the region. Not only do they sell all manner of fly-fishing tackle and offer advice about good spots to try your luck, but they also operate a guide service and rent waders and boats.

Continuing west, the highway passes under the **Vermilion Cliffs,** so named for their deep red coloring. At the base of these cliffs are huge boulders balanced on narrow columns of eroded soil. The balanced rocks give the area a very otherworldly appear-ance. In recent years, these cliffs have been the site of attempts to reintroduce California condors to the Grand Canyon. So far, most of the birds released here have survived and are slowly becoming accustomed to these new surroundings after having been raised in captivity. Along this unpopulated stretch of road are a couple of very basic lodges.

Seventeen miles west of Marble Canyon, you'll see a sign for **House Rock Ranch.** This wildlife area, managed by the Arizona Game and Fish Department, is best known for its herd of bison (American buffalo). From the turnoff it's a 22-mile drive on a gravel road to reach the ranch.

## NORTH OF THE PARK

If you'd like to learn more about the pioneer history of this remote and sparsely pop-ulated region of the state (known as the Arizona Strip), continue west from Jacob Lake 45 miles on Ariz. 389 to **Pipe Spring National Monument** (☎ **520/643-7105**), which preserves an early Mormon fort. During the summer, there are living history demonstrations here. The monument is open daily (except Thanksgiving, Christmas, and New Year's Day) from 8am to 5pm, and admission is $2 per adult.

# WHERE TO STAY
## INSIDE THE PARK
✪ **Grand Canyon Lodge.** Amfac Parks & Resorts, 14001 E. Iliff Ave., Aurora, CO 80014. ☎ **303/297-2757** or 520/638-2611 (for same-day reservations). Fax 303/297-3175. www.amfac.com. 200 units. $65–$95 double in room or cabin. JCB, MC, V (advance reservations); AE, DISC, JCB, MC, V (at the lodge). Closed Oct 15–May 15.

Perched right on the canyon rim, this classic mountain lodge is listed on the National Register of Historic Places and is as impressive a lodge as you will find in any national park. The stone-and-log main lodge building has a soaring ceiling and a viewing room set up with chairs facing a wall of glass. On either side of this room are flagstone terraces set with rustic chairs that face out toward the canyon. The guest rooms vary from standard motel rooms to rustic mountain cabins to comfortable modern cabins. Our favorites are the little cabins, which, though cramped and paneled with dark wood, capture the feeling of a mountain retreat better than any of the other rooms. A few rooms have views of the canyon, but most are tucked back away from the rim.

A large dining hall with two walls of glass serves straightforward American food and is open daily for all three meals. There are also a saloon and a snack bar outside the lodge's front entrance. There's a tour desk in the lodge's lobby.

## OUTSIDE THE PARK
In addition to this hotel, and the other lodges mentioned below, you'll find numerous budget motels in Fredonia, Arizona (30 miles west of Jacob Lake), and Kanab, Utah (37 miles west of Jacob Lake).

**Jacob Lake Inn.** Jacob Lake, AZ 86022. ☎ **520/643-7232.** Fax 520/643-7235. www.jacoblake.com. 44 units. May 15–Nov $69–$77 double in cabins, $85–$88 double in rooms; Dec–May 15 $39 double in cabins, $49–$55 double in rooms. AE, DC, DISC, MC, V. Pets accepted.

Located 30 miles north of the entrance to the North Rim, the Jacob Lake Inn consists of motel rooms and rustic cabins. The motel rooms are quite a bit nicer than the cabins, which have old carpets and cramped bathrooms with showers (no tubs). Just off the lobby is a coffee shop and adjacent is a more formal dining room. A bakery counter sells delicious cookies and fudge, and the general store sells snacks. Recreational facilities include basketball and volleyball courts and a playground. This lodge stays open in winter and is a base for cross-country skiers and snowmobilers. There's also a gas station here.

**Kaibab Lodge.** P.O. Box 2997, Flagstaff, AZ 86003. ☎ **800/525-0924** or 520/638-2389 (May 15–Oct 31 only). Fax 520/527-9398 or 520/638-9864. www.canyoneers.com. 29 units. Mid-May to late Oct $70–$120 double. DISC, MC, V. Closed late Oct to mid-May. Pets accepted.

Located 5 miles north of the entrance to the Grand Canyon's North Rim, the Kaibab Lodge was built around 1926 and is situated on the edge of a large meadow where deer can often be seen grazing. Nights here are cool even in summer, and a favorite pastime of guests is to sit by the fireplace in the lobby. The rooms are in small rustic cabins set back in the pines from the main lodge building. The lodge's dining room serves all meals, and the kitchen also prepares box lunches. There are hiking-equipment and mountain-bike rentals, a whirlpool spa, a tour desk, and a gift shop.

## EN ROUTE TO THE PARK
If you don't have a reservation at one of the three lodges at or near the North Rim, you may want to stop at one of the lodges recommended below and continue on to

the North Rim the next morning. Lodges near the canyon fill up early in the day if they aren't already fully booked with reservations made months in advance.

**Cliff Dwellers Lodge.** U.S. 89A (HC67-30), Marble Canyon, AZ 86036. ☎ **800/433-2543** for reservations, or 520/355-2228. Fax 520/355-2229. 21 units. A/C. Apr–Sept $56–$66 double; Oct–Mar $39 double. DISC, MC, V. Pets accepted.

To give you some idea of how remote an area this is, the Cliff Dwellers Lodge is marked on official Arizona state maps. There just isn't much else out here, so a single lodge can be as important as a town. The newer, more expensive rooms here are standard motel rooms and have combination bathtub/showers, while the older rooms, in a stone-walled building, have more character but showers only. A small restaurant provides meals. The lodge is close to some spectacular balanced rocks and it's about 11 miles east to Lees Ferry. The views here are great.

**Lees Ferry Lodge.** U.S. 89A (HC67-Box 1), Marble Canyon, AZ 86036. ☎ **520/355-2231.** 11 units. A/C. $50–$75 double. MC, V.

Located at the foot of the Vermilion Cliffs, 3½ miles west of the Colorado River, the Lees Ferry Lodge, built in 1929 of native stone and rough-hewn timber beams, is a small place with rustic accommodations. However, the rafters and anglers who stay here don't seem to care much about the condition of the rooms, and besides, the patio seating area in front of all the rooms has fabulous views of the Vermilion Cliffs. Unfortunately, the highway is only a few yards away, so traffic noises occasionally disturb the tranquillity. There's a small dining room on the premises.

**Marble Canyon Lodge.** Marble Canyon, AZ 86036. ☎ **800/726-1789** or 520/355-2225. Fax 520/355-2227. 60 units. A/C TV. $60–$125 double. AE, DISC, MC, V. Pets accepted.

Located just 4 miles from Lees Ferry, the Marble Canyon Lodge was built in the 1920s and is popular with rafters preparing to head down the Grand Canyon. The room styles vary considerably in size and age, with some rustic rooms in old stone buildings and other newer motel-style rooms as well. You're right at the base of the Vermilion Cliffs here, and the views are great. There's a cozy restaurant and a trading post (be sure to have some Marble Canyon cake).

## CAMPGROUNDS

Located just north of Grand Canyon Lodge, the **North Rim Campground,** with 82 sites and no hookups for RVs, is the only campground at the North Rim. The campground opens in mid-May and may stay open past the mid-October closing of other North Rim visitor facilities. Reservations can be made up to 3 months in advance by calling the **National Park Reservation Service** (☎ **800/365-2267**). The fee is $15 per site per night.

There are also two nearby campgrounds outside the park in the Kaibab National Forest. These are **DeMotte Park Campground,** which is the closest to the park entrance and has only 23 sites, and **Jacob Lake Campground,** which is 30 miles north of the park entrance and has 56 sites. Both campgrounds charge $10 per night and do not take reservations. You can also camp anywhere in the Kaibab National Forest as long as you're more than ¼ mile from a paved road or water source. So if you can't find a site in a campground, simply pull off the highway in the national forest and park your RV or pitch your tent.

The **Kaibab Camper Village,** P.O. Box 3331, Flagstaff, AZ 86003 (☎ **520/643-7804**), is a privately owned campground in the crossroads of Jacob Lake, 30 miles north of the park entrance. This campground has 60 RV sites and 25 tent sites. Rates are $12 per night for tent sites and $22 per night for RV sites with full hookups. Make reservations well in advance.

# The Four Corners Region: Land of the Hopi & Navajo

**W**ay up in the northeast corner of Arizona is a spot that's unique in the United States. Neither canyon, nor mountain, nor ancient ruin, this spot is unusual because here four states—Arizona, New Mexico, Colorado, and Utah—come together. But the name Four Corners refers to more than just a spot where you can stand in four states at the same time. The name also applies to the huge surrounding area, including a large piece of northeastern Arizona.

Most of the land in the Four Corners region of Arizona is Navajo and Hopi reservation land, and it's also some of the most spectacular countryside in the state, with majestic mesas, rainbow-hued deserts, towering buttes, multicolored cliffs, deep canyons, a huge cliff-rimmed reservoir, and even a meteorite crater. Among the most spectacular of these are the 1,000-foot buttes of Monument Valley. For years these evocative and colorful monoliths have symbolized the Wild West of cowboys, John Wayne movies, and car commercials.

In the name of progress, almost the entire length of the Colorado River in Arizona has been dammed, and among these vast artificial lakes, Lake Powell, created by the damn at Glen Canyon, is the most scenic. This lake is also one of the biggest tourist attractions in the Southwest. The bitter fight to preserve Glen Canyon is a thing of the past, and today the lake is popular with boaters, anglers, water-skiers, and sightseers from all over the world. This lake, with its miles of water mirroring steep canyon walls hundreds of feet high, is one of northern Arizona's curious contrasts—a vast artificial reservoir in the middle of barren desert canyons.

The Navajo and Hopi peoples who have lived on these lands for hundreds of years have adapted different means of surviving in the arid Four Corners region. The Navajo, with their traditional log homes scattered across the countryside, have become herders of sheep, goats, and cattle. The Hopi, on the other hand, have congregated in villages atop mesas and built houses of stone. They farm the floors of narrow valleys at the feet of their mesas in much the same way the indigenous peoples of the Southwest have done for centuries.

These two tribes are, however, only the most recent Native Americans to inhabit what many consider to be a desolate, barren wilderness. The ancient Anasazi left their mark throughout the canyons of the Four Corners region, with cliff dwellings dating from 700 years and more, the most spectacular in Arizona being the ruins in Canyon de Chelly and Navajo national monuments. No one is sure why the

Anasazi moved up into the cliff walls, but there is speculation that unfavorable growing conditions brought on by drought may have forced them to use every possible inch of arable land. The cliff dwellings were mysteriously abandoned in the 13th century, and with no written record, the disappearance of the Anasazi may forever remain a mystery.

The Hopi, who believe that the Anasazi were their ancestors, have had their villages for centuries on the tops of mesas in northeastern Arizona. They claim that Oraibi, on Third Mesa, is the oldest continuously inhabited community in the United States. Whether or not this is true, several of the Hopi villages are quite old, and for this reason they have become tourist attractions. Most of the villages are built on three mesas, known simply as First, Second, and Third Mesa, which are numbered from east to west. These villages have always maintained a great deal of autonomy, which over the years has led to fighting. The appearance of missionaries and the policies of the Bureau of Indian Affairs have also created conflicts among and within villages. Today the Hopi Reservation is completely surrounded by the much larger Navajo Reservation.

Roughly the size of West Virginia, the Navajo Reservation covers an area of 25,000 square miles in northeastern Arizona, as well as parts of New Mexico, Colorado, and Utah. It's the largest Native American reservation in the United States and is home to nearly 200,000 Navajo. Though there are now modern towns with supermarkets, shopping malls, and hotels on the reservation, many Navajo still follow a pastoral lifestyle as herders of goats and sheep. As you travel the roads of the Navajo Reservation, you'll frequently encounter these flocks as well as herds of cattle and horses. These animals have free range of the reservation and often graze beside the highways.

Unlike the pueblo tribes such as the Hopi and Zuni, the Navajo are relative newcomers to the Southwest. Their Athabascan language is most closely related to the languages spoken by Native Americans in the Pacific Northwest, Canada, and Alaska. It's believed that the Navajo migrated southward from northern Canada beginning around A.D. 1000, arriving in the Southwest sometime after 1400. At this time the Navajo were still hunters and gatherers, but contact with the pueblo tribes, who had long before adopted an agricultural lifestyle, began to change the Navajo into farmers. When the Spanish arrived in the Southwest in the early 17th century, the Navajo acquired horses, sheep, and goats through raids and adopted a pastoral way of life, grazing their herds in the high plains and canyon bottoms.

The continued use of raids, made even more successful with the acquisition of horses, put the Navajo in conflict with the Spanish settlers who were beginning to encroach on Navajo land. In 1805, the Spanish sent a military expedition into the Navajo's chief stronghold, Canyon de Chelly, and killed 115 people, who, by some accounts, may have been all women, children, and old men. This massacre didn't stop the conflicts between the Navajo and Spanish settlers. In 1846, when this region became part of the United States, American settlers encountered the same problems that the Spanish had. Military outposts were established to protect the new settlers, and numerous unsuccessful attempts were made to establish peace. In 1863, after continued Navajo attacks, a military expedition led by Col. Kit Carson burned crops and homes late in the summer, effectively obliterating the Navajo's winter supplies. Thus defeated, the Navajo were rounded up and herded 400 miles to an inhospitable region of New Mexico near Fort Sumner. This march became known as the Long Walk and had a profound influence on the Navajo. Living conditions at Fort Sumner were deplorable, and the land was unsuitable for farming. In 1868, the Navajo were allowed to return to their homeland.

Upon returning home, and after continued clashes with white settlers, the Navajo eventually settled into a lifestyle of herding. In recent years the Navajo have had to turn to different livelihoods. Though weaving and silver work have become lucrative businesses, the amount of money they garner for the tribe as a whole is not significant. Many Navajo now take jobs as migrant workers, and gas and oil leases on the reservation provide more income.

Though the reservation covers an immense area, much of it is of no value other than as scenery. Fortunately, the Navajo are recognizing the income potential of their spectacular land. Monument Valley is operated as a tribal park, and there's also a Navajo-owned marina on Lake Powell in Utah.

As you travel the Navajo reservation you may notice small hexagonal buildings with rounded roofs. These are *hogans,* the traditional homes of the Navajo, and are usually made of wood and earth. The doorway of the hogan always faces east to greet the new day. At the Canyon de Chelly and Navajo National Monument visitor centers you can look inside hogans that are part of the parks' exhibits. If you take a tour at Canyon de Chelly or Monument Valley, you may have an opportunity to visit a hogan that is still someone's home. Most Navajo now live in modest houses or mobile homes, but a family will usually also have a hogan for religious ceremonies.

All over the Navajo Reservation, you'll see stalls set up beside the road and at scenic overlooks. While you can sometimes find quality merchandise and bargain prices at these roadside stalls, you'll usually find better quality at trading posts, museum and park gift shops, and established shops where you receive some guarantee of the quality of the pieces for sale.

The Navajo and Hopi reservations cover a vast area and are laced with a network of good paved roads, as well as many unpaved roads that are not always passable to cars without four-wheel drive. The main things to keep in mind when driving in this area are to keep your car gassed up, since distances are great, and to keep an eye out for livestock on the road, especially at night.

Before taking a photograph of a Navajo, always ask permission. If permission is granted, a tip of $1 or more is expected. Photography is not allowed at all in the Hopi villages. The Navajo Reservation observes daylight saving time, unlike the rest of Arizona, so remember to set your watch forward an hour if you're visiting in the summer. The Hopi reservation is on Arizona time. Also keep in mind that *alcohol is not allowed on the reservation.*

## 1  Winslow

55 miles E of Flagstaff; 70 miles S of Second Mesa; 33 miles W of Holbrook

It's hard to imagine a town that could build its entire tourist fortunes on a mention in a pop song, but that is exactly what Winslow has done for a couple of decades now ever since the Eagles sang about "standin' on a corner in Winslow, Arizona," in their hit song "Take It Easy." They're even building an official Standin' on a Corner Park (scheduled for dedication in late 1999). Exactly which corner that fellow was standin' on isn't so important these days, and Eagles fans get their pictures taken on lots of corners around town.

Popular songs aside, Winslow can claim a couple of more significant attractions. Right in town is one of the Southwest's historic railroad hotels, La Posada, which has been recently renovated. Twenty miles west of town is a mile-wide Meteor Crater. And east of town is Homolovi Ruins State Park, which has ancient ruins as well as extensive petroglyphs.

### ESSENTIALS

**GETTING THERE**   Winslow is on I-40 at the junction with Ariz. 87, which leads north to the Hopi mesas and south to Payson.

**Amtrak** (☎ 800/872-7245) passenger trains stop in Winslow on East Second Street (at La Posada).

**VISITOR INFORMATION**   For more information on the area, contact the **Winslow Chamber of Commerce,** 300 W. North Rd., Winslow, AZ 86047 (☎ 520/289-2434; www.winslowchamber@cybertrails.com).

### METEOR CRATER: THE ORIGINAL DEEP IMPACT

West of Winslow 20 miles at exit 233 off I-40, you'll come to a 570-foot-deep **Meteor Crater** (☎ 520/289-2362), which is billed as "this planet's most penetrating natural attraction" and is the best-preserved impact crater on earth. This gaping hole in the barren desert landscape was created 49,000 years ago when a meteorite estimated to be about 100 feet in diameter slammed into the ground at 45,000 miles per hour. Standing on a platform on the crater rim, it's difficult to imagine the instant devastation that occurred when this meteorite struck the earth. So closely does this crater resemble craters on the surface of the moon that in the 1960s, NASA used this area as a training site for Apollo program astronauts.

The land the crater is on is privately owned, and on the rim you'll find a small museum, part of which is dedicated to the exploration of space. An Apollo space capsule is also on display. The rest of the museum is devoted to astrogeology and includes a meteorite weighing nearly three-quarters of a ton.

Admission is $8 for adults, $7 for senior citizens, $4 for children 6 to 17, and free for children 5 and under. From May 15 to September 15, hours are daily from 6am to 6pm; from September 16 to May 14, hours are daily from 8am to 5pm.

## OTHER WINSLOW AREA ATTRACTIONS

In downtown Winslow, near that famous corner, you'll find the little **Old Trails Museum,** 212 N. Kinsley St. (☎ 520/289-5861), which has exhibits on Route 66 and the Harvey Girls, who once worked in the nearby La Posada Resort. From April to September, the museum is open Tuesday through Saturday from 1 to 5pm; other months it's open only Tuesday, Thursday, and Saturday. Admission is free.

Even if you aren't planning on staying the night at the restored **La Posada Resort,** 303 E. Second St. (☎ 520/289-4366), you should be sure to stop by just to see this historic railway hotel. Self-guided tours are available for a $2 donation, and guided tours ($5 for adults, $2 for children under 18) are also available.

On the windswept plains north of Winslow (1.3 miles north of I-40 at Exit 257), you'll find **Homolovi Ruins State Park** (☎ 520/289-4106), which preserves more than 300 ancient Anasazi archaeological sites, several of which have been partially excavated. Though these ruins are not nearly as impressive as those at Wupatki or Walnut Canyon, a visit here will give you a better understanding of the interrelationship of the many ancient pueblos of this region. Also in the park are numerous petroglyphs; ask directions at the visitor center. Admission is $4 per vehicle (up to four people, then $1 per person). The ruins are open from sunrise to sunset, though the visitor center is only open from 8am to 5pm daily. There is also a campground here.

## WHERE TO STAY

In addition to the historic hotel mentioned here, you'll find lots of budget chain motels in Winslow. These include the **Best Western Adobe Inn,** 1701 N. Park Dr. (☎ 520/289-4638), charging $50 to $69 double; **Comfort Inn,** 520 Desmond St. (☎ 520/289-9581), charging $48 to $70 double; **Econo Lodge,** 1706 N. Park Dr. (☎ 520/289-4687), charging $49 to $109 double; and **Super 8 Motel,** 1916 W. Third St. (☎ 520/289-4606), charging $43 to $45 double. See appendix B for toll-free central reservation numbers.

✪ **La Posada.** 303 E. 2nd St., on U.S. Rte. 66, Winslow, AZ 86047. ☎ **520/289-4366.** Fax 520/289-3873. www.laposada.org. 23 units. TV TEL. $69–$89 double. Rates include continental breakfast. AE, DC, DISC, MC, V. Pets accepted, $5 fee.

Designed by Mary Elizabeth Jane Colter, who designed many of the buildings on the South Rim of the Grand Canyon, this railroad hotel opened in 1930 and was the last hotel built in the Southwest by tourism pioneer Fred Harvey. Today the hotel is being restored and is itself reason enough to stay in Winslow. In designing the hotel, Colter created an entire fictitious history surrounding the building, and consequently, La Posada has the feel of an old Spanish hacienda. In the large lobby, you'll now find an old railway luggage cart and the original safe from the hotel. There are also several pieces of original furniture as well as reproductions of pieces that were once found in the hotel. The nicest guest rooms at this time are the large rooms that are named for various famous guests of the hotel—Clark Gable, Howard Hughes, Gary Cooper, Charles Lindbergh, even the Marx brothers. The management's artistic flare comes across in these rooms, one of which (the Frank & Joanne Randall Room) has wide plank floors, murals, a fireplace, a rustic bed and armoire, art deco chairs, and a kilim rug. The bathroom is a classic of black-and-white tile and still has the original fixtures. By mid-1999, there should be more rooms available here, as well as a restaurant.

## 2 The Hopi Reservation

250 miles NE of Phoenix; 67 miles N of Winslow; 100 miles SW of Canyon de Chelly; 140 miles SE of Page/Lake Powell

Completely surrounded by the Navajo Reservation, the Hopi Reservation has at its center the grouping of mesas that are home to the Hopi pueblos. This remote region of Arizona, with its flat-topped mesas and rugged, barren landscape, is the center of the universe for the Hopi peoples.

The handful of villages that make up the Hopi pueblos are ancient and independent communities that have today been brought together under the guidance of the Hopi Tribal Council. This land has been inhabited by the Hopi and their ancestors for nearly 1,000 years, and many aspects of the ancient pueblo culture remain intact. However, much of the Hopi culture is hidden from the view of non-Hopi. Though the Hopi perform elaborate religious and social dances throughout the year, many of these dances are no longer open to outsiders.

*Important note:* When visiting the Hopi pueblos, remember that you are a guest and your privileges can be revoked at any time. Respect all posted signs at village entrances, and remember that *photographing, sketching, and recording are all prohibited in the villages and at ceremonies.* Also, kivas (ceremonial rooms) and ruins are off-limits.

## ESSENTIALS

**GETTING THERE**   This section of Arizona is one of the state's most remote regions. Distances are great but the highways are generally in good condition. Ariz. 87 leads from Winslow to Second Mesa, while Ariz. 264 runs from Tuba City in the west to the New Mexico state line in the east.

The **Navajo Transit System** (☎ 520/729-4002) operates a bus service Monday through Friday throughout the Navajo and Hopi reservations with service between the following towns: Farmington, Gallup, and Crown Point (all in New Mexico) and Window Rock, Kayenta, Chinle, and Tuba City. The route between Window Rock and Tuba City stops at several of the Hopi villages, including Second Mesa.

**VISITOR INFORMATION**   For more information before you leave home, contact the **Hopi Tribal Council,** P.O. Box 123, Kykotsmovi, AZ 86039 (☎ 520/734-3000). The Hopi Cultural Preservation Office home page Web address is www.nau.edu/~hcpo-p/.

Because each of the Hopi villages is relatively independent, you might want to contact the **Community Development Office** of a particular village for specific information on that village: **Bacavi** (☎ 520/734-9360), **First Mesa** (☎ 520/737-2670), **Hotevilla** (☎ 520/734-2420), **Kykotsmovi** (☎ 520/734-2474 or 520/734-2244), **Mishongnovi** (☎ 520/737-2520), **Moenkopi** (☎ 520/283-8051), **Polacca** (☎ 520/737-2670), and **Shipaulovi** (☎ 520/737-2570). These offices are open Monday through Friday from 8am to 5pm.

## EXPLORING THE WORLD OF THE HOPI

Start your visit to the Hopi pueblos at the **Hopi Cultural Center,** on Ariz. 264 (☎ 520/734-6650) in Second Mesa. This museum, motel, and restaurant is the tourism headquarters for the area. Here you can visit the museum and learn about the Hopi culture and its history. Be sure to take notice of signs indicating when villages are open to visitors. The museum is open Monday through Friday from 8am to 5pm and in the summer on Saturday and Sunday from 9am to 3pm. Admission is $3 for adults and $1 for children.

Though it's possible to get permission to visit most Hopi villages, the easiest to visit is ✪ **Walpi,** on First Mesa. Guided tours of this tiny village are offered daily in the winter from about 9:30am to 4pm, and in the summer daily from 9am to 6pm. Admission is $5 per adult, $4 ages 10 to 17, and $3 seniors and ages 5 to 10, although at press time, higher rates were being considered. To sign up for a tour, drive up to the top of First Mesa (in Polacca, take the road that says to First Mesa villages) and continue driving straight through the village at the top of the mesa until you see the **Information Office** (☎ 520/737-2262) and the signs for the tour. The 40-minute tours are led by Hopis who will tell you the history of the village and explain a bit about the local culture. On the third weekend in September, a harvest festival, with 2 days of dancing, is held and, as of this writing, is open to the public.

## THE VILLAGES

**FIRST MESA**    At the foot of First Mesa is **Polacca,** a settlement founded in the late 1800s by Walpi villagers who wanted to be closer to the trading post and school.

At the top of First Mesa is the village of **Walpi,** which was located lower on the slopes of the mesa until the Pueblo Rebellion of 1680 brought on fear of reprisal by the Spanish. The villagers moved Walpi to the very top of the mesa so that they could better defend themselves in the event of a Spanish attack. Walpi looks much like the Anasazi villages of the Arizona canyons, with small stone houses that seem to grow directly from the rock of the mesa top and ladders jutting from the roofs of kivas. The view stretches for hundreds of miles around.

**Sichomovi,** lower down on the mesa, was founded in 1750 as a colony of Walpi, while **Hano,** adjacent to Walpi, was founded by Tewa peoples either seeking refuge from the Spanish or offering aid to the people of Walpi.

**SECOND MESA**    Second Mesa is today the center of tourism in Hopiland, as the Hopi country is called, and this is where you'll find the Hopi Cultural Center.

Villages on Second Mesa include **Shungopavi,** which was moved to its present site after Old Shungopavi was abandoned in 1680 following the Pueblo Revolt against the Spanish.

Below Shungopavi is **Gray Spring.** The Snake Dance (actually a rain dance, and considered one of the most spectacular Native American ceremonies) is performed here in even-numbered years.

**Mishongnovi,** which means "place of the black man," is named for the leader of a clan that came here from the San Francisco Peaks around A.D. 1200. This village was also abandoned in 1680 and moved to its present location. The Snake Dance is held here in odd-numbered years.

**Shipaulovi** may also have been founded after the Pueblo Revolt of 1680.

**THIRD MESA**    **Oraibi,** which the Hopi claim is the oldest continuously occupied town in the United States, is located on Third Mesa. The village dates from 1150 and, according to legend, was founded by people from Old Shungopavi. A Spanish mission was established in Oraibi in 1629, and the ruins are still visible north of the village. Today Oraibi is a mix of old stone houses and modern ones, usually of cinderblock. With permission, you can wander around in Oraibi, where you'll likely be approached by village women offering to sell you various local crafts.

For centuries Oraibi was the largest of the Hopi villages, but in 1906 a schism occurred over Bureau of Indian Affairs policies and many of the villagers left to form **Hotevilla.** This latter village is considered the most conservative of the Hopi villages and has had frequent confrontations with the federal government.

**Kykotsmovi,** also known as Lower Oraibi or New Oraibi, was founded in 1890 by villagers from Oraibi who wanted to be closer to the school and trading post.

**Bacavi** was founded in 1907 by villagers who had helped found Hotevilla but who later decided that they wanted to return to Oraibi. The people of Oraibi would not let them return, and rather than go back to Hotevilla, they founded a new village.

**MOENKOPI**    One last Hopi village, **Moenkopi,** is located 40 miles to the west. Founded in 1870 by people from Oraibi, Moenkopi sits in the center of a wide green valley where plentiful water makes farming more reliable. Moenkopi is only a few miles from Tuba City off U.S. 160.

## CULTURAL TOURS

Perhaps the best way to see the Hopi mesas is on a guided small-group tour. With a guide, you will likely learn much more about this rather insular culture than you ever could on your own. Tour companies also frequently use local guides and stop at the homes of working artisans. This all adds up to a more in-depth and educational visit to one of the oldest cultures on the continent.

Some companies offering Hopi tours include **Crossing Worlds,** P.O. Box 623, Sedona, AZ 86339 (☎ **800/350-2693** or 520/649-3060; www.crossingworlds.com), **Discovery Passages,** 1161 Elk Trail (P.O. Box 630), Prescott, AZ 86303 (☎ **520/ 717-0519**), **Native Highways Tour Company,** P.O. Box 1804, Sedona, AZ 86339 (☎ **888/282-8474** or 520/282-8474; www.nativehwytours.com), and **Secret Mountain Tours,** 85 Arrowhead Dr., Sedona AZ 86351 (☎ **520/284-2140**). One-day tours to the Hopi Mesas run about $100 to $135 per person.

## DANCES & CEREMONIES

The Hopi have developed the most complex religious ceremonies of any of the Southwest tribes. Masked kachina dances, for which they are most famous, are held from January to July, while the equally well-known Snake Dances are held from August through December.

**Kachinas,** whether in the form of dolls or as masked dancers, are representative of the spirits of everything from plants and animals to ancestors and sacred places. There are more than 300 kachinas that appear on a regular basis in Hopi ceremonies, and another 200 that appear occasionally. The kachina spirits are said to live in the San Francisco Peaks to the south and at Spring of the Shadows in the east. According to legend, the kachinas lived with the Hopi long ago, but the Hopi people made the kachinas angry, causing them to leave. Before leaving, though, the kachinas taught the Hopi how to perform their ceremonies. Today the kachina ceremonies serve several purposes. Most important, they bring clouds and rain to water the all-important corn crop, but they also ensure health, happiness, long life, and harmony in the universe. The kachina season lasts from the winter solstice until shortly after the summer solstice. These months are marked by various kachina dances and ceremonies, with men wearing the elaborate costumes and masks of whichever kachinas have been chosen to appear. Clowns known as *koyemsi, koshares,* and *tsukus* entertain spectators between the more serious dances, with ludicrous and sometimes lewd mimicry, bringing a lighthearted counterpoint to the very serious nature of the kachina dances.

Preparations for the dances take place in the kivas (circular ceremonial rooms) that are entered from the roof by means of a ladder. The kachina dancers often bring carved wooden kachina dolls to village children to introduce them to the various kachina spirits.

Despite the importance of the kachina dances, it's the **Snake Dance** that has captured the attention of many non-Hopis. The Snake Dance is held only every other year in any given village and involves the handling of both poisonous and nonpoisonous snakes. The ceremony takes place over 16 days with the first 4 days dedicated to collecting all the snakes from the four cardinal directions. Later, footraces are held from the bottom of the mesa to the top. On the last day of the ceremony, the actual Snake Dance is performed. Men of the Snake Society form pairs of dancers—one to carry the snake in his mouth and the other to distract the snake with an eagle feather. When all the snakes have been danced around the plaza, they are rushed down to their homes at the bottom of the mesa to carry the Hopi prayers for rain to the spirits of the underworld.

The best way to find out about attending dances or ceremonies is to call the **Community Development Office** of the individual villages (see phone numbers under "Visitor Information," above). At press time, most villages prohibited non-Hopis at religious dances but allowed them at social dances. This closure of the religious dances is due to the disrespectful attitude of some visitors.

## SHOPPING

Most visitors come to the reservations to shop for Hopi crafts. There are literally dozens of small shops selling crafts and jewelry of different quality, and some homes have signs indicating that they sell crafts—you never know what you might discover by following such signs. Shops often sell the work of only a few individuals, so you should stop at several to get some idea of the variety of work available. Also, if you tour Walpi or wander around in Oraibi, you will be approached by villagers selling various crafts, including kachinas. The quality is not usually as high as those sold in shops, but then, neither are the prices.

One of the best places to stop to get a quick education in Hopi art and crafts is **Tsakurshovi** (no phone), a tiny shop 1½ miles east of the Hopi Cultural Center on Second Mesa. This shop has an amazing selection of crafts, old-style kachina dolls, native herbs, coil and wicker plaque baskets, and "Don't Worry Be Hopi" T-shirts. The owners are very friendly and are happy to share their knowledge and expertise with visitors.

If you're in the market for Hopi silver jewelry, stop in at **Hopi Arts and Crafts-Silvercraft** (☎ 520/734-2463), 100 yards from the Hopi Cultural Center on Second Mesa. This arts-and-crafts cooperative shows work by artisans from all the villages of the Hopi mesas. The best time to shop here is in the summertime when the selection is most extensive. The **Honani Crafts Gallery** (☎ 520/737-2238), at the intersection of Highway 264 and the road up to Second Mesa, sells both silver and the less common gold jewelry.

If you're interested in kachina dolls, be sure to visit the **Monongya Gallery** (☎ 520/734-2344), a big blue and gray building on Ariz. 264 in Oraibi (west of the Hopi Cultural Center). This store usually has one of the largest selections of kachina dolls in the area and holds a Christmas Eve sale at 50% off.

Also in Oraibi you'll find **Old Oraibi Crafts** (no phone), which sells artwork and crafts based on kachina images. At Keams Canyon, almost 30 miles east of the cultural center, you'll find another great place to shop for kachina dolls. **McGee's Indian Art** (☎ 520/738-2295) is adjacent to a grocery store and has been a trading post for more than 100 years. There's always an outstanding selection of the best quality kachina dolls here.

## WHERE TO STAY & DINE

The restaurant at the Hopi Cultural Center has a good salad bar and tasty traditional meals such as Hopi stew with hominy, lamb, and green chile and piki bread (a paper-thin bread made from blue corn). Prices here are very reasonable, considering the remoteness of the location. If you've brought your food along, there are some picnic tables with an amazing view just east of Oraibi on top of the mesa.

# A Native American Crafts Primer

The Four Corners region is taken up almost entirely by the Navajo and Hopi reservations, so Native American crafts are ubiquitous here. You'll see jewelry for sale by the side of desolate, windswept roads, Navajo rugs for sale in tiny trading posts, and Hopi kachinas being sold out of village homes. If you decide you want to take home a work by a local craftsperson, the information below will help you make an informed purchase. It is also now possible to shop for Native American crafts on the Internet at **www.hopimarket.com**.

**Hopi Kachinas**   These elaborately decorated wooden dolls are representations of spirits of plants, animals, ancestors, and sacred places. Traditionally, they were given to children to initiate them into the pantheon of kachina spirits, who play important roles in ensuring rain and harmony in the universe. In recent years kachinas have become popular with collectors of Native American crafts, and Hopi kachina carvers have changed their style to cater to the new market. Older kachinas were carved from a single piece of cottonwood, sometimes with arms simply painted on. This older style of kachina is much simpler and stiffer than the currently popular style that emphasizes action poses and realistic proportions. A great deal of carving and painting goes into each kachina, and prices today are in the hundreds of dollars for even the simplest. Currently gaining popularity with tourists and collectors are the *tsuku,* or clown, kachinas, which are usually painted with bold horizontal black and white stripes. The *tsukus* are often depicted in humorous situations or carrying slices of watermelon.

**Navajo Silver Work**   While the Hopi create overlay silver work from sheets of silver and the Zuni use silver work simply as a base for their skilled lapidary or stone-cutting work, the Navajo silversmiths highlight the silver itself. Just as rug weaving did not begin until the latter part of the 19th century, silversmithing did not catch on with the Navajo until the 1880s, when Lorenzo Hubbell decided to hire Mexican silversmiths as teachers. When tourists began visiting the area after 1890, the demand for Navajo jewelry increased. The earliest pieces of Navajo jewelry were replicas of Spanish ornaments, but as the Navajo silversmiths became more proficient, they began to develop their own designs. Sandcasting, stamp work, repoussé, and file-and-chisel work give Navajo jewelry its unique look. The squash-blossom necklace, with its horseshoe-shaped pendant, is perhaps the most distinctive Navajo jewelry design. Wide bracelets and concha belts are also popular.

**Hopi Overlay Silver Work**   Overlay silver work has come to be considered the characteristic Hopi style of silver work, but only since World War II have the Hopi been making this sort of jewelry almost exclusively. After the war the GI bill provided the funds for Hopi soldiers to study silversmithing at a school founded by the famous Hopi artist Fred Kabotie. The overlay process basically uses two

**Hopi Cultural Center Restaurant & Inn.** P.O. Box 67, Second Mesa, AZ 86043. ☎ **520/734-2401.** Fax 520/734-6651. 30 units. TV TEL. Apr 1–Sept 30 $85–$90 double; Oct 1–Mar 31 $65–$70 double. AE, MC, V.

Though it isn't much, this is the only lodging for miles around—so be sure you have a reservation before heading up here for an overnight visit. The rooms are comfortable and modern if a bit spartan. The restaurant serves American and traditional Hopi meals, including piki bread. There's also a museum.

sheets of silver, one with a design cut from it. Heat fuses the two sheets, forming a raised image. Designs used in overlay jewelry are often borrowed from other Hopi crafts such as baskets and pottery, as well as from ancient Anasazi pottery designs. Belt buckles, earrings, bolo ties, and bracelets are all popular.

**Hopi Baskets**    Though the Tohono O'odham of the deserts of central and southern Arizona are better known for their basketry, the Hopi also produce beautiful work. Wicker plaques and baskets are made on Third Mesa from rabbit brush and sumac and are colored with bright aniline dyes. Coiled plaques and baskets, using dyed yucca fibers, are created on Second Mesa. Yucca-fiber sifters are made by plaiting over a willow ring. This style of basket is made throughout the reservation.

**Hopi Pottery**    With the exception of undecorated utilitarian pottery that's made in Hotevilla on Third Mesa, most Hopi pottery is produced on First Mesa. Contemporary Hopi pottery comes in a variety of styles including a yellow-orange ware that's decorated with black-and-white designs. This style is said to have been introduced by the potter Nampeyo, a Tewa from the village of Hano who stimulated the revival of Hopi pottery in 1890. A white pottery with red-and-black designs is also popular. Hopi pottery designs tend toward geometric patterns.

**Navajo Rugs**    After they acquired sheep and goats from the Spanish, the Navajo learned weaving from the pueblo tribes, and by the early 1800s their weavings were widely recognized as being the finest in the Southwest. The Navajo women primarily wove blankets, but by the end of the 19th century the craft began to die out when it became more economical to purchase a ready-made blanket. When Lorenzo Hubbell set up his trading post, he immediately recognized a potential market in the East for the woven blankets if they could be made heavy enough to be used as rugs. Having great respect for Hubbell, the Navajo adapted his ideas and soon began doing a brisk business. Although today the cost of Navajo rugs, which take hundreds of hours to make, has become almost prohibitively expensive, there are still enough women practicing the craft to keep it alive and provide plenty of rugs for shops and trading posts all over Arizona.

The best rugs are those made with homespun yarn and natural vegetal dyes. However, commercially manufactured yarns and dyes are being used more and more in order to keep costs down. There are more than 15 regional styles of rugs and quite a bit of overlapping and borrowing. Bigger and bolder patterns are likely to cost quite a bit less than very complex and highly detailed patterns. Navajo rug auctions are held at Crown Point, New Mexico, about 60 miles east of Window Rock.

**Quality Inn Tuba Trading Post, Restaurant & RV Park.** At the junction of U.S. 160 and Ariz. 264 (P.O. Box 247), Tuba City, AZ 86045. ☎ **800/228-5151** or 520/283-4545. 80 units. A/C TV TEL. Apr–Oct $95–$140 double; Nov–Mar $75–$105 double. AE, DISC, MC, V.

If you can't get a room at the Hopi Cultural Center, this is the next nearest acceptable motel and at that, it's 62 miles from Second Mesa. Located on the Navajo Reservation adjacent to the historic Tuba City Trading Post, the motel offers comfortable, modern rooms. Its restaurant serves Mexican and American meals. There's also an RV park.

## 3 The Petrified Forest & Painted Desert

25 miles E of Holbrook; 90 miles E of Flagstaff; 118 miles S of Canyon de Chelly; 180 miles N of Phoenix

Though petrified wood can be found in almost every state, the "forests" of downed logs here in northeastern Arizona are by far the most spectacular. A 27-mile scenic drive winds through the petrified forest and a small corner of the Painted Desert, providing a fascinating high desert experience.

Petrified wood has intrigued people for years and when, in the 1850s, it was discovered scattered like kindling across this section of Arizona, enterprising people began exporting it wholesale to the East. By 1900 so much had been removed that in 1906 several areas were set aside as the Petrified Forest National Monument.

It may be hard to believe when you drive across this arid landscape, but at one time this area was a vast humid swamp. That was 225 million years ago, when dinosaurs and huge amphibians ruled the earth and giant now-extinct trees grew on the high ground around the swamp. Fallen trees were washed downstream and gathered in piles in still backwaters and were eventually covered over with silt, mud, and volcanic ash. As water seeped through this soil, it dissolved the silica in the volcanic ash and redeposited this silica inside the cells of the logs. Eventually the silica recrystalized into stone to form petrified wood.

This region was later inundated with water, and thick deposits of sediment buried the logs ever deeper. Eventually, the land was transformed yet again as a geologic upheaval thrust the lake bottom up above sea level. This upthrust of the land cracked the logs into the segments we see today. Wind and water gradually eroded the landscape to create the many colorful and spectacular features of northern Arizona, including the Painted Desert, and the petrified logs were once again exposed on the surface of the land.

Throughout the region you'll see petrified wood in all sizes and colors, natural and polished, being sold in gift stores. This petrified wood comes from private land. No piece of petrified wood, no matter how small, may be removed from Petrified Forest National Park.

## ESSENTIALS

**GETTING THERE**   The north entrance to Petrified Forest National Park is 25 miles east of Holbrook on I-40. The south entrance is 20 miles east of Holbrook on U.S. 180.

There is **Amtrak** passenger service to Winslow, 33 miles west of Holbrook. Call ☎ **800/872-7245** for schedules and rate information.

**VISITOR INFORMATION**   For further information on the Painted Desert or the Petrified Forest, contact the **Petrified Forest National Park,** P.O. Box 2217, Petrified Forest National Park, AZ 86028 (☎ **520/524-6228**). The park is open daily from 8am to 6pm (closed on Christmas and shorter hours in winter), and admission is $10 per car.

For information on Holbrook and the surrounding region, contact the **Holbrook Chamber of Commerce,** 100 E. Arizona St., Holbrook, AZ 86025 (☎ **800/ 524-2459** or 520/524-6558).

## EXPLORING A UNIQUE LANDSCAPE

Although Petrified Forest National Park has both a north and a south entrance, it is probably better to start at the southern entrance and work your way north. This way, you'll see the most impressive displays of petrified logs early in your visit. The north end of the park is where you'll find Painted Desert overlooks.

The park has two visitor centers, and both have maps and books about the region and issue the free permits necessary to backpack and camp in the park's wilderness areas. The **Rainbow Forest Museum,** at the south end of the park, is open daily from 8am to 6pm (shorter hours in winter). Exhibits, including letters written by people who had taken pieces of petrified wood and who later felt guilty and returned the stones, chronicle the area's geologic and human history.

The **Painted Desert Oasis Visitor Center** is at the north end of the park and is open daily from 8am to 6pm (shorter hours in winter). A 17-minute film here explains the process by which wood becomes fossilized. Connecting the two visitor centers is a 27-mile scenic road with more than 20 overlooks.

Starting at the southern end of the park, there is the **Giant Logs self-guided trail.** This trail starts behind the Rainbow Forest Museum, and a booklet explaining the numbered stops is available at the front desk. The trail lives up to its name, with huge logs strewn about the hilly area. Almost directly across the parking lot from the Rainbow Forest Museum is the entrance to the **Long Logs** and **Agate House** areas. On the Long Logs trail, you can see more big trees, while at Agate House you will see the ruins of a pueblo built from wood that was turned into colorful agate. Minerals such as iron, manganese, and carbon are what give petrified wood its distinctive colors.

Heading north, you pass by the unusual formations known as **The Flattops.** These structures are caused by the erosion of softer soil deposits from beneath a harder and more erosion-resistant layer of sandstone. The Flattops area is one of the park's wilderness areas. The **Crystal Forest** is the next stop to the north and is named for the beautiful amethyst and quartz crystals that were once found in the cracks of petrified logs. Concern over the removal of these crystals was what led to the protection of the petrified forest.

At the **Jasper Forest Overlook** you can see logs that include petrified roots, while at **Blue Mesa** pieces of petrified wood form capstones over easily eroded clay soils. As wind and water wear away at the clay beneath a piece of stone, the balance of the stone becomes more and more precarious until it eventually comes toppling down. At the **Agate Bridge** stop, the soil has been washed away under a petrified log creating a natural agate bridge.

Erosion has played a major role in the formation of the Painted Desert, and to the north of Blue Mesa you'll see some of the most interesting erosional features of the area. It's quite evident why these hills of sandstone and clay are known as **The Teepees.** The layers of different color are due to different types of soils and stone and to minerals dissolved in the soil.

Human habitation of the area dates from more than 2,000 years ago, and at **Newspaper Rock** you can see petroglyphs left by generations of Native Americans. At **Puerco Indian Ruins** you can see the homes of the people who made the carvings before the area's abandonment around 1400.

North of Puerco Ruins, the road crosses the Santa Fe Railroad and then I-40. From here to the Painted Desert Visitor Center, there are eight overlooks onto the southernmost edge of the **Painted Desert.** Named for the vivid colors of the soil and stone that cover the land here, the Painted Desert is a Technicolor dreamscape of pastel colors washed across a barren expanse of eroded hills. The colors are created by minerals dissolved in the sandstone and clay soils that were deposited during different geologic periods. There's a picnic area at Chinde Point overlook, and at Kachina Point, where you'll also find the **Painted Desert Inn Museum,** open daily 8am to 5pm. From here, there's access to the park's other wilderness area.

At the north end, the **Painted Desert Oasis** provides a full-service cafeteria, and at the south end of the park there's a snack bar serving sandwiches and ice cream.

# OTHER REASONS TO LINGER IN HOLBROOK

Though the Petrified Forest National Monument is the main reason for visiting this area, you may also want to stop at the **Navajo County Historical Society Museum,** 100 E. Arizona St. (☎ 520/524-6558), in downtown Holbrook. This old and dusty museum, in the town's historic courthouse, has exhibits on local history, but is most interesting for having the town's old jail cells on display. From June to August, the Holbrook Chamber sponsors Native American dancers weekday evenings on the lawn in front of the museum.

Although it is against the law to collect petrified wood inside Petrified Forest National Park, there are several **rock shops** in Holbrook where you can buy pieces of petrified wood in all shapes and sizes. These shops also sell plenty of other types of rocks as well. You'll find them lined up along the main street through town.

Three miles west of town, you'll find the **International Petrified Forest/Museum of the Americas/Dinosaur Park,** 1001 Forest Dr. (☎ 520/524-9178), at exit 292 off I-40. This warehouse-size rock shop also happens to have an impressive collection of fossils and pre-Columbian artifacts from North and South America.

If you're a **Route 66** fan, you'll also find plenty to keep you entertained here. Hopi Drive, the town's main street, is old Route 66, and it is here that you will find the Wigwam Motel (see below). At **Julien's Roadrunner,** 109 W. Hopi Dr. (☎ 520/524-2388), you can investigate all manner of memorabilia, from Route 66 Highway signs to enameled replicas of old advertising signs for Mobil Gas and the Santa Fe Railroad. West of Holbrook at exit 269 off I-40, the **Jack Rabbit Trading Post** is another fun Route 66–era tourist trap worth a stop if you're a fan of the old highway. Here you'll find all kinds of fun, kitschy stuff straight out of the 1960s.

Also here in town (on the north side of I-40), you'll find **McGee's Gallery,** 2114 N. Navajo Blvd. (☎ 520/524-1977), a Native American crafts gallery with a wide selection of typical crafts at reasonable prices.

If you're interested in **petroglyphs** (see appendix A, "Arizona in Depth"), you may want to schedule a visit to the **Rock Art Canyon Ranch** (☎ 800/524-2459 or 520/288-3260), which is located southwest of Holbrook on part of the old Hashknife Ranch, which was the largest ranch in the country during the late 19th century. Within the bounds of this ranch are hundreds of Anasazi petroglyphs pecked into the rocks of Chevelon Canyon. Ranch visits are more than just a chance to see petroglyphs; they might include wagon rides, horseback riding, swimming, and rockhounding. Cowboy lunches and dinners, complete with music and storytelling, are also part of the Rock Art Canyon Ranch experience (available between mid-May and mid-October). Tours are scheduled year-round, except for Sundays and Easter, Thanksgiving, and Christmas; guests can opt for their choice of the above described activities, and prices vary depending on the activities and the size of the group.

# WHERE TO STAY

Holbrook is the nearest town to Petrified Forest National Monument. In addition to the unique Wigwam Motel listed below, you'll find several budget chain motels, including the **Comfort Inn,** 2602 Navajo Blvd. (☎ 520/524-6131), charging $42 to $65 double; **Days Inn,** 2601 Navajo Blvd. (☎ 520/524-6949), charging $39 to $49 double; **Econo Lodge,** 2596 Navajo Blvd. (☎ 520/524-1448), charging $40 to $50 double; **Motel 6,** 2514 Navajo Blvd. (☎ 520/524-6101), charging $34 double; and **Super 8 Motel,** 1989 Navajo Blvd. (☎ 520/524-2871), charging $44 to $51 double.

✪ **Wigwam Motel.** 811 W. Hopi Dr. (P.O. Box 788), Holbrook, AZ 86025. ☎ 520/524-3048. Fax 520/524-2119. 15 units. A/C TV TEL. $32–$37 double. MC, V. Pets accepted.

If you're willing to sleep on a saggy mattress for the sake of reliving a bit of Route 66 history, don't miss this collection of concrete wigwams (teepees, actually). This unique motel was built in the 1940s when unusual architecture was springing up all along famous Route 66. Owned by the same family since it was built, the Wigwam was renovated a few years back. However, you'll still find the original rustic furniture and colorful bedspreads in the small wigwam-shaped buildings. There's also a small museum here at the motel.

## WHERE TO DINE

If you're just looking for some simple diner fare, check out **Joe & Aggie's Café,** 120 W. Hopi Dr. (☎ **520/524-6540**), with old Route 66 diner fare, friendly owners, good salsa, and plenty of Route 66 decor around the dining room.

**Butterfield Stage Co.** 609 W. Hopi Dr. ☎ **520/524-3447.** Main courses $9–$18. AE, MC, V. Daily 4–10pm. STEAK/SEAFOOD.

It's natural to assume that finding a decent meal in an out-of-the-way town might be nearly impossible, so the Butterfield Stage Co. is a pleasant surprise. The owners are from the former Yugoslavia, and we're not sure how they got to Holbrook, but we do know that meals here are pretty good, with a soup and salad bar that is usually fresh. Tables have historical panels with amusing information to read while waiting for your pepper steak or filet mignon. The restaurant is named for the famous overland stagecoach line that carried the mail from St. Louis to San Francisco in the mid–19th century.

## 4  The Window Rock & Ganado Areas

190 miles E of Flagstaff; 68 miles SE of Canyon de Chelly National Monument; 74 miles NE of Petrified Forest National Park; 91 miles E of Second Mesa

Window Rock, the capital of the Navajo nation, is less than a mile from the New Mexico state line and is named for a huge natural opening in a sandstone cliff just outside town. Today that landmark is preserved as the **Window Rock Tribal Park,** which is located 2 miles north of Ariz. 264. At one time there was a spring at the base of Window Rock, and water from the spring was used by medicine men performing the Tohee Ceremony, a water ceremony intended to bring the rains.

As the Navajo nation's capital, Window Rock is the site of government offices, a museum and cultural center, and a zoo. About a half hour's drive west of Window Rock is the community of Ganado, the location of two historic sites—St. Michael's Mission and the Hubbell Trading Post. Window Rock's Navajo Nation Inn makes a good base for exploring this corner of the reservation.

## ESSENTIALS

**GETTING THERE**   To reach Window Rock from Flagstaff, take I-40 east to Lupton and go north on Indian Route 12.

There is **Amtrak** passenger service to Winslow, south of the reservation. Call ☎ 800/872-7245 for schedules and fares.

The **Navajo Transit System** operates bus service Monday through Friday throughout the Navajo nation with service between the cities of Farmington, Gallup, and Crown Point (all in New Mexico), and Window Rock, Kayenta, Chinle, and Tuba City. Call ☎ 520/729-4002 for schedule information.

**TIME**   The Navajo nation observes daylight saving time, contrary to the rest of Arizona, so if you are coming from elsewhere in Arizona, the time here will be 1 hour later in months when daylight saving is in effect.

**MONEY**    ATMs are few and far between in this area, but there is one at the Navajo Nation Inn.

**VISITOR INFORMATION**    For more information before visiting, contact the Navajoland Tourism Department, P.O. Box 663, Window Rock, AZ 86515 (☎ **520/ 871-7371** or 520/871-6436).

**SPECIAL EVENTS**    Unlike the village ceremonies of the pueblo-dwelling Hopi, Navajo religious ceremonies tend to be held in the privacy of family hogans. However, there are numerous fairs, powwows, and rodeos held throughout the year, and the public is welcome to attend. The biggest of these is the **Navajo Nation Fair** (☎ **520/ 871-6478**), held in Window Rock in early September each year. At this fair there are traditional dances, a rodeo, a powwow, a parade, a Miss Navajo Pageant, and arts-and-crafts exhibits and sales. Other important fairs on the Navajo Reservation include the **Shiprock Navajo Fair** (☎ **505/368-1081**) at Shiprock, New Mexico, in late September to early October (the most traditional of all Navajo fairs) and the **Western Navajo Fair** (☎ **520/283-3284**) at Tuba City, Arizona, in mid-October.

## HUBBELL TRADING POST

Located just outside the town of Ganado, 26 miles west of Window Rock, the **Hubbell Trading Post National Historic Site** (☎ **520/755-3475**) is the oldest continuously operating trading post on the Navajo Reservation. The trading post was established in 1876 by Lorenzo Hubbell, who did more to popularize the arts and crafts of the Navajo people than any other person. In the visitor center you can watch Navajo weavers in the slow process of creating a rug.

The rug room is filled with a variety of traditional and contemporary Navajo rugs. Though it's possible to buy a small 12-by-18-inch rug for around $100, most cost in the thousands of dollars. There are also baskets, kachinas, and several cases of jewelry by Navajo, Hopi, and Zuni in another room. Glance around the general store, and you'll see basic foodstuffs (not much variety here) and bolts of cloth used by Navajo women for sewing their traditional skirts and blouses.

Trading posts have long been more than just a place to trade crafts for imported goods. They were for many years the main gathering spot for meeting people from other parts of the reservation and served as a sort of gossip fence and newsroom. You can tour the grounds on your own or take a guided tour. There's no admission fee. From May to October, hours are daily from 8am to 6pm; in other months, daily 8am to 5pm.

## OTHER SIGHTS

**The Navajo Nation Museum.** W. Ariz. 264, Window Rock (across from the Navajo Nation Inn). ☎ **520/871-6673.** Admission sometimes free; other times it varies, depending on exhibits. Oct–May Mon–Fri 8am–5pm; June–Sept, may be open on Sat 10am–4pm.

Sponsored by the Navajo Nation Historic Preservation Society, this new museum and cultural center is housed in a large modern building patterned after a traditional hogan. Inside you may find the *Chilchinbeto* rug, at 24 feet by 28 feet one of the largest Navajo rugs ever made. You'll also find temporary exhibits of contemporary crafts and art, as well as exhibits on contemporary Navajo culture, a library, and gift shop. There are also plans to eventually add an exhibit of historical Navajo artifacts and old photos.

**Navajo Nation Zoo & Botanical Park.** Ariz. 264, Window Rock. ☎ **520/871-6573.** Free admission. Daily 8am–5pm. Closed Jan 1 and Dec 25.

Located in back of the Navajo Nation Inn, this zoo and botanical garden features animals and plants that are significant in Navajo history and culture. Bears, cougars, and wolves are among the animals you'll see here. The setting, which includes several sandstone "haystack" rocks, is very dramatic, and some of the animal enclosures are quite large and incorporate natural rock outcroppings. Also exhibited are examples of different styles of hogans. Well worth a stop.

**St. Michael's Historical Museum.** St. Michael's, just south of Ariz. 264. ☎ **520/871-4171.** Free admission. Memorial Day–Christmas daily 9am–5pm. Closed the rest of the year.

Located in the town of St. Michael's, 4 miles west of Window Rock, this historical museum chronicles the lives and influence of Franciscan friars who started a mission in this area in the 1670s. The museum is in a small building adjacent to the impressive stone mission church.

## A TOUR FROM THE NAVAJO PERSPECTIVE

The best way to understand the Navajo culture is through the eyes of a Navajo. Stanley M. Perry, a Navajo Indian born and raised on the reservation, is a storyteller and guide who will accompany you in your vehicle to tour the Window Rock, Canyon de Chelly, and Monument Valley areas. He can be reached at (☎ **520/871-2484,** best after 7pm). The rate is $100 per day for up to four people; for larger groups, rates depend on the number in the party.

## SHOPPING

The Hubbell Trading Post, though it is a National Historic Site, is still an active trading post and has an outstanding selection of rugs, as well as lots of jewelry (see above).

In Window Rock, be sure to visit the **Navajo Arts and Crafts Enterprise** (☎ **520/ 871-4090**), which is adjacent to the Navajo Nation Inn and has been operating since 1941. Here you'll find silver-and-turquoise jewelry, Navajo rugs, sandpaintings, baskets, pottery, and Native American clothing.

## WHERE TO STAY

**Navajo Nation Inn.** 48 W. Hwy. 264 (P.O. Box 2340), Window Rock, AZ 86515. ☎ **800/ 662-6189** or 520/871-4108. Fax 520/871-5466. 54 units. A/C TV TEL. $54–$73 double; $77 suite. AE, DC, MC, V. Pets accepted ($50 deposit).

Located on the edge of Window Rock, the administrative center of the Navajo Reservation, the Navajo Nation Inn is an older motel with rustic pine furniture in the guest rooms. The restaurant and coffee shop are open daily serving American and traditional Navajo dishes.

## WHERE TO DINE

In Window Rock, your best bet for a meal is at the **Navajo Nation Inn,** but you'll also find McDonald's and KFC fast-food restaurants. In Ganado, you can get good, inexpensive cafeteria-style food at **Cafe Sage** (☎ **520/755-3411,** ext. 292) on the grounds of Ganado's health clinic, which is across Ariz. 264 and ½ mile east of the trading post.

## 5  Canyon de Chelly

222 miles NE of Flagstaff; 68 miles NW of Window Rock; 110 miles SE of Navajo National Monument; 110 miles SE of Monument Valley Navajo Tribal Park

It's hard to imagine narrow canyons less than 1,000 feet deep being more spectacular than the Grand Canyon, but in some ways ✪ **Canyon de Chelly National Monument** is just that. Gaze down from the rim of Canyon de Chelly at an ancient Anasazi cliff dwelling as the whinnying of horses and clanging of goat bells drifts up from far below, and you will be struck by the continuity of human existence. For more than 2,000 years people have called these canyons home, and today there are more than 100 prehistoric dwelling sites in the area.

Canyon de Chelly National Monument consists of two major canyons—Canyon de Chelly (which is pronounced canyon de *shay* and is derived from the Navajo word *tségi,* meaning "rock canyon") and *Canyon del Muerto* (Spanish for "Canyon of the Dead")—and several smaller canyons. The canyons extend for more than 100 miles through the rugged slick-rock landscape of northeastern Arizona, draining the seasonal runoff from the snowmelt of the Chuska Mountains.

Canyon de Chelly's smooth sandstone walls of rich reds and yellows contrast sharply with the deep greens of corn, pasture, and cottonwood on the canyon floor. Vast stone amphitheaters form the caves in which the ancient Anasazi built their homes, and as you watch shadows and light paint an ever-changing canyon panorama, it's easy to see why the Navajo consider these canyons sacred ground. With mysteriously abandoned cliff dwellings and breathtaking natural beauty, Canyon de Chelly is certainly as worthy of a visit as the Grand Canyon.

From Memorial Day to Labor Day there are interpretive programs here at the national monument. Check at the **visitor center** for daily activities, such as campfire programs and natural-history programs, that might be scheduled.

## ESSENTIALS

**GETTING THERE**    From Flagstaff, the easiest route to Canyon de Chelly is to take I-40 to U.S. 191 to Ganado. At Ganado, drive west on Ariz. 264 and then pick up U.S. 191 again heading north to Chinle. If you're coming down from Monument Valley or Navajo National Monument, Indian Route 59, which connects U.S. 160 and U.S. 191, is an excellent road with plenty of beautiful scenery.

Chinle, 3 miles from the entrance to Canyon de Chelly National Monument, is served by the **Navajo Transit System** (☎ **520/729-4002** for schedules and fares).

**VISITOR INFORMATION**    Before leaving home you can contact **Canyon de Chelly National Monument,** P.O. Box 588, Chinle, AZ 86503 (☎ **520/674-5500**).

**SPECIAL EVENTS**    The **Central Navajo Fair** is held in Chinle each year in August.

**ADMISSION**    Park admission is free.

## SEEING THE CANYON

Your first stop at Canyon de Chelly should be the **visitor center,** which is open daily May through September from 8am to 6pm (on daylight saving time) and October through April from 8am to 5pm. In front of the visitor center is an example of a traditional crib-style hogan, a hexagonal structure of logs and earth that Navajo use both as a home and as a ceremonial center. Inside, a small museum acquaints visitors with the history of Canyon de Chelly, and there's often a silversmith demonstrating Navajo jewelry-making techniques. From here most people tour the canyon by car.

Very different views of the canyon are provided by the North Rim and South Rim drives. The North Rim Drive overlooks Canyon del Muerto, while the South Rim Drive overlooks Canyon de Chelly. Each of the rim drives is around 20 miles in each direction, and with stops it can easily take 3 hours to visit each rim.

### THE NORTH RIM DRIVE

The first stop on the North Rim is the Ledge Ruin Overlook. On the opposite wall, about 100 feet up from the canyon floor, you can see the Ledge Ruin. This site was occupied by the Anasazi between A.D. 1050 and 1275. Nearby, at the Dekaa Kiva

Viewpoint, you can see a lone kiva (circular ceremonial building). This structure was reached by means of toeholds cut into the soft sandstone cliff wall.

The second stop is at the **Antelope House Overlook.** The Antelope House ruin takes its name from the paintings of antelopes on a nearby cliff wall. It's believed that the paintings were done in the 1830s. Beneath the ruins of Antelope House, archaeologists have found the remains of an earlier pit house dating from A.D. 693. Though most of the Anasazi cliff dwellings were abandoned sometime after a drought began in 1276, Antelope House had already been abandoned by 1260, possibly because of damage caused by flooding. Across the wash from Antelope House, an ancient tomb, known as the Tomb of the Weaver, was discovered in the 1920s by archaeologists. The tomb contained the well-preserved body of an old man wrapped in a blanket of golden eagle feathers and accompanied by cornmeal, shelled and husked corn, pine nuts, beans, salt, and thick skeins of cotton. Also visible from this overlook is Navajo Fortress, a red sandstone butte that the Navajo once used as a refuge from attackers. A steep trail leads to the top of Navajo Fortress, and through the use of log ladders that could be pulled up into the refuge, the Navajo were able to escape their attackers.

The third stop is at **Mummy Cave Overlook,** named for two mummies that were found in burial urns below the ruins. Archaeological evidence indicates that this giant amphitheater consisting of two caves was occupied for 1,000 years from A.D. 300 to 1300. In the two caves and on the shelf between there are 80 rooms, including three kivas. The central structure between the two caves is interesting because it includes a three-story building characteristic of the architecture in Mesa Verde in New Mexico. Archaeologists speculate that a group of Anasazi migrated here from New Mexico. Much of the original plasterwork of these buildings is still intact and indicates that the buildings were colorfully decorated.

The fourth and last stop on the North Rim is at the **Massacre Cave Overlook.** The cave received its name after an 1805 Spanish military expedition killed more than 115 Navajo at this site. The Navajo at the time had been raiding Spanish settlements that were encroaching on Navajo territory. Accounts of the battle at Massacre Cave differ. One account claims that there were only women, children, and old men taking shelter in the cave, though the official Spanish records claim 90 warriors and 25 women and children were killed. Also visible from this overlook is Yucca Cave, which was occupied about 1,000 years ago.

## THE SOUTH RIM DRIVE

The South Rim Drive climbs slowly but steadily along the South Rim of Canyon de Chelly, and at each stop you're a little bit higher above the canyon floor.

The first stop is at **Tségi Overlook.** *Tségi* means "rock canyon" in Navajo, and that's just what you'll see when you gaze down from this viewpoint. A short narrow canyon feeds into Chinle Wash, which is formed by the streams cutting through the canyons of the national monument.

The second stop is at the **Junction Overlook,** so named because it overlooks the junction of Canyon del Muerto and Canyon de Chelly. Visible here is the Junction Ruin, with its 10 rooms and one kiva. The Anasazi occupied this ruin during the great pueblo period, which lasted from around 1100 until the Anasazi disappeared shortly before 1300. Also visible is First Ruin, which is perched precariously on a long narrow ledge. In this ruin are 22 rooms and two kivas.

The third stop, at **White House Overlook,** provides the only opportunity for descending into Canyon de Chelly without a guide or ranger. The ✪ **White House Ruins Trail** descends 600 feet to the canyon floor, crosses Chinle Wash, and approaches the White House Ruins. These buildings were constructed both on the canyon floor and 50 feet up the cliff wall in a small cave. Though you cannot enter

# Fred Harvey & His Girls

Unless you grew up in the Southwest and can remember back to pre–World War II days, you may never have heard of Fred Harvey and the Harvey Girls. However, if you spend much time in northern Arizona, you're likely to run into quite a few references to the Harvey Girls and their boss.

Fred Harvey was the southwest's most famous mogul of railroad tourism, an early promoter of tourism and the service industries as the future of the Grand Canyon State. Harvey, who was working for a railroad in the years shortly after the Civil War, had developed a distaste for the food served at railroad stations. He decided he could do a better job, and in 1876, opened his first Harvey House railway-station restaurant for the Santa Fe Railroad. At the time of his death in 1901, Harvey operated 47 restaurants, 30 diners, and 15 hotels across the West.

The women who worked as waitresses in the Harvey House restaurants came to be known as Harvey Girls. Known for their distinctive black dresses with white aprons and black bow ties, Harvey Girls had to adhere to very strict behavior codes and were the prim and proper women of the late 19th- and early 20th-century American West. In fact, in the late 19th century, they were considered the only real "ladies" in the West, aside from school teachers. So celebrated were they in their day that in the 1940s, Judy Garland starred in a Technicolor MGM musical called *The Harvey Girls*. Garland played a Harvey Girl who battles the evil town dancehall queen (played by Angela Lansbury) for the soul of the local saloonkeeper.

the ruins, you can get close enough to get a good look. You're not allowed to wander off this trail, and please respect the privacy of those Navajo living here. It's a 2½-mile round-trip hike and takes about 2 hours. Be sure to carry water. If you aren't inclined to hike the trail, you can view the ruins from the overlook. This is one of the largest ruins in the canyon and contains 80 rooms. It was inhabited between 1040 and 1275. Notice the black streaks on the sandstone walls above the White House Ruins. These streaks were formed by seeping water that reacted with the iron in the sandstone. Iron is what gives the walls their reddish hue. Anasazi artists used to chip away at this black patina to create petroglyphs. Later the Navajo would use paints to create pictographs, painted images of animals, and records of historic events such as the Spanish military expedition that killed 115 Navajo at Massacre Cave. Many of these petroglyphs and pictographs can be seen if you take one of the guided tours into the canyon.

The fourth stop is at **Sliding House Overlook.** These ruins are built on a narrow shelf and appear to be sliding down into the canyon. Inhabited from about 900 until 1200, Sliding House contained between 30 and 50 rooms. This overlook is already more than 700 feet above the canyon floor, with sheer walls giving the narrow canyon a very foreboding appearance.

**Wild Cherry Overlook** and **Face Rock Overlook,** the next two stops, provide further glimpses of the ever-deepening canyon. Here you gaze 1,000 feet down to the bottom of the canyon. The last stop on the South Rim is one of the most spectacular: **Spider Rock Overlook.** This viewpoint overlooks the junction of Canyon de Chelly and Monument Canyon, and at this wide spot in the canyon stands the monolithic pinnacle called Spider Rock. Rising 800 feet from the canyon floor, the freestanding twin towers of Spider Rock are a natural monument, a geologic wonder. Across the canyon from Spider Rock stands the similarly striking **Speaking Rock,** which is connected to the far canyon wall.

## ALTERNATIVE WAYS OF SEEING THE CANYON

Access to the floor of Canyon de Chelly is restricted, and in order to enter the canyon *you must be accompanied by either a park ranger or an authorized guide* (unless you're on the White House Ruins trail). **Navajo guides** charge $10 to $15 per hour with a 3-hour minimum and will lead you into the canyon on foot or in your own four-wheel-drive vehicle. To hire a guide, check at the visitor center, which maintains a list of guides, or contact **de Chelly Tours** (☎ 520/674-3772 or 520/674-5433). The latter company charges $15 per hour to go out in your own 4x4 vehicle. If they supply the vehicle, it's $100 total for 3 people.

Another way to see Canyon de Chelly and Canyon del Muerto is from one of the **four- or six-wheel-drive trucks** that operate out of **Thunderbird Lodge** (☎ 800/ 679-2473 or 520/674-5841). These trucks are equipped with seats in the bed and stop frequently for photographs and to visit ruins, Navajo farms, and rock art. Tours cost $35.75 per person for a half-day, ($27.50 for children 11 and under); all-day tours are $57.50 for all ages. Half-day tours leave at 9am and 2pm in summer, at 9am and 1pm in winter; full-day trips leave at 9am and return at 5pm (summer only). Locals call these ✪ **shake-and-bake tours,** and in summer they really live up to the name.

If you'd rather use a more traditional means of transportation for your tour of the inner canyon, you can go on a guided horseback ride. Stables offering horseback tours into the canyon include **Justin Tso Horse Rental** (☎ 520/674-5678), which charges $10 per hour per person for a horse and $10 per hour per group for a guide (2-hour minimum).

## SHOPPING

The large **Thunderbird Lodge Gift Shop** (☎ 520/674-5841) in Chinle is well worth a stop while you're in the area. It has a huge collection of rugs, as well as good selections of pottery and plenty of souvenirs. In the canyon wherever visitors gather (at ruins and petroglyph sites), you're likely to encounter craftspeople selling jewelry and other types of handiwork. These craftspeople, most of whom live here in the canyon, accept cash, personal checks, and travelers' checks but not credit cards.

## WHERE TO STAY & DINE

In addition to the motels listed below, another lodging option in the Canyon de Chelly area is **Coyote Pass Hospitality,** P.O. Box 91-B, Tsaile, AZ 86558 (☎ 520/ 724-3383; www.navajocentral.org/cppage.htm), which operates a very rustic sort of bed-and-breakfast operation. Guests stay in a traditional dirt-floored hogan and receive a traditional breakfast in the morning. For an additional cost, you can arrange dinner for the night of your arrival. Rates are $85 for one person and $15 for each additional person. At the time of making the reservation, guests may also arrange for customized, off-the-beaten path Navajo cultural and historic tours with the hosts.

**Best Western Canyon de Chelly Inn.** 100 Main St. (P.O. Box 295), Chinle, AZ 86503. ☎ **800/327-0354** or 520/674-5875. Fax 520/674-3715. 99 units. A/C TV TEL. $56–$112 double. DISC, MC, V.

Located in the center of Chinle, this modern motel is the farthest from the park of the three hotels here in town and should be a last choice. The rooms are medium to large and have beamed ceilings and coffeemakers. The restaurant is large and reminiscent of a suburban chain restaurant, and the menu features moderately priced American and Navajo meals. There's also an indoor swimming pool.

**Holiday Inn—Canyon de Chelly.** Indian Rte. 7 (P.O. Box 1889), Chinle, AZ 86503. ☎ **800/HOLIDAY** or 520/674-5000. Fax 520/674-8264. 108 units. A/C TV TEL. May–Aug $99–$109 double; Sept–Apr $69–$109 double. AE, CB, DC, DISC, JCB, MC, V.

This is the newest hotel in Chinle and is located between the town and the entrance to Canyon de Chelly National Monument. The hotel is on the site of an old trading post, which is incorporated into the restaurant and gift shop building. The guest rooms all have patios or balconies and big windows and bathrooms, and most face the cottonwood-shaded pool courtyard. The hotel's restaurant serves moderately priced American and Navajo meals. Room service is available when the restaurant is open.

✪ **Thunderbird Lodge.** P.O. Box 548, Chinle, AZ 86503. ☎ **800/679-BIRD** or 520/ 674-5841. Fax 520/674-5844. www.tbirdchelly.com. 72 units. A/C TV TEL. $93–$98 double; $135 suite. Lower rates Nov–Mar. AE, CB, DC, DISC, MC, V.

Built on the site of an early trading post right at the mouth of Canyon de Chelly, the Thunderbird Lodge is the most appealing of the hotels in Chinle and is the closest to the national monument. The pink adobe construction is reminiscent of ancient pueblos, and the guest rooms have rustic furniture and Navajo sandpaintings on the walls. The rooms come in two sizes, with either two double beds or two queen-size beds, and ceiling fans and air conditioners keep the rooms cool in the hot summer months. The original trading-post building now serves as the lodge cafeteria, where American and Navajo meals are served. The lodge also has a tour desk, gift shop, and rug room.

## CAMPGROUNDS

Adjacent to the Thunderbird Lodge is the **Cottonwood Campground,** which doesn't take reservations but neither is there a fee. In the summer the campground has water and rest rooms, but in the winter you must bring your own water and only portable toilets are available. On South Rim Drive 10 miles east of the Canyon de Chelly Visitor Center, you'll also find the private **Spider Rock Campground** (☎ 520/ 674-8261), which charges about $10 per night for campsites. The next nearest campgrounds are at **Tsaile Lake** and **Wheatfields Lake,** both of which are south of the town of Tsaile on Indian Route 12. Tsaile is at the east end of the North Rim Drive.

## 6  Monument Valley & Navajo National Monument

Monument Valley Navajo Tribal Park: 200 miles NE of Flagstaff; 60 miles NE of Navajo National Monument; 110 miles NW of Canyon de Chelly; 150 miles E of Page

Navajo National Monument: 140 miles NE of Flagstaff; 90 miles E of Page; 60 miles SW of Monument Valley; 110 miles NW of Canyon de Chelly

Nature, in her role as sculptor, has created a garden of monoliths and spires in the north-central part of the Navajo Reservation. You may not be aware of it, but you have almost certainly seen ✪ **Monument Valley** before. This otherworldly landscape has been an object of fascination for years and has served as backdrop for countless movies, including John Ford's *Stagecoach* (1938) and *Thelma and Louise* (1992), with Susan Sarandon and Geena Davis, as well as for television shows and commercials.

Located 30 miles north of Kayenta just across the Utah state line, Monument Valley is a vast flat plain punctuated by natural cathedrals of sandstone. These huge monoliths rise up from the sagebrush with sheer walls that capture the light of the rising and setting sun and transform it into fiery hues. Evocative names reflect the shapes the sandstone has taken as the forces of nature have eroded it: The Mittens, Three Sisters, Camel Butte, Elephant Butte, the Thumb, and Totem Pole are some of the most awe-inspiring natural monuments. A 17-mile unpaved loop road winds among these 1,000-foot-tall buttes and mesas.

Human habitation has also left its mark. Within the park there are more than 100 ancient Anasazi archaeological sites, ruins, and petroglyphs dating from before A.D. 1300. The Navajo have been living in the valley for generations, herding their sheep through the sagebrush scrublands, and some families continue to live here today.

**Navajo National Monument,** though set in a less spectacular landscape, is no less interesting. It is here that you will find some of the largest cliff dwellings in Arizona. Located 30 miles west of Kayenta and 60 miles northeast of Tuba City, Navajo National Monument encompasses three of the best-preserved Anasazi cliff dwellings in the region: Betatakin, Keet Seel, and Inscription House. It's possible to visit both Betatakin and Keet Seel, but fragile Inscription House is closed to the public. The name Navajo National Monument is a bit misleading. Although the Navajo people do inhabit the area now, it was the ancient Anasazi who built the cliff dwellings. The Navajo arrived centuries after the Anasazi had abandoned the area.

The inhabitants of Tsegi Canyon were ancestral Hopi and Pueblo peoples known as the Kayenta Anasazi. The Anasazi began abandoning their well-constructed homes around the middle of the 13th century, for reasons unknown. Tree rings suggest that a drought in the latter part of the 13th century prevented the Anasazi from growing sufficient crops. However, in Tsegi Canyon there's another theory for the abandonment. The canyon floors were usually flooded each year by spring and summer snowmelt, which made farming quite productive, but in the mid-1200s weather patterns changed and streams running through the canyons began cutting deep into the soil, forming deep, narrow canyons called arroyos, which lowered the water table and made farming much more difficult.

## ESSENTIALS

**GETTING THERE**    From Flagstaff, Navajo National Monument can be reached by taking U.S. 89 north to U.S. 160; Monument Valley Navajo Tribal Park is a bit farther on U.S. 160 and then north on U.S. 163.

The **Navajo Transit System** operates bus service Monday through Friday throughout the Navajo nation with service between the cities of Farmington, Gallup, and Crown Point (all in New Mexico) and Window Rock, Kayenta, Chinle, and Tuba City. Call ☎ **520/729-4002** for schedule information.

**MONEY**    ATMs are few and far between in this area, but there is one at the grocery store below Gouldings Lodge and one at the Basha's in Kayenta.

**VISITOR INFORMATION**    For more information on Monument Valley, contact **Monument Valley Navajo Tribal Park,** P.O. Box 360289, Monument Valley, UT 84536 (☎ **435/727-3287**). The park is open April to September, daily from 7am to 6pm; October to March, daily from 8am to 5pm. Admission is $2.50 for adults, $1 for seniors, and free for children 7 and under. Please note, the National Park Services Golden Eagle Passport isn't valid here because Monument Valley is a private park.

For more information on the national monument, contact **Navajo National Monument,** HC 71, Box 3, Tonalea, AZ 86044-9704 (☎ **520/672-2366**). The park is open daily. There's no lodge at the national monument, but there is a campground. Park admission is free.

## MONUMENT VALLEY NAVAJO TRIBAL PARK

This is big country, and, like the Grand Canyon, is primarily a point-and-shoot experience. Because this is reservation land and people still live in Monument Valley, backcountry or off-road travel is prohibited unless you have a licensed guide. So basically the only way to see the park is from the overlook at the visitor center; by driving the park's scenic (but very rough) dirt road; or by taking a four-wheel-drive, horseback, or guided-hiking tour.

At the valley overlook parking area in Monument Valley Navajo Tribal Park, you'll find a small museum, gift shop, restaurant, snack bar, campground, and numerous local Navajo guides who offer tours of the park.

If you want to do a four-wheel-drive tour, try **Roland's Navajoland Tours** (☎ **800/368-2785** or 520/697-3524). Owner Roland Cody Dixon offers three different four-wheel-drive tours of Monument Valley. **Sacred Monument Tours** (☎ **435/727-3218**) also offers Jeep tours, as well as hiking and horseback tours. Expect to pay $12 to $70 for most jeep tours (depending on the length of the tour and whether a meal is served).

If you want to see the park on foot, you can arrange a hiking tour through **Fred's Adventure Tours** (☎ **435/739-4294**), **Black's Hiking/Van Tours** (☎ **435/739-4226**), or **Totem Pole Guided Tours** (☎ **800/345-TOUR** or 435/727-3313). A day-long guided hike will run you about $45 to $75, and can be physically demanding.

If nothing but the cowboy thing will do for you in this quintessential Wild West landscape, you've got some options. **Ed Black's Monument Valley Trail Rides** (☎ **435/739-4285**) is located near the visitor center and charges $30 for a 1½-hour ride and $100 for an all-day ride.

Another option is to book with **Goulding's Tours,** P.O. Box 360001, Monument Valley, UT 84536 (☎ **435/727-3231**). This company has its office on the edge of the valley at Goulding's Lodge (see below), just a few miles from the park entrance. Half-day tours are $30 for 8 years and older; full-day tours are $60 for adults and $45 for children 8 and older, free for 7 and under.

Before leaving the area, you might also want to visit **Goulding's Museum and Trading Post** at Goulding's Lodge. This old trading post was the home of the Gouldings for many years and is set up as they had it back in the 1920s and 1930s. There are also displays about the many movies that have been shot here. The trading post is usually open in the summer daily from 7:30am to 9pm, with shorter hours in other months; admission is by donation. Also in the area is the **Oljato Trading Post & Museum** (☎ **435/727-3210**), which is located 11 miles west of Monument Valley on the very scenic stretch of road that leads past Gouldings. Although this trading post, which dates back to 1921, is in Utah, it was originally located in Arizona. The old building still has a classic trading post feel and few tourists ever venture out this way. There's also a small museum here.

## NAVAJO NATIONAL MONUMENT

Unlike Monument Valley, a visit to Navajo National Monument requires physical effort. The shortest distance you'll have to walk here is 1 mile, which is the round-trip distance from the visitor center to the Betatakin overlook. However, if you want to actually climb around inside these ruins, you're looking at strenuous day-long or overnight hikes.

Your first stop should be the **visitor center,** which has informative displays on the ancestral Pueblo and Navajo cultures, including numerous artifacts from Tsegi Canyon. You can also watch a couple of short films or a slide show. The center is open daily from 8am to 5pm (daylight savings time), and closed on New Year, Christmas, and Thanksgiving.

✪ *Betatakin,* which means "ledge house" in Navajo, is the only one of the three ruins that can be seen easily. Built in a huge amphitheater-like alcove in the canyon wall, Betatakin was occupied only from 1250 to 1300, and at its height of occupation may have housed 125 people.

A 1-mile round-trip paved trail from the visitor center leads to overlooks of Betatakin. The strenuous 5-mile round-trip hike to Betatakin itself is led by a ranger, takes about 6 hours, and involves descending more than 700 feet to the floor of Tsegi Canyon and later returning to the rim. This hike is conducted from early May through October and leaves from the visitor center. All hikers should carry 2 quarts of water. This very popular hike is limited to 25 people per tour; many people line up at the visitor center an hour or more before the center opens.

✪ *Keet Seel,* which means "broken pieces of pottery" in Navajo, has a much longer history than Betatakin, with occupation beginning as early as A.D. 950 and continuing until 1300. At one point Keet Seel may have housed 150 people.

The 17-mile round-trip hike or horseback ride to Keet Seel is quite strenuous. Hikers may stay overnight at a primitive campground near the ruins. You must carry enough water for your trip, since none is available along the trail. Only 20 people a day are given permits to visit Keet Seel, and the trail is open only from Memorial Day to Labor Day.

## WHERE TO STAY & DINE

In addition to the lodgings listed here, you'll find numerous budget motels 22 miles north of Monument Valley in Mexican Hat, Utah.

**Anasazi Inn at Tsegi Canyon.** U.S. 160 (P.O. Box 1543), Kayenta, AZ 86033. ☎ **520/ 697-3793.** Fax 520/697-8249. 57 units. A/C TV. May–Oct $50–$$95 double; Nov–Apr $35–$50 double. AE, CB, DC, DISC, MC, V. Pets accepted.

Located about halfway between Kayenta and Navajo National Monument, the Anasazi Inn at Tsegi Canyon is a very basic motel made up mostly of old mobile homes that have been converted into tiny motel rooms. However, it's the closest lodging to Navajo National Monument. If your standards aren't too high, this motel should be fine for you. Think of it as a last resort or option to camping. There's a small dining room attached to the motel.

**Best Western Wetherill Inn Motel.** P.O. Box 175, Kayenta, AZ 86033. ☎ **800/ 528-1234** or 520/697-3231. Fax 520/697-3233. 54 units. A/C TV TEL. May 1–Oct 15 $98 double; Oct 16–Nov 15 and Mar 1–Apr 30 $70 double; Jan 1–Feb 28 and Nov 16–Dec 31 $55 double. AE, DC, DISC, MC, V.

Located in Kayenta 1 mile north of the junction of U.S. 160 and U.S. 163 and 20 miles south of Monument Valley, the Wetherill Inn Motel offers neither the convenience of Goulding's Lodge nor the amenities of the nearby Holiday Inn. However, the rooms here are comfortable enough and do have coffeemakers. There's a cafe next door that serves Navajo and American food.

**Country of Many Hogan Bed & Breakfast.** ℅ P.O. Box 2984, Tuba City, AZ 86045 ☎ **520/283-4125.** $125 single or double. Rates include Navajo breakfast. DISC, MC, V.

Anyone accustomed to camping may want to consider spending the night in this traditional Navajo hogan. You'll sleep on sheepskins spread on the floor and awake in the morning to a traditional Navajo breakfast that includes tea made from local plants. The hogan is located 10 miles southwest of Monument Valley Navajo Tribal Park on Navajo Rte. 6450. If you make arrangements in advance, you can also experience a traditional sweat lodge. Guided horse and hiking tours are offered, and campsites are available for $15 per night. Dinners can be arranged here with prior notice.

✪ **Goulding's Lodge.** P.O. Box 360001, Monument Valley, UT 84536-0001. ☎ **435/ 727-3231.** Fax 435/727-3344. www.gouldings.com. 62 units. A/C TV TEL. Mar 15–Oct 15 $101–$140 double; Oct 16–Mar 14 $68–$79 double. AE, CB, DC, DISC, MC, V.

This is the only lodge actually located in Monument Valley, and it offers superb views from the private balconies of the guest rooms, which are furnished with Southwestern decor. And while the setting is memorable, the service can be somewhat lacking. A restaurant serves Navajo and American dishes, and the views from the restaurant are enough to make any meal an event. The hotel also has a seasonal indoor pool, tour desk, museum, gift shop, coin laundry, and gas station.

**Holiday Inn—Kayenta.** At the junction of U.S. 160 and U.S. 163 (P.O. Box 307), Kayenta, AZ 86033. ☎ **800/HOLIDAY** or 520/697-3221. Fax 520/697-3349. 160 units. A/C TV TEL. Apr–Oct $99–$129 double; Nov–Mar $69–$79 double. AE, DC, DISC, MC, V.

Located in the center of Kayenta, 23 miles south of Monument Valley and 29 miles east of Navajo National Monument, this Holiday Inn is very popular with tour groups and is almost always crowded. Though the grounds are dusty and a bit run-down, the rooms are spacious and clean and most have new carpets. We like the poolside rooms best. Part of the motel's restaurant is designed to look like an Anasazi ruin. The menu offers both American and Navajo meals, and room service is available. The hotel also has an outdoor pool and a tour desk in the gift shop.

## CAMPGROUNDS

If you're headed to Monument Valley Navajo Tribal Park, you can camp in the park at the **Mitten View Campground** (☎ 435/727-3353), which charges about $10 per night per site April to September and $5 October to March, or just outside the park at **Goulding's Campground** (☎ 435/727-3231), which charges about $14 to $22 per night, is open March 15 to October 15, and even has an indoor swimming pool.

There's also a free campground at **Navajo National Monument** (☎ 520/672-2366), west of Kayenta via U.S. 160 and Ariz. 564. There are only 31 campsites here, plus an overflow area containing about a dozen more (summer only). In summer the spaces are usually full by dark.

## DRIVING ON TO COLORADO OR NEW MEXICO: THE FOUR CORNERS MEET

Other attractions you might want to visit while you're in this part of the state include the **Four Corners Monument Navajo Tribal Park** (☎ 520/871-6647), north of Teec Nos Pos in the very northeast corner of the state. This is the only place in the United States where the corners of four states come together, and you can stand in four states at the same time. Those states are Arizona, Colorado, Utah, and New Mexico, and the point where they come together is marked by a cement pad surrounded by flags. In the park you'll find a picnic ground and crafts vendors. The park is open daily from 7am to 8pm between May and late August and from 8am to 5pm between late August and April. Admission is $2.50 for adults, $1 seniors, free for children 7 and under.

Also in the area, in the community of Teec Nos Pos, you'll find the **Teec Nos Pos Trading Post** (☎ 520/656-3224) and **Foutz Teec Nos Pos Arts and Crafts** (☎ 520/656-3228), both of which have good selections of rugs and other crafts.

## DRIVING ON TO FLAGSTAFF OR THE GRAND CANYON

On the west side of the reservation, in Tuba City, you'll find the **Tuba Trading Post** (☎ **520/283-5441**) on the corner of Main Street and Moenave Street. This octagonal trading post was built in 1906 of local stone and is designed to resemble a Navajo hogan. The trading post serves both as a small market and as a store selling Native American crafts, with an emphasis on Pendleton blankets, books, music, and jewelry. On the western outskirts of Tuba City, on U.S. 160, you'll find **Van's Trading Co.** (☎ **520/283-5343**), in the corner of a large grocery store, which has a dead-pawn auction on the 15th of each month at 3pm. This auction provides opportunities to buy older pieces of Navajo silver-and-turquoise jewelry.

West of Tuba City and just off U.S. 160, you can see **dinosaur footprints** preserved in the stone surface of the desert. There are usually a few people waiting at the site to guide visitors to the best footprints. These guides will expect a tip.

The **Cameron Trading Post** (☎ **520/679-2231**), 16 miles south of the junction of U.S. 160 and U.S. 89, is also well worth a visit. The main trading post is filled with souvenirs, but it has large selections of rugs and jewelry as well. In the adjacent stone-walled gallery, you'll find museum-quality Native American artifacts (with prices to match). The trading post also includes a motel (see chapter 7 for details).

Between Cameron and Flagstaff, keep an eye out for **Sacred Mountain Trading Post** (☎ **520/679-2255**), which though small, has the look and feel of a trading post of 50 years ago. The shelves are full of Navajo pottery.

## 7  Lake Powell & Page

272 miles N of Phoenix; 130 miles E of the Grand Canyon North Rim; 130 miles NE of Grand Canyon South Rim

Imagine the Grand Canyon filled with water instead of air, and you have a pretty good picture of Lake Powell. Had the early Spanish explorers of Arizona suddenly come upon this lake after traipsing for months across desolate desert, they would have either taken it for a mirage or fallen to their knees and rejoiced. Surrounded by hundreds of miles of parched desert land, this reservoir, created by the damming of the Colorado River at Glen Canyon, seems unreal when first glimpsed. Yet real it is, and, like a magnet, it draws everyone in the region toward its promise of relief from the heat.

Though construction began on the Glen Canyon Dam in 1960 and was completed in 1963, it took another 17 years for Lake Powell to reach capacity. Today the lake is a huge water playground frequented by boaters, water skiers, and anglers. One of the natural wonders of the world can be found on the shores of Lake Powell—**Rainbow Bridge,** called *nonnozhoshi,* or "the rainbow turned to stone," by the Navajo is the largest natural bridge on earth and stretches 275 feet across a side canyon of Lake Powell.

Construction of the Glen Canyon Dam came about despite the angry outcry of many who felt that this canyon was even more beautiful than the Grand Canyon and should be preserved in its natural state. Preservationists lost this battle, and today houseboats and skiers cruise where birds and waterfalls once filled the canyons with their songs. These days, however, most people seem to agree that Lake Powell is as amazing a sight as the Grand Canyon, and the lake draws almost as many visitors each year as its down-river neighbor.

The town of Page, a work camp constructed to house the workers who built the dam, has now become much more than just a construction camp and, with its many motels and restaurants, is the best place from which to explore Lake Powell.

# ESSENTIALS

**GETTING THERE**    Page is connected to Flagstaff by U.S. 89. Ariz. 98 leads south-east onto the Navajo Indian Reservation and connects with U.S. 160 to Kayenta and Four Corners.

   **Sunrise Airlines** (☎ **800/347-3962**) flies from Phoenix to the Page Airport, 1 mile east of town on Ariz. 98.

**VISITOR INFORMATION**    For further information on Page and Lake Powell, contact the **Page/Lake Powell Chamber of Commerce,** 644C N. Navajo Dr., Suite C (P.O. Box 727), Page, AZ 86040-0727 (☎ **888/261-7243** or 520/645-2741); or the **John Wesley Powell Museum and Visitor Center,** 6 N. Lake Powell Blvd. (P.O. Box 547), Page, AZ 86040 (☎ **520/645-9496;** www.powellmuseum.org).

**GETTING AROUND**    Rental cars are available at the Page Airport from **Avis** (☎ **800/331-1212** or 520/645-2024). Call **Lake Powell Taxi** (☎ **520/645-8540**) if you need a cab.

## GLEN CANYON NATIONAL RECREATION AREA

Until the flooding of Glen Canyon formed Lake Powell, this area was one of the most remote regions in the contiguous 48 states. However, with the construction of Glen Canyon Dam across a stretch of the Colorado River less than ⅓ mile wide, this remote and rugged landscape became one of the country's most popular national recreation areas. Today the lake and much of the surrounding land is designated the Glen Canyon National Recreation Area and attracts nearly four million visitors each year. The otherworldly setting amid the slick-rock canyons of northern Arizona and southern Utah is a tapestry of colors, the blues and greens of the lake contrasting with the reds and oranges of the surrounding sandstone cliffs. This interplay of colors and vast, desert landscapes easily makes Lake Powell the most beautiful of Arizona's many reservoirs.

   Built to provide water for the desert communities of the Southwest and West, **Glen Canyon Dam** stands 710 feet above the bedrock and contains almost 5 million cubic yards of concrete. The dam also provides hydroelectric power, and deep within its massive wall of concrete are huge power turbines. Most visitors to the area are, however, more interested in water-skiing and powerboating than they are in drinking water and power production. Without the dam, however, there would be no lake, so any visit to this area ought to start with a tour of the dam and a stop at the **Carl Hayden Visitor Center** (☎ **520/608-6404**), which is located beside the dam (on U.S. 89 just north of Page) and is open daily from 8am to 5pm (to 7pm from May to October). Here you can learn about the construction of the dam and then descend into the dam itself for a free guided tour that takes about an hour. Keep in mind that these tours must start at least 1 hour before the visitor center closes. A visit to the dam helps add a bit of perspective to an appreciation of Lake Powell's many recreational pursuits.

   More than 500 feet deep in some places, and bound by nearly 2,000 miles of shoreline, Lake Powell is a maze of convoluted canyons where rock walls often rise hundreds of feet straight out of the water. In places, long, winding canyons are so narrow that there isn't even room to turn a motorboat around. It is this otherworldly meeting of rock and water that has made this lake one of the most popular destinations in the Southwest.

   For more information before leaving home, you can contact the **Glen Canyon National Recreation Area,** P.O. Box 1507, Page, AZ 86040 (☎ **520/608-6200**). Admission to the national recreation area is $5 per car (pass good for 1 week), and there is also a $10-per-week boat fee if you bring your own boat. In addition to the Carl Hayden Visitor Center mentioned above, there is the **Bullfrog Visitor Center,** in Bullfrog, Utah (☎ 801/684-7400). This visitor center is open daily from 8am to 4pm and is usually closed in the colder months.

## BOAT & AIR TOURS

There are few roads penetrating the Glen Canyon Recreation Area, so the best way to appreciate this rugged region is by boat. If you don't have your own boat, you can at least see a small part of the lake on a boat tour. There are a variety of boat tours that depart from **Wahweap Marina** (☎ 800/528-6154 or 520/645-2433). Three times daily, the paddle wheeler *Canyon King* embarks on a 1-hour tour ($10 for adults, $7 for children) that, unfortunately, doesn't really show you much more of the lake than you can see from shore. The *Canyon King* also does sunset dinner cruises ($56). A better choice for anyone with limited time or finances would be the Navajo Tapestry Cruise ($35 for adults, $27 for children) or the Antelope Canyon Cruise ($22 for adults, $18 for children). However, to see the most of the lake, opt for the full-day tour to Rainbow Bridge (see below for details).

The Glen Canyon National Recreation Area covers an immense area, much of it inaccessible by car and only partially accessible by boat. If you'd like to see more of the area than is visible from car or boat, consider taking an air tour with **Sunset Airlines** (☎ 800/245-8668), which offers several air tours of northern Arizona and southern Utah, including flights over Rainbow Bridge, the Escalante River, the Grand Canyon, Canyonlands, Bryce Canyon, Monument Valley, and the Navajo nation. Sample rates are $71 for a 30-minute flight over Rainbow Bridge and $150 for a 90-minute flight over Monument Valley.

## RAINBOW BRIDGE NATIONAL MONUMENT

Roughly 50 miles up Lake Powell from Wahweap Marina and Glen Canyon Dam, in a narrow side canyon of the lake, rises **Rainbow Bridge,** the world's largest natural bridge and one of the most spectacular sights in the Southwest. Preserved in Rainbow Bridge National Monument, this natural arch of sandstone stands 290 feet high and spans 275 feet. Carved by wind and water over the ages, Rainbow Bridge is an awesome reminder of the powers of erosion that have sculpted this entire region into the spectacle it is today.

Rainbow Bridge is accessible only by boat or on foot (13-mile hike minimum), and traveling there by boat is by far the more popular route. **Lake Powell Resorts and Marinas** (☎ 800/528-6154 or 520/645-2433) offers daily half-day ($69 for adults, $49 for children) and full-day ($92 for adults, $62 for children) boat tours to Rainbow Bridge. The latter tours include box lunches and exploring one or more other major canyons along the way.

Rainbow Bridge National Monument is administered by Glen Canyon National Recreation Area, and information is available from sources mentioned above for the recreation area. For information on hiking to Rainbow Bridge, contact the **Navajo Parks and Recreation Department,** P.O. Box 9000, Window Rock, AZ 86515 (☎ 520/871-6647).

## ANTELOPE CANYON

If you've spent any time in Arizona, chances are you've seen photos of a narrow canyon only a few feet wide. The sandstone walls of the canyon seem to glow with an inner light in these photos, and beams of sunlight slice down through the darkness of this deep slot canyon. Sound familiar? If you have seen such a photo, chances are you were looking at ✪ **Antelope Canyon** (also known as Corkscrew Canyon). Located 2½ miles outside of Page off Ariz. 98 (at milepost 299), this famous photogenic canyon lies on the Navajo Indian Reservation at the end of a rough dirt and sand road. There are currently two options for visiting Antelope Canyon. The most convenient and reliable way is to take a 1½-hour tour with **Lake Powell Jeep Tours** (☎ 520/645-5501), **Photographic Tours** (☎ 520/645-8579 or 520/645-9102), or **Grand Circle Adventures Scenic Tours** (☎ 520/645-5594), all of which charge $26.50 per person (lower rates for children). Alternatively, you can drive out to the trailhead and hire a Navajo guide through **Antelope Canyon Tours** (☎ 520/698-3384), which usually has guides at the trailhead whenever the weather is safe for hiking into the canyon; or call them ahead of time. The guide will then drive you to the canyon from the parking area. This latter option will cost you $5 for a visitor's permit and $12.50 for the guide to drive you from the highway to the canyon and then pick you up again after your hike. Just remember that if there is even the slightest chance of rain anywhere in the region, you should not venture into this canyon, which is subject to flash floods. In the past, people who have ignored bad weather have been killed by flash floods in this canyon. For more information, contact the **Navajo Parks and Recreation Department,** P.O. Box 9000, Window Rock, AZ 86515 (☎ 520/871-6647).

## WATER SPORTS

While simply exploring the lake's maze of canyons on a narrated tour is satisfying enough for many visitors, houseboating, waterskiing, riding personal watercraft, and fishing are still the most popular activities, and five marinas (only Wahweap is in Arizona) help boaters explore the lake. You can bring your own boat or rent one here. At the **Wahweap Marina** (☎ 800/528-6154 or 520/645-2433) you can rent various types of boats, personal watercraft, and water skis and head out on your own to have some fun on the water. Rental rates in the summer high season range from about $140 to $360 per day. In the low season, rates range from about $80 to $215 per day. Weekly rates are also available. Small boats and personal watercraft can be rented from **Lake Powell Water World,** 920 Hemlock St. (☎ 520/645-8845), and from **Doo Powell,** 130 Sixth Ave. (☎ 800/350-1230 or 520/645-1230). For information on renting houseboats, see "Houseboats," below.

If roaring engines aren't your speed, you might want to consider exploring Lake Powell in a sea kayak. While afternoon winds can sometimes make paddling difficult, mornings are often quiet. With a narrow sea kayak, you can even explore canyons too small for powerboats. You can rent sea kayaks from **Red Rock Cyclery & Sea Kayaks,** 819 N. Navajo Dr. (☎ 520/645-1479). A one-person kayak rents for $40 per day, and a two-person kayak rents for $50 a day. Kayak rentals are also available from **Twin Finn Diving Center,** 811 Vista Ave. (☎ 520/645-3114). Sea kayaks rent for $45 per day, and sit-on-top kayaks rent for $35 per day.

While most of Glen Canyon National Recreation Area consists of the impounded waters of Lake Powell, within the recreation area there is also a short stretch of the Colorado River that still flows swift and free. If you'd like to see this stretch of river, try a float trip from Glen Canyon Dam to Lees Ferry. These raft trips are operated by **Wilderness River Adventures** (☎ 800/992-8022) between March and October and cost $51 for adults and $44 for children 12 and under for a half-day trip. All-day trips are also available ($71 adults, $64 children). Make reservations at least 2 weeks in advance.

If you have a boat (either your own or a rental), avail yourself of some excellent year-round **fishing.** Smallmouth, largemouth, and striped bass, as well as walleye, catfish, and crappie, are all plentiful. Because the lake lies within both Arizona and Utah, you'll need to know which state's waters you're fishing in whenever you cast your line out, and you'll need the appropriate license. (Also, be sure to pick up a copy of the Arizona and Utah state fishing regulations or ask about applicable regulations at any of the marinas on the lake.) You can arrange licenses to fish the entire lake at **Wahweap Lodge and Marina** (☎ 520/645-2433), which also sells bait and tackle and can provide you with a bit of advice on fishing this massive reservoir. Other marinas on the lake also sell licenses, bait, and tackle. The best season is March through November, though walleye are most often caught during the cooler months. Throughout the year there are numerous fishing tournaments.

If you'd rather try your hand at catching enormous rainbow trout, try downstream of the Glen Canyon Dam, where cold waters provide ideal conditions for trout to grow big. Unfortunately, there isn't much access to this stretch of river. You'll need a trout stamp to fish for these trophy trout.

If you're just looking for a good place to go for a swim near Wahweap Lodge, take the Coves Loop just west of the marina. Of the three coves, the third one is the best, with a sandy beach. The Chains area, another good place to jump off the rocks and otherwise lounge by the lake, is just outside Page down a rough dirt road just before you reach Glen Canyon Dam. The view underwater at Lake Powell is as scenic as the view above it, and if you're interested in exploring the underwater regions of the canyon, contact **Twin Finn Diving Center,** 811 Vista Ave. (☎ 520/645-3114), which charges $45 a day for scuba gear and also rents snorkling equipment.

## MORE OUTDOOR FUN

While most activity within the national recreation area centers around water, the short hike to the **Horseshoe Bend** viewpoint is very worthwhile (be sure to bring your camera). Horseshoe Bend is a huge loop of the Colorado River, and the viewpoint is hundreds of feet above the water on the edge of a sheer cliff. Far below, you can often see people camped at a riverside campsite that is accessible only by boat. It's about ½ mile to the viewpoint from the trailhead, which is located 5 miles south of the Carl Hayden Visitor Center on U.S. 89 just south of milepost 545.

At Lees Ferry, 39 miles from Page at the southern tip of the national recreation area, you'll find three short trails (Cathedral Wash, River Trail, and Spencer Trail), as well as the southern trailhead for the famed **Paria Canyon,** a favorite of canyoneering backpackers. This latter trail is 37 miles long and follows the meandering route of a narrow slot canyon for much of its length. Most hikers start from the northern trailhead, which is in Utah on U.S. 89. At the Carl Hayden Visitor Center, you can also pick up brochures that describe several area day hikes.

The 27-hole **Lake Powell National Golf Course,** 400 Clubhouse Dr. (☎ 520/645-2023), is one of the most spectacular golf courses in the state. The fairways wrap around the base of the red sandstone bluff atop which sits the town of Page. In places, walls of eroded sandstone come right down to the greens, and alongside one fairway, water is pumped up the rock to create a waterfall. The views stretch to forever. Greens fees are $60 in the warmer months, and tee times can be booked up to 1 week in advance.

## OTHER AREA ATTRACTIONS

**John Wesley Powell Memorial Museum & Visitor Information Center.** 6 N. Lake Powell Blvd. ☎ 520/645-9496. Free admission; requested donation $1. May–Oct daily 8am–6pm; Nov–Dec 15 and Feb 17–Apr Mon–Fri 9am–5pm. Closed Dec 16–Feb 16.

In 1869, John Wesley Powell, a one-armed Civil War veteran, and a small band of men spent more than three months fighting the rapids of the Green and Colorado rivers to become the first people to travel the length of the Grand Canyon. It is for this intrepid—some said crazy—adventurer that Lake Powell is named and to whom this small museum is dedicated. Besides documenting the Powell expedition with photographs, etchings, and artifacts, the museum displays Indian artifacts from

Anasazi pottery to contemporary Navajo and Hopi crafts. The exhibit of fluorescent minerals is particularly interesting, and there are several informative videos that are regularly screened in the museum's small auditorium. The museum also acts as an information center for Page, Lake Powell, and the region, and has a small gift shop.

# WHERE TO STAY
## HOUSEBOATS

✪ **Lake Powell Resorts and Marinas.** P.O. Box 56909, Phoenix, AZ 85079. ☎ **800/528-6154**, or 602/278-8888 in Phoenix. Fax 602/331-5258. www.visitlakepowell.com. May to mid-Oct $1,681–$4,657 per week; mid-Oct to Apr $1009–$2,794 per week (3-, 4-, 5-, and 6-night rates also available). AE, DISC, MC, V.

Although there are plenty of hotels and motels in and near Page, the most popular accommodations here are not waterfront hotel rooms but houseboats, which function as floating vacation homes. With a houseboat, which is as easy to operate as a car, you can explore Lake Powell's beautiful red-rock country, far from any roads. No special license or prior experience is necessary, and plenty of hands-on instruction is offered before you leave the marina. Because Lake Powell houseboating is extremely popular with people from all over the world, it's important to make reservations as far in advance as possible, especially if you plan to visit in the summer.

Houseboats range in size from 36 to 59 feet, sleep anywhere from 6 to 12 people, and come complete with hot showers, refrigerator/freezer, heating system (more expensive houseboats also have heat pumps or evaporative coolers), stove, oven, and gas grill. Kitchens come equipped with everything you'll need to prepare meals. The only things you'll really need to bring are bedding and towels.

## HOTELS/MOTELS
### Expensive

✪ **Courtyard by Marriott.** 600 Clubhouse Dr. (P.O. Box 4150), Page, AZ 86040. ☎ **800/851-3855**, 800/321-2211, or 520/645-5000. Fax 520/645-5004. 153 units. A/C TV TEL. Mar–Oct $97–$109 double; Nov–Apr $54–$79 double. AE, CB, DC, DISC, MC, V.

Located at the foot of the mesa on which Page is built and adjacent to the Lake Powell National Golf Course, this hotel is the closest you'll come to a golf resort in this corner of the state and is the top in-town choice. The rooms are larger than those at most motels, and there are king-size beds, separate seating areas, dressing areas, and mirrored closet doors. You'll pay a premium for views of the golf course or lake.

**Dining/Diversions:** Moderately priced meals are served in a casual restaurant that has a terrace overlooking the distant lake. There's also an adjacent lounge.

**Amenities:** The adjacent 18-hole golf course has great views of the surrounding landscape. There's also an outdoor pool, a whirlpool, and an exercise room, room service, and valet/laundry service.

**Wahweap Lodge.** 100 Lakeshore Dr. (Mailing address: P.O. Box 56909, Phoenix, AZ 85079). ☎ **800/528-6154**, 520/645-2433, or 602/278-8888 in Phoenix. Fax 602/331-5258. 350 units. A/C TV TEL. Apr–Oct $153–$164 double, $251 suite; Nov–Mar $107–$115 double, $176 suite. AE, DC, DISC, MC, V. Pets accepted.

The Wahweap Marina is a sprawling complex 4 miles north of Glen Canyon Dam on the shores of Lake Powell. As the biggest and busiest hotel in the area, Wahweap features many of the amenities and activities of a resort. The guest rooms are arranged in several long two-story wings, and all the rooms have either a balcony or a patio. However, only half the rooms have lake views. The west wing has the better view (the east wing overlooks the Navajo coal-fired power plant). This place stays packed with tour groups from around the world and getting a reservation can be difficult.

**Dining/Diversions:** The Rainbow Room (see "Where to Dine," below) offers fine dining with a sweeping panorama of the lake and desert. The menu is equally divided between American standards and Southwestern fare. A snack bar near the boat ramp provides light meals, snacks, ice cream, and cookies, and a lounge serves cocktails with a view.

**Amenities:** Two outdoor pools, whirlpool, boat ramp, boat rentals, boat tours, float trips, room service.

## Moderate

**Best Western Arizonainn.** 716 Rimview Dr. (P.O. Box 250), Page, AZ 86040. ☎ **800/ 826-2718** or 520/645-2466. Fax 520/645-2053. 103 units. A/C TV TEL. Apr–Oct $80–$140 double; Nov–Mar $52–$77 double. AE, DC, DISC, MC, V. Pets accepted ($10 charge).

Perched right at the edge of the mesa on which Page is built, this modern motel has a fine view across miles of desert. Half the rooms have views, and of course, these are more expensive. The hotel offers free coffee in the lobby, an airport shuttle, an outdoor pool with a 100-mile view, a whirlpool, and an exercise room.

**Best Western at Lake Powell.** 208 N. Lake Powell Blvd., Page, AZ 86040. ☎ **888/ 794-2888** or 520/645-5988. Fax 520/645-2578. 132 units. A/C TV TEL. Apr to mid-Oct $59–$109 double; mid-Oct to Mar $49–$69 double. AE, DC, DISC, MC, V.

This hotel lies on the edge of town overlooking Lake Powell and is right next door to the Arizonainn. The rooms are comfortable and modern, and you'll find a pool with a great view, a hot tub, and an exercise room. There's no restaurant on the premises, but breakfast is available. The hotel also offers a free airport shuttle.

**Lake Powell Motel.** U.S. 89 near Wahweap Marina (mailing address: P.O. Box 56909, Phoenix, AZ 85079). ☎ **800/528-6154,** 520/645-2477, or 602/278-8888 in Phoenix. Fax 602/331-5258. 25 units. A/C TV TEL. $85 double. AE, DC, DISC, MC, V. Closed Nov–Mar. Pets accepted. Drive 3 miles west of the Wahweap Marina or 4 miles north of the Glen Canyon Dam on U.S. 89.

Located on a barren hill set back from the lake, the Lake Powell Motel offers an alternative away from the traffic and lights of downtown Page and the bustle of activity at the Wahweap Marina. The accommodations are standard motel rooms with two queen-size beds.

## CAMPGROUNDS & RV PARKS

There are campgrounds and RV facilities at Wahweap and Lees Ferry in Arizona and at Bullfrog, Hite, and Halls Crossing in Utah. At Wahweap, there are separate campgrounds for tenters and for RVers. Some scrubby trees provide a bit of shade at the tenting campground, but the winds and sun make this a rather bleak spot in summer. However, because of the lake's popularity, these campgrounds stay packed for much of the year. Reservations are not taken.

## WHERE TO DINE

**Butterfield Stage Co.** 704 Rimview Dr. ☎ **520/645-2467.** Main courses $15–$19. AE, MC, V. Daily 3:30–9 or 10pm. STEAKS/AMERICAN.

Located adjacent to the Best Western Arizonainn, this steak house is the only in-town restaurant with a view. Although the view is somewhat marred by the number of power lines that stretch out from the dam, it's still the best in town. Sunrises and sunsets are gorgeous. Steaks and seafood are the menu mainstays.

✪ **The Dam Bar & Grille.** 644 N. Navajo Dr. ☎ **520/645-2161.** Reservations recommended in summer. Main courses $5–$24. AE, MC, V. Mon–Sat 11am–11pm, Sun 3– 11pm (shorter hours in winter). AMERICAN.

Page's first and only theme restaurant is a warehouse-size space that is designed to conjure up images of the Glen Canyon Dam. Big industrial doors are the first hint that this is more than the usual small-town dining establishment. Inside, cement walls, hard hats, and a big transformer that sends out neon bolts of "electricity" all put you in a dam good mood. Sandwiches, pastas, and steaks dominate the menu, with a smattering of seafood. There's also a large lounge area with an interesting bar menu. Next door is an affiliated nightclub.

**Rainbow Room.** In the Wahweap Lodge, Lakeshore Dr. ☎ **520/645-2433.** Reservations not accepted. Main courses $6–$8 at lunch, $15–$19 at dinner. AE, DC, DISC, MC, V. Daily 6am–10am, 11am–3pm, and 5–9pm (10pm in summer). AMERICAN/SOUTHWEST.

Because of the sweeping vistas of Lake Powell through the walls of glass, the Rainbow Room at the Wahweap Lodge is Page's premier restaurant. As such, be prepared for a wait; this place feeds busloads of tourists from around the world daily. The menu features American dishes, such as blackened catfish and Caesar salad, but there are also specials and dishes such as pine nut–crusted trout. If you're heading out on the water for the day, the kitchen will fix you a box lunch.

**Zapata's.** 614 N. Navajo Dr. ☎ **520/645-9006.** Main courses $7.50–$13.50. AE, DC, DISC, MC, V. Mon–Fri 11am–9pm, Sat noon–9pm. MEXICAN.

Zapata's, a little place in the shopping plaza diagonally across the intersection from the Powell Museum, serves some of the best Mexican food in town and also fixes good margaritas. The food served here is Sonoran style, and you can count on finding spicy chile verde burritos and somewhat milder, though flavorful, chicken enchiladas. Rice and beans, which are usually pretty generic in Mexican restaurants, are tasty too. At lunch there is a limited selection of specials for about $6. The crowd here is usually more local than tourist.

# Eastern Arizona's High Country

When most people think of Arizona, they think of deserts and saguaro cacti. However, that's only part of the picture. Arizona actually has more mountainous country than Switzerland and more forest than Minnesota, and most of these mountains and forests are here in the highlands of eastern Arizona.

In this sparsely populated region, towns with such apt names as Alpine, Lakeside, and Pinetop have become summer retreats for the people who live in the state's low-lying, sun-baked deserts. Folks from Phoenix and its surrounding cities discovered long ago how close the cool mountain forests were to the desert. In only a few hours you can drive up from the cacti and creosote bushes to the meadows and pine forests of the White Mountains.

Dividing the arid lowlands from the cool pine forests of the highlands is the Mogollon Rim (pronounced *Mug*-ee-un by the locals), a 2,000-foot-high escarpment that stretches for 200 miles from central Arizona into New Mexico. Along this impressive wall, the climatic and vegetative change is dramatic. Imagine sunshine at the base and snow squalls at the top, and you have an idea of the Mogollon Rim's variety. This area was made famous by Western author Zane Grey, who lived in a cabin near Payson and set many of his novels in this scenic yet often-overlooked part of Arizona. Fans of Zane Grey's novels can follow in the author's footsteps and also visit a small museum dedicated to him.

Trout fishing, hiking, horseback riding, and hunting are the main warm-weather pastimes of eastern Arizona, and when winter weather reports from up north have Phoenicians dreaming about snow (it's true, they really do), many head up this way to the White Mountains for a bit of skiing. Sunrise Park Resort, operated by the White Mountain Apache Tribe, is the state's biggest and busiest downhill ski area, and there are plenty of cross-country ski trail systems in the region as well.

A large chunk of eastern Arizona—1,664,874 acres to be exact—is Apache Reservation land. Recreational activities abound on the reservation, but just remember that the Apache tribe requires visitors to have reservation fishing permits and outdoor recreation permits. Fishing is particularly popular on the reservation, which isn't surprising considering that there are 400 miles of trout streams and 25 lakes stocked with rainbow and brown trout.

## 1 Payson & the Mogollon Rim

94 miles NE of Phoenix; 90 miles SW of Winslow; 90 miles SE of Flagstaff; 100 miles W of Pinetop-Lakeside

Payson, 94 miles from Phoenix and 5,000 feet above sea level, is one of the closest places for Phoenicians to find relief from the summer heat. Payson may not be quite high enough to be considered the mountains, but it certainly isn't the desert (summer temperatures are 20° cooler than in the Valley of the Sun). The 2,000-foot-high, 200-mile-long Mogollon Rim is only 22 miles north of town, and the surrounding Tonto National Forest provides opportunities for hiking, swimming, fishing, and hunting. In recent years, retirees have discovered the nearly perfect climate of Payson. Summer highs are usually in the 80s or 90s, while winter highs are usually in the 50°-to-60°F range.

## ESSENTIALS

**GETTING THERE**   Payson is 94 miles from Phoenix on Ariz. 87, the Beeline Highway. Ariz. 87 also connects Payson to Winslow, which is 90 miles away. Ariz. 260 runs east from Payson, climbing the Mogollon Rim and continuing into the White Mountains.

The **Payson Express** operates one bus a day between Phoenix and Payson and charges $25 to $35 one way; call ☎ **520/474-5254** or 602/256-6464 in Phoenix, for further information. The **White Mountain Passenger Line** also offers service between Phoenix, Payson, and Show Low. The fare from Phoenix to Payson is $22 one-way; phone ☎ **520/537-4539** in Show Low or **602/275-4245** in Phoenix for more information.

**VISITOR INFORMATION**   For more information on Payson, contact the **Rim Country Regional Chamber of Commerce,** 100 W. Main St. (P.O. Box 1380), Payson, AZ 85547 (☎ **800/672-9766** or 520/474-4515).

**SPECIAL EVENTS**   The ✪ **World's Oldest Continuous Rodeo** takes place each year on the third weekend in August, while another **PRCA Rodeo** is held in May. In June there's the annual **Blues Festival,** and in September there's the **State Championship Old Time Fiddler's Contest.**

## ENJOYING THE OUTDOORS

The area's most popular attraction is **Tonto Natural Bridge State Park** (☎ **520/476-4202**), which is located 15 miles north of Payson on Ariz. 87 and preserves the largest natural travertine bridge in the world. Discovered in 1877 by a gold prospector named David Gowan while he was being chased by Apaches, the bridge is 183 feet high and 150 feet across at its widest point. This state park preserves not only the bridge, but a historic lodge built by Gowan's nephew and the nephew's sons. Today the lodge has been restored to the way it looked in 1927 but is not open for overnight accommodations. Admission to the park is $5 per car. The park is open daily from 9am to 5pm in winter, 8am to 6pm in spring and fall, and 8am to 7pm Memorial Day to Labor Day.

If you'd like to go horseback riding between Memorial Day and late September, contact **O.K. Corral Stables** (☎ **520/476-4303**) in Pine, which is 14 miles north of Payson on Ariz. 87, or **Kohl's Ranch Stables,** located on Highway 260 17 miles north of Payson (☎ **520/478-4211**). Rates start at around $20 for a 1-hour ride.

In the winter, cross-country skiers will find ski rentals and 30 kilometers of groomed trails at **Forest Lakes Touring Center and Cabins,** 36 miles east of Payson on Ariz. 260 (☎ **520/535-4047**).

## Eastern Arizona's High Country

The **Highline Trail** is a 51-mile-long hiking trail along the lower slope of the Mogollon Rim. You can find out more about this and other area trails at the **Payson Ranger Station** (☎ **520/474-7900**) on Ariz. 260 at the east end of town. At the ranger station, you can also find out about area trails open to mountain bikes.

## MORE TO SEE & DO

About 5 miles north of town, off Ariz. 87 on Houston Mesa Road, you can visit the ruins of **Shoofly Village,** in the Tonto National Forest. This village was first occupied nearly 1,000 years ago by peoples related to the Hohokam and Salado cultures and contained 87 rooms. Today only rock foundations remain, but an interpretive trail helps bring the site to life.

To learn a bit more about the history of the area, stop in at the **Rim Country Museum,** 700 Green Valley Pkwy. (☎ **520/474-3483**), which has displays on the region, as well as a special Zane Grey exhibit. The museum, which is located in Green Valley Park, is open Wednesday through Sunday from noon to 4pm and admission is $3 adults, $2.50 seniors, and $2 students 12 to 17 years old.

You'll find more Zane Grey memorabilia at the **Zane Grey Museum of Payson,** 503B W. Main St. (☎ **520/474-6243**). The museum is open Monday through Saturday from 11am to 4pm and Sunday from 1 to 4pm, and admission is free.

Other attractions in the Payson area include the small **Payson Zoo,** located less than 7 miles east of town on Ariz. 260 (☎ **520/474-5435**). It's a good place to bring the kids, who will enjoy seeing animals from around the world, many of which have appeared in films, TV shows, and commercials. Open daily 10am to 3pm in summer;

Friday through Wednesday 10am to 3pm in winter. Admission is $4 for adults and $1 for children 12 and under.

If you feel lucky, you can spend some time and money at the **Mazatzal Casino** (☎ **800/777-PLAY**) ½ mile south on Ariz. 87. The casino is run by the Tonto Apaches.

## SCENIC DRIVES

Scenic drives through this region are also among the favorite pastimes of visitors. One of the most popular drives is along the top of the Mogollon Rim on 45-mile-long **Forest Road 300.** On the road, which clings to the edge of the Mogollon Rim, there are numerous views of the forest far below and plenty of places to stop, including lakes, picnic areas, trailheads, and campgrounds. This is a good gravel road in summer and can be negotiated in a standard passenger car. However, in winter, the road is not maintained. To access the rim road, head east on Ariz. 260 or north on Ariz. 87 for 30 miles and watch for signs.

About 15 miles north of Payson on Ariz. 87, you'll find the village of **Pine** and another 3 miles beyond this, the village of **Strawberry.** Here, in a quiet setting in the forest, you'll find a few antiques and crafts shops, and, in Pine, a small museum that chronicles the history of this area. In Strawberry, on the road that leads west from the center of the village, is the old Strawberry schoolhouse, a restored log building dating from 1885.

Another interesting drive starts west of the old Strawberry schoolhouse. If you continue west on this road, you will be on the Fossil Creek Road, a gravel road leading down a deep and spectacular canyon. It's a bit of a hair-raising drive, but if you like views, it's well worth the white knuckles and dust. At the bottom, **Fossil Creek** offers swimming and fishing.

## WHERE TO STAY
### IN TOWN

✪ **Majestic Mountain Inn.** 602 E. Ariz. 260, Payson, AZ 85541. ☎ **800/408-2442** or 520/474-0185. Fax 520/472-6097. 50 units. A/C TV TEL. $64–$150 double. AE, CB, DC, DISC, MC, V.

Although it's located in town, this motel is built in an attractive, modern mountain-lodge design that makes it the most appealing place to stay right in Payson. There's a large stone chimney and fireplace in the lobby, and several of the deluxe rooms have fireplaces of their own. These deluxe rooms also have tile floors and double whirlpool tubs facing the fireplaces. The standard rooms aren't as spacious or luxurious, but are still quite comfortable. There's also a seasonal outdoor swimming pool.

### OUTSIDE TOWN

**Christopher Creek Lodge.** Ariz. 260 (Star Rte., Box 119), Payson, AZ 85541. ☎ **520/478-4300.** 24 units. $45–$85 double. MC, V. Pets accepted ($20 deposit).

Located 21 miles east of Payson on Ariz. 260, the Christopher Creek Lodge is a family-oriented rustic mountain retreat. You can choose between motel-style rooms with sleeping lofts; large Spartan creek-side cabins complete with full kitchen, woodstove, and sleeping loft; or duplex cabins with woodstoves, sliding glass doors, and picnic tables in the dining areas. All the accommodations are under the trees, and Christopher Creek runs along the edge of the property. For Phoenicians fleeing the heat of summer, this is one of the nearest escapes.

✪ **Kohl's Ranch Lodge.** E. Ariz. 260, Payson, AZ 85541. ☎ **800/331-KOHL** or 520/478-4211. Fax 520/478-0353. 49 units. A/C TV TEL. May 1–Sept 30 $95–$105 double, $230–$250 cabin; Oct 1–Apr 30 $75–$85 double, $200–$225 cabin. AE, DISC, MC, V. Pets accepted.

Located 17 miles east of Payson on Ariz. 260, Kohl's Ranch is surrounded by pine forest on the banks of Tonto Creek and is the most comfortable mountain retreat in the area. Though the main lodge building looks like an aging mountain motel from the outside, this casual family-oriented resort makes an excellent base for exploring the Mogollon Rim region. All the guest rooms here feature a contemporary rustic look, and all the cabins and some of the smaller lodge rooms have fireplaces. The creek-side cabins are the best accommodations, but they seem somewhat overpriced. The dining room is done up like an old log cabin, and there's a lounge in the main lodge and a cowboy bar and pool hall across the parking lot. The hotel offers horseback riding, mountain-bike rentals, an outdoor pool, a fitness room, volleyball, horseshoes, bocce ball, a video arcade, and a playground.

**The Opal Ranch Inn Bed & Breakfast.** 2160 Moonlight Dr. (HC 4, Box 29), Payson, AZ 85541. ☎ **520/472-6193.** 3 units. $60–$80 double. Rates include full breakfast. MC, V. Take Ariz. 260 east 4 miles to Star Valley, turn right on Moonlight Dr. and continue 2½ miles to the inn.

Located only 5½ miles outside Payson in the community of Star Valley, this blindingly white contemporary B&B sits on 5 acres of pastures and forest that abut the Tonto National Forest. From the big sunroom, there are great views of surrounding mountains, rocky outcroppings, and forests. After a hearty farm breakfast, you can visit with the inn's many farm animals and pets and then head out into the national forest on trails that start at the edge of the property. Guest rooms are simply furnished in a mix of country and Southwestern lodge styles.

## CAMPGROUNDS

East of Payson on Ariz. 260 are several national forest campgrounds, where camping is on a first-come, first served basis. These campgrounds include (from west to east) Lower Tonto Creek Campground, Upper Tonto Creek Campground, and Christopher Creek Campground.

Information is available from the **Payson Ranger Station** (☎ **520/474-7900**) on Ariz. 260 at the east end of town

## WHERE TO DINE

In addition to the restaurant listed below, you might want to check out the **Heritage House Garden Tea Room,** 202 W. Main St. (☎ **520/474-5501**), which was in the process of changing hands at press time. This combination crafts store and ladies' lunch spot has long been one of the more popular restaurants in Payson.

**The Oaks Restaurant & Lounge.** 302 W. Main St. ☎ **520/474-1929.** Reservations recommended for dinner. Main courses $4–$7 at lunch, $12–$17 at dinner. AE, DISC, MC, V. Sun and Wed–Thurs 11am–2pm and 5–8pm, Fri–Sat 11am–2pm and 5–9pm. AMERICAN.

Taking its name from the grove of oak trees spreading over it, the Oaks Restaurant is a quiet, upscale place for a meal in Payson, and the large patio dining area beside the grassy front lawn is a great spot for lunch or dinner on a warm night. The dinner menu is short and to the point: straightforward preparations of steaks and seafood, complemented by a selection of primarily California wines. The Caesar salad is good, as are the various cakes. The lunch menu features a variety of hot and cold sandwiches as well as several salads.

## 2  Pinetop-Lakeside

185 miles NE of Phoenix; 140 miles SE of Flagstaff; 50 miles S of Holbrook; 90 miles NE of Payson

With dozens of motels and cabin resorts strung out along Ariz. 260 as it passes through town, Pinetop-Lakeside, actually two towns that grew together over the years, is the busiest town in the White Mountains. At first glance it is easy to dismiss Pinetop-Lakeside as too commercial, what with all the strip malls, budget motels, and old cabin resorts, but this area has spent a lot of years entertaining families during the summer months, and it still has plenty of things to keep visitors busy. You just have to look a little harder than you might in other White Mountains communities.

With Apache-Sitgreaves National Forest on one side of town and the unspoiled lands of the White Mountain Apache Indian Reservation on the other, Pinetop-Lakeside is well situated for anyone who enjoys getting outside. Several lakes with good fishing; nearly 200 miles of hiking, mountain biking, and cross-country ski trails; horseback riding stables; and downhill skiing are all nearby, which makes this area a good base for a visit to the White Mountains. Although summer is the busy season up here, Pinetop-Lakeside becomes a ski resort in the winter. Sunrise ski area is only 30 miles away, and on weekends the town is packed with skiers.

Pinetop-Lakeside is definitely the family destination of the White Mountains, so if you're looking for a romantic weekend or to just get away from it all, continue farther into the White Mountains to Greer or Alpine.

## ESSENTIALS

**GETTING THERE**    Pinetop and Lakeside are both located on Ariz. 260.

**Sunrise Airlines** (☎ **888/394-1851** or 520/532-8888) provides regularly scheduled air service between Scottsdale Airport and Show Low. Fares range from $151 to $191 round-trip.

**White Mountain Passenger Lines** has regularly scheduled service to Show Low from Phoenix. The fare is $40 each way. For the schedule, call ☎ **520/537-4539** in Show Low or **602/275-4245** in Phoenix.

**GETTING AROUND**    Rental cars are available in Show Low from **Enterprise Rent-a-Car** (☎ **520/537-5144**).

**VISITOR INFORMATION**    For information on this area, contact the **Pinetop-Lakeside Chamber of Commerce,** 674 E. White Mountain Blvd. (P.O. Box 4220), Lakeside, AZ 85935 (☎ **520/367-4290;** www.pinetop.com). For more information on the White Mountain Apache Reservation, contact the **White Mountain Apache Tribe Office of Tourism,** P.O. Box 710, Fort Apache, AZ 85926 (☎ **520/338-1230**).

## ENJOYING THE OUTDOORS

Old forts and casinos aside, it is the outdoors (and the cool weather) that really draws people up here. Fishing, hiking, mountain biking, and horseback riding are among the most popular activities in the Pinetop-Lakeside area.

If you want to saddle up, call **Porter Mountain Stable,** 4048 Porter Mountain Rd. (☎ **520/368-5306**), or **Pinetop Lakes Stables,** Buck Springs Road (☎ **520/ 369-1000**) for trail rides. A 1-hour ride at either stable is $18.

In the forests surrounding Pinetop-Lakeside is the 180-mile **White Mountain Trail system.** Many of these trails are easily accessible (in fact some are right in town) and are open to hikers and mountain bikers. The trails at **Woodland Lake Park** are among our favorites. The park is just off Ariz. 260 near the east side of Pinetop and has 6 miles of trails, including a paved trail around the lake. For a panoramic vista of the Mogollon Rim, you can hike the short **Mogollon Rim Nature Walk** off Ariz. 260 on the west side of Lakeside. For another short but pleasant stroll, check out the **Big Springs Environmental Study Area,** which is on Woodland Road in Lakeside. This quiet little preserve encompasses a small meadow through which flows a spring-fed stream. There is often good bird watching here. You can spot more birds at **Woodland Lake Park** in

Pinetop and at **Jacques Marsh,** 2 miles north of Lakeside on Porter Mountain Road. For more information on area trails, contact the **Lakeside Ranger Station** (☎ 520/ 368-5111) on Ariz. 260 in Lakeside or the **Pinetop-Lakeside Chamber of Commerce,** 674 E. White Mountain Blvd., Lakeside (☎ 520/367-4290).

If you're up here to catch the big one, you've got plenty of options. Area lakes hold native Apache trout, as well as stocked rainbows, browns, and brookies. This is also the southernmost spot in the United States where you can fish for Arctic graylings. Right in the Pinetop-Lakeside area, try **Rainbow Lake,** which is a block south of Ariz. 260 in Lakeside and has boat rentals available; **Woodland Lake,** in Woodland Lake Park, which is toward the east end of Pinetop and just south of Ariz. 260; or **Show Low Lake,** which is east of Lakeside and north of Ariz. 260. On the nearby White Mountain Apache Indian Reservation, there is good fishing in **Hawley Lake** and at **Horseshoe Lake,** both of which are east of Pinetop-Lakeside and south of Ariz. 260. Be sure to get your reservation fishing license ($6 per day). They're available at **Pinetop Sporting Goods,** Hudson Plaza, Ariz. 260, Pinetop (☎ 520/367-5050); the **Hon Dah Service Station** (☎ 520/369-4311) at the junction of Ariz. 260 and Ariz. 73; and **Hawley Lake Resort Store** (☎ 520/335-7511), south of Ariz. 260 between Hon Dah and Sunrise.

Several golf courses in the area are open to the public, including **Pinetop Lakes Golf Club** (☎ 520/369-4531), Buck Springs Road, Pinetop-Lakeside; **Silver Creek Golf Club** (☎ 520/537-2744), Bourdon Ranch Road, Show Low; and the **Show Low Country Club** (☎ 520/537-4564), Ariz. 260 and Old Linden Road, Show Low.

About 50 miles south of Show Low, U.S. 60 crosses a bridge over the narrow, scenic canyon of the Salt River. This stretch of the Salt River is a favorite of white-water rafters, and there are several companies that offer rafting trips of varying lengths on this stretch of the river. Some of these companies include **Far Flung Adventures** (☎ 800/231-7238 or 520/425-7272; www.farflung.com), **Sun Country Rafting** (☎ 800/272-3353 or 602/493-9011), and **Mild to Wild Rafting** (☎ 800/567-6745).

## MORE TO SEE & DO

**Fort Apache Historic Park** (☎ 520/338-4625), in the town of Fort Apache, centers around Old Fort Apache, which, along with the White Mountain Apache Reservation, was established in 1870 by the U.S. government. The park, which is located approximately 22 miles south of Pinetop on Ariz. 73, now encompasses almost 300 acres, including more than 20 buildings, prehistoric ruins, a reconstructed Apache village, petroglyphs, and the Apache Museum/Cultural Center. The cultural center is open Monday through Friday from 8am to 5pm (also on Saturday in the summer). Here you'll find interpretive films such as *The Geronimo Experience* and arts and crafts demonstrations on weekends. Admission is $3 for adults and children 6 and older and $2 for seniors.

Also in this area, you'll find **Kinishba Ruins,** which are up a gravel road 1 mile west of Fort Apache on Ariz. 73. This 200-room pueblo ruin is more than 1,000 years old and was visited by Coronado when he passed through this region in search of the Seven Cities of Cíbola. Get directions to the ruins at the cultural center.

For more information on visiting the White Mountain Apache Reservation, contact the **White Mountain Apache Office of Tourism** (☎ 520/338-1230), which is also in Fort Apache Historic Park.

If you're looking for something to do after dark, you can head out to the **Hon-Dah Casino** (☎ 800/WAY-UP-HI or 520/369-0299), which is owned and operated by the White Mountain Apache Tribe. It's open daily around the clock and is at the junction of Ariz. 73 and Ariz. 260, about 4 miles east of Pinetop.

## WHERE TO STAY

In addition to accommodations listed below, area chain motels include the **Best Western Inn of Pinetop,** 404 S. White Mountain Blvd., Pinetop (☎ **520/ 367-6667**), charging $69 to $109 for a double; and the **Econo Lodge,** 458 White Mountain Blvd., Pinetop (☎ **520/367-3636**), charging $59 to $109 for a double.

**Hon-Dah Resort.** 777 Ariz. 260 (P.O. Box 3250), Pinetop, AZ 85935. ☎ **800/WAY-UP-HI** or 520/369-0299. Fax 520/369-0382. 130 units. A/C TV TEL. $79–$109 double; $150–$180 suite. Rates include continental breakfast. AE, DISC, MC, V.

This hotel, adjacent to the Hon-Dah Casino a few miles east of Pinetop-Lakeside, is the largest and most luxurious in the White Mountains these days. As with most casino hotels, this place is designed to impress. The portico is big enough to hold a basketball court, and inside the front door, there's an artificial rock wall on which are mounted stuffed animals including a cougar, bobcat, bear, ducks, and even a bugling elk. Guest rooms are for the most part very large with big bathrooms and refrigerators. Amenities include two restaurants and two lounges, a year-round outdoor swimming pool with heated water in winter, and a whirlpool and a sauna. The casino, however, is the hotel's main draw. For kids, there's a video arcade.

**Lake of the Woods.** Ariz. 260 (P.O. Box 777), Lakeside, AZ 85929. ☎ **520/368-5353.** 27 units. TV. $48–$158 cabin for 2; $87–$285 house for 2. DISC, MC, V.

Located on its own private lake right on Ariz. 260, Lake of the Woods is a rustic mountain resort that caters to families. The kids can fish in the lake, play in the snow, or row a boat. The resort also offers a whirlpool, sauna, exercise equipment, table tennis, pool table, shuffleboard, horseshoes, a playground, and coin-operated laundry. Cabins and houses range from tiny to huge, with rustic and modern side by side. The smallest sleep two or three, while the largest house sleeps 18. Several have kitchens and fireplaces. Some are on the edge of the lake while others are tucked away under the pines—be sure to request a location away from the busy highway. Cabins vary considerably in their quality; ask for a newer cabin.

✪ **Rawhide & Roses.** 5130 S. Flores Dr. (P.O. Box 1153), Lakeside, AZ 85929. ☎ **520/ 537-0216.** 3 units. A/C TV. $90–$120 double (discounts for 2nd and 3rd nights). Rates include full breakfast. DISC, MC, V. From the hospital on Ariz. 260 west of Pinetop-Lakeside, go south on Cub Lake Rd., turn left on Flores Dr. and left again on S. Flores Dr.

Set among tall pines at the end of a rutted gravel road, this large log home is a surprising escape from the commercial clutter of Pinetop-Lakeside's main drag. Here, amid the pines, you'll find very tasteful Eddie Bauer–style decor and furnishings. Seemingly everywhere you turn in this house, there is rock and wood. In the living room there's a big stone fireplace, and in the dining room, an antler chandelier hangs above an alligator juniper table. In the high-ceilinged game room, you'll find a pool table, and out on the deck, there's a hammock for lazy afternoons. A split-log open staircase leads up to the second floor and to the three guest rooms, each of which has its own fireplace. Despite the name, Geronimo's Room, with its fireplace and adjacent rock-surrounded whirlpool tub, is the inn's most romantic room.

✪ **Sierra Springs Ranch.** H.C. 62, Box 32100, Pinetop, AZ 85935. ☎ **800/492-4059** or 520/369-3900. Fax 520/369-0741. www.sierraspringsranch.com. 9 units. TV. $175 cabin for 2; $225 and up for larger cabins. 2-night minimum stay (longer minimum on holidays and in summer). AE, MC, V.

Located off a gravel road east of Pinetop, the Sierra Springs Ranch is the most upscale property around and is as idyllic a mountain retreat as you'll find in Arizona. Set in a wide clearing in the forest, each of the nine cabins is a little bit different, but all are large and comfortable (the largest cabin sleeps 13). Our favorite is the honeymoon cottage, which is built of logs and has a stone fireplace. All the cabins have full kitchens, which make up for the lack of a restaurant on the premises.

On the ranch grounds you'll find a trout pond and meadows, a tennis court, and a walking/jogging path. Fishing gear, tennis racquets, and bicycles are all available for guests to use.

## CAMPGROUNDS

There are four campgrounds in the immediate Pinetop-Lakeside area, including Show Low Lake, Fool Hollow, Lewis Canyon, and Lakeside. Of these, **Show Low Lake County Park** (☎ 520/537-4126) and **Fool Hollow Lake Recreation Area** (☎ 520/537-3680) are the nicest. There are also numerous campgrounds nearby on the White River Apache Indian Reservation. For information about these campgrounds, contact the **White Mountain Wildlife and Outdoor Recreation Division** (☎ 520/338-4385) or the **Fort Apache Office of Tourism** (☎ 520/338-1230).

## WHERE TO DINE

In addition to the places mentioned below and a few basic burger and steak places in town, there's **Lauth's Country Store,** on Ariz. 260 at the east end of Pinetop (☎ 520/367-2161), where you can get an inexpensive breakfast and a variety of burgers and sandwiches made with applewood-smoked meats. Also, the food at the Hon-Dah Casino gets praises from locals, but the prices are only cheap if you can resist the temptation to spend some time at the slot machines.

**Charlie Clark's Steak House.** Ariz. 260 at Penrod Ave., Pinetop. ☎ **520/367-4900.** Main courses $10–$20. AE, DC, MC, V. Daily 5–9pm in summer (off-season hours vary).

Charlie Clark's has been serving up thick, juicy steaks since 1938 and is the oldest steakhouse in the White Mountains. Mesquite-broiled steaks and chicken, as well as seafood and prime rib, fill the menu; in the lounge there's a large-screen TV and a pool table. This has long been a local favorite and is steeped in traditional White Mountains atmosphere, but in spite of these things, you'll also find such items on the menu as escargot and oysters Rockefeller and a list of wines. To find Charlie Clark's, just look for the building with the buggy, wagon, and fake horse on the roof.

**The Christmas Tree Restaurant.** 455 Woodland Rd., Lakeside. ☎ **520/367-3107.** Reservations recommended on weekends. Main courses $7–$30. DISC, MC, V. Wed–Sun 5–9pm. AMERICAN/CONTINENTAL.

Located in a quiet setting off the main drag, this country restaurant serves good old-fashioned American food as well as a few standard continental offerings. Chicken and dumplings are the specialty of the house, but you can also get a good New York steak accompanied by your choice of seafood. Meals are large and filling and come with everything from delicious pickled beets to Boston clam chowder. As the name implies, a Christmas theme prevails here year-round, and there's also a country gift store.

## 3  Greer & Sunrise Park

51 miles SE of Show Low; 98 miles SE of Holbrook; 222 miles NE of Phoenix

The tiny community of Greer, set in the lush meadows on either side of the Little Colorado River, and surrounded by forests, holds the distinction of being the most picturesque mountain village in Arizona. The elevation of 8,525 feet assures plenty of snow in winter and pleasantly cool temperatures in summer, and together these two factors have turned Greer into a very popular vacation village. In the past few years Greer has begun to take on the appearance of an upscale mountain getaway town and has become quite popular with wealthy, in-the-know Phoenix residents. Modern log homes are springing up all over the valley, but Greer is still free of the sort of strip-mall developments that have forever changed the character of Payson and Pinetop-Lakeside.

The Little Colorado River, which flows through the middle of Greer on its way to the Grand Canyon, is little more than a babbling brook up here. Still, it's well known for trout fishing, which is one of its main draws. Several lakes and ponds in the area also provide good fishing. In winter there are more than 12 miles of cross-country ski trails around Greer, and ice-skating, ice fishing, and sleigh rides are also popular. Additionally, Greer happens to be the closest town to the Sunrise ski area, which is what gives the village its ski resort atmosphere. There are several rustic mountain lodges and a number of rental-cabin operations here.

## ESSENTIALS

**GETTING THERE**    From Phoenix, take U.S. 87 north to Payson and then go east on Ariz. 260, or take U.S. 60 east from Phoenix through Globe and Show Low to Ariz. 260 east. Greer is just a few miles south of Ariz. 260 on Ariz. 373.

**VISITOR INFORMATION**    For information on the Greer area, contact the **Round Valley Chamber of Commerce,** P.O. Box 31, Springerville, AZ 85938 (☎ **520/333-2123**).

## ENJOYING THE OUTDOORS

Winter is one of the busiest seasons in Greer, since it is so close to the **Sunrise Park Resort** ski area (☎ **520/735-7669**). Located just off Ariz. 260 on Ariz. 273, this ski area, the largest and most popular in Arizona, is operated by the White Mountain Apache Tribe. The ski area usually opens in November, though winter thaws and long stretches without snow can make winters a bit unreliable (snowmaking machines enhance the sometimes sparse natural snowfall). Though there are some good advanced runs, beginner and intermediate skiers will be in heaven. We've rarely seen so many green runs starting from the uppermost lifts of a ski area, all of which translates into a very family-oriented ski area. At the top of 11,000-foot Apache Peak is a day lodge providing meals and a view that goes on forever. There's also a ski school that offers lessons for everyone from beginners to advanced skiers. Lift tickets are $34 for adults and $19 for children. Ski rentals are available here and at numerous shops in Pinetop-Lakeside.

There are also more than 13.5 kilometers of groomed cross-country ski trails at Sunrise. These trails begin at the **Sunrise Sports Center,** which is located in the service station at the turnoff for the downhill area, and wind their way through forests of ponderosa pines and across high snow-covered meadows. There are also good opportunities for cross-country skiing in Greer, which has 35 miles of developed trails. At 8,500 feet, the alpine scenery here is quiet and serene. You can also go for a sleigh ride near Sunrise. They're offered by **Lee Valley Outfitters** (☎ **520/735-7454**), which charges $8 for a 20-minute ride or $15 for a 45-minute ride.

Come summer the cross-country ski trails in Greer become **mountain-bike trails,** and when combined with the nearby **Poll Knoll trail system,** provide mountain bikers with 35 miles of trails of varying degrees of difficulty.

This area offers some of the finest mountain **hiking** in Arizona, and most popular of all the area trails is the trail up 11,590-foot **Mount Baldy,** which is the second-highest peak in Arizona. This peak lies on the edge of the White Mountain Apache Indian Reservation and is sacred to the Apaches. Consequently, the summit is off limits to non-Apaches. There are two trailheads for the hike up Mount Baldy. The most popular and scenic route begins 6 miles south of Sunrise Ski Resort (off the gravel extension of Ariz. 273) and follows the West Fork of the Little Colorado River.

This trail climbs roughly 2,000 feet and is moderately strenuous, although the high elevation often leaves lowland hikers gasping for breath.

To explore the Greer area from the back of a horse, contact **Lee Valley Outfitters** (☎ 520/735-7454), which is located between Greer and Ariz. 260 and offers rides of varying lengths ($18 for 1 hour, $28 for 2 hours, $60 for 4 hours with lunch). This company also does hay rides and cookout rides.

The three Greer Lakes on the outskirts of town—Bunch, River, and Tunnel reservoirs—are popular fishing spots. All three lakes hold brown and rainbow trout. On River Reservoir, try fishing the shallows at the south end. On Tunnel Reservoir, you can often do well fishing from shore, especially if fly-fishing, but there is a boat launch. However, it is Big Lake, south of Greer, that has the biggest fishing reputation around these parts. Fishing is also good on Sunrise Lake, but be sure to get a White Mountain Apache Indian Reservation fishing license (available at the Sunrise service station). If you'd like a guide to take you out for a day of fishing the Arizona high country, contact **Troutback Flyfishing Guide Service,** P.O. Box 864, Show Low, AZ 85902 (☎ **800/903-4092** or 520/532-3474), which charges $175 per day for one angler and $225 for two anglers.

**Sunrise Lake,** near the Sunrise ski area, is a popular spot in the summer when boat rentals (including small sailboats) are available.

## A MUSEUM

The **Butterfly Lodge Museum** (☎ 520/735-7514) is a restored historic cabin built in 1914. Once owned by James Willard Schultz (a writer) and his son Hart Merriam Schultz (a painter), the museum is a memorial to these two unusual and creative individuals who once called Greer home. The museum, which is located just off Ariz. 373 between Ariz. 260 and Greer, is open Memorial Day through Labor Day Friday through Sunday from 10am to 5pm.

## WHERE TO STAY
### In Greer

**Cattle Kate's Bed and Breakfast.** 80 N. Main St. (P.O. Box 21), Greer, AZ 85927. ☎ **520/ 735-7744.** Fax 520/735-7386. 9 units. $69–$95 double; $135 suite. Rates include full breakfast. MC, V. Children under 16 discouraged.

Consisting of several new log buildings with a classic mountain feel, Cattle Kate's seems to have patterned itself after the nearby Greer Lodge and is every bit as comfortable. The rooms, though Spartanly furnished in classic Western style, have high ceilings and look out on small trout ponds (fly-fishing lessons available) and the meadows along the Little Colorado River. In the large breakfast room, an elk head is mounted over the fireplace and an antler chandelier hangs from the ceiling. The only real drawback here is that you are right on the main road through Greer; however, this road is rarely very busy.

**Greer Lodge.** 44 Main St. (P.O. Box 244), Greer, AZ 85927. ☎ **888/475-6343** or 520/ 735-7216. Fax 520/735-7720. 18 units. $120 double; $75–$120 cabin for 2; $210–$280 house. AE, DISC, MC, V.

Located only 20 minutes from the Sunrise ski area and with its own trout ponds and section of the Little Colorado River, this old lodge is popular with both skiers and anglers. Rooms in the main lodge all have nice views of the mountains or river but tend to get quite a lot of noise from the lobby (which doubles as a TV room). If you're seeking quiet, request a cabin, although these have not been well maintained in recent years. The hotel also offers ice-skating, croquet, volleyball, horseshoes, a barbecue area, and fishing ponds.

**The Peaks at Greer.** P.O. Box 132, Greer, AZ 85927. ☎ 800/556-9997 or 520/735-7777. Fax 520/735-7204. 19 units. $99–$109 double; $149–$159 suite; $119 cabin for 2. Rates include continental breakfast. AE, DISC, MC, V. Pets accepted in cabins.

Located on a hill just past Greer Lodge, this is the most luxurious of Greer's handful of full-service hotels. In the high-ceilinged lobby, there are huge overstuffed chairs in front of the fireplace and exposed log beams overhead. Guest rooms are new, and many are quite large. Suites have their own fireplaces, as do the much more rustic cabins, which are quite a bit older than the rest of the hotel. The restaurant here is one of the best in town, and there is also a small bar with a big deck and good views. Amenities include a hot tub and game room.

✪ **Red Setter Bed & Breakfast Inn.** P.O. Box 133, Greer, AZ 85927. ☎ 888/99-GREER or 520/735-7441. Fax 520/735-7425. www.redsetterinn.com. 12 units. $130–$195 double. Rates include full breakfast. AE, MC, V.

If you're headed up to the mountains for a romantic weekend getaway, this three-story log lodge, the most luxurious in Greer, should be your first choice. Several of the guest rooms have fireplaces and whirlpool tubs that make them just right for a quiet weekend together. Other rooms have vaulted ceilings, some with skylights. The inn is built on the bank of the Little Colorado River, which is only steps away from the decks of some rooms. If you stay for 2 nights or more, you'll receive a complimentary picnic lunch to take with you on an outing. Cases full of antique toys and a game room with old arcade games make this inn fun as well as romantic. There is also a housekeeping "cottage" with four bedrooms, three bathrooms, and three fireplaces.

✪ **Snowy Mountain Inn.** P.O. Box 337, Greer, AZ 85927-0377. ☎ 520/735-7576. Fax 520/735-7705. www.snowymountain.net. 14 units. $85–$100 double; $110–$225 cabin or house. Room rates include continental breakfast. 2- to 5-night minimums during busy times. MC, V. Short-haired pets accepted during summer.

Set back from the main road down a gravel driveway and shaded by tall pines, the Snowy Mountain Lodge has a very remote yet very comfortable feel about it. For couples, the lodge rooms are a good deal. Some of these rooms have gas fireplaces and/or whirlpool tubs. The large modern cabins are perfect for family vacations and come with gas fireplaces, porches, and sleeping lofts; some have private hot tubs. Surrounding the log cabins and main lodge building are 100 acres of private forest, so guests have plenty of room to roam. The 1½-acre trout pond here is one of the largest in the area. The inn also has its own gourmet restaurant, which occasionally even serves kangaroo (see "Where to Dine," below, for details).

**White Mountain Lodge Bed & Breakfast and Cabins.** 140 Main St. (P.O. Box 143), Greer, AZ 85927. ☎ 888/493-7568 or 520/735-7568. Fax 520/735-7498. 11 units. $65–$95 double; $85–$95 cabin for 2. 2-night minimum on weekends, 3 nights on holidays. Lodge room rates include full breakfast. DC, DISC, MC, V. Pets accepted ($20 charge).

Situated on the road into Greer with a view across an open, marshy stretch of the valley, this recently remodeled lodge was built in 1892 and is the oldest building in Greer (though you'd never know it to look at it). Knotty pine throughout gives the lodge a classic cabin feel, though the many large windows prevent the rooms from feeling too dark. Guest rooms are done up either in a Southwestern or country theme, and our favorite has a king-size bed and a view up the valley. However, the cabins, which are perfect for families or two couples, are even more comfortable. One has a stone fireplace and a porch swing.

## IN MCNARY

**Sunrise Park Resort Hotel.** Hwy. 273, near intersection of Hwy. 260 (P.O. Box 217), McNary, AZ 85930. ☎ **800/55-HOTEL** or 520/735-7669. Fax 520/735-7315. www. sunriseskipark.com. 94 units. A/C TV TEL. Winter $59–$125 double, $195–$295 suite; summer $59–$72 double, $140 suite. AE, DC, DISC, MC, V.

Located 20 miles outside Greer in McNary, this is the closest lodge to the Sunrise ski area and thus is a favorite of downhill skiers. About half the rooms overlook Sunrise Lake, and the suite has a whirlpool tub. The lounge is a cozy place to gather after a day of skiing or hiking, and in the dining room, you'll find some surprising menu items such as chicken piccata, steak au poivre, and smoked duck and wild mushroom pasta. The hotel also offers a ski area shuttle bus, tiny indoor swimming pool, indoor and outdoor whirlpools, sauna, exercise room, volleyball, rental bikes, video arcade, and baby-sitting. The hotel has been undergoing renovation and is beginning to look a little less run-down than it has in the past few years.

## CAMPGROUNDS

In the immediate vicinity of Greer, there are three campgrounds on Apache-Sitgreaves National Forest. There are also several campgrounds nearby on the White Mountain Apache Indian Reservation (no reservations accepted). Reservations can be made at the Rolfe C. Hoyer campground 1 mile north of Greer on Ariz. 373 and at the Winn Campground 12 miles southwest of Greer on Ariz. 273 (the road past Sunrise Ski Resort) by calling the **National Recreation Reservation Service** line (☎ **800/280-CAMP**). Benny Creek, 2 miles north of Greer, does not take reservations. Because of its proximity to Greer and the Greer lakes, Rolfe C. Hoyer is the top choice in the area.

## WHERE TO DINE

**Amberon's at Greer Lodge.** 44 Main St. ☎ **520/735-7216.** Reservations suggested. Main courses $5–$8 at lunch, $9–$24 at dinner. AE, MC, V. Summer daily 7–10:30am, 11am–2:30pm, and 5–9pm. Winter hours Thurs–Fri 5–9pm; Sat 7–10am, 11am–2pm, and 5–9pm; Sun 7–10am. Hours may vary. AMERICAN/CONTINENTAL.

You couldn't wish for a prettier location than this one for a meal in the mountains. This multilevel restaurant has walls of glass that look out over a river, meadows, and a trout pond, and in the winter there's a cozy fireplace. Unfortunately, meals are not always up to the quality of the view. Dinner fare includes various treatments of chicken, lamb, shrimp, and prime rib, including some Southwestern flavorings. There's also a children's menu. The wine list has some reasonably priced wines.

✪ **Snowy Mountain Inn.** North of Greer on Ariz. 373. ☎ **520/735-7576.** Reservations required. Main courses $12–$21. MC, V. Fri–Sat and holidays 5:30–8pm. CONTINENTAL/ AMERICAN/AUSTRALIAN.

How often do you find kangaroo on a menu in the United States? Not too often, so it comes as even more of a shock to run across it way out here in little old Greer. The explanation, however, is simple: One of the owners (who also happens to be the chef) of this combination lodge and restaurant is from down under. You'll also find New Zealand lamb on the menu, and though neither of these meats is always available, you just may luck into a culinary adventure on the night of your visit. There are all kinds of Continental dishes here as well. To accompany meals, there is an excellent wine list. The restaurant's decor reflects the owners' global travels. *Note:* If the restaurant doesn't have any reservations by mid-afternoon, it may not open that evening. Also, the restaurant may be open Wednesday and Thursday in summer, so give it a try.

## 4 Springerville & Eagar

56 miles E of Show Low; 82 miles SE of Holbrook; 227 miles NE of Phoenix

Together, the adjacent towns of Springerville and Eagar constitute the northeastern gateway to the White Mountains. Though the towns themselves are at the foot of the mountains, the vistas from around the two towns take in all of the area's peaks. Springerville and Eagar like to play up their Wild West background, and, in fact, John Wayne liked the area so much that he had a ranch along the Little Colorado River just west of Eagar. Today large ranches still run their cattle on the windswept plains north of the two towns.

However, it was volcanic activity between 300,000 and 700,000 years ago that gave the land north of Springerville and Eagar its distinctive character. This area is known as the Springerville Volcanic Field—the third largest volcanic field of its kind in the continental United States (the San Francisco Field near Flagstaff and the Medicine Lake Field in California are both larger). The Springerville Volcanic Field covers an area bigger than the state of Rhode Island and contains 405 extinct volcanic vents. However, it is the many cinder cones dotting the landscape that give this region such a distinctive appearance. For a brochure outlining a tour of the volcanic field, contact the Round Valley Chamber of Commerce (see "Visitor Information," below).

One other thing you might be curious about is that big dome—it's the Round Valley Ensphere, one of the only domed high school football stadiums in the country.

## ESSENTIALS

**GETTING THERE**  Springerville and Eagar are in the northeast corner of the White Mountains at the junction of U.S. 60, U.S. 180/191, and Ariz. 260. From the Phoenix area, there are two routes: Ariz. 87 north to Payson and then Ariz. 260 east, or U.S. 60 east to Globe and then north to Show Low and on to Springerville (alternatively you can take Ariz. 260 from Show Low to Springerville). From Holbrook, take U.S. 180 southeast to St. Johns and U.S. 180/191 south to Springerville. From southern Arizona, U.S. 191 is slow but very scenic.

**VISITOR INFORMATION**  For information on the Springerville and Eagar areas, contact the **Round Valley Chamber of Commerce,** P.O. Box 31, Springerville, AZ 85938 (☎ **520/333-2123**).

## ANASAZI RUINS

✪ **White Mountain Archaeological Center/Raven Site Ruin.** H.C. 30, Box 30, St. Johns, AZ 85936. ☎ **888/333-5859** or 520/333-5857. Daily 10am–5pm (guided tours at 11am and 2pm). Hands-on programs $59 adults, $37 children 9–17 (children under 9 not accepted); tours $4 adults, $3 seniors and children 12–17; petroglyph hikes $18 adults, $15 children. 12 miles. north of Springerville off U.S. 180/191.

If you've ever dreamed about being an archaeologist, you've got a chance to do just that here in eastern Arizona. This field school and research center is located on a 5-acre pueblo site where Mogollon and Anasazi artifacts have been found. Hands-on archaeological programs allow visitors to assist in excavating this site while learning the basics of archaeology. Tours of the ruins, both guided and self-guided, and hikes to a nearby area rich in petroglyphs are also offered.

**Casa Malpais Archaeological Park.** 318 Main St., Springerville. ☎ **520/333-5375.** Guided tours $4 adults, $3 students and seniors, $1 children under 12. Daily 9am–4pm (due to shortage of staff, weekends are most reliable).

These Mogollon culture ruins, just outside Springerville, can also be visited, though you won't be able to do any digging. Casa Malpais is unique in that the pueblo, which dates

## Cowboy Golf

If you've spent much time in Arizona souvenir shops, you've probably seen humorous drawings of cowboys playing golf on the range. Well, each year in June, the **X Diamond Ranch** (☎ **520/333-2286**) west of Springerville actually does hold a charity cowboy golf tournament. What sets cowboy golf apart from regular golf? Well, first of all, the caddies are horses. Then there's the golfers' attire—cowboy boots, blue jeans, and cowboy hats. And, of course, there are the coffee-can holes and the tall-grass fairways, which are really just cow pastures, filled with all the hazards one would expect in a cow pasture. (A chip shot on this golf course can be a very messy affair!)

from A.D. 1250 and was occupied until about 600 years ago, was built to take advantage of existing caves. Many of these caves form a system of catacombs under the pueblo. The Casa Malpais museum is located downtown and it is from here that tours start.

**Lyman Lake State Park.** 18 miles north of Springerville. ☎ **520/337-4441.** Admission $4 per car; tours $2 per person. Park, daily; tours, Memorial Day–Labor Day (Sat–Sun).

Within this state park are the early Anasazi ruins of Rattlesnake Point Pueblo, as well as petroglyphs that date back to 10,000 B.C. Some of the petroglyphs are only accessible by boat, and during the summer months you can see them on guided tours.

### OTHER AREA MUSEUMS

Also in the area are a couple of small museums worth a look if you have the time. The **Reneé Cushman Art Collection** (☎ **520/333-4514**) is housed in the L.D.S. (Mormon) Church in Springerville and consists of one woman's personal collection of European art and antiques. Among the works in the collection are an etching attributed to Rembrandt and three pen-and-ink drawings by Tiepolo. The antique furniture dates back to the Renaissance. The museum is open by appointment only.

Local history and old automated musical instruments are the focus of the **Little House Museum** (☎ **520/333-2286**), located 7 miles west of Eagar on South Fork Road, off Ariz. 260. The museum is open late May through Labor Day; 90-minute tours in which visitors learn about colorful characters and events of Wild West days are offered Thursday through Monday. In winter, tours are by appointment only. Tours cost $4 for adults and $1.50 for children 12 and under.

### OUTDOOR ACTIVITIES

If you're interested in fishing, contact **Troutback Flyfishing Guide Service,** P.O. Box 864, Show Low, AZ 85902 (☎ **520/532-3474**), which charges $175 per day for one angler and $250 for two. Alternatively, you can head out to the **X Diamond Ranch,** P.O. Box 791, Springerville, AZ 85938 (☎ **520/333-2286**), which maintains a section of the Little Colorado River as a fishing habitat. A half day of fishing here will cost $25 and a full day will cost $35.

**Lyman Lake State Park** (☎ **520/337-4441**), 18 miles north of Springerville, is also popular for lake fishing. And if it's high summer and you feel like swimming, this is the place to take a dip or even plan a day of waterskiing or sailing.

### WHERE TO STAY

✪ **Paisley Corner Bed & Breakfast.** 287 N. Main St. (P.O. Box 458), Eagar, AZ 85938. ☎ **520/333-4665.** www.wmbba.com. 4 units. $65–$95 double. Rates include full breakfast. MC, V.

This lovingly restored 1910-vintage colonial-revival house in Eagar is one of the most authentic B&Bs we've visited and as such is one of our favorites in the state. (For *authentic*, read Victorian antiques and dark color schemes.) However, in contrast there is also a room done up to resemble an old soda fountain, complete with vintage juke-boxes and an old telephone booth in one corner. The inn's kitchen features a 1910 gas stove and looks as though it came straight out of a 1920s Sears and Roebuck catalog. Guest rooms on the second floor have antique beds, and two have bathrooms with claw-foot tubs and old pull-chain toilets.

**South Fork Guest Ranch.** P.O. Box 627, Springerville, AZ 85938. ☎ **888/333-3565** or 520/333-4455. Fax 520/333-4466. www.skioddessy.com. 14 cabins. $35–$120 double. MC, V.

Located just a few miles west of Eagar on Ariz. 260 at the confluence of the Little Colorado River and South Fork Creek, this 38-acre guest ranch is a popular summer vacation spot for families looking to get away from it all. The cabins vary from the very basic to luxurious, complete with king-size beds and fireplaces. The creek-side cabins are your best bet. Peace and tranquillity are the stock in trade here with trout fishing a favorite activity of guests.

**X Diamond Ranch.** P.O. Box 791, Springerville, AZ 85938. ☎ **520/333-2286.** Fax 520/333-5009. 5 units. $90–$125 double. MC, V.

Long known for its Little House Museum and trout fishing on the Little Colorado River, this ranch now also rents a variety of cabins ranging from an updated old log cabin to a couple of new cabins. Cabins have porches and good views. Ranch activities include fishing, horseback riding (including cattle drives), and tours of the ranch's two archaeological sites (there's a resident archaeologist). The ranch is located off Ariz. 260 between Eagar and Greer (take County Road 4124). There's no restaurant on the premises, but cabins have full kitchens.

## CAMPGROUNDS

**Lyman Lake State Park** (☎ **520/337-4441**), 18 miles north of Springerville on U.S. 180/191, is a good place to camp and is very popular in summer. Reservations are not taken, but except for the July 4th weekend, getting a campsite usually isn't a problem.

## WHERE TO DINE

There aren't a whole lot of dining options in this area. You might try **Booga Red's,** 521 Main St., Springerville (☎ **520/333-2640**); or **A Little Taste of Texas Bar-B-Q,** 1133 E. Main St., Springerville (☎ **520/333-3086**).

## 5 The Coronado Trail

Alpine: 28 miles S of Springerville & Eagar; 95 miles N of Clifton & Morenci; 75 miles E of Pinetop-Lakeside

If you are not prone to car sickness, you may want to take a leisurely drive down the Coronado Trail (U.S. 191). This is one of the most remote and little-traveled paved roads in the state, winding southward from Springerville and Eagar to the Clifton and Morenci area. Because this road is so narrow and winding, it is slow going—the sort of road meant for people who aren't in a hurry to get anywhere anytime soon.

The Coronado Trail is named for the Spanish explorer Francisco Vásquez de Coronado, who came to Arizona in the early 1540s in search of gold. Though he never found it, his party did make it as far north as the Hopi pueblos and would have traveled through this region on their march northward from Mexico. Centuries later the discovery of huge copper reserves would make the fortunes of the towns of Clifton and Morenci, which lie at the southern end of the Coronado Trail.

However, it is **Alpine,** at the northern end of the Coronado Trail (28 miles south of the end of Ariz. 260 at the junction of U.S. 180 and U.S. 191), that is the main base for today's explorers, who tend to be outdoor types in search of uncrowded trails and trout streams where the fish are still biting. In Alpine, which is not far from the New Mexico state line, you'll find a few basic lodges and restaurants and easy access to the region's many trails.

This area is known as the Alps of Arizona, and Alpine's picturesque setting in the middle of a wide grassy valley at 8,030 feet certainly lives up to this image. Alpine is surrounded by **Apache–Sitgreaves National Forest,** which has miles of hiking trails and several campgrounds. In spring, wildflowers abound, and the trout fishing is excellent. In summer, there's hiking on forest trails. In autumn, the aspens in the Golden Bowl on the mountainside above Alpine turn a brilliant yellow, and in winter, there's cross-country skiing and ice fishing.

## ESSENTIALS

**GETTING THERE**   Alpine is located 28 miles south of Springerville and Eagar at the junction of U.S. 191, which continues south to Clifton and Morenci, and U.S. 180, which leads east into New Mexico.

**VISITOR INFORMATION**   For more information on this area, contact the **Alpine Area Chamber of Commerce,** P.O. Box 410, Alpine, AZ 85920 (☎ 520/339-4330). For outdoors information, contact the Apache–Sitgreaves National Forest's **Alpine Ranger District,** P.O. Box 469, Alpine, AZ 85920 (☎ 520/339-4384).

## ENJOYING THE OUTDOORS

Fall, when the aspens turn the mountainside gold, is probably the most popular time of year in this area—there are only a few places in Arizona where fall color is worth a drive, and this is one of them.

Not far outside Alpine, there is cross-country skiing at the **Williams Valley Winter Recreation Area,** which doubles as a mountain-biking trail system in summer. On the first weekend in January, there are dog sled races in Alpine.

In Alpine you can also play a round of golf at the **Alpine Country Club** (☎ 520/339-4944), which is 3 miles east of town off U.S. 180. At 8,500 feet in elevation, this is one of the highest golf courses in the country.

If you're looking for fish to catch, try **Luna Lake,** which is east of Alpine off U.S. 180. Here at the lake, you'll also find some easy to moderate mountain-bike trails that usually offer good wildlife-viewing opportunities.

The best hiking in the area is the trail up **Escudilla Mountain** just outside Alpine. It is here that you'll see some of the best displays of aspens in the autumn.

Summer or winter, **Hannagan Meadows,** 23 miles south of Alpine, is the place to be. Here you'll find excellent hiking, mountain biking, and cross-country ski trails. Hannagan Meadows also provides access to the **Blue Range Primitive Area,** which is popular with hikers. The Eagle Trail, which starts 5 miles south of Hannagan Meadows off Eagle Creek Road is another good place to spot wildlife.

## WHERE TO STAY & DINE

Between Springerville/Eagar and Clifton/Morenci, there are nearly a dozen National Forest Service campgrounds. One particularly popular spot is **Luna Lake Campground** just east of Alpine on U.S. 180. The **Hannagan Meadows Campground** (no reservations) is also popular and makes a good base for exploring the Coronado Trail. Reservations are taken for Luna Lake Campground by calling the **National Recreation Reservation Service** (☎ 800/280-2267). For information on these campgrounds, contact the **Alpine Ranger District** (☎ 520/339-4384).

If you're looking for someplace to eat, you'll find a couple of basic restaurants in Alpine.

**Tal-Wi-Wi Lodge.** U.S. 191 (P.O. Box 169), Alpine, AZ 85920. ☎ **520/339-4319.** Fax 520/339-1962. www.AZ-high-country.com/talwiwi. 20 units. $65–$95 double. 2-night minimum on holidays. AE, MC, V. Dogs accepted ($5).

Located 3 miles north of Alpine on U.S. 191, the Tal-Wi-Wi Lodge is nothing fancy (just a rustic lodge popular with anglers and hunters), but it's the best place to stay in the Alpine area. The deluxe rooms come with their own hot tub or woodstove (one room comes with both), and these heat sources are well appreciated on cold winter nights (Alpine is often the coldest town in Arizona). The furnishings in the guest rooms are rustic and comfortable, and the wood-paneled walls and large front porches give the lodge a classic country flavor. The lodge's dining room serves country breakfasts and dinners.

# Tucson 9

Melding Hispanic, Anglo, and Native American roots, Tucson is a city with a strong sense of identity, aware of its desert setting, confident in its style. Back in the days of urban renewal, Tucson's citizens turned back the bulldozers and managed to preserve at least some of the city's old Mexican character. Likewise, today, in the face of the sort of sprawl that has turned Phoenix into something like another Los Angeles, advocates for controlled growth are fighting hard to preserve both Tucson's desert environment and the city's unique character. Today the struggle to retain an identity distinct from other southwestern cities continues, and despite long, drawn-out attempts to breathe life into the city's downtown, the Tucson Downtown Arts District has, in the past year, lost much of its vibrancy as shops have moved out and restaurants have closed down. But this only means that one small part of the city is waiting once again to have its day in the sun.

Founded by the Spanish in 1775, Tucson is built on the site of a much older Native American village. The city's name comes from the Pima Indian word *chukeson,* which means "spring at the base of black mountain," a reference to the peak now known simply as "A Mountain." From 1867 to 1877, Tucson was the territorial capital of Arizona, but eventually the capital was moved to Phoenix. Consequently, Tucson did not develop as quickly as Phoenix and holds fast to its Hispanic and Western heritage.

Despite its position as Arizona's second city, Tucson supports an active cultural life, with symphony, ballet, opera, and theater companies and many festivals celebrating aspects of local life. However, it's the city's natural surroundings that set Tucson apart. Four mountain ranges ring the city, and in those mountains and their foothills are giant saguaro cacti, an oasis, one of the finest zoos in the world, a ski area, and miles of hiking and horseback-riding trails. Understandably, the Tucson lifestyle is oriented toward the outdoors.

History, culture, and nature are the major attractions, but with its mild, sunny climate and mountain vistas, Tucson is a natural for resorts. The city may not yet have as many world-class resorts as the Valley of the Sun, but the ones in Tucson definitely boast the finer views.

# Tucson at a Glance

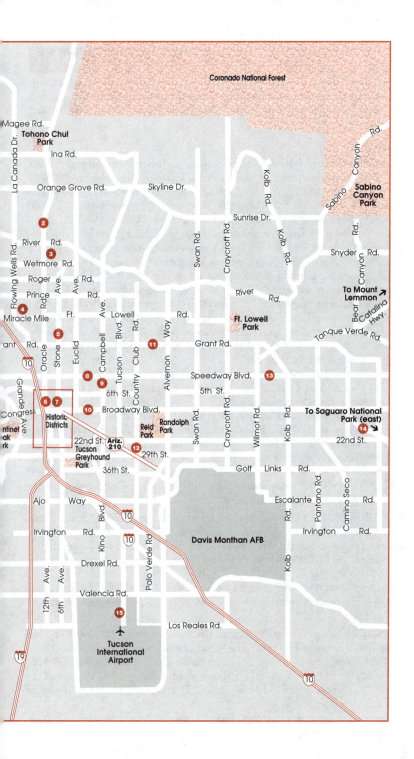

Coronado National Forest

Magee Rd.
**Tohono Chul Park**
Ina Rd.

La Canada Dr.

Orange Grove Rd.
Skyline Dr.

Kolb Rd.
Sunrise Dr.

**2**

River Rd.
**3**
Wetmore Rd.
Roger Ave. Rd.
Prince Rd.
**4**
Miracle Mile

Flowing Wells Rd.

Swan Rd.
Craycroft Rd.
River Rd.

Sabino Canyon Rd.
**Sabino Canyon Park**

Snyder Rd.

Bear Canyon Rd.

**To Mount Lemmon** ↗
Catalina Hwy.
Tanque Verde Rd.

Ft. Lowell Rd.
**Ft. Lowell Park**

Grant Rd.

**5**
Euclid
Campbell Ave.
Tucson Blvd.
Country Club Rd.
**11**
Way
Alvernon

Oracle
Stone

**10**

**8** **9**
6th St.

**6** **7**
**Historic Districts**

Grande Ave.
Congress
ntinel ak rk

Grant Rd.

Speedway Blvd.
**13**
5th St.

**10** Broadway Blvd.

**Reid Park**
**Randolph Park**
Swan Rd.
Craycroft Rd.
Wilmot Rd.
Kolb Rd.

**To Saguaro National Park (east)** ↘
**14**

22nd St. **Ariz. 210**
**Tucson Greyhound Park**
**12**
29th St.
36th St.

22nd St.

Ajo Way
**10**
Irvington Rd.
**10**

Kino Blvd.

Palo Verde Rd.

Drexel Rd.

12th Ave.
6th Ave.

Valencia Rd.
**15**
✈
**Tucson International Airport**

Golf Links Rd.

Escalante Rd.
Pantano Rd.
Camino Seco Rd.

Irvington Rd.

Kolb

**Davis Monthan AFB**

Los Reales Rd.

**19**

**10**

285

# 1  Orientation

Not nearly as large and spread out as Phoenix and the Valley of the Sun, Tucson is small enough to be convenient, yet large enough to be sophisticated. Compared to Phoenix, the mountains ringing the city of Tucson are bigger and closer to town, and the desert is equally close.

## ARRIVING

**BY PLANE**   Located 6 miles south of downtown, **Tucson International Airport** (☎ 520/573-8000) is served by many airlines, including **Aero México** (☎ 800/ 237-6639), **America West** (☎ 800/235-9292), **American** (☎ 800/433-7300), **Continental** (☎ 800/525-0280), **Delta** (☎ 800/ 843-9378), **Northwest** (☎ 800/ 225-2525), **Southwest** (☎ 800/435-9792), and **United** (☎ 800/241-6522).

At the airport you'll find car-rental desks, regularly scheduled shuttle vans to downtown, and taxis. In the baggage-claim area is a **visitor information center** where you can pick up brochures about Tucson and reserve a hotel room if you haven't done so already.

Many resorts and hotels in Tucson provide airport shuttle service and will pick you up and return you to the airport either for free or for a competitive fare, so check with your hotel. **Arizona Stagecoach** (☎ 520/889-1000) operates a daily 24-hour van service to downtown Tucson and the foothills resorts. You'll find the vans outside the center of the baggage-claim area. Fares for two people range from $15 to downtown to up to $32 to the foothills resorts. To return to the airport, it's best to call at least a day before your scheduled departure.

You'll also find taxis waiting in the same area, or you can call **Yellow Cab** (☎ 520/ 624-6611) or **Allstate Cab** (☎ 520/798-1111). A taxi to downtown costs around $16 and to the resorts about $24 to $38.

**Sun Tran** (☎ 520/792-9222), the local public transit, operates a bus service to and from the airport, though you'll have to make a transfer to reach downtown. The bus at the airport is no. 25 (ask for a transfer when you board); at the Roy Laos Transit Center you should transfer to no. 16 for downtown. The fare is 85¢. Route 25 from the airport operates daily Monday through Friday between about 6:30am and 7:30pm, on Saturday between about 7:30am and 7:30pm, and on Sunday between about 8:30am and 7:30pm. Departures are every hour.

**BY CAR**   **I-10,** the main east-west interstate across the southern United States, passes through Tucson as it swings north to Phoenix. **I-19** connects Tucson with the Mexican border at Nogales. **Arizona 86** heads southwest into the Papago Indian Reservation, and **U.S. 89** leads north toward Florence and eventually connects with **U.S. 60** into Phoenix.

If you're headed downtown, take the Congress Street exit off I-10. If you're headed for one of the foothills resorts north of downtown, you'll probably want to take the Ina Road exit.

**BY TRAIN**   Tucson is served by **Amtrak** passenger rail service (☎ 800/872-7245 in the United States and Canada). The Sunset Limited, which runs between Miami and Los Angeles, stops in Tucson. The **train station** is at 400 E. Toole Ave. (☎ 520/ 623-4442) in the heart of downtown Tucson and is within walking distance of the Tucson Convention Center, El Presidio Historic District, and a few hotels. You'll find taxis waiting to meet the train.

**BY BUS**   **Greyhound Lines** (☎ 800/231-2222 or 520/792-3475) connects Tucson to the rest of the United States through its extensive system. The bus station is at 2 S. Fourth Ave., across the street from the Hotel Congress in the Downtown Arts District.

## VISITOR INFORMATION

The **Metropolitan Tucson Convention and Visitors Bureau (MTCVB),** 130 S. Scott Ave., Tucson, AZ 85701 (☎ **800/638-8350** or 888/2-TUCSON; www. arizonaguide.com/visittucson), is an excellent source of information on Tucson and environs. You can contact the bureau before leaving home or stop in at the visitor center, which is stocked with brochures and has helpful people at the desk to answer your questions. The visitor center is open Monday through Friday from 8am to 5pm and on Saturday and Sunday from 9am to 4pm.

## CITY LAYOUT

**MAIN ARTERIES & STREETS**    Tucson is laid out on a grid that's fairly regular in the downtown areas but becomes less orderly the farther you go from the city center. In the foothills, where Tucson's most recent growth has occurred, the grid system breaks down completely because of the hilly terrain. Major thoroughfares are spaced at 1-mile intervals, with smaller streets filling in the squares created by the major roads.

The **main east-west roads** are (from south to north) 22nd Street, Broadway Boulevard, Speedway Boulevard, Grant Road (with Tanque Verde Road as an extension), and Ina Road/Skyline Drive. The **main north-south roads** are (from west to east) Miracle Mile/Oracle Road, Stone/Sixth Avenue, Campbell Avenue, Country Club Road, and Alvernon Road. **I-10** cuts diagonally across the Tucson metropolitan area from northwest to southeast.

In **downtown Tucson,** Congress Street and Broadway Boulevard are the main east-west streets and Stone Avenue, Fourth Avenue, and Sixth Avenue are the main north-south streets.

**FINDING AN ADDRESS**    Because Tucson is laid out on a grid, finding an address is relatively easy. The zero (or starting) point for all Tucson addresses is the corner of Stone Avenue, which runs north and south, and Congress Street, which runs east and west. From this point, streets are designated either north, south, east, or west. Addresses usually, but not always, increase by 100 with each block, so that an address of 4321 E. Broadway Blvd. should be 43 blocks east of Stone Avenue. In the downtown area, many of the streets and avenues are numbered, with numbered streets running east and west and numbered avenues running north and south.

**STREET MAPS**    The best way to find your way around Tucson is to pick up a map at the visitor information center at the airport or at the MTCVB (see "Visitor Information," above) for $2. The MTCVB also offers a free map in the *Tucson Official Visitors Guide.* The maps handed out by car-rental agencies are not very detailed, but will do for some purposes. Local gas stations also sell detailed maps.

## Neighborhoods in Brief

**El Presidio Historic District**    Named for the Spanish military garrison that once stood on this site, the neighborhood is bounded by Alameda Street on the south, Main Avenue on the west, Franklin Street on the north, and Church Avenue on the east. El Presidio was the city's most affluent neighborhood in the 1880s, and many large homes from that period have been restored and now house restaurants, arts-and-crafts galleries, and a bed-and-breakfast inn. The Tucson Museum of Art anchors the neighborhood.

**Barrio Histórico District**    Another 19th-century neighborhood, the Barrio Histórico is bounded on the north by Cushing Street, on the west by the railroad tracks, on the south by 18th Street, and on the east by Stone Avenue. The Barrio Histórico is characterized by Sonoran-style adobe row houses that directly abut the street with no yards, a style typical in Mexican towns. Although a few restaurants and art galleries dot the neighborhood, most restored buildings serve as offices. This is still a borderline neighborhood where restoration is a slow, ongoing process, so try to avoid it late at night.

**Armory Park Historic District**   Bounded by 12th Street on the north, Stone Avenue on the west, 19th Street on the south, and Second Avenue and Third Avenue on the east, the Armory Park neighborhood was Tucson's first historic district. Today this area is undergoing a renaissance but isn't yet an entirely safe place to wander after dark.

**Downtown Arts District**   This neighborhood encompasses a bit of the Armory District, a bit of El Presidio District, and the stretch of Congress Street and Broadway Boulevard west of Toole Avenue. Although the area is home to several galleries, nightclubs, and hip cafes, as of 1999, it had lost most of its best businesses and was struggling to survive as an arts district. Today it is mostly frequented by the young and the homeless.

**Fourth Avenue**   Running from University Boulevard in the north to Ninth Street in the south, Fourth Avenue is Tucson's hippest shopping district (although a little run-down and not tending upward as one would expect). Businesses cater to University of Arizona students with boutiques selling ethnic clothing and shops offering handcrafted items from around the world. Twice a year, in spring and late fall, the street is closed to traffic for a colorful street fair. With plenty of bars and restaurants, this street sees a lot of after-dark foot traffic that keeps it pretty safe.

**The Foothills**   Encompassing a huge area of northern Tucson, the foothills contain the city's most affluent neighborhoods. Elegant shopping plazas, modern malls, world-class resorts, golf courses, and expensive residential neighborhoods are surrounded by hilly desert at the foot of the Santa Catalina Mountains.

## 2 Getting Around

### BY CAR

Unless you plan to stay by the pool or on the golf course, you'll probably want to rent a car. See "Getting Around," in chapter 2, for details on renting a car in Arizona. Luckily, rates are fairly economical, especially if you can skip the collision-damage waiver. At press time, Budget was charging $169 per week or $41 per day for a compact car with unlimited mileage in Tucson.

The **car-rental agencies** below have offices at Tucson International Airport: **Alamo** (☎ 800/327-9633), **Avis** (☎ 800/331-1212), **Budget** (☎ 800/279-3734), **Dollar** (☎ 800/800-4000), **Enterprise** (☎ 800/736-8222, **Hertz** (☎ 800/654-3131), **National** (☎ 800/227-7368), and **Thrifty** (☎ 800/367-2277). Several companies have offices in other parts of the city as well, so be sure to ask if they have a more convenient location for pickup or drop-off of your car.

Downtown Tucson is still a relatively easy place to find a parking space, and parking fees are low. There are two huge parking lots at the south side of the Tucson Convention Center, a couple of small lots on either side of the Tucson Museum of Art (one at Main Avenue and Paseo Redondo, south of El Presidio Historic District, and one at the corner of Council Street and Court Avenue), and parking garages beneath the main library and El Presidio Park. You'll also find plenty of metered parking on the smaller downtown streets. Almost all Tucson hotels and resorts provide free parking.

Lanes on several major avenues in Tucson change direction at rush hour to facilitate traffic flow, so pay attention to signs hung over the street. These tell you the time and direction of traffic in the lanes.

## BY PUBLIC TRANSPORTATION

**BY BUS**    Covering much of the Tucson Metropolitan area, **Sun Tran** (☎ 520/792-9222) public buses cost only 85¢ for adults, 60¢ for students, 35¢ for senior citizens, and are free for children 5 and under. Monthly bus passes are available.

Bus stops are marked by signs that provide information on which buses stop there, the major streets they serve, and their final destinations. The **Downtown-Ronstadt Transit Center,** at the corner of Congress Street and Sixth Avenue, is served by about 30 regular and express bus routes to all parts of Tucson.

The bus system does not extend to such tourist attractions as the Arizona–Sonora Desert Museum, Old Tucson, Saguaro National Park, or the foothills resorts and, consequently, is of limited use to visitors. However, Sun Tran does provide a shuttle for sports games and special events. Call ☎ **520/792-9222** for information.

**BY TROLLEY**    Though they don't go very far, the restored electric streetcars of **Old Pueblo Trolley** (☎ 520/792-1802) are a fun way to get from the Fourth Avenue shopping district to the University of Arizona. The trolleys operate on Friday from 6pm to 10pm, on Saturday from noon to midnight, and on Sunday from noon to 6pm. The fare is $1 for adults and 50¢ for children 6 to 12; children under 5 ride free. All-day passes are $2.50 for adults and $1.25 for children.

## BY TAXI

If you need a taxi, you'll have to phone for one. **Yellow Cab** (☎ **520/624-6611**) and **Allstate Cab** (☎ **520/798-1111**) provide service throughout the city. Fares start at about $1.25, and after that it's $1.50 per mile. Although distances in Tucson are not as great as those in Phoenix, it's still a good 10 or more miles from the foothills resorts to downtown Tucson, so expect to pay at least $10 for any taxi ride. Most resorts offer or can arrange taxi service to the major tourist attractions around Tucson.

Shoppers should keep in mind that several Tucson shopping malls offer free shuttle service from hotels and resorts. Be sure to ask at your hotel before paying for a ride to a mall.

## ON FOOT

Downtown Tucson is compact and easily explored on foot. Many old streets in the downtown historic neighborhoods are narrow and much easier to appreciate if you leave your car in a parking lot. On the other hand, several major attractions, including the Arizona–Sonora Desert Museum, Old Tucson Studios, Saguaro National Park, and Sabino Canyon, require quite a bit of walking, often on uneven footing, so be sure to bring a good pair of walking shoes.

# Fast Facts: Tucson

**American Express**    The local American Express representative in the Tucson area is Bon Voyage Travel, with 10 offices. One is located at 3375 N. Campbell Ave., at Ft. Lowell Road (☎ **520/795-8991**), open Monday through Friday from 8:30am to 5:30pm.

**Baby-sitters**    Most hotels can arrange a baby-sitter for you, and many resorts feature special programs for children on weekends and throughout the summer.

If your hotel can't help, call **A-1 Messner Sitter Service** (☎ 520/881-1578), which will send a sitter to your hotel.

**Car Rentals**   See "Getting Around," earlier in this chapter.

**Climate**   See "When to Go," in chapter 2.

**Dentist**   Call the **Arizona State Dental Association** (☎ 800/866-2732) for a dentist referral.

**Doctor**   For a doctor referral, call ☎ 800/230-CARE.

**Emergencies**   For fire, police, or medical emergency, phone ☎ 911.

**Eyeglasses**   **Alvernon Optical** has several stores around town where you can have your glasses repaired or replaced. Locations include 440 N. Alvernon Way (☎ 520/327-6211), 7043 N. Oracle Rd. (☎ 520/297-2501), and 7123 E. Tanque Verde Rd. (☎ 520/296-4157).

**Hospitals**   The **Tucson General Hospital** is at 3838 N. Campbell Ave. (☎ 520/318-6300); the **Tucson Medical Center** is at 5301 E. Grant Rd. (☎ 520/327-5461); and the **University Medical Center** is at 1501 N. Campbell Ave. (☎ 520/694-0111).

**Information**   See "Visitor Information" in "Orientation," earlier in this chapter.

**Internet Access**   The hot spot in downtown Tucson is **The Library of Congress** at the Hotel Congress, 311 E. Congress St. (☎ 520/622-2708).

**Lost Property**   If you lose something and you don't know where, try the **Tucson Police Department Found-Recovered Property Office** (☎ 520/791-4458). If you lose something at the airport, call ☎ 520/573-8156; if you lose something on a Sun Tran bus, call ☎ 520/792-9222.

**Newspapers/Magazines**   The *Arizona Daily Star* is Tucson's morning daily, and the *Tucson Citizen* is the afternoon daily. The *Tucson Weekly* is the city's weekly news-and-arts journal; it's published on Thursday. **Crescent Tobacco and News,** 200 E. Congress St. (☎ 520/622-1559) and 7037 E. Tanque Verde Rd. (☎ 520/296-3102), carries newspapers and magazines from all over the country.

**Pharmacies**   Walgreens has stores all over Tucson. Call ☎ 800/WALGREENS for the Walgreens pharmacy that's nearest you or that's open 24 hours a day.

**Photographic Needs**   **NuArt Photo,** at 7090 N. Oracle Rd. (☎ 520/797-2493), and El Con Mall, 3601 E. Broadway Blvd. (☎ 520/327-7062), can supply camera needs or repairs.

**Police**   In case of an emergency, phone ☎ 911.

**Post Office**   There's a post office in downtown Tucson at 141 S. Sixth Ave. (☎ 800/275-8777), open Monday through Friday from 8:30am to 5pm and on Saturday from 9am to noon.

**Radio**   KXCI (91.3 FM) has an alternative mix of programming and is a favorite with local Tucsonans, while **KUAT** (90.5 FM) has all-classical programming and is a good station for news. **KUAZ** (89.1 FM) is National Public Radio.

**Safety**   Tucson is surprisingly safe for a city of its size. However, the Downtown Arts District isn't all that lively after dark, and you should be particularly alert in this area if you're down here for a performance of some sort. An exception is on the nights of Downtown Saturday Night festivities. Just to the south of downtown Tucson lies a poorer section of the city that's best avoided after dark unless you are certain of where you're going. Otherwise, take the same precautions you would in any other city.

When driving, be aware that many streets in the Tucson area are subject to flooding when it rains. Heed warnings about possible flooded areas and don't try to cross a low area that has become flooded. Find an alternative route instead.

**Taxes**   In addition to the 5% state sales tax, Tucson levies a 2% city sales tax. State car-rental tax is 5% (plus there are other taxes and surcharges on car rentals). The hotel room tax is 9.5% (plus $1 per day occupancy tax).

**Taxis**   See "Getting Around," earlier in this chapter.

**Television**   You can get Channels 4 (NBC), 6 (PBS), 9 (ABC), 11 (Fox), 13 (CBS), and 58 (Warner Brothers).

**Transit Information**   For information on **Sun Tran** public buses, phone ☎ **520/792-9222.**

**Weather**   Phone ☎ **520/881-3333** for the local weather forecast.

## 3  Where to Stay

Though Phoenix still holds the title of Resort Capital of Arizona, Tucson is not far behind, and this city's resorts boast much more spectacular settings than many comparable resorts in Phoenix and Scottsdale. Also, as far as nonresort accommodations go, Tucson has a wider variety of accommodations than Phoenix—partly because several historic neighborhoods around Tucson are becoming home to bed-and-breakfast inns. The presence of several guest ranches within a 20-minute drive of Tucson also adds to the city's diversity of accommodations. Business and budget travelers are well served with all-suite and conference hotels, as well as plenty of budget chain motels.

If you're looking to stay in a bed-and-breakfast inn while in Tucson, you can contact several agencies. The **Arizona Association of Bed and Breakfast Inns,** P.O. Box 22086, Phoenix, AZ 86002-2086 (☎ **800/284-2589;** www.bbonline.com/az/aabbi/index.html), has several members in Tucson. **Advance Reservations Inn Arizona/Mi Casa-Su Casa Bed & Breakfast Reservation Service,** P.O. Box 950, Tempe, AZ 85280-0950 (☎ **800/456-0682** or 480/990-0682), will book you into one of its many homestays in the Tucson area (or elsewhere in the state), as will **Arizona Trails Bed & Breakfast Reservation Service,** P.O. Box 18998, Fountain Hills, AZ 85269-8998 (☎ **888/799-4284** or 480/837-4284; fax 480/816-4224; www.arizonatrails.com), which also books tour and hotel reservations.

At the more expensive hotels and resorts, summer room rates, usually in effect from May to September or October, are roughly half what they are in winter. Temperatures usually aren't unbearable in May or September, which makes these good times to visit if you're looking to save money on an Arizona vacation. Different hotels change their rates on different dates and these rates change from year to year, so always ask when rates are scheduled to go up or down.

Most hotels also offer special packages, weekend rates, various discounts, and free accommodations for children, so it also helps to ask when you reserve. Also keep in mind that nearly all hotels have no-smoking and wheelchair-accessible rooms.

In the following listings, price categories are based on the rate for a double room (with tax included) in high season (most resorts and hotels charge the same for a single or double room). Keep in mind that the rates listed are what hotels call "rack rates." Various discounts are often available that will reduce these rates (AAA, AARP, and so on), so be sure to ask if any specials or discounted rates are available. Also, if you aren't coming to Tucson specifically for the winter gem and mineral shows, then you'll save quite a bit on your room if you avoid the last week in January and the first 2 weeks in February, when hotels around town generally charge exorbitant rates.

# Tucson Accommodations

Adobe Rose Inn 24
Arizona Inn 23
Best Western
  Ghost Ranch Lodge 8
Best Western Inn at
  the Airport 10
Canyon Ranch 33
Catalina Park Inn 21
Clarion Hotel Tucson Airport 11
Clarion Hotel & Suites
  Santa Rita 18
Days Inn Tucson 16
Doubletree Guest Suites 28
Doubletree Hotel at
  Reid Park 33
El Presidio Bed & Breakfast Inn 19
Elysian Grove Market 17
Hacienda del Sol
  Guest Ranch Resort 6
Hawthorn Suites Ltd. 30
Hotel Congress 20
La Tierra Linda Guest
  Ranch Resort 1
The Lodge at Ventana
  Canyon 31
The Lodge on the Desert 25
Loews Ventana Canyon
  Resort 32
Motel 6 12 13
Motel 6—Tucson/
  Congress Street 15
Motel 6—Tucson/
  22nd Street 14
Omni Tucson National
  Golf Resort & Spa 2
Sheraton El Conquistador
  Resort & Country Club 3
Smuggler's Inn 27
Starr Pass Golf Resort 9
Sunstone Guest Ranch 29
Super 8—Tucson/Downtown 22
Super 8—Tucson/East 26
Westin La Paloma 5
Westward Look Resort 4
Windmill Inn at
  St. Philip's Plaza 7

NA-0262

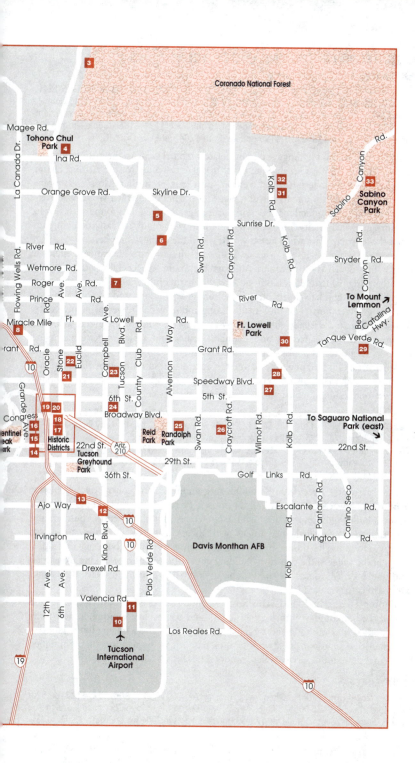

Coronado National Forest

**3**

Magee Rd.

**Tohono Chul Park** **4**

Ina Rd.

La Canada Dr.

Orange Grove Rd.

Skyline Dr.

Kolb Rd. **32**
**31**

Sabino Canyon Rd.

**33**

**Sabino Canyon Park**

**5**

Sunrise Dr.

Craycroft Rd.

Swan Rd.

Kolb Rd.

**6**

Flowing Wells Rd.

River Rd.

Wetmore Rd.

Roger Rd.

Prince Rd.

Ave.

Ave. Rd.

**7**

Snyder Rd.

Bear Canyon Rd.

**To Mount Lemmon**

Catalina Hwy.

Miracle Mile

**8**

Ft. Lowell Rd.

Campbell Ave.

Lowell Blvd.

Country Club Rd.

Way

River Rd.

**Ft. Lowell Park**

Tanque Verde Rd.

**30**

**29**

rant Rd.

**10**

Oracle

Stone

**22**

Euclid

**21**

**23**

Tucson

6th St.

**24**

Country Club

Alvernon

Grant Rd.

Speedway Blvd.

5th St.

**28**

**27**

Swan Rd.

Craycroft Rd.

Wilmot Rd.

Kolb Rd.

**To Saguaro National Park (east)**

Grande Ave.

**19** **20**

Congress

**16**

**18**

**15**

**17**

**14**

**Historic Districts**

Broadway Blvd.

**Reid Park** **25**

**Randolph Park**

**26**

22nd St.

Ariz. 210

**Tucson Greyhound Park**

29th St.

36th St.

22nd St.

**13**

Ajo Way

**12**

Irvington Rd.

**10**

Kino Blvd.

Drexel Rd.

12th Ave.

6th Ave.

Valencia Rd.

**11**

**10**

**Tucson International Airport**

Palo Verde Rd.

Los Reales Rd.

Golf Links Rd.

**Davis Monthan AFB**

Escalante Rd.

Pantano Rd.

Camino Seco Rd.

Irvington Rd.

Kolb Rd.

**19**

**10**

293

# DOWNTOWN & THE UNIVERSITY AREA
## EXPENSIVE

**✪ Arizona Inn.** 2200 E. Elm St., Tucson, AZ 85719. ☎ **800/933-1093** or 520/325-1541. Fax 520/320-2182. 82 units, 3 houses. A/C TV TEL. Mid-Jan to mid-Apr $195–$245 double, from $247 suite; mid-Apr to May 31 $170–$230 double, from $207 suite; June 1 to mid-Sept $98–$110 double, from $120 suite; mid-Sept to mid-Dec $130–$186 double, from $184 suite; mid-Dec to mid-Jan $150–$196 double, from $204 suite. AE, DC, MC, V.

With its pink stucco buildings and immaculately tended gardens, the historic Arizona Inn, opened in 1930, is an absolute oasis. If you're searching for old Arizona charm but also demand modern levels of comfort, then look no further. Most guest rooms here have original furniture (much of it made for the inn by disabled World War I veterans) as well as reproductions of period furnishings. Strolling the grounds, relaxing in the antiques-filled library lounge, or cozying into your room, it's easy to conjure up those slower paced days when guests would spend the entire winter here.

Guest rooms are often very spacious, and most suites have private patios or enclosed sunporches, as well as sitting rooms. Although bathrooms are generally fairly small and have their original fixtures, this only adds to the charm of the rooms. Some rooms also have fireplaces, and hair dryers, irons, and ironing boards are standard.

**Dining/Diversions:** The inn's main dining room, which serves primarily continental cuisine, is a casually elegant hall with plenty of outdoor seating as well. The lounge is filled with greenery and Audubon prints, and a pianist performs in the evening. There's also a poolside bar and restaurant.

**Amenities:** Outdoor pool (the warmest in Tucson and surrounded by fragrant flowering trees and vines), two tennis courts, croquet court, modern and well-equipped exercise room, saunas, table tennis, concierge, room service, massages.

**Doubletree Hotel at Reid Park.** 445 S. Alvernon Way, Tucson, AZ 85711. ☎ **800/222-TREE** or 520/881-4200. Fax 520/323-5225. 306 units. A/C TV TEL. Early Jan to early Apr $119–$165 double, $250–$475 suite; mid-Apr to mid-May and late Sept to mid-Dec $89–$119 double, $175–$375 suite; late May to mid-Sept $59–$79 double, $150–$375 suite; late Dec to early Jan $69–$99 double, $150–$375 suite. AE, CB, DC, DISC, MC, V. Pets accepted ($50 deposit).

Located across the street from Randolph Park municipal golf course, the Doubletree is midway between the airport and downtown Tucson and can be thought of as an in-town budget golf resort. Although the hotel does a lot of convention business and sometimes feels crowded, the gardens, with their citrus trees and roses, are almost always tranquil. The rooms are divided between a nine-story building that offers views of the valley and a two-story building with patio rooms overlooking the garden and pool area. All rooms are comfortably appointed with contemporary furnishings and have coffee-makers.

**Dining/Diversions:** The Cactus Rose Restaurant serves Southwestern cuisine (and one of the best Sunday brunches in Tucson), and the Javelina Cantina, a more lively place, serves Mexican food and megamargaritas. There's also a quieter lobby lounge.

**Amenities:** Outdoor pool, whirlpool, exercise room, six tennis courts, boutiques, car-rental desk, room service, valet/laundry service.

## MODERATE

**Adobe Rose Inn.** 940 N. Olsen Ave., Tucson, AZ 85719. ☎ **800/328-4122** or 520/318-4644. Fax 520/325-0055. 5 units. A/C TV. Mid-Dec to May $95–$125 double; June to Aug $65–$75 double; Sept to mid-Dec $75–$95 double. Rates include full breakfast. AE, DC, DISC, MC, V.

Located in a quiet residential neighborhood only a few blocks from the University of Arizona campus, this B&B, with its strikingly angular adobe buildings, has the feel of a little village. Our favorite room is right off the entrance hall and has a brick floor, beehive fireplace, and colorful stained-glass windows. For extra privacy, you can opt for the room in the cottage out back. Almost the first thing you see as you step through the front door is the blue of the swimming pool outside a large picture window. There's also a hot tub. Furnishings throughout the inn are of peeled lodge-pole pine logs for a sort of contemporary Southwestern rustic look.

**Catalina Park Inn.** 309 E. 1st St., Tucson, AZ 85705. ☎ **800/792-4885** or 520/792-4541. www.catalinaparkinn.com. 6 units. A/C TV TEL. $95–$125 double (lower rates in summer and fall). Rates include full breakfast. DISC, MC, V.

Located just a few blocks from the Fourth Avenue shopping district and overlooking a shady park, this bed-and-breakfast inn has the look of a Mediterranean villa. Built in 1927, the home has been lovingly restored by owners Mark Hall and Paul Richard, and many interesting and playful touches enliven the classic interior (a crystal chandelier in a bathroom, beautifully lit display cases in the living room, a formal dining room, and a rustic breakfast room). The huge basement room is one of our favorites. Not only does it conjure up the inside of an adobe, but there's a whirlpool tub in a former cedar closet and a separate toilet room with a display of colorful Fiesta ware. Two of the rooms are in a separate cottage across the back garden, and these offer more contemporary styling than do the rooms in the main house. Two upstairs rooms have balconies.

✪ **El Presidio Bed & Breakfast Inn.** 297 N. Main Ave., Tucson, AZ 85701. ☎ **800/349-6151** or 520/623-6151. Fax 520/623-3860. 3 units. TV TEL. $95–$115 double. Rates include full breakfast. 2-night minimum in winter season. No credit cards.

Built in 1886 and lovingly restored by innkeeper Patti Toci and her husband, Jerry, El Presidio is a mix of Victorian and adobe architectural styles. This old house, located only steps from the Tucson Museum of Art, Old Town Artisans, and El Charro Cafe, is the quintessential Tucson territorial home and is now filled with interesting antiques. There is one high-ceilinged guest suite in the main house, while the other two, both with kitchenettes, are arranged around a shady courtyard at the center of which is a Mexican-style fountain. All three suites are decorated with antiques and original art (much of it by Jerry), and have kitchenettes. In addition to the filling breakfast in the sunroom, there are complimentary drinks, fruit, and treats in the afternoon and evening.

**Elysian Grove Market.** 400 W. Simpson St., Tucson, AZ 85701. ☎ **520/628-1522.** www.bbonline.com/az/elysiangrove. 2 units. $75 double. Rates include continental or Mexican breakfast. No credit cards. Well-supervised pets accepted.

Located in the Barrio Histórico just a block away from El Tiradito shrine, this former general store (the building still has the old store name painted on the front wall) is now an unusual little inn filled with rustic Mexican antiques and Hispanic folk art. The two suites consists of high-ceilinged living rooms that incorporate all manner of salvaged architectural details, colorful textiles, folk art, and original grocery store fixtures (including an old walk-in meat locker that has now been turned into a kitchen). Each suite has a bedroom on the ground level and a second bedroom (rather dark but cool) down a flight of steps. Although this funky barrio B&B isn't for everyone, the old Mexican atmosphere and abundance of art will appeal to travelers searching for a place with the feel of old Tucson. There are plans to add two more bathrooms so that every room will have its own private bathroom.

✪ **The Lodge on the Desert.** 306 N. Alvernon Way, Tucson, AZ 85711. ☎ **800/456-5634** or 520/325-3366. Fax 520/327-5834. www.lodgeonthedesert.com. 39 units. A/C TV TEL. Jan to mid-May $128–$205 double, $205–$225 suite; mid-May to mid-Sept $52–$105 double, $92–$115 suite; mid-Sept to mid-Dec $88–$145 double, $128–$160 suite. Rates include full breakfast Jan to mid-May only. AE, CB, DC, DISC, MC, V. Pets accepted ($50 deposit).

Dating from 1936, the Lodge on the Desert was, until a couple of years ago, a dated hotel that appealed primarily to families that had been coming here for generations. However, under new management, the hotel is being transformed into a romantic getaway. The lodge consists primarily of hacienda-style adobe buildings in a garden compound shaded by palm, orange, and eucalyptus trees, and the neatly manicured lawns and flower gardens offer a lush and relaxing retreat. In the rooms—some with tile floors, others carpeted—you'll find a mix of contemporary and Southwestern furnishings, as well as coffeemakers and hair dryers. Many rooms also have beamed ceilings or fireplaces (though the fireplace rooms sometimes smell of smoke). **Cielos,** the hotel's elegant restaurant, still seems to be searching for its niche in the city's restaurant scene, and the pool (the original) is very small, though it has a good view of the Catalinas.

## INEXPENSIVE

In addition to the inexpensive hotels listed below, you'll find dozens of budget chain motels along I-10 as it passes through downtown Tucson. Among the better choices are **Days Inn Tucson,** 222 S. Freeway, Exit 258 (☎ **520/791-7511**), charging $55 to $129 double; **Motel 6—Tucson/Congress Street,** 960 S. Freeway, Exit 258 (☎ **520/628-1339**), and **Motel 6—Tucson/22nd Street,** 1222 S. Freeway, Exit 259 (☎ **520/624-2516**), both charging $36 to $51 double; and **Super 8—Tucson/Downtown,** 1248 N. Stone St., Exit 257 (☎ **520/622-6446**), charging $47 to $92 double. See the appendix for a list of toll-free numbers.

✪ **Best Western Ghost Ranch Lodge.** 801 W. Miracle Mile, Tucson, AZ 85705. ☎ **800/456-7565** or 520/791-7565. Fax 520/791-3898. www.ghostranchlodge.com. 83 units. A/C TV TEL. Jan–Apr $78–$110 double; May–June and Nov–Dec $54–$96 double; July–Oct $42–$78 double. Rates include continental breakfast. AE, CB, DC, DISC, MC, V. Pets accepted.

Although Miracle Mile was once Tucson's main drag, today it's looking a bit shabby. One exception is the Ghost Ranch Lodge, which opened in 1941 and was for many years one of Tucson's desert resorts catering to northern visitors who stayed for the winter. If you're looking for affordable Old Tucson, this is it. Situated on 8 acres, the lodge has a justly famous cactus garden, orange grove, and extensive lawns that together create an oasis atmosphere. The guest rooms were refurbished recently but retain a bit of Western flavor, with beamed ceilings, painted brick walls, and patios covered by red-tile roofs. The lodge's dining room serves Southwestern-style meals and offers dining on a poolside patio or inside with a view of the Santa Catalina Mountains. Facilities include a small pool and a whirlpool.

**Clarion Hotel & Suites Santa Rita.** 88 E. Broadway Blvd., Tucson, AZ 85701. ☎ **800/CLARION** or 520/622-4000. Fax 520/620-0376. www.presidiohotels.com. 153 units. A/C TV TEL. Jan–Apr $99 double, $119–$149 suite; May–Sept $59 double, $99–$109 suite; Oct–Dec $79 double, $109–$149 suite. Rates include continental breakfast. AE, DISC, MC, V. Pets accepted.

Although this hotel, located only a block from the convention center and close to El Presidio Historic District, isn't exactly luxurious, you'd never know that it's nearly 100 years old. Completely remodeled and updated a few years ago, the Clarion stays busy with conventioneers, but it can also be a good choice for vacationers looking for an economical downtown location. Benefits of staying here include the complimentary breakfast, an evening cocktail hour, and free local phone calls. Best of all, however, is that this hotel is home to Cafe Poca Cosa, Tucson's most innovative (and colorful) Mexican restaurant. In the guest rooms, you might find such touches as ergonomic office chairs, hair dryers, coffeemakers, refrigerators, microwaves, and irons and ironing boards. Facilities include saunas and a surprisingly pleasant little pool in a lushly landscaped courtyard.

---

### ⓘ  Family-Friendly Hotels

**Loews Ventana Canyon Resort** *(see p. 299)*   With a playground, kids club, croquet court, table tennis, basketball hoop, and its own waterfall, this resort has plenty to keep the kids busy. There's also a hiking trail that starts from the edge of the property, and Sabino Canyon Recreation Area is just a free shuttle away.

**Smuggler's Inn** *(see p. 298)*   Built around a large central courtyard with a very tropical feel, this hotel is a good choice for families on a budget. In addition to a pool and whirlpool, there are lawns for the kids to play on and a meandering pond that's home to fish and ducks

**Westin La Paloma** *(see p. 300)*   Kids get their own lounge and games room, and in the summer and during holiday periods there are special programs for the kids so parents can have a little free time. There's also a great water slide in the pool area.

**Guest Ranches**   The Tucson area has several guest ranches, most of which are family oriented. Kids can play cowboy to their heart's content, riding the range and singing songs by campfire.

---

✪ **Hotel Congress.** 311 E. Congress St., Tucson, AZ 85701. ☎ **800/722-8848** or 520/622-8848. Fax 520/792-6366. www.hotcong.com. 40 units. TEL. $32–$75 double. $14 per person in shared hostel rooms. AE, MC, V. Pets accepted.

Located in the heart of downtown Tucson, the Hotel Congress, built in 1919 to serve railroad passengers, once played host to John Dillinger. Today the hotel, conveniently located near the Greyhound and Amtrak stations, operates as a budget hotel and youth hostel and is particularly popular with European backpack travelers. Although the hotel is far from luxurious, the lobby has been restored to its original Southwestern elegance (straight out of a film noir set). With antique telephones and old radios that really work, guest rooms remain true to their historical character, so don't expect anything fancy (like TVs). Some bathrooms have bathtubs only, and others have showers only. There's a classic little diner/cafe off the lobby (think Edward Hopper meets Gen X), as well as a tiny though very genuine Western bar. At night the Club Congress is a very popular dance club (guests can pick up free earplugs at the front desk). There's even a cybercafe called the Library of Congress.

## EAST TUCSON
### MODERATE

**Doubletree Guest Suites.** 6555 E. Speedway Blvd., Tucson, AZ 85710. ☎ **800/222-TREE** or 520/721-7100. Fax 520/721-1991. www.dtguestsuites.com. 304 suites. A/C TV TEL. Mid-Sept to mid-Jan $144–$154 double; mid-Jan to early Apr $94–$114 double; early Apr to mid-May $94–$114 double; mid-May to mid-Sept $75–$85 double. Rates include full breakfast (lower rates without breakfast). AE, DISC, MC, V. Pets accepted ($25 nonrefundable fee).

With surprisingly reasonable rates throughout the year, this all-suite hotel is a good choice for both those who need plenty of space and those who want to be in the east-side business corridor. The five-story brick building is arranged around two long garden courtyards, one of which has a large pool and whirlpool. The pool and gardens, along with the full breakfast and evening cocktail hour, are the best reasons for vacationers to stay here. The two-room suites feature contemporary furnishings and all have refrigerators, coffeemakers, hair dryers, and irons and ironing boards (most also have microwaves). Food in the hotel's restaurant is uneven, but the cookies you get at check-in are great! An exercise room (and access to a nearby health club), room service, and valet/laundry service round out the amenities here.

**Hawthorn Suites Ltd.** 7007 E. Tanque Verde Rd., Tucson, AZ 85715. ☎ **800/527-1133** or 520/298-2300. Fax 520/298-6756. www.hawthorn.com. 90 units. A/C TV TEL. Jan–Mar $99–$125 double; Apr–May and Oct–Dec $79–$89 double; June–Sept $59–$69 double. Rates include full breakfast. AE, CB, DC, DISC, MC, V. Pets accepted ($25 nonrefundable fee).

Though it looks rather stark from the outside, the Hawthorn Suites Ltd., which is built around four tranquil and lushly planted garden courtyards, is surprisingly pleasant inside. Most rooms are quite large and have coffeemakers and irons and ironing boards (some also have kitchenettes). There's no restaurant on the premises, but numerous excellent restaurants are nearby (Tanque Verde is Tucson's restaurant row), which makes this a good choice for a foodie on a budget. Facilities include a pool and whirlpool (and access to a nearby fitness center). Local phone calls are free, and there's a complimentary cocktail reception each evening.

✪ **Smuggler's Inn.** 6350 E. Speedway Blvd. (at Wilmot), Tucson, AZ 85710. ☎ **800/525-8852** or 520/296-3292. Fax 520/722-3713. E-mail: smugglers@rtd.com. 150 units. A/C TV TEL. Mid-Jan to Mar $99–$119 double, $125–$135 suite; Apr–May $89–$119 double, $125 suite; June–Sept $79 double, $89 suite; Oct–Dec $89–$119 double, $99 suite. AE, CB, DC, DISC, MC, V.

Built around an attractive garden and pond, the Smuggler's Inn is a very comfortable and economically priced hotel, and the neatly trimmed lawns and tall palm trees give the garden a very tropical look. There's nothing about this place to remind you that you're in the middle of the desert, but the grounds are much nicer than you'll find at most other comparably priced hotels in the area. Amid these tropical surroundings you'll find the pool, whirlpool, and putting green. Guest rooms are spacious, and all have modern furnishings and a balcony or patio. There are also such amenities as coffeemakers and video games on the TVs. A fairly recent renovation has kept the rooms in good shape. There's a cocktail lounge here, but at press time, the restaurant was no longer open for business. Room service and golf and health club privileges are available.

✪ **Sunstone Guest Ranch.** 2545 N. Woodland Rd., Tucson, AZ 85749. ☎ **520/749-1928.** Fax 520/749-2456. www.azstarnet.com/~sunston. 11 units. A/C TEL. Sept 1–May 31 $125 double; June 1–Aug 31 $95 double. Rates include breakfast. MC, V.

Although not exactly a guest ranch, this inn offers a beautiful ranchlike setting in a pocket of grassland surrounded by desert and suburbs. Though you'll feel as if you're on a remote spread, the gourmet dining of Tucson's restaurant row is only a 10-minute drive away. Basically, it's the best of both worlds—a little bit of country and a little bit of city. Accommodations are in a pair of 1920s baked-adobe buildings fronted by long verandas. Rooms are large and decorated in modern Southwest style with the occasional Mission-style antique. Bathrooms, though small, are functional. Surrounding these buildings are lush green lawns and huge old mesquite trees that keep the grounds delightfully shady. A heated pool, whirlpool, tennis court and basketball courts, and horseshoe pits provide plenty of recreational opportunities.

## THE FOOTHILLS
### VERY EXPENSIVE

**The Lodge at Ventana Canyon.** 6200 N. Clubhouse Lane, Tucson, AZ 85750. ☎ **888/GRAN-BAY** or 520/577-1400. Fax 520/577-4065. 49 units. A/C TV TEL. Oct to late Jan and Apr to early May $295–$345 1-bedroom suite, $495–$595 2-bedroom suite; late Jan to Mar $395–$455 1-bedroom suite, $595–$695 2-bedroom suite; late May to Sept $125–$175 1-bedroom suite, $215–$255 2-bedroom suite; Oct to early Jan $295–$345 1-bedroom suite, $395–$495 2-bedroom suite. AE, DC, DISC, MC, V.

Golf is the name of the game at this small boutique resort, which is set within a gated country-club community at the base of the Santa Catalina Mountains. Though small, the lodge manages to offer plenty of big-resort amenities and places an emphasis on its personal service. Although there are a dozen tennis courts here, this resort appeals almost exclusively to avid golfers, thanks to the two highly acclaimed and spectacular Tom Fazio golf courses. (The Mountain Course's third hole plays across a deep ravine and is one of the most photographed holes in the West.) The accommodations are in spacious suites, most with walls of windows so you can enjoy the views of the Catalinas. Furnishings are modern Mission style, and all suites include small kitchens and large bathrooms with two sinks, separate changing rooms, and oversize tubs (sometimes old-fashioned footed tubs). Some suites also have balconies, cathedral ceilings, and spiral stairs that lead to sleeping lofts.

**Dining/Diversions:** The dining room, a few steps from the lobby, offers fine dining with a view of the Catalinas. Drinks are served in two lounges, and there's also a poolside snack bar.

**Amenities:** In addition to the golf courses and tennis courts, there are a pool, whirlpools, exercise and aerobics rooms, steam rooms, saunas, a beauty salon, and a pro shop. A concierge, room service, golf and tennis lessons, massages and other spa treatments, baby-sitting, and valet/laundry service are also available.

✪ **Loews Ventana Canyon Resort.** 7000 N. Resort Dr., Tucson, AZ 85750. ☎ **800/ 234-5117** or 520/299-2020. Fax 520/299-6832. www.loewsventanacanyon@loewshotels. com. 398 units. A/C TV TEL. Early Jan to late May $199–$405 double, $600–$2,400 suite; late May to early Sept $109–$150 double, $255–$1,200 suite; early Sept to early Jan $219–$320 double, $600–$1,850 suite. AE, CB, DC, DISC, MC, V. Valet parking $11; self-parking free.

For breathtaking scenery, fascinating architecture, and superb resort amenities (including two excellent Tom Fazio golf courses and a full-service spa), no other Tucson resort can compare with Loews Ventana Canyon. The Santa Catalina Mountains rise up in rugged contrast to the genteel comforts of this haven of luxury, and despite its many amenities, the resort is firmly planted in the desert and uses desert plants in much of its landscaping. Of particular appeal is a short nature trail that leads to a cascading waterfall. Flagstone floors in the lobby and tables with boulders for bases give the resort's public rooms a rugged but luxurious appeal.

The guest rooms, all of which were recently renovated, are designed to impress. Beds angle out from corners and drapes hang from headboards. Private balconies overlook either the city lights or the mountains, and some rooms have fireplaces. Bathrooms are designed for convenience and comfort, with tiny TVs, hair dryers, telephones, travertine floors, and bathtubs built for two.

**Dining/Diversions:** The Ventana Room (see "Where to Dine," below), is one of the finest restaurants in Tucson, while the Flying V is popular for its large decks overlooking the golf course and city lights. There's also a casual cafe with a waterfall view and a poolside snack bar. The lobby lounge serves afternoon tea and then becomes an evening piano bar.

**Amenities:** Two 18-hole golf courses, two pools with mountain views, whirlpools, eight lighted tennis courts, croquet court, jogging track, nature trails, health spa (including a lap pool, aerobics room, exercise machines and free weights, steam rooms, saunas, and full assortment of spa treatments and services), beauty salon, bike rentals, car-rental desk, tour desk, concierge, 24-hour room service, valet/laundry service, playground, and kids club.

**Omni Tucson National Golf Resort & Spa.** 2727 W. Club Dr. (off Magee Rd.), Tucson, AZ 85742. ☎ **800/528-4856** or 520/297-2271. Fax 520/297-7544. 167 units. A/C MINIBAR TV TEL. Mid-Jan to late Mar $255–$285 double, $275–$365 suite; late Mar to late May

$169–$205 double, $189–$265 suite; late May to mid-Sept $89–$115 double, $99–$165 suite; mid-Sept to Dec $165–$185 double, $185–$265 suite. AE, CB, DC, DISC, MC, V.

As the name implies, golf is the driving force behind most stays at this boutique resort, which is the site of the annual Tucson Open PGA golf tournament. If you haven't got your own set of clubs, you might feel a bit out of place here. Then again, you could just avail yourself of the full-service health spa, which is one of the best in Arizona. There are also two pools and a tennis complex.

Most of the spacious guest rooms cling to the edges of the golf course and have their own patios or balconies. Hand-carved doors and Mexican tile counters in the bathrooms give the rooms a Spanish colonial feel, though furnishings have a classically modern Mediterranean style. For convenience there are two sinks and large dressing areas in all the rooms. Aside from the least expensive rooms, the accommodations here are the best and most luxurious in Tucson.

**Dining/Diversions:** A clublike gourmet dining room serves good regional American fare, while a second restaurant, downstairs from the lobby, serves reasonably priced Southwestern fare. A lobby lounge provides distant views of the Santa Catalina Mountains, and an upscale, clublike sports bar looks out over the golf course.

**Amenities:** Championship 27-hole golf course, four lighted tennis courts, two pools, basketball and volleyball courts, pro shop, and full-service health spa (with exercise machines, free weights, an aerobics room, steam rooms, saunas, whirlpools, and numerous skin and body treatments), concierge, 24-hour room service, valet/laundry service.

**Sheraton El Conquistador Resort & Country Club.** 10000 N. Oracle Rd., Tucson, AZ 85737. ☎ **800/325-7832** or 520/544-5000. Fax 520/544-1228. www.sheratonelconquistador.com. 428 units. A/C MINIBAR TV TEL. Jan 1–Mar 31 $239–$349 double, $314–$1,250 suite; Apr 1–May 27 $169–$259 double, $234–$1,250 suite; May 28–Sept 21 $79–$159 double, $124–$1,250 suite; Sept 22–Dec 31 $154–$319 double, $229–$1,250 suite. AE, CB, DC, DISC, MC, V. Pets accepted.

With the Santa Catalina Mountains rising up directly behind the property, this resort in Tucson's northern foothills boasts one of the most spectacular settings in the state. Just keep in mind that if you stay here, you'll be at least 30 minutes from downtown. The majority of the guest rooms are built around a central courtyard with a large pool and manicured lawns. However, this area is often taken over by conventions, and those seeking peace and quiet may want to opt for a room in the separate casitas area, which has its own pool. While golf on the resorts' three courses is the favorite pastime here, nongolfers have plenty of options, too.

Guest rooms feature Southwestern-influenced contemporary furniture and have spacious marble bathrooms. All rooms also have coffeemakers, hair dryers, irons and ironing boards, and a balcony or patio. In most suites, you'll also find a fireplace. For the full Tucson experience, ask for a mountain-view room.

**Dining/Diversions:** In the lively Mexican restaurant, strolling mariachis entertain, while in the steakhouse, cowboy vittles and cancan dancers are the order of the day. A casual cafe offers patio dining and moderate prices. The country club's restaurant capitalizes on its outstanding view.

**Amenities:** Three golf courses (45 holes total), 31 lighted tennis courts, seven indoor racquetball courts, four pools, six whirlpools, sauna, two health clubs, jogging trails, volleyball and basketball courts, rental bikes, car-rental desk, tour desk, concierge, room service, valet/laundry service, baby-sitting, massages, shopping shuttle, horseback riding, and children's programs in summer.

✪ **Westin La Paloma.** 3800 E. Sunrise Dr., Tucson, AZ 85718. ☎ **800/WESTIN-1** or 520/742-6000. Fax 520/577-5878. 487 units. A/C MINIBAR TV TEL. Jan 1 to late May $299–$399 double, from $490 suite; late May to early Sept $119–$139 double, from $290 suite; early Sept to Dec 31 $219–$259 double, from $390 suite. AE, CB, DC, DISC, EURO, JCB, MC, V.

If grand scale is what you're looking for in a resort, this is the place. Everything about the Westin is big—big portico, big lobby, big lounge, big pool area, big views. La Paloma, a collection of sunset-pink mission-revival buildings, sits in the middle of Tucson's prestigious foothills neighborhoods and offers sweeping panoramas from its hilltop perch and from the surrounding golf course. While adults appreciate the resort's tennis courts, exercise facilities, and abundant poolside lounge chairs, kids love the 170-foot water slide.

Guest rooms are situated in 27 low-rise buildings surrounded by desert landscaping. Couples should opt for the king rooms, which have the bed angled out from the corner of the room to best take in the views (ask for a mountain or golf course view if you don't mind spending a bit more). Bathrooms are extremely spacious, with separate tubs and showers, two sinks, and telephones.

**Dining/Diversions:** French-inspired Southwestern cuisine is the specialty at Janos, one of Tucson's finest restaurants (see "Where to Dine," below). There's also casual dining with a view just off the lobby. Snack bars are convenient to tennis and golf, and there's even a swim-up bar and grill. The lobby lounge provides great views and evening piano music.

**Amenities:** 27-hole golf course, three swimming pools (one for adults only), water slide, three whirlpools, 12 tennis courts, racquetball court, golf and tennis pro shops, volleyball and croquet courts, bike rentals, children's lounge and game room, shopping arcade, Personal Services Center offering spa treatments, health club (with exercise machines, aerobics room, and steam room), concierge, 24-hour room service, valet service.

## EXPENSIVE

✪ **Hacienda del Sol Guest Ranch Resort.** 5601 N. Hacienda del Sol Rd., Tucson, AZ 85718. ☎ **800/728-6514** or 520/299-1501. Fax 520/299-5554. www.haciendadelsol.com. 30 units, 3 casitas. A/C TV TEL. Jan 1 to Apr 30 $155 double, $250 suite, $295–$395 casita; May and mid-Sept to mid-Nov $130 double, $210 suite, $240–$310 casita; June to mid-Sept $90 double, $140 suite, $170–$210 casita; mid-Nov to Dec 31 $175 double, $270 suite, $315–$415 casita. AE, MC, V.

With its colorful Southwest styling, historic character, mature desert gardens, and ridge-top setting, Hacienda del Sol is one of the most distinctive hotels in Tucson. The small resort, once a guest ranch (and later a private girls' school), exudes the sort of Old Tucson atmosphere available only at a couple of other lodgings in the city. The basic rooms have rustic and colorful Mexican character, with a decidedly artistic flare; while not exactly luxurious, they are evocative of Spanish posadas and old Mexican inns. These rooms are in the lodge's oldest buildings, which are set around flower-filled courtyards. If you prefer more modern, comfortable, and very spacious accommodations, ask for a suite, and if you want loads of space and the chance to stay where Katherine Hepburn and Spencer Tracy may have once stayed, ask for a casita.

**Dining/Diversions:** With views over the foothills and large terraces for alfresco dining, The Grill is one of Tucson's most popular restaurants (see "Where to Dine," below). There's also an adjacent lounge.

**Amenities:** The small pool has a great view of the Catalinas. Also available are tennis and croquet courts, a whirlpool, horseback riding, nature walks, and massages.

✪ **Westward Look Resort.** 245 E. Ina Rd., Tucson, AZ 85704. ☎ **800/722-2500** or 520/297-1151. Fax 520/297-9023. www.westwardlook.com. 244 units. A/C MINIBAR TV TEL. Mid-Jan to Apr $170–$395 double; May $150–$249 double; June to mid-Sept $85–$199 double; mid-Sept to early Jan $150–$239 double. AE, CB, DC, DISC, MC, V. Pets accepted ($50 refundable deposit).

Built in 1912 as a dude ranch, the Westward Look is the oldest resort in Tucson and one of the most reasonably priced resorts in the city. Set in the Catalina foothills, the resort is surrounded by desert, and although it doesn't have its own golf course, it does offer privileges at the nearby Raven Golf Club. Guests can also enjoy tennis courts, a fitness center, jogging trails, and a full-service health spa. Recent renovations have left the resort looking every bit as stylish as other major resorts in the area. If you aren't a golfer but do enjoy resort amenities, this is one of your best Tucson choices.

The guest rooms, all of which were recently renovated, are quite large and have private patios or balconies and coffeemakers and hair dryers. Spanish colonial–style furnishings with an antique look give rooms here a classic, Southwestern flavor. Many also have exposed-beam ceilings and great views of the city.

**Dining/Diversions:** The Gold Room restaurant features walls of glass that provide sweeping views of Tucson and serve reliably excellent continental and Southwestern cuisine. A casual bar and grill, with live music on weekends, benefits from the same views.

**Amenities:** Three pools, eight tennis courts, three whirlpools, basketball and volleyball courts, a jogging trail, pro shop, large fitness center and full-service health spa (offering a wide variety of spa treatments and exercise, tai chi, and yoga classes), rental bikes, tour desk, concierge, room service, valet/laundry service, tennis lessons, horseback riding, guided hikes, baby-sitting.

## MODERATE

**Windmill Inn at St. Philip's Plaza.** 4250 N. Campbell Ave., Tucson, AZ 85718. ☎ **800/ 547-4747** or 520/577-0007. Fax 520/577-0045. www.windmillinns.com. 122 units. A/C TV TEL. Mid-Jan to mid-Apr $135 double; mid-Apr to May and mid-Sept to mid-Jan $103 double; June to mid-Sept $67 double. AE, DC, DISC, MC, V.

Located in St. Philip's Plaza, which has several great restaurants and an array of upscale shops, this hotel has both a good location and spacious accommodations. All the rooms are suites and contain couches, work desks, two TVs, three telephones (one in the bathroom), double vanities, wet bars, small refrigerators, and microwaves. Basically there's everything to make the business traveler or vacationer comfortable for a long stay, and local phone calls are free. Amenities here include an outdoor pool, whirlpool, lending library, and complimentary use of bicycles (the Rillito River bike path starts in back of the hotel).

# WEST OF DOWNTOWN
## EXPENSIVE

**La Tierra Linda Guest Ranch Resort.** 7501 N. Wade Rd., Tucson, AZ 85743. ☎ **888/ 872- 6241** or 520/744-7700. Fax 520/579-9742. www.latierralinda.com. 16 units. A/C TV TEL. Mid-Dec to mid-May $165 double, from $215 suite; mid-May to mid-Sept $100 double, from $125 suite; mid-Sept to mid-Dec $125 double, from $160 suite. Rates include full breakfast. AE, DISC, MC, V.

Set on 30 acres in northwestern Tucson and adjacent to Saguaro National Park, this guest ranch was recently renovated and is now a surprisingly resortlike property. Originally opened as a dude ranch back in the 1930s, La Tierra Linda went through many incarnations before its most recent facelift. The grounds benefit immensely from the mature desert landscaping, including a huge old tamarisk tree and many citrus trees and saguaros. Guest rooms vary a lot in size and layout and the suites, which provide you with plenty of extra room, are generally worth the added expense. Throughout the property, there's lots of interesting stonework incorporated into the buildings. A viewing deck provides an excellent view of Sobrero Peak in the Tucson Mountains.

**Dining/Diversions:** The Ranch House Grill, in the main ranch house, of course, serves economically priced Southwestern fare. There's also a small bar with the feel of a mine shaft.

**Amenities:** There's a small outdoor pool, a whirlpool in a stone-walled gazebo, a tennis court, volleyball court, horseshoe pits, and horseback riding.

**Starr Pass Golf Suites.** 3645 W. Starr Pass Blvd., Tucson, AZ 85745. ☎ **800/503-2898** or 520/670-0500. Fax 520/670-0427. www.starrpasstucson.com. 105 units. A/C TV TEL. Mid-Jan to Mar $169 double, $299 suite, $419 casita; Apr to mid-May $129 double, $189 suite, $279 casita; mid-May to Sept $79 double, $129 suite, $189 casita; Oct and mid-Dec to early Jan $139 double, $199 suite, $299 casita. Nov to mid-Dec and early to mid-Jan $109 double, $169 suite, $239 casita. AE, CB, DC, DISC, MC, V.

Located off West 22nd Street, 3 miles west of I-10, Starr Pass is both the closest golf resort to downtown and the most economically priced golf resort in the city. This is a condominium resort, and you won't find the sort of service you get at Tucson's other resorts, but on the other hand, you won't pay nearly as much either. Accommodations are in privately owned Santa Fe–style casitas that can be broken down into a master suite and a standard hotel-style room or that can be rented as two-bedroom units. The master suites are the larger and more comfortable rooms and have fireplaces, washers and dryers, full kitchens with tile floors, wrought-iron breakfast-bar stools and bed frames, and a general Southwestern styling throughout. Bathrooms are large and have separate showers and tubs. The smaller rooms are a bit cramped and much less lavish in their appointments.

**Dining:** The dining room here looks out over the golf course and surrounding hills and serves a mix of continental and Southwestern dishes at reasonable prices.

**Amenities:** The desert-style 18-hole golf course is best known for its 15th hole, which plays through a pass that was once a stagecoach route. There's also a large pro shop, outdoor pool, exercise room, two tennis courts, whirlpool spa, hiking/biking trails, and valet/laundry service.

## MODERATE

✪ **Casa Tierra.** 11155 W. Calle Pima, Tucson, AZ 85743. ☎ **520/578-3058.** Fax 520/578-8445. 4 units. Aug 15–July 15 $95–$135 double; $200 suite. Rates include a full vegetarian breakfast. MC, V. Closed July 15–Aug 15.

If you've come to Tucson to be in the desert and you really want to be a *part* of the desert, then there's no doubt about where you should stay. Casa Tierra, a modern adobe home built to look as if it has been here since Spanish colonial days, is surrounded by 5 acres of cactus and *palo verde*. The inn, which is situated on the west side of Saguaro National Park, has fabulous views of a landscape full of saguaros. There are also stunning sunsets and views of the mountains to the north. Surrounding a landscaped central courtyard is a covered seating area; the guest rooms are off of it. The outdoor whirlpool spa makes a perfect stargazing spot, and there's also a very well-equipped exercise room.

## NEAR THE AIRPORT
### MODERATE

**Best Western Inn at the Airport.** 7060 S. Tucson Blvd., Tucson, AZ 85706. ☎ **800/772-3847** or 520/746-0271. Fax 520/889-7391. 149 units. A/C TV TEL. Jan–Mar $69–$139 double; Apr–May $59–$99 double; June to mid-Sept $49–$89 double; mid-Sep to Dec $59–$99 double. Rates include continental breakfast. AE, CB, DC, DISC, MC, V.

If you're the type who likes to get as much sleep as possible before getting up to catch a plane, this motel right outside the airport entrance will do it for you—there's no place closer. Although you'll have the drawback of airport noise, there are a great range of amenities at surprisingly reasonable rates. In addition to the buffet breakfast, an evening beer and wine social hour is also complimentary. The rooms are comfortable and have small refrigerators and hair dryers. The restaurant and the lounge assure that guests don't go hungry or thirsty. There's a small courtyard pool and a whirlpool, as well as a fitness room and a tennis court.

**Clarion Hotel Tucson Airport.** 6801 S. Tucson Blvd., Tucson, AZ 85706. ☎ **800/526-0550** or 520/746-3932. Fax 520/889-9934. 191 units. A/C TV TEL. Jan–Apr $79–$129 double; May–Aug $55–$79 double; Sept–Oct $69–$89 double; Nov–Dec $69–$99 double. Rates include full breakfast. AE, CB, DC, DISC, MC, V.

Located just outside the airport exit, this low-rise hotel provides convenience and some great amenities, including a nightly complimentary cocktail reception and late-night snacks. The rooms are generally quite large, and the "king" rooms are particularly comfortable. The poolside rooms, in addition to being convenient for swimming and lounging, have small refrigerators. The restaurant offers moderately priced meals in casual surroundings, and the menu is rather eclectic. There's also an adjacent lounge. A pool, whirlpool, exercise room, concierge, room service, valet service, and complimentary airport shuttle are all available.

### INEXPENSIVE

There are numerous budget motels near the Tucson Airport. These include **Motel 6,** 755 E. Benson Hwy., Exit 262 off I-10 (☎ **520/622-4614**), and **Motel 6,** 1031 E. Benson Hwy., Exit 262 (☎ **520/628-1264**), both charging $36 to $49 double; and **Super 8—Tucson/East,** 1990 S. Craycroft Rd., Exit 265 off I-10 (☎ **520/790-6021**), charging $46 to $90 double. See appendix B for a list of toll-free numbers.

## OUTLYING AREAS
### NORTH OF TUCSON

✪ **"Across The Creek" at Aravaipa Farms.** 89395 Aravaipa Rd., Winkelman, AZ 85292. ☎ **520/357-6901.** 2 units. $225 double. Rates include all meals. No credit cards.

Located 60 miles north of Tucson on one of the only year-round streams in southern Arizona, this B&B is a romantic getaway near one of the state's most spectacular desert wilderness areas. Because the inn is 3 miles up a gravel road and then across a stream (high-clearance vehicle recommended), it's a long way to a restaurant. Consequently, innkeeper Carol Steele, who formerly operated restaurants in the Scottsdale area, provides all meals. Guests entertain themselves hiking in the nearby Aravaipa Canyon Wilderness, bird watching, and cooling off in Aravaipa Creek. The two casitas here are eclectically designed and decorated in a mix of international folk art, rustic Mexican furniture, and original works of art. There are tile floors, stone-walled showers, and shady verandas. For either a romantic getaway or a vigorous weekend exploring the desert, this inn makes an ideal base.

**C.O.D. Ranch.** P.O. Box 241, Oracle, AZ 85623. ☎ **800/868-5617** or 520/615-3211. Fax 520/896-2271. www.codranch.com. 9 units. $125–$190 per house. MC, V.

Located 45 minutes north of Tucson, this lodge is primarily used by groups and family reunions, but, with its two restored 1880s adobe houses and remote setting overlooking the San Pedro Valley, the C.O.D. is an ideal spot for a tranquil getaway between the desert and the mountains. The ranch has been lovingly restored by Steve Malkin. Four of the casitas have full kitchens, and two have fireplaces. The decor is a mix of rustic Mexican furnishings and contemporary art by regional artists (Malkin was once a resident at a nearby artists community). Within a few miles of the ranch, you'll find the Arizona Trail, which will eventually stretch the length of the state.

Horseback rides on this trail can be arranged. At an additional cost and with prior arrangement, meals can be provided for guests staying more than 1 night.

**The Triangle L Ranch.** P.O. Box 900, Oracle, AZ 85623. ☎ **888/782-9572** or 520/896-2804. www.trianglelranch.com. 4 units. $95–$125 double. AE, DISC, MC, V.

Set on 75 acres on the edge of Oracle, this charming place was the first guest ranch in southern Arizona and looks as if it could have been built for a John Wayne movie. There's the squeaky windmill slowly turning in the wind, a mesquite-fenced corral, cactus thickets, and four white cottages with bright blue trim. The cottages date from the late 1800s and early 1900s, and all are furnished with antiques. For the best views, request the Hill House. In the main ranch house, where breakfast is served either in the country kitchen or on the patio overlooking the iris garden, you'll find more antiques, some of which are original to the ranch. Owners Margot and Tom Beeston, who have lived here for more than 20 years, are always happy to share their personal interests—wildlife rehabilitation and the construction and repair of stringed musical instruments—with their guests.

## SOUTH OF TUCSON

**Santa Rita Lodge.** HC 70, Box 5444, Sahuarita, AZ 85629. ☎ **520/625-8746.** Fax 520/648-1186. www.maderacanyon.com. 12 units. $73–$93 double in the lodge, $83–$93 double in cabins. AE, MC, V. Pets accepted Sept–Feb only.

Located in the shade of Madera Canyon, this lodge is used almost exclusively by bird watchers, and getting a room here in late spring, when the birds are out in force, can be difficult. Book early. The rooms and cabins are large and fairly comfortable; natural history programs and guided bird walks are offered between February and August.

## SPAS

**Canyon Ranch Health Resort.** 8600 E. Rockcliff Rd., Tucson, AZ 85750. ☎ **800/726-9900** for information, 800/742-9000 for reservations, or 520/749-9000. Fax 520/749-7755. www.canyonranch.com. 180 units. A/C TV TEL. Late Sept to early June 4-night package from $4,400 double; early June to late Sept 4-night package from $3,400 double. Rates include all meals and a variety of spa services and programs. AE, DC, DISC, MC, V. No children under 14 accepted (with exception of infants in the care of personal nannies).

Canyon Ranch, one of America's premier health spas, offers the sort of complete spa experience that's available at only a handful of places around the country (and then only to those who can afford it). On staff are doctors, nurses, psychotherapists and counselors, fitness instructors, massage therapists, and tennis, golf, and racquetball pros. Services offered include health and fitness assessments; health, nutrition, exercise, and stress-management consultations, seminars, presentations, and evaluations; fitness classes and activities; massage therapy; herbal and aroma wraps; facials, manicures, pedicures, haircuts, and styling; private sports lessons; makeup consultations; cooking demonstrations; and art classes. There are a variety of spacious and very comfortable accommodations.

**Dining:** Three gourmet low-calorie meals are served daily with options for total daily caloric intake. Because this is a health spa, no alcoholic beverages are served.

**Amenities:** 62,000-square-foot spa complex that includes seven gyms, aerobics and strength-training rooms, squash and racquetball courts, yoga/meditation room, saunas, steam rooms, inhalation rooms, whirlpools, cold plunges, private sunbathing areas, and skin care and beauty salons. Additional facilities include a new aquatic center plus several other pools, eight tennis courts, and a basketball court. A concierge is available and airport transfers are included in the rates.

**Miraval.** 5000 E. Via Estancia Miraval, Catalina, AZ 85739. ☎ **800/232-3969** or 520/825-4000. Fax 520/792-5870. www.miravalresort.com. 106 units. A/C MINIBAR TV TEL. Oct to mid-May $750–$1,000 double, $1,200–$1,700 suite for 2; mid-May to Sept $300–$850 double, $1,200–$1,400 suite for 2. Rates include all meals and a variety of spa services and programs. AE, DISC, MC, V.

Focusing on what it calls "life balancing," Miraval emphasizes stress management, self-discovery, and relaxation rather than facials and mud baths. To this end, activities at the all-inclusive resort include meditation, tai chi, and yoga, but for more active types, there is also hiking, mountain biking, and rock climbing (on an outdoor climbing wall). Of course, such desert classics as horseback riding, tennis, volleyball, and swimming are also available. However, staying busy isn't really the objective here; learning a new way of living your life is the ultimate goal at Miraval.

Throughout the resort, Southwestern styling predominates, and lots of original art hangs on the walls. However, no amount of art can equal the views of the Santa Catalina Mountains to be had from the grounds here. Guest rooms, many of which have mountain views, are done in a Southwestern style and have very large bathrooms that, for the most part, have showers but no tubs.

**Dining:** With two restaurants and two snack lounges, no one need fear going hungry here. However, rest assured that everything served is healthful as well as delicious.

**Amenities:** Two exercise pools and a three-tiered leisure pool surrounded by waterfalls and desert landscaping are among the most popular facilities here, but you'll also find a superbly equipped exercise room, rock-climbing wall, tennis courts, volleyball court, riding stables, whirlpool spas, saunas, and steam rooms. Miraval offers lifestyle management workshops, fitness/nutrition consultations, cooking demonstrations, exercise classes, an "equine experience" program, massage, skin care and facials, and a confidence-building course. Airport transfers are also included in the rates.

## GUEST RANCHES

**Lazy K Bar Ranch.** 8401 N. Scenic Dr., Tucson, AZ 85743. ☎ **800/321-7018** or 520/744-3050. Fax 520/744-7628. www.lazykbar.com. 23 units. A/C. $185–$275 double; $225–$300 suite. Rates include all meals. 3-night minimum. AE, DISC, MC, V. Closed mid-June to Aug.

Homesteaded in 1933 and converted to a dude ranch in 1936, the Lazy K Bar Ranch covers 160 acres adjacent to Saguaro National Park. There are plenty of nearby hiking and riding trails, and if you have a hankering for city life, it isn't difficult to reach downtown (20 minutes away). The guest rooms vary in size and comfort level. The newest are the most comfortable, with exposed brick walls and sliding glass doors that open onto patios. The ranch-oriented activities at the Lazy K include horseback riding twice daily, hayrides, lunch rides, cookouts. There are also nature talks and star viewing.

**Dining:** Meals are served family style in a dining room that features Mexican tile floors and an open-pit fireplace. The food is hearty American ranch style with cookouts some nights. Each evening there's a happy hour at the ranch's BYOB bar.

**Amenities:** Horseback riding and lessons, pool, whirlpool, two tennis courts, volleyball and basketball courts, horseshoe pits, stables, mountain bikes. Complimentary airport transfer, Sunday shuttle to the Arizona–Sonora Desert Museum.

✪ **Tanque Verde Ranch.** 14301 E. Speedway Blvd., Tucson, AZ 85748. ☎ **800/234-DUDE** or 520/296-6275. Fax 520/721-9426. 75 units. A/C TEL. Mid-Dec to Apr $315–$415 double; May–Sept $250–$330 double; Oct to mid-Dec $260–$345 double. Rates include all meals. AE, DISC, MC, V.

Far and away the most luxurious guest ranch in Tucson (some people say this is a resort with horses), Tanque Verde Ranch, founded in the 1880s, still has some of its original buildings. The ranch borders both Saguaro National Park and the Coronado National Forest, which assures plenty of room for guided horseback rides. In addition to riding, the bird watching here is excellent (more than 220 species have been seen on the ranch) and birders are well served. There are also nature trails, wildlife viewing ramadas (shaded patios), and a nature center with displays of live snakes and other desert critters. The guest rooms are spacious and comfortable, but don't expect a TV here—ranch policy encourages guests to participate in various activities. Many rooms have fireplaces and patios, and the bathrooms are large. The new casitas are absolutely huge and are among the most luxurious accommodations in the state.

**Dining/Diversions:** The large dining room, which overlooks the Rincon Mountains, sets impressive buffets. There are also breakfast horseback rides, poolside luncheons, and cookout rides. An old foreman's cabin houses a cantina.

**Amenities:** Indoor and outdoor pools, riding stables, five tennis courts, exercise room, saunas, whirlpool, horseshoes, basketball and volleyball courts, tennis pro shop, rodeo arena, nature trails, complimentary riding and tennis lessons, evening lectures and performances, nature hikes, children's programs, baby-sitting, and complimentary airport shuttle with 4-night stay.

**White Stallion Ranch.** 9251 W. Twin Peaks Rd., Tucson, AZ 85743. ☎ **888/977-2624** or 520/297-0252. Fax 520/744-2786. www.wsranch.com. 35 units. A/C. Oct 1–Dec 18 $224–$250 double; $268–$296 suite; Dec 19–May 31 $244–$288 double, $312–$350 suite. Rates include all meals. Weekly rates available. 4-night minimum stay in winter. No credit cards. Closed June–Sept.

Set on 3,000 acres of desert just over the hill from Tucson, the White Stallion Ranch is perfect for those who crave wide-open spaces. Operated since 1965 by the True family, this spread has a more authentic ranch feel than any other guest ranch in the area. Two fast rides and two slow rides are offered daily, and a petting zoo keeps kids entertained. The guest rooms vary considerably in size and comfort from the tiny, spartan single rooms to deluxe two-bedroom suites.

**Dining/Diversions:** All meals, mostly traditional, familiar American fare, are served family style in the main dining room, which is housed in a 90-year-old building. There's also an honor bar with cowhide stools and a longhorn steer head on the wall.

**Amenities:** Horseback riding and lessons, outdoor pool, indoor hot tub, two tennis courts, basketball and volleyball courts, nature trails, rental bikes, games room, hayrides, guided nature walks and hikes, airport pickup, tours available at additional charge, baby-sitting.

## 4  Where to Dine

A few years back, Tucson's mayor declared the city the Mexican restaurant capital of the universe. Though Mexico City might want to contest that claim, it isn't far off the mark. There's historic Mexican at El Charro Cafe, nouveau Mexican at Café Poca Cosa, Mexico City Mexican at La Parilla Suiza, and family style Mexican at Casa Molina. If you like Mexican food, you'll be in heaven; if you don't, there are dozens of other restaurants serving everything from the finest French cuisine to innovative American, Italian, and Southwestern food. Southwestern cuisine is almost as abundant in Tucson as Mexican food, and you should be sure to dine at a Southwestern restaurant early in your visit. It can be brilliantly creative, and after trying it you may want *all* your meals to be Southwestern. Keep in mind, however, that this food tends to be both pricey and spicy.

# Tucson Dining

NA-0263

308

Coronado National Forest

Magee Rd.

Tohono Chul
Park 8 10

Ina Rd. 9

11

Orange Grove Rd.

Skyline Dr.

La Canada Dr.

19

20

Sunrise Dr.

21

Kolb Rd.

Sabino Canyon Rd.

Sabino
Canyon
Park

Swan Rd.

Craycroft Rd.

Kolb Rd.

River Rd.

Flowing Wells Rd.

Wetmore Rd.

18

Roger Rd.

17

Prince Rd.

Campbell Ave.

Stone Ave.

Oracle Rd.

Euclid Ave.

Snyder Rd.

Bear Canyon Rd.

To Mount
Lemmon

Catalina Hwy.

Miracle Mile

Ft. Lowell Rd.

23

River Rd.

Ft. Lowell
Park

36

Grant Rd.

Tanque Verde Rd.

12

16

15

25

14

26

24

Way

34

35

37

33

38

Alvernon Way

27

Tucson Blvd.

28

Country Club Rd.

29

Speedway Blvd.

39

13

6th St.

30

32

31

5th St.

40

Swan Rd.

Craycroft Rd.

Broadway Blvd.

Wilmot Rd.

42

Kolb Rd.

To Saguaro National
Park (east)

41

22nd St.

Grande Ave.

Congress

43

Reid
Park

Randolph
Park

22nd St.

Ariz
210

Tucson
Greyhound
Park

29th St.

36th St.

Golf Links Rd.

Ajo Way

Blvd.

10

Escalante Rd.

Pantano Rd.

Camino Seco Rd.

Irvington Rd.

10

Kino Blvd.

Irvington Rd.

Drexel Rd.

Palo Verde Rd.

Davis Monthan AFB

Kolb Rd.

12th Ave.

6th Ave.

Valencia Rd.

Los Reales Rd.

10

19

Tucson
International
Airport

**309**

Foodies fond of the latest culinary trends will find plenty of places to satisfy their cravings. Try almost any of the restaurants along East Tanque Verde Road, which is Tucson's restaurant row. Elsewhere around the city, trendsetting restaurants include Pastiche, Firecracker, and Wildflower. On the other hand, if you're on a tight dining budget you may want to avoid the trendy places and instead look for early bird dinners, which are particularly popular with retirees. Though these economical early evening dinners are more often offered during the summer months, some places have them year-round.

# DOWNTOWN & THE UNIVERSITY AREA
## EXPENSIVE

✪ **Arizona Inn.** 2200 E. Elm St. ☎ **520/325-1541.** Reservations recommended. Main courses $5–$15 at lunch, $20–$28 at dinner. AE, DC, MC, V. Mon–Sat 7–10am, 11:30am–2pm, and 6–10pm; Sun 7–10am, 11am–2pm (brunch), and 6–10pm. NEW AMERICAN.

The dining room at the Arizona Inn, one of the state's first resorts, has established itself as a consistently excellent restaurant with reasonable prices. The rose-pink stucco pueblo-style buildings are surrounded by neatly manicured gardens that have aged gracefully, and it's romantic to dine in the twinkle lighted courtyard or overlooking the colorful gardens on the bar patio. The menu is not extensive, but every dish, such as Chilean sea bass with prosciutto-wrapped shrimp, is perfectly prepared. Flavors are predominantly Southwestern, with hints of Mediterranean and Asian. Because the Arizona Inn is a class act and doesn't have to work too hard to impress, presentation is artistic but not overly so, and fresh ingredients are emphasized more than sauces. The bouillabaisse is beautiful yet simple and home-made ice cream, such as ginger-cappuccino and mango sorbet, are fabulous. On weekends, you might catch some live music. Lunches include quiche, pastas, salads, and sandwiches.

## MODERATE

**The Barrio Food & Drink.** 135 S. 6th Ave. ☎ **520/629-0191.** Reservations recommended for dinner. Main courses $8–$18. AE, DC, MC, V. Mon 11am–3pm, Tues–Thurs 11am–10pm, Fri 11am–midnight, Sat noon–midnight, Sun 4–9pm. SOUTHWESTERN.

Located at the edge of the Barrio Histórico, this neighborhood restaurant is popular with downtown professionals and the art crowd. On the whole, the food is pleasantly spicy and served with zippy Southwestern accents. If you're not too hungry, one of the little plates, such as the tasty Anaheim chile stuffed with black beans, garlic, and goat cheese on a red-pepper cream sauce will do. For fans of burgers, the jalapeño burger is thick, juicy, and just spicy enough. Looking for an interesting melange of flavors? Try the pork tenderloin with a mango-ginger chutney.

✪ **Café Poca Cosa.** Clarion Hotel & Suites Santa Rita, 88 E. Broadway Blvd. ☎ **520/ 622-6400.** Reservations highly recommended. Main courses $7.50–$9 at lunch, $11.50–$17 at dinner. MC, V. Mon–Thurs 11am–9pm, Fri–Sat 11am–10pm. MEXICAN.

Created by owner-chef Suzana Davila, the food here is not just *any* Mexican food; it's imaginative and different, and the flamboyant atmosphere of red and purple walls and Mexican/Southwestern artwork is equally unusual. The cuisine here—which has been compared to the dishes dreamed up in *Like Water for Chocolate*—consists of creations such as beef marinated in tequila and then grilled, and chicken with a green *mole* (pronounced *mole*-ay) sauce made with pistachios. The menu changes daily, but there is always something wonderful to try. The service staff is courteous and friendly and will recite the menu for you in both Spanish and English. This lively restaurant is an excellent value, especially at lunch.

Another (smaller and simpler) Café Poca Cosa, 20 S. Scott St., is open for breakfast and lunch Monday through Friday from 7:30am to 2:30pm.

# North-of-the-Border Margaritaville

Jimmy Buffet may have had a problem keeping his flip-flops on after a few margaritas, but he certainly knew a good thing when he tasted it. Nothing takes the heat out of a hot desert day like an icy, limey margarita. While the rest of the country is busy sipping single malts and designer martinis, Tucson has quietly become a north of the border Margaritaville.

Today, with dozens of premium tequilas making their way north from Mexico, tequila is no longer something to be slammed back as quickly as possible with enough salt and lime to hide its flavor. A margarita makes far better use of salt and lime, which, when combined with a dash of Triple Sec or Cointreau, produce the perfect drink for the desert. When the tequila in a margarita is a premium *reposado* (rested or aged), 100% blue agave tequila and the lime juice is fresh squeezed instead of from a bottle or a margarita mix, you have the makings of the perfect margarita. Of course the question of on the rocks or frozen is a matter of personal taste; we prefer our margaritas on the rocks. It allows the flavors to better express themselves. And, yes, with salt. However, we do make an exception for prickly pear margaritas. These hot pink concoctions, made with the fruit of the prickly pear cactus, are best when they're served blended.

The following are some restaurants and bars that we think make the best margaritas in Tucson and where you, too, can ponder the question, Is this the perfect margarita?

**Café Poca Cosa,** 88 E. Broadway Blvd. (☎ **520/622-6400**). Great food, great atmosphere, and you never wonder if the bartender forgot the tequila in your margarita.

**Casa Molina,** 6225 E. Speedway Blvd. (☎ **520/886-5468**). Long the most popular margaritas in Tucson, strong. They go well with the cheap Mexican meals here. No pretension.

**Cottonwood Cafe,** 60 N. Alvernon Way (☎ **520/326-6000**). Big selection of premium tequilas, rich and limey margaritas. Cool building, great patio.

**Cushing Street Bar & Grill,** 343 S. Meyer Ave. (☎ **520/622-7984**). Housed in a vintage adobe building, this place positively oozes Old Tucson style. However, beware the premium margarita here, it's made without any lime!

**Flying V Bar & Grill,** in Loews Ventana Canyon Resort, 7000 N. Resort Dr. (☎ **520/299-2020**). While the prickly pear margaritas here aren't necessarily better than others around town, the view from the deck is superb. Not only does all of Tucson spread out below you, but you can watch the golfers double bogey the 18th hole of the Canyon Course.

**¡Toma!,** 311 N. Court Ave. (☎ **520/622-1922**). Another downtown favorite next door to El Charro Cafe, Tucson's famous *carne seca* restaurant. These margaritas are just plain good.

**The Dish Bistro & Wine Bar.** 3200 E. Speedway Blvd. (at the Rumrunner). ☎ **520/326-1714.** Reservations highly recommended. Main courses $14.50–$25, smaller dishes $7–$12. AE, DC, MC, V. Mon–Sat 5–10pm. NEW AMERICAN.

Located in the rear of the Rumrunner Wine and Cheese Co. (and also part of the same operation), this tiny, minimalist restaurant is brimming with urban chic. On a busy night, the space could be construed as either cozy or crowded, so if you like it more on the quiet side, come early or late. The chef has a well-deserved reputation for daring, and turns out such dishes as a cambozola and mascarpone cheese soufflé; colorful and well-composed salads; porcini mushroom ravioli in a garlic broth with fresh arugula; and pork chops with a roasted cashew and chile sauce. Naturally, the wine list is also great, and the servers, who are well informed about the menus, will be happy to help you choose a bottle. Dishes come from small to large to suit your appetite.

✪ **El Charro Café.** 311 N. Court Ave. ☎ **520/622-1922.** Reservations recommended for dinner. Main courses $5–$14. AE, CB, DC, DISC, MC, V. Sun–Thurs 11am–9pm, Fri–Sat 11am–10pm. SONORAN MEXICAN.

El Charro, located in an old stone building in El Presidio Historic District, claims to be Tucson's oldest family operated Mexican restaurant. A front porch has been glassed in for a greenhouselike dining area overlooking the street, and there's also dining downstairs. Look at the roof of El Charro as you approach, and you might see a large metal cage containing beef drying in the sun. This is the main ingredient in *carne seca,* El Charro's well-known specialty (like beef jerky), which is oft copied but never duplicated at other Mexican restaurants around town. You'll rarely find *carne seca* on a Mexican menu outside Tucson, so indulge in it while you're here. *A warning:* The cafe can be packed at lunch, so arrive early or late.

Other El Charro Cafe branches can be found in the Tucson International Airport (☎ **520/573-8222**) and at 6310 E. Broadway (☎ **520/745-1922**). The family also runs the adjacent ¡Toma!, a colorful bar/cantina next door.

✪ **Kingfisher.** 2564 E. Grant Rd. ☎ **520/323-7739.** Reservations recommended on weekends. Main courses $7–$10 at lunch, $12–$20 at dinner. AE, DC, DISC, MC, V. Mon–Fri 11am–midnight, Sat–Sun 5pm–midnight. SEAFOOD.

If you're serious about seafood, head for the Kingfisher. The freshest seafood, artfully blended with bright flavors and imaginative ingredients, is deftly prepared as appetizers, sandwiches, and main dishes. You may have difficulty deciding whether to begin with Umpqua Bay oysters (there's a full-service raw bar), seared ahi tuna salad, or the delicately smoked red trout—so why not tackle them all? Fans of outstanding salads will flip over the warm cabbage salad with mesquite bacon and spiced pecans, and meat eaters as well as vegetarians will find items on the menu. The atmosphere is upscale and lively, and the bar and late-night menu are a hit with night owls.

**La Cocina/Two Micks Cantina.** 201 N. Court St. ☎ **520/622-0351.** Reservations recommended. Main courses $6–$8.50 at lunch, $11–$17 at dinner. AE, CB, DC, DISC, MC, V. Mon 11am–2pm, Tues–Fri 11am–2pm and 4:30–9pm; Sat 11am–3pm and 4:30–9pm; Sun 4:30–8pm. SOUTHWESTERN.

Housed in the same historic 1850s adobe building as the Old Town Artisans shopping plaza, La Cocina is one of the few good restaurants left in downtown Tucson. Its convenience to both shopping and the Tucson Museum of Art makes it imminently recommendable. The restaurant's tree-shaded patio dining area, in the courtyard of the old adobe, is surrounded by colorful gardens and is an excellent place for a light lunch (salads and sandwiches). The more formal indoor dining room, decorated with regional artwork, is most popular in the evening, when you might start your meal with black bean chili with mesquite grilled beef or chicken tortilla soup, then move on to tequila glazed prawns or a New York strip steak. On the far side of the courtyard from the dining room is the restaurant's rustic cantina.

**Le Bistro.** 2574 N. Campbell Ave. ☎ **520/327-3086.** Reservations recommended for dinner. Main courses $5.25–$9 at lunch, $8–$18 at dinner. AE, DISC, MC, V. Mon–Fri 11am–2:30pm and 5–10pm, Sat–Sun 5–10pm. FRENCH/EUROPEAN.

Etched mirrors, lace, and live trees full of twinkling lights set the scene for some casual bistro cuisine. European specialties include the likes of duck pâté, roast quail, blackened sea scallops, and bouillabaisse. Salads are quite good, there are dozens of choices for wine, and prices are reasonable. On the extravagant side is the showcase of desserts, with names such as Tuxedo (a double-chocolate mousse), Opera (a creation with hazelnut and mocha crème), and bombe (a chocolate-covered mountain of cream puffs), which frequently stops passersby dead in their tracks. The bar here is a good place to come for a glass of wine and one of these rich, decadent desserts.

**Pastiche.** 3025 N. Campbell Ave. ☎ **520/325-3333.** Reservations recommended. Main courses $7–$20. AE, DISC, MC, V. Mon–Sat 11:30–midnight, Sun 4:40pm–midnight. NEW AMERICAN.

Situated in a shopping plaza with lots of Tucson character, this high-energy bistro is currently one of *the* places to dine in Tucson. The colorful artwork and vibrant contemporary food fairly scream *trendy*. However, the main reason for the restaurant's popularity is probably its variety of menu offerings. There are small plates, split plates, sandwiches, and full-size entrees—something to satisfy every appetite. Duck breast salad with crunchy wontons is terrific, as are the bold flavors of fusilli pasta with andouille sausage and Gorgonzola cheese. The crowded bar is a popular watering hole that also turns out some tasty margaritas.

**Presidio Grill.** 3352 E. Speedway Blvd. ☎ **520/327-4667.** Reservations recommended. Main courses $8–$12 at lunch, $15–$21 at dinner. AE, DC, DISC, MC, V. Sun–Thurs 11am–10pm, Fri–Sat 11am–midnight. AMERICAN REGIONAL.

This ever-trendy restaurant, modern and upbeat in both cuisine and interior design, is located in the Rancho Center shopping plaza, along busy Speedway Boulevard. Whether you want seafood, pasta, or something from the grill, the dishes here show a variety of international influences. The shrimp cocktail, with Absolut Citron–marinated grilled shrimp and horseradish sauce is a great starter. For a heartier dish, try the Presidio chicken pasta with prosciutto, garlic, poblano chiles, fresh basil, and roma tomatoes on linguine (which was featured on the cover of *Bon Appétit* magazine). The restaurant is usually packed at lunchtime during the week, so make a reservation if possible. On Sundays breakfast is served from 10am to 1pm from a long menu. There's a good selection of wines and liquors.

## INEXPENSIVE

**Cushing Street Bar & Grill.** 343 S. Meyer Ave. at Cushing St. (across from the Tucson Convention Center). ☎ **520/622-7984.** Reservations recommended. Main courses $6–$17. AE, MC, V. Daily 11am–midnight (bar open until 1am). CONTEMPORARY AMERICAN.

Though the menu has become rather mundane in recent times, this restaurant, located at the edge of the old Barrio neighborhood, is still appealing, though primarily for the fact that it's in a restored historic adobe building. Saltillo tile floors and lots of antique touches make this a fascinating place. The courtyard patio is classically stark and a great place for a wintertime lunch. An assortment of burgers, sandwiches, pastas, and dishes such as meat loaf and mashed potatoes make this place popular with all ages, and the bar and live jazz keep the joint jumpin'.

**La Indita.** 622 N. 4th Ave. ☎ **520/792-0523.** Main courses $4–$8. DISC, MC, V. Mon–Fri 11am–9pm, Sat 6–9pm, Sun 9am–9pm. REGIONAL MEXICAN.

It's just a little family run business serving Tohono-Tarascan Mexican-style food, but the home cooking here is cheap and authentic. House and daily specials such as chilies rellenos, chicken mole, and chicken enchiladas with green sauce are all popular. There are also plenty of vegetarian dishes such as spinach-and-nut enchiladas and mushroom tacos. This place is a favorite of college students.

**Miami Tropical Cafeteria.** 1045 E. 6th St. ☎ **520/623-8020.** Main courses $4–$6.25. No credit cards. Mon–Sat 11am–7pm. CUBAN.

With just a few tables in a storefront near the University of Arizona, this casual place feels like a Cuban restaurant straight out of Miami. The cheerful proprietor will dish you up a daily special from the steam table (perhaps chicken seasoned with olives, garlic, and bay leaves accompanied by black beans and rice). The Cuban sandwich is a meat- and cheese-filled baguette, pressed and warmed on the grill. Exotic drinks are often unidentifiable but are well worth trying, as are fruit shakes of mango, banana, and *guanabana*.

✪ **Native Café & Coffee House.** 3073 N. Campbell Ave. ☎ **520/881-8881.** Salads and sandwiches $5–$9. DC, DISC, MC, V. Mon–Thurs 8am–9pm, Fri–Sat 8am–11pm, Sun 8am–4:30pm. NATURAL FOODS.

With a mellow, arty atmosphere and a comfortable patio, the Native Café is a good place for a leisurely light meal or snack. Opulent salads brimming with the freshest of veggies, and delicious sandwiches garnished with huge, crunchy sunflower sprouts are the norm here (the sandwiches are basically salads between slices of handcrafted bread). There are plenty of choices for everyone from vegans to meat eaters—and it's all healthful and impeccably fresh. You can also choose among juices, smoothies, or coffees to go with a sweet treat of banana nut bread or cardamom cinnamon coffee cake.

**Pronto.** 2955 E. Speedway Blvd. ☎ **520/326-9707.** Soups, salads, and sandwiches $5–$9. MC, V. Mon–Thurs 11am–3pm and 5–9pm, Fri 11am–3pm and 5–10pm, Sat 9am–3pm and 5–10pm, Sun 9am–3pm. CONTEMPORARY AMERICAN/MEDITERRANEAN.

This restaurant is a good example of what can be done to recycle a fast-food establishment. It still retains the walk-up counter, but now boasts a creative, contemporary menu and hip decor. Come here if you want your food fast, good, and cheap. You can get not only burgers and lots of sandwiches but also favorites such as vegetarian lasagna, pizza, and penne with chicken and Gorgonzola cream sauce. There's also a kids' menu with items such as Parmesan and butter pinwheel sandwiches. Very reasonably priced wines.

# EAST TUCSON
## EXPENSIVE

**Cielos.** At Lodge on the Desert, 306 N. Alvernon Way. ☎ **520/325-3366.** Reservations recommended. Main courses $13–$23. AE, DISC, MC, V. Daily 7–10:30pm, 11am–2pm, and 5–10pm. CONTINENTAL.

Arriving at Cielos is like taking a step back to a more tranquil time. Against a backdrop of rosy terra cotta walls, the colorful gardens, table candlelight, and fragrant woods burning in the open fireplaces create a romantic ambience. Ask for a table on the terrace, where you'll have garden and fireplace views. Cielos tends to be popular with an older clientele, and perhaps for that reason the menu has become more conservative of late. Look for familiar favorites such as well-prepared pork tenderloin or filet mignon with whipped potatoes and a port wine sauce. Salads are simple yet tasty. The wine list, both by the glass and by the bottle, is fairly reasonably priced, as are the entrees.

**Le Rendez-Vous.** 3844 E. Ft. Lowell Rd. (at Alvernon Way). ☎ **520/323-7373.** Reservations recommended. Main courses $7–$11 at lunch, $14–$26 at dinner. AE, DC, DISC, MC, V. Tues–Fri 11:30am–2pm; Tues–Sun 6–10pm. FRENCH.

While this rather casual French restaurant serves all the usual dishes you would expect (escargots, pâté, vichyssoise, veal sweetbreads), it has become legendary among Tucson's foodies for its phenomenal duck à l'orange, and you would be remiss if someone at your table didn't order this dish. However, rest assured that there are also other dishes worth ordering here. To leave more room for a selection from the pastry tray, you can even order from the limited spa menu. At lunch, try the classic *moules marinieres* (mussels cooked in white wine) and the ultimate spinach salad. You might expect such rich and savory fare to be served amid rarefied elegance, but instead, Le Rendez-Vous is housed in an unpretentious little stucco cottage and the atmosphere is strictly bistro.

**The Ranchers Club.** In the Sheraton Tucson Hotel & Suites, 5151 E. Grant Rd. ☎ **520/ 323-6262** or 520/321-7621. Reservations recommended. Main courses $7.25–$12 at lunch, $15.50–$26 at dinner. AE, CB, DC, DISC, MC, V. Mon–Fri 11:30am–2pm, Mon–Sat 5:30–10pm. STEAK/SEAFOOD.

There's no question as to where to get one of the best steaks in Tucson: The Ranchers Club. But before you saddle up the palomino and trot over, you might want to know that the interior is liberally accented by stuffed animal heads, like a private men's club of yore. The Ranchers Club glorifies the Old West with its decor of old saddles, chaps, and steer horns, while antiques and brocade chairs lend the dining room a touch of elegance. Certified Black Angus beef is grilled over aromatic mesquite fire, adding subtle flavors to the meats. Seafood and poultry is also available.

## MODERATE

✪ **Cottonwood Café.** 60 N. Alvernon Way (north of Broadway). ☎ **520/326-6000.** Reservations recommended especially for patio dining. Main courses $6–$11 at lunch, $11–$20 at dinner. AE, DC, DISC, MC, V. Daily 11:15am–3pm and 5:30–10pm. SOUTH-WESTERN.

Located in a beautifully renovated old hacienda in a park-like setting, the Cottonwood Cafe turns out some of the boldest flavors in town, making this one of Tucson's most popular Southwestern restaurants. Portions are generous, and wine prices moderate. There's also an outstanding selection of tequilas (think margarita on the palm-shaded patio). The "absolutely fiery" chicken, the restaurant's signature dish, made with a habanero-mango glaze, is definitely for fire-eaters only. At lunch, the Zuni roll—smoked turkey, scallions, Havarti cheese, and boar bacon in a flour tortilla with raspberry chipotle sauce—is complex and delicious. A late-night menu goes until about 11pm, and there's live jazz and blues throughout the week in the adjacent Cottonwood Club.

**Dakota Café.** 6541 E. Tanque Verde Rd. (at Traildust Town near the Pinnacle Peak Steak-house). ☎ **520/298-7188.** Reservations recommended on weekends, especially for the patio. Main courses $6–$10 at lunch, $9–$18 at dinner. AE, CB, DC, DISC, MC, V. Mon–Thurs 11am–9pm, Fri–Sat 11am–10pm. INTERNATIONAL.

Located in a mock cow town favored by families with small children, this restaurant, with its bold paint job and halogen lighting, lures a fairly sophisticated and adult crowd. Start your meal out on the patio with fruity apricot iced tea (very refreshing on a hot day) and tempura coconut shrimp with chutney marmalade. The grilled Ahi tuna sandwich with herbed aioli and pickled ginger is tasty and well textured and comes with a generous side of pasta salad. For dinner, we like the grilled lamb sauced with prickly pear and port wine. The food here is hearty yet inventive enough to try on a regular basis, and vegetarians will find many meatless choices. Reasonable prices and a comfortable atmosphere add up to a good value.

**Fuego.** 6958 E. Tanque Verde Rd. (in Santa Fe Square). ☎ **520/886-1745.** Reservations recommended. Main courses $15–$19. AE, MC, V. Sun–Thurs 5–9pm, Fri–Sat 5–11pm. CONTEMPORARY AMERICAN/SOUTHWEST.

The name Fuego means fire, and there really *are* flambéed dishes on the menu here, especially among the extensive list of appetizers. Overall, though, the food here is more Southwestern than fiery. The atmosphere is slightly formal but unpretentious, with tables set fairly close together. Waiters bustle about serving such uniquely flavored dishes as the signature Field of Greens salad, with blue cheese, chile-roasted walnuts, and dried cranberries, or prickly pear pork tenderloin that is so tender you can cut it with a fork. Great sauces, such as a rich, smoky chipotle cream sauce on chicken capellini, also issue from this kitchen. Artful food presentation can be amusing, if a little difficult to approach with a fork. Lively yet intimate, Fuego appeals to couples, families, and retirees alike, and as for attire, casual to dressy fits in just fine.

**Keaton's Arizona Grill.** 7401 N. La Cholla Blvd. (in the Foothills Mall). ☎ **520/297-1999.** Reservations recommended on weekends. Main courses $6–$14 at lunch, $9–$18 at dinner. AE, DISC, MC, V. Daily 11am–10pm. CONTEMPORARY AMERICAN.

Keaton's, located adjacent to a shopping mall in the northern suburbs, is a great place for innovative and moderately priced food. The unpretentious setting is casual yet classy, with cozy lighting and booths, a comfortable spot for conversation with friends. Be forewarned, however, that both the crunchy sourdough and the zucchini bread at Keaton's are so good that it's virtually impossible to save room for your meal (just say no to more bread). To balance out your overly zealous attack on the bread basket, try the chicken salad with sun-dried cherries or the applewood house-smoked salmon. If you were able to control yourself, consider the barbecued baby back ribs or pasta with mesquite-grilled chicken and poblano chile pesto. You might not want to miss the great selection of margaritas and martinis served here.

**Vivace Restaurant.** 4811 E. Grant Rd. ☎ **520/795-7221.** Reservations recommended. Main courses $12–$20. AE, DC, MC, V. Mon–Thurs 11:30am–9pm, Fri–Sat 11:30am–10pm, Sun 5–9pm. NORTHERN ITALIAN.

Run by the same folks who gave Tucson Scordato's restaurant, this Italian restaurant serves reasonably priced creative dishes in a casual but upscale setting in a shopping plaza. The restaurant can be noisy at times, owing to its popularity—the crowd is mixed, both young and old. First, crusty bread comes with a basil-infused olive oil. Then one of the possible appetizers is a large luscious antipasto platter for two containing garlicked spinach, roasted red peppers, artichoke hearts, and marinated goat cheese. The dish is visually appealing and tastes as good as it looks. The bustling wait staff doesn't waste time in getting your order from the open kitchen to you. Pasta dishes, such as penne with sausage and roasted-pepper sauce, come served on a very large dish. Salads are generous, the wine list is good and reasonable, and the server will recite a long litany of desserts: mango sorbet, crème brûlée, and the lightest ever flourless chocolate cake.

## INEXPENSIVE

**Casa Molina.** 6225 E. Speedway Blvd. (near the northwest corner with Wilmot Rd.). ☎ **520/886-5468.** Reservations recommended. Dinners $12–$18, à la carte $3–$12. AE, DC, DISC, MC, V. Daily 11am–10pm. MEXICAN.

For years this has been Tucson's favorite family run Mexican restaurant. You can't miss it—just watch for the larger-than-life-size bull and bullfighter in front. Casa Molina sports a festive atmosphere and is usually abuzz with families, groups, and couples. The margaritas are among the best in town, and the *carne seca* (sun-dried beef) shouldn't be missed. Lighter eaters will enjoy a layered topopo salad made with tortillas, refried beans, chicken, lettuce, celery, avocado, tomato, and jalapeños. The food is good, and the service is efficient; the only complaint is that prices are a little on the high side for Mexican cookery. The patio is pleasant in almost any weather.

There are other locations at 3001 N. Campbell Ave. (☎ **520/795-7593**) and 4240 E. Grant Rd. (☎ **520/326-6663**).

**La Parilla Suiza.** 5602 E. Speedway Blvd. ☎ **520/747-4838.** Main courses $5.50–$15. AE, DC, DISC, MC, V. Sun–Thurs 11am–10pm, Fri–Sat 11am–11pm. MEXICAN.

Most Mexican food served in the United States is limited to Sonoran style, originating just south of the border. Actually, however, the cuisine of Mexico is nearly as varied as that of China, and the meals served at La Parilla Suiza are based on the style popular in Mexico City, where most of the chain's restaurants are located. Many menu items are sandwiched between two flour tortillas, much like a quesadilla, but the charcoal broiling of meats and cheeses lends the sandwiches special status. Fried green scallions with lime is a favorite appetizer.

There's another La Parilla Suiza at 2720 N. Oracle Rd. (☎ **520/624-4300**).

**Little Anthony's Diner.** 7010 E. Broadway Blvd. (in back of the Gaslight Plaza). ☎ **520/ 296-0456.** Burgers and sandwiches $4–$7. MC, V. Mon–Thurs 11am–9pm, Fri 11am–11pm, Sat 8am–11pm, Sun 8am–10pm. AMERICAN.

This is a place for kids, although big kids like us also enjoy the 1950s music and decor. The staff is good with children, and there's a video-games room and a rocket ship outside to ride. How about a jailhouse rock burger or hound dog hot dog with a tower of onion rings? Daily specials and bottomless soft drinks make feeding the family fairly inexpensive. Beer and wine are also served, and Friday and Saturday nights there's a DJ along with the dinner. The gaslight melodrama theater next door makes a perfect night out for the family.

## THE FOOTHILLS
### EXPENSIVE

**Anthony's in the Catalinas.** 6440 N. Campbell Ave. ☎ **520/299-1771.** Reservations highly recommended. Main courses $9–$15 at lunch, $20–$30 at dinner. AE, DC, MC, V. Mon–Fri 11am–2pm and 5:30–9pm, Sat–Sun 5:30–9pm. NEW AMERICAN/CONTINENTAL.

Anthony's, housed in a modern Italianate-style building overlooking the city, exudes Southwestern elegance from the moment you drive under the portico and let the valet park your car. The waiters are smartly attired in tuxedos, and guests (the cigar and single-malt Foothills set) are nearly as well dressed. In such a rarefied atmosphere you'd expect only the finest meal, and that's exactly what you get. Shrimp stuffed with horseradish and wrapped in bacon with a caper sauce is a fitting beginning, followed by the likes of lamb Wellington baked in puff pastry with pâté and prosciutto. Wine is not just an accompaniment but a reason for dining out at Anthony's; at more than 70 pages, the wine list may be the most extensive in the city. Don't miss out on the next best part of a meal here (after the wine): the day's soufflé (order early).

**Daniel's Restaurant & Trattoria.** In St. Philip's Plaza, 4340 N. Campbell Ave. ☎ **520/ 742-3200.** Reservations recommended. Main courses $17–$28.50. AE, CB, DC, DISC, MC, V. Daily 5–10pm. NORTHERN ITALIAN/MEDITERRANEAN.

Although the elegant atmosphere here translates into a good place for a business lunch or a romantic evening out (you might want to dress up a bit), what stands out most is the contemporary northern Italian cuisine, which varies from the simple to the complex. Service is attentive but nonintrusive, and a basket of bread that appears as soon as you're seated includes fresh baked focaccia, breadsticks, and herb-flavored olive oil. For an appetizer, we recommend the intriguing flavors of the smoked-salmon napoleon, which is layered with cream cheese and shaved sweet potato and garnished with capers and red onion. No less extravagant is the mesquite-grilled beef tenderloin with kalamata olive sauce and spicy eggplant relish, but save room for the warm chocolate truffle cake and vanilla-bean gelato. An outstanding wine list emphasizes Italian wines and includes about 40 wines by the glass, many of them fairly inexpensive. Lots of single malts, too.

**The Gold Room.** In the Westward Look Resort, 245 E. Ina Rd. ☎ **520/297-1151.** Reservations recommended. Main courses $9–$16 at lunch, $17.50–$34 at dinner. AE, DC, DISC, MC, V. Mon–Sat 7–11am, 11:30am–2pm, and 5:30–10pm; Sun 7–10:30am, 11:30–2pm (brunch) and 5:30–10pm. NEW AMERICAN/CONTINENTAL.

Located in the Westward Look Resort, the Gold Room is a tastefully casual restaurant featuring Southwestern ranch decor and a terrace for alfresco dining. Despite the casual decor, the place settings are elegant and the service is very professional. Satisfying all tastes, the menu is equally divided between classic dishes (filet mignon and roast rack of lamb) and regional specialties, all of which are beautifully presented. We favor the regional cuisine—tender mesquite-grilled buffalo with purple Peruvian potatoes or blue corn–encrusted pork chops—which emphasizes flavor over fire. The length of the wine list is staggering, and there's a welcome range of prices. Desserts are delectably rich and amusingly presented—the chocolate bombé is an event in itself. Lunch prices are less expensive than those at dinner, but the restaurant is most remarkable at night when the cityscape of Tucson twinkles below.

✪ **The Grill.** At the Hacienda del Sol Guest Ranch Resort, 5601 N. Hacienda del Sol Rd. ☎ **520/529-3500.** Reservations recommended. Main courses $18–$34. AE, CB, DC, DISC, MC, V. Daily 5–10pm, Sun brunch 10am–2pm. NEW AMERICAN.

Located in a 1920s hacienda-style building at a former foothills dude ranch, The Grill has been one of Tucson's hottest restaurants for a couple of years now. Not only do you get well-prepared grilled meats and vegetables, you also get great views of the city and a classically styled southwestern setting. For openers, consider the roasted tomato soup, which comes with grilled zucchini and goat cheese crostini and is among the most satisfying starters on the menu. The dry-aged angus New York strip steak is the most popular entree, but anyone seeking greater creativity would do well to opt for the applewood-smoked breast of duck with apple-cranberry relish. To top things off, try one of the extravagant desserts, such as mango, lemon, and raspberry sorbets in a chocolate tulip. The patio overlooks the Catalinas and the fairways of the Westin La Paloma's golf course.

**Janos.** At the Westin La Paloma, 3770 E. Sunrise Dr. ☎ **520/615-6100.** Reservations highly recommended. Main courses $24–$36; 5-course tasting menu $65 ($100 with wines); summer sampler $14–$16. AE, DC, MC, V. Mon–Sat 5:30–9pm. SOUTHWESTERN/REGIONAL.

Housed in a separate building just outside the front door of the luxurious Westin La Paloma resort, Janos has long been Tucson's most celebrated restaurant. This is about as formal a restaurant as you'll find in this otherwise very casual city, and the tuxedoed wait staff looks as if it could be a symphony orchestra moonlighting for the night. The surroundings are positively baronial, with overtones of Spanish colonial decor. The menu here changes both daily and seasonally, and the wine list is award-winning. Chef Janos shows his enthusiasm in creating complex dishes such as a Napoleon of potato crisps, Dungeness crab, salmon gravlax, and guacamole, along with dramatically presented entrees such as pistachio-crusted rack of lamb with couscous and fig baklava. At least one vegetarian entree with sophisticated embellishments appears on the menu nightly. During the summer there's a low-priced sampler menu that is one of Tucson's best values.

**McMahon's Prime Steakhouse.** 2959 N. Swan Rd. ☎ **520/327-7463.** Reservations recommended. Main courses $17–$44. AE, DC, DISC, MC, V. Mon–Thurs 11:30am–10pm, Fri 11:30am–11pm, Sat 5–11pm, Sun 5–10pm. STEAKS/SEAFOOD.

If a perfectly done steak is your idea of a memorable meal out, then you'll enjoy McMahon's. With a decidedly nineties opulence that's a far cry from steakhouses of yore, McMahon's boasts an atmosphere that's calculated to impress. A large glass-walled wine room dominates the main dining room, which is ringed with large plush booths. You can drop a bundle on dinner here, but no more than you'd spend at such high-end restaurants as Janos, the Tack Room, or the Ventana Room. The main difference is that here your choices are simpler: steak, seafood, or steak and seafood. You'd be wasting a night out, though, if you didn't order a steak; the aged prime-beef steaks here are the best we've ever had. Though the steaks come with a wedge of iceberg lettuce, everything else is à la carte. For those whose tastes run to after-dinner entertainments, there is a separate piano lounge and cigar bar.

✪ **The Tack Room.** 7300 E. Vactor Ranch Trail. ☎ **520/722-2800.** Reservations recommended. Main courses $26.50–$37.50. AE, CB, DC, DISC, MC, V. May to mid-Jan Tues–Sun 6–10pm; mid-Jan to Apr daily 6–10pm. SOUTHWESTERN/NEW AMERICAN.

Housed in an older Southwestern-style hacienda with a casually elegant atmosphere, The Tack Room is Tucson's most prestigious restaurant. This is a place to feel pampered. From the time that little marinated salads appear on the table to the moment the last bit of chocolate is savored , service (by a bevy of tuxedoed waiters) is attentive and discreet. Although the filet mignon (perhaps served with a charred tomato and oregano sauce) is the most popular dish on the menu, plump Guaymas shrimp shows up regularly in various incarnations and is always delicious. Crispy yet succulent duck, topped with pistachios and sitting on a pile of not-too-sweet fig-and-orange chutney, is another perennial favorite here. Coffee, which comes with a condiment tray that includes whipped cream and crumbled Belgian chocolate, could double as desert, but don't let it. Of course, you'll pay for all this, but you'll leave truly satisfied with your dining experience.

**Ventana Room.** In Loews Ventana Canyon Resort, 7000 N. Resort Dr. ☎ **520/299-2020.** Reservations highly recommended. Jacket recommended for men. Main courses $26–$38; chef's 5-course tasting menu $75 without wine, $125 with wine; 4-course spa menu $55. AE, CB, DC, DISC, MC, V. Daily 6–10pm, closed Tues July–Aug. NEW AMERICAN.

With the spectacular setting and waterfall at the head of Ventana Canyon, it would be worth eating at the Ventana Room even if the food weren't so good. *Ventana* means "window" in Spanish, and the views through the windows here feature either the canyon waterfall or the twinkling lights of the city below. Ethereal strains of a harp set the mood. Perhaps the best dish on the menu is the velvety textured fillet of Dover sole with truffles. The house smoked salmon, translucent and moist, is nearly as appealing. Baby spinach Caesar salad on a Parmesan wafer is another standout. With creations such as the indecently rich signature crème brûlée surrounded by raspberry sauce, you might not want to let the dessert cart pass you by. In this rarified atmosphere, you will be pampered by a bevy of wait staff, including a well-informed sommelier, whose service is professional and unobtrusive.

## MODERATE

**Café Terra Cotta.** In St. Philip's Plaza, 4310 N. Campbell Ave. (at River Rd.). ☎ **520/577-8100.** Reservations recommended. Main courses $12–$22. AE, DC, DISC, MC, V. Sun–Thurs 11am–9:30pm, Fri–Sat 11am–10:30pm. SOUTHWESTERN.

Located in the upscale St. Philip's Plaza shopping center, Café Terra Cotta is Arizona's original Southwestern restaurant, and for many years, one of Tucson's most highly acclaimed. The combination of a casual atmosphere and creative cooking appeals to trendy Tucsonans, who stop by for dinner or to pick up gourmet food to go. A large brick oven is used to make imaginative pizzas, while salads, sandwiches, small plates, and main dishes flesh out the long menu. With so many choices, it's often difficult to decide, but we can recommend the grilled eggplant and portobello sandwich with red bell peppers, basil, and goat cheese on focaccia and the pork tenderloin *adobado* (spicy red sauce) with apricot-chile conserve. For dessert, the chocolate mousse pie requires a Herculean effort to resist.

**Firecracker.** 2990 N. Swan Rd. (at Ft. Lowell). ☎ **520/318-1118.** Reservations recommended. Main courses $8–$18. Sunset dinners 4–6pm daily. AE, DISC, MC, V. Sun–Thurs 4–10pm, Fri–Sat 4pm–10:30pm. PAN ASIAN.

With a menu that knows no boundaries and a wild decor that includes flames issuing from torches atop the building and faux tree trunks in the bar, Firecracker is currently one of Tucson's hot spots. Large portions and very reasonable prices contribute to this restaurant's popularity. The spicy-chicken lettuce-cup appetizers (sort of roll-your-own burritos) are a fun finger-food starter. Seafood is definitely the strong suit here, and the huge wok-charred chunks of salmon covered with cilantro pesto is just about the best thing on the menu (and at only $11 is a great deal). Needless to say, the coconut crème brûlée is rich and creamy and deliciously unhealthful. Expect a wait even if you have a reservation.

✪ **Flying V Bar & Grill.** In Loews Ventana Canyon Resort, 7000 N. Resort Dr. ☎ **520/299-2020.** Reservations recommended at dinner. Main courses $10–$16 at lunch, $16–$23 at dinner. AE, DC, DISC, MC, V. Tues–Sun 11am–2:30pm and 5–10pm, appetizers daily 2:30–5pm. SOUTHWESTERN.

If it's bold Southwestern fare you're after, you won't do better than the Flying V. Take a seat out on the large deck and watch the koi in the pond below or the golfers struggling not to double bogey on the 18th hole of the Canyon Course. Mixing creative Southwestern and gourmet Mexican, this is just about the only menu in Tucson that competes with the flair of downtown's Café Poca Cosa. There aren't too many places where you'll find ostrich fajitas, venison nachos, and duck tacos. Even the soups get creative; the flavorful chicken posole comes with a pastry cup of *crema* (sort of like sour cream) to drop into the middle of the bowl. The guacamole prepared table side is a lot of fun, as are the hot pink prickly pear margaritas. Keep an eye out for stray golf balls, and don't miss the red-chile onion rings.

**Ovens.** At St. Philip's Plaza, corner of Campbell Ave. at River Rd. ☎ **520/577-9001.** Reservations recommended. Main courses $8–$19. AE, DC, MC, V. Sun–Thurs 11am–9:30pm, Fri–Sat 11am–10pm. INTERNATIONAL.

Sort of a clone of Café Terra Cotta (see above), Ovens is located across the plaza from the aforementioned cafe—which is fine because you can never have too much of a good thing. Here at Ovens, the wood-fired oven turns out pizzas topped with practically every imaginable ingredient, from green chiles to grilled eggplant sauced with *chipotle* (a smoky jalapeño flavor). Or if you'd rather, there are salads, handmade pasta dishes, and grilled meats and fish. Like the cafe across the way, there is also an outdoor patio on the mall and a lounge inside, where you can sample one of their many wines by the glass. Whimsical art on the walls lend a playful atmosphere.

✪ **Wildflower.** 7037 N. Oracle Rd. (in the Casa Adobes Shopping Plaza between Oracle and Ina rds.). ☎ **520/219-4230.** Reservations recommended. Main courses $7.50–$10 at lunch, $11–$20 at dinner. AE, DC, DISC, MC, V. Sun–Thurs 11am–3pm and 5–9pm; Fri–Sat 11am–3pm and 5–10pm. NEW AMERICAN.

Stylish comfort foods in gargantuan proportions are the order of the day at this chic and casually elegant north Tucson bistro. A huge wall of glass creates minimalist drama, and large flower photographs on the walls enhance the bright and airy decor. The marinated Chinese chicken salad tossed with Napa cabbage and wontons and the heaping plate of fried calamari with mizuna greens are both well worth trying. Dinner

---

### ⓘ  Family-Friendly Restaurants

**Hidden Valley Inn** *(see p. 322)*   It's a false-fronted cow town in bright colors with an authentic dance hall and stable, which are the dining rooms. Kids will love the miniature action dioramas of funny Western scenes.

**Little Anthony's Diner** *(see p. 317)*   This is a place for kids, although big kids like us also enjoy the 1950s music and decor. The staff is good with children, and there's a video-games room and a rocket ship outside to ride. The gaslight melo-drama theater next door makes a perfect night out for the family.

**Pinnacle Peak Steakhouse** *(see p. 322)*   Dinner here is a Wild West event, with an entire Western town outside and a carousel. Kids love it.

---

offers similar appetizers and entrees as at lunch. These run the gamut from roasted sturgeon with black caviar essence to a simple roasted chicken. Pasta and salmon also both show up in various guises. With so many tempting, reasonably priced dishes to sample, Wildflower is a foodie's delight.

## INEXPENSIVE

✪ **El Corral Restaurant.** 2201 E. River Rd. ☎ **520/299-6092.** Reservations not accepted. Complete dinner $8–$12; kids' meals $2.25–$4. AE, DC, DISC, MC, V. Mon–Thurs 5–10pm, Fri–Sun 4:30–10pm. STEAKS.

Owned by the same folks who brought you Tucson's Pinnacle Peak Steakhouse, El Corral is another inexpensive steakhouse, and very popular with retirees and families. The restaurant doesn't accept reservations, so expect long lines or come before or after regular dinner hours. The hacienda building has flagstone floors and wood paneling that make it dark and cozy, while outside in the bright sunlight a cactus garden flourishes. In keeping with the name, there's a traditional corral fence of mesquite branches around the restaurant parking lot. Prime rib is the house specialty, but there are also steaks, chicken, pork ribs, and burgers for the kids.

**Tohono Chul Tea Room.** 7366 N. Paseo del Norte (1 block west of the corner of Ina Rd. and Oracle Rd. in Tohono Chul Park). ☎ **520/797-1222.** Reservations accepted for 6 or more. Main courses $5–$8. AE, MC, V. Daily 8am–5pm. REGIONAL AMERICAN.

Located in a brick territorial-style building in 37-acre Tohono Chul Park, this is one of the most tranquil restaurants in the city. The garden setting provides a wonderful chance to experience the desert. Before or after lunching on a grilled raspberry-chipotle chicken sandwich or some tortilla soup, you can wander through the park's desert landscaping admiring the many species of cacti. The tearoom's patios, sur-rounded by natural vegetation and plenty of flowers in pots, are frequented by many species of birds. The adjacent gift shop is packed with Mexican folk art, nature theme toys, household items, T-shirts, and books. For a description of the park, see "Parks, Gardens & Zoos" under "Seeing the Sights."

## WEST TUCSON

**Scordato's.** 4405 W. Speedway Blvd. ☎ **520/792-3055.** Reservations highly recom-mended. Main courses $16–$21. AE, CB, DC, DISC, MC, V. Daily 5–9pm. ITALIAN.

It's a long way out to Scordato's, but that doesn't bother the loyal clientele of retirees, business types, and families who enjoy the setting near Saguaro National Park. The restaurant looks a bit like a lost Italian villa searching for the Mediterranean coast, with saguaros standing next to cypresses out front. Inside, a semiformal atmosphere reigns, with plush carpets, comfortable brocade chairs, and big windows that allow diners to enjoy desert views in comfort. Despite the crystal chandeliers and tapestries on the walls, casually dressy is the key for attire here. The menu contains many tempting choices, although it's difficult to move beyond the variety of veal dishes. Veal Stresa, stuffed with prosciutto and mozzarella and then sautéed in marsala and white-wine sauce is a favorite. For an appetizer, we like the scampi sauté. The extensive wine list will satisfy the wine connoisseur.

## COWBOY STEAKHOUSES

✪ **Hidden Valley Inn.** 4825 N. Sabino Canyon Rd. ☎ **520/299-4941.** Reservations not accepted. Main courses $6–$20. MC, V. Daily 11am–3pm and 4:30–10pm. STEAKS.

Kids will love this brightly colored, false-fronted cow town, whose most entertaining feature are the walls of glass cases containing miniature action dioramas of humorous Western scenes. A very authentic dance hall and stable serve as dining rooms, and the Red Garter Saloon is a place for adults to imbibe. This steakhouse is the kind where people come to celebrate a family birthday and inevitably leave with large doggie bags. Cowpuncher-size steaks and barbecued ribs are the main attraction, although there are also some seafood and chicken choices.

**L'il Abner's Steakhouse.** 8500 N. Silverbell Rd. ☎ **520/744-2800.** Reservations recommended on weekends. Main courses $11–$21. MC, V. Sun–Thurs 5–10pm, Fri–Sat 5–11pm. Take I-10 to the Cortaro Farms Rd. exit; then go west on Cortaro Farms Rd. and north on Silverbell Rd. STEAKS.

This steakhouse, which used to be an old stagecoach stop, is almost as rustic as in the days of the Wild West, though the suburbs are just across the street these days. The steaks are cooked over a mesquite fire and eaten (with all the beans, bread, and salsa your heart desires) at picnic tables. Friday and Saturday nights are extra lively with country music and dancing.

**Pinnacle Peak Steakhouse.** 6541 E. Tanque Verde Rd. ☎ **520/296-0911.** Reservations not accepted. Main courses $2.25–$14. AE, DC, DISC, MC, V. Winter Mon–Thurs 5–10pm, Fri–Sun 4:30–10pm; summer daily 5–10pm. STEAKS.

Located in the Trail Dust Town, a Wild West–themed shopping and dining center, the Pinnacle Peak Steakhouse specializes in family dining in a fun cowboy atmosphere. Be prepared for crowds—this place is very popular with tour buses. Stroll the wooden sidewalks past the opera house and saloon to the grand old dining rooms of the Pinnacle Peak Steakhouse. You'll be surprised at the authenticity of the restaurant, which really does resemble a dining room in Old Tombstone or Dodge City. During the winter months, the longest waits for a table will be around 7pm, so try to come either earlier or later.

## QUICK BITES, CAFES & COFFEEHOUSES

A student hangout near the University of Arizona, **Café Paraíso,** 820 E. University Blvd. (☎ **520/624-1707**), has a shady and cool patio and delectable salads and sandwiches. **Cuppuccinos,** 3400 E. Speedway Blvd. (☎ **520/323-7205**), bills itself as a Seattle-style coffeehouse, and **The Epic Café,** 745 N. Fourth Ave. (☎ **520/624-6844**), is a good hangout place with wild artwork, delicious scones, and other light fare. Look for the mural out front. For eight-layer cakes and light food in an edgy atmosphere, we buzz on over to **The Cup** at Club Congress, 311 E. Congress St. (☎ **520/798-1618**). With comfy couches and a place to plug in your laptop, the **Coffee X Change,** 2415 N. Campbell Ave. (☎ **520/327-6784**) makes a good stop between downtown and the foothills. The **Bristol Espresso Bus,** a 1937 British double-decker bus and probably the oldest double-decker bus in the U.S., is parked at

5775 E. Broadway (no phone), waiting to serve you espresso. The bus will probably be closed during the summer.

You can't beat the cheap breakfast specials on our favorite bagels at **The Bagelry,** 5319 E. Speedway Blvd. (☎ **520/322-0223**) and 2575 N. Campbell Ave. (☎ **520/ 881-6674**). When we need a quick lunch, we dart over to **Baggins Gourmet Sandwiches** for a delicious sandwich. Baggins has several locations, three of which are at Kolb Road and Speedway Boulevard (☎ **520/290-9383**), Campbell Avenue and Ft. Lowell Road (☎ **520/327-1611**), and Church Avenue and Pennington Street (☎ **520/792-1344**). Call for the one nearest you. **Beyond Bread,** 3055 North Campbell Ave. (☎ **520/322-9965**), will make you up the likes of a turkey and brie sandwich on their ultrafresh bread. The best pizza in town can be had at **Magpies Gourmet Pizza,** at Fourth Avenue and Fifth Street (☎ **520/628-1661**), Speedway Boulevard and Swan Road (☎ **520/795-5977**), Broadway Boulevard and Pantano Road (☎ **520/751-9949**), and Ina and Oracle roads (☎ **520/297-2712**). **Reay's Ranch Markets** is a good place to get picnic supplies. They have organic fruit, delicious baked goods, cheese, meats, and wine, the kind of things you'd expect from a specialty market. They're located at 3360 E. Speedway Blvd. (☎ **520/795-9844**), 7133 Oracle and Ina rds. (☎ **520/297-5394**), and in the foothills at Sunrise Drive and Swan Road (☎ **520/299-8858**).

# 5  Seeing the Sights

## THE TOP ATTRACTIONS

While there are plenty of interesting things to see and do all over the Tucson area, anyone interested in the desert Southwest or the cinematic Wild West should head over to the western edge of the city immediately. Here is not only the west section of Saguaro National Park (with the biggest and best stands of saguaro cactus) but also the Arizona–Sonora Desert Museum (one of Arizona's most popular attractions) and Old Tucson Studios (film site for hundreds of westerns over the years). Together these three attractions make a great day's outing.

## THE TUCSON AREA'S (MOSTLY) NATURAL WONDERS

✪ **Arizona–Sonora Desert Museum.** 2021 N. Kinney Rd. ☎ **520/883-2702** or 520/ 883-1380. Admission $8.95 adults, $1.75 children 6–12, free for children 5 and under. Oct–Feb daily 8:30am–5pm; Mar–Sept daily 7:30am–6pm. From downtown Tucson, go west on Speedway Blvd., which becomes Gates Pass Rd., and follow the signs.

Don't be fooled by the name. This is a zoo, and it's one of the best in the country. Also, don't be surprised to find yourself spending more hours here than you intended. The Arizona–Sonora Desert Museum is located 14 miles west of Tucson between Tucson Mountain Park and Saguaro National Park West.

The Sonoran Desert encompasses much of central and southern Arizona as well as parts of northern Mexico. In this desert are not only arid lands but also forested mountains, springs, rivers, and streams. The full spectrum of Sonoran Desert life— from plants to insects to fish to reptiles to mammals—is on display here in natural settings. There are black bears and mountain lions, beavers and otters, frogs and fish, tarantulas and scorpions, prairie dogs and javelinas (wild boar). In addition, there's a simulated cave with exhibits on prehistoric desert life. Our favorite exhibit is an aviary holding a dozen species of hummingbird. The tiny birds buzz past your ears and stop only inches in front of your face. A separate aviary contains many other bird species. Docents explain everything from the life cycle of the saguaro cactus to the feeding habits of the tarantula. Two restaurants, Ironwood Terraces (cafeteria style) and the Ocatillo Cafe (a sit-down restaurant), serve excellent food and are well worth a stop.

# Tucson Attractions

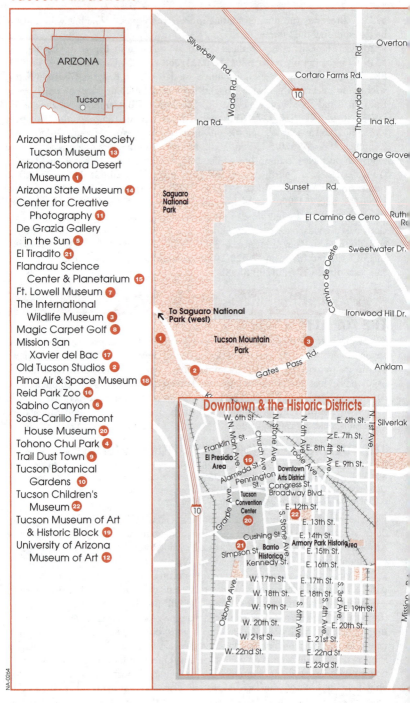

ARIZONA

Tucson

Arizona Historical Society
 Tucson Museum 13
Arizona-Sonora Desert
 Museum 1
Arizona State Museum 14
Center for Creative
 Photography 11
De Grazia Gallery
 in the Sun 5
El Tiradito 21
Flandrau Science
 Center & Planetarium 15
Ft. Lowell Museum 7
The International
 Wildlife Museum 3
Magic Carpet Golf 8
Mission San
 Xavier del Bac 17
Old Tucson Studios 2
Pima Air & Space Museum 18
Reid Park Zoo 16
Sabino Canyon 6
Sosa-Carillo Fremont
 House Museum 20
Tohono Chul Park 4
Trail Dust Town 9
Tucson Botanical
 Gardens 10
Tucson Children's
 Museum 22
Tucson Museum of Art
 & Historic Block 19
University of Arizona
 Museum of Art 12

Silverbell Rd.
Wade Rd.
Cortaro Farms Rd.
Overton
10
Thornydale
Ina Rd.
Ina Rd.
Orange Grove
Saguaro
National
Park
Sunset    Rd.
El Camino de Cerro
Ruth
Rd
Camino de Oeste
Sweetwater Dr.
To Saguaro National
Park (west)
Ironwood Hill Dr.
1
Tucson Mountain
Park
3
2
Gates    Pass    Rd.
Anklam

## Downtown & the Historic Districts

W. 6th St.
N. Stone Ave.
N. 6th Ave.
N. 4th Ave.
E. 6th St.
Silverlak
E. 7th St.
W. Main St.
Franklin St.
Church Ave.
Toole Ave.
N. Stone Ave.
E. 8th St.
E. 9th St.
El Presidio
Area
19
Downtown
Arts District
Alameda St.
Pennington
St.
Congress St.
Broadway Blvd.
Grande Ave.
Tucson
Convention
Center
E. 12th St.
22
20
S. Stone Ave.
E. 13th St.
10
Cushing St.
E. 14th St.
Armory Park Historic Area
21
Simpson St.
Barrio
Historico
E. 15th St.
Kennedy St.
E. 16th St.
Osborne Ave.
W. 17th St.
E. 17th St.
S. 3rd Ave.
W. 18th St.
E. 18th St.
S. 4th Ave.
S. 6th Ave.
W. 19th St.
E. 19th St.
W. 20th St.
E. 20th St.
W. 21st St.
E. 21st St.
Mission
W. 22nd St.
E. 22nd St.
E. 23rd St.

NA-0264

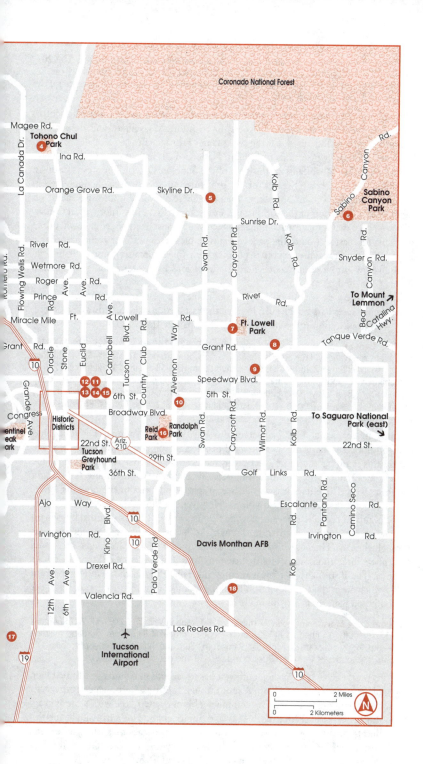

Coronado National Forest

Magee Rd.
Tohono Chul Park
4
Ina Rd.
La Canada Dr.

Orange Grove Rd.
Skyline Dr.
5

Sabino Canyon Rd.
Sabino Canyon Park
6

River Rd.
Wetmore Rd.
Roger Rd.
Prince Rd.
Miracle Mile
Grant Rd.

Flowing Wells Rd.
Romero Rd.

Kolb Rd.
Craycroft Rd.
Swan Rd.

Sunrise Dr.

Snyder Rd.

To Mount Lemmon

Bear Canyon Rd.
Catalina Hwy.

River Rd.
Ft. Lowell Park
7

Tanque Verde Rd.

Oracle
Stone
Ft. Lowell Rd.
Euclid Ave.
Campbell Ave.
Tucson Blvd.
Country Club Rd.
Alvernon Way
Grant Rd.
8

Speedway Blvd.
9

10
12 11
13 14 15
6th St.
5th St.
Broadway Blvd.
Reid Park
16
Randolph Park
22nd St.
Ariz. 210
29th St.

Historic Districts
Grande Ave.
Congress
Sentinel Peak Park

Tucson Greyhound Park
36th St.

Swan Rd.
Craycroft Rd.
Wilmot Rd.
Kolb Rd.

To Saguaro National Park (east)

22nd St.

Golf Links Rd.
Escalante Rd.
Irvington Rd.

Pantano Rd.
Camino Seco Rd.

Ajo Way
Irvington Rd.
Kino Blvd.
Palo Verde Blvd.
10
10

Davis Monthan AFB

Kolb Rd.

Drexel Rd.
Valencia Rd.
12th Ave.
6th Ave.

18

Tucson International Airport

Los Reales Rd.

17
19

10

0        2 Miles
0        2 Kilometers

N

325

✪ **Saguaro National Park.** East district visitor center, 3693 S. Old Spanish Trail. ☎ **520/ 733-5153.** West district visitor center, 2700 N. Kinney Rd. ☎ 520/733-5158. $4 per car, $2 per hiker (charged on the east section only). Park open daily 7am–sunset; visitor centers daily 8:30am–5pm; open to hikers 24 hours a day.

The saguaro cactus has been called the monarch of the desert and is the quintessential symbol of the American desert. Coyotes, foxes, squirrels, javelinas, and the region's Tohono O'odham Indians all eat the sweet fruit of the saguaro.

Since 1933 the two sections of Saguaro National Park have protected the saguaro and all the other inhabitants of this part of the Sonoran Desert. The west section is the more popular both because of its proximity to the Arizona–Sonora Desert Museum and Old Tucson Studios and because there are more impressive stands of saguaros in this section of the park. In the area near the Red Hills Information Center is a water hole that attracts wild animals, which you're most likely to see at dawn, dusk, or night. The east section of the park contains an older area of forest at the foot of the Rincon Mountains. This section is popular with hikers because most of it has no roads. There's also a visitor center here. Both sections have loop roads, nature trails, hiking trails, and picnic grounds.

To reach the west section, take Speedway Boulevard west from downtown Tucson (it becomes Gates Pass Boulevard); to reach the east section, take Speedway Boulevard east, then head south on Freeman Road to Old Spanish Trail.

**Sabino Canyon.** 5900 N. Sabino Canyon Rd. ☎ **520/749-2861** or 520/749-2327 for moonlight reservations. Free admission. Sabino Canyon tram ride, $6 adults, $2.50 children 3–12, free for children 2 and under; Bear Canyon tram ride, $3 adults, $1 children 3–12, free for children 2 and under. Park, daily dawn–dusk. Sabino Canyon tram rides, daily 9am–4:30pm; Bear Canyon tram rides, daily 9am–4pm (both trams more limited in summer). Take Grant Rd. east to Tanque Verde Rd., continuing east; at Sabino Canyon Rd., turn north and watch for the sign.

Located in the Santa Catalina Mountains of Coronado National Forest, Sabino Canyon is a desert oasis that has attracted people and animals for thousands of years. Today this is by far the most spectacular and accessible corner of the desert in the Tucson area, containing not only impressive desert scenery, but hiking trails and a stream as well. These days it is the chance to splash and swim in the canyon's waterfalls and pools that attracts most visitors. However, for those who prefer just to gaze at the beauty of crystal-clear water flowing through a rocky canyon guarded by saguaro cacti, there's a narrated tram ride through the lower canyon at frequent intervals through the day. There are also many trails and picnic tables. Moonlight tram rides take place three times each month between April and December (but not July or August). The Bear Canyon tram is used by hikers heading to the picturesque Seven Falls, which are at the end of a 2.6-mile hiking trail. Bring at least 1 quart of water per person if you plan to do any hiking here.

**Colossal Cave Mountain Park.** 22 miles east of Tucson in Vail. ☎ **520/647-7275.** Admission $7.50 adults, $4 children 6–12. Mar 16–Sept 15 Mon–Sat 8am–6pm, Sun and holidays 8am–7pm; Sept 16–Mar 15 Mon–Sat 9am–5pm, Sun and holidays 9am–6pm. Take Old Spanish Trail southeast from east Tucson or take I-10 and get off at the Vail exit.

It seems nearly every cave in the Southwest has its legends of bandits and buried loot, and Colossal Cave is no exception. A tour through this dry cavern, which isn't exactly colossal, but still pretty impressive, combines a bit of Western lore with a bit of geography for an experience that both kids and adults enjoy. Not surprisingly for this desert location, this is a dry cave, which means that the stalactites, stalagmites, and other formations are no longer actively growing. The 45-minute tour of the cave covers about half a mile, and the temperature is a comfortable 70° to 72°F.

# HISTORIC ATTRACTIONS BOTH REAL & REEL

**Old Tucson Studios.** 201 S. Kinney Rd. ☎ **520/883-0100.** Admission $14.95 adults, $9.45 children 4–11 (Pima County residents $12.95 adult and $8.95 children). Daily 10am–6pm. Closed Thanksgiving and Dec 25. Take Speedway Blvd. west, continuing in the same direction when it becomes Gates Pass Blvd., and turn left on S. Kinney Rd.

Despite the name, this is not the historic location of the old city of Tucson—it's a Western town originally built as the set for the 1939 movie *Arizona*. In the years since then, Old Tucson has been used during the filming of John Wayne's *Rio Lobo, Rio Bravo,* and *El Dorado;* Clint Eastwood's *The Outlaw Josey Wales;* Kirk Douglas's *Gunfight at the O.K. Corral;* Paul Newman's *The Life and Times of Judge Roy Bean;* and, more recently, *Tombstone* and *Geronimo.*

Today, however, Old Tucson is far more than just a movie set. In addition to serving as a site for frequent film, TV, and advertising productions (call ahead to find out if any filming is scheduled), it has become a Wild West theme park with diverse family oriented activities and entertainment. Throughout each day there are staged shootouts in the streets, stunt shows, cancan performances, medicine shows, and other performances. There are also train rides, stagecoach rides, kiddie rides, a circus act, video games, restaurants, and gift shops.

A fire destroyed much of Old Tucson in early 1995, and many of the original buildings were lost. However, the town has since been rebuilt. Though it isn't quite the same Old Tucson it once was, it looks just as old as it ever did (movie sets can look pretty authentic). The new Old Tucson includes plenty of educational shows that explain the history of the West from both the white and Native American perspectives. Several multimedia and video presentations complement the various live performances.

✪ **Mission San Xavier del Bac.** 1950 W. San Xavier Rd. ☎ **520/294-2624.** Free admission. Daily 8am–5:30pm. Take I-19 south to Exit 92 and turn right.

Called the White Dove of the Desert, Mission San Xavier de Bac, a blindingly white adobe building rising from a sere, brown landscape, is considered the finest example of mission architecture in the Southwest. The beautiful church, which was built between 1783 and 1797, incorporates Moorish, Byzantine, and Mexican Renaissance architectural styles. However, the church was never actually completed, which becomes clear when the two bell towers are compared. One is topped with a dome, while the other has none. The mission underwent an extensive restoration in recent years, and much of the elaborate interior decoration has taken on a new luster. Restored murals cover the interior walls, and behind the altar are colorful and elaborate decorations. To the left of the main altar, in a glass sarcophagus, is a statue of Saint Francis Xavier, the mission's patron saint, who is believed to answer the prayers of the faithful. A visit to the San Xavier's new museum provides a bit of historical perspective and a chance to explore a bit more of the mission. To the east of the church, atop a small hill, you'll find not only an interesting view of the church but also a replica of the famous grotto in Lourdes, France. This is an active Roman Catholic church serving the San Xavier Indian Reservation. Masses are held daily at 8:30, Saturday at 5:30pm, and Sunday at 11am and 12:30pm.

# MORE TO SEE & DO
## ART MUSEUMS

In addition to the museums and galleries listed below, you need only look around you as you drive through Tucson to see some of the city's most memorable art. Tucson abounds in outdoor murals and public art. Two of the most impressive are the Farmer John Meats mural at 1102 W. Grant Rd. and the Truly Nolan bee mural at 3620 E. Speedway Blvd.

**Tucson Museum of Art & Historic Block.** 140 N. Main Ave. ☎ **520/624-2333.** Admission $2 adults, $1 students and seniors, free for children 12 and under; free for everyone Tues. Mon–Sat 10am–4pm, Sun noon–4pm. Closed Mon June–Aug and all national holidays. All downtown-bound buses.

The Tucson Museum of Art is situated in a large modern building surrounded by historic adobes and a spacious plaza frequently used to display sculptures. The museum boasts an excellent collection of pre-Columbian art, representing 3,000 years of life in Mexico and Central and South America, and a large collection of Western art, depicting cowboys, horses, and the wide-open spaces of the American West. In addition, the museum hosts temporary exhibitions, such as the annual *American Women Artists and the West.* The museum has also preserved five historic homes on this same block, and these are open to the public. See "History Museums & Landmark Buildings," below, for details. A renovation in 1997 added 7,000 square feet of new gallery space to the museum.

✪ **The University of Arizona Museum of Art.** University of Arizona campus, Park Ave. and Speedway Blvd. ☎ **520/621-7567.** Free admission. Labor Day to mid-May Mon–Fri 9am–5pm, Sun noon–4pm; mid-May to Labor Day Mon–Fri 10am–3:30pm, Sun noon–4pm. Closed major holidays. Bus: 1, 4, 5, 6, 9X, 102, 103, or 250.

With European and American works from the Renaissance to the 20th century, this collection is even more extensive and diverse than that of the Tucson Museum of Art. Tintoretto, Rembrandt, Piranesi, Picasso, O'Keeffe, Warhol, and Rothko are all represented here. Another attraction, the *Retable of Ciudad Rodrigo,* consists of 26 paintings from 15th-century Spain and was originally placed above a cathedral altar. The museum also has an extensive collection of 20th-century sculpture that includes more than 60 clay and plaster models and sketches by Jacques Lipchitz.

✪ **Center for Creative Photography.** University of Arizona campus, east of the corner of Park Ave. and Speedway Blvd. ☎ **520/621-7968.** $2 suggested donation. Mon–Fri 9am–5pm, Sat–Sun noon–5pm. Bus: 1, 4, 5, 6, 9X, 102, 103, or 250.

Have you ever wished you could see an original Ansel Adams print up close, or perhaps an Edward Weston or a Richard Avedon? You can at the Center for Creative Photography. Originally conceived by Ansel Adams, the center now holds more than 500,000 negatives, 200,000 study prints, and 60,000 master prints by the world's greatest photographers, making it one of the best and largest collections in the world. Although the center mounts excellent photography exhibits year-round, it's also a research facility that preserves the complete photographic archives of various photographers, including Adams. Prints may be examined in a special room. It's highly recommended that you make an appointment and decide beforehand whose works you'd like to see. You're usually limited to two photographers per visit.

**De Grazia Gallery in the Sun.** 6300 N. Swan Rd. ☎ **800/545-2185** or 520/299-9191. Free admission. Daily 10am–4pm.

Southwestern artist Ettore "Ted" De Grazia is a Tucson favorite son, and his gallery, set in an adobe home in the foothills, is a Tucson landmark. De Grazia is said to be the most reproduced artist in the world because many of his impressionistic images of big-eyed children were used as greeting cards during the 1950s and 1960s. Connected to the gallery is a small adobe chapel that De Grazia built in honor of the missionary explorer Father Eusebio Kino. No original works are for sale, but there are many reproductions and other objects with De Grazia images.

## HISTORY MUSEUMS & LANDMARK BUILDINGS

In addition to the museums and buildings listed below, downtown Tucson has a couple of historic neighborhoods, which are described in "A Walking Tour," below.

Among the more interesting buildings are those maintained by the Tucson Museum of Art and located on the block surrounding the museum. These restored homes date from between 1850 and 1907 and are all built on the former site of the Tucson presidio. A map and descriptive brochures about the houses are available at the museum's front desk, and free guided tours of the historic block are available.

**Arizona Historical Society Tucson Museum.** 949 E. 2nd St. ☎ **520/628-5774.** Free admission or by donation. Mon–Sat 10am–4pm, Sun noon–4pm. Closed major holidays. Bus: 1, 4, 5, 6, 9X, 102, 103, or 250.

As Arizona's oldest historical museum, this repository of all things Arizonan is a treasure trove for the history buff. If you've never explored a real mine, you can do the next best thing by looking at the museum's full-scale reproduction of an underground mine tunnel. You'll also see an assayer's office, miner's tent, stamp mill, and blacksmith's shop in the mining exhibit. A transportation exhibit, displaying stagecoaches and horseless carriages that revolutionized life in the Southwest, and temporary exhibits, such as a display on 19th-century medicine in Arizona, give a pretty good idea of what it was like back then. The museum has a research library and a good gift shop.

**Arizona State Museum.** University of Arizona campus, University Blvd. and Park Ave. ☎ **520/621-6302.** Free admission. Mon–Sat 10am–5pm, Sun noon–5pm. Closed major holidays. Bus: 1, 4, 5, 6, 9X, 102, 103, or 250.

Founded in 1893, the Arizona State Museum houses an extensive collection of artifacts from prehistoric and contemporary Native American cultures of the Southwest. A Paleo-Indian exhibit displays 12,000-year-old spear points that were found embedded in the bones of mammoths, now long extinct, and a large exhibit covers the Hohokam, an ancient farming culture that lived in the desert and built extensive networks of irrigation canals before disappearing mysteriously around 1450. Across the street in the North Building, an exhibit explores the lifestyles and cultural traditions of Indians living in Arizona today. Excellent temporary exhibits are regularly scheduled here.

**Sosa-Carillo-Frémont House Museum.** 141 S. Granada Ave. (in the Tucson Convention Center complex). ☎ **520/622-0956.** Free admission. Wed–Sat 10am–4pm. Closed all major holidays. All downtown-bound buses.

Located on the shady grounds of the modern Tucson Convention Center, the Sosa-Carillo-Frémont House is a classic example of Sonoran-style adobe architecture. Originally built in 1858 as a small adobe house, the structure was enlarged after 1866. In 1878 it was rented to territorial governor John Charles Frémont, who had led a distinguished military career as an explorer of the West. The building has been restored in the style of this period, with the living room and bedrooms opening off a large central hall known as a *zaguán*. All rooms are decorated with period antiques. The flat roof is made of pine beams called *vigas,* covered with saguaro cactus ribs, and topped by a layer of hard-packed mud. From November through March, this museum also offers Saturday tours ($5) of historic Tucson.

**Fort Lowell Museum.** 2900 N. Craycroft Rd. ☎ **520/885-3832.** Free admission. Wed–Sat 10am–4pm. Closed all major holidays. Bus: 34.

Located in Fort Lowell Park on the site of a former cavalry outpost, this museum chronicles the history of life at the fort. Some of the ruins of the original fort can still be seen. Before it was a fort, this site was a Hohokam village, and artifacts uncovered from archaeological digs around the surrounding park lands are also on display.

## SCIENCE & TECHNOLOGY MUSEUMS

**Flandrau Science Center & Planetarium.** University of Arizona campus, Cherry Ave. and University Blvd. ☎ **520/621-STAR.** Admission to exhibits $3 adults, $2 children 13 and

# Saguaros & Their Spiny Friends

From the diminutive hedgehog to the stately saguaro, the cacti of the Sonoran Desert display a fascinating variety of shapes and sizes. While your first thought is usually to give them a wide berth, Arizona's cacti are worth a closer inspection, especially in the spring, when their large, waxy flowers paint the desert with splashes of color. May is probably the best all-around month for seeing cactus flowers, but you can see them in April and June as well.

The best natural areas to see cacti (it's OK to say cactuses, too) are Saguaro National Park (outside Tucson), Organ Pipe National Monument (100 miles west of Tucson), Sabino Canyon Park (in Tucson), Picacho Peak (near Casa Grande), and South Mountain Park (in Phoenix). To learn more about cacti, visit the Desert Botanical Garden in Phoenix, Boyce Thompson Southwestern Arboretum in Superior, or Tucson Botanical Gardens.

**Saguaro Cactus**   The saguaro (pronounced sa-*hwah*-ro) is the largest cactus of Arizona's Sonoran Desert and grows nowhere else on earth. Reaching heights of as much as 50 feet, saguaros are the redwoods of the desert, and often grow in dense stands that resemble forests. Saguaros are a slow-growing cactus; a 6-inch-tall cactus might be 10 years old, and it can take 75 years for a saguaro to sprout its first branch. The oldest-known saguaros are around 200 years old, and some have more than 40 arms.

To support their great size in such an arid environment, saguaros have a highly efficient root system that can be as large as 100 feet in diameter. These roots soak up water quickly and store it in the spongy interior of the cactus. After a rainstorm, a mature saguaro can weigh as much as 7 tons and survive for up to 2 years without another drop of water. Supporting this great mass is an internal framework of sturdy ribs, while the exterior of the cactus is pleated so that it can expand and contract as it takes up and loses water.

Each spring, waxy white flowers sprout from the tips of saguaro arms. These flowers are pollinated by white-winged doves and lesser long-nosed bats that come from hundreds of miles away in Mexico just for saguaro flowering season. Other animals that rely on saguaros include Gila woodpeckers and elf owls that nest in holes in saguaro trunks.

The Tohono O'odham people, natives of the Sonoran Desert, have long relied on saguaro cactus fruit as an important food source, even making a traditional

under. Telescope viewing free. Planetarium $5 adults, $4.50 seniors and students, $4 children 13 and under. Daytime daily 9am–5pm; evenings Wed–Sat 7–9pm. Telescope viewing Wed–Sat 7–10pm (weather permitting). Closed major holidays. Bus: 9.

Located on the campus of the University of Arizona, the Flandrau Planetarium offers stargazers a chance to learn more about the universe. The planetarium theater presents programs on the stars as well as very popular laser shows set to music. Exhibit halls contain a mineral collection (the largest in the state) and hands-on science exhibits for people of all ages. On clear nights, you can gaze through the planetarium's 16-inch telescope. (Arizona has become a magnet for stargazers, and several famous telescopes are near Tucson. See "Starry Starry Nights," in chapter 10, for information on the Kitt Peak National Observatory.)

**The International Wildlife Museum.** 4800 W. Gates Pass Rd. ☎ **520/617-1439** or 520/629-0100. Admission $6 adults, $4.75 seniors and students, $2 children 6–12, free for ceremonial wine from the red, seedy pulp. So important has the saguaro harvest been in the past that the Tohono O'odham consider the saguaro harvest as the start of the new year.

**Organ Pipe Cactus**   This close relative of the saguaro takes its name from its many trunks, which give it the appearance of an old pipe organ. The organ pipe cactus is even more frost sensitive than the saguaro and lives only in an area 100 miles west of Tucson on either side of the Mexican border. This population of stately cacti has been preserved in a national monument.

**Barrel Cactus**   When mature, these cacti look much as their name implies and can be confused with young saguaros. However, the barrel cactus can be distinguished by its fishhook-shaped spines which are usually yellow or red. This is the cactus that for years has been touted as a source of life-giving water to anyone lost in the desert. The liquid in this cactus's spongy interior is actually quite bitter and foul tasting. However, the same spongy pulp, when cooked in sugar water, becomes very tasty.

**Cholla Cactus**   The cholla (pronounced *choi*-yah) is the most dreaded of all the Arizona cacti. Its spines are long, plentiful, sharp, and brittle. To brush up against a cholla is to experience certain pain. Here in Arizona, there are several species of cholla, most of which resemble small trees. They go by such graphic names as jumping cholla, which is said to throw pieces of its spiny branches at unwary passersby; teddy bear cholla, which is so covered with spines that it looks fuzzy; and chain fruit cholla, on which fruit hang in fragile, spiny chains. The chollas are favored nesting spots of cactus wrens and doves. Give chollas a wide birth.

**Prickly Pear Cactus**   This is one of the largest and most widespread families of cacti and can be found throughout the United States, not just in the desert. They are also among the most commercially important cacti. The flat stems or pads (known as *nopales* in Spanish) of one species are used in Mexican cooking and can be found both fresh and canned in markets in Arizona. The fruit of the prickly pear is also edible and is relished by both humans and animals. Here in Arizona, it's possible to find prickly pear jams and jellies, as well as prickly pear ice cream and prickly pear margaritas.

children 5 and under. Mon–Fri 9am–5pm, Sat–Sun 10am–6pm. Closed Thanksgiving, Dec 25. 5 miles west of I-10 on Speedway Blvd.

This castlelike building (modeled after a French Foreign Legion fort) on the road that leads to the Arizona–Sonora Desert Museum is a natural-history museum filled with stuffed animals in lifelike poses and surroundings. Animals from all over the world are displayed, and there are exhibits of extinct animals including the Irish elk and the woolly mammoth. There is also an interesting insect exhibit.

**Pima Air & Space Museum.** 6000 E. Valencia Rd. ☎ **520/574-0462.** Admission $7.50 adults, $6.50 seniors and military, $4 children 10–17, free for children under 10. Daily 9am–5pm. Closed Thanksgiving, Dec 25. Take the Valencia Rd. exit from I-10 and then drive east 2 miles to the museum entrance.

Located just south of Davis Monthan Air Force Base, the Pima Air & Space Museum houses one of the largest collections of historic aircraft in the world. On display are

---

**❓ Did You Know?**

- The University of Arizona was established in Tucson to appease the citizenry after the territorial capital was moved to Phoenix.
- Mount Lemmon, named for the woman who first climbed it, is the site of the southernmost ski area in the continental United States.
- Tucson is the sunniest city in the country.
- The Sonoran Desert is the only place in the world where the saguaro cactus grows, and Saguaro National Park outside Tucson has the greatest concentration of these plants.
- Singer Linda Ronstadt is part of a Tucson family very active in local politics; a public bus station is named for one of the Ronstadts.
- There are more astronomical observatories within a 50-mile radius of Tucson than in any other area of comparable size in the world.

---

more than 250 aircraft that together cover the evolution of American aviation. A 20,000-square-foot building houses part of the collection, though most of the aircraft are outside. The collection includes replicas of the Wright brothers' 1903 Wright Flyer, and the X-15, the world's fastest aircraft. World War II bombers and later jet fighters are popular attractions. Tours are available. The museum also now offers guided tours of Davis Monthan's AMARC (Arizona Maintenance and Regeneration Center) facility, which also goes by the name of The Boneyard. Here, thousands of mothballed planes are lined up in neat rows under the Arizona sun. Tours last just under an hour and cost $5 for adults, $3.50 for seniors, and $3 for children. Tour reservations should be made 2 or 3 days in advance.

**Titan Missile Museum.** Duval Mine Rd., Green Valley (Exit 69 from I-19). ☎ **520/625-7736.** Admission $7.50 adults, $6.50 seniors, $4 children 10–17, free for children under 10. May 1–Oct 31, Wed–Sun 9am–5pm; Nov 1–Apr 30, daily 9am–5pm. Closed Thanksgiving, Dec 25. Take I-19 south to Green Valley.

Operated by the Pima Air & Space Museum and located south of Tucson in the retirement community of Green Valley, this museum is a deactivated intercontinental ballistic missile (ICBM) silo and is the only such museum in the world. Tours lead you down into the silo itself so you can get a firsthand look at what it would be like to have your finger on the button. Advance reservations are recommended.

## PARKS, GARDENS & ZOOS

See "Seeing the Sights," at the beginning of this section, for full details on the Arizona–Sonora Desert Museum, the region's premier zoo.

**Reid Park Zoo.** Lake Shore Lane and 22nd St. (between Country Club Rd. and Alvernon Way). ☎ **520/791-4022.** Admission $4 adults, $2.50 seniors, 75¢ children 5–14, free for children 4 and under. Daily 9am–4pm. Closed Dec 25. Bus: 7 or 14.

Although small and overshadowed by its neighbor, the Arizona–Sonora Desert Museum, the Reid Park Zoo is an important breeding center for several endangered species. Among the animals in the zoo's breeding programs are giant anteaters, white rhinoceroses, tigers, ruffed lemurs, and zebras. A new South American exhibit features a capybara (the largest rodent in the world), piranhas, and black jaguars. Get here early when the animals are more active and before the crowds hit. There's also a good playground in the adjacent park.

## ⭐ Frommer's Favorite Tucson Experiences

**Visiting the Arizona–Sonora Desert Museum.** One of the world's finest zoos, the museum focuses exclusively on the animals and plants of the Sonoran Desert of southern Arizona and northern Mexico.

**Taking a Full-Moon Desert Hike.** There's no better time to explore the desert than at night (when the desert comes alive) under a full moon. Drive to the east or west section of Saguaro National Park for your hike, where the parking lots at the east ends of Speedway and Broadway are open 24 hours a day. It's also possible to park on Old Spanish Trail outside the main entrance to the east unit of the park. There are places on the west side where you can park outside gates and walk into the park as well.

⭐ **Making the Drive to Mount Lemmon.** From the desert, the road twists and turns up into the Santa Catalina Mountains, with cactus and *palo verde* gradually replaced by pine and juniper. You'll have breathtaking views of Tucson along the way.

**Spending Time in Sabino Canyon.** Biking, hiking, swimming, birding— Sabino Canyon has it all. The canyon, carved by a creek that flows for most of the year, is an oasis in the desert. Though popular with both locals and tourists, it still offers delightful opportunities for escaping the city.

**Bird Watching in Madera Canyon.** Located south of the city in the Santa Rita Mountains, this canyon attracts many species of birds, some of which can only be seen in a handful of other spots in the United States. Even if you're not into birding, there are hiking trails and lots of shade here.

⭐ **Tucson Botanical Gardens.** 2150 N. Alvernon Way. ☎ **520/326-9686.** Admission $4 adults, $3 seniors, free for children under 12. Daily 8:30am–4:30pm; Memorial Day–Labor Day 7:30am–4:30pm. Closed Jan 1, July 4, Thanksgiving, and Dec 24–25. Bus: 11.

Located amid residential neighborhoods in midtown Tucson, these gardens are an oasis of greenery and, though small, are well worth a visit if you are interested in desert plant life, landscaping, or gardening. On the 5½-acre grounds are several small gardens that not only have visual appeal but are also historic and educational. If you live in the desert, you might want to visit just to learn about harvesting rainfall for your desert garden and designing a water-conserving landscape. The sensory garden stimulates all five senses, while in another garden traditional Southwestern crops are grown for research purposes. In the greenhouse, you'll see "useful" plants from tropical forests. There's a gift shop here as well.

**Tohono Chul Park.** 7366 N. Paseo del Norte. ☎ **520/575-8468.** Admission by suggested donation, $2. Grounds, daily 7am–sunset. Exhibit house, Mon–Sat 9:30am–5pm, Sun 11am–5pm. Tearoom, daily 8am–5pm. Off Ina Rd. west of the intersection with Oracle Rd.

Though this public park is fairly small, it provides an excellent introduction to the plant and animal life of the desert. You'll see a forest of cholla cactus and a garden of small and complex pincushion cactus. The park includes an ethnobotanical garden; a garden for children that encourages them to touch, listen, and smell; a demonstration garden; natural areas; an exhibit house for art displays; a tea room that is great for breakfast, lunch, or afternoon tea; and a very good gift shop. From mid-February through April, the wildflower displays here are gorgeous, and guided tours are offered.

# The Shrine That Stopped a Freeway

The southern Arizona landscape is dotted with roadside shrines, symbols of the region's Hispanic and Roman Catholic heritage. Most are simple crosses decorated with plastic flowers and dedicated to people who have been killed in auto accidents. However, one shrine in particular stands out from all the rest. It is Tucson's El Tiradito (The Castaway), which is dedicated to a sinner, and not too long ago stopped a freeway.

El Tiradito, located on South Granada Avenue at West Cushing Street, is the only shrine in the United States dedicated to a sinner buried in unconsecrated soil. Several stories tell of how this shrine came to be, but the most popularly accepted tells of a young shepherd who fell in love with his mother-in-law some time in the 1880s. When the father-in-law found his wife in the arms of this young man, he shot the son-in-law. The young shepherd stumbled from his in-laws' house and fell dead beside the dusty street. Because he had been caught in the act of adultery and died without confessing his sins, his body could not be interred in the church cemetery, so he was buried where he fell.

The people of the neighborhood soon began burning candles on the spot to try to save the soul of the young man, and eventually people began burning candles in hopes that their own wishes would come true. They believed that if the candle burned through the night their prayers would be answered. The shrine eventually grew into a substantial little structure and in 1927 was dedicated by its owner to the city of Tucson. In 1940, the shrine became an official Tucson monument.

However, such status was not enough to protect the shrine from urban renewal, and when the federal government announced that it would level the shrine when it built a new freeway through the center of Tucson, the city's citizens were outraged. Their activities and protest led the shrine to be named to the National Register of Historic Places. Thus protected, the shrine could not be destroyed, and the freeway was moved a few hundred yards to the west.

To this day, devout Catholics from the surrounding neighborhood still burn candles at the shrine that stopped a freeway.

## ESPECIALLY FOR KIDS

In addition to the museums listed below, two of the greatest places to take kids in the Tucson area are the Arizona–Sonora Desert Museum and Old Tucson Studios. Kids will also get a kick out of the tram ride at Sabino Canyon, the Reid Park Zoo, the International Wildlife Museum, Flandrau Science Center and Planetarium, and the Pima Air & Space Museum. All are described in detail above.

They'll also enjoy **Trail Dust Town,** 6541 E. Tanque Verde Rd., a Wild West–themed shopping and dining center. It has a full-sized carousel, a scaled down train to ride, shoot-out shows, and a minigolf course next door. Basically, it's a sort of scaled down Old Tucson. If the kids are into miniature golf, they'll probably love **Magic Carpet Golf,** 6125 E. Speedway Blvd. (☎ 520/885-3691), as much as we do. Putt balls under and around a sphinx, a skull, a giant Easter Island head, and a huge snake.

**Tucson Children's Museum.** 200 S. 6th Ave. ☎ **520/792-9985.** Admission $5 adults, $4 seniors, $3 children 2–16, free for children under 2; free for everyone on the 3rd Sun of each month. Tues–Fri 9:30am–5pm, Sat 10am–5pm, Sun noon–5pm. Closed Jan 1, Easter Sunday, Thanksgiving, Dec 25. All downtown-bound buses.

This museum is located in the old Carnegie Library in downtown Tucson and is filled with fun and educational hands-on activities. Exhibits change every year or so, but have included a doctor's office, a fire station, and a bubble factory. Weekends generally feature special performances and programs.

**Valley of the Moon.** 2544 E. Allen Rd. ☎ **520/323-1331.** Admission varies. No regular hours.

This folk art construction of rock and cement was built back in the 1920s and been slowly undergoing restoration for more than 25 years. The diminutive fantasy world created by George Phar delights children and adults with its blend of rock and imagination. Because the Valley of the Moon is operated by volunteers, there is no set schedule for when it is open, but several times a year there are guided tours. Call for information.

## DOWNTOWN SATURDAY NIGHT
Throughout the year, on the first and third Saturday of each month, the Downtown Arts District—which includes East Pennington Street, East Congress Street, and East Broadway Boulevard between Fourth Avenue and Stone Avenue—comes alive from 7 to 10pm. On these nights there are art gallery openings, music performances on the street and in cafes, and late-evening shopping. However, with recent closures of many of the neighborhood's shops and restaurants, these Saturday night events are not nearly as lively as they once were. For more information, call the **Tucson Arts District Partnership** (☎ **520/624-9977**).

# A Walking Tour
# El Presidio & Barrio Histórico Districts

**Start:** Old Town Artisans.
**Finish:** Hotel Congress.
**Time:** 5 hours.
**Best Times:** Weekends, when restaurants aren't packed at lunch.
**Worst Times:** Summer, when it's just too hot to do any walking.

Tucson has a long and varied cultural history, which is most easily seen on a walking tour of the downtown historic districts. Start your explorations in the El Presidio Historic District, which is named for the Presidio of San Augustín del Tucson (1775), the Spanish garrison that once stood here to protect the San Xavier del Bac Mission from the Apaches. For many years this was the heart of Tucson, and though no original buildings are still standing, there are numerous buildings from the mid–19th century.

After finding a parking space at the large public parking lot at the corner of Court Avenue and Council Street, walk south on Court Avenue to the corner of Washington Street. Here you'll find Tucson's premier crafts market:

1. **Old Town Artisans,** 186 N. Meyer Ave. In this adobe building dating from 1862 are numerous rooms full of handmade Southwestern crafts (see "Shopping," below, for details). The central courtyard has shady gardens. You could spend hours browsing through the amazing assortment of crafts here but keep in mind that you've still got a long walk ahead of you. Across Meyer Avenue from this building's southwest corner is:

2. **La Casa Cordova,** 175 N. Meyer Ave., which dates from about 1848 and is one of the oldest buildings in Tucson. Although the art museum owns five historic homes on this block, this is the only one that has been restored to look as it might

have in the late 1800s. Each year from November to March, there is a very elaborate *nacimiento*, a Mexican folk-art nativity scene, with images from the Bible and Latin American history all rolled up into one miniature landscape full of angels, greenery, and Christmas lights. Through a colorful gate just to the south of La Casa Cordova is the entrance to the:

3. **Tucson Museum of Art** (see above for details). This modern building houses collections of pre-Columbian and Western art, as well as exhibits of contemporary works. A visit to the museum will not only allow you to see plenty of art, but you should also be able to see inside a couple of historic buildings that now house some of the museum's galleries. After touring the museum, walk back up N. Meyer Avenue and at the end of the block you will find the:

4. **Romero House,** which was built in 1868 and may incorporate part of the original presidio wall. This house was altered numerous times over the years and at one time served as a gas station. The Romero House now contains the Tucson Museum of Art School.

From the Romero House, turn left onto Washington Street and then left again onto Main Avenue. The first building you'll come to on this side of the art museum's historic block is the:

5. **Corbett House,** 180 N. Main Ave., a restored mission revival–style building that was built in 1906. The house, which is set back behind a green lawn, is strikingly different from the older, Sonoran-style adobe homes on this block. Today, the Corbett House has been furnished with mission-style furniture and Tiffany lamps and is open for tours. Next door to this home stands the:

6. **Stevens House,** 150 N. Main Ave., a Sonoran-style row house completed in 1866. At press time, this building was being restored so that it could eventually house the museum's pre-Columbian and Spanish colonial art collections. Next door is the:

7. **Fish House,** 120 N. Main Ave., which was built in 1867 on the site of old Mexican barracks. Named for Edward Nye Fish, a local merchant, this building now houses the museum's Western art collection. Some of the walls of this house are two feet thick and ceilings in some places are made from old packing crates.

From here, head back up Main Avenue and at the far end of the next block, you will come to the:

8. **Julius Kruttschnidt House,** 297 N. Main Ave., which dates from 1886 and now houses El Presidio Bed and Breakfast Inn. Victorian trappings, including a long veranda, disguise the adobe origins of this unique and beautifully restored home.

Across Main Avenue from the B&B stands the:

9. **Steinfeld Mansion,** 300 N. Main Ave., which was built in 1900 in California mission–revival style and was designed by Henry Trost, Tucson's most noted architect. This building served as the original Owl's Club, a gentlemen's club for some of Tucson's most eligible turn-of-the-century bachelors. Another block north on Main Avenue stands the:

10. **Owl's Club Mansion,** 378 N. Main Ave., which was built in 1902 and was also designed by Henry Trost in the mission-revival style, albeit with a great deal of ornamentation. This impressive mansion replaced the Steinfeld House as home to the bachelors of the Owl's Club.

**TAKE A BREAK** If you started your tour late in the morning, you're probably hungry by now. Backtrack down Main Avenue, cross the street, and walk east on Franklin Street to Court Avenue. Turn right onto Court, and you will come to **El Charro Cafe,** Tucson's oldest Mexican restaurant. Be sure to order *carne seca*, the house specialty. (See "Where to Dine," above, for details.)

N

0    1/8 Mile
0    1/8 Kilometer

Armory Park Historic District

finish here

10th St.

23

4th    Ave.

5th    Ave.

12th St.

13th St.

14th St.

6th    Ave.

6th    Ave.

Toole    Ave.

St.

Scott    Ave.

22

Congress    St.

Broadway    Blvd.

Stone

20

19

Stone    Ave.

Ave.

Church    Ave.

Council    Ave.

Council    St.

St.

Stone

21

Meyer    Ave.

Court    Ave.

Court    St.

Washington    St.

Meyer    St.

Pennington    St.

El Presidio Park

12

11

14

13    15

Barrio Historico District

Simpson    St.

S. Meyer Ave.    18

Main Ave.

16

17

Cushing    St.

1

4    2    3

5    6    7

Alameda

start here

8

Main    Ave.

9

Franklin    St.

10

Paseo Redondo

Granada    Ave.

Congress    St.

Main-Granada Ave.

10

10

LEGEND

✝ Church
○ Take a break

Santa    Cruz    River

1 Old Town Artisans
2 La Casa Cordova
3 Tucson Museum of Art
4 Romero House
5 Corbett House
6 Stevens House
7 Fish House
8 Julius Kruttschnidt House
9 Steinfeld Mansion
10 Owl's Club Mansion
11 El Presidio Park
12 Pima County Courthouse
13 Tucson Convention Center
14 La Placita Village
15 Sosa-Carillo-Frémont House
16 El Tiradito
17 Elysian Grove Market
18 America West Primitive and Modern Art
19 Tucson Police Department
20 Temple of Music and Art
21 St. Augustine Cathedral
22 Carnegie Library
23 Hotel Congress

NA-0366

337

From here, continue south on Court Avenue and cross Alameda Street to reach:

**11. El Presidio Park,** once the parade ground for the presidio and now a shady gathering spot for everyone from the homeless to downtown office workers.

Just to the east of the park is the very impressive:

**12. Pima County Courthouse,** 115 N. Church St. Built in 1928, the courthouse incorporates Moorish, Spanish, and Southwestern architectural features, including a colorful tiled dome. A portion of the original presidio wall is in a glass case on the second floor.

From the courthouse, continue south 2 blocks and you will come to the:

**13. Tucson Convention Center,** a sprawling complex that includes a sports arena, grand ballroom, concert hall, theater, pavilions, meeting halls, gardens, restaurants, and craft and souvenir vendors. It is also here that you will find:

**14. La Placita Village,** 110S. Church Ave., a complex of offices and restaurants that was designed to resemble a Mexican village. This complex incorporates the Samaniego House, a Sonoran-style row house that dates from the 1880s. Near the fountains in the center of the convention center complex is the historic:

**15. Sosa-Carillo-Frémont House,** 151 Granada Ave., an adobe structure built in the 1850s and later the home of territorial governor John C. Frémont. The restored building is open to the public and is furnished in the style of the period.

Continue south through the grounds of the convention center complex and you will come to Cushing Street, across which lies the Barrio Histórico District. With its 150 adobe row houses, this is the largest collection of 19th-century Sonoran-style adobe architecture in the United States. However, the entire neighborhood was almost razed in the name of urban renewal and highway construction. About half of the downtown, including the neighborhoods that once stood on the site of today's convention center, was razed before the voices for preservation and restoration were finally heard. In fact, if it had not been for the activism of the residents of the Barrio Histórico, Interstate 10 would now run right through much of this area.

Start your exploration of the northern (and more restored) blocks of this neighborhood by crossing Cushing Street and then turning down Main Avenue, where you will find, on the west side of the street in the first block:

**16. El Tiradito.** This is the only shrine in the United States dedicated to a sinner buried in unconsecrated soil. People still light candles here in hope of having their wishes come true (see "The Shrine That Stopped a Freeway" box above). Continuing south to the corner of W. Simpson Street, you will see the:

**17. Elysian Grove Market,** 400 W. Simpson St. This dilapidated looking old adobe building is actually one of the most interesting and artistically decorated bed-and-breakfast inns in the city (see "Where to Stay" above).

Wander a while through the Barrio Histórico District, admiring the Sonoran-style homes that are built right out to the street. Many of these homes sport colorfully painted facades, signs of the ongoing renovation of this neighborhood.

Before leaving the Barrio, you may want to stop in at:

**18. America West Primitive and Modern Art,** 363 S. Meyer Ave. Not only will you get a glimpse inside one of these buildings, but the collection of art for sale in this gallery is fascinating.

☕ **TAKE A BREAK**   If you didn't eat at El Charro or are in need of a pick-me-up, stop in at the **Cushing Street Bar & Grill,** 343 S. Meyer Ave. at Cushing Street. The restaurant is housed in a historic adobe building and serves Southwestern and American food in a jazzy atmosphere.

From the corner of Cushing Street and S. Meyer Avenue, walk 2 blocks east to S. Stone Avenue, where you'll find the:

**19. Tucson Police Department,** 270 S. Stone Ave. While most people like to give police stations a wide berth, this one is worth a visit. In the lobby you'll find a display of John Dillinger memorabilia (Dillinger's capture took place not long after an eventful stay at the nearby Hotel Congress). Continue another block east on Cushing Street and you will come to the:

**20. Temple of Music and Art,** 330 S. Scott Ave, which was built in 1927 as a movie and stage theater and is the home of the Arizona Theatre Company (see "Tucson After Dark," below, for details). From here, walk north on S. Scott Avenue, turn left on McCormick St./13th Street and then right onto S. Stone Avenue, which will bring you to:

**21. St. Augustine Cathedral,** which was built in 1896 and is modeled after the Cathedral of Queretaro, Mexico. Above the door of the cathedral, you'll see a statue of Saint Augustine as well as symbols of the Arizona desert—the horned toad, the saguaro, and the yucca. From here walk east on Corral Street, turn left on S. Scott Avenue, then right on 12th Street and right again on S. Sixth Avenue to reach the front of the old:

**22. Carnegie Library,** which dates from 1901 and was designed by Henry Trost. The building now houses the Tucson Children's Museum (see "Especially for Kids," above, for details). From here head north on S. Sixth Avenue for two blocks and turn right on Congress Street. In one block, you will see on the far side of the street the:

**23. Hotel Congress,** 311 E. Congress St., which was built as a railroad hotel in 1919 and once played host to John Dillinger, infamous public enemy number one. Today the restored budget hotel is popular with European travelers and students and has a classically Western-styled lobby. There's also a cybercafe and a regular cafe here. The lobby is well worth a stroll through.

## 6  Organized Tours

To get a thorough overview of Tucson, you can take a 6½-hour tour with **Old Pueblo Tours** (☎ 520/795-7448). The tour includes visits to A Mountain, the downtown historic districts, De Grazia's Gallery in the Sun, the Arizona Historical Society Tucson Museum, and Mission San Xavier del Bac. The tour is $40 for adults and $15 for children 16 and under.

**Tucson Tours** (☎ 520/297-2911) offers 1½-hour guided city tours for $18. The tours head up to the top of A Mountain for an overview of the city, then visit the three downtown historic districts and the University of Arizona. The same company also offers a shuttle service to the Arizona–Sonora Desert Museum and Old Tucson Studios and tours to Mission San Xavier del Bac, Bisbee, Tombstone, Nogales, and Sedona.

To learn more about the history of Tucson, see if you can attach yourself to one of Ken Scoville's **Old Pueblo Walking Tours** (☎ 520/323-9290) of downtown (he usually does tours for groups). Mr. Scoville is a wealth of information about the city and offers tours that focus on the original presidio site, El Presidio Historic District, and Tucson after the arrival of the railroad. Two-hour tours cost $12.50 and are offered November to May or on request; call for a reservation first.

Laurel Cooper at **Desert Paths Tours** (☎ 520/327-7235) has a Ph.D. in anthropology and many years' experience in leading history, art, and culture-oriented field trips. She offers customized tours of the Saguaro National Monument and Southeastern Arizona, among other places.

If you'd like to learn more about the native peoples who lived in the Tucson area hundreds of years ago, take a tour with the **Center for Desert Archaeology** (☎ 520/885-6283; www.cdarc.org; E-mail: connie@desert.com), a nonprofit educational and research organization that can take you to view petroglyphs in the foothills of the Tucson Mountains or Hohokam sites in Catalina State Park. Tours cost $40 for a half day and $70 for a full day and are usually led by Connie Allen-Bacon, who is a wealth of information on the ancient residents of this region. The Hohokam sites tour also includes the chance to throw a spear using an *atlatl* and also a chance to grind mesquite beans in an ancient mortar and pestle.

For a look at a completely different sort of excavation, head south from Tucson 15 miles to the **ASARCO Mineral Discovery Center,** Pima Mine Road exit off I-19 (☎ 520/625-7513), where you can tour a huge open-pit copper mine and learn about copper mining past and present. The Mineral Discovery Center is open Tuesday through Saturday 9am to 5pm and admission is free. One-hour mine tours, which leave the Discovery Center every 20 to 30 minutes, are $6 for adults, $5 for seniors, and $4 for children 5 to 12.

Tours of the Sabino Canyon Ruin are offered by the **Old Pueblo Archaeology Center** (☎ 520/798-1201), which also offers opportunities to assist in the excavation of the site. Two-hour tours provide an introduction to the site and cost $10. Day-long programs that include an orientation, a tour of the ruin site, 4 to 5 hours of excavation, and time in the lab cost $69 (2-day programs are $130 and 3-day programs are $189). The center also has a special archaeology program for children.

If you want to get out into the wilds or crave a taste of pioneer history, **High Desert Convoys** (☎ 800/93-TOURS or 520/323-3386) will take you out in a four-wheel-drive World War II vehicle. The company offers trips to a ghost town, a trip to some remote petroglyphs, and a tour that includes a hike to a cave. Prices range from $45 to $75.

**Trail Dust Jeep Tours** (☎ 520/747-0323), which charges $49 for a half-day tour, will take you into the desert on a private Jeep trail. Along the way you stop to visit a 1,000-year-old archaeological site. With **Sunshine Jeep Tours** (☎ 520/742-1943), which charges $48 for adults, you'll head out through the saguaros northwest of Tucson and also visit an archaeological site.

## 7 Outdoor Pursuits

**BALLOONING  Balloon America** (☎ 520/299-7744; www.balloonridesusa. com) offers breakfast flights over the foothills of the Santa Catalina Mountains, with free pickups at selected resorts and a champagne toast at the end of the flight. Flights cost $135 to $250 per person and the ballooning season runs from October to June. **Southern Arizona Balloon Excursions** (☎ 520/624-3599) offers similar flights for $125 per person ($110 between Thanksgiving and Christmas).

**BIKING**    Tucson is one of the best bicycling cities in the country, and the dirt roads and trails of the surrounding national forest and desert are perfect for mountain biking. Bikes can be rented for between $15 (a basic road bike) and $40 (a full-suspension mountain bike) a day at the following bike shops: **Full Cycle,** 3232 E. Speedway Blvd. (☎ 520/327-3232); **Bargain Basement Bike,** 428 N. Fremont Ave. (☎ 520/628-1015), which is near the university; or **Broadway Bicycles,** 140 S. Sarnoff Dr. (☎ 520/296-7819), which is out in east Tucson just south of Broadway and east of Pantano Road. Any of these bike stores can also set you up with a bicycling map of the area.

If you'd rather confine your pedaling to paved surfaces, there are some great options around town. The number-one choice in town for cyclists in halfway decent shape is the road up **Sabino Canyon** (see "Seeing the Sights," above). Keep in mind, however, that bicycles are only allowed on this road 5 days a week and then only before 9am and after 5pm, 5 days a week (the road's closed to bikes all day on Wednesday and Saturday). For a much easier ride, try the **Rillito River Park path,** a 4-mile trail that parallels River Road and the usually dry bed of the Rillito River between Campbell Avenue and La Cholla Boulevard. If you've got knobby tires, you can continue west on this trail after the pavement ends. Another option close to downtown is the 4-mile **Santa Cruz River Park path,** which extends from West Grant Road to 29th Street. Once again this trail parallels a usually dry riverbed.

**BIRD WATCHING**    Southern Arizona has some of the best bird watching in the country, and though the best spots are south of Tucson, there are a few places around the city that birders will enjoy seeking out. **Agua Caliente County Park,** 4002 N. Soldier Trail, at the corner of Roger Road in the northeast corner of the city, is just about the best place in the city to see birds. The year-round warm springs here are a magnet for dozens of species, including waterfowl, great blue herons, black phoebes, soras, and vermilion flycatchers. To find the park, follow Tanque Verde Road east 6 miles from the intersection with Sabino Canyon Road and turn left onto Soldier Trail. Watch for signs.

Other good places include **Sabino Canyon Recreation Area** and the path to the waterfall at **Loews Ventana Canyon Resort.**

However, the best area bird watching is in ✪ **Madera Canyon National Forest Recreation Area** (☎ 520/281-2296), which is about 40 miles south of the city, in the Coronado National Forest. Because of the year-round water to be found here, Madera Canyon attracts a surprising variety of bird life. Avid birders flock to this canyon from around the country in hopes of spotting more than a dozen species of hummingbirds, an equal number of flycatchers, warblers, tanagers, buntings, grosbeaks, and many rare birds that are not found in any other state.

However, before birding became a hot activity, this canyon was popular with families looking for a way to escape the heat down in Tucson, and the shady picnic areas and trails still get a lot of use by those who don't carry binoculars. If you're heading out here for the day, arrive early—parking is very limited. To reach Madera Canyon, take Exit 39 off I-19; from the exit, it's another 12 miles southeast. The canyon is open daily from dawn to dusk for day use, but there is also a campground ($10 per night). On weekends a $2 donation is requested for use of the recreation area. For information on the canyon's Santa Rita Lodge, see "Where to Stay," in this chapter.

**GOLF**    Although there aren't quite as many golf courses in Tucson as in Phoenix, this is still a golfer's town. For last-minute tee-time reservations, contact **Standby Golf** (☎ **520/882-2665**).

In addition to the public and municipal links, there are numerous resort courses that allow nonguests to play. Perhaps the most famous of these are the two 18-hole courses at ✪ **Ventana Canyon Golf and Racquet Club,** 6200 N. Clubhouse Lane (☎ 520/ 577-1400). These Tom Fazio–designed courses offer challenging desert target–style play that is nearly legendary. The third hole on the Mountain Course here is one of the most photographed holes in the west ($170 winter; $80 summer). However, as famous as Ventana Canyon courses are, it is the 27-hole ✪ **Omni Tucson National Golf Resort and Spa,** 2727 W. Club Dr. (☎ 520/575-7540), a traditional course, that is perhaps more familiar to golfers—as the site of the annual Tucson Open ($135 winter; $55 summer). The **El Conquistador Country Club,** 10555 N. La Cañada Dr. (☎ **520/544-1800**), with two 18-hole courses and a nine-hole course, offers stunning (and very distracting) views of the Santa Catalina Mountains ($125 winter; $50 summer). At the **La Paloma Resort and Country Club,** 3660 E. Sunrise Dr. (☎ **520/299-1500**), golfers will find 27 holes designed by Jack Nicklaus ($155 winter; $75 summer). At ✪ **Starr Pass Golf Club,** 3645 W. Starr Pass Blvd. (☎ **520/ 670-0400**), players are seduced by the deceptively difficult 15th hole that plays right through the narrow Starr Pass, which was once a stagecoach route ($120 winter; $45 summer).

There are also many other public courses around town. The **Raven Golf Club at Sabino Springs,** 9777 E. Sabino Greens Dr. (☎ **520/749-3636**), incorporates stands of cactus and rocky outcroppings into the course layout ($135 winter; $55 summer). At the **Golf Club at Vistoso,** 955 W. Vistoso Highlands Dr. (☎ **520/797-9900**), you'll find a championship desert course ($125 winter; $55 summer). **Heritage Highlands Golf & Country Club,** 4949 W. Heritage Club Blvd. (☎ **520/579-7000**), is a new championship desert course at the foot of the Tortolita Mountains ($99 winter; $30 to $45 summer). **The Links at Continental Ranch,** 8480 N. Continental Links Dr. (☎ **520/744-7443**), is a rolling links-style course reminiscent of Scottish courses ($49 to $59 winter; $29 to $36 summer).

Tucson Parks and Recreation operates five municipal golf courses, of which the **Randolph North** and **Dell Urich,** 600 S. Alvernon Way (☎ **520/325-2811**), are the premier courses. The former is the site of the LPGA Open. Other municipal courses include **Trini Alvarez/El Rio,** 1400 W. Speedway Blvd. (☎ **520/623-6783**); **Silverbell,** 3600 N. Silverbell Rd. (☎ **520/743-7284**); and **Fred Enke,** 8251 E. Irvington Rd. (☎ **520/ 296-8607**). Nonresident greens fees for 18 holes are $26.50 to $28.50 between November and May ($16.50 to $18.50 in summer). Golf carts are available for $16.

**HIKING**   Tucson is nearly surrounded by mountains, most of which are protected as city and state parks, national forest, or national park, and within these public areas are hundreds of miles of hiking trails.

**Saguaro National Park** flanks Tucson on both the east and west with units accessible off Old Spanish Trail east of Tucson and past the end of Speedway Boulevard west of the city. In these areas you can observe Sonoran Desert vegetation and wildlife and hike among the huge saguaro cacti for which the park is named. For saguaro-spotting the west unit is the better choice.

**Tucson Mountain Park,** also at the end of Speedway Boulevard, is adjacent to Saguaro National Park and preserves a similar landscape. The parking area at Gates Pass, on Speedway, is a favorite sunset spot.

**Sabino Canyon,** off Sabino Canyon Road, is Tucson's most popular recreation area. A cold mountain stream here cascades over waterfalls and forms pools that make great swimming holes. The ✪ **Seven Falls Trail,** which follows Bear Canyon deep into the mountains, is a 5.2-mile round-trip hike and is the most popular hike in the recreation area. You can take a tram to the trailhead or add extra miles by hiking from the main parking lot.

With Tucson's city limits pushing right out to the boundary of the Coronado National Forest, there are some excellent hiking options in Tucson's northern foothills. The **Ventana Canyon Trail** begins at a parking area adjacent to the Loews Ventana Canyon Resort (off Sunrise Drive west of Sabino Canyon Road) and leads into the Ventana Canyon Wilderness. Over near the Westward Look Resort, there is the **Pima Canyon Trail,** which also leads into the Ventana Canyon Wilderness and is reached off of Ina Road just east of Oracle Road. Both of these trails provide classic desert canyon hikes of whatever length you feel like hiking (a dam at 3 miles on the latter trail makes a good turn-around point).

**Catalina State Park,** 11570 N. Oracle Rd. (☎ **520/628-5798**), is set on the rugged northwest face of the Santa Catalina Mountains, between 2,500 and 3,000 feet high. Hiking trails here lead into the Pusch Ridge Wilderness; however, the favorite park day hike is to Romero Pools, a refreshing destination on a hot day. Admission to the park is $5. There are also horseback riding stables adjacent to the park, and within the park there is an ancient Hohokam ruin. Guided hikes are offered in the cooler months.

One of the reasons Tucson is such a livable city is the presence of the cool (and, in winter, snow-covered) pine forests of 8,250-foot Mount Lemmon. Within the **Mount Lemmon Recreation Area,** at the end of the Catalina Highway, there are many miles of hiking trails, and the hearty hiker can even set out from down in the lowland desert and hike up into the alpine forests. For a more leisurely hike, drive to the top to start your hike. Keep in mind, however, that in winter, when the weather is pleasant in Tucson, people may be skiing up here. There is a $5-per-vehicle charge to use any of the sites within this recreation area. Even if you only plan to pull off at a roadside parking spot and ogle the view of the desert far below, you'll need to stop at the roadside ticket kiosk at the base of the mountain and pay your fee.

**HORSEBACK RIDING**   If you want to play cowboy or just go for a leisurely ride through the desert, there are plenty of stables around Tucson where you can saddle up. In addition to renting horses and providing guided trail rides, all the stables below also offer sunset rides with cookouts. Though reservations are not always required, they're a good idea. You can also opt to stay at a guest ranch and do almost as much riding as your muscles can stand.

**Pusch Ridge Stables,** 13700 N. Oracle Rd. (☎ **520/825-1664**), is adjacent to Catalina State Park and Coronado National Forest. Rates are $20 for 1 hour, $35 for 2 hours. This stable also has a satellite stable at the Sheraton El Conquistador.

In the same area, you'll find **Walking Wind Stables,** 10811 N. Oracle Rd. (☎ **520/742-4422**) at Catalina State Park. Rates here are $18 for 1 hour, $35 for 2 hours, and $55 for 3 hours. Reservations are required.

**Desert-High Country Stables,** 6501 W. Ina Rd. (☎ **520/744-3789**), is located 2 miles west of I-10 and offers a variety of rides in the Tucson Mountains and Saguaro National Park West. Rates range from $18 for 1 hour to $85 for a full day. Reservations are requested.

If just riding the range isn't enough for you, then you should contact **Rocky Mountain Cattle Moo-vers** (☎ **800/826-9666**) and sign on for a cattle drive. These aren't genuine cattle drives, but you will be movin' them doggies up the trail a piece. Prices range from $80 for a breakfast cattle drive to $210 for an all-day cattle drive. If your idea of fun is doing the city slicker thing, call the **Cocoraque Ranch,** 6255 N. Diamond Hills Lane (☎ **520/682-8594**). This working cattle ranch dates from the 1890s and now offers cattle drives. Rates depend on the number of people, and there is a 10-person minimum, though it is sometimes possible to join another group. Trail rides ($15 for 1 hour, $25 for 2 hours) are also available. The ranch is located near the Arizona–Sonora Desert Museum and Old Tucson Studios.

**IN-LINE SKATING**   You can rent in-line skates at **Peter Glen's,** 5626 E. Broadway Blvd. (☎ **520/745-4514**), for $3 an hour or $12 per day, including protective equipment. Good places to skate include Reid Park and the Rillito River Wash between North Campbell Avenue and North Oracle Road (just south of River Road).

**SKIING**   Located 1 hour (35 miles) from Tucson, **Mount Lemmon Ski Valley** (☎ **520/576-1321**) is the southernmost ski area in the United States and offers 15 runs for experienced downhill skiers as well as beginners. The season here isn't very reliable, and locals recommend not using your own skis or snowboard (too many exposed rocks). The ski area often only opens after a new dump of snow (at which time the Mount Lemmon Highway is usually closed), so be sure to call the road condition information line (☎ **520/547-7510**) before driving up. The ski season runs from December to April. Full-day lift tickets are $28 for adults and $12 for children. Half-day rates are $23 for adults, $9 for children.

**TENNIS**   The **Randolph Tennis Center,** 50 S. Alvernon Way (☎ **520/791-4896**), convenient to downtown, offers 25 lighted courts. During the day, court time is $2 per person; at night it's $6 per court. Many of the city's hotels and resorts provide courts for guest use.

**WHITE-WATER RAFTING**   The desert may seem like a strange place to think about rafting, but within 2 hours of the city, you can be rafting on the Class II waters of the Gila River. **Chandelle Ski and Travel** (☎ **800/242-6335** or 520/577-1824) offers trips on the Gila River 60 miles north of Tucson. Trip price for a half-day run is $59 per person, including lunch.

**WILDFLOWER VIEWING**   Bloom time varies from year to year, but April and May are good times to view native wildflowers in the Tucson area. While the crowns of white blossoms worn by saguaro cacti are among the most visible blooms in the area, other cacti are far more colorful. Saguaro National Park and Sabino Canyon are among the best local spots to see saguaros, other cacti, and various other wildflowers in bloom. If you feel like heading farther afield, the wildflower displays at Picacho Peak State Park, between Tucson and Casa Grande, are considered the most impressive in the state.

## 8 Spectator Sports

**BASEBALL**   The **Colorado Rockies** (☎ **520/327-9467**) pitch spring-training camp in March at Hi Corbett Field, 3400 E. Camino Campestre, in Reid Park (at South Country Club Road and East 22nd Street). Tickets are $4 to $12. Both the **Chicago White Sox** and the **Arizona Diamondbacks** have their spring training camps and exhibition games at Tucson Electric Park, 2500 E. Ajo Way (☎ **520/434-1159**), which is on the south side of the city near the airport. Tickets for all three teams are available through the **Dillard's** department store box office (☎ **800/638-8350**).

This is also where you can watch the **Tucson Sidewinders** (☎ **520/434-1021**), the Arizona Diamondbacks AAA team in the Pacific Coast League. The season runs from April to August, and tickets are $3 to $8.

**FOOTBALL**   The **University of Arizona Wildcats** (☎ **520/621-2287**), a PAC-10 team, play at UA's Arizona Stadium.

**GOLF TOURNAMENTS**   In mid-March, women golfers compete for big prizes at the **Welch's/Circle K LPGA Championship** (☎ **520/791-5742**), which is held at the Randolph North Golf Course. Daily tickets are $10. The **Touchstone Energy Tucson Open** (☎ **800/882-7660**), Tucson's main PGA tournament, is held in mid-February at the Omni Tucson National Golf Resort and Spa. Daily tickets are around $15.

**GREYHOUND RACING**   Greyhounds race year-round at **Tucson Greyhound Park,** 36th Street at Fourth Avenue (☎ **520/884-7576**). Admission is $1.25. To reach the track, take Exit 261 off I-10.

**HORSE RACING**   **Rillito Park** (☎ **520/293-5011** during racing season, or 520/740-2690 other months), on First Avenue between River and Limberlost roads, was the birthplace of both the photo finish and organized quarter-horse racing and has now been restored for both quarter-horse and thoroughbred racing. The ponies run on weekends in February and March, and admission is $2 to $3.

**TENNIS TOURNAMENTS**   The **Allstate Celebrity Golf & Tennis Classic** (☎ **520/623-6165**) takes place at the Randolph Tennis Center at Randolph Park in mid- to late April, when more than 40 celebrity tennis players take on the locals. There's also a golf tournament and a celebrity golf shootout. Tickets are $5.

# 9  Day Spas

If you'd rather opt for a massage than a round on the links, consider spending a few hours at a day spa. While full-service health spas can cost $400 to $500 or more per person per day, for less than $100, you can avail yourself of a spa treatment or two (massages, facials, seaweed wraps, loofah scrubs, and the like) and maybe even get to spend the day lounging by the pool at some exclusive resort. Spas are also great places to while away an afternoon if you couldn't get a tee time at that golf course you wanted to play or if it happens to be raining. While spas in general still cater primarily to women, those mentioned below also have special programs for men.

For variety of services and gorgeous location, you just can't beat the Spa & Tennis Center at **Loews Ventana Canyon Resort,** 7000 N. Resort Dr. (☎ **520/299-2020**), which is wedged between the rugged Catalinas and manicured fairways of some of the most fabled golf courses in the state. Soothed by the scent of aromatherapy, you can treat yourself to herbal wraps, mud body treatments, seaweed body masks, different styles of massage, specialized facials, complete beauty salon services, and much more. Treatments run $45 to $125. With any body treatment, you also get use of the spa's fitness facilities and pool and can attend any fitness classes being held the day of your treatment.

For an equally luxurious day at the spa, you can also opt to visit the **Omni Tucson National Golf Resort & Spa,** 2727 W. Club Dr. (☎ **520/575-7559**) off Magee Road in the northwestern foothills. Services and prices here are comparable to those at Loews, and once again, with any body treatment or massage, you have full use of the spa's facilities. Try the hot stone massage!

With five locations around the Tucson area, **Gadabout Day Spa** offers the opportunity to slip a relaxing visit to a spa into a busy schedule. Mud baths, facials, and massages as well as hair and nail services are available. You'll find Gadabout at the following locations: St. Philip's Plaza, 1990 E. River Rd. (☎ **520/577-2000**); 6393 E. Grant Rd. (☎ **520/885-0000**); Rancho Center, 3382 E. Speedway Blvd. (☎ **520/ 325-0000**); Canyon Ranch, 8600 Rockcliff Rd. (☎ **520/749-1002**); and Plaza Escondida, 7888 N. Oracle Rd. (☎ **520/742-0000**). Fifty-minute body treatments and massages range in price from $50 to $145. There are also longer treatments, as well as half-day and full-day spa getaways.

# 10  Shopping

Tucsonans have a very strong sense of their place in the Southwest, and this is reflected in the city's shopping scene. Southwestern clothing, food, crafts, furniture, and art abound (and often at reasonable prices), as do shopping centers built in a Southwestern architectural style.

Although Tucson is overshadowed by Scottsdale and Phoenix, the city provides a very respectable diversity of merchants. Its population center has moved steadily northward for some years, so it is in the northern foothills that you'll find most of the city's large enclosed shopping malls as well as expensive shops selling the best-quality merchandise.

On Fourth Avenue, between Congress Street and Speedway Boulevard, more than 100 shops, galleries, and restaurants make up the **North Fourth Avenue historic shopping district.** The buildings here were built in the early 1900s, and there has been an attempt to keep the neighborhood humming and maintain Tucson's downtown vitality. Through the underpass at the south end of Fourth Avenue is Congress Street, the heart of the **Downtown Arts District,** where there are a few art galleries. However, despite the city's best efforts for several years now, neither of these neighborhoods seems to have caught on very fast with Tucson shoppers, and both neighborhoods seem to be primarily hangouts for college students.

**El Presidio Historic District** around the Tucson Museum of Art is the city's center for crafts shops. This area is home to Old Town Artisans and the Tucson Museum of Art museum shop. The **"Lost Barrio"** on the corner of Southwest Park Avenue and 12th Street (a block off Broadway) is a good place to look for Mexican imports and Southwestern-style home furnishings at good prices. Stores include Rústica, Colonial Frontiers, and Magellan Trading.

## ANTIQUES

In addition to the shops listed below, you'll find concentrations of antiques shops along Speedway Boulevard between Swan and Craycroft roads and along Grant Road between Campbell Avenue and Alvernon Way.

**Antique Center.** 5001 E. Speedway Blvd. ☎ **520/323-0319.**

This mall has 90 dealers and claims to be the largest antiques mall in southern Arizona. For sale are all manner of collectibles and antiques, including Aunt Jemima figures, old radios and telephones, and lots of copper and glassware collectibles.

## ART

One of the best ways to take in the downtown Tucson art gallery scene is on the free Thursday night docent-led ArtWalk tours that take place between 5:30 and 7:30pm. These walks are held between September and May and are sponsored by the **Tucson Arts District Partnership** (☎ 520/624-9977). Call for information on tour starting point.

**Americas.** 6420 N. Campbell Ave. (corner of Skyline Dr. and N. Campbell Rd.). ☎ **520/ 529-7002.**

Located right below Anthony's restaurant, this very small shop specializes in very expensive Native American artifacts (mostly pre-1940s) such as pots, Apache and Pima baskets, 19th-century plains Indian beadwork, Navajo weavings, and antique kachinas. They've recently added both historic and contemporary jewelry.

**America West Primitive & Modern Art.** 363 S. Meyer Ave. ☎ **520/623-4091.**

Although this gallery in the Barrio Histórico specializes in works by Native Americans, you'll also find pre-Columbian art and pieces from Africa, Oceania, and Asia. This is museum-quality work. An appointment is requested, but drop-ins are also welcome.

**Dinnerware Contemporary Art Gallery.** 135 E. Congress St. ☎ **520/792-4503.**

*Contemporary* is the key word at this gallery in the downtown arts district. Artists represented here tend to have a very wide range of styles and media, so you never know what you'll find. However, you can be sure it will be at the cutting edge of Tucson art.

**El Presidio Gallery.** 7000 E. Tanque Verde Rd. (at Santa Fe Sq.). ☎ **520/733-0388.**

This is one of Tucson's premier galleries and deals primarily in traditional paintings of the Southwest, although some contemporary works are also available. A second location is at St. Philip's Plaza, 4340 N. Campbell Ave. (☎ **520/529-1220**).

**Eleanor Jeck Galleries.** 4280 N. Campbell Ave. (at River Rd. in St. Philip's Plaza). ☎ **520/ 299-2139.**

Featuring brilliant and whimsical contemporary paintings, this gallery also carries art glass, sculpture, large-format ceramics, and art jewelry.

✪ **Etherton Gallery.** 135 S. 6th Ave. ☎ **520/624-7370.**

For more than 15 years this gallery has been presenting some of the finest new art to be found in Tucson, including contemporary and historic photographs. Etherton Gallery, a favorite of museums and serious collectors, isn't afraid to present work with strong themes. The gallery also has exhibition space upstairs from the B&B Café at the Temple of Music and Art, 330 S. Scott Ave.

**Mark Sublette Medicine Man Gallery.** In Santa Fe Square, 7000 E. Tanque Verde Rd. ☎ **520/722-7798.**

There's a large body of well-chosen contemporary Western art in this gallery, as well as an excellent selection of Native American crafts. The shop is located near the El Presidio Gallery, above. See "Native American Arts & Crafts" below for more details.

✪ **Philabaum Contemporary Art Glass.** 711 S. 6th Ave. ☎ **520/884-7404.**

Visitors can stop by Tom Philabaum's glass studio to watch vases, perfume bottles, and bowls being blown, then browse the gallery full of lovely art glass pieces by Philabaum and more than 100 other artists from around the country.

## BOOKS

Chain bookstores in the Tucson area include **Barnes & Noble,** 5130 E. Broadway Blvd. (☎ **520/512-1166**) and 7325 N. La Cholla Blvd. (☎ **520/742-6402**); and **Borders,** 4235 N. Oracle Rd. (☎ **520/292-1331**).

**Settlers West Book & Print Gallery.** 3061 N. Campbell Ave. ☎ **520/323-8838.**

An impressive selection of books about the West, both for adults and for children, is the main attraction here, but there are also lots of interesting prints of Western themes.

## CRAFTS

**Details & Green Shoelaces.** 2990 N. Swan Rd. (in Plaza Palomino). ☎ **520/323-0222.**

If you enjoy crafts with a sense of humor, you'll get a kick out of this place. Imaginative and unexpected objets d'art turn up in the form of clocks, ceramics, glass, and other mediums.

**Obsidian Gallery.** 4340 N. Campbell Ave. (at River Rd. in St. Philip's Plaza). ☎ **520/577-3598.**

Contemporary crafts by artists of national renown fill this gallery. You'll find luminous art glass, unique and daring jewelry, imaginative ceramics, and much more.

✪ **Old Town Artisans.** 186 N. Meyer Ave. ☎ **800/782-8072** or 520/623-6024.

Housed in a restored 1850s adobe building covering an entire city block of El Presidio Historic District are 15 rooms brimming with traditional and contemporary Southwestern designs by more than 400 artisans.

**Pink Adobe Gallery.** 6538 E. Tanque Verde Rd. (in La Plaza Shoppes). ☎ **520/298-5995.**

This contemporary crafts gallery sells unique and whimsical works produced by artists from all over the United States. On a recent visit there were hand-tinted photos, painted-tin folk art, ceramics, one-of-a-kind pieces of furniture, and cases full of unique jewelry. They also feature fine-crafted Judaica.

**Tucson Museum of Art Shop.** 140 N. Main Ave. ☎ **520/624-2333.**

The museum's gift shop offers a colorful and changing selection of Southwestern arts and crafts, mostly by local and regional artists.

## FASHIONS

See also "Western Wear," below.

### FOR BOTH MEN & WOMEN

**The Buffalo Exchange.** 2001 E. Speedway Blvd. ☎ **520/795-0508.**

A big hit with the college students, this resale shop has grown into a chain with stores across the West. Browse through racks of resale and new clothing at fairly reasonable prices, and you're sure to find something to fit your needs. This is a good place to pick up a pair of cowboy boots if you're heading out on the trail. There's another Buffalo Exchange at 7045 E. Tanque Verde Rd. (☎ **520/885-8392**).

## FOR MEN

**Individual Man.** In St. Philip's Plaza, 4320 N. Campbell Ave. ☎ **520/577-2121.**

Unique ties, silk and other natural-fiber shirts, and cotton slacks are colorful and casual, with styles by American and Italian designers including Tuliano, Axis, Jhane Barnes, and New Man.

## FOR WOMEN

**Jasmine.** 423 N. 4th Ave. ☎ **520/629-0706.**

Natural fibers, including washable silks and some hand-loomed fabrics are the specialty here. There are plenty of styles to browse from on the crowded racks, from classic to exotic. There are Southwestern accessories and jewelry to go with the clothes. There's a second store at 3025 N. Campbell (☎ **520/323-1771**).

**Maya Palace.** In Plaza Palomino, El Mercado de Boutiques, 6332 E. Broadway Blvd. ☎ **520/748-0817.**

This shop features lushly ethnic but very wearable women's clothing in natural fabrics. The friendly staff helps customers put together a complete look, from casual to dressy, or young to older. A second shop is at 2960 N. Swan Rd. (☎ **520/325-6411**).

✪ **Rochelle K Fine Women's Apparel.** 5350 E. Broadway Blvd. in The Plaza at Williams Centre (southwest corner of Broadway and Craycroft). ☎ **520/745-4600.**

With everything from the latest in the little black dress to casual and drapey silks and linens, Rochelle K attracts a well-heeled clientele. There are also beautiful accessories and jewelry.

## GIFTS/SOUVENIRS

**B&B Cactus Farm.** 11550 E. Speedway Blvd. ☎ **520/721-4687.**

This plant nursery is devoted exclusively to cacti and succulents. The store can pack your purchase for traveling or can ship it anywhere in the United States. The farm is worth a visit just to see the amazing variety of cacti on display. It's a good place to stop on the way to or from Saguaro National Monument east.

✪ **Picánte.** 2932 E. Broadway. ☎ **520/320-5699.**

There's a plethora of Hispanic-theme icons and accessories here, including *milagros,* Day of the Dead skeletons, Mexican crosses, jewelry, greeting cards, and folk art from around the world.

**Tohono Chul Gift Shop and Tea Room.** 7366 N. Paseo del Norte (1 block west of the corner of Ina Rd. and Oracle Rd. in Tohono Chul Park). ☎ **520/797-1222.**

This gift shop is packed with Mexican folk art, nature theme toys, household items, T-shirts, and books and makes a good stop after a visit to the surrounding Tohono Chul Park, which is landscaped with desert plants. Add a meal at the park's tea room, and you've got a good afternoon's outing. For a description of the park, see "Parks, Gardens & Zoos" under "Seeing the Sights."

## JEWELRY

In addition to the stores mentioned below, see the Obsidian Gallery under "Crafts" in this section.

**Beth Friedman Jewelry.** 186 N. Meyer Ave. ☎ **520/622-5013.**

Located in the Old Town Artisans complex, this shop primarily sells jewelry by Native American craftspeople and international designers. The shop also carries some extravagant cowgirl getups in velvet, lace, and denim.

✪ **Turquoise Door.** In St. Philip's Plaza, 4330 N. Campbell Ave. (at River Rd.). ☎ **520/ 299-7787.**

The Southwestern contemporary jewelry here is among the most stunning in the city and is made with opals, diamonds, lapis lazuli, amethyst, and the ubiquitous turquoise. There are also baskets, sculptures, bronzes, and rugs.

## MALLS/SHOPPING CENTERS
**Foothills Mall.** 7401 N. La Cholla Blvd. ☎ **520/742-7191.**

This large foothills mall went out of business a few years back but has now been revived as an outlet mall and discount shopping center. You'll find a Nike Factory Store, Off 5th Saks Fifth Avenue Outlet, and Donna Karan Company Store.

✪ **Plaza Palomino.** 2970 N. Swan Rd. ☎ **520/795-1177.**

Built in the style of a Spanish hacienda with a courtyard and fountains, this shopping center is home to some of Tucson's fun little specialty shops, galleries, and restaurants. A courtesy hotel shuttle (☎ **520/750-0365**) is available.

✪ **St. Philip's Plaza.** 4280 N. Campbell Ave. (at River Rd.). ☎ **520/529-2775.**

This upscale Southwestern-style shopping center includes three excellent restaurants, a luxury beauty salon, and numerous shops and galleries, including Bahti Indian Arts and Turquoise Door jewelry. A great one-stop Tucson outing locale.

**The Tucson Mall.** 4500 N. Oracle Rd. ☎ **520/293-7330.**

The foothills of northern Tucson have become shopping-center central, and this is the largest of the malls. You'll find more than 200 merchants in this busy two-story skylit complex.

## MEXICAN & LATIN AMERICAN IMPORTS
In addition to the shops mentioned below, the **"Lost Barrio"** on the corner of Southwest Park Avenue and 12th Street (a block off Broadway) is a good place to look for Mexican imports and Southwestern-style home furnishings at good prices.

**Antigua de Mexico.** 7037 N. Oracle Rd. (in the Casa Adobes Plaza). ☎ **520/742-7114.**

This is a place for arts and crafts from Mexico—big household items such as oversized ceramics and painted plates, wooden and wrought-iron furniture, and punched metal framed mirrors and frames. Smaller items include crucifixes and candlesticks. There are plans afoot for this business to close at this location and reopen in a new warehouse/showroom at 3295 W. Orange Grove Rd. The new showroom should offer similar items and also craft demonstrations. Call the above number for more information.

**La Buhardilla ("The Attic").** 2360 E. Broadway Blvd. ☎ **520/622-5200.**

OK, so you just cashed out of your place in California, you bought a big house, and you need some sizable furniture to fill up all that space. Buhardilla has it—the hand-carved Spanish Baroque furniture is big—10-foot-high carved wood doors and larger-than-life-size carvings of angels and archangels. There are also Latin American art and crafts pieces to accessorize all that furniture.

# NATIVE AMERICAN ARTS & CRAFTS

**Bahti Indian Arts.** In St. Philip's Plaza, 4300 N. Campbell Ave. ☎ 520/577-0290.

Family owned for more than 40 years, this store sells fine pieces—jewelry, baskets, sculpture, paintings, books, weavings, kachina dolls, Zuni fetishes, and much more.

**Indian Territory.** 5639 N. Swan Rd. (on the northwest corner with Sunrise Dr.). ☎ 520/577-7961.

Despite the location in the foothills in a shopping plaza, it's a bit like an old museum in here, with hardwood floors and antique display cases full of Plains and Southwest Indian arts and crafts and regalia. Though much of the store is devoted to new works, you'll also find rare old pieces such as beaded gauntlets and moccasins. Get owner Neil Hicks to show you some of the amazing items here, but don't come on Monday when the store is closed.

✪ **Mark Sublette Medicine Man Gallery.** In Santa Fe Square, 7000 E. Tanque Verde Rd. ☎ 520/722-7798.

Collectors of old Navajo rugs seem to agree that this rug shop has the best and biggest selection in the city and perhaps even the entire state. There are also Mexican and other Hispanic textiles, Acoma pottery, basketry, and other Indian crafts, as well as art work by cowboy artists.

**The Kaibab Shops.** 2841 N. Campbell Ave. ☎ 520/795-6905.

This store has been in business for almost 50 years and offers one of the best selections of Native American arts and crafts in Tucson. You can also find high-quality jewelry, Mexican pottery, home furnishings, glassware, kachinas, and antique *retablos* (paintings of saints on sheet metal).

✪ **Morning Star Traders.** 2020 E. Speedway Blvd. (next door to the Plaza Hotel). ☎ 520/881-2112.

With hardwood floors and a museum-like atmosphere, this store features museum-quality goods: antique Navajo rugs, kachinas, furniture, and a huge selection of old Native American jewelry. This just may be the best store of its type in the entire state.

An adjoining shop, **Morning Star Antiques,** at 2000 E. Speedway Blvd. (☎ 520/881-3060), carries an astounding selection of antique Spanish mission and Mexican furniture, as well as WPA, Mennonite, and South American pieces.

**Silverbell Trading.** In Casas Adobes Plaza, 7007 N. Oracle Rd. ☎ 520/797-6852.

Not your usual run-of-the-mill crafts store, this shop specializes in regional Native American artwork such as baskets and pottery and carries unique items that the shop's owner has obviously sought out. Small items such as stone Navajo corn maidens, Zuni fetishes, and animals carved from sandstone shouldn't be overlooked.

# TOYS

✪ **Yikes! Toy Store.** 2930 E. Broadway. ☎ 520/320-5669.

If you love wild and wacky toys that are as much fun for adults as they are for kids, you won't want to miss Yikes!, which has a huge selection of rubber bugs, lizards, snakes, and frogs, as well as yo-yos, marbles, wind-up toys, and other absurd playthings.

# WESTERN WEAR

**Arizona Hatters.** 3600 N. 1st Ave. ☎ 520/292-1320.

Arizona hatters carries important names in cowboy hats, from Stetson to Bailey to Tilles. They do custom fitting and shape the hat to the wearer's head and face. You'll also find fancy beaded hatbands, shirts, and belts here.

**The Corral Western Wear.** 4525 E. Broadway Blvd. (just west of Swan Rd.). ☎ **520/ 322-6001.**

Standard cowboy gear and accoutrements for the more flamboyant wrangler such as turquoise cowboy hats and brightly colored cowboy boots are stocked here. This is the oldest Western-wear store in Tucson.

**Western Warehouse.** 3030 E. Speedway Blvd. ☎ **520/327-8005.**

If you want to put together your Western-wear ensemble under one roof, this is the place. It's the largest Western-wear store in Tucson and can deck you out in jeans, hats, boots, and Native American jewelry. There are also branches at 3719 N. Oracle Rd. (☎ **520/293-1808**) and 6701 E. Broadway Blvd. (☎ **520/885-4385**).

## 11  Tucson After Dark

Tucson after dark is a much easier landscape to negotiate than the vast cultural sprawl of the Phoenix area. Instead of having numerous performing arts centers all over the suburbs as in the Valley of the Sun, Tucson has a more concentrated nightlife scene. The **Downtown Arts District** is the center of all the action, with the Temple of Music and Art, the Tucson Convention Center Music Hall, a small avant-garde theater, and several nightclubs. The **University of Arizona campus,** only a mile away, is another hot spot for entertainment.

The best place to look for entertainment listings is in the ***Tucson Weekly.*** Here you'll find thorough listings of concerts, theater and dance performances, and club offerings. The newspaper is free and can be picked up in convenience stores and record stores, among other places. The "Starlight" section of the Thursday edition of ***The Arizona Daily Star*** is another good source.

## THE CLUB & MUSIC SCENE
### MARIACHI MUSIC

Tucson is the mariachi capital of the United States, and no one should visit without spending at least one evening listening to some of these strolling minstrels. Luckily, there are at least two restaurants in town that feature mariachi music several nights each week.

**El Mariachi Restaurant.** 106 W. Drachman St. ☎ **520/791-7793.** No cover.

Although the music is just as good and the view of the stage better, El Mariachi just doesn't have the atmosphere you'll find at La Fuente. The band International Mariachi America performs Wednesday through Sunday night (closed Monday and Tuesday), and the menu features steaks, shrimp, and Mexican food in the $10 to $18 range. Shows are at 7 and 9pm. Reservations are recommended.

✪ **La Fuente.** 1749 N. Oracle Rd. ☎ **520/623-8659.** Closed Mon June–Labor Day. No cover.

La Fuente is the largest Mexican restaurant in Tucson and serves up good food, but what really draws the crowds is the live mariachi music. The music starts at 6pm, and if you just want to listen and not have dinner, you can hang out in the lounge. During the summer, the mariachis perform Thursday through Sunday; the rest of the year, performances are Wednesday through Sunday.

### COUNTRY

**Cactus Moon Café.** 5470 E. Broadway Blvd. (on the east side of town at the corner of Craycroft Rd.). ☎ **520/748-0049.** Cover $1–$4.

A younger to middle-aged crowd frequents this large and glitzy nightclub primarily for country music. However, Sundays are currently '80s retro night.

**The Maverick, King of Clubs.** 4702 E. 22nd. St. (at Swan Rd.). ☎ **520/748-0456.** No cover.

This country-and-Western place is tiny, which as far as a lot of people are concerned makes The Maverick a great place to go dancing. Basically it attracts an older crowd, but there's usually a mix of people. The house band plays Tuesday through Saturday.

**The New West/Gotham.** 4385 W. Ina Rd. ☎ **520/744-7744.** Cover $3–$21.

Once upon a time this huge place was a bowling alley. These days, however, the club splits its attentions between the country-music crowd and rock 'n' rollers. In the New West part of the club you can still line dance the night away, and there are regularly scheduled live shows by touring bands. There's also a Hooters sports bar associated with the club.

## ROCK, BLUES & REGGAE

**Berky's Bar.** 5769 E. Speedway Blvd. ☎ **520/296-1981.** Cover $3 Fri–Sat.

There's live music wailing 7 nights a week in this dark and smoky tavern. Monday nights are open jam night, so you never know who or what you might hear.

**The Boondocks.** 3306 N. 1st Ave. ☎ **520/690-0991.** Cover $2–$10.

Long a popular dive bar, this place north of downtown is now one of the city's best spots to hear live blues and reggae. There's even a swing night complete with dance lessons. Just look for the giant Chianti bottle out front.

**Chicago Bar.** 5954 E. Speedway Blvd. ☎ **520/748-8169.** Cover $3 Wed–Sat.

Transplanted Chicagoans love to watch their home teams on the TVs at this neighborhood bar, but there's also live music nightly. Sure, blues gets played a lot, but so do reggae and rock and about everything in between.

✪ **Club Congress.** 311 E. Congress St. ☎ **520/622-8848.** Cover $3–$15.

Just off the lobby of the restored Hotel Congress (now a budget hotel and youth hostel), Club Congress is Tucson's main alternative-music venue. There are usually a couple of nights of live music each week.

**The Rialto Theatre.** 318 E. Congress St. ☎ **520/740-0126.** Tickets $5–$25.

This recently renovated 1919 vaudeville theater, though not a nightclub, is now Tucson's main venue for performances by bands that are too big to play Club Congress (Los Lobos, Big Bad Voodoo Daddy, NRBQ).

## JAZZ

For their musical edification, serious jazz fans in Tucson turn to the **Tucson Jazz Society** (☎ **520/743-3399**), which sponsors a wide variety of performances throughout the year (including those at the Cottonwood Club, below). Give them a call to find out about any upcoming events. You'll also catch live jazz on the weekends at the **Cushing Street Bar and Grill,** 343 S. Meyer Ave. (☎ **520/622-7984**), a popular downtown restaurant.

✪ **Cottonwood Club.** 60 N. Alvernon Way. ☎ **520/326-6000.** Cover $2–$4.

Every Sunday from 7:30pm to 11:30pm, this club, affiliated with one of the city's better Southwestern-style restaurants, becomes a jazz club. The Sunday night jazz jams are sponsored by the Tucson Jazz Society. There's live jazz and blues other nights as well—call for a schedule.

## A COMEDY CLUB

**Laffs Comedy Caffè.** The Village, 2900 E. Broadway Blvd. ☎ **520/323-8669.** Cover Wed–Thurs, and Sun $5; Fri–Sat $8.

This stand-up comedy club has local comedians and professional comedians from around the country performing Wednesday through Sunday nights. They have a full bar and a full menu.

## DANCE CLUBS/DISCOS

**DV8.** 5851 E. Speedway Blvd. ☎ **520/885-3030.** Cover $3.

Playing alternative, '80s retro, and techno dance music, this big club attracts a young crowd. The cheap drinks assure that the club stays packed.

**Metro.** 296 N. Stone Ave. ☎ **520/622-4700.** Cover $3–$5.

It's big, it's loud, it's crowded, and under one name or another, this space has long been a favorite of the college crowd. Currently there are two distinctly different dance clubs under one roof here. One area has high-energy dance music while the other has alternative and Top 40.

# THE BAR, LOUNGE & PUB SCENE
## BARS & LOUNGES

**The Arizona Inn.** 2200 E. Elm St. ☎ **520/325-1541.**

If you're looking for a quiet, comfortable scene, the jazz or acoustic music in the Audubon Lounge at the Arizona Inn is sure to soothe your soul. The gardens here are beautiful.

**Cascade Lounge.** In Loews Ventana Canyon Resort, 7000 N. Resort Dr. ☎ **520/299-2020.**

This is Tucson's ultimate piano bar. With a view of the Catalinas and a caviar-and-pâté happy hour (weeknights 5 to 7pm), the plush lounge is perfect for romance or relaxation at the start or end of a night on the town. A couple of nights each week, a harpist performs instead of a pianist, and on the weekends, you'll find a band here.

**Kon Tiki.** 4625 E. Broadway. ☎ **520/323-7193.**

If you know who Martin Denny is, then you must be part of the cocktail nation. Well, this is an original, still sporting that Tahitian motif from way back in the 1950s (there are even live parrots in an aviary behind the bar). The crowd is young, urban, but not necessarily professional.

**Presidio Grill.** 3352 E. Speedway Blvd. ☎ **520/327-4667.**

With its hip contemporary decor, Presidio Grill attracts a young upscale crowd. Though best known as one of the city's premier restaurants, the bar is a great place for a cocktail.

✪ **¡Toma!** 311 N. Court Ave. ☎ **520/622-1922.**

Located in El Presidio Historic District and owned by the family that operates El Charro Café next door, this cafe has a humorous, festive atmosphere complete with a Mexican hat fountain/sculpture in the courtyard. Drop by for cheap margaritas during the daily happy hour from 4 to 7pm. On Friday and Saturday nights there is live mariachi or other Latin-inspired music.

## PUBS & BREW PUBS

**Breckenridge Brewery.** 1980 E. River Rd. (at River Rd. and Campbell Ave. in St. Philip's Plaza). ☎ **520/577-0800.**

This cavernous brew pub (part of a Colorado chain) is in an upscale shopping plaza. It may be more glitz than local pub, but its motto, "Life's too short to drink cheap beer!" leaves no question about where its priorities lie.

**Frog & Firkin.** 874 E. University Blvd. ☎ **520/623-7507.**

This pub in an old house near UA is giving Gentle Ben's a run for its money. Not only are there plenty of great brews on tap, but you can also get good hard cider. There's live rock a few nights a week, and the crowd is primarily college students.

**Gentle Ben's Brewing Co.** 865 E. University Blvd. ☎ **520/624-4177.**

Located just off the UA campus, Gentle Ben's, a big modern place with plenty of outdoor seating, is Tucson's favorite microbrewery. The crowd is young and active, and there are daily food and drink specials.

**Nimbus Brewing.** 3850 E. 44th St. (2 blocks east of Palo Verde Rd.). ☎ **520/745-9175.**

Located in a warehouse district on the south side of Tucson, this brewpub is basically the front room of Nimbus's brewing and bottling facility. The furniture is straight out of Goodwill, but the beer is good, and there's live rock and jazz several nights a week. Hard to find, and definitely a local scene.

**Pusch Ridge Restaurant & Brewery.** 5861 N. Oracle Rd. ☎ **520/888-7547.**

If you're up on the north side of town and looking to quaff a few handcrafted beers, check out Pusch Ridge, which usually has seven of its own brews on tap. There's live blues and jazz a couple of nights a week.

## COCKTAILS WITH A VIEW

Just about all the best views in town are at foothills resorts, but luckily they don't mind sharing with nonguests. In addition to those listed below, the lounge at Anthony's in the Catalinas has a great view. See "Where to Dine," earlier in this chapter, for details.

**Desert Garden Lounge.** In the Westin La Paloma, 3800 E. Sunrise Dr. ☎ **520/742-6000.**

If you'd like a close-up view of the Santa Catalina Mountains, drop by the Desert Garden Lounge (at sunset perhaps). The large lounge, with its multicolored hardwood floors, affects a sort of Casablanca ambience, and there's live piano music on weeknights.

✪ **Flying V Bar & Grill.** In Loews Ventana Canyon Resort, 7000 N. Resort Dr. ☎ **520/299-2020.**

If you can't afford the lap of luxury, you can at least pull up a chair. Set it next to a waterfall just outside the front door of this popular resort watering hole for a view over the golf course and Tucson far below. The view is one of the best in the city.

**Lookout Bar & Grille.** In the Westward Look Resort, 245 E. Ina Rd. ☎ **520/297-1151.**

The Westward Look is one of Tucson's oldest resorts and took to the hills long before it became the fashionable place to be. The nighttime view of twinkling city lights and stars is unmatched. On weekend nights there's live music.

## SPORTS BARS

**Famous Sam's.** 3620 N. 1st Ave. ☎ **520/292-0314.**

With 10 branches around the city, Famous Sam's keeps a lot of Tucson's sports fans happy with their cheap prices and large portions. Other convenient locations include 1830 E. Broadway Blvd. (☎ **520/884-0119**), 7930 E. Speedway Blvd. (☎ **520/290-9666**), and 4801 E. 29th St. (☎ **520/748-1975**).

**Trophies.** In the Sheraton Tucson Hotel & Suites, 5151 E. Grant Rd. ☎ **520/323-6262.**

On weekends and any time there's an Arizona sports team playing, this place gets packed. If you want some sports camaraderie, check it out.

## GAY & LESBIAN BARS

To find out about other gay bars around town, keep an eye out for *The Observer,* Tucson's newspaper for the gay, lesbian, and bisexual community. You'll find it at **Antigone Books,** 411 N. Fourth Ave. (☎ **520/792-3715**), as well as at the bars listed here.

**Ain't Nobody's Bizness.** 2900 E. Broadway Blvd. ☎ **520/318-4838.**

Located in a small shopping plaza in midtown, this somewhat upscale bar is *the* lesbian gathering spot in Tucson and has been for several years. There's a dance floor, two pool tables, and a quiet smoke-free room where you can duck out of the noise.

**Hours.** 3455 E. Grant Rd. ☎ **520/327-3390.**

With a dance floor, fireplace, and pool table, this casual neighborhood bar is one of Tucson's most popular gay and lesbian hangouts, though straights sometimes make the scene also. If you're lookin' to do some boot scootin', this is the place.

**IBT's.** 616 N. 4th Ave. ☎ **520/882-3053.**

Located on funky Fourth Avenue, IBT's has long been the most popular gay dance bar in town. The music ranges from eighties retro to techno, and there are regular drag shows. There's always an interesting crowd.

## THE PERFORMING ARTS

To a certain extent, Tucson is a clone of Phoenix when it comes to the performing arts. Three of Tucson's major performance companies—the Arizona Opera Company, Ballet Arizona, and the Arizona Theatre Company—spend half their time in Phoenix. This means that whatever gets staged in Phoenix also gets staged in Tucson. This city does, however, have its own symphony, and Tucson manages to sustain a diversified theater scene as well.

The best way to purchase tickets in Tucson is directly from the company's box office, but tickets to many concerts and theater performances are also available at **Dillard's** department store box offices or by calling the Dillard's telephone reservation line (☎ **800/638-4253**). Tickets to Tucson Convention Center events and other venues around town may be available by calling the TCC box office at ☎ **520/791-4266.** **Ticketmaster** (☎ **520/321-1000**) also sells tickets to some Tucson performances.

## CLASSICAL MUSIC, OPERA & DANCE

Both the **Tucson Symphony Orchestra** (☎ **520/882-8585**), which is the oldest continuously performing symphony in the Southwest, and the **Arizona Opera Company** (☎ **520/293-4336**), the state's premier opera company, perform at the Tucson Convention Center (TCC) Music Hall, 260 S. Church Ave. Symphony tickets run $10 to $29, and opera tickets run about $17 to $70.

Tucson's dance scene is dominated by **Ballet Arizona** (☎ **888/322-5538**), which splits its season between Tucson and Phoenix. Productions usually include well-known ballets as well as new works by regional choreographers, and performances are at different venues around town, including the Tucson Convention Center. Most tickets are $16 to $40.

If your interests run more to modern dance, find out if **Orts Theatre of Dance** (☎ **520/624-3799**) or **Tenth Street Danceworks** (☎ **520/795-6980**) will be performing in town during your visit.

## THEATER

Tucson doesn't have a lot of theater companies, but what few it does have stage a surprisingly diverse sampling of both classic and contemporary plays.

**Arizona Theatre Company (ATC)** (☎ 520/622-2823), which performs at the Temple of Music and Art, 330 S. Scott Ave., splits its time between here and Phoenix and is the state's top professional theater company. Each season sees a mix of comedy, drama, and Broadway-style musical shows; tickets cost about $19 to $33.

For experimental theater, there's the **Invisible Theatre,** 1400 N. First Ave. (☎ 520/882-9721), a tiny theater in a converted laundry building that has been home to Tucson's most experimental theater for 25 years (it also does off-Broadway shows and musicals). Tickets go for $11 to $18.

The West just wouldn't be the West without good old-fashioned melodramas, and the **Gaslight Theatre,** 7010 E. Broadway Blvd. (☎ 520/886-9428), is where evil villains, stalwart heroes, and defenseless heroines pound the boards. You can boo and hiss, cheer and sigh as the predictable stories unfold on stage. It's all great fun for kids and adults. Tickets are $13.95 for adults, $11.95 for students and senior citizens, and $6 for children 12 and under. Performances are held Wednesday through Sunday, with two shows nightly on Friday and Saturday and a Sunday matinee.

## PERFORMING ARTS CENTERS & CONCERT HALLS

Tucson's largest performance venue is the **Tucson Convention Center Music Hall,** 260 S. Church Ave. (☎ 520/791-4266). It's the home of the Tucson Symphony Orchestra and is where the Arizona Opera Company and Ballet Arizona usually perform when they're in town. This hall also hosts many touring companies. The box office is open Monday through Friday from 10am to 6pm.

However, the **Temple of Music and Art,** 330 S. Scott Ave. (☎ 520/622-2823 or 520/884-8210), a restored historic theater dating from 1927, is the centerpiece of the Tucson theater scene. The 605-seat Alice Holsclaw Theatre is the Temple's main stage, but there's also the 90-seat Cabaret Theatre. You'll also find an art gallery, a gift shop, and a restaurant here. Free tours of the Temple of Art and Music are given on Saturday mornings. The box office is open Monday through Friday from 10am to 6pm (it's also open Saturday and Sunday and later in the evening Tuesday through Friday during performance weeks).

**Centennial Hall,** University Boulevard and Park Avenue (☎ 520/621-3341), on the UA campus, is Tucson's other main performance hall and stages performances by touring national musical acts, international performance companies, and Broadway shows. A large stage and excellent sound system permit large-scale productions. The box office is open Monday through Friday from 10am to 5pm and Saturday from noon to 5pm.

Also downtown, you'll find the **Tucson Center for the Performing Arts,** 408 S. Sixth Ave. (☎ 520/792-8480), which stages a wide variety of performances, providing an alternative stage for small productions and concerts.

The **Center for the Arts,** Pima Community College (West Campus), 2202 W. Anklam Rd. (☎ 520/206-6988), is another good place to check for classical music performances. It offers a wide variety of shows, including performances by Ballet Arizona and the Tucson Symphony Chamber Orchestra. The box office is open Monday through Friday from 10am to 4pm.

## OUTDOOR VENUES & SERIES

Weather permitting, Tucsonans head to Reid Park's **DeMeester Outdoor Performance Center,** at Country Club Road and East 22nd Street (☎ 520/791-4079), for performances under the stars. This amphitheater is the site of performances by the Parks and Recreation Community Theatre and other production companies, as well as frequent music performances.

The **Tucson Jazz Society** (☎ 520/743-3399), which manages to book a few well-known jazz musicians each year, sponsors different outdoor music series at various locations around the city with the summer series at St. Philip's Plaza shopping center being the most popular. Over the course of the year the society presents around 40 concerts. Tickets are $11 to $25.

There are also various outdoor concert series downtown throughout the year. The most popular of these are the concerts held in conjunction with the Downtown Saturday/Downtown Saturday Night events. Check in the *Tucson Weekly* for details.

## FILM

**The Loft Cinema.** 3233 E. Speedway Blvd. ☎ **520/795-7777.**

If *Star Wars* wasn't your idea of the best movie ever made, this is the place for you. The screen here is one of the largest around, just right for watching a new independent or foreign release.

**The Screening Room.** 127 E. Congress St. ☎ **520/622-2262.**

Operated by the Arizona Center for Media Arts, this theater in the downtown arts district specializes in classic art-house films and contemporary independent and foreign films. This is the place to catch *That Obscure Object of Desire, The Night of the Iguana,* or *Woman in the Dunes* one more time.

## CASINOS

**Casino of the Sun.** 7406 S. Camino de Oeste. ☎ **800/344-9435** or 520/883-1700.

Located 15 miles southwest of Tucson and operated by the Pascua Yaqui tribe, this is southern Arizona's largest casino and offers slot machines, keno, bingo, and a card room.

**Desert Diamond Casino.** 7350 S. Nogales Hwy. ☎ **520/294-7777.**

Operated by the Tohono O'odham tribe and located only 3 miles away from Mission San Xavier del Bac, this casino offers the same variety of slot and video poker machines found at other casinos in the state. A card room, bingo, and keno round out the options here.

## 12  A Side Trip from Tucson

For a day's excursion, you can combine a visit to Biosphere 2 with some hiking or horseback riding in Catalina State Park.

✪ **Biosphere 2 Visitor Center.** Ariz. 77, mile marker 96.5. ☎ **800/828-2462** or 520/825-1289. www. bio2.edu. Admission $12.95 adults, $8.95 children 6–17, free for children 5 and under. Discounts for students and seniors. Daily 8:30am–7pm. Closed Dec 25. Take Oracle Rd. north out of Tucson and continue north on Ariz. 77 until you see the Biosphere sign.

For 2 years, beginning in September 1991, four men and four women were locked inside this airtight, 3-acre greenhouse in the desert 35 miles north of Tucson near the town of Oracle. During their tenure in Biosphere 2 (earth is considered Biosphere 1), they conducted experiments on how the earth, basically a giant greenhouse, manages to support all the planet's life forms. Though there are no longer people living in Biosphere 2, similar experiments continue. This giant science project is also a major tourist attraction.

Tours of the facility are offered daily, including a tour of part of the interior of Biosphere 2. You can learn about the project at an orientation center and then take a guided tour that includes the Ocean Viewing Gallery, the test module, Biome Ecology Laboratories, and multimedia presentations. An interactive display area provides entertainment for children. Whether you consider it science or a tourist attraction, there's plenty to see and do. Also on the grounds are a hotel, restaurant, cafe, bookstore, and gift shop.

# 10 Southern Arizona

Although southern Arizona has its share of prickly pears and saguaros, much of this region has more in common with the Texas plains than it does with the Sonoran Desert. In the southeastern corner of the state, the mile-high grasslands, punctuated by forested mountain ranges, have long supported vast ranches where cattle range across wide-open plains. Perhaps because of this prime ranch land, it was here that much of America's now-legendary Western history took place. Wyatt Earp and the Clantons shot it out at Tombstone's O.K. Corral, Doc Holliday played his cards, and Cochise and Geronimo staged the last Indian rebellions. Cavalries charged, and prospectors searched for the mother lode. Today, ghost towns litter the landscape of southeastern Arizona, but the past is kept alive by people searching for a glimpse of the Wild West.

Long before even the prospectors and outlaws arrived in this corner of the state, this region had gained historical importance as the first part of the Southwest explored by the Spanish. This first Spanish expedition, led by Francisco Vásquez de Coronado in 1540, marched up the San Pedro River valley past present-day Sierra Vista, where today a national memorial commemorates his unfruitful search for the Seven Cities of Cíbola. These cities were rumored to be filled with gold and precious jewels, but all Coronado found were simple Indian pueblos. Nearly 150 years later Father Eusebio Francisco Kino would found a string of Jesuit missions across the Pimeria Alta, a region that would later become northern Mexico and southern Arizona. Converting the Indians and building mission churches, Father Kino left a long-lasting mark on this region. Today two of the missions founded by Father Kino—San Xavier del Bac (see chapter 9, "Tucson") and San José de Tumacacori (see the section on Amado, Tubac, and Tumacacori, below)—still stand.

Today, more than 450 years after Coronado marched through this region, the valley of the San Pedro River is undergoing something of a population explosion, especially in the town of Sierra Vista, where retirement communities now sprawl across the landscape. Nearby, in the once nearly abandoned copper-mining town of Bisbee, famous for its Bisbee Blue turquoise, a different sort of boom is underway. Urban refugees and artists have been taking up residence and opening art galleries and B&Bs, making this one of the most interesting small towns in the state.

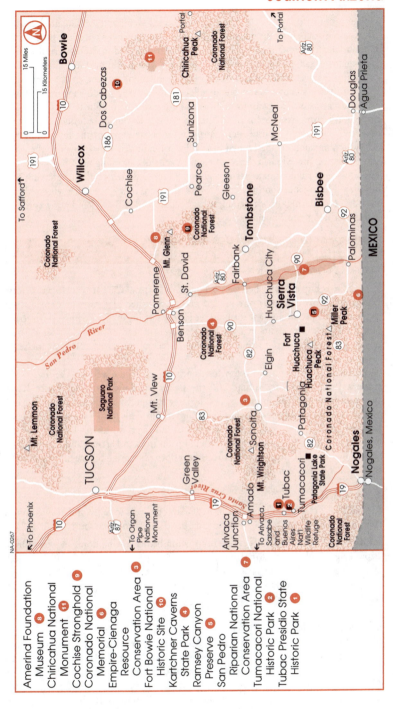

15 Miles
15 Kilometers

Bowie
Portal
To Portal
Chiricahua Peak △
Coronado National Forest
Dos Cabezas
Ariz 80
Douglas
Agua Prieta
**11**
**10**
181
Sunizona
McNeal
191
MEXICO
Willcox
186
Cochise
Pearce
Gleeson
Ariz 80
Bisbee
191
To Safford
Coronado National Forest
191
191
Coronado National Forest
**8**
Mt. Glenn △
**9**
Tombstone
92
Palominas
San Pedro River
Pomerene
Mt. Glenn △
St. David
Fairbank
Huachuca City
**90**
**7**
Sierra Vista
**4**
90
Benson
Ariz 80
Coronado National Forest
92
Miller Peak △
**6**
**5**
Fort Huachuca
Huachuca Peak △
83
Saguaro National Park
Coronado National Forest
Mt. View
**10**
82
Elgin
TUCSON
Mt. Lemmon △
Coronado National Forest
**3**
Sonoita
83
Patagonia
Coronado National Forest
Mt. Wrightson △
Patagonia Lake State Park
Nogales
Nogales, Mexico
Green Valley
Coronado National Forest
82
To Phoenix
Santa Cruz River
Ariz 87
To Organ Pipe National Monument
Amado
Tumacacori
Tubac
19
**1**
**2**
19
Arivaca Junction
To Arivaca, Sasabe and Buenos Aires Nat'l Wildlife Refuge
Coronado National Forest

NA-0267

San Pedro River

359

The combination of low deserts, high plains, and even higher mountains has given this region a fascinating diversity of landscapes. Giant saguaros cover the slopes of the Sonoran Desert throughout much of southern Arizona, and in the western reaches of this region, organ pipe cacti, similar to saguaros, reach the northern limit of their range. In the cool mountains, cacti give way to pines and passing clouds bring snow and rain. Narrow canyons and broad valleys, fed by the rain and snowmelt, provide habitat for an astounding variety of birds and other wildlife unique to the region. This is the northernmost range for many species of birds usually only found south of the border. Consequently, southeastern Arizona has become one of the most important bird-watching spots in the United States. Even nonbirders can appreciate the possibility of seeing more than a dozen different species of hummingbirds.

The region's mild climate has also given rise to the state's small but growing wine industry. Throughout southeastern Arizona, there are now quite a few vineyards and wineries, and touring the wine country has become a favorite weekend getaway for residents of Tucson and Phoenix.

## 1 Organ Pipe National Monument

135 miles S of Phoenix; 185 miles SE of Yuma; 140 miles W of Tucson

Located roughly midway between Yuma and Tucson, ✪ **Organ Pipe Cactus National Monument** is one of Arizona's least visited and most remote national monuments. This monument is a preserve for the rare organ pipe cactus, which resembles the saguaro cactus in many ways. However, instead of forming a single main trunk, organ pipes form many trunks, some 20 feet tall, that resemble, you guessed it, organ pipes.

This is a rugged region with few towns or services. To the west lies the inaccessible **Cabeza Prieta Wildlife Refuge** and the **Barry M. Goldwater Air Force Range** (a bombing range), and to the east lies the large Papago Indian Reservation. The only services and motels in the area are to be found in Ajo. This former company town was built around a now-abandoned copper mine, and the downtown plaza has the look and feel of a Mexican town square, with tall palm trees and arched and covered walkways. On a hot day, the ice-cream parlor here does a booming business. Be sure to gas up your car before leaving Ajo.

### ESSENTIALS

**GETTING THERE**  From Tucson, take Ariz. 86 west to Why and turn south on Ariz. 85. From Yuma, take I-8 east to Gila Bend and then drive south on Ariz. 85.

**VISITOR INFORMATION**  For information before leaving home, contact **Organ Pipe Cactus National Monument,** Route 1, Box 100, Ajo, AZ 85321-9626 (☎ **520/387-6849;** www.nps.gov/orpi). There is a visitor center open daily from 8am to 5pm, although the park itself is open 24 hours a day.

**ADMISSION**  Park admission is $4 per car.

### SEEING THE MONUMENT

Two well-graded one-way gravel roads loop through the park. The Puerto Blanco Drive is a 53-mile loop, while the Ajo Mountain Drive is only 21 miles long. On the Puerto Blanco Drive, you'll pass **Quitobaquito Spring,** which was relied upon by Native Americans and pioneers as the only year-round source of water for miles around. This large spring offers great bird-watching opportunities, but cars are subject to break-ins (a highway is only 100 yards from the parking lot). Quitobaquito Springs can also be reached at the end of a 15-mile two-way section of the Puerto Blanco

Drive. Guides available at the park's visitor center explain natural features of the landscape along both the loop roads. There are also a number of hiking trails along both of these roads.

## WHERE TO STAY

The nearest lodgings are in Ajo, where there are several old and very basic motels as well as a couple of B&Bs. There are also plenty of budget chain motels in the town of Gila Bend, 70 miles to the north of the monument. There is one campground within the park (although nonvehicle camping is allowed in the backcountry with a permit). Campsites are $8 per night.

**The Guest House Inn Bed & Breakfast.** 700 Guest House Rd., Ajo, AZ 85321. ☎ **520/ 387-6133.** 4 units. A/C. $79 double. Rates include full breakfast. DC, MC, V.

Built in 1925 as a guest house for mining executives, this B&B has attractive gardens in the front yard, a mesquite thicket off to one side, and a modern Southwestern feel to its interior decor. Guest rooms are cool and dark, which is often appreciated in the desert heat here in Ajo. However, there are also sunrooms on both the north and the south side of the house.

**The Mine Manager's House.** 601 W. Greenway Dr., Ajo, AZ 85321. ☎ **520/387-6505.** Fax 520/387-6508. 5 units. A/C. $75–$105 double. Rates include full breakfast. MC, V.

Perched high on a hill overlooking the town of Ajo, this B&B boasts commanding views that take in the abandoned open-pit mine on the outskirts of town. As the name implies, this was once the home of the mine's manager, built in 1919. The inn is thoroughly unpretentious, and a stay here is a bit like a visit to your retired aunt and uncle's house. Although it may seem like an odd theme for the middle of the desert, the Nautical Room is the most fun of the inn's rooms.

## 2  Amado, Tubac & Tumacacori

45 miles S of Tucson; 21 miles N of Nogales; 84 miles W of Sierra Vista

Located in the fertile valley of the Santa Cruz River 45 miles south of Tucson, Tubac and Tumacacori together sum up the early experiences of the Spanish, who were the first Europeans to settle in this region. Established in 1691 by Fr. Eusebio Francisco Kino, Tumacacori was one of the first Spanish missions in what would eventually become Arizona. At that time, Tubac was a Pima village, but by the 1730s, the Spanish had begun settling here in the region they called Pimeria Alta. After a Pima uprising in 1751, Spanish forces were sent into the area to protect the settlers, and, in 1752, Tubac became a *presidio* (fort). Between 1752 and the present, seven different flags have flown over Tubac, including those of Spain, Mexico, the United States, the New Mexico Territory, the Confederacy, the U.S. Territory of Arizona, and the state of Arizona.

Though the European history of this area is more than 300 years old, the area's human habitation actually dates far back into prehistory. Archaeologists have found evidence that there have been people living along the nearby Santa Cruz River for

## Impressions

*It has a melancholy appearance. The walls of the church still stand, no roof, and only the upright piece of the cross. It looks desolate indeed.*

—A traveler named Hays, upon seeing the ruins of Tumacacori in 1849 nearly 10,000 years. The Hohokam dwelled in the area from about A.D. 300 until their mysterious disappearance around 1500, and when the Spanish arrived around 200 years later, they found the Pima people inhabiting this region.

Tubac's other claim to fame is as the site from which Juan Bautista de Anza III, the second commander of the presidio, set out in 1775 to find an overland route to California. De Anza led 240 settlers and more than 1,000 head of cattle on this grueling expedition, and when the group finally reached the coast of California, they founded the settlement of San Francisco. One year later, the garrison was moved from Tubac to Tucson, and, with no protection, settlers moved away from the area. Soldiers were once again stationed here beginning in 1776, but lack of funds caused the closure of the presidio when, in 1821, Mexican independence brought Tubac under a new flag. It was not until this region became U.S. territory that settlers returned to the area, and by 1860, Tubac was the largest town in Arizona.

Today, Tubac is one of Arizona's largest arts communities. The town's old buildings house more than 80 shops selling fine arts, crafts, and unusual gifts, and although some are touristy, others are gems worth seeking out. This concentration of shops, artists' studios, and galleries makes Tubac one of southern Arizona's most popular destinations, and a small retirement community is beginning to develop in the area. After visiting Tubac Presidio State Historic Park and Tumacacori National Monument to learn about the area's history, you'll probably want to spend some time browsing through these interesting shops. Keep in mind, however, that many of the local artists leave town during the summer, so it's best to visit on weekends then. The busy season is from October to May, and during these months shops are open daily.

The tiny community of Amado is the site of a couple of good restaurants and an inn. But Amado's most interesting attraction is probably a building built in the shape of a giant cow skull. Recently reopened as a restaurant, it's on the west side of I-19 at Exit 48.

## ESSENTIALS

**GETTING THERE** Amado, Tubac, and Tumacacori are all due south of Tucson on I-19.

**VISITOR INFORMATION** For further information about Tubac and Tumacacori, contact the **Tubac Chamber of Commerce,** P.O. Box 1866, Tubac, AZ 85646 (☎ **520/398-2704;** www.tubacaz.com).

**SPECIAL EVENTS** The **Tubac Festival of the Arts** is held each year in February. Artists from all over the country participate. In October, on the weekend nearest to the 23rd, **De Anza Days** commemorate Captain Juan Bautista de Anza's 1775 trek to found San Francisco.

## ART & HISTORY IN THE SANTA CRUZ VALLEY

**Tumacacori National Historical Park.** Frontage Rd. ☎ **520/398-2341.** Admission $2 per person or $4 per carload, free for children 16 and under. Daily 8am–5pm. Closed Thanksgiving and Dec 25. Take I-19 to Exit 29; you'll find Tumacacori 3 miles south of Tubac.

We in the United States often forget our Spanish heritage, but these mission ruins are a silent reminder of the role that Spanish missionaries played in settling the Southwest. The Tumacacori mission was founded by Jesuit missionary and explorer Fr. Eusebio Francisco Kino in 1691 to convert the Pima people. Much of the old adobe mission church still stands, and the Spanish architectural influences can readily be seen. A small museum contains exhibits on mission life and the history of the region.

On weekends, Native American and Mexican craftspeople give demonstrations of indigenous arts. The **Tumacacori Fiesta,** a celebration of Indian, Hispanic, and Anglo cultures, is held the first weekend of December.

**Tubac Presidio State Historic Park.** Presidio Dr. ☎ **520/398-2252.** Admission $2 adults, $1 children 7–13, free for children 6 and under. Daily 8am–5pm. Closed Dec 25.

The Tubac Presidio has a long and fitful history. Though the Tumacacori mission was founded in 1691, it was not until 1752 that the Tubac Presidio was established in response to a Pima uprising. In 1775, the presidio's military garrison was moved to Tucson and, with no protection from raiding Apache, most of Tubac's settlers also left the area. A military presence was reestablished in 1787, but after Mexican independence in 1821, insufficient funds led to the closing of the presidio. Villagers once again abandoned Tubac because of Apache attacks. After the Gadsden Purchase, Tubac became part of the United States and was again resettled.

Though little but buried foundation walls remains of the old presidio, Tubac Presidio State Historic Park has exhibits that explain the history of the presidio. There are displays on the Spanish soldiers, Native Americans, religion, and contemporary Hispanic culture in southern Arizona. Also on the grounds is the old Tubac School, which was built in 1885 and is the oldest schoolhouse in Arizona.

From October through March on Sundays between 1 and 4pm, there are living history presentations. Among the characters you'll meet are Spanish soldiers, settlers, and friars.

**Tubac Center of the Arts.** 9 Plaza Rd. ☎ **520/398-2371.** $1 donation suggested. Early Sept to late May Tues–Sat 10am–4:30pm, Sun 1–4:30pm; Mid-Nov to mid-Apr same hours plus Mon 10am–4:30pm. Closed June–Aug and major holidays.

Tubac is an arts community, and this Spanish colonial building serves as its center for cultural activities. Throughout the season there are workshops, traveling exhibitions, juried shows, an annual craft show, theater and music performances, and a gift shop. The quality of the art at these shows is generally better than what's to be found in the surrounding shops.

## SHOPPING

With so many shops and tastes, it's hard to recommend specific stops in the Tubac area. But if you want to take the flavor of the area home, stop in at **The Chile Pepper** (☎ **520/398-2921**) on Tubac Road in downtown Tubac for gourmet foods with a Southwestern accent. Down near Tumacacori National Historical Park, you'll find all things hot (chiles, hot sauces, salsas) arranged on the shelves of the ✪ **Santa Cruz Chile and Spice Co.** (☎ **520/398-2591**), which is a combination store and packing plant. There's also an amazing assortment of familiar and obscure spices for sale. In the back, you can see various herbs being prepared and packaged. The shop is closed on Sunday.

The **Sonora Trading Company** (☎ **520/398-9016**), in Plaza Antigua on Tubac Street in downtown Tubac, is another interesting shop that specializes in carved Zuni fetishes. Some of the better fine art in Tubac is found at the **Karin Newby Gallery,** Mercado de Baca, 19 Tubac Rd. (☎ **520/398-9662**).

## ENJOYING THE OUTDOORS

Linking Tubac with Tumacacori is the 8-mile-long **Anza Trail,** which follows the Santa Cruz River for much of its route and passes through forests and grasslands. This trail is part of the Juan Bautista de Anza National Historic Trail, which stretches from Nogales to San Francisco. Along the trail is an excavation of part of the Spanish colonial settlement of Tubac. However, bird watching is the most popular activity along the trail. The most convenient trailhead is beside Tubac Presidio State Historic Park. An interesting way to see this trail is on horseback rides offered by **Rex Ranch** (☎ **520/398-2696**), which charges $30 for a 2-hour horseback ride (offered mid-October to mid-May).

If golf is more your speed, you can play a round at the **Tubac Golf Resort** (☎ **520/398-2021**), just north of Tubac off East Frontage Road. Greens fees range from $18 to $59.

## WHERE TO STAY

✪ **Amado Territory Inn Bed & Breakfast.** 3001 E. Frontage Rd. (P.O. Box 81), Amado, AZ 85645. ☎ **888/398-8684** or 520/398-8684. Fax 520/398-8186. www.amado-territory-inn.com. 10 units. A/C. Nov–June $105–$135 double, $250 suite; July–Oct $90–$105 double, $175 suite. Rates include full breakfast. MC, V. No children under 12.

This modern inn just off I-19 in the crossroads of Amado is built in the territorial style and succeeds in capturing the feel of old Arizona ranch houses. A spacious high-ceilinged lobby has a big leather couch in front of the fireplace—welcome warmth on cool winter nights. Guest rooms are furnished in a mix of reproduction East Coast antiques and Mexican rustic furnishings, much the way homes would have been furnished in Arizona 100 years ago. While a bit Spartan, the rooms have plenty of character, and those on the second floor have balconies with views across the farm fields of the Santa Cruz Valley. The suite is a large apartment with a full kitchen. Breakfast is served in a sunny breakfast room, and there's a flagstone patio out back under the mesquite trees. Next door, there's a similarly designed restaurant affiliated with the inn.

**The Rex Ranch.** P.O. Box 636, Amado, AZ 85645. ☎ **800/547-2696** or 520/398-2914. Fax 520/398-8229. www.rexranch.com. 22 units. A/C TEL. Oct–May $125–$225 double; June–Sept $105–$205 double. AE, CB, DC, DISC, MC, V.

Just getting to this remote and economical health spa is something of an adventure, since you have to drive *through* the Santa Cruz River to reach it. With its classic Southwestern styling and location adjacent to the de Anza Trail, this place is truly a getaway, and though not all of the guest rooms are as attractively decorated as the public areas, the more recently renovated rooms are quite comfortable. Primarily a health spa, the family-run ranch offers a wide variety of spa treatments and massages. The attractive little dining room is one of this area's best restaurants. Horseback riding and mountain bike rentals are available.

**Tubac Golf Resort.** 1 Otero Rd. (P.O. Box 1297), Tubac, AZ 85646. ☎ **800/848-7893** or 520/398-2211. Fax 520/398-9261. www.arizonaguide.com/tubac. 46 units. A/C TV TEL. $72–$135 double; $89–$180 casita. AE, MC, V.

The Tubac Golf Resort is built on the Otero Ranch, which, in 1789, became the first Spanish land grant in the Southwest. The old ranch stables, which now house the resort's restaurant, are the ranch's oldest buildings and date from the turn of the century. Red-tile roofs and brick archways remind you that this was once a Spanish hacienda. The guest rooms come in two sizes, but most have brick walls and shuttered windows. The casitas have two patios, tile bathroom counters, beamed ceilings, and beehive fireplaces. Newer rooms are worth requesting.

The dining room, in the old ranch stables, has booths that resemble horse stalls, and the menu focuses on mesquite-broiled steaks and seafood. A wall of glass looks out from the lounge to the golf course and mountains beyond. Facilities include an 18-hole golf course (used in the film *Tin Cup*), a swimming pool, hot tub, a tennis court, volleyball and bocci ball, and a pro shop.

**Valle Verde Ranch Bed & Breakfast.** ¼ mi. south of Tubac on E. Frontage Rd. (P.O. Box 157), Tumacacori, AZ 85640. ☎ and fax **520/398-2246**. 3 units, 2 casitas. TV. $80–$95 double; $100–$135 casita. Rates include full breakfast (in rooms) and continental breakfast (in casitas). No credit cards. Closed Memorial Day through October. No children.

Built in 1937, this mission-revival ranch house fairly jumps out of the brown landscape with its pink walls and blue trim, while inside the cool darkness characteristic of mission architecture is welcome on hot afternoons. The interior of the main house is straight out of a 1940s Hollywood movie, and European furnishings predominate in the guest rooms. In one of the casitas you'll find a whirlpool bath, but if you don't stay in that particular one, you can still relax in the inn's outdoor whirlpool spa. Though it is only ¼ mile out of town, this inn feels as though it is miles away from civilization.

## WHERE TO DINE

In addition to the restaurants mentioned below, the **Tubac Golf Resort** has a good restaurant. See "Where to Stay," above, for details.

**Amado Café.** 3001 E. Frontage Rd., Amado (Exit 48 off I-19). ☎ **520/398-9211.** Main courses $6–$8 at lunch, $10–$20 at dinner. AE, DISC, MC, V. Tues–Sun 11:30am–2pm and 5–8pm. Closed Mon–Tues in summer and also for 2–3 weeks in July. GREEK/AMERICAN.

There aren't a lot of dining options out here, so this restaurant, in a handsome territorial-style building just off I-19, is an addition to the community. The best part of the experience is sitting out back on the rustic flagstone patio, listening to the gurgling fountain, and contemplating the view of the mountains in the distance. The menu includes sandwiches, salads, and more filling fare such as leg of lamb and prime rib. The family that owns the restaurant is Greek, so such dishes as Greek salad, a gyro sandwich, and stuffed grape leaves are good bets. The dessert tray usually has some tempting treats, including baklava.

✪ **Cantina Romantica.** At the Rex Ranch, 6 miles north of Tubac in the community of Amado. ☎ **520/398-2914.** Reservations recommended for dinner. Main courses $6.50–$9 at lunch, $18–$23 at dinner. AE, CB, DC, DISC, MC, V. Tues–Sat 10am–2pm and 5–9pm, Sun brunch 10am–2pm. SOUTHWESTERN/CONTEMPORARY AMERICAN.

Located in a historic adobe hacienda, Cantina Romantica is a culinary oasis in this neck of the woods. The chef arrived here by way of other famous restaurant kitchens in Tucson and brings a metropolitan flair to the menu, which includes the likes of pecan-crusted pork and grilled citrus chicken with Guaymas shrimp in a tequila prickly pear sauce. A gargantuan grilled chicken salad and a vegetarian portobello mushroom, avocado, and Brie sandwich are both delicious sensory overloads. The setting is rustic and colorful, and the inn is reached by driving *through* the Santa Cruz River.

**Cow Palace.** 28802 S. Nogales Hwy. (Exit 48 off I-19). ☎ **520/398-2201.** Main courses $6–$18. DISC, MC, V. Daily 8am–9pm. STEAKS.

Located across I-19 from the Amado Café (see above), this long red building has a steer on the roof, which signals its status as an institution for steak. Another claim to fame is that John Wayne frequented the place. Inside there are plenty of deer heads and wagon wheels and a smoky Wild West bar. You can get your three squares here, from chorizo and eggs for breakfast to salads and burgers for lunch to sizzling steaks for dinner. A couple of alternatives to steak include fried shrimp or fried chicken. A classic road house: not fancy, but filling.

## A SIDE TRIP FOR FABULOUS BIRD WATCHING & OTHER OUTDOOR PURSUITS

If you are a bird watcher, you'll definitely want to make the trip over to ✪ **Buenos Aires National Wildlife Refuge,** P.O. Box 109, Sasabe, AZ 85633 (☎ **520/823-4251**), which is about 28 miles from Tubac. To get to the refuge, first head north from Tubac on I-19 to Arivaca Junction and then drive west on a winding but paved two-lane road. The refuge begins just outside the small community of Arivaca.

# Starry, Starry Nights

Southern Arizona likes to brag about how many sunny days it has each year, but those clear sunny days also give way to clear starry nights. The absence of lights in the surrounding desert makes the night sky here as brilliant as anywhere on earth. This fact has not gone unnoticed by the world's astronomers—the Tucson vicinity has a greater concentration of astronomical observatories than any other region on earth, and Southern Arizona has come to be known as the Astronomy Capital of the World.

Many of these observatories are open to the public. In addition to the ones listed below, the Flandrau Science Center in Tucson also offers public viewings (see "Seeing the Sights" in chapter 9 for details). In Flagstaff, there are also public viewing programs at the Lowell Observatory (see the Flagstaff section in chapter 6 for details).

## Observatories

✪ **Kitt Peak National Observatory.** Off Ariz. 86. ☎ **520/318-8200,** or 520/318-8726 for stargazing reservations. Admission by donation ($2 suggested). Nighttime stargazing program (reservations required) $35 adults; $25 students, seniors, and children under 18. Daily 9am–4pm (tours at 10 and 11:30am and 1:30pm). Closed Jan 1, Thanksgiving, and Dec 24–25. Take Ariz. 86 southwest from Tucson for about 40 miles to the turnoff for Kitt Peak.

Kitt Peak National Observatory is the largest and most famous of the astronomical observatories in this region. Located in the Quinlan Mountains, 56 miles southwest of Tucson, the observatory sits atop 6,882-foot Kitt Peak. There are five major telescopes operating at Kitt Peak, including the McMath telescope, the world's largest solar telescope. This telescope's system of mirrors channels an image of the sun deep into the mountain before reflecting it back up to the observatory, where scientists study the resulting 30-inch-diameter image. The 158-inch Mayall telescope features a 30,000-pound quartz mirror and is used for studying distant regions of the universe. This is the area's only major observatory to offer public nighttime viewing. Day visitors must be content with a visitor center and museum that provide information on the facility. A box meal is provided with evening stargazing programs; day visitors will need to pack a lunch.

**Fred Lawrence Whipple Observatory.** Near Amado. ☎ **520/670-5707.** Tours $7 adults, $2.50 children ages 6–12, no children under age 6 allowed. Reservations are required and can be made up to 4 weeks in advance. Visitor center Mon–Fri 8:30am–4:30pm; tours

Your first stop should be at **Arivaca Cienega,** ¼ mile east of Arivaca. *Ciénaga* is a Spanish word for "marsh." This particular marsh is fed by seven springs that provide year-round water and consequently attract an amazing variety of bird life. This is one of the few places in the United States where you can see a gray hawk. Vermilion flycatchers are also common here. A boardwalk leads across the marsh.

Other good birding spots within the refuge include **Arivaca Creek,** 2 miles west of Arivaca, and **Aguirre Lake,** ½ mile north of the refuge headquarters and visitor center, which is located off Ariz. 286 north of Sasabe. The visitor center is also a good place to spot one of the refuge's rarest birds, the masked bobwhite quail. These quail disappeared from Arizona in the late 19th century but have been reintroduced in the refuge. Other birds you might spot outside the visitor center include Bendire's thrasher, Chihuahuan mid-Mar to Nov Mon, Wed, and Fri 9am to 3pm. Take I-19 south from Tucson to exit 56, then follow the eastside frontage road south 3 miles to Elephant Head Rd. Turn left on this road and then right on Mt. Hopkins Rd. Continue 7 miles to visitor center.

Located atop 8,550-foot Mt. Hopkins, this is the largest observatory operated by the Smithsonian Astrophysical Observatory. Tours last 6 hours, and no food is available here, so be sure to bring a picnic lunch.

**Mt. Graham International Observatory & Discovery Park's Gov Aker Observatory.** Near Safford. ☎ **520/428-6260.** Tours $30. Reservations required; call at least 2 weeks in advance. Tours offered mid-May to mid-Nov (weather permitting) Sat 10am–4pm. Mt. Graham Observatory also open to the public Fri–Sat 3–9pm.

This controversial observatory, one of the nation's newest, stands atop Mt. Graham and is partly operated by The Vatican and partly by the University of Arizona. The facilities include the Vatican Advanced Technology Telescope, the Heinrich Hertz Sub-millimeter Telescope, and the Large Binocular Telescope, which was still under construction at press time. When completed, this last telescope will be the most powerful on earth. Tours of the facility last 6 hours but do not include actual viewing through the telescopes.

## Accommodations

**Skywatcher's Inn.** ℅ 420 S. Essex Lane, Tucson, AZ 85711-4522. ☎ **520/745-2390.** Fax 520/745-2390. www.communiverse.com/skywatcher. 3 units. $89 double. Rates include full breakfast. MC, V. Pets accepted with limitations.

Situated on the grounds of the privately owned Vega-Bray Observatory, an amateur observatory with six telescopes and a planetarium, this has to be the most unusual lodging in the state of Arizona. The inn provides guests not only with a bed for the night, but also with a chance to observe both the night sky and the sun through the observatory's telescopes. Although experienced amateur astronomers can rent the facilities for $35 per night, inexperienced guests should opt for one of the astronomer-assisted programs, which range in price from $85 to $120 per night per group. The observatory also includes a small science and astronomy museum, and on the grounds there are two ponds, a 1½-mile nature trail that provide good bird-watching opportunities, and a whirlpool spa. A kitchen is available to guests. The inn is located 4 miles outside Benson; call for directions.

ravens, canyon towhees, and green-tailed towhees. Other wildlife in the refuge includes pronghorn antelopes, javelinas, coatimundis, white-tailed deer, mule deer, and coyotes.

The visitor center is open daily from dawn to dusk. There is also a refuge information center in Arivaca, though this center is only open when volunteers are available to staff it.

Guided birding and other tours at the refuge are offered weekends throughout the year. Call for details; reservations are required. There is primitive camping within the refuge at more than 100 designated spots along rough gravel roads. At the refuge information center, there's a catalog that shows pictures of the campsites and provides accessibility information. Look for the brown campsite signs along the road and bring water. There is also good mountain biking on these roads. If you're looking for a strenuous

---

**Factoid**

To find out what, if any, rare birds have been spotted at the time of your visit, call the Tucson Audubon Society's Rare Bird Alert Hotline (☎ **520/798-1005**).

---

hike, try the **Mustang Trail,** which has its trailhead 2 miles west of Arivaca. The trail climbs up from Arivaca Creek into the surrounding dry hills and makes for a 5-mile round-trip hike.

If you enjoy scenic drives and don't mind gravel roads, you won't want to pass up the opportunity to drive the Ruby Road through Coronado National Forest to **Peña Blanca Lake** and **Nogales.** This road winds its way through the mountains just north of the Mexican border, passing Arivaca Lake and the privately owned ghost town of Ruby before reaching picturesque Peña Blanca Lake, where there are a couple of camp-grounds and the paved road picks up again.

## WHERE TO STAY

✪ **Rancho de la Osa.** P.O. Box 1, Sasabe, AZ 85633. ☎ **800/872-6240** or 520/823-4257. Fax 520/823-4238. www.guestranches.com/ranchodelaosa. 18 units. $300 double; $375 suite. 3- to 4-night minimum. Rates include all meals and horseback riding. DISC, MC, V.

Steeped in history and sharing a fence line with the Mexican border, this ranch dates from roughly 200 years ago and was one of the last Spanish haciendas built in what later became the United States. Today the ranch is owned by Richard and Veronica Schultz, who gave up their law practices in Scottsdale to live out their dream of restoring and operating a historic ranch. As avid art collectors, the Schultzes have brought to the ranch an artistic aesthetic unknown at other guest ranches in the state. The adobe buildings, painted in vibrant shades of pink and turquoise with blue trim, are arranged around a large eucalyptus-shaded *zócalo* ("central square") much as a Mexican village might be. Guest rooms, which are in sun-baked adobe buildings, are furnished with rustic Mexican antiques, and each has received a distinctive paint job. Most also have fireplaces and patios. Meals are gourmet Southwestern fare served at a massive table that is original to the ranch (guests are asked to dress for dinner), and there is also a rustic little saloon in what may be the oldest building in the state. In the main lodge, there are a number of seating areas with big, comfortable chairs and plenty of art on the walls. Although horseback riding is the traditional favorite activity, the ranch also attracts a good number of bird watchers due to its proximity to Buenos Aires National Wildlife Refuge. A swimming pool and whirlpool are refreshing after a long day of riding the range on the ranch's purebred quarter horses. This guest ranch feels completely removed from the hustle and bustle of late-20th-century America, and the artistic flare with which it has been restored makes it a unique getaway.

## 3 Nogales

175 miles S of Phoenix; 63 miles S of Tucson; 65 miles W of Sierra Vista

Situated on the Mexican border, the twin towns of Nogales, Arizona, and Nogales, Sonora, Mexico (known jointly as Ambos Nogales) form a bustling border town. All day long U.S. citizens cross into Mexico to shop for bargains on hand-crafted items and duty-free imports from around the world, while Mexican citizens cross into the United States to buy products not available in their own country. Nogales is also the busiest produce port in the world. During the harvest season more than 700 truck-loads of produce cross into the United States from Mexico per day.

## ESSENTIALS

**GETTING THERE**    Nogales is the last town on I-19 before the Mexican border. Arizona 82 leads northeast from town toward Sonoita and Sierra Vista.

**Greyhound** (☎ **800/231-2222**) offers service between Nogales and Tucson/Phoenix. There's also bus service from Mexico. The bus station is at 35 N. Terrace Ave.

**VISITOR INFORMATION**    For further information on Nogales, contact the **Nogales–Santa Cruz County Chamber of Commerce,** Kino Park Place, Nogales, AZ 85621 (☎ **520/287-3685**).

## EXPLORING NORTH & SOUTH OF THE BORDER

Most people who visit Nogales, Arizona, are here to cross the border to Nogales, Mexico. The favorable exchange rate makes shopping in Mexico very popular with Americans, though most of the items for sale in Mexico are actually cheaper in Tucson. Many people now cross the border specifically to purchase prescription drugs, and pharmacies line the streets near the border crossing.

If you'd like to learn more about the history of this area, stop by the **Pimeria Alta Historical Society,** at the corner of Grand Avenue and Crawford Street (☎ **520/287-4621**), near the border crossing in downtown Nogales. The historical society maintains a small museum, library, and archives on this region of northern Mexico and southern Arizona, which was once known as Pimeria Alta. It's open Saturday from 10am to 4pm. Admission is by donation.

**Bazaar de Mexico** at 82 N. Terrace Ave. (☎ **520/287-5253**), diagonally across from the bus station, has an interesting selection of Mexican folk art, with prices just about as good as you'll find over the border.

Just a couple of miles outside Nogales on the road to Patagonia, you'll see signs for the **Arizona Vineyard Winery** (☎ **520/287-7972**), open daily 10am to 5 or 6pm. You may not think of Arizona as wine country, but the Spanish began growing grapes and making wine as soon as they arrived in the area several centuries ago. You can taste free samples of white burgundy, Grand Canyon White, Road Runner White, Desert Dust, and Rattlesnake Red, among others.

As you can probably guess, Nogales, Mexico, is a typical border town filled with tiny shops selling Mexican crafts and souvenirs and dozens of restaurants serving simple Mexican food. Some of the better deals are on wool rugs, which cost a small fraction of what a Navajo rug will cost, but are not nearly as well made. Pottery is another popular buy. Our personal favorites are the ceramic sinks and the hand-blown drinking glasses and pitchers.

All the shops and restaurants in Nogales, Mexico, are within walking distance of the border, so unless you're planning to continue farther into Mexico, it's not a good idea to take your car. There are numerous pay parking lots and garages on the U.S. side of the border where your vehicle will be secure for the day. If you should take your car into Mexico, be sure to get Mexican auto insurance before crossing the border—your U.S. auto insurance is not valid. There are plenty of insurance companies set up along the road leading to the border.

Most shops and restaurants in Nogales, Mexico, accept U.S. dollars. You may bring back $400 worth of merchandise duty free, including 1 liter of liquor (if you are 21 or older). U.S. citizens need only a driver's license to walk across the border. (For those under the driving age, birth certificates are recommended, but not required.)

## WHERE TO STAY

In addition to the golf resort listed below, you'll find numerous budget chain motels in Nogales, including the **Best Western Time Motel,** 921 N. Grand Ave. (☎ **520/287-4627**), charging $36 to $59 double; **Motel 6,** 141 W. Mariposa Rd.

(☎ **520/281-2951**), charging $42–$46 double; and **Super 8 Motel,** 547 W. Mariposa Rd. (☎ **520/281-2242**), charging $51 to $58 double.

✪ **Rio Rico Resort & Country Club.** 1069 Camino Caralampi, Rio Rico, AZ 85648. ☎ **800/288-4746** or 520/281-1901. Fax 520/281-7132. 180 units. A/C TV TEL. $100–$185 double; $175–$230 suite. AE, CB, DC, DISC, MC, V.

Located a few miles north of Nogales, Rio Rico is a secluded hilltop golf resort that attracts quite a few retirees contemplating relocating to this area. If you're looking for someplace where you can feel that you've gotten away from it all, this is a good bet. While the setting is far from the madding crowd, the accommodations and amenities are the equal of many of the resorts in Tucson, and the views are almost as good. All the guest rooms have excellent views over the golf course and desert (third-floor rooms have the best views) and come with coffeemakers, hair dryers, and irons/ironing boards. An abundance of Mexican tile work gives these rooms a little sense of place, too.

**Dining/Diversions:** The resort's dining room, which has those same great views, serves a mix of Southwestern and Mediterranean dishes, and the lavish Sunday brunch is extremely popular. There is also a large, adjacent lounge.

**Amenities:** An 18-hole golf course, Olympic-size pool, whirlpool, sauna, exercise room, four tennis courts, pro shop, horseback riding ($20 for 1 hour).

## WHERE TO DINE

✪ **La Roca Restaurant.** Calle Elias 91, Nogales, Mexico. ☎ **888/527-0220** toll free in the U.S., or (52) 631/2-08-91. Main courses $8–$16. MC, V. Daily 11am–midnight. MEXICAN.

La Roca is as unexpected a restaurant as you're ever likely to find in a border town. Built into a cliff and cool as a cave, the restaurant conjures up images of colonial Mexico. White-jacketed waiters provide a level of professional service found only in the most expensive restaurants north of the border. Folk art and large paintings in the spacious rooms seem to make the interior glow, and at night the place is lit with candles ensconced on the stone walls. The Guaymas shrimp and chicken mole are our longtime favorites. The shrimp are reliably succulent, and the mole sauce is a brilliantly flavorful balance between chile and chocolate. Don't miss the margaritas—small but zesty with lime and full of tequila.

To find La Roca, walk through the border checkpoint, continue 100 feet or so, cross over the railroad tracks on your left, and continue walking away from the border. Within a block, you'll see a narrow street angling toward the big rock wall to your left. The restaurant is about 100 feet down this street.

**Las Vigas Steak Ranch.** 180 W. Loma St. ☎ **520/287-6641.** Main courses $5–$6 at lunch, $6–$11 at dinner. AE, MC, V. Tues–Thurs 10am–9pm, Fri 10am–9:30pm, Sat 8am–9:30pm, Sun 8am–9pm. Head down Grand Ave. toward the border; before you get to downtown Nogales, watch for Arroyo Blvd., which forks to the right; Las Vigas is just past the fork on W. Loma St. STEAKS/SONORAN MEXICAN.

This Western-style building has a covered sidewalk in front and old photos and paintings covering the walls inside. Antiques give Las Vigas a very rustic feel, and a G-gauge model train chugs around the dining room. Meals are inexpensive and filling, and there are daily specials during the week. Steaks are accompanied by a salad bar, beans, baked potato, and tortillas. Breakfast comes both Mexican and Western style.

## 4 Patagonia & Sonoita

Patagonia: 171 miles SE of Phoenix; 60 miles SE of Tucson; 50 miles SW of Tombstone; 19 miles NW of Nogales

The small communities of Patagonia and Sonoita have become favorite weekend get-aways for Tucsonians. The mild climate, bed-and-breakfast inns, and wineries are the main attractions for many. However, it's Sonoita Creek that manages to attract visitors from all over the country. This creek is one of only a few in the region that flows throughout the year, and consequently attracts an amazing variety of bird life and bird watchers.

Most people heading out to explore the Patagonia-Sonoita wine country have heard about the area's excellent restaurants and are looking forward to dining at a few of these establishments. However, be forewarned that almost all of the restaurants in the area are closed on Monday and Tuesday. Bird watchers should also take note that the Patagonia–Sonoita Creek Sanctuary is also closed on Monday and Tuesday.

## ESSENTIALS

**GETTING THERE**    Sonoita is at the junction of Ariz. 83 and Ariz. 82. Patagonia is 12 miles southwest of Sonoita on Ariz. 82.

**VISITOR INFORMATION**    For further information on Patagonia and Sonoita, contact the Patagonia Community Association, **Patagonia Visitors Center,** P.O. Box 241, Patagonia, AZ 85624 (☎ **520/394-0060**). The visitor center is located in the center of town at 305 McKeown Ave., in the building with Mariposa Bookstore and next to the lobby of the Stage Stop Inn.

## BIRD WATCHING, WINE TASTING & OTHER AREA ACTIVITIES

Patagonia, 18 miles north of Nogales on Ariz. 82, is a historic old mining and ranching town 4,000 feet up in the Patagonia Mountains. Surrounded by higher mountains, the little town has for years been popular with film and television crews. Among the films that have been shot here are *Oklahoma, Red River, A Star Is Born,* and *David and Bathsheba.* Television programs filmed here have included *Little House on the Prairie, The Red Badge of Courage,* and *The Young Riders.* Today, however, bird watching and tranquillity draw people to this remote town.

The **Patagonia–Sonoita Creek Preserve** (☎ **520/394-2400**) is a nature preserve owned by the Nature Conservancy and protects 1½ miles of Sonoita Creek riparian (riverside) habitat, which is important to migratory birds. More than 250 species of birds have been spotted on the preserve, which makes this a very popular spot with birders from all over the world. Among the rare birds that may be seen here are 22 species of flycatchers, kingbirds, and phoebes, and the Montezuma quail. A forest of cottonwood trees, some of which are 100 feet tall, lines the creek and is one of the best remaining examples of such a forest in southern Arizona. At one time these forests grew along all the rivers here. The sanctuary is located just outside Patagonia on a dirt road that parallels Ariz. 82. Hours are Wednesday to Sunday from 7:30am to 4pm. On Saturday mornings at 9am, there are naturalist-guided walks through the preserve; reservations aren't required. If the reserve should be closed when you visit, you are welcome to bird along the road bordering the preserve from dawn to dusk.

Avid birders will also want to visit the **Empire-Cienaga Resource Conservation Area** (☎ **520/722-4289**), which has grasslands, wetlands, and oak forests. This is a good place to look for the rarely seen gray hawk. Access is off Ariz. 83—10 miles north of Sonoita.

**Patagonia Lake State Park** (☎ **520/287-6965**), located 11 miles south of Patagonia off Ariz. 82, is a popular boating and fishing lake formed by the damming of Sonoita Creek. The lake is 2½ miles long and is stocked in the winter with trout. Bass, crappie, bluegill, and catfish can also be found in the lake. Park facilities include a picnic ground, a campground, and a swimming beach.

Sonoita proper is little more than a crossroads with a few shops and restaurants. Surrounding the community are miles of rolling grasslands that are primarily cattle ranches. However, recent years have seen the planting of several wine vineyards in the area, and the Sonoita area is slowly becoming Arizona's wine country. The **R. W. Webb Winery** (and Dark Mountain Brewery) (☎ **520/762-5777**), the most accessible of the area's wineries, does a fairly nice sherry. Its attractive little tasting room is located 27 miles north of Sonoita at Exit 279 off I-10. In the ghost town of Elgin, you'll find the **Village of Elgin Winery** (☎ **520/455-9309**), and 3 miles south of Elgin, **Sonoita Vineyards** (☎ **520/455-5893**) on Canelo Road. **Callaghan Vineyards** (☎ **520/455-5322**) is open for tastings with more limited hours than other tasting rooms. They're usually open Sundays from 10am to 4pm from November to May. This vineyard is located 5 miles south of Elgin; call for directions. In "downtown" Patagonia, the **Santa Cruz Winery** (☎ **520/394-2888**) is located at 315 McKeown Ave.

Despite the proliferation of vineyards in the area, this is still ranch country. If you'd like to ride the open range, there are a couple of area horseback riding stables that will get you back in the saddle again. In Patagonia, contact **Arizona Trail Tours** (☎ **800/477-0615;** www.rosemart.com/az-tr-tours/), which offers everything from 2½-hour rides ($40) to 4-day pack trips ($750). These rides head up into the Patagonia Mountains and the San Rafael Valley. In Sonoita, contact **Sonoita Stables** (☎ **520/455-9266**), which offers 1-hour to half-day rides into the Empire-Cienega Resource Conservation Area on Peruvian Paso horses. Rates range from $20 for 1 hour to $70 for a half day. Expect to see antelope on your ride.

# WHERE TO STAY
## IN PATAGONIA

✪ **Circle Z Ranch.** P.O. Box 194, Patagonia, AZ 85624. ☎ **888/854-2525** or 520/394-2525. www.circlez.com. 24 units. $274–$324 double; $610–$755 cottage (sleeping 4–6 people). Rates include all meals and horseback riding. 3-night minimum. Lower weekly rates, special long-weekend rates, and lower rates for ages 17 and under. No credit cards. Closed May 16–Nov 1.

Located on Ariz. 82 between Nogales and Patagonia, this guest ranch has been in business since 1925 and is the oldest working cattle ranch in Arizona. Over the years it has served as a backdrop for numerous movies and TV shows, including *Gunsmoke* and John Wayne's *Red River*. The 6,000-acre ranch on the banks of Sonoita Creek is bordered by the Nature Conservancy's Patagonia–Sonoita Creek Sanctuary, Patagonia State Park, and the Coronado National Forest. Miles of trails and a remuda of nearly 80 ranch-bred horses assure everyone of getting in plenty of riding in a variety of terrains from desert hills to grasslands to the riparian forest along the creek. The adobe cabins, some of which are stuccoed and some of which have their adobe blocks exposed, provide that authentic ranch feel that is appreciated by guests hoping to find a genuine bit of the Old West. There is a wide variety of accommodation styles, including large cottages for families. Kids get to eat with the wranglers, and there's a special kids' cantina complete with video games, jukebox, and a pool table. A pool and tennis court are also here.

**Duquesne House B&B–Gallery.** 357 Duquesne Ave. (P.O. Box 772), Patagonia, AZ 85624. ☎ **520/394-2732.** 4 units. $75 double. Rate includes full breakfast. No credit cards.

This old adobe building with a long shady porch across the front was built at the turn of the century as a miner's boarding house and has been renovated and converted into a B&B. Each guest room has its own entrance off the front porch and both sitting room and bedroom. Our personal favorite has an ornate woodstove and claw-foot bathtub. At the back of the house is a screened porch that overlooks the garden and a fishpond. The owner of the B&B also owns a local art gallery, and artists will feel right at home here.

**Stage Stop Inn.** 303 W. McKeown St. (P.O. Box 777), Patagonia, AZ 85624. ☎ **800/ 923-2211** inside Arizona, or 520/394-2211. 43 units. A/C TV TEL. $69 double. AE, DISC, MC, V.

Though nothing fancy, this small hotel in the center of town is large enough that it usually has a few rooms available. Furnishings are motel basic, but there's a small pool in the courtyard if you happen to be here in the heat of summer. A bit of Western styling adds a touch of character to the lobby, where you'll usually find information on local attractions and activities.

## IN SONOITA

**Sonoita Inn.** P.O. Box 99, Sonoita, AZ 85637. ☎ **520/455-5935.** Fax 520/455-5069. www.sonoitainn.com. 18 units. A/C TV TEL. $99–$145 double. Rates include continental breakfast. AE, DC, DISC, MC, V.

Housed in a barnlike building at the intersection of Ariz. 82 and Ariz. 83, the Sonoita Inn plays up the area's ranching history. The building was originally built by the owner of the famed Triple Crown–winning thoroughbred Secretariat, but in 1999 was converted into an inn. The large lobby, with its wooden floors, huge fireplace, and ranch brands for decoration, is cool and dark; breakfasts and afternoon snacks are served here. Guest rooms feature rustic beds, Indian rugs, and big windows, with 1950s-inspired bedspreads for a retro cowboy touch. All of the rooms are named for local ranches. Although the inn is right on Sonoita's main road, the fascinating interior decor more than makes up for the less-than-quiet location. The inn's owners are also rebuilding their adjacent steakhouse, which was destroyed by a fire.

**The Vineyard Bed & Breakfast.** 92 S. Los Encinos Rd. (P.O. Box 1227), Sonoita, AZ 85637. ☎ **520/455-4749.** 4 units. $85 double; $95 casita. Rates include full breakfast. No credit cards.

Set atop a hill just south of Sonoita, the heart of southeast Arizona's wine country, this B&B is in a pink adobe ranch house that was built in 1916. There are expansive views from the property, and the vineyards for which the inn is named are in the process of being replanted after having been killed by Texas root rot. The sweeping views of plains and mountains are the biggest selling point of this inn, so if you're looking for high, wide, and handsome, this is it. The house itself has an unpretentious farm/ranch feel. The casita is well worth the little extra it costs and has its own patio and Saltillo tile floors. Inn pets include a talking parrot, peacocks, a burro, and very friendly black labs. There's also a whirlpool.

# WHERE TO DINE
## IN PATAGONIA

✪ **Cose Buone.** 436 Naugle Ave. ☎ **520/394-2366.** Reservations highly recommended. $18 for 3-course meal. AE, MC, V. Fri–Tues 5:30 until closing. Closed early June to early Sept. ITALIAN.

It's not often you have a fine dining experience in a building that also houses a Laundromat, but here it is. Intimate seating (there are only 20 chairs), and a relaxed atmosphere (the owner is willing to stop and chat) combine for an experience that seems worlds away from the urban glitz to the north. The menu changes weekly, but the first course might be a full-flavored antipasto of assorted untraditional vegetables, including a dollop of creamy mashed potatoes, or a rustic mushroom soup. For *secondi*, expect risotto or pasta, and for a third course a spicy, robust planked beef with onion rings sautéed in port and hot cherry peppers. A finale of light and airy tiramisu is liberally dusted with cocoa powder. Add an extensive and reasonably priced list of wines, with an emphasis on Italian vintages, and you'll think you've died and gone to Tuscany.

**Marie's European Cuisine.** 340 Naugle Ave. ☎ **520/394-2812.** Reservations recommended. Main courses $10–$14. MC, V. Wed–Sat 5–9pm, Sun 1–7pm. EUROPEAN.

Located in the center of Patagonia, this little restaurant sits behind a low wall in a colorful cottage with a few tiled tables and folk art in a "secret garden" setting. The menu offers simple yet very flavorful rustic European food and ranges the continent from the Adriatic to the Baltic. Marie is the chef here and whips up the likes of leek tart, broccoli soufflé, chicken with olives and dried fruit in white-wine sauce, roast lamb so tender it cuts with a fork, and even stuffed cabbage. Don't miss the chicken pâté or the house-blended Château Marie wine. Portions are large, but if you want vegetables, order a salad. This is a small two-person operation, so be prepared to relax.

**Velvet Elvis Pizza Company.** 292 Naugle Ave. ☎ **520/394-2102.** Pizzas $12–$22. MC, V. Wed–Sun noon–8pm. ITALIAN.

While Marie's and Cose Buone are just the sort of restaurants you might expect to find in wine country, Velvet Elvis strikes a very different chord. Faux-finished walls ooze artiness, and paeans to pop culture here include shrines to both the Virgin Mary and Elvis. There's even a genuine velvet Elvis painting on display. This casual hangout features pizzas heaped with veggies, cheeses, and meats. Add a salad for even more vegetables (your mom would be proud) and accompany it with a microbrew or an espresso.

## In Sonoita

**Café Sonoita.** 3280 Ariz. 82. ☎ **520/455-5278.** Reservations recommended for dinner for 5 or more. Main courses $6–$13. MC, V. Wed 5–8pm, Thurs–Sat 11am–2:30pm and 5–8pm, Sun 8am–2:30pm. INTERNATIONAL.

A tiny place with just a handful of tables, this cafe is a great favorite with locals—some even keep their personal coffee mugs on a rack behind the counter. In spite of the casual atmosphere, the kitchen here actually turns out some very tasty and creative dishes, and the prices are great. For dinner, try pan-seared salmon with Elgin blackberry sauce, sautéed jumbo shrimp with bacon and basil, or a bowl of *posole*. Lunchtime sandwiches are huge and delicious. You'll find Café Sonoita in an old building at the east end of Sonoita.

**Karen's Wine Country Café.** 3266 Ariz. 82. ☎ **520/455-5282.** Reservations recommended. Main courses $7–$9 at lunch, $17–$19 at dinner. Chef's wine dinner $39.95. MC, V. Daily 11am–4pm, Thurs–Sat 5–8pm. SOUTHWESTERN.

With crisp blue-and-white tablecloths and wraparound windows, this bright room looks out on panoramic rangeland that, framed by the windows, seems almost surreal. The view is of the Empire Cienaga Ranch, a grassland ringed by mountain ranges—you might see antelope grazing here. And inside, instead of dusty, beer-drinking cowboys, there are well-dressed urbanites sipping wine and grazing on focaccia. You can order dishes such as grilled chicken glazed with honey-jalapeño sauce, or pork tenderloin with blue cheese. Salads are good and liberally dosed in vinaigrette dressing (which is a specialty here, along with local jams and jellies, all available for purchase). This being wine country, local wines are highlighted in the chef's wine dinner.

## 5 Sierra Vista & the San Pedro Valley

189 miles SE of Phoenix; 70 miles SE of Tucson; 33 miles SW of Tombstone; 33 miles W of Bisbee

At 4,620 feet above sea level, surrounded by deserts and mountains, Sierra Vista is blessed with the perfect climate—never too hot, never too cold. However, because it's a long way from any population centers and is not on an interstate, few people know about Sierra Vista. If it weren't for the U.S. Army's Fort Huachuca, it's likely that no one would have ever settled here, but when Camp Huachuca (later to become Fort

Huachuca) was founded in 1877, the seeds of Sierra Vista were sown. Today, however, retirees, free from the necessity of living where there are jobs available, have discovered the climate and settled down.

Though the town itself is modern and has very little character, the surrounding countryside has much to offer. Within a few miles' drive of town are a national conservation area, a national memorial, and a Nature Conservancy preserve. No other area of the United States attracts more attention from birders, who come in hopes of spotting some of the 300 bird species that have been sighted here in southeastern Arizona. With its many inexpensive motels, Sierra Vista makes a good base for exploring all of this region.

## ESSENTIALS

**GETTING THERE**   Sierra Vista is located at the junction of Ariz. 90 and Ariz. 92 about 35 miles south of I-10.

**America West** (☎ **800/235-9292**) has regular flights from Phoenix to the Fort Huachuca Airport (also called the Sierra Vista Airport), 2100 Airport Dr.

**VISITOR INFORMATION**   For further information on Sierra Vista, contact the **Sierra Vista Convention and Visitors Bureau,** 21 E. Wilcox Dr., Sierra Vista, AZ 85635 (☎ **800/288-3861** or 520/458-6940; www.sierravistachamber.org). Follow the signs for Visitor Information/Chamber of Commerce. Turn onto Carmichael Avenue from Fry Boulevard; the office is 1 block off Fry Boulevard.

## ATTRACTIONS AROUND BENSON

✪ **Kartchner Caverns State Park.** Off Ariz. 90, 10 miles south of Benson. ☎ **602/542-4174.** www.pr.state.az.us. Admission $10 per car to enter the park and visit aboveground exhibits; cave tours $12 adults, $4 children 7–13, free for children under 7. Call ahead for reservations. Hours not yet established at press time.

These caverns, discovered in 1974 and kept secret for 14 years to protect them, are among the largest and most beautiful caverns in the country. Seven acres of the caverns are being opened to the public, and within this area are two huge rooms each larger than a football field, with ceilings more than 100 feet high. Countless still-growing features such as soda straws, "cave bacon," stalactites, and stalagmites decorate these chambers.

The difficulty in preparing the caves for the public has caused numerous delays in the opening date. However, by November 1999, the caverns should finally be open and will likely be the biggest news in these parts since the shoot-out at the O.K. Corral. The park will include a campground ($15 per night), and there are plans for an exhibit hall and multimedia presentation as well. Arizona State Parks is expecting the caverns to become one of the biggest attractions in southern Arizona, so we recommend making tour and accommodation reservations ahead of your visit.

**San Pedro & Southwestern Railroad.** 796 E. Country Club Dr., Benson. ☎ **800/269-6314** or 520/586-2266. Tickets for the 3½-hour rides are $28 round-trip for adults, $25 for seniors, and $19 for children kindergarten–12th grade. To reach the train depot, take I-10 east to Exit 303 in Benson, drive through town and take U.S. 80 south 1 mile, and then turn left on Country Club Dr. Call ahead for the current schedule. Reservations required.

Railroad buffs and anyone else who wants to see the San Pedro River valley from a different perspective may want to check out this train excursion that runs between Benson and the ghost town of Charleston. Along the route the train passes ghost towns (including the town of Fairbank where the train stops to allow passengers to look around at the old adobe buildings), Spanish outpost ruins, stamp mill ruins, and abandoned ranches. Much of the trip is within the San Pedro Riparian National Conservation Area. In addition to desert scenery, the historical narration provides fascinating background on this region, including stories from Tombstone's glory days.

**Singing Wind Bookshop.** ☎ 520/586-2425. See text below for directions.

Located far off the beaten path down a dirt road outside the town of Benson, this remarkable bookstore is the brainchild of Winifred Bundy, who, with her late husband, began the business 20 years ago with only a couple of shelves of books. Now the inventory is well into the thousands, and although the emphasis is on the Southwest, almost any category you can think of, plus fiction and children's books, can be found. Despite the shop's remote location on Bundy's ranch, it attracts book lovers from around the world. To reach Singing Wind Bookshop, take Exit 304 from I-10 in Benson. Drive north 2¼ miles and take a right (east) at the sign that says SINGING WIND ROAD (and the black mailbox full of buckshot holes). Drive to the end, opening and closing the green gate.

## ATTRACTIONS AROUND SIERRA VISTA

**Fort Huachuca Museum.** Inside the Fort Huachuca U.S. Army base, Grierson Rd., Sierra Vista. ☎ 520/533-5736. Free admission ($2 donation suggested). Mon–Fri 9am–4pm, Sat–Sun 1–4pm.

Fort Huachuca, an army base located at the mouth of Huachuca Canyon northeast of Sierra Vista, was established in 1877 and, though it has been closed a couple of times, is active today. The buildings of the old post have been declared a National Historic Landmark, and one is now a museum dedicated to the many forts that dotted the Southwest in the latter part of the 19th century. One of the most interesting aspects of the exhibits is the quotes by soldiers that give an idea of what it was like to serve in the Southwest in the latter half of the 19th century. Near the museum stands a row of Victorian officers' quarters. Also nearby is the **U.S. Army Military Intelligence Museum.**

**Arizona Folklore Preserve.** 44 Ramsey Canyon Rd. (Ariz. 92 south of Sierra Vista). ☎ 520/378-6165. Admission by donation. Showtimes Sat–Sun 2pm. Reservations required.

Set beneath the shady cottonwoods and sycamores of Ramsey Canyon, the Arizona Folklore Preserve is an ongoing project, the brainchild of Dolan Ellis, Arizona's official state balladeer, and his wife, Rose. Ellis, who started out with the folk group The New Christy Minstrels, was first appointed state balladeer back in 1966 and has been writing songs about Arizona for more than 30 years. As the name implies, the objective of the center is to preserve the folklore of Arizona, and, to that end, Ellis takes to the stage most weekends to sing his songs of life in Arizona. He also often welcomes guests to the stage (currently in an old house on the property). In the past there have been cowboy poets, folk artists, a fiddle maker, saddle makers, and musicians. If all goes according to plan, there will eventually be a small but impressive theater tucked amid the trees here.

## BIRDING HOT SPOTS & OTHER NATURAL AREAS

Birding has become big business in this area over the past few years, with birders' B&Bs, bird refuges, and even birding festivals. The **Southwest Wings Birding Festival** (☎ 800/288-3861 or 520/459-EVNT) is held in Sierra Vista each year in August.

If you'd like to join a guided bird walk along the San Pedro River or up Carr Canyon in the Huachuca Mountains, an owl-watching night hike, or a hummingbird banding session, contact the **Southeastern Arizona Bird Observatory,** P.O. Box 5521, Bisbee, AZ 85603-5521 (☎ 520/432-1388; www.sabo.org). Most of these activities take place between March and May and cost between $8 and $20 (hummingbird banding sessions are by donation). Workshops and tours are also offered.

In addition to the birding hot spots listed below, there are a few other spots in the area that serious birders should not miss. **Garden Canyon,** on Fort Huachuca, has 8 miles of trails, and 350 species of birds have been sighted. There are also Indian pictographs along one of the trails through the canyon. This is a good place to look for elegant trogons and Mexican spotted owls. Get directions to Garden Canyon at the fort's front gate, and be prepared to show your license, vehicle registration, and proof of vehicle insurance. The canyon is open to the public daily during daylight hours but is sometimes closed due to military maneuvers, so you must check with the **Range Control Office** (☎ 520/533-7100 or 520/533-7093) before heading out here.

South of Ramsey Canyon off Ariz. 92, you'll find **Carr Canyon,** which has a road that climbs up through the canyon to some of the higher elevations in the Huachuca Mountains. This is a good place to look for buff-breasted flycatchers, red crossbills, and red-faced warblers.

The **Sierra Vista Wastewater Wetlands,** 3.1 miles east of Ariz. 92 on Ariz. 90, is a good place to see yellow-headed blackbirds, ducks, peregrines, and harriers from fall through spring.

✪ **Ramsey Canyon Preserve.** 27 Ramsey Canyon Rd. (off Ariz. 92 south of Sierra Vista). ☎ **520/378-2785.** $5 suggested donation (free for Nature Conservancy members). Mar–Oct daily 8am–5pm; Nov–Feb Mon–Fri 9am–5pm, Sat–Sun 8am–5pm. Closed Thanksgiving, Christmas, and New Year's Day.

In late spring, a buzzing fills the air in Ramsey Canyon, but it's not mosquitoes; it's the buzzing of curious hummingbirds. Wear bright red clothing when you visit this preserve, and you're certain to attract the curious little avian dive bombers, which will mistake you for the world's largest flower. Located 5 miles south of Sierra Vista off Ariz. 92, this wildlife preserve is owned by the Nature Conservancy and is internationally known as home to 14 species of hummingbirds—more than anywhere else in the United States.

Covering only 280 acres, the preserve is situated in a wooded gorge in the Huachuca Mountains. A short nature trail leads through the canyon, with an explanatory guidebook that points out the reasons for and difficulties in preserving Ramsey Canyon; a second trail leads higher up the canyon. There are guided walks as well. Ramsey Creek is a year-round stream, a rarity in this region, and attracts a wide variety of wildlife, including bears, bobcats, and nearly 200 species of birds. April and May are the busiest times of year here, and August and May are the best times to see hummingbirds.

The preserve was closed for much of 1999 so that renovation of the visitor center and expansion of the parking area could take place. At press time, the preserve was scheduled to reopen in October 1999. Because the preserve is very popular and has limited parking, it has in the past been necessary to make parking reservations in advance. This system may or not be in effect after the preserve reopens; call to make sure. To avoid parking problems, you can stay at the preserve's adjacent bed-and-breakfast inn (see "Where to Stay," below, for details).

✪ **San Pedro Riparian National Conservation Area.** Ariz. 90. ☎ **520/458-3559.** Free admission. Parking areas open sunrise to sunset.

Located 8 miles east of Sierra Vista, the San Pedro Riparian National Conservation Area is a rare example of a natural riverside habitat. Over the past 100 years the Southwestern landscape has been considerably altered by the human hand. Most deleterious of these changes has been the loss of 90% of the region's free-flowing year-round rivers and streams that once provided water and protection to myriad plants, animals, and even humans. Fossil findings from this area indicate that people were living along this river

11,000 years ago. At that time this area was not a desert, but a swamp, and the San Pedro River is all that remains of this ancient wetland. (Today there isn't much water on the surface, because most of the river water has flowed underground since an earthquake a century ago.) The conservation area is particularly popular with birders, who have a chance of spotting more than 300 species of birds here. Also living in this region are 80 species of mammals, 14 species of fish, and 40 species of amphibians and reptiles.

There are three main parking areas for the conservation area at the bridges over the San Pedro River on Ariz. 92, Ariz. 90, and Ariz. 82. This last parking area is at the ghost town of Fairbank. At the Ariz. 90 parking area, the San Pedro House, a 1930s ranch, operates as a visitor center and bookstore. It's open daily from 9:30am to 4:30pm.

**Coronado National Memorial.** Montezuma Canyon Rd. ☎ **520/366-5515.** Free admission. Daily 8am–5pm.

About 20 miles south of Sierra Vista is a 5,000-acre memorial dedicated to Francisco Vásquez de Coronado, the first European to explore this region. Coronado, leading more than 700 people, left Compostela, Mexico, on February 23, 1540, in search of the fabled Seven Cities of Cíbola. These cities were said to be rich in gold and jewels, and Coronado had dreams of becoming wealthy from his expedition. Coronado led his band of weary men and women up the valley of the San Pedro River sometime between 1540 and 1542. The forested Montezuma Pass, in the center of the memorial, is situated at 6,575 feet and provides far-reaching views of Sonora, Mexico, to the south, the San Pedro River to the east, and several mountain ranges and valleys to the west. A visitor center tells the story of Coronado's fruitless quest for riches and features a wildlife observation area where you might see some of the memorial's 140 or more species of birds.

## OTHER OUTDOOR ACTIVITIES

The near-perfect climate of Sierra Vista has made this a popular retirement community in recent years, and it has also made Sierra Vista a great place to play golf. You can play a round at the **Pueblo del Sol Country Club,** St. Andrew's Drive (☎ **520/ 378-6444**), which is off Ariz. 92 on the east side of town and has a great view of the Huachuca Mountains.

Hikers will find numerous trails within the Huachuca Mountains, which rise up to the west of Sierra Vista. There are trails at Garden Canyon near Fort Huachuca, at Ramsey Canyon Preserve, at Carr Canyon in Coronado National Forest, and at Coronado National Memorial. See "Birding Hot Spots & Other Natural Areas," above, for details on all of these natural areas. For information on hiking in the Coronado National Forest, contact the **Sierra Vista Ranger District** (☎ **520/378-0311**) at 5990 S. Hwy. 92, 8 miles south of Sierra Vista in Hereford.

## WHERE TO STAY
### IN BENSON

If you're looking for someplace to stay close to Kartchner Caverns, try the **Holiday Inn Express,** 630 South Village Loop, Benson, AZ 85602 (☎ **888/263-CAVE** or 520/586-8800), which charges $52 to $69 for a double.

### IN SIERRA VISTA

In addition to the moderately priced Sierra Vista hotel listed below, you'll find numerous budget chain motels in Sierra Vista. These include the **Motel 6,** 1551 E. Fry Blvd. (☎ **520/459-5035**), charging $36 to $38 for a double; and **Super 8 Motel,** 100 Fab Ave. (☎ **520/459-5380**), charging $47 to $52 for a double. See appendix B for toll-free numbers.

**Windemere Hotel & Conference Center.** 2047 S. Hwy. 92, Sierra Vista, AZ 85635. ☎ **800/825-4656** or 520/459-5900. Fax 520/458-1347. 149 units. A/C TV TEL. $68–$86 double; $150–$195 suite. Rates include full breakfast. AE, CB, DC, DISC, MC, V. Pets accepted ($50 deposit).

This modern three-story conference hotel on the south side of town is one of Sierra Vista's best lodgings and one of the closest to Ramsey Canyon. However, it is much more popular with conventions than with avid bird watchers. The guest rooms feature contemporary furnishings, coffeemakers, refrigerators, irons/ironing boards, large closets, and plenty of counter space in the bathrooms. There's a casual restaurant, a lounge, an outdoor pool, and a whirlpool. The hotel also offers room service, complimentary evening cocktail hour, and access to a nearby health club.

## IN HEREFORD

**Casa de San Pedro.** 8933 S. Yell Lane, Hereford, AZ 85615. ☎ **800/588-6468** or 520/366-1300. Fax 520/366-0701. www.naturesinn.com. 10 units. A/C. Mar to early June $119 double (2-night minimum); remainder of year $100 double. Rates include full breakfast. DISC, MC, V.

Built with bird-watching tour groups in mind, this modern inn is set on the west side of the San Pedro River on 10 acres of land that border the river. While the setting doesn't have as much historical character as that of the San Pedro River Inn (see below), the rooms are large, modern, hotel-style accommodations. Built in the territorial style around a courtyard garden, the inn has a large common room where birders gather to swap tales of the day's sightings. This is by far the most upscale inn in the region.

**✪ The Nature Conservancy's Ramsey Canyon Inn Bed & Breakfast.** 29 Ramsey Canyon Rd., Hereford, AZ 85615. ☎ and fax **520/378-3010.** 6 units; 2 apts. $105–$125 double (including full breakfast); $125–$135 apt. (breakfast not included). MC, V.

Located just outside the gates of the Nature Conservancy's Ramsey Canyon Preserve and operated by the conservancy, this inn is the most convenient lodging choice for avid birders. The inn's property straddles Ramsey Creek. Guest rooms are in the main house, while apartments are in small cabins reached by a footbridge over the creek. Hummingbird feeders set up on the inn's front porch attract 14 species of hummers. A large country breakfast is served in the morning, and in the afternoon you're likely to find a fresh pie made with fruit from the inn's orchard. Breakfast is not included in the apartment rates because they have their own kitchens. Very popular, book early.

**San Pedro River Inn.** 8326 S. Hereford Rd., Hereford, AZ 85615. ☎ and fax **520/366-5532.** www.sanpedroriverinn.com. 4 units. $95 double. Rates include continental breakfast. $5 fee for dogs and horses. No credit cards.

With the character of a small guest ranch, this family-friendly inn is a casual place that will please avid birders who prefer old Arizona character over spotless modern accommodations. Located on the east side of the San Pedro Riparian National Conservation Area, the four cottages here are set beneath huge old cottonwood trees. Surrounding the grounds are acres of grasslands and expansive vistas. All the cottages, which are rather eclectically furnished, have kitchens so you can do your own cooking.

## CAMPGROUNDS

You'll find two Coronado National Forest campgrounds—Reef Townsite and Ramsey Vista—in Carr Canyon south of Sierra Vista off Ariz. 92. At Fort Huachuca there are a few campsites and a rustic cabin available in Garden Canyon. To reserve a site or the cabin, contact the **Sportsmen Center** (☎ **520/533-7085**) on base.

## WHERE TO DINE

Because Sierra Vista is home to a military base and many of the servicemen have Asian wives, the town supports quite a number of good Asian restaurants, with an emphasis on Chinese, Japanese, and Korean cuisine.

**The Outside Inn.** 4907 S. Ariz. 92. ☎ **520/378-4645.** Reservations recommended. Main courses $6–$7 at lunch, $13–$21 at dinner. AE, MC, V. Mon–Fri 11am–1:30pm and 5–9pm, Sat 5–9pm. STEAKS/SEAFOOD/ITALIAN.

It's difficult to find a decent meal in Sierra Vista, but your best hope is The Outside Inn, which has long been the special occasion/formal restaurant in town. Located south of town just north of the turnoff for Ramsey Canyon, it's a country cottage in the midst of malls; inside, there's a couple of casual dining rooms and a patio area. The dinner menu includes fare such as salmon with spinach fettuccine, rack of lamb, and blackened swordfish or mahimahi. The lunch menu offers a variety of salads and sandwiches, and desserts are American favorites such as mud pie and cheesecake.

## 6 Tombstone

181 miles SE of Phoenix; 70 miles SE of Tucson; 24 miles N of Bisbee

"The town too tough to die" is today one of Arizona's most popular tourist attractions, though we'll leave it up to you to decide whether it deserves its reputation (either as a tough town or as a tourist attraction). Although the name Tombstone alone would be enough to interest most visitors, this old mining town's claim to fame is that of the Wild West—"cowboys and Indians" and the cavalry. It was here in Tombstone that a livery stable known as the O.K. Corral once stood. When Wyatt Earp, his brothers Virgil and Morgan, and Doc Holliday took on the outlaws Ike Clanton and Frank and Tom McLaury on October 26, 1881, the ensuing gun battle sealed the fate of this town.

Tombstone was named by Ed Schieffelin, a silver prospector who had been warned against venturing into this region, which at the time was home to Apache tribes who were fighting to preserve their homeland. Schieffelin was warned that the land would be his tombstone, so when he discovered a mountain of silver here, he named it Tombstone. Within a few years Tombstone was larger than San Francisco. Between 1880 and 1887, an estimated $37 million worth of silver was mined here. Such wealth created a sturdy little town, and as the Cochise County seat of the time, Tombstone boasted a number of imposing buildings, including the county courthouse, which is now an Arizona state park. In 1887, the silver mines were flooded by an underground river. Despite attempts to pump the water out, the mines were never reopened, and the population rapidly dwindled.

Today the historic district consists of both original buildings that went up after the town's second fire and newer structures built in keeping with the architectural styles of the time. Most of them house souvenir shops and restaurants, which should give you some indication that this place is a classic tourist trap, but kids (and adults raised on Louis L'Amour and John Wayne) love it, especially when the famous shoot-out is reenacted.

## ESSENTIALS

**GETTING THERE**   From Tucson, take I-10 east to Benson, from which U.S. 80 heads south to Tombstone. From Sierra Vista, take Ariz. 90 north to Ariz. 82 heading east.

**VISITOR INFORMATION**   Contact the **Tombstone Office of Tourism,** P.O. Box 917, Tombstone, AZ 85638 (☎ **800/457-3423**). There's also a **visitor information**

If you're interested in learning more about Arizona's most notorious town, consider reading *Tombstone's Early Years* (Bison Books, 1995), by John Myers.

**center** on the corner of Allen Street and Fourth Street that's run by the Tombstone Chamber of Commerce (☎ 520/457-3929; www.cityoftombstone.com).

**SPECIAL EVENTS**   Tombstone's biggest annual celebrations are **Territorial Days,** held the third weekend of March; **Wyatt Earp Days,** held in late May; and **Helldorado Days,** held on the third weekend in October. The latter celebrates the famous gunfight at the O.K. Corral and includes countless shoot-outs in the streets, mock hangings, a parade, and contests.

## GUNSLINGERS & SALOONS: IN SEARCH OF THE WILD WEST

As portrayed in novels, movies, and TV shows over the years, the shoot-out has come to epitomize the Wild West, and nowhere is this great American phenomenon more glorified than here in Tombstone, where the star attraction is the famous ✪ **O.K. Corral.** Located on Allen Street near the corner of Third Street, the O.K. Corral, site of a brief gun battle, has taken on mythic proportions over the years despite the brevity of the shoot-out that took place here. Today fans of Western lore flock to this site as if on a pilgrimage. Inside the corral, you'll find life-size figures set up in the spots where all the famous gunslingers are thought to have been standing when the fight took place. Next door you'll find **Tombstone's Historama,** a sort of multimedia affair that rehashes the well-known history of Tombstone's "bad old days." Admission is $2.50 at both places.

However, you need not settle for static figures and dioramas. All over Arizona there are regular reenactments of gunfights, with the sheriff in his white hat always triumphing over the bad guys in black hats, and nowhere else in the state are there so many modern-day gunslingers entertaining so many people with their blazing six-guns as in Tombstone. Shoot-outs occur fairly regularly around town between noon and 4pm. Expect to pay about $4 for any of these shows.

When the smoke cleared in 1881, three men lay dead. They were later carted off to the **Boot Hill Graveyard** on the edge of town. The cemetery is open to the public and is entered through a gift shop on U.S. 80 just north of town. The graves of Clanton and the McLaury brothers, as well as those of others who died in gunfights or by hanging, are well marked. Entertaining epitaphs grace the gravestones here; among the most famous is that of Lester Moore—"Here lies Lester Moore, 4 slugs from a 44, No Les, no more."

When the residents of Tombstone weren't shooting each other in the streets, they were likely to be found in the saloons and bawdy houses that lined Allen Street. The most famous of these is the **Bird Cage Theatre,** so named for the cagelike cribs (actually what most people would think of as box seats) that are actually suspended from the ceiling. These velvet-draped cages were used by prostitutes to ply their trade. Also here in the Bird Cage, you can see the poker table where the longest running poker game in the west was played. For old Tombstone atmosphere, this place is hard to beat.

The town's other famous drinking and gambling emporium is the **Crystal Palace,** a popular watering hole at the corner of Allen and Fifth streets. The high-ceilinged saloon, built in 1879, has been completely restored and is a hangout for the town's costumed actors and other would-be cowboys and cowgirls.

Tombstone has long been a tourist town, and its streets are lined with souvenir shops; however, there are also several small museums scattered around town. At the **Rose Tree Inn Museum,** at Fourth and Toughnut streets, you can see what may be the world's largest rose bush (a "Lady Banksia" rose, actually more of a tree). The shrub is indeed impressive as it sprawls across an arbor and covers 8,000 square feet. Inside the museum, you'll see antique furnishings from Tombstone's heyday in the 1880s.

The most imposing building in town is the **Tombstone Courthouse State Park,** at the corner of Third and Toughnut streets. Built in 1882, the courthouse is now a state historic park and museum, containing artifacts, photographs, and newspaper clippings chronicling Tombstone's lively past. In the courtyard, the gallows that once ended the lives of outlaws and bandits still stands.

At the **Tombstone Epitaph Museum,** on Fifth Street between Allen and Fremont streets, you can inspect the office of the town's old newspaper. To see what life was like for the common folk in the old days, pay a visit to the **Pioneer Home Museum,** on Fremont Street (U.S. 80) between Eighth and Ninth streets.

Of the dozens of shops in town, one that stands out is **G. F. Spangenberg,** 17 S. Fourth St. (☎ 520/457-9229), a gun shop dealing in antique and modern six-shooters, as well as other guns, holsters, and the sundry necessities of the cowboy life. This is the town's most authentic shop and has been in business since 1880. One other shop well worth a visit is the **Tombstone Smithy,** 302 E. Fremont St. (☎ **520/457-2326**), where a wide variety of Western-theme metalwork is crafted. Here you'll find such imagery as petroglyphs and gun-totin' cowboys.

At several places along Allen Street, you can hop aboard a reproduction **stagecoach or covered wagon,** and for a few dollars get a narrated tour of town. With their rubber tires, these wagons and stagecoaches are much more comfortable than the originals.

## WHERE TO STAY

**Best Western Lookout Lodge.** U.S. 80 W. (P.O. Box 787), Tombstone, AZ 85638. ☎ **800/652-6772** or 520/457-2223. Fax 520/457-3870. www.tombstone1880.com/bwlookoutlodge. 40 units. A/C TV TEL. $59–$80 double. Rates include continental breakfast. AE, CB, DC, DISC, MC, V. Pets accepted ($5 a night plus deposit).

The biggest and most comfortable motel in Tombstone is located 1 mile north of town overlooking the Dragoon Mountains. Stone walls, porcelain doorknobs, Mexican tiles in the bathrooms, and old-fashioned "gas" lamps give the spacious rooms an Old West feel. In summer the pool is very welcome after a long hot day. Ask for a room with a view of the Dragoon Mountains.

**Priscilla's Bed & Breakfast.** 101 N. 3rd St. (P.O. Box 700), Tombstone, AZ 85638. ☎ **520/457-3844.** E-mail: priscilla@tombstone1880.com. 4 units, 1 with private bathroom. $55 double with shared bathroom, $69 double with private bathroom. Rates include full breakfast. AE, MC, V.

Located 2 blocks from the O.K. Corral, this small Victorian farmhouse has been completely restored and is set behind its original white picket fence. Built in 1904, the home reflects a less notorious period of Tombstone's past, a time when lawyers could build houses such as this. Lace curtains hang in the windows, and throughout the house, oak trim and oak furniture set a Victorian mood.

| Impressions |
| --- |

*From the hygienic point of view, whiskey and cold lead are mentioned as the leading diseases at Tombstone.*

—A Tombstone visitor in the 1880s

# Ghosts of the Past

The late 19th century were boom years in southeastern Arizona. Throughout the region, mining camps and towns flourished (and often disappeared just as quickly). While the most famous of the region's mining boom towns, Tombstone, may be the town too tough to die (or is it too much a tourist trap to die?), there were many other towns, some even tougher than Tombstone, that are today little more than ruins amid the cactus and mesquite. While there isn't always much to see in a ghost town, it can be fun exploring these forgotten boomtowns of the Wild West. The following are some of the most easily accessible and picturesque ghost towns of the region. There are also several interesting ghost towns (Duquesne, Harshaw, Mowry, and Washington Camp) 10 to 20 miles south of Patagonia, but these are all on gravel roads that aren't always in the best condition.

**Dos Cabezas:** Located 15 miles southeast of Willcox on Ariz. 186, this town is home to a few live residents. You can still see the old 1885 Wells Fargo stage stop and ruins of old adobe buildings.

**Fairbank:** Located near the San Pedro River on Ariz. 82 west of Tombstone, Fairbank was a railroad supply town in the 1880s and has several adobe buildings in good condition. The ghost town is now a destination for the San Pedro & Southwestern Railroad.

**Gleeson:** Located 16 miles east of Tombstone on a gravel road, Gleeson developed around a turquoise mine first used by Native Americans before the arrival of settlers and later used by Tiffany's for its jewelry.

**Pearce:** Located 30 miles south of Willcox just off U.S. 191, this ghost town still has a general store, post office and handful of residents. In the 1890s, there was a productive gold mine here that supported a population of 2,000 people.

If you'd like to see some of this region's ghost towns from a restored Willys four-by-four, contact Jon Lauderbaugh at **High Desert Adventures** (☎ **520/586-9309;** www.highdesertadventures.com), which offers tours into various mountain ranges in the area. Tours range from $45 to $65. Lauderbaugh, a former radio announcer, will regale you with stories of when the West was wild. He also offers petroglyph tours.

**Tombstone Boarding House.** 108 N. Fourth St. (P.O. Box 906), Tombstone, AZ 85638. ☎ **520/457-3716.** Fax 520/457-3038. 8 units. $65–$80 double. Rates include full breakfast. AE, MC, V.

Housed in two whitewashed 1880s adobe buildings with green trim, this inn is located 2 blocks from busy Allen Street in a quiet residential neighborhood. The main house was originally the home of Tombstone's first bank manager, while the guest rooms are in an old boarding house. Rooms are comfortable and very clean, with good beds and country decor. Hardwood floors and antiques lend a period feel to these rooms. Two guest rooms have claw-foot tubs, and one is in an old miner's cabin.

## WHERE TO DINE

**Don Teodoro's Mexican Restaurant.** 15 N. 4th St. ☎ **520/457-3647.** Reservations not taken; phone 30 minutes ahead. Main courses $4–$10. MC, V. Sun–Thurs 11am–9pm, Fri–Sat 11am–10pm. SONORAN MEXICAN.

We heard the sweet strains of a guitar wafting through Tombstone, and followed the sound to Don Teodoro's, a little restaurant with a real south-of-the-border atmosphere (and with live music many nights of the week). We dined on the plastic-enclosed patio, and the experience as a whole was slightly better than the food, which consisted of adequately prepared dishes such as burritos, chile rellenos, and *carne asada*. What's really good is the Sonoran-style enchilada, a thick corn tortilla covered with enchilada sauce and jack cheese; the tortilla soup is okay, but too salty. This is actually one of the better options for dining in Tombstone.

**OK Café**, 220 E. Allen St. (corner of 3rd and Allen sts.). ☎ **520/457-3980.** Main courses $4–$7. Credit cards not accepted. Daily 7am–2pm. AMERICAN.

Sure it's touristy, since it's on the main drag in Tombstone, but we really enjoy the buffalo burgers and homemade soups. Along with buffalo burgers, you'll also find ostrich, emu, and veggie burgers, and, of course, beef burgers, as well as chicken and BLTs. It's also a good place for breakfast—the service is bustling and the people who work here are friendly.

## 7 Bisbee

205 miles SE of Phoenix; 94 miles SE of Tucson; 24 miles NW of Douglas

Arizona has a wealth of ghost towns that boomed on mining profits but then quickly went bust when the mines played out. Between 1880 and 1975, the mines in Bisbee produced $6.1 billion worth of metals. When the Phelps Dodge Company shut down its copper mines here, Bisbee nearly went the way of other abandoned mining towns, but because it's the Cochise County seat, it was not fated to disappear into the desert dust. And since the town stopped growing in the early part of this century, it's one of the best-preserved turn-of-the-century towns anywhere in the Southwest. Old brick buildings line the narrow winding streets of the old section of town. Television and movie producers have discovered these well-preserved streets, and in recent years Bisbee has doubled as New York City, Spain, Greece, Italy, and, of course, the Old West.

The rumor of silver in "them thar hills" is what first attracted prospectors to the area in 1877, and within a few years the diggings attracted the interest of some San Francisco investors, among them Judge DeWitt Bisbee, for whom the town is named. However, it was copper and other less-than-precious metals that would make Bisbee's fortune. With the help of outside financing, large-scale mining operations were begun in 1881 by the Phelps Dodge Company. By 1910, the population had climbed to 25,000, and Bisbee was the largest city between New Orleans and San Francisco. The town boasted that it was the liveliest spot between El Paso and San Francisco—and the presence of nearly 50 saloons and bordellos along Brewery Gulch backed up the boast.

Tucked into a narrow valley surrounded by red hills a mile high in the Mule Mountains, Bisbee today has a very cosmopolitan air. Many artists now call the town their home, and urban refugees have been dropping out of the rat race to restore the town's old buildings and open small inns, restaurants, and art galleries. Between the rough edges left over from its mining days and this new cosmopolitan atmosphere, Bisbee is rapidly becoming one of Arizona's most interesting towns.

This interesting growth may be coming to a halt, however, as Phelps Dodge begins mining once again in the area. Residents of Bisbee are concerned that dynamiting in an open-pit mine might cause damage to homes and belongings and may even cause rock slides on the steep hillsides around town. Whether Bisbee will remain a tourist town or revert to a mining town is yet to be seen.

## ESSENTIALS

**GETTING THERE** Bisbee is on U.S. 80, which begins at I-10 in the town of Benson, 45 miles east of Tucson.

If you think dining at good restaurants is an integral part of any vacation, you shouldn't head down this way on a Monday or Tuesday. Most of the best restaurants in southeastern Arizona are closed on those days of the week. To be absolutely certain of getting good food during your visit, plan to come between Thursday and Sunday, but you should be on your way somewhere else by Sunday afternoon because most of the good restaurants aren't open Sunday night either.

**VISITOR INFORMATION**   For further information on Bisbee, contact the **Bisbee Chamber of Commerce,** 7 Main St. (P.O. Box BA), Bisbee, AZ 85603 (☎ **520/432-5421**).

**SPECIAL EVENTS**   Each year Bisbee puts on the Mile High Chili Cook-Off in April, coaster races on the Fourth of July, Brewery Gulch Days in September, a Gem and Mineral Show in October, a Historic Homes tour on Thanksgiving weekend, and an Arts Festival in the spring and fall. Ask the Bisbee Chamber of Commerce for specific information.

## EXPLORING THE TOWN

At the Bisbee Chamber of Commerce visitor center, located in the middle of town, you can pick up walking-tour brochures that will lead you past the most important buildings and sites in town. There's parking available around the downtown area.

Your first stop should be the **Bisbee Mining and Historical Museum,** 5 Copper Queen Plaza (☎ **520/432-7071**), which is housed in the 1897 Copper Queen Consolidated Mining Company office building. This small museum features an exhibit on the history of Bisbee and other exhibits that change annually. The museum is open daily from 10am to 4pm, and admission is $3 for adults, $2.50 for seniors, and free for anyone 17 and under.

For another look at early life in Bisbee, visit the **Muheim Heritage House,** 207 Youngblood Hill (☎ **520/432-7071**), which was built between 1902 and 1915 and has an unusual semicircular porch. Inside, the house is decorated with period furniture. You'll find the historic home up Brewery Gulch. The Muheim House is open Friday through Monday from 10am to 4pm, and a $2 donation is suggested.

On the second floor of the **Copper Queen Library,** across the street from the visitor center, are some great old **photographs** that give a pretty good idea of what the town looked like within the last century.

If you climb up to the top of **OK Street,** there's a path that will take you up to a hill above town for an excellent panorama of the jumble of old buildings. Atop this hill are numerous small colorfully painted shrines built into the rocks and filled with candles, plastic flowers, and pictures of the Virgin Mary. It's a steep climb on a rocky, very uneven path, but the views and the fascinating little shrines make it well worth the effort. After you've seen the old town, you might want to drive out to the Warren district, where the wealthier citizens of Old Bisbee built their homes.

You can also see what it was like to work inside one of Bisbee's copper mines by taking one of the ✪ **Queen Mine Tours** (☎ **520/432-2071**). You can choose either the underground Queen Mine tour or the surface mine and historic tour. Tours are offered daily from 9am to 3:30pm. Underground Queen Mine tours cost $10 for adults, $3.50 for children 7 to 15, $2 for children 3 to 6; surface mine and historic tours cost $7 per person; children under 3 are admitted free. You'll find the ticket office and mine just south of the Old Bisbee business district at the U.S. 80 interchange.

If you're interested in a personally guided tour of the area, contact **Mary's Walking Tours** (☎ 520/432-9039).

There are lots of interesting ✪ **shops and galleries** in Bisbee—all you have to do is walk around to explore—but there are a couple of places we especially like. **Optimo Custom Hat Works,** 47 Main St. (☎ **520/432-4544**), sells Panama hats woven by hand in Ecuador and custom fitted with finesse. The hats sold here range in price from about $20 for a low-grade model to several thousand dollars for a grade 20 "fino fino" (but many are much more reasonably priced). One of the best galleries in town is **Jane Hamilton Fine Art,** 29 Main St. (☎ 520/432-3660), showing a wide variety of art styles. If you're interested in having a look at some of the quality jewelry that is created from the minerals mined in the Bisbee area, stop by **Czar Minerals** (☎ 520/432-2698), up at the top of Tombstone Canyon Road and Clausen Avenue, or **Bisbee Blue** (☎ 520/432-5511), at the Lavender Pit View Point on Ariz. 80. At the former, the specialty is gold- and silversmithing; the latter is an exclusive dealer of the famous Bisbee Blue turquoise, which is a by-product of copper mining and comes from the Lavender Pit mine. The proprietor here will be happy to tell you about the stones.

## WHERE TO STAY

✪ **Bisbee Grand Hotel.** 61 Main St. (P.O. Box 825), Bisbee, AZ 85603. ☎ **800/421-1909** or 520/432-5900. 13 units. $55–$78 double; $95–$150 suite. Rates include breakfast. AE, CB, DC, DISC, MC, V.

The Bisbee Grand Hotel is the sort of place you'd expect Wyatt Earp and his wife to patronize. At street level there's a historic saloon with a high pressed-tin ceiling and an 1880s back bar from Tombstone. Upstairs are beautifully decorated turn-of-the-century guest rooms. The Oriental Suite has a ceiling fan, an incredibly ornate Chinese wedding bed, a claw-foot tub, and a skylight; the Victorian Suite has a red-velvet canopy bed. Other, smaller rooms are equally attractive and sport their own themes, and while they all have private bathrooms, some of these are not in the room but across the hall. For 1890s atmosphere, this hotel can't be beat. There are also two additional suites across the street; one of them has a full kitchen. (Guests staying in this suite don't receive breakfast.)

**Copper Queen Hotel.** 11 Howell Ave. (P.O. Drawer CQ), Bisbee, AZ 85603. ☎ **800/247-5829** or 520/432-2216. Fax 520/432-4298. 45 units. TV TEL. $70–$135 double. AE, DC, DISC, MC, V.

Located in the center of Bisbee, the Copper Queen Hotel was built just after the turn of the century by the Copper Queen Mining Company and in those years played host to such notables as Theodore Roosevelt and General "Black Jack" Pershing. Today, the atmosphere here is casual and authentic. The old safe behind the check-in desk has been there for years, as has the oak rolltop desk. Spacious halls, with their own lounges, lead to guest rooms furnished with antiques. Rooms vary considerably in size (the smallest being quite cramped), and while most have been renovated and are attractively furnished, the renovation is an ongoing project. Ask for a renovated room. The hotel's dining room serves continental and Southwestern fare, and out front there's a terrace for alfresco dining. And what would a mining-town hotel be without its saloon? For cooling off, there's even a swimming pool.

✪ **High Desert Inn.** 8 Naco Rd. (P.O. Box 145), Bisbee, AZ 85603-9998. ☎ **800/281-0510** or 520/432-1442. Fax 520/432-1410. www.highdesertinn.com. 6 units. A/C TV TEL. $70–$95 double. DISC, MC, V.

Though small, this is Bisbee's most luxurious hotel, housed in the former Cochise County Jail (ca. 1901). The guest rooms vary in size, but all feature high ceilings, new carpets, and contemporary furnishings including wrought-iron headboards on the beds. The small bathrooms have lace shower curtains and modern fixtures. The inn's dining room is one of the best restaurants in town.

**The Inn at Castle Rock.** 112 Tombstone Canyon Rd. (P.O. Box 1161), Bisbee, AZ 85603-2161. ☎ **800/566-4449** or 520/432-4449. Fax 520/432-7868. www.theinn.org. 15 units. $59–$89 double. Rates include full breakfast. AE, DC, DISC, MC, V. Pets accepted ($10).

This funky B&B right on the main road into Bisbee was built in 1890 as a miners' boarding house, and today the bright-red two-story inn, with verandas on both floors, is a warren of casually furnished small rooms affecting such themes as a sultan's harem. A shady patio, bar, and dining room add to the appeal of this unusual place. Most unusual of all is the flooded mine shaft in the middle of the dining room! Definitely not for everyone, this inn attracts a young, artistic clientele who appreciate the owners' unusual sense of style.

**Shady Dell RV Park.** 1 Douglas Rd. (P.O. Box 1432), Bisbee, AZ 85603. ☎ **520/432-3567.** 6 units. $25–$75 per trailer (1–2 people). No credit cards. No pets or children under 10.

Yes this really is an RV park, but you'll find neither shade nor dell at this roadside location just south of the Lavender Pit mine. What you will find are eight vintage trailers that have been lovingly restored by owners Ed Smith and Rita Personett. Although the trailers don't have their own private bathrooms (there's a bathhouse in the middle of the RV park), they do have all kinds of vintage decor and furnishings (even tapes of period music and radio shows). After numerous write-ups in national publications, the Shady Dell has become so famous that reservations need to be made far in advance. Also here at the Shady Dell is **Dot's Diner,** a 1957 vintage diner that fits right in with the vintage trailers. Call ☎ **520/432-2046** for directions.

## WHERE TO DINE

In addition to the restaurants listed below, the dining room of **The Inn at Castle Rock** offers meals amid unusual surroundings—it's worth dining here to see the mine shaft turned gold fish pond in the middle of the room. The dining room at the **Copper Queen Hotel** is another good hotel dining room to try, especially on nights when other restaurants in town are closed or too crowded. (See above for both.) The **Quartermoon Coffeehouse** (☎ 520/432-9088) at 1 OK St. in Lyric Plaza is a favorite locals hangout where you might find impromptu music or poetry. For good coffee and a mining-theme decor, check out the **Bisbee Coffee Co.** (☎ 520/432-7879), at the Convention Center. For burgers and homemade sweet potato pie in a 1957 vintage diner, drop by **Dot's Diner,** 1 Douglas Rd. (☎ 520/432-2046), which is open Tuesday through Saturday. Call for directions.

✪ **Café Roka.** 35 Main St. ☎ **520/432-5153.** Reservations recommended. Main courses $12.50–$18.50. AE, MC, V. Wed–Sat 5–9pm. CONTEMPORARY CALIFORNIAN.

Ask almost anyone in southern Arizona where to eat in Bisbee, and this is where they'll send you. Café Roka offers good value, as well as imaginatively prepared food. Every main course comes with a soup, salad, and sorbet, and the presentation is quite elegant. You'll find a lively mix of locals and out-of-towners here having dinner or sitting at the bar in the middle of the room. It's a sophisticated and surprising find in out-of-the-way Bisbee. On the menu you'll find the likes of grilled halibut with red pepper, kalamata olives, and white truffle relish. Flourless chocolate cake with raspberry sauce is a delicious ending. On some evenings jazz musicians perform, and local artists display their works.

**High Desert Inn Restaurant.** 8 Naco Rd. ☎ **520/432-1442.** Reservations recommended. Main courses $12.50–$17.50. DISC, MC, V. Thurs–Sat (and major holiday Sundays) 5:30–9pm; Sun brunch 10am–2pm. INTERNATIONAL.

Along with Café Roka, this is the most upscale restaurant in Bisbee. It's housed in what was formerly the Cochise County Jail—the back patio used to be the jail cells. In a genteel, romantically lit setting, you'll dine on food that draws its inspiration from around the globe. Such dishes as roasted chicken with mesquite bacon in a red wine–mushroom sauce, pork chops with a mango-orange-chipotle sauce, and seared and roasted fillet of salmon with herb-and-black-pepper crust are representative of the sorts of dishes that show up on the menu here.

## 8 Exploring the Rest of Cochise County

Willcox: 192 miles SE of Phoenix; 81 miles E of Tucson; 74 miles N of Douglas.

This is the land that Apache chief Cochise once called home and that he and his men fought hard to keep. The region's high plains attracted cattle ranchers early on, and to this day ranching is a mainstay of the local economy. Today it's the spectacular scenery of the Chiricahua and Dragoon mountains that lure many visitors. Others come to add to their bird-watching life lists.

In the southern part of this region lies the town of Douglas, which is an important gateway to Mexico. Unless you're heading to Mexico, there aren't many reasons to visit Douglas. But if you do find yourself passing through town, be sure to stop in at the historic Gadsden Hotel (see "Where to Stay," below, for more information).

## ESSENTIALS

**GETTING THERE**   Willcox is located on I-10, with Ariz. 186 heading southeast toward Chiricahua National Monument.

**VISITOR INFORMATION**   For more information on this area, contact the **Willcox Chamber of Commerce and Agriculture,** 1500 N. Circle I Rd., Willcox, AZ 85643 (☎ 800/200-2272 or 520/384-2272).

**SPECIAL EVENTS**   **Wings over Willcox,** a festival celebrating the return to the area of more than 12,000 sandhill cranes and other migratory birds, takes place in January. For information, contact the Willcox Chamber of Commerce and Agriculture (☎ **520/384-2272**).

## IN WILLCOX

**Rex Allen Museum.** 155 N. Railroad Ave. ☎ **520/384-4583.** $2 per person, $3 per couple, or $5 per family. Daily 10am–4pm.

If you grew up in the days of singing cowboys, then you're probably familiar with Willcox's favorite hometown star. It was Rex Allen who made famous the song "Streets of Laredo," and here at the small museum dedicated to Allen, you'll find plenty of Rex Allen memorabilia as well as a Cowboy Hall of Fame exhibit. Each year in October, Willcox celebrates Rex Allen Days.

**Museum of the Southwest.** In the Willcox Chamber of Commerce Visitor Center, 1500 N. Circle I Rd. ☎ **520/384-2272.** Free admission. Mon–Sat 9am–5pm, Sun 1–5pm. Take Exit 340 (Rex Allen Dr.) off I-10.

If you want to learn more about the history and geology of southeastern Arizona, stop by the this small museum. There are exhibits on pioneers, the U.S. Army, and the Chiricahua Apaches.

## SOUTHWEST OF WILLCOX

While Chiricahua National Monument claims the most spectacular scenery in this corner of the state, there are a couple of areas southwest of Willcox in the Dragoon

Mountains that are almost as impressive. The first of these, **Texas Canyon,** lies right along I-10 between Benson and Willcox and can be enjoyed from the comfort of a speeding car. Here, huge boulders are scattered across a rolling desert landscape. South of the community of Dragoon, which is now known for its many pistachio farms (most of which are open to the public), lies a much less accessible area of the Dragoon Mountains. It is not without good reason that this corner of these mountains has come to be called **Cochise Stronghold.** This rugged jumble of still more giant boulders is almost as spectacular as the nearby Chiricahua National Monument and is reached by a rough gravel road, at the end of which you'll find a campground, picnic area, and hiking trails. A hike among these incredible rock formations is an opportunity to muse on the history of this area.

The Apache peoples first moved into this region of southern Arizona sometime in the early 16th century. They pursued a hunting and gathering lifestyle that was supplemented by raiding neighboring tribes for food and other booty. When the Spanish arrived in the area, the Apache acquired horses and became even more efficient raiders. They attacked Spanish, Mexican, and eventually American settlers, and despite repeated attempts to convince them to give up their hostile way of life, the Apache refused to change. Not long after the Gadsden Purchase of 1848 made Arizona U.S. soil, more people than ever before began settling in the region. The new settlers immediately became the object of Apache raids and eventually the U.S. Army was called in to put an end to the attacks.

By the mid-1880s only Cochise and Geronimo and their Chiricahua Apache were continuing to attack settlers and fight the U.S. Army. Cochise used this rugged section of the Dragoon Mountains as his hideout and managed to elude capture for years, the granite boulders and pine forests making it impossible for the army to track him and his followers. Cochise eventually died and was buried at an unknown spot somewhere in the area now called Cochise Stronghold.

More Native American history is on display at the following museum.

✪ **Amerind Foundation Museum.** Dragoon. ☎ **520/586-3666.** Admission $3 adults, $2 seniors and children 12–18, free for children 11 and under. Sept–May daily 10am–4pm; June–Aug Wed–Sun 10am–4pm. Closed major holidays. 64 mi. east of Tucson between Benson and Willcox, take the Triangle T-Dragoon exit (Exit 318) from I-10 and continue 1 mile east.

It may be out of the way and difficult to find, but this museum is well worth seeking out. Established in 1937, the Amerind Foundation is dedicated to the study, preservation, and interpretation of prehistoric and historic Indian cultures. To that end the foundation has compiled the nation's finest private collection of archaeological artifacts and contemporary items. There are exhibits about the dances and religious ceremonies of the major Southwestern tribes, including the Navajo, Hopi, and Apache, and exhibits that contain archaeological artifacts amassed from the numerous Amerind Foundation excavations over the years. Many of the pieces came from right here in Texas Canyon. Fascinating ethnology exhibits include amazingly intricate beadwork from the Plains tribes, a case full of old Zuni fetishes, Pima willow baskets, old kachina dolls, 100 years of Southwestern tribal pottery, and Navajo weavings. The art gallery displays works by 19th- and 20th-century American artists, such as Frederic Remington, whose works focused on the West. The museum store is small but has a surprisingly good selection of books and Native American crafts and jewelry.

## SOUTHEAST OF WILLCOX

If you'd like to explore the Chiricahua Mountains on horseback, contact **Sunglow Guest Ranch** (☎ **520/824-3334**), which offers rides of anywhere from 1 hour ($18) to all day ($85). Lessons are also available. Reservations are required. This guest ranch also offers overnight ranch-to-ranch horseback rides (see "Area Guest Ranches," below, for details) and stagecoach rides in the Chiricahua Forest.

The **Fort Bowie Vineyard,** 156 N. Jefferson St., Bowie (☎ **520/847-2593**), has a wine-tasting room and also sells locally grown pecans and walnuts.

**Fort Bowie National Historic Site.** Off Ariz. 186. ☎ **520/847-2500.** Free admission. Visitor center, daily 8am–5pm; grounds, daily dawn–dusk. Closed Christmas. From Willcox drive southeast on Ariz. 186, and after about 20 miles, watch for the signs; it's another 8 miles up a dirt road to the trailhead. Alternatively, drive east from Willcox to Bowie and drive 11 miles south on Apache Pass Rd. From the trailhead, it is a 1½-mile hike to the fort.

The Butterfield Stage, which carried mail, passengers, and freight across the Southwest in the mid-1800s, followed a route that passed through the heart of Apache territory in the Chiricahua Mountains. Fort Bowie was established in 1862 near the mile-high Apache Pass to ensure the passage of this slow-moving stage as it traversed this difficult region, and to protect the water source for cavalry going east to fight the Confederate army in New Mexico. Later, it was from Fort Bowie that federal troops battled Geronimo until the Apache chief finally surrendered in 1886. Today there's little left of Fort Bowie but some crumbling adobe walls, but the hike along the old stage route to the ruins conjures up the ghosts of Geronimo and the Indian Wars.

✪ **Chiricahua National Monument.** Ariz. 186, 30 miles southwest of Willcox. ☎ **520/824-3560.** Admission $6. Visitor center open daily 8am–5pm.

Sea Captain, China Boy, Duck on a Rock, Punch and Judy—these may not seem like appropriate names for landscape features, but this is no ordinary landscape. These gravity-defying rock formations—called "the land of the standing-up rocks" by the Apache and the "wonderland of rocks" by the pioneers—are the equal of any of Arizona's many amazing rocky landmarks. Rank upon rank of monolithic giants seem to have been turned to stone as they marched across the forested Chiricahua Mountains. Big Balanced Rock and Pinnacle Balanced Rock threaten to come crashing down at any moment. Formed about 25 million years ago by a massive volcanic eruption, these rhyolite (a very acidic, volcanic rock) badlands were once the stronghold of renegade Apache. If you look closely at Cochise Head peak, you can even see the famous chief's profile. If you're in good physical condition, don't miss the chance to hike the ✪ **Heart of Rocks Trail,** which can be accessed from several trailheads. However, no matter where you start, you'll have to hike 7 to 10 miles to see this spectacular scenery.

Within the monument are a visitor center, campground, picnic area, many miles of hiking trails, and a scenic drive that provides views of many of the most unusual rock formations.

## IN & NEAR DOUGLAS

In addition to the historic site listed below, the town of Douglas abounds in old buildings, and though not many of them are restored, they hint at the diverse character of this community. Just across the border from Douglas is Agua Prieta, Sonora, where Pancho Villa lost his first battle. Whitewashed adobe buildings, old churches, and sunny plazas provide a contrast to Douglas. Curio shops and Mexican restaurants abound. At the **Douglas Chamber of Commerce,** 1125 Pan American Ave. (☎ **888/315-9999** or 520/364-2477), you can pick up a map to the town's historic buildings, as well as a rough map of Agua Prieta.

**Slaughter Ranch Museum.** ☎ **520/558-2474.** Admission $3 adults, children under 14 free. Wed–Sun 10am–3pm. From Douglas, go east on 15th St., which runs into Geronimo Trail; keep going east for 15 miles.

About 15 miles east of Douglas on a gravel road is the verdant San Bernardino Valley. In 1884, former Texas Ranger John Slaughter bought the valley and turned it into a cattle ranch, one of the finest in the West. Slaughter later went on to become the sheriff of Cochise County and helped rid the region of the unsavory characters who had flocked to the many mining towns of this remote part of the state. Today the ranch is a National Historic Landmark and has been restored to its turn-of-the-century look. Long shady porches, whitewashed walls, and dark green trim give the ranch a well-manicured look, while inside, antique furnishings present a picture of a very comfortable life.

## BIRDING HOT SPOTS

To the east of Chiricahua National Monument, on the far side of the Chiricahuas, lies ✪ **Cave Creek Canyon,** one of the most important bird-watching spots in America. It's here that the colorful, elegant trogon reaches the northern limit of its range. Other rare birds that have been spotted here include sulfur-bellied flycatchers and Lucy's, Virginia's, and black-throated gray warblers. Stop in at the visitor center for information on the best birding spots in the area. If you'd like a guide to help you identify the area's many bird species, contact David Jasper (☎ 520/558-2307). Cave Creek Canyon lies just outside the community of Portal and in summer can be reached by driving over the Chiricahuas from the national monument on graded gravel roads. However, in the winter you'll have to drive around the mountains, which entails going south to Douglas and then 60 miles north to Portal or north to I-10 and then south 35 miles to Portal.

The ✪ **Cochise Lakes** (actually the Willcox sewage ponds) are another great bird-watching spot in this region. Here bird watchers can see a wide variety of waterfowl and shorebirds including avocets and sandhill cranes. To find the ponds, head south out of Willcox on Ariz. 186, turn right onto Rex Allen Jr. Drive at the sign for the Twin Lakes golf course, and go past the golf course.

Between October and March, as many as 12,000 sandhill cranes gather in the Sulphur Springs Valley south of Willcox, and in January, the town holds the Wings over Willcox celebration of these majestic birds. One good place to see sandhill cranes is at the Whitewater Draw Wildlife Area on Coffman Road southwest of the town of Elfrida, which is a little more than midway between Willcox and Douglas on U.S. 191. The Sulphur Springs Valley is also well known for its large wintering population of raptors, including ferruginous hawks and prairie falcons.

North of Willcox, at the end of a 30-mile-long gravel road, lies the **Muleshoe Ranch Cooperative Management Area** (☎ 520/586-7072), a Nature Conservancy preserve that contains seven perennial streams. These streams support endangered aquatic life as well as riparian zones that attract a large number of bird species. To reach the ranch, take Exit 340 off I-10 and go south; take a right on Bisbee Avenue and then take another right onto Airport Road. After 15 miles watch for a fork in the road and take the right fork. If the road is dry, it is usually passable in passenger cars. The headquarters, which includes the visitor's center, is open mid-February to mid-May daily from 8am to 5pm. Mid-May to mid-February the headquarters is closed Tuesday and Wednesday. The backcountry is accessible all year-round 24-hours a day. Overnight accommodations in casitas ($70 to $100) are available by reservation, but are closed June through August.

## WHERE TO STAY
### IN & NEAR WILLCOX

Budget chain motels are the only options right in Willcox. These include the **Best Western Plaza Inn,** 1100 W. Rex Allen Dr. (☎ 520/384-3556), charging $69 to $109 double; **Days Inn,** 724 N. Bisbee Ave., off I-10 at Exit 340 (☎ 520/384-4222), charging $35 to $50 double; **Motel 6,** 921 N. Bisbee Ave., off I-10 at Exit 340 (☎ **520/384-2201**), with rates of $38 double; and **Super 8,** 1500 Fort Grant Rd. (☎ **520/384-0888**), charging $48 double. See appendix B for toll-free numbers.

✪ **Cochise Hotel.** P.O. Box 27, Cochise, AZ 85606. ☎ **520/384-4314** or 520/384-3156. 5 units. $50–$65 double. Rates include full breakfast. No credit cards. Take Exit 331 off I-10 onto Ariz. 191 and drive south 5 miles to Cochise.

Built in 1882, this historic hotel is about the most authentic in the state. The atmosphere is totally uncontrived, and though all the rooms have private bathrooms, the rooms are as simply furnished as travelers on the Southern Pacific Railroad might have found them 100 years ago. In the hotel's parlor, you'll find a working Victrola (guests often end up dancing to old 78 records) and a velvet sofa said to have belonged to Jenny Lind. On 2-day notice the hotel can prepare dinners of either baked chicken ($8) or grilled steaks ($10). Although this hotel is certainly not for everyone, it is a genuine step back in time. If you're a light sleeper, bring earplugs; the trains still run right past the front door.

## IN DOUGLAS

✪ **Gadsden Hotel.** 1046 G Ave., Douglas, AZ 85607. ☎ **520/364-4481.** Fax 520/364-4005. www.theriver.com/gadsdenhotel. 156 units. A/C TV TEL. $38–$60 double; $70–$85 suite. AE, CB, DC, DISC, MC, V.

There aren't many reasons to stay in the quiet border town of Douglas; this hotel is about it. Built in 1907, the Gadsden bills itself as "the last of the grand hotels," and its listing on the National Register of Historic Places backs up that claim. The marble lobby, though dark, is a classic. Vaulted stained-glass skylights run the length of the ceiling, and above the landing of the wide Italian marble stairway is a genuine Tiffany stained-glass window. Though the carpets in the halls are well worn and rooms aren't always spotless, many rooms have been renovated and refurnished. The bathrooms are, however, a bit worse for the wear. The lounge is a popular local hangout, with more than 200 cattle brands painted on the walls. The dining room serves Mexican and American food, and there's also a coffee shop.

## IN PORTAL

**Portal Peak Lodge, Portal Store & Cafe.** P.O. Box 364, Portal, AZ 85632. ☎ **520/558-2223.** Fax 520/558-2473. 16 units. A/C TV. $65 double. AE, DISC, MC, V.

This motel-like lodge is located behind the general store/cafe in the hamlet of Portal. The guest rooms are fairly new and face each other across a wooden deck. All have two double beds and coffeemakers. Meals are available in the adjacent cafe. If you are seeking utterly predictable accommodations, you'll find them here.

✪ **Southwestern Research Station, The American Museum of Natural History.** P.O. Box 16553, Portal, AZ 85632. ☎ **520/558-2396.** Fax 520/558-2396. 15 units. $122 double 1st night ($116 subsequent nights; discounts for children). Rates include 3 meals. No credit cards.

Located far up into Cave Creek Canyon, this is a field research station that takes guests when the accommodations are not filled by scientists doing research here in the canyon. As such it is the best place in the area for serious bird watchers, who will find the company of researchers to be a fascinating addition to a stay here. Accommodations are in simply furnished cabins scattered around the open grounds of the research center. Spring and fall are the easiest times to get reservations and the best times for bird watching.

## AREA GUEST RANCHES

**Grapevine Canyon Ranch.** P.O. Box 302, Pearce, AZ 85625. ☎ **800/245-9202** or 520/826-3185. Fax 520/826-3636. www.gcranch.com. 12 units. $300 cabin for 2; $340 casita for 2. Rates include all meals. 3-night minimum. Various weeklong packages available. AE, DISC, MC, V. No children under 12 accepted.

This ranch is located in the foothills of the Dragoon Mountains adjacent to Cochise Stronghold about 35 miles southwest of Willcox and can be either a quiet hideaway where you can enjoy the natural setting or a place to experience traditional ranch life—horseback riding, rounding up cattle, mending fences. The landscape of mesquite and yucca conjures up images of the high chaparral, and a wide variety of rides are offered, with an emphasis on those for experienced riders. The small cabins (with only showers in their bathrooms) and larger casitas (with combination baths) are set under groves of manzanita and oak trees, and there are decks from which you can view wildlife and the night sky. Unfortunately, furnishings and carpets are old, and rooms lack Western character. There's a swimming pool, and if you don't care to go horseback riding, complimentary sightseeing is included.

✪ **Sunglow Guest Ranch.** HCR 1 Box 385, Turkey Creek Rd., Pearce, AZ 85625. ☎ and fax **520/824-3334.** www.sunglowranch.com. 10 units, including 1 house. $65–$85 double; $140 for 4 in house. DISC, MC, V.

Located in the western foothills of the Chiricahua Mountains roughly 40 miles southeast of Willcox, this remote and tranquil ranch is surrounded by Coronado National Forest. A small lake lies just downhill from the ranch buildings, and rising up behind this lake are the peaks of the Chiricahuas. Back in the 1880s, Sunglow was a logging boom town, but all that remains today is an adobe cottage said to have been the home of outlaw Johnny Ringo's girlfriend. Today the old adobe building is the ranch's dining hall. A reproduction of an old mission church serves as a recreation hall and lounge. Guest rooms are all quite large and have kitchenettes, and most also have woodstoves. However, you won't find TVs or telephones in the rooms. This guest ranch is much less structured than so many others in the state and consequently rates are also much lower. Horseback riding is an additional $18 per hour for guests ($25 per hour for riding lessons). There are also several emus here at the ranch, but many guests are much more interested in the many species of wild birds that can be seen on the ranch and in the nearby hills. Meals are available if arranged in advance ($24 per person per day). Daily maid service is not provided.

## CAMPGROUNDS

Campgrounds in the area include one at **Chiricahua National Monument** (☎ 520/824-3560) on Ariz. 186 and a small campground at **Cochise Stronghold** in the Coronado National Forest on the road to Portal. For information on these national forest campgrounds, contact the **Douglas Ranger District** (☎ 520/364-3468). Reservations are not accepted for any of these campgrounds.

# WHERE TO DINE
## IN WILLCOX

Right across the parking lot from the Willcox Chamber of Commerce Visitor Center/Museum of the Southwest (off I-10 at Exit 340), you'll find **Stout's Cider Mill** (☎ 520/384-3696), which makes delicious concoctions with apples. There's cider, cider floats, "cidersicles," apple cake, and the biggest (and contender for the best) apple pie in the world. It's open daily 8am to 6pm.

## IN DOUGLAS

**The Grand Café.** 1119 G Ave. ☎ **520/364-2344.** Reservations not necessary. Main courses $6–$14. MC, V. Sun–Thurs 10am–10pm, Fri–Sat 10am–11pm. SONORAN MEXICAN.

The most interesting part of this cafe is the flamboyant interior and the Marilyn Monroe pictures all over the walls. There are plenty of familiar Mexican choices—enchiladas, tacos, fajitas, and posole, a chile stew with hominy and beef or pork—with steak and the occasional Italian dish thrown in for good measure. We like the chicken mole, if it's available, with an appetizer of grilled green onions. The guacamole had cottage cheese in it, which seemed rather strange, but the green corn tamales are quite good.

## NORTH TOWARD PHOENIX: THE SAFFORD AREA & MOUNT GRAHAM

Roughly 50 miles north of Willcox, off U.S. 191, lie the Pinaleño Mountains and 10,717-foot **Mount Graham** in a unit of Coronado National Forest. Mount Graham has for decades been a favorite summer vacation spot for desert dwellers. Its cool heights offer respite from the heat. Campgrounds and hiking trails provide places to stay and activities while on the mountain. The mountain is also the site of an astronomical observatory, (see the box, "Starry, Starry Nights" above for details). This observatory, funded partly by the University of Arizona and partly by the Vatican, was built despite concerns that the mountaintop was the last remaining habitat of 400 endangered Mount Graham red squirrels.

To the northwest of Mount Graham, at the end of a 45-mile gravel road, lies the **Aravaipa Canyon Wilderness,** through which flows the perennial Aravaipa Creek. This scenic canyon is bordered on both ends by the Nature Conservancy's **Aravaipa Canyon Preserve** (☎ 520/828-3443). Together these natural areas protect Arizona's healthiest population of native desert fishes, as well as cougars, desert bighorn sheep, bobcats, and 200 species of birds. Permits are required for hiking in the canyon and should be requested 13 weeks in advance of your visit (this place is popular). The Nature Conservancy has a guest house on its property here at the east end of the canyon.

Not far from the turnoff for Mount Graham and just south of Safford, you'll find **Roper Lake State Park** (☎ 520/428-6760), which has a hot spring, a campground, and a lake with a swimming beach. The day-use fee is $4 and camping is $10 to $15. There's also good bird watching here and at the nearby Dankworth Ponds (where you'll find another hot spring). The park is off U.S. 191 south of Safford about 6 miles (the pond is another 2 miles farther south).

In this same area you'll find the **Kachina Mineral Springs Spa** (☎ 520/428-7212) on Cactus Road (6 miles south of Safford in the shadow of Mt. Graham). Here you can soak in hot mineral waters, enjoy a sweat wrap, and get a massage. A soak costs $5 and massages range from $25 for 30 minutes to $55 for 1½ hours.

In Safford itself, **Discovery Park,** 1651 Discovery Park Blvd. (☎ 520/428-6260), is an interesting stop for both kids and adults. This science park includes the Gov Aker Observatory (open Thursday through Saturday from 3 to 9pm), which provides opportunities for exploring the heavens. There are plans to add other science-oriented attractions within the park.

Twenty miles northeast of Safford off U.S. 70, you'll find the **Gila Box Riparian National Conservation Area,** another popular hiking area. As at Aravaipa Canyon, this area preserves the landscape around a perennial stream, in this case the upper reaches of the Gila River.

For more information on the Safford area, contact the **Graham County Chamber of Commerce,** 1111 Thatcher Blvd., Safford, AZ 85546 (☎ 520/428-2511), or the **Bureau of Land Management,** Safford District Office, 711 14th Ave., Safford, AZ 85546 (☎ 520/348-4400).

# Western Arizona

**S**eparating Arizona from California and Nevada are 340 miles of Colorado River waters, most of which are impounded in huge reservoirs that provide the water and electricity to such sprawling Southwestern boomtowns as Phoenix and Las Vegas. Because of this watery border, this region has come to be known as Arizona's West Coast.

Lake Havasu, Lake Mohave, and Lake Mead are the largest and most popular of these reservoirs, and due to convolutions in the landscape, these lakes offer thousands of miles of shoreline. In some ways Arizona's West Coast is actually superior to California's Pacific Ocean coastline. Though there aren't many waves on this stretch of the Colorado River, both the weather and the water are warmer than in California. Consequently, water sports of all types are extremely popular, and the fishing is some of the best in the country.

While the Colorado River has always been the lifeblood of this region, it was not water that first attracted settlers to this rugged region. A hundred years ago, prospectors ventured into this sun-baked landscape hoping to find gold in the desert's mountains. Some actually did hit pay dirt. Mining towns sprang up over night, only to be abandoned a few years later when the gold ran out. Today, Oatman is the most famous of these mining boom towns, though it has too many people and wild burros to be called a ghost town (there's even an active mine or two here).

People are still venturing into this region in hopes of striking it rich, but now they head for the casinos in Laughlin, Nevada, just across the Colorado River from Bullhead City, Arizona. Here a miniature version of Las Vegas has grown up on the Nevada shore of the Colorado River.

As with any warm coastline, Arizona's West Coast is lined with lakefront resorts, hotels, RV parks, and campgrounds. Arizona's West Coast is for the most part a vacation destination for desert residents, so you won't find any hotels or resorts even remotely as upscale or expensive as those in Phoenix, Tucson, or Sedona. You will, however, find plenty of houseboats for rent. These floating vacation homes are immensely popular for family and group vacations. With a houseboat, you can get away from the crowds. When you find a remote cove, the best fishing, or the most spectacular views, you can just drop anchor and kick back. You can even houseboat to the London Bridge, which is no longer falling down, but instead bridges a backwater of Lake Havasu and is now one of Arizona's biggest tourist attractions.

## Kingman

90 miles SE of Las Vegas; 180 miles SW of Grand Canyon Village; 150 miles W of Flagstaff; 30 miles E of Laughlin

Though Lt. Edward Fitzgerald Beale, leading a special corps of camel-mounted soldiers, passed through this area in 1857, Kingman was not founded until 1882, by which time the railroad had already arrived in this region. Gold and silver were discovered in the nearby mountains in the 1870s, and mining continued well into the 1920s until the mines became unprofitable and were abandoned (although a few mines are still operating today).

During the 1930s, Kingman was a stop on the road to the promised land of California, as tens of thousands of unemployed people followed Route 66 from the Midwest to Los Angeles. Route 66 has long since been replaced by I-40, but the longest remaining stretch of the old highway runs between Kingman and Ash Fork. Over the years Route 66 has taken on legendary qualities, and today people come from all over the world searching for pieces of this highway's historic past.

Remember Andy Devine? No? Well, Kingman is here to tell you all about its squeaky-voiced native-son actor. Devine starred in hundreds of short films and features in the silent-screen era, but he's perhaps best known as cowboy sidekick Jingles on the 1950s TV Western *Wild Bill Hickok.* In the 1950s, and 1960s, he hosted *Andy's Gang,* a popular children's TV show. In the 1960s, he played Captain Hap on the popular program *Flipper.* Devine died in 1977, but here in Kingman his memory lives on—in a room in the local museum, on an avenue named after him, and, every October, when the town celebrates Andy Devine Days.

## ESSENTIALS

**GETTING THERE**  Kingman is on I-40 at the junction with U.S. 93 from Las Vegas. One of the last sections of old Route 66 (Ariz. 66) connects Kingman with Seligman, Arizona.

**America West** (☎ 800/235-9292) flies between Phoenix and Kingman Airport.

There is **Amtrak** (☎ 800/872-7245) passenger service to Kingman from Chicago and Los Angeles. The railway station is at 120 W. Andy Devine Ave. in downtown Kingman.

**VISITOR INFORMATION**  For more information about Kingman, contact the **Kingman Area Chamber of Commerce,** 333 W. Andy Devine Ave. (P.O. Box 1150), Kingman, AZ 86402-1150 (☎ 520/753-6106; www.arizonaguide.com/visitkingman). The chamber of commerce also operates the Tourist Information Center in the restored 1907 powerhouse at 120 W. Andy Devine Ave. This center is open daily from 9am to 6pm.

## EXPLORING THE KINGMAN AREA

There isn't much to do right in Kingman, but while you're in town, you can learn more about local history at the **Mohave Museum of History and Arts,** 400 W. Beale St. (☎ 520/753-3195). There's also plenty of Andy Devine memorabilia on display. The museum is open Monday through Friday from 9am to 5pm and on Saturday and Sunday from 1 to 5pm. Admission is $3. After touring the museum, take a drive or a stroll around downtown Kingman to view the town's many historic buildings. (You can pick up a map at the museum.)

If you're interested in historic homes, you can tour the **Bonelli House,** 430 E. Spring St., a two-story stone home that was built in 1915 and is now furnished much as it may have been when it was constructed. The house is open to the public

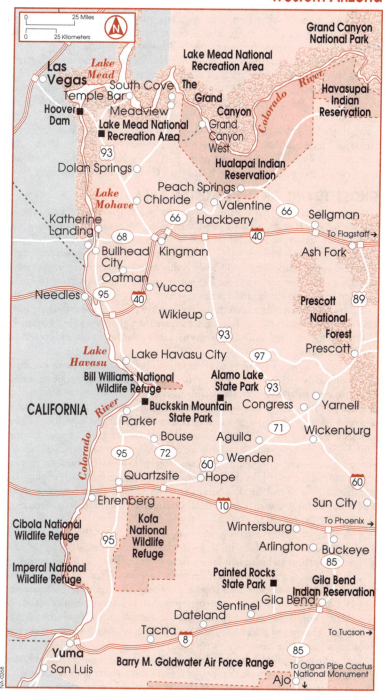

# Western Arizona

**25 Miles**
**25 Kilometers**
N

Lake Mead National
Recreation Area

*Lake
Mead*

Las
Vegas

South Cove
Temple Bar

**The
Grand**

Havasupai
Indian
Reservation

Hoover
Dam

Meadview

**Canyon**

Grand
Canyon
West

Lake Mead National
Recreation Area

93

Hualapai Indian
Reservation

Dolan Springs

*Lake
Mohave*

Peach Springs

Chloride

Valentine

Seligman

Katherine
Landing

66

Hackberry

66

40

To Flagstaff →

68

Bullhead
City

Kingman

Ash Fork

Oatman

Prescott

89

Needles

95

Yucca

40

National

Wikieup

Forest

93

Prescott

*Lake
Havasu*

Lake Havasu City

97

Bill Williams National
Wildlife Refuge

**Alamo Lake
State Park**

93

**CALIFORNIA**

*Colorado River*

Buckskin Mountain
State Park

Congress

Yarnell

Parker

71

Wickenburg

Bouse

Aguila

95

72

Wenden

60

Quartzsite

Hope

60

Ehrenberg

10

Sun City

Cibola National
Wildlife Refuge

Kofa
National
Wildlife
Refuge

Wintersburg

To Phoenix →

Arlington

Buckeye

Imperial National
Wildlife Refuge

95

85

**Painted Rocks
State Park**

**Gila Bend
Indian Reservation**

Sentinel

Gila Bend

Dateland

Tacna

8

To Tucson →

Yuma

85

San Luis

**Barry M. Goldwater Air Force Range**

To Organ Pipe Cactus
National Monument

Ajo

NA-0268

Thursday through Monday from 1 to 4pm, but before heading over to the Bonelli House, check at the Mohave Museum of History and Arts to see if there will be a guide to show you around the historic home. Admission is by donation.

A new **Route 66 Museum** is also under construction in the renovated powerhouse at 120 W. Andy Devine Ave. However, at press time, the Historic Route 66 Association of Arizona (☎ 520/753-5001) had not yet been able to raise enough money to finish the museum, though there were hopes that it would open some time in 1999.

When you're tired of the heat and want to cool off, head southeast of Kingman to **Hualapai Mountain Park,** on Hualapai Mountain Road (☎ 520/757-0915), which is at an elevation of 7,000 feet and offers picnicking, hiking, camping, and rustic rental cabins that were built in the 1930s by the Civilian Conservation Corp.

## GHOST TOWNS OF THE KINGMAN AREA

Located 30 miles southwest of Kingman on what was once Route 66 is the busy little ghost town of **Oatman,** a classic Wild West ghost town tourist trap full of shops selling tacky souvenirs. Founded in 1906 when gold was discovered here, Oatman quickly grew into a lively town of 12,000 people and was an important stop on Route 66—even Clark Gable and Carole Lombard once stayed here (on their honeymoon, no less). However, when the U.S. government closed down many of Arizona's gold-mining operations in 1942 because gold was not essential to the war effort, Oatman's population plummeted. Today there are fewer than 250 inhabitants, and the once-abandoned old buildings have been preserved as a ghost town. The historic look of Oatman has attracted filmmakers for years; among the movies filmed here was *How the West Was Won*.

One of the biggest attractions of Oatman is its population of almost-wild burros. These animals, which roam the streets of town begging for handouts, are descendants of burros used by gold miners. Be careful—they bite!

There are daily staged shoot-outs in the streets and dancing to country music on weekend evenings. Special events include bed races in January, a Fourth of July high-noon sidewalk egg fry, a Labor Day burro biscuit toss, and a December Christmas bush festival (bushes along the highway are decorated with tinsel and Christmas ornaments). Saloons, restaurants, and a very basic hotel (where you can view the room that Clark and Carole rented on their wedding night) provide food and lodging if you decide you'd like to soak up the Oatman atmosphere for a while. For more information, contact the **Oatman Chamber of Commerce,** P.O. Box 423, Oatman, AZ 86433 (☎ 520/768-6222).

**Chloride,** yet another almost-ghost town, is located about 20 miles northwest of Kingman. The town was founded in 1862 when silver was discovered in the nearby Cerbat Mountains, and is named for a type of silver ore that was mined here. By the 1920s, there were 75 mines and 2,000 people in Chloride. When the mines shut down in 1944, the town lost most of its population. Today there are about 300 residents.

Much of the center of the town has been preserved as a historic district and includes the oldest continuously operating post office in Arizona, the old jail, the Silverbelle Playhouse, and the Jim Fritz Museum. Many of the downtown buildings now serve as studios and shops for artists and craftspeople.

On the first and third Saturday of each month, Chloride comes alive with **staged gunfights** in the streets (at high noon, of course) and an afternoon **vaudeville show** at the Tennessee Saloon (at 2pm). On the last Saturday in June, the town celebrates **Old Miners' Day** with a parade, shoot-outs, melodramas, music, and dancing.

Chloride's biggest attractions are the **Chloride murals,** painted by Western artist Roy Purcell in 1966. The murals are painted on the rocks on a hillside about a mile outside of town. To find them, drive through town on Tennessee Avenue and continue onward after the road turns to dirt. You can also see old petroglyphs created by the Hualapai tribe on the hillside opposite the murals.

For more information about Chloride, contact the **Chloride Chamber of Commerce,** P.O. Box 268, Chloride, AZ 86431 (☎ 520/565-2204).

## WHERE TO STAY

In addition to the accommodations listed below, most of the budget chain motels have lodgings in Kingman. These include the **Days Inn—Kingman,** 3023 E. Andy Devine Ave. (☎ 520/753-7500), charging $40 to $70 double; **Motel 6,** 3351 E. Andy Devine Ave. (☎ 520/757-7151), charging $30 to $36 double; and **Super 8 Motel,** 3401 E. Andy Devine Ave. (☎ 520/757-4808), charging $35 to $46 double. See appendix B for toll-free numbers.

✪ **Brunswick Hotel.** 315 E. Andy Devine Ave., Kingman, AZ 86401. ☎ 520/718-1800. Fax 520/718-1801. www.hotel-brunswick.com. 22 units, 13 with private bathroom. A/C TV TEL. $25 single with shared bathroom, $50 double with private bathroom; $75–$95 suite. Rates include deluxe continental breakfast. AE, DISC, MC, V.

Built in 1909 and located in downtown Kingman, the Brunswick Hotel reopened in 1997 after a complete renovation and is Kingman's only historic lodging (and the only historic hotel in at least a hundred mile radius). Back when the hotel's imposing tufa-stone building was constructed, the railroad was the lifeblood of this town, and inside you'll find rooms furnished with antiques and vintage character from those days. The guest rooms vary considerably in size, and most of those with shared bathrooms have only single beds. The rooms are quite comfortable, and suites are extremely spacious. Although the railroad tracks are right across the street, triple-paned windows keep the rooms pretty quiet. The restaurant on the premises serves excellent continental fare, and there is a small bar at the back of the high-ceilinged lobby. New owners have brought more than 3 decades of hotel experience to the management of this hotel.

**Quality Inn—Kingman.** 1400 E. Andy Devine Ave., Kingman, AZ 86401. ☎ 800/869-3252 or 520/753-4747. 98 units. A/C TV TEL. $49–$59 double. Rates include continental breakfast. AE, CB, DC, DISC, MC, V.

Andy Devine Avenue used to be the famous Route 66, and this motel, located 2 miles south of I-40, cashes in on the fame of this historic highway. There are antique gas pumps and other Route 66 memorabilia in the motel lobby and a breakfast room done up like a 1950s soda shop. The rooms here are a bit cramped but are clean and have coffeemakers and two sinks in the bathrooms. The motel also offers an outdoor pool, whirlpool, sauna, and fitness room.

## WHERE TO DINE

If you're desperate for an espresso, try **Oldtown Coffeehouse,** 616 E. Beale St. (☎ 520/753-2244), in an old cottage in downtown Kingman. Need a microbrew? Try the Iguana Amber Ale at **Your Mother's,** 301 N. Fourth St. (☎ 520/753-3615), a brew pub and restaurant in the historic 1904 Elks Lodge building.

**DamBar & Steak House.** 1960 E. Andy Devine Ave. ☎ 520/753-3523. Reservations recommended on weekends and in summer. Lunch items $5–$13; main courses $6–$17 at dinner. AE, MC, V. Daily 11am–10pm. STEAK.

Operated by the same people who run Murphy's in Prescott, this steak house has long been Kingman's favorite place for dinner out. It's hard to miss the DamBar—just watch for the steer on the roof of a rustic wooden building as you drive along Andy Devine Avenue. Inside, the atmosphere is very casual, with sawdust on the floor and wooden booths. Mesquite-broiled steaks are the name of the game here, but there are

# Get Your Kicks on Route 66

It was the Mother Road, the Main Street of America, and for thousands of Midwesterners devastated by the dust bowl days of the 1930s, Route 66 was the road to a better life. On the last leg of its journey from Chicago to California, Route 66 meandered across the vast empty landscape of northern Arizona.

Officially dedicated in 1926, Route 66 was the first highway in America to be uniformly signed from one state to the next. Less than half of the highway's 2,200-mile route was paved, and in those days the stretch between Winslow and Ash Fork was so muddy in winter that drivers had their cars shipped by railroad between those two points. By the 1930s, however, the entire length of Route 66 had been paved, and the westward migration that characterized the Great Depression was under way.

The years following World War II saw Americans take to Route 66 in unprecedented numbers, but this time for a different reason. Steady jobs, a new prosperity, and reliable cars made travel a pleasure, and Americans set out to discover the West—many on the newly affordable family vacation. Motor courts, cafes, and tourist traps sprang up along its length, and these businesses turned to increasingly more eye-catching signs and billboards in order to lure passing motorists. Neon lights abounded, looming out of the dark Western nights on lonely stretches of highway.

By the 1950s, Route 66 just couldn't handle the amount of traffic it was seeing. With President Eisenhower's initiation of the National Interstate Highway System, Route 66 was eventually replaced by a four-lane divided highway. Many of the towns along the old highway were bypassed, and motorists stopped frequenting such roadside establishments as Pope's General Store and the Oatman Hotel. Many closed, and others were replaced by their more modern equivalents. Some, however, have managed to survive, and they appear along the road like strange time capsules from another era, vestiges of Route 66's legendary past.

The **Wigwam Motel** is one of the most distinctive Route 66 landmarks. For many miles out from the town of Holbrook, billboards along I-40 beckon weary motorists to "sleep in a wigwam." The wigwams in question (actually teepees) were built out of concrete around 1940, and still contain many of their original furnishings. Also in Holbrook are several rock shops with giant signs—and life-size concrete dinosaurs—that date from Route 66 days. Nighttime here comes alive with vintage neon.

Continuing west, between Winslow and Flagstaff, you'll find a landmark that made it into *Forrest Gump*. The Twin Arrows truck stop, now little more than an old cafe just off the interstate, has as its symbol two giant arrows constructed from telephone poles.

Flagstaff, the largest town along the Arizona stretch of Route 66, became a major layover spot. Motor courts flourished on the road leading into town from the east. Today this road has been officially renamed Route 66 by the city of Flagstaff, and many of the old motor courts remain. Though you probably wouldn't want to stay in many of these old motels, their neon signs were once beacons in the night for tired drivers. Downtown Flagstaff has quite a few shops where you can pick up Route 66 memorabilia.

About 65 miles west of Flagstaff begins the longest remaining stretch of old Route 66. Extending for 160 miles from Ash Fork to Topock, this lonely blacktop passes through some of the most remote country in Arizona (and also goes right through the town of Kingman). In the community of Seligman, at the east end of this stretch of the highway, you'll find the **Snow Cap Drive-In,** where owner Juan Delgadillo serves up fast food and quick wit amid outrageous decor. You can't miss it. Next door at **Angel's Barber Shop,** which is owned by Juan's brother Angel, you'll be entertained by one of the Route 66's most famous residents and an avid fan of the old highway. Angel still cuts hair, and his one-chair barbershop's walls are covered with photos and business cards of happy customers, many of whom traveled thousands of miles to get their hair cut here. Angel's place also serves as something of a Route 66 information center and souvenir shop, and Angel is president emeritus of the Route 66 Association of Arizona.

After leaving Seligman, the highway passes through such waysides as Peach Springs, Truxton, Valentine, and Hackberry. Before reaching Peach Springs, you'll come to **Grand Canyon Caverns,** once a near-mandatory stop for families traveling Route 66. At Valle Vista, near Kingman, the highway goes into a curve that continues for 7 miles. Some people claim it's the longest continuous curve on a U.S. highway.

After driving through the wilderness west of Seligman, Kingman feels like a veritable metropolis, and its bold neon signs once brought a sigh of relief to the tired and the hungry. Today there are dozens of modern motels in Kingman, but our favorite is the **Quality Inn** on Andy Devine Avenue. The lobby here is filled with Route 66 memorabilia, and a breakfast room is done up like a 1950s malt shop. **Mr. D'z Route 66 Diner,** a modern rendition of a 1950s diner (housed in an old gas station/cafe), serves burgers and blue plate specials and usually has a few classic cars parked out front. Across the street you'll find the newly restored Powerhouse, which dates from 1907 and is now home to the Kingman Area Chamber of Commerce Tourist Information Center, a 1950s-style malt shop, and the **Historic Route 66 Association of Arizona** (☎ **520/753-5001**), which has been raising money for years to open a Route 66 Museum here in Kingman's old powerhouse. Each year in late April or early May, Kingman is the site of the **Route 66 Fun Run Weekend,** which consists of a drive along 150 miles of old Route 66 between Topock and Seligman.

The last stretch of Route 66 in Arizona heads southwest out of Kingman through the rugged Sacramento Mountains. This stretch of the old highway passes through **Oatman,** once almost a ghost town after the local mining industry collapsed and the new interstate pulled money out of town. Today mock gun-fights and nosy wild burros (watch out, they bite) entice motorists to stop, and shops playing up Route 66's heritage line the wooden sidewalks.

Dropping down out of the mountains, the road once crossed the Colorado River on a narrow metal bridge. The bridge is still there, but now it carries a pipeline instead of traffic, and cars must return to the bland I-40 to continue their journey into the promised land of California.

plenty of other hearty dishes as well (Louisiana catfish, margarita grilled chicken, baby back ribs).

**Hubb's Café.** At the Hotel Brunswick, 315 E. Andy Devine Ave. ☎ **520/718-1800.** Lunch items $4–$11; main courses $9–$16 at dinner. AE, DISC, MC, V. Wed–Mon 7am–9pm. CONTINENTAL.

Hubb's is a welcome addition to dining options in Kingman. The downtown restaurant, located in an authentically restored historic 1909 hotel, has a surprising asset—a chef from Belgium. He lends his expert touch to such dishes as a terrine, a velvety and delicious paté sometimes served with mango sauce, and scallops *waterzooi*, a traditional Belgium dish that is rich, creamy, and flavorful. If these sound too exotic for your tastes, you'll also find steak, chicken, and pastas on the menu. Desserts are calculated to be small enough so that you end your dinner feeling satisfied, not stuffed. This is also a good place for breakfast and lunch.

**Mr. D'z.** 105 E. Andy Devine Ave. ☎ **520/718-0066.** Sandwiches $3–$7; blue plate specials $7–$9. AE, DC, DISC, MC, V. Tues–Sun 10am–8pm. AMERICAN.

This 1990s version of a vintage roadside diner is housed in an old gas station now painted an eye-catching turquoise and pink. The retro color scheme continues inside where you can snuggle into a pink-and-turquoise booth or grab a stool at the counter. This place is a big hit with car buffs and people doing Route 66, and there are usually a some hot rods and vintage cars in the parking lot. Punch in a few 1950s tunes on the jukebox, order up a Corvette burger and a root beer float, and you've got an instant trip down memory lane Route 66 style.

**Portofino Ristorante Italiano.** 318 Oak St. ☎ **520/753-7504.** Lunch items $5–$7; main courses $8–$15 at dinner. MC, V. Mon–Fri 11am–2pm and 5–9pm, Sat 5–9pm. ITALIAN.

Housed in an old territorial-style cottage in the historic section of downtown Kingman, this friendly Italian restaurant is a favorite spot in Kingman for a meal. Displays of cheeses, wines, and liqueurs around the restaurant lend an authentic and rustic feel to the dining room, and once you peruse the menu, you'll know you're in for a meal the likes of which you're not likely to find very often in these parts. You might start with fresh mozzarella with tomato and basil. From there you can move on to a selection from the long pasta menu, such as fettuccine *tutto mare* with shrimp, scallops and baby clams in spicy white-wine sauce, or the short selection of filling main courses. Of course, there's an excellent and very light and airy tiramisu with which to finish things off.

## 2 Lake Mead National Recreation Area

30 miles SE of Las Vegas; 70 miles NW of Kingman; 256 miles NW of Phoenix

Constructed between 1931 and 1935, Hoover Dam was the first major dam on the Colorado River, and by providing huge amounts of electricity and water to Arizona and California, it set the stage for the phenomenal growth the region experienced in the second half of the 20th century. But Lake Mead, the massive reservoir impounded by Hoover Dam's gargantuan cement wall, provides far more than just water and power. As the focal point of Lake Mead National Recreation Area, it is one of Arizona's (and Nevada's) favorite aquatic playgrounds. Every year more than eight million people visit this national recreation area to boat, ski, fish, swim, and camp on both Lake Mead and Lake Mohave. This latter lake, impounded by Davis Dam, is much smaller than Lake Mead but also lies within the boundaries of the National Recreation Area, which encompasses parts of both Arizona and Nevada.

## ESSENTIALS

**GETTING THERE**    U.S. 93, which runs between Las Vegas and Kingman, crosses over Hoover Dam, and traffic backups at the dam can be horrendous. Don't be surprised if you get stuck for an hour just trying to get across the dam. Several small secondary roads lead to various marinas on the lake. There are also many miles of unpaved roads within the recreation area. If you have a high-clearance vehicle or four-wheel-drive, these roads can take you to some of the least visited shores of the two lakes.

**VISITOR INFORMATION**    For more information, contact the **Lake Mead National Recreation Area,** 601 Nevada Hwy., Boulder City, NV 89005-2426 (☎ **702/293-8906**), or stop by the **Alan Bible Visitor Center** (☎ **702/293-8990**), between Hoover Dam and Boulder City, Nevada.

## DAM, LAKE & RIVER TOURS

Standing 726 feet tall, from bedrock to the roadway atop it, and tapering from a thickness of 660 feet at its base to only 45 feet at the top, **Hoover Dam** is the tallest concrete dam in the western hemisphere. Behind this massive dam lie the waters of **Lake Mead,** which, at 110 miles long and with a shoreline of more than 550 miles, is the largest artificial lake in the United States. U.S. 93 runs right across the top of the dam, and there's a visitor center that chronicles the dam's construction. The visitor center is open daily from 8:30am to 5:30pm (closed Thanksgiving and Christmas). Two different guided tours of the dam are offered. The basic tours last 35 minutes and cost $8 for adults, $7 for seniors, and $2 for children ages 6 to 16. The Hardhat Tour, a more behind-the-scenes tour, lasts about an hour and costs $25.

If you'd like to tour the lake and the dam, book passage on one of **Lake Mead Cruise's** (☎ **702/293-6180**) paddle-wheeler excursions on the *Desert Princess.* These cruises leave from Lake Mead Cruises Landing off Lakeshore Drive on the Nevada side of Hoover Dam. Day tours, which go to the dam, last 1½ hours and are $16 for adults and $6 for children ages 2 to 11. There are also weekend breakfast cruises ($21 adults and $10 children), dinner cruises ($29 adults and $15 children), and weekend dinner-and-dancing cruises ($43).

One of the most interesting ways to see a remote section of Lake Mohave is to take a kayak trip with **Back Bay Canoes & Kayaks,** 1450 Newberry Dr. (at Ariz. 95), Bullhead City (☎ **888/KAYAKEN** or 520/758-6242), which offers trips through Black Canyon (just below Hoover Dam) to Willow Beach. Trips cost $55 per person. This company also offers full-day and half-day river trips in the Laughlin-Bullhead City area. **Black Canyon Raft Tours** (☎ **702/293-3776**) offers 3-hour motorized raft trips down this same stretch of the river. Trips cost $65 for adults, $35 for children ages 5 to 12 (includes lunch, but transportation to and from Las Vegas and area hotels costs extra). This is an easy float trip rather than a white-water run.

## OUTDOOR RECREATION

As you would expect, swimming, fishing, waterskiing, sailing, windsurfing, and power-boating are the most popular activities within Lake Mead National Recreation Area. On Arizona shores, there are designated swimming beaches at Lake Mohave's Katherine Landing (outside Bullhead City) and Lake Mead's Temple Bar (north of Kingman off U.S. 93). Picnic areas can be found at these two areas and also at Willow Beach on Lake Mohave and more than half a dozen spots on the Nevada side of Lake Mead.

**Fishing** for monster striped bass (up to 50 lb.) is one of the most popular activities on Lake Mead, and while Lake Mohave's striped bass may not reach these awesome proportions, fish in the 25-pound range are not uncommon. However, largemouth bass and even rainbow trout are also plentiful within the National Recreation Area's waters due to the diversity of habitats. Try for big rainbows in the cold waters that flow out from Hoover Dam through Black Canyon and into Lake Mohave. Trout are stocked during winter and spring in several places around both Lake Mead and Lake Mohave. To fish from shore, you'll need a fishing license from either Arizona or Nevada (depending on which shore you're fishing from). To fish from a boat, you'll need a license from one state and a special use stamp from the other.

The fishing season for striped bass starts around the beginning of April when the water starts to warm up. If you don't have your own boat, try fishing from the shore of Lake Mohave near Davis Dam, where the water is deep. Anchovy pieces work well as bait, but be sure to put some shot on your line to get it down to the depths where the fish are feeding. You can get bait, tackle, licenses, and fishing tips at the **Lake Mohave Resort marina** at Katherine Landing.

In Arizona, **marinas** can be found at Katherine Landing on Lake Mohave (just outside Bullhead City), near the north end of Lake Mohave at Willow Beach (best access for trout angling), and at Temple Bar on Lake Mead. There is also a boat ramp at South Cove, north of the community of Meadview at the east end of Lake Mead. This latter boat ramp is the closest to the Grand Canyon end of Lake Mead. On the Nevada side of Lake Mohave, you'll find a marina at Cottonwood Cove, and on the Nevada side of Lake Mead, you'll find marinas at Boulder Beach, Las Vegas Bay, Callville Bay, and Echo Bay. These marinas offer resorts, restaurants, general stores, campgrounds, and boat rentals. At both **Temple Bar** (☎ **520/767-3211**) and **Lake Mohave Resort** (☎ **520/754-3245**), you can rent ski boats, fishing boats, and patio boats for between $75 and $250 per day. Personal watercraft are also available and rent for $50 an hour or $270 a day.

Despite the area's decided water orientation, there's also quite a bit of mountainous desert here, land that's home to bighorn sheep, roadrunners, and other wildlife. This land was also once home to several indigenous tribes who left reminders of their presence in **petroglyphs.** The best place to see these carvings is at Grapevine Canyon, which is due west of Laughlin, Nevada, in the southwest corner of the National Recreation Area. To reach Grapevine Canyon, take Nev. 163 west from Laughlin to milepost 13 and turn right on the marked dirt road. From the highway, it's about 1½ miles to the turnoff for the parking area. From here it is less than ¼ mile to the petroglyph-covered jumble of rocks at the mouth of Grapevine Canyon. Covering the boulders here are thousands of cryptic symbols, as well as ancient illustrations of bighorn sheep. To see these petroglyphs, you'll have to do a lot of scrambling, so wear sturdy shoes (preferably hiking boots).

For information on other **hikes,** contact any of the ranger stations within the National Recreation Area (Katherine Landing, Cottonwood Cove, Temple Bar, Las Vegas Bay, Callville Bay, Echo Bay, or Overton Beach).

## WHERE TO STAY

All three of the accommodations listed below are operated by Seven Crown Resorts, which also operates two other resorts on the Nevada side of the lake. For more information, contact **Seven Crown Resorts** (☎ **800/752-9669**).

### HOUSEBOATS

**Seven Crown Resorts.** Mailing address: P.O. Box 16247, Irvine, CA 92623-9801. ☎ **800/752-9669.** www.sevencrown.com. A/C. $1,150–$2,750 per week. DISC, MC, V.

Why pay extra for a lake-view room when you can rent a houseboat that always has a 360° water view? There's no better way to explore Lake Mead than on one of these floating vacation homes. You can cruise for miles, tie up at a deserted cove, and have a wilderness adventure with all the comforts of home. Houseboats come complete with full kitchens, air-conditioning, and room to sleep up to 14 people. The scenery here isn't quite as spectacular as on Lake Powell, Arizona's other major houseboating lake.

## MOTELS

**Lake Mohave Resort.** Katherine Landing, Bullhead City, AZ 86430. ☎ **800/752-9669** or 520/754-3245. 51 units. A/C TV TEL. Mar–Oct $60–$83 double; Nov–Feb $35–$65 double. DISC, MC, V. Pets accepted, $5 day.

Just up Lake Mohave from Davis Dam and only a few minutes outside Bullhead City, the Lake Mohave Resort is an older motel, but the huge rooms are ideal for families on vacation. Most of the rooms have some sort of view of the lake, which is across the road from the motel. Tail O' the Whale, the resort's nautical-theme restaurant and lounge, overlooks the marina where giant carp loll just below the surface waiting for people to feed them. The resort also offers boat rentals, a convenience store, and a tackle-and-bait store.

**Temple Bar Resort.** Temple Bar, AZ 86443. ☎ **800/752-9669** or 520/767-3211. 22 units. A/C TV TEL. $43–$89 double. DISC, MC, V. Pets accepted ($5 per night plus $25 deposit).

Though basically just a motel, the Temple Bar Resort has a wonderfully remote setting that will have you thinking you're on vacation in Baja California. With a beach right in front, great fishing nearby, and 40 miles of prime skiing waters extending out from the resort, this place makes an excellent getaway. Directly across from Temple Bar is the huge Temple monolith from which this area gets its name. A restaurant and lounge overlook the lake and provide economical meals. The resort offers ski rentals, powerboat rentals, shuffleboard, boccie, horseshoes, and a convenience store. There are also four very basic fishing cabins here that share shower rooms and toilets.

## CAMPGROUNDS

In Arizona, there are campgrounds at Katherine Landing on Lake Mohave and at Temple Bar on Lake Mead. Both of these campgrounds have been heavily planted with trees so they provide some semblance of shade during the hot, but popular, summer months. In Nevada, you'll find campgrounds at Cottonwood Cove on Lake Mohave and at Boulder Beach, Las Vegas Bay, Callville Bay, and Echo Bay on Lake Mead.

## 3  Bullhead City & Laughlin, Nevada

30 miles W of Kingman; 216 miles NW of Phoenix; 60 miles N of Lake Havasu City

You may find it difficult at first to understand why anyone would ever want to live in Bullhead City. According to the U.S. Weather Service, this is the hottest town in the country, with temperatures regularly topping 120°F during the summer. However, to understand Bullhead City, you need only gaze across the Colorado River at the gambling mecca of Laughlin, Nevada, where the slot machines are always in action and the gaming tables are nearly as hot as the air outside. Laughlin, Nevada, is the southernmost town in Nevada and is therefore the closest place to Phoenix to do some serious gambling. This makes Bullhead City one of the busiest little towns in Arizona.

Laughlin is a perfect miniature Las Vegas. High-rise hotels loom above the desert like so many glass mesas, miles of neon lights turn night into day, and acres of asphalt are always covered with cars and RVs as hordes of hopeful gamblers go searching for Lady Luck. Cheap rooms and meals lure people into spending on the slot machines what they save on food and a bed. It's a formula that works well. Why else would anyone endure the heat of this remote desert?

## ESSENTIALS

**GETTING THERE**  From Phoenix, take U.S. 60, which becomes U.S. 93, north-west to I-40. From Kingman, take Ariz. 68 west to Bullhead City.

The Bullhead City–Laughlin Airport is in Bullhead City and is served by **America West** (☎ 800/235-9292).

There are also shuttle bus services operating between Laughlin and the Las Vegas airport. For information or a reservation, call **Super Shuttle** (☎ **800/801-8687** or 520/704-9000), which charges $28 one-way.

**VISITOR INFORMATION**  For more information on Bullhead City and Laughlin, Nevada, contact the **Bullhead Area Chamber of Commerce,** 1251 Hwy. 95, Bullhead City, AZ 86429 (☎ **800/987-7457** or 520/754-4121). For information in Laughlin, stop by the **Laughlin Visitor Bureau,** 1555 S. Casino Dr. (P.O. Box 502), Laughlin, NV 89029 (☎ **800/452-8445** or 702/298-3321).

**GETTING AROUND**  Car rentals are available in Bullhead City/Laughlin from **Avis** (☎ **800/831-2847** or 520/754-4686), **Enterprise** (☎ **800/325-8007** or 520/754-2700), **Hertz** (☎ **800/654-3131** or 520/754-4111), and **Thrifty** (☎ **800/ 367-2277** or 520/704-0193). **Citizens Area Transit (CAT)** provides public bus service within Laughlin. The fare is $1.50. There is also a shuttle service that operates between the casinos, and a ferry that shuttles gamblers back and forth across the river from Bullhead City to Laughlin.

## CASINOS & OTHER INDOOR PURSUITS

Laughlin is a very popular weekend destination for Phoenicians and other Arizonans, who have limited gambling in their own state. The casinos of Laughlin are known for having liberal slots—that is, the slot machines pay off frequently. There's also keno, blackjack, poker, craps, off-track betting, and sports betting. If you want to learn how to play a game that requires a bit more thinking than slot machines, you can take a lesson in poker, blackjack, or craps at most of the casinos. All the hotels in Laughlin offer live entertainment of some sort, including an occasional headliner (Roy Clark, Doobie Brothers, Mills Brothers), but gambling is still the main event after dark as far as most people are concerned.

If you'd like to learn more about the history of this area, visit the **Colorado River Museum,** 355 Hwy. 95, Bullhead City (☎ 520/754-3399), which is located ½ mile north of the Laughlin Bridge. The museum is open April to June, September, and October Tuesday to Saturday from 9:30am to 2:30pm; November to March daily 9:30am to 2:30pm; closed July and August. Admission is free.

## BOAT TOURS

If you'd like to get away from the noise of the casinos and see a bit of the Colorado River, there are daily "paddle wheeler" cruises available at the **Flamingo Hilton** and **Edgewater** (☎ 800/228-9825). These cruises cost $11 for adults and $6 for children (dinner cruises for $26 are also available). At the **Riverside Resort** (☎ **702/ 298-2535**), you can take a tour to Davis Dam, which is about the same length as the "paddle wheeler" tours and costs $10 for adults and $6 for children. Alternatively, you can opt for a more luxurious cruise from **Harrah's** (☎ **702/298-4600**) on a modern blue-water yacht. These cruises cost only $12.95 for adults and $7.95 for children age 12 and under.

If you'd rather look at natural surroundings instead of casino towers, consider booking a jet-boat tour with **London Bridge Jet Boat Tours** (☎ **888/505-3545** or 702/298-5498). The trip leaves from Laughlin's Pioneer Casino and goes down river to Lake Havasu City to see London Bridge. On the way, the boat passes through scenic

Topock Gorge. These powerful boats cruise at up to 40 m.p.h. and make the 58-mile trip in 2 hours. Round-trip fares are $49 for adults and $30 for children ages 3 to 12.

## OUTDOOR RECREATION

If you'd like to rent a personal watercraft yourself and play around a bit on the river, there are rental kiosks along the waterfront behind the casinos. Try **Del Rio Beach Club,** at Harrah's Casino, 2900 S. Casino Dr. (☎ **800/74-BEACH** outside Nevada, or 702/298-6828) in Laughlin. Expect to pay $55 to $70 an hour.

If you'd like to do some guided kayaking, contact **Back Bay Canoes & Kayaks,** 1450 Newberry Dr., Bullhead City (☎ **888/KAYAKEN** or 520/758-6242), which offers full-day and half-day river kayak trips in the Laughlin-Bullhead City area. **Desert River Outfitters** also offers guided trips in sit-on-top ocean kayaks starting at about $30 per person. They also rent canoes.

If you're interested in doing a little fishing and want to have a guide show you some local hot spots, contact **Desert Recreation** (☎ **702/298-6828**), which operates out of Harrah's Casino and charges $75 per person. For information on fishing in nearby Lake Mohave, see the "Lake Mead National Recreation Area" section above. If you'd rather just feed the fish, check out the carp that hang out at the dock behind the Edgewater Hotel & Casino. There are machines dispensing carp chow so you can feed these aquatic vacuums.

In Laughlin golfers can play a round at the scenic and challenging **Emerald River Golf Course** (☎ **702/298-0061**), which is 2 miles south of Harrah's. Greens fees range from $65 to $75. The **Mojave Resort Golf Club,** 9905 Aha Macav Pkwy. (☎ **702/535-4653**), adjacent to the Avi Resort & Casino, is the area's newest golf course and charges greens fees of $50 to $75. In Bullhead City, try the **Desert Lakes Golf Course** (☎ **520/768-1000**), 15 miles south of town off Ariz. 95 on Joy Lane in Fort Mohave. Greens fees range from $60 to $65. Greens fees are usually lower during the hot summer months. There are also three 9-hole courses near Bullhead City. These include **Riverview Resort & Golf Club,** 2000 E. Ramar Rd. (☎ **520/763-1818**); **Chaparral Country Club,** 1260 E. Mohave Dr. (☎ **520/758-6330**); and **Willow Spring Golf Course,** 8011 Hwy. 95, Mohave Valley (☎ **520/768-4414**).

Bird watching is excellent in **Havasu National Wildlife Refuge,** which is a wintering area for many species of waterfowl. However, much of this refuge lies within the scenic Topock Gorge and is accessible only by boat. The most accessible birding areas are along the marshes in the vicinity of the communities of Golden Shores and Topock, which are both north of the I-40 bridge over the Colorado. Topock Gorge, which is one of the most scenic stretches of the lower Colorado River, is a 15-mile stretch of the Colorado River that is bordered by multicolored cliffs that rise up from the river.

## WHERE TO STAY & DINE
### IN BULLHEAD CITY

Bullhead City has numerous budget chain motels, including **Super 8,** 1616 Ariz. 95 (☎ **520/763-1002**), charging $25 to $30 for a double. See appendix B for toll-free numbers.

### IN LAUGHLIN, NEVADA

Laughlin, Nevada, currently has 10 huge hotel-and-casino complexes, 8 of which are right on the west bank of the Colorado River (the 9th is across the street from the river, and the 10th is on the river but several miles south of town). All offer cheap rooms (usually $15 to $30 on weeknights) to lure potential gamblers. In addition to huge casinos with hundreds (even thousands) of slot machines and every sort of gaming table, these hotels all have several restaurants (with ridiculously low prices in at least one restaurant, which usually has long lines), bars and lounges (usually with live country or pop music nightly), swimming pools, video arcades for kids, ferry service to parking lots on the Arizona side of the river, valet parking, room service, car-rental desks, airport shuttles, gift shops, and gaming classes. The only real difference between most of these places is the theme each has adopted for its decor.

Should you wish to stay at one of these hotels, here's the information you'll need:

**Avi Hotel & Casino,** 10000 Aha Macav Pkwy. (P.O. Box 77011), Laughlin, NV 89029-7011 (☎ 800/284-2946 or 702/535-5555)

**Colorado Belle Hotel & Casino,** 2100 S. Casino Dr., Laughlin, NV 89028 (☎ 800/47-RIVER or 702/298-4000)

**Edgewater Hotel & Casino,** 2020 S. Casino Dr. (P.O. Box 30707), Laughlin, NV 89028 (☎ 800/67-RIVER or 702/298-2453)

**Flamingo Hilton,** 1900 S. Casino Dr., Laughlin, NV 89029 (☎ 800/FLAMINGO or 702/298-5111)

**Golden Nugget,** 2300 S. Casino Dr., Laughlin, NV 89028 (☎ 800/237-1739 or 702/298-7111)

**Harrah's Laughlin,** 2900 S. Casino Dr., Laughlin, NV 89028 (☎ 800/447-8700 or 702/298-4600)

**Pioneer Hotel & Gambling Hall,** 2200 S. Casino Dr. (P.O. Box 29664), Laughlin, NV 89029 (☎ 800/634-3469 or 702/298-2442)

**Ramada Express,** 2121 S. Casino Dr., Laughlin, NV 89029 (☎ 800/243-6846 or 702/298-4200)

**River Palms Resort & Casino,** 2700 S. Casino Dr. (P.O. Box 77700), Laughlin, NV 89028-7700 (☎ 800/835-7903 or 702/298-2242)

**Riverside Resort Hotel & Casino,** 1650 S. Casino Dr. (P.O. Box 500), Laughlin, NV 89029 (☎ 800/227-3849 or 702/298-2535)

## WHERE TO DINE

The dozens of inexpensive casino hotel restaurants are usually the top choice of visitors to Laughlin and Bullhead City. Cheap steaks, prime ribs, and all-you-can-eat buffets are the specialties of these places.

## 4 Lake Havasu & the London Bridge

200 miles NW of Phoenix; 60 miles S of Bullhead City; 61 miles S of Kingman; 150 miles S of Las Vegas

Once upon a time London Bridge really was falling down, but that was before Robert McCulloch, founder of Lake Havasu City, hit upon the brilliant idea of buying the bridge in the late sixties and having it shipped to his undertouristed little town in the middle of the Arizona desert. Today the London Bridge sits like a mirage on the banks of Lake Havasu. An unlikely place for a bit of British heritage, true, but Lake Havasu City and the London Bridge have become the second most popular tourist destination in Arizona (only the Grand Canyon attracts more visitors).

Lake Havasu was formed in 1938 by the building of the Parker Dam, but it wasn't until 1963 that the town of Lake Havasu City was founded by McCulloch. Not too many people were keen on spending time out in this remote corner of the desert, where summer temperatures are often over 110°F. Despite its name, Lake Havasu City at the time was little more than an expanse of desert with a few mobile homes on it. It was then that McCulloch began looking for ways to attract more people to his little city on the lake. His solution proved to be a stroke of genius.

In recent years, Lake Havasu City has become very popular with college students across Arizona, especially during spring break. The city is sort of a Fort Lauderdale in the desert, and businesses cater primarily to young partiers. Be prepared for a lot of noise if you are here on a weekend or during a holiday.

## ESSENTIALS

**GETTING THERE**   From Phoenix, take I-10 west to Ariz. 95 north. From Las Vegas, take U.S. 93 south to Kingman and then I-40 west to Ariz. 95 south.

**America West** (☎ 800/235-9292) has regular flights to Lake Havasu City from Phoenix.

The **Havasu/Vegas Express** (☎ 800/459-4884 or 520/453-4884) operates a shuttle van between Lake Havasu City and Las Vegas. Fares are $49 one-way and $87 round-trip.

**VISITOR INFORMATION**   For more information on this area, contact the **Lake Havasu Area Chamber of Commerce/Lake Havasu Tourism Bureau,** 314 London Bridge Rd., Lake Havasu City, AZ 86403 (☎ 800/242-8278 or 520/453-3444; www.arizonaguide.com/lakehavasu).

**GETTING AROUND**   Taxi service is available from **City Transit Service** (☎ 520/453-7600). Car rentals are available from **Avis** (☎ 800/831-2847 or 520/764-3001) and **Enterprise Rent-a-Car** (☎ 800/325-8007 or 520/453-0033). There is also the **River City Trolley,** a trolley-style bus that loops past many of the city's shopping centers and motels (with a stop at Shugrue's at the Island Mall at the island side of the London Bridge).

## LONDON BRIDGE

In the mid-1960s, the British government decided to sell the London Bridge, which was indeed falling down—or, more correctly, sinking—into the Thames River because of too much heavy car and truck traffic. McCulloch and his partner paid $2,460,000 for the famous bridge; had it shipped 10,000 miles to Long Beach, California; and then trucked it to Lake Havasu City. Reconstruction of the bridge was begun in 1968, and the grand reopening was held in 1971. Oddly enough, the 900-foot-long bridge was not built over water; it just connected desert to more desert on a peninsula jutting into Lake Havasu. It wasn't until after the bridge was rebuilt that a mile-long channel was dredged through the base of the peninsula, thus creating an island offshore from Lake Havasu City.

The London Bridge has a long history, though the bridge that now stands in Arizona is not very old by British standards. The first bridge over the Thames River in London was probably a pontoon bridge built by the Romans in A.D. 43. However, the first written record of a London Bridge comes from the mention of a suspected witch being drowned at the bridge in 984. In 1176, the first stone bridge over the Thames was built. They just don't build 'em like that bridge anymore—it lasted for more than 600 years but was eventually replaced in 1824 by the bridge that now stands in Lake Havasu City.

At the base of the bridge sits **English Village,** which is done up in proper English style and has shops, restaurants, and a waterfront promenade. It's here that you'll find several cruise boats and small-boat rental docks.

## LAND, RIVER & LAKE TOURS

There are several companies offering different types of boat tours on Lake Havasu. **Bluewater Charters** (☎ 888/855-7171 or 520/855-7171) offers jet-boat tours that leave from the London Bridge and spend 2 hours cruising up the Colorado River to the Topock Gorge, a scenic area 25 miles from Lake Havasu City. The tours are $35 for adults, $32 for seniors, $17.50 for children 10 to 16, and free for children 9 and under.

You can also cruise on the *Dixie Belle* (☎ 520/453-6776), a small replica paddle-wheel riverboat. Cruises are $12 for adults and $5 for children 6 to 12.

One of the most interesting and beautiful boat tour destinations is Copper Canyon, a flooded canyon 9 miles from Lake Havasu City. The *Kon Tiki*, a pontoon boat berthed at English Village, makes the trip regularly and charges $10 for adults and $5 for children 6 to 12.

For an even more scenic tour, but one that entails a bit of effort, contact **Western Arizona Canoe and Kayak Outfitter** (☎ 520/855-6414 or 520/680-9719), which offers kayak trips through the beautiful and rugged Topock Gorge, where you can see ancient petroglyphs and possibly bighorn sheep. Trips start at $44 per person. **Jerkwater Canoe Company** (☎ 520/768-7753) offers a similar Topock Gorge trip, and also arranges other canoe trips of varying lengths. With Jerkwater, the Topock Gorge trip is $35 per person. Another popular trip is through Black Canyon, but advance planning is required to get the necessary permit. Both companies provide boats, paddles, life jackets, maps, and shuttles to put-in and take-out points, but no guide (the maps make it easy for you to find your own way). Some trips also include additional overnight campground or bunkhouse bed-and-breakfast fees.

If you'd like to explore the desert surrounding Lake Havasu City, you can arrange a four-wheel-drive tour through **Outback Off-Road Adventures** (☎ 520/680-6151), which charges $65 for a half-day tour and $130 for a full-day tour.

## WATER SPORTS

While the London Bridge is what made Lake Havasu City, these days water sports on 45-mile-long Lake Havasu are the area's real draw. Whether you want to go for a swim, take a leisurely pedal-boat ride under the London Bridge, go parasailing, or spend the day waterskiing, there are plenty of places to arrange to get wet.

The best beach in the area is the **London Bridge Beach,** in a county park behind the Island Inn Resort off West McCulloch Boulevard. This park has a sandy beach, lots of palm trees, and views of both the London Bridge and the distant desert mountains. There are also picnic tables and a snack bar, which make this park a great place to spend the whole day. There are more beaches at the **Windsor Beach Unit of Lake Havasu State Park,** 2 miles north of the London Bridge, and **Cattail Cove State Park,** 15 miles south of Lake Havasu City. Lake Havasu State Park also has 20 miles of shoreline to the south of Lake Havasu City, but there are no roads to this shoreline. If you have your own boat, you'll find lots of secluded little beaches.

The cheapest way to get out on the water in Lake Havasu also happens to involve the greatest expenditure of energy. At the **Fun Center** (☎ 520/453-4386) in English Village you can rent pedal boats and aqua cycles for $15 an hour. If kayaking or canoeing is more your style, contact **Western Arizona Canoe and Kayak Outfitter** (☎ 520/855-6414), which rents canoes and kayaks on the lake beginning at $25 a day.

If you didn't bring your own boat, you can rent one at **Resort Boat Rentals,** in English Village beside the bridge (☎ 520/453-9613 or 520/855-7171). The company offers half- and full-day rentals of ski boats (starting at $190 per day) and pontoon boats (starting at $150 per day). Ski boats come with water skis or knee board. Boats are also available at **Lake Havasu Marina,** 1100 McCulloch Blvd. (☎ 520/855-2159), and at **Fun Time Boat Rentals,** 655 Kiowa Blvd. (☎ 800/680-1003 or 520/680-1003).

Two- and three-passenger WaveRunners are available from **Jet Ski Rentals,** 660 Kiowa Ave. (☎ **520/680-8100**) and the **Water Sports Center,** Nautical Inn Resort, 1000 McCulloch Blvd. (☎ **520/453-6212**). Rates range from $45 to about $55 an hour. WaveRunners are also available at the Fun Center in English Village.

If your main reason for getting out on the water is to catch some fish, you'll likely come away from a visit to Lake Havasu with plenty of fish stories to tell. Striped bass, also known as stripers, are the favorite quarry of anglers here. These fish have been known to reach almost 60 pounds in these waters, so be sure to bring the heavy tackle. Largemouth bass in the 2- to 4-pound range are also fairly common, and giant channel catfish of up to 35 pounds have been caught in Topock Marsh. The best fishing starts in midspring when the water begins to warm up, but there is also good winter fishing. If you want to hire a fishing guide, call Jim Ocker (☎ **520/680-1873**); his rate is about $100 per day for the first person, $50 each for the second and third person. Or check at the Lake Havasu Area Chamber of Commerce for a list of guides.

## GOLF

And what would an Arizona desert community be without its golf courses? Lake Havasu City has four, all of which are open to the public. Panoramic views are to be had from each of the courses here, and there's enough variety to accommodate golfers of any skill level.

**London Bridge Golf Club,** 2400 Club House Dr. (☎ **520/855-2719**), with two 18-hole courses, is the area's premier championship course. High-season greens fees (with cart) top out at $69 (with cart) on the West Course and $50 on the East Course. The **Havasu Island Golf Course,** 1000 McCulloch Blvd. (☎ **520/855-5585**), is a 4,012-yard, par-60 executive course with lots of water hazards. The 9-hole **Queens Bay Golf Course,** 1477 Queen's Bay Rd. (☎ **520/855-4777**), at the London Bridge Resort, is the most accessible and easiest of the area courses.

Golfers also won't want to miss the ✪ **Emerald Canyon Golf Course,** 72 Emerald Canyon Dr., Parker (☎ **520/667-3366**), which is about 30 miles south of Lake Havasu City. This municipal course is the most spectacular course in the region and plays through rugged canyons and past red-rock cliffs, from which there are views of the Colorado River. One hole even has you hitting your ball off a cliff to a green 200 feet below you! Greens fees range from about $28 on weekdays in summer to about $42 daily in fall, winter, and spring.

## WHERE TO STAY
### HOUSEBOATS

**Havasu Springs Resort.** 2581 Hwy. 95, Parker, AZ 85344. ☎ **520/667-3361.** Fax 520/667-1098. Mar 1–Sept 9 $1,855–$2,432 per week; Sept 10–Feb 28 $1,166–$1,690 per week. No credit cards.

One of the most popular ways to enjoy Lake Havasu is on a rented houseboat. You can spend your days motoring from one good fishing or swimming hole to the next, and there are beaches and secluded coves where you can drop anchor and stay for days. If you feel like doing a bit of sightseeing or shopping, you can cruise right up to the London Bridge. Houseboats come in several sizes, with the large boats providing much more luxury. Boats sleep 10 to 12 people and are very popular with families.

### HOTELS & MOTELS

**Bridgeview Motel.** 101 London Bridge Rd., Lake Havasu City, AZ 86403. ☎ **520/855-5559.** Fax 520/855-5564. 37 units. A/C TV TEL. $40–$80 double. MC, V.

If you're just looking for a clean and inexpensive place to stay, this motel fits the bill and offers a view of the bridge. It's also quiet here (usually), and there's a small pool.

**Island Inn.** 1300 W. McCulloch Blvd., Lake Havasu, AZ 86403. ☎ **800/243-9955** or 520/680-0606. Fax 520/680-4218. 117 units. A/C TV TEL. Mar 1–Oct 31 $65–$95 double, $130–$180 suite; Nov 1–Feb 28 $49–$59 double, $98 suite. AE, DISC, MC, V. Pets accepted with extra charge.

This is one of the newest hotels in Lake Havasu City and is located across the London Bridge from downtown. Though it's not right on the water, the Island Inn is close to one of the area's best public beaches. The rooms are large and Spartan, and they seem to have seen a lot of wear and tear. Most rooms have balconies, and those on the upper floors have the better views (and higher prices). Facilities include an outdoor pool and a whirlpool.

✪ **London Bridge Resort.** 1477 Queens Bay, Lake Havasu City, AZ 86403. ☎ **800/624-7939** or 520/855-0888. Fax 520/855-9209. 120 units. A/C TV TEL. S$79 studio; $129–$199 1- or 2-bedroom condo. Higher rates on holidays. AE, DC, DISC, MC, V.

It doesn't take much to figure out that this resort was built after the London Bridge made its historic move to the Arizona desert. Merrie Olde England was once the theme here, with Tudor half-timbers jumbled up with turrets, towers, ramparts, and crenellations. However, England is giving way to the tropics and the desert as the resort strives to please its young, partying clientele (who tend to make a lot of noise and leave the hotel looking much the worse for wear). Though the bridge is just out the hotel's back door, and a replica of Britain's gold State Coach is inside the lobby, guests seem more interested in the three pools, the tropical-theme outdoor nightclub, and the Mexican cantina. Even the dining room now serves Southwestern food. The rooms are large, and have been getting a Southwestern face-lift. In addition to the three pools, recreational options include an executive golf course, tennis courts, whirlpools, and a beach. Note that this hotel is now a time-share facility.

## CAMPGROUNDS

In the Lake Havasu City area, there are two state park campgrounds. **Lake Havasu State Park's Windsor Beach Unit** (☎ 520/855-2784) is 2 miles north of the London Bridge on London Bridge Road and **Cattail Cove State Park** (☎ 520/855-1223) is 15 miles south of Lake Havasu City off Ariz. 95. The former campground has no hookups and charges $12 per night per vehicle, and the latter charges $10 or $15 for a full hookup per vehicle. In addition to sites in these campgrounds, there are 200 boat-in campsites within Lake Havasu and Cattail Cove state parks.

## WHERE TO DINE

✪ **Chico's Tacos.** In the Basha's Center, 1641 McCulloch Blvd. ☎ **520/680-7010.** Main courses $2.25–$6. MC, V. Sun–Thurs 10:30am–9pm, Fri–Sat 10:30am–10pm. MEXICAN.

This Mexican fast-food place is great for a quick, cheap bite to eat. The *carne asada* and chicken *carbón* are excellent, and there's a fresh salsa bar for you to do your own doctoring of your meal. Be forewarned that the burritos are big and messy!

✪ **City of London Arms Pub & Restaurant.** 422 English Village. ☎ **520/855-8782.** Reservations recommended. Main courses $8–$20. AE, DC, DISC, MC, V. Sun–Thurs 11am–9pm, Fri–Sat 11am–10pm. PUB FARE/STEAKS.

A British pub atmosphere reigns here, with a Tudor-style interior and British comfort food on the menu—fish-and-chips, steak-and-mushroom pie, and bangers and mash. It's a cool retreat from the blazing sun, and kind of an odd place in which to find oneself (since this is the desert). This pub was actually built by the City of London, and here you'll be competing with other tourists on the London Bridge scene for a table either inside or on the patio overlooking the river. If you desire something non-British, take heart—the menu includes seafood, steaks, pizza, and pasta. For dessert, don't pass up the trifle. The restaurant serves Guiness stout, but this is also a brew pub serving a half dozen different beers and ales brewed on the premises.

**Shugrue's.** 1425 McCulloch Blvd. (at the Island Mall). ☎ **520/453-1400.** Reservations recommended. Main courses $8–$23. AE, DC, MC, V. Daily 11am–3pm and 4:30–9pm (sometimes later on weekend nights). STEAK/SEAFOOD.

Located just across the London Bridge from the English Village shopping complex, Shugrue's seems to be popular as much for its view of the London Bridge as it is for its food. The large restaurant has been built so that most diners get a view of the bridge. In addition to the seafood, prime rib, burgers, and sandwiches, there's a short list of pastas. This place is a favorite of vacationing retirees and families—there's also a children's menu including such items as chicken tenders or a minipizza. Shugrue's operates the Barley Brothers Brewery and Grill in the same shopping center as well.

# DRIVING DOWN TO YUMA
## THE PARKER AREA

About 16 miles south of Lake Havasu City stands the **Parker Dam,** which holds back the waters of Lake Havasu and is said to be the deepest dam in the world because 73% of its 320-foot height is below the riverbed. Beginning just above the dam and stretching south to the town of Parker is one of the most beautiful stretches of the lower Colorado River. Just before you reach the dam, you'll come to the **Bill Williams National Wildlife Refuge,** which preserves the lower reaches of the Bill Williams River. This refuge offers some of the best bird watching in western Arizona. Keep your eyes out for vermilion flycatchers, Yuma clapper rails, soras, Swainson's hawks, and white-faced ibises.

Continuing south, you'll come to a dam overlook and the Take-Off Point boat launch, where you can also do some fishing from shore. Below the dam, the river becomes narrow, and red-rock canyon walls close in. Though this narrow gorge is lined with mobile home parks, the most beautiful sections have been preserved in two units of **Buckskin Mountain State Park** (☎ 520/667-3231). Both units—Buckskin Point and River Island—have campgrounds ($15 for campsites and $20 for cabanas at Buckskin and $12 at River Island) as well as day-use areas ($7) that include river beaches and hiking trails leading into the Buckskin Mountains. In this area is the spectacular Emerald Canyon Golf Course (see "Golf," above, for details).

South of this area, the highway leaves the banks of the river, and the scenery becomes far less memorable. However, in the town of Parker, you might want to stop at the **Colorado River Indian Tribes Museum,** Second Avenue and Mohave Road (☎ 520/669-9211), which is south of downtown Parker on the outskirts of town. The museum is dedicated to preserving the history of several of the Colorado River's tribes. Included here is a large collection of Chemehuevi baskets, as well as pottery, beadwork, and jewelry. The museum is open Monday through Friday from 8am to 5pm with a lunch closure from noon to 1pm. Admission is free. To find the museum, follow signs to the hospital and then go 1.3 miles farther on Mohave Road.

For more information on the Parker area, contact the **Parker Area Chamber of Commerce,** 1217 California Ave., Parker, AZ 85344 (☎ 520/669-2174).

## THE QUARTZSITE AREA

For much of the year, the community of **Quartzite** is little more than a few truck stops at an interstate off-ramp. However, the population explodes each year with the annual influx of winter visitors (also known as snowbirds), and from early January to mid-February the community is the site of numerous gem-and-mineral shows that attract more than a million rock hounds. Among these shows is the ✪ **Quartzsite Pow Wow,** which is held the first weekend in February and is the largest gem-and-mineral show in the world. If you're passing through during these months, you might want to check out one of these shows. During the winter months, Quartzite sprouts thousands of vendor stalls as flea markets and the like are erected along the town's main streets. A variety of interesting food makes this a great place to stop for lunch or dinner. For more information, contact the **Quartzsite Chamber of Commerce,** 1495 Main Event Lane (P.O. Box 85), Quartzsite, AZ 85346 (☎ **520/927-5600**).

For information on parking your RV in the desert outside Quartzsite, contact the **Bureau of Land Management,** Yuma Field Office, 2555 East Gila Ridge Rd., Yuma, AZ 85365 (☎ **520/317-3200**). Alternatively, you can get information and camping permits at the Long-Term Visitor Area entrance stations just south of Quartzsite on U.S. 95. The season here runs from September 15 to April 15, with permits going for $100 for the season and $20 for 7 consecutive days.

If ancient rock art interests you, be sure to watch for Plomosa Road as you travel between Parker and Quartzsite. Off this road, you'll find a 30-foot-long intaglio (or geoglyph) known as the **Bouse Fisherman.** This primitive image of a person spearing fish was formed by scratching away the rocky crust of the desert soil. Its origin and age are unknown, but it is believed to have been created centuries ago by native peoples and may depict the god Kumastamo, who created the Colorado River by thrusting a spear into the ground. To find this intaglio, drive 8 miles up Plomosa Road, which is approximately 6 miles north of Quartzsite, and watch for a wide parking area on the north side of the road. From here, follow the trail ¼ mile over a small hill.

Right in Quartzsite you'll find **Hi Jolly's Last Camp,** the pyramid-shaped stone monument and tomb of Hadji Ali (Hi Jolly), the Syrian camel driver who tended the camels of the U.S. Army's experimental camel corps from 1856 to 1864. You'll find the monument at the west end of town off Main Street, and though it's not particularly impressive, it commemorates a fascinating desert experiment of the 19th century.

There are only three places in Arizona where palm trees grow wild, and if you'd like to visit one of these spots, watch for the Palm Canyon turnoff 18 miles south of Quartzsite. Palm Canyon lies within the boundaries of the **Kofa National Wildlife Refuge,** which was formed primarily to protect the desert bighorn sheep that live here in the rugged Kofa Mountains. The palms are 8 miles off U.S. 95 in a narrow canyon a short walk from the end of the well-graded gravel road, and though there are only a couple of dozen trees, the hike to see them provides an opportunity to experience these mountains up close. Keep your eyes peeled for desert bighorn sheep. Incidentally, the Kofa Mountains took their name from the King of Arizona Mine. For maps and more information, contact the **Kofa National Wildlife Refuge,** 356 W. First St., Yuma, AZ 85364 (☎ **520/783-7861**).

## 5 Yuma

180 miles SW of Phoenix; 180 miles E of San Diego; 240 miles W of Tucson

Though you may never have heard of Yuma, Arizona, it was once one of the most important towns in the Southwest. Known as the Rome of the Southwest, all roads led to Yuma Crossing—the shallow spot along the Colorado River where Yuma was founded. Quechan Indians, Spanish missionaries and explorers, Kit Carson and his mountain men, '49ers heading for the gold fields of California, pioneers, and soldiers all passed through this narrows. Despite its location in the middle of the desert, Yuma

was also a busy port town when shallow
orado River from the Gulf of California
wars of the 1870s and 1880s, military su
forts and camps throughout the Southw
California in the 1870s, it also passed th
San Diego with Tucson and Phoenix, cro

Hotter than Phoenix, Yuma often reco
and the U.S. Weather Service says that Yu
Yuma's warm winters have made it the
snowbirds, who drive their RVs from as fa

photos of many of the 3,049 me
the years. After the prison wa
housing for the homeless

**Arizona Historical S**
**782-1841.** Free ad

If you'd like to
home, wh
dens a
exce

## ESSENTIALS

**GETTING THERE** Yuma is on I-8, w
Casa Grande, Arizona.

The Yuma Airport is at 2191 32nd St. and is served by **America West** (☎ **800/ 235-9292**).

There's **Amtrak** (☎ **800/872-7245**) passenger service to Yuma from Los Angeles and New Orleans. The station is on Gila Street.

**VISITOR INFORMATION** For more information about Yuma, contact the **Yuma Convention and Visitors Bureau,** 377 S. Main St., Yuma, AZ 85364 (☎ **800/ 293-0071** or 520/783-0071).

**GETTING AROUND** For a taxi, call **Yuma City Cab** (☎ **520/782-0111**). Rental cars are available in Yuma from **Avis** (☎ **800/331-1212** or 520/726-5737), **Budget** (☎ **800/527-0700** or 520/344-1822), **Enterprise** (☎ **800/325-8007** or 520/ 344-5444), and **Hertz** (☎ **800/654-3131** or 520/726-5160).

## HISTORIC SITES

✪ **Yuma Crossing State Historic Park.** 201 N. 4th Ave. (at the Colorado River). ☎ **520/ 329-0471.** Admission $3 adults, $2 children 7–13, free for children 6 and under. Daily 10am–5pm (closed Tues–Wed in summer). Closed Dec 25.

In 1865, Yuma Crossing, the narrow spot in the Colorado River where the town of Yuma sprang up, became the site of the military's Quartermaster Depot. Yuma was a busy river port during this time, and after supplies shipped from California were unloaded, they went to military posts throughout the region. When the railroad arrived in Yuma in 1877, the Quartermaster Depot began losing its importance in the regional supply network, and by 1883, the depot had been closed. Today the depot's large wooden buildings have been restored, and though they are now set back from the current channel of the Colorado River, it's easy to imagine being stationed at this hot and dusty outpost in the days before air-conditioning. Exhibits tell the story of those who lived and worked at Yuma Crossing, and a short video documents the town's story.

**Yuma Territorial Prison State Historic Park.** 1 Prison Hill Rd. ☎ **520/783-4771.** Admission $3 adults, $2 children 7–13, free for children 6 and under. Daily 8am–5pm. Closed Dec 25.

Yuma is one of the hottest places in the world, so it comes as no surprise that the Arizona Territory chose this bleak spot for a prison (although there is a nice view of the confluence of the Gila and Colorado rivers from Prison Hill). The prison first housed convicts in 1876 but operated for only 33 years before being replaced by a larger prison. Despite the thick stone walls and iron bars, this prison was considered a model penal institution in its day. It even had its own generating plant for electricity and a ventilation system. The prison museum has some interesting displays, including

and 29 women who were incarcerated at Yuma over
shut down, the building served as a high school and as
during the Depression.

**ociety Century House Museum.** 240 S. Madison Ave. ☎ **520/**
mission; $2 suggested donation. Tues–Sat 10am–4pm.

find out more about pioneer life in Yuma, stop by this territorial-period
ch is full of historical photographs and artifacts and surrounded by lush gar-
d aviaries full of exotic birds. Adjacent to the museum is the Garden Cafe, an
ent lunch spot.

## DOWNTOWN YUMA

Historic downtown Yuma isn't exactly a bustling place, and it doesn't abound in historic flavor, but the south-of-the-border atmosphere is well worth a visit. Huge well-shaped ficus trees provide deep shade, and at the center of the shopping district is a plaza similar to those found in towns all over Mexico. Funky and inexpensive crafts and antiques shops occupy an occasional storefront. An alleyway of shops off Main Street (at 224 Main St., across from Lutes Casino) has a potpourri of small tourist-oriented stores. Within just a couple of blocks of downtown, you can play in the sand or go for a stroll in Colorado River Crossing Beach Park, along the bank of the Colorado River. The park is at the north end of Madison Street.

## CAMELS, DATES & DESERT TOURING

A hundred years ago, there were camels wandering the deserts near here. No, they weren't native camels, they were just turned loose by the army after an experimental camel corps was disbanded. Today there are still camels, as well as other rare and interesting desert wildlife, in Yuma at the ✪ **Saihati Camel Farm,** 15672 S. Ave. 1E (☎ **520/627-2553**). Guided tours are offered October to May, Monday through Saturday at 10am and 2pm. Admission is $3, and reservations are recommended.

Date palms, that other symbol of the Middle East, also flourish here in the heat of the Arizona desert. Dates are among the most ancient of cultivated tree crops and were grown in the Middle East as far back as 3000 B.C. Right in Yuma, you'll find **Ehrlich's Date Garden,** 868 Ave. B (☎ **520/783-4778**), which sells nearly a dozen varieties of organically grown dates, as well as organic oranges. Prices are incredibly low, and the old-fashioned fruit stand is open daily from 9am to 5pm.

The Colorado River has been the lifeblood of the Southwestern desert for centuries, and today there's a wealth of history along its banks. **Yuma River Tours,** 1920 Arizona Ave. (☎ **520/783-4400**), operates narrated jet-boat tours from Yuma to the Imperial Wildlife Refuge (great bird watching) and an extended trip to Draper. Along the way, you'll learn about the homesteaders, boatmen, Native Americans, and miners who relied on the Colorado River. Tours, including lunch, cost $52 to $69. Alternatively, you can take a 3-hour paddle-wheel trip on the *Colorado King I* (☎ **520/782-2412**). Tours are $30 to $39 for adults and $20 for children 12 and under.

While the river was the reason for Yuma's existence, it was the railroad that finally forced the town to abandon its connection to the Colorado. Today, you can ride the rails on the historic **Yuma Valley Railway** (☎ **520/783-3456**), which offers 34-mile excursions along the Colorado River between October and May. Along the way you may spot birds and other wildlife on the banks of the river, and you'll get views of Mexico across the river and rich agricultural lands on this side. Passengers ride in a 1922 Pullman coach pulled by a 1952 Davenport-Beshler diesel-electric engine. Fares are $11 for adults, $10 for seniors, and $6 for children ages 4 to 16. There are also picnic and steak runs.

If you're a bird watcher, an angler, or a canoeist, you'll want to spend some time along the Colorado River north of Yuma. Here you'll find the **Imperial and Cibola National Wildlife Refuges,** with their lakes and marshes. Plenty of bird species, good fishing and canoeing, and several campgrounds make this a popular area. For more information on this area, contact the Imperial Refuge (☎ **520/783-3371**) or the Cibola Refuge (☎ **520/857-3250**). One of the best ways to explore the Imperial National Wildlife Refuge is from a canoe. Boats can be rented from **Martinez Lake Resort** (☎ **520/783-9589**) for $32 a day plus shuttle and delivery charges. Both 1- and 2-day canoe trips are possible along this stretch of the lower Colorado, which features rugged, colorful mountains and quiet backwater areas.

## GOLF

Golf courses cater to the snowbirds who descend on this area every winter. The **Mesa del Sol Golf Club,** 10583 Camino del Sol (☎ **520/342-1283**), off I-8 at the Fortuna Road exit, is the most challenging local course open to the public. On the other hand, the **Desert Hills Golf Course,** 1245 W. Desert Hills Dr. (☎ **520/344-GOLF**), has been rated the best municipal course in the state. Other area courses include the **Arroyo Dunes Golf Course,** 32nd Street and Avenue A (☎ **520/726-8350**), and the **Cocopah Bend RV Resort,** 6800 Strand Ave. (☎ **520/343-1663**). The 9-hole **Ironwood Public Golf Course,** 2945 W. Eighth St. (☎ **520/343-1466**), is worth a round if you're only in the mood for a quick nine holes.

## WHERE TO STAY
### MODERATE

**Best Western Inn Suites Hotel.** 1450 S. Castle Dome Ave., Yuma, AZ 85365-1732. ☎ **800/922-2034** or 520/783-8341. Fax 520/783-1349. 166 units. A/C TV TEL. $79–$159 double. Rates include continental breakfast. AE, DC, DISC, MC, V. Pets accepted.

If you've come to Yuma to escape the cold weather up north and want to enjoy some active sports, this hotel may be just what you're looking for. It has a pool, whirlpool, exercise room, and tennis courts, and there's a golf course nearby. The rooms are divided between studios and one- and two-bedroom suites; all have microwave ovens, coffeemakers, refrigerators, and hair dryers. P. J.'s Poolside Café serves breakfast, sandwiches, snacks, and cocktails. The hotel also offers complimentary afternoon cocktails.

**La Fuente Inn.** 1513 E. 16th St., Yuma, AZ 85365. ☎ **800/841-1814** or 520/329-1814. Fax 520/343-2671. 96 units. A/C TV TEL. $78–$99 double. Rates include continental breakfast. AE, CB, DC, DISC, MC, V.

Conveniently located just off the interstate at 16th Street, this appealing hotel is done in Spanish-colonial style with red-tile roof, pink stucco walls, and a fountain out front. The theme continues in the lobby with rustic furnishings and a tile floor. French doors open onto the pool terrace and a large courtyard, around which the guest rooms are arranged. Standard rooms feature modern motel furnishings, while the well-designed suites offer much more space. The hotel also offers complimentary evening happy hour, whirlpool, fitness room (and use of a nearby fitness center).

**Shilo Inn.** 1550 S. Castle Dome Rd., Yuma, AZ 85365-1702. ☎ **800/222-2244** or 520/782-9511. Fax 520/783-1538. 134 units. A/C TV TEL. $79–$105 double; $121–$155 suite. Rates include full breakfast. AE, CB, DC, DISC, MC, V. Small supervised pets accepted ($7).

Located on the edge of town overlooking farmland and desert, the Shilo Inn is Yuma's most luxurious hotel, and the neatly manicured gardens provide an oasis of greenery in this dry landscape. The guest rooms have comfortable chairs, couches, and patios, as well as microwaves, refrigerators, and VCRs. In the bathrooms you'll find plenty of counter space and a hair dryer. The hotel's more expensive rooms are those with a view of the desert. For long-term stays, there are also suites with kitchenettes. The hotel's casual dining room offers both indoor and terrace dining, and to one side of the dining room is a lounge that often has live music on weekends. The hotel also offers room service, a large pool, whirlpool, exercise room, sauna, and steam room.

## INEXPENSIVE

In addition to numerous older budget motels, Yuma has several newer budget chain motels. These include the **Airport Travelodge,** 711 E. 32nd St. (☎ **520/726-4721**), charging $54 to $74 double; **Days Inn,** 1671 E. 16th St. (☎ **520/329-7790**), charging $50 to $90 double; **Motel 6,** with one location at 1445 E. 16th St. (☎ **520/782-9521**), charging $36 to $48 double and another location at 1640 S. Arizona Ave (☎ **520/782-6561**), charging $34 to $46 double; and **Super 8,** 1688 S. Riley Ave. (☎ **520/782-2000**), charging $53 to $76 double. See appendix B for toll-free numbers.

## WHERE TO DINE

**California Bakery Company.** 284 S. Main St. ☎ **520/782-7335.** Reservations recommended. Lunch items $5–$8; main courses $8–$25 at dinner. AE, MC, V. Mon–Wed 8am–9pm, Thurs–Sat 8am–10pm. REGIONAL AMERICAN.

With decor more like what you'd find in Scottsdale or Santa Monica, this cavernous restaurant seems out of place in downtown Yuma, but the contemporary setting is quite welcome in this otherwise very traditional town. The owners seem to want to cover all the bases; within these walls you'll find a bakery, an espresso bar, a bar, and a restaurant (and there's live music on weekends). The menu isn't quite as contemporary as the interior decor, but you can get linguine with fresh mussels, grilled chicken with a "secret" tequila-orange sauce, pecan-encrusted catfish, and lamb shanks braised in wine sauce. The smoked salmon rolls are a nibble-perfect appetizer. Definitely a step above burgers and fries.

✪ **The Garden Cafe.** 250 Madison Ave. ☎ **520/783-1491.** Main courses $5–$8.25. AE, MC, V. Tues–Fri 9am–2:30pm, Sat–Sun 8am–2:30pm. BREAKFAST/SANDWICHES/SALADS.

In back of the Century House Museum, you'll find Yuma's favorite breakfast and lunch cafe. Set amid quiet terraced gardens and large aviaries full of singing birds, The Garden Cafe provides a welcome respite from Yuma's heat. On the hottest days, misters spray the air with a gentle fog that keeps the gardens cool. There's also an indoor dining area. The menu consists of various delicious sandwiches, daily special quiches, salads, and rich desserts. Pancakes with lingonberry sauce are a breakfast specialty. On Sunday there's a brunch buffet. This place is a favorite of the ladies' lunch crowd and retirees.

✪ **Lutes Casino.** 221 S. Main St. ☎ **520/782-2192.** Main courses $3–$6. No credit cards. Mon–Fri 9am–8pm, Fri–Sat 9am–9pm, Sun 9am–6pm. BURGERS/SANDWICHES.

You won't find any slot machines or poker tables at Lutes Casino anymore, just lots of very serious domino players (this is the state's only domino parlor). Today Lute's is a dark and cavernous pool hall, but it's better known as a family restaurant serving the best hamburgers in town. You don't need to see a menu—just walk in and ask for a special, or *especial* (this is a bilingual joint). What you'll get is a cheeseburger/hot dog combo. Then cover your special with Lute's own secret-recipe hot sauce to make it truly special.

# Appendix A: Arizona in Depth

**D**espite the searing summer temperatures in the deserts that cover much of Arizona, people have been lured to this state for generations. In the 16th century, the Spanish came looking for gold—but settled for saving souls. In the 19th century, cattle ranchers came (despite frightful tales of spiny cactus forests) and found that a few corners of the state were covered with lush grasslands. At the same time, sidetracked '49ers were scouring the hills for gold (and found more than the Spanish did). However, boom towns—both cattle and mining— soon went bust. Despite occasional big strikes (such as the silver strike at Tombstone), mining didn't prove itself until the early 20th century, and even then, the mother lode was not gold or silver, but rather copper, which Arizona has in such abundance that it's called the Copper State.

In the 1920s and 1930s, Arizona struck a new vein of gold. The railroads made travel to Arizona easy, and the word of the mild winter climate spread to colder corners of the nation. Among the first "vacationers" were people suffering from tuberculosis. These "lungers," as they were known, rested and recuperated in the dry desert air. It didn't take long for the perfectly healthy to realize that they, too, could enjoy winter in Arizona, and wintering in the desert soon became fashionable with wealthy northerners.

Today it's still the golden sun that lures people to Arizona. Scottsdale, Phoenix, Tucson, and Sedona are home to some of the most luxurious and expensive resorts in the country, and more are under construction. The state has also seen a massive influx of retirees, many of whom have found the few pockets of Arizona where the climate is absolutely perfect—not too hot, not too cold, and plenty of sunshine.

Although it's the Grand Canyon that attracts the most visitors to Arizona, the state has plenty of other natural wonders. The largest natural travertine bridge in the world, the largest meteorite crater, the spectacular red-rock country of Sedona, the sandstone buttes of Monument Valley, and "forests" of saguaro cacti are just a few of the state's other natural spectacles.

The human hand has also left its mark on Arizona. More than 1,000 years ago, the Anasazi, Sinagua, and Hohokam tribes built villages on mesas, in valleys, and in the steep cliff walls of deep canyons. In more recent years, much larger structures have risen in canyons across the state. The Hoover and Glen Canyon dams on the Colorado River are among the largest dams in the country and have created the nation's largest and most spectacular reservoirs, although at the expense of the rich riparian areas that once filled the now flooded desert canyons. Today these reservoirs are among the state's most popular destinations, especially with Arizonans, who flock to the water with an amazing variety of high-powered watercraft.

Just as compelling as its sunshine, resorts, and reservoirs are the tall tales of Arizona's fascinating history. This is the Wild West, the land of cowboys and Indians, of prospectors and ghost towns, coyotes and rattlesnakes. Scratch the glossy surface of modern, urbanized Arizona and you'll strike real gold—the story of the American West.

## 1 The Natural Environment

Though the very mention of Arizona may cause some people to turn the air conditioner on full blast, this state is much more than a searing landscape of cactus and creosote bush. From the baking shores of the lower Colorado River to the snowcapped heights of the San Francisco Peaks, Arizona encompasses virtually every climatic zone. Cactus flowers bloom in the spring, and mountain wildflowers have their turn in summer. In autumn the aspens color the White Mountains golden, and in winter snows blanket the higher elevations from the north rim of the Grand Canyon almost to the Mexican border.

But it's the Sonoran Desert, with its massive saguaro cacti, that most people associate with Arizona, and it is here in the desert that the state's two largest cities—Phoenix and Tucson—are found. In large part due to the relatively plentiful rains here, the Sonoran Desert is among the world's most biologically diverse deserts. Rain falls both during the winter and the late-summer monsoon season (when clamorous thunderstorms send flash floods surging down arroyos). Before the coming of dams and deep wells, many rivers and streams flowed year-round and nurtured a surprising variety of plants and animals. Today only a few rivers and creeks still flow unaltered through the desert. These include Sonoita and Aravaipa creeks and the San Pedro, Verde, and Hassayampa rivers. The green riparian areas along these watercourses are characterized by the rare cottonwood-willow forest and serve as magnets for wildlife, harboring rare birds as well as fish species that are unique to Arizona.

The saguaro cactus, which can stand 40 feet tall and weigh several tons, is the Sonoran Desert's most conspicuous native inhabitant. Massive and many-armed, these are the cacti of comic strips and Hollywood Westerns. But there are also many other lesser-known species of cactus, such as the organ pipe cactus (closely related to the saguaro), the barrel cactus, and various species of prickly pears and chollas, all of which have adapted to this harsh environment by storing water in their stems, growing without leaves, and both protecting and shading themselves with spines. Despite spiny defenses, cacti are still a source of food and shelter for many species of desert animals. Bats sip the nectar from saguaro flowers, and in the process act as pollinators. Javelinas, which are similar to wild pigs and are also known as collared peccaries, chow

### Impressions

*Do nothing to mar its grandeur . . . keep it for your children, your children's children, all who come after you, as the one great sight which every American should see.*

—Pres. Theodore Roosevelt, after visiting the Grand Canyon in 1903

# Arizona: Hollywood Back Lot

Spectacular landscapes, rugged deserts, ghost towns, and the cowboy mystique have, over the years, made Arizona the location for hundreds of films. From obscure B Westerns starring long-forgotten singing cowboys to the seminal works of John Ford, Arizona has provided a stunning backdrop to stories of life in the Wild West. This state has become so associated with the Old West that Europeans, Asians, and Australians come from halfway around the world to walk where John Wayne once swaggered and where Clint Eastwood cultivated his outlaw image.

Arizona's landscape is so varied that over the years it has managed to double for Texas, Kansas, Mexico, foreign planets, a postapocalyptic earth, and even New York. It has represented the past, the present, and the future. Production companies working on movies, television shows, and commercials have traveled to every corner of the state to find just the right setting for their productions.

A movie set was built in Tucson in 1939 for the filming of the movie *Arizona,* and when the filming was over, the set was left to be used in other productions. Today this mock-Western town is known as Old Tucson Studios and is still used for film and video productions. Movies that have been filmed here include *Tombstone;* John Wayne's *Rio Lobo, Rio Bravo,* and *El Dorado;* Clint Eastwood's *The Outlaw Josey Wales;* Kirk Douglas's *Gunfight at the O.K. Corral;* and Paul Newman's *The Life and Times of Judge Roy Bean.*

Though John Ford was not the first to film at Monument Valley, he made this otherworldly landscape a trademark of his filmmaking, using the valley as the backdrop for such films as *Stagecoach, She Wore a Yellow Ribbon, My Darling Clementine, Rio Grande,* and *The Searchers.* Other Westerns filmed here have included *How the West Was Won, The Legend of the Lone Ranger,* and *Mackenna's Gold.* The valley has also shown up in such non-Western films as *Back to the Future III, 2001: A Space Odyssey, Thelma and Louise,* and *Forrest Gump.* The red rocks of Sedona have also attracted many filmmakers over the years. *Broken Arrow, 3:10 to Yuma, The Riders of the Purple Sage,* and *The Call of the Canyon* were all filmed in Sedona and the nearby Oak Creek Canyon.

Patagonia, in southeastern Arizona, is another town that has served as a backdrop for quite a few films, including *Oklahoma, Red River, McClintock, Broken Lance, David and Bathsheba,* and *A Star Is Born,* and television programs including *Little House on the Prairie, The Young Riders,* and *Red Badge of Courage.*

down on the prickly pear fruit—spines and all. Gila woodpeckers nest in holes in saguaro trunks, while cactus wrens build their nests in the branches of the cholla cactus.

Just as cacti have adapted to the desert, so, too, have the animals that live here. Many desert animals spend the sweltering days in burrows and only venture out in the cool of the night. Under cover of darkness, rattlesnakes and great horned owls hunt kangaroo rats, coyotes howl, and javelinas root about for anything edible. Gila lizards, among the only poisonous lizards in the world, drag their ungainly bodies through the dust, while tarantulas tiptoe silently in search of unwary insects.

Outside the desert regions there is great diversity as well. In the southern part of the state, small mountain ranges rise abruptly from the desert floor, creating refuges for plants and animals that require cooler climates. It is these so-called mountain or sky islands that harbor the greatest varieties of bird species in the continental United States. Birds from both warm and cold climates find homes in such oases as Ramsey, Madera, and Cave Creek canyons.

Although rugged mountain ranges crisscross the state, only a few rise to such heights that they support actual forests. Among these are the Santa Catalinas outside Tucson, the White Mountains along the state's eastern border, and the San Francisco Peaks north of Flagstaff. However, it's atop the Mogollon Rim and the Kaibab Plateau that the ponderosa pine forests cover the greatest areas. The Mogollon Rim is a 2,000-foot-high escarpment that stretches from central Arizona all the way into New Mexico. The ponderosa pine forest here is the largest in the world and is dotted with lakes well known for their fishing. The Mogollon Rim area is also home to large herds of elk. At over 8,000 feet in elevation, the Kaibab Plateau is even higher than the Mogollon Rim, yet it is through this plateau that the Grand Canyon cuts.

This then is the natural environment of Arizona, a land of extremes where summer temperatures in the Sonoran Desert top 120°F while snow still lies atop the San Francisco Peaks. Life here has adapted to these extremes in fascinating ways that are still being deciphered by biologists throughout the state.

## 2  Arizona Today

Combining aspects of Indian, Hispanic, and European cultures, Arizona is one of the most culturally diverse states in the country. Here the Old West and the "New West" coexist. While the wealthy residents of Scottsdale raise Arabian horses as investments, the Navajos of the Four Corners region still raise sheep for sustenance and wool, herding their flocks from the backs of hard-working horses. Vacationers on Lake Powell water-ski through flooded canyons while cowboys in the southeast corner of the state still ride the range, mending fences and rounding up cattle.

Although Arizonans are today more likely to drive Hondas and Toyotas than to ride pintos and appaloosas, Western wear is still the preferred fashion of rich and poor alike. Cowboy boots, cowboy hats, blue jeans, and bolo ties are acceptable attire at almost any function in Arizona. Horses are still used on ranches around the state, but most are kept simply for recreational or investment purposes. In Scottsdale, one of the nation's centers of Arabian horse breeding, horse auctions attract a well-heeled (read lizard-skin-booted) crowd, and horses sell for tens of thousands of dollars. Even the state's dude ranches, which now call themselves "guest ranches," have changed their image, and many are as likely to offer tennis and swimming as horseback riding.

A long legacy of movies being filmed here has further blurred the line between the real West and the Hollywood West. More city slickers wander the streets of the Old Tucson movie set and videotape shoot-outs at the O.K. Corral than ever saddle up a palomino or ride herd on a cattle drive. Even dinner has been raised to a cowboy entertainment form at Arizona's many Wild West steakhouses, where families are entertained by cowboy bands, staged gunfights, hayrides, and sing-alongs, all in the name of reliving the glory days of "cowboys and Indians."

For Arizona's Indians, those were days of hardship and misery, and today the state's many tribes continue to strive for the sort of economic well-being enjoyed by the state's nonnative population. However, traditional ways are still alive, though tribes must struggle to preserve their unique cultures—their languages, religious beliefs and ceremonies, livelihoods, and architecture.

Arizona is home to the largest Indian reservation in the country—the Navajo nation—as well as nearly two dozen other smaller reservations. As elsewhere in the United States, poverty and alcoholism are major problems on Arizona reservations. However, several of the state's tribes have, through their arts and crafts, managed to both preserve some of their traditional culture and share it with nonnatives. Among these tribes are the Navajo, known for their rugs and silver jewelry; the Hopi, known for their pottery and kachinas; the Zuni, known for their inlaid stone jewelry; and the Tohono O'odham, known for their baskets.

Lately, however, many nonnatives have been visiting reservations not out of an interest in learning about another culture, but to gamble. Throughout the state, casinos have opened on reservation land, and despite the controversies surrounding such enterprises, many native peoples are finally seeing some income on their once-impoverished reservations.

Many of the people who visit these new casinos are senior citizens, who are among the fastest growing segment of Arizona's population. The mild winter climate in Arizona has attracted tens of thousands of retirees to the state over the past few decades. Many of these winter residents, known as snowbirds, park their RVs outside such warm spots as Yuma and Quartzsite. Others, however, have come to stay and have settled in retirement communities such as Sun City and Green Valley.

This graying of the population, combined with strong ranching and mining industries, has made Arizona one of the most conservative of states. Though by today's standards Barry Goldwater could almost be considered a liberal, his conservative politics were so much a part of the Arizona mindset that the state kept him in the Senate for 30 years.

However, recent years have been more characterized by political controversies than the traditional battle between conservatives and liberals. When Arizona, under Gov. Evan Mecham, chose not to recognize the Martin Luther King Jr. holiday, the state was branded racist and lost millions of dollars in potential income from conventions and sporting events (including the Super Bowl) that, in protest, chose not to come to Arizona. The state finally acquiesced to public opinion and agreed to observe the holiday, which is perhaps one reason why Phoenix finally was able to host the Super Bowl in 1996.

The controversial Governor Mecham was convicted in 1988 of illegally loaning state funds to his automobile dealership and of trying to block an investigation into charges that an aide made a death threat against a grand jury witness. (Mecham was succeeded by Rose Mofford, the state's first woman governor.)

Within 3 years controversy again threw Arizona into the national limelight as Charles Keating was convicted of defrauding Lincoln Savings and Loan customers of $250 million. At least some of the money went into the ostentatious Phoenician resort in Scottsdale and a smaller sister hotel, the Crescent, in Phoenix.

In 1997, politics and fraud once again made Arizona headlines as Gov. Fife Symington was convicted in federal court of defrauding a bank when he was a real estate developer. The conviction led to Symington's resignation as governor.

Arizona's environmental politics have also seen their share of battles in recent years. Though many people think of the desert as a wasteland in need of transformation, others see it as a fragile ecosystem that has been endangered by the encroachment of civilization. Although saguaro cacti throughout the state are protected by law, the deserts they grow in are not. In Tucson, environmentalists have for several years been fighting (with limited success) to stop the suburban sprawl that's pushing farther and farther into saguaro country. The balance in this battle tipped in favor of preservation when rare ferruginous pygmy owls were found nesting in the Tucson area.

Way up at the north end of the state, remote Grand Canyon National Park is suffering from its own popularity. With more than 5 million visitors a year, the park now sees summer traffic jams and parking problems that have made a visit an exercise in patience. However, in 1998 Grand Canyon National Park finally announced plans to develop a combination light rail and alternative-fuel bus system for transporting visitors to and around the South Rim and Grand Canyon Village. By having day-use visitors leave their cars outside the park and take the light rail to the South Rim, much of the park's traffic congestion should be alleviated. This new transportation system is not expected to be completed until 2002, but by late 2000 the new Canyon View Information Plaza should be open to the public. It will serve as the new visitor information center for the park.

Likewise, attempts are being made to restore the Colorado River at the bottom of the Grand Canyon to a closer approximation of the river it once was. In early 1996, an attempt to duplicate the traditional spring floods that the Colorado River experienced before the construction of the Glen Canyon Dam demonstrated that a more controlled use of waters from Lake Powell could be beneficial to the Grand Canyon. The goal of the experiment was to try to duplicate the sort of seasonal deposition of sand and silt that used to occur along the riverbanks before the construction of the dam. The experiment was successful, and it is likely that this seasonal artificial flooding will become a part of future river policy.

Efforts at preserving the state's environment make it clear that Arizonans value the outdoors, but a ski boat in every driveway doesn't mean that the arts are ignored. Although it hasn't been too many years since evening entertainment in Arizona meant dance-hall girls or a harmonica by the campfire, Phoenix and Tucson have become centers for both the visual and the performing arts. The two cities share both an opera company and a ballet company, and the Valley of the Sun is also home to a number of symphony orchestras and theater companies. Early 1999 saw the opening of both the Scottsdale Museum of Contemporary Art and a newly expanded Heard Museum. In Tucson, the Tucson Museum of Art has also undergone a facelift and expansion.

Small towns around the state are also supporting the arts. Whole communities such as Jerome, Tubac, and Bisbee, all nearly ghost towns at one time, have been reborn as arts communities. Where miners and outlaws once walked, artists now offer their creations for sale.

Tourism continues to boom in Arizona, and after a decade-long construction lull, new resorts are in the works in both the Valley of the Sun and Tucson. In particular, the north Scottsdale area, which has seen a residential building boom in recent years, is now seeing the construction of luxury resorts. Downtown Phoenix has now positioned itself as the state's sports and entertainment Mecca, with Bank One Ballpark, the America West Arena, and numerous sports bars, nightclubs, and even a combination barbecue joint and sports bar operated by former rock star Alice Cooper.

In Arizona today, the New West and the Old West are coming to grips with each other. Hopi perform their age-old dances atop their mesas, urban cowboys and cowgirls line dance in nightclubs around the state, grizzled wranglers lead vacationing Germans on horseback rides across open range, and ranchers find that they have something in common with environmentalists—saving Arizona's ranch lands.

## 3 History 101

Over the past five centuries, the land now known as Arizona has been Native American territory and part of New Spain, Mexico, and the United States. Early explorers and settlers saw little profit in the desert wasteland, but time proved them wrong: mineral resources, cattle grazing, and particularly cotton (after dams began providing irrigation water) all became important income sources. In this century, the economy has moved from the three Cs (copper, cattle, and cotton) to a service industries–based economy, with tourism as one of its major resources.

**EARLY HISTORY** Arizona is the site of North America's oldest cultures and one of the two longest continuously inhabited settlements in the United States (the Hopi village of Oraibi). However, the region's human habitation dates back much further even than the ancient culture that built Oraibi. More than 11,000 years ago, Paleo-Indians known as the Clovis people lived in southeastern Arizona. In this region of the state, stone tools and arrowheads of the type credited to the Clovis people have been found. A mammoth-kill site has also been discovered and has become an important source of information about these people, some of the earliest inhabitants of North America.

Few records exist of the next 9,000 years of Arizona's history, but by about A.D. 200, wandering bands of hunter-gatherers began living in Canyon de Chelly in the north. These people would come to be known as the *Anasazi*, a Navajo word that means "the ancient ones." The earliest Anasazi period, from A.D. 200 to 700, is called the Basket Maker period because of the numbers of baskets that have been found in Anasazi ruins from this time. During this period the Anasazi gave up hunting and gathering and took up agriculture, growing corn, beans, squash, and cotton on the canyon floors in northeastern Arizona.

During the Pueblo period, between 700 and 1300, the Anasazi began building multistory pueblos (villages) and cliff dwellings. Despite decades of research, it is still unknown why the

### Dateline

- **9700 B.C.** Paleo-Indians (the Clovis people) in southeastern Arizona are among the earliest recorded inhabitants of North America.
- **A.D. 200** The Anasazi people move into Canyon de Chelly.
- **450** Hohokam peoples farm the Salt and Gila river Valleys, eventually building 600 miles of irrigation canals.
- **650** The Sinagua cultivate land northeast of present-day Flagstaff.
- **1100s** Hopi tribes build Oraibi village, the oldest continuously occupied village in the United States; the Anasazi build cliff dwellings in Canyon de Chelly; the Sinagua build Wupatki.
- **1250** The Sinagua abandon Wupatki and other pueblos.
- **1300** The Anasazi abandon cliff dwellings in Canyon de Chelly and Tsegi Canyon.
- **1350** The Hohokam build Casa Grande in the Gila River valley.
- **1400s** The Navajo peoples migrate south from Canada to northeastern Arizona.
- **1450** The Hohokam abandon lowland desert villages; the Sinagua abandon Verde Valley villages.
- **1539** Marcos de Niza ventures into present-day Arizona from Mexico (New Spain) in search of the Seven Cities of Cíbola.
- **1540s** Francisco Vásquez de Coronado leads an expedition to Arizona in search of gold.

*continues*

- **1691** Jesuit Fr. Eusebio Kino begins converting Native Americans.
- **1751** The mission of Tumacacori and the presidio of Tubac are established, the first European settlement in Arizona.
- **1776** A Spanish garrison is posted in Tucson to protect the mission of San Xavier del Bac.
- **1821** Mexico gains independence from Spain and takes control of Arizona.
- **1848** Most of present-day Arizona is ceded to the United States following the Mexican-American War.
- **1853** In the Gadsden Purchase, the United States acquires the remainder of Arizona from Mexico.
- **1862** Arizona becomes the Confederate Territory of Arizona but is reclaimed by the Union later that same year.
- **1863** Arizona becomes a U.S. territory.
- **1886** Geronimo surrenders to the U.S. Army.
- **1911** Theodore Roosevelt Dam, on the Salt River, enables irrigation and development of the desert.
- **1912** Arizona becomes the 48th state.
- **1919** Grand Canyon National Park established.
- **1936** Hoover Dam completed.
- **1948** Arizona Indians receive the right to vote.
- **1963** U.S. Supreme Court upholds Arizona's claim to Colorado River water.
- **1974** Construction begins on the Central Arizona Project aqueducts.
- **1975** Raul Castro becomes the first Hispanic governor of Arizona.
- **1981** Arizona judge Sandra Day O'Connor becomes the first woman appointed to the U.S. Supreme Court.

*continues*

Anasazi began living in niches and caves high on the cliff walls of the region's canyons. It may have been to conserve farmland as their population grew and required larger harvests or for protection from flash floods or attacks by hostile neighbors. Whatever the reason, the Anasazi cliff dwellings were all abandoned by 1300. It's also unknown why the villages were abandoned, but a study of tree rings indicates that the region experienced a severe drought between 1276 and 1299, which suggests that the Anasazi left in search of more-fertile farmland. Keet Seel and Betatakin, at Navajo National Monument, and the many ruins in Canyon de Chelly, are Arizona's best-preserved Anasazi ruins.

During the Anasazi Basket Maker period, another culture was beginning to develop in the fertile plateau northeast of present-day Flagstaff and southward into the Verde River valley. The *Sinagua,* a Spanish name that means "without water," built their stone pueblos primarily on hills and mesas such as those at Tuzigoot near Clarkdale and Wupatki near Flagstaff. They also built cliff dwellings at places such as Walnut Canyon and Montezuma Castle. However, by the mid–13th century, Wupatki had been abandoned by the Sinagua, and by the early 15th century Walnut Canyon and pueblos in the lower Verde Valley region had also been abandoned.

By A.D. 450 the Hohokam culture, from whom the Sinagua learned irrigation, had begun to farm the Gila and Salt river valleys between Phoenix and Casa Grande. Over a period of 1,000 years, they constructed a 600-mile network of irrigation canals, some of which can still be seen today. Because the Hohokam built their homes of earth, few Hohokam ruins remain. However, one building, the Casa Grande ruin, has been well preserved, and throughout the desert the Hohokam left **petroglyphs** (rock carvings) as a lasting reminder that they once dwelt in this region. By the 1450s, the tribe had abandoned its villages and disappeared without a sign, hence the name *Hohokam,* a Tohono O'odham word meaning "all used up" or "the people who have gone." Archaeologists believe that the irrigation of desert soil for hundreds of years had left a thick crust of alkali on the surface, which made farming impossible.

**HISPANIC HERITAGE** The first Europeans to visit the region may have been a motley crew of shipwrecked Spaniards among whom was a black man named Estévan de Dorantes. This unfortunate group spent 8 years wandering from a beach in Florida to a Spanish village in Mexico. These wanderers arrived back in Spanish territory with a fantastic story of seven cities filled with goldsmiths, where doorways were encrusted with jewels. No one is sure whether they actually passed through Arizona, but their story convinced the viceroy of New Spain (Mexico) to send a small expedition, led by Fr. Marcos de Niza and Estévan de Dorantes, into the region. Father de Niza's report of finding the fabled Seven Cities of Cíbola also inspired Don Francisco Vásquez de Coronado to set off in search of wealth. However, instead of fabulously wealthy cities, Coronado found only pueblos of stone and mud. A subordinate expedition led by Garcia Lopez de Cárdenas stumbled upon the Grand Canyon, while another group of Coronado's men, led by Don Pedro de Tovar, visited the Hopi mesas.

In the 150 years that followed, only a handful of Spaniards visited Arizona. In the 1580s and 1600s, Antonio de Espejo and Juan de Oñate explored northern and central Arizona and found indications that there were mineral riches in the region. In the 1670s, the Franciscans founded several missions among the Hopi pueblos, but the Pueblo Revolt of 1680 obliterated this small Spanish presence.

- **1985** The Central Arizona Project begins delivering water to Phoenix.
- **1988** Gov. Evan Mecham removed from office.
- **1991** A California jury finds Charles Keating guilty of defrauding Arizona investors who had deposited funds with Lincoln Savings and Loan.
- **1992** A Tucson jury awards $3 billion in damages to investors who were defrauded in the failed Lincoln Savings and Loan.
- **1996** After the state finally recognizes the Martin Luther King Jr. holiday, Super Bowl XXX is played in Tempe's Sun Devil Stadium.
- **1997** Gov. Fife Symington is convicted of bank fraud and resigns as governor.
- **1998** Former Arizona Sen. Barry Goldwater, one of America's most influential and outspoken conservative leaders, dies. Bank One Ballpark, with retractable roof, opens in Phoenix.

In 1687, Fr. Eusebio Francisco Kino, a German-educated Italian Jesuit, began establishing missions in the Sonoran Desert region of northern New Spain. In 1691, he visited the Pima village of Tumacacori. Father Kino taught the inhabitants European farming techniques, planted fruit trees, and gave the natives cattle, sheep, and goats to raise. However, it was not until 1751, in response to a Pima rebellion, that the permanent mission of Tumacacori and the presidio (military post) of Tubac were built. Together these two Spanish outposts became the first European settlements in Arizona.

In 1775, a group of settlers led by Juan Bautista de Anza set out from Tubac to find an overland route to California, and in 1776 this group founded the city of San Francisco. That same year the Tubac presidio was moved to Tucson. As early as 1692 Father Kino had visited the Tucson area and by 1700 had laid out the foundations for the first church at the mission of San Xavier del Bac. However, it was not until sometime around 1783 that construction of the present church, known as the White Dove of the Desert, began.

In 1821, Mexico won its independence from Spain, and Tucson, with only 65 inhabitants, became part of Mexico. Mexico at that time extended all the way to northern California, but in 1848 most of this land, except for a small section of southern Arizona that included Tucson, became U.S. territory in the wake of the Mexican-American War. Five years later, in 1853, Mexico sold the remainder of southern Arizona to the United States in a transaction known as the Gadsden Purchase.

**INDIAN CONFLICTS** At the time that the Spanish arrived in Arizona, the tribes living in the southern lowland deserts were peaceful farmers, while in the mountains of the east lived the Apache, a hunting-and-gathering tribe that frequently raided neighboring tribes. In the north, the Navajo, relatively recent immigrants to the region, fought over land with the neighboring Hopi (who were also fighting among themselves) and Ute.

Coronado's expedition through Arizona and into New Mexico and Kansas was to seek gold. To that end he attacked one pueblo, killed the inhabitants of another, and forced still others to abandon their villages. Spanish-Indian relations were never to improve, and the Spanish were forced to occupy their new lands with a strong military presence. Around 1600, three hundred Spanish settlers moved into the Four Corners region, which at the time supported a large population of Navajo. The Spanish raided Navajo villages to take slaves, and angry Navajo responded by stealing Spanish horses and cattle.

For several decades in the mid-1600s, missionaries were tolerated in the Hopi pueblos, but the Pueblo tribes revolted in 1680, killing the missionaries and destroying the missions. Encroachment by farmers and miners moving into the Santa Cruz Valley in the south caused the Pima people to stage a similar uprising in 1751, attacking and burning the mission at Tubac. This revolt led to the establishment of the presidio at Tubac that same year. When the military garrison moved to Tucson, Tubac was quickly abandoned because of frequent raids by Apaches. In 1781, the Yuman tribe, whose land at the confluence of the Colorado and Gila Rivers had become a Spanish settlement, staged a similar uprising that wiped out the settlement at Yuma.

By the time Arizona became part of the United States, it was the Navajo and the Apache who were proving most resistant to white settlers. In 1864 the U.S. Army, under the leadership of Col. Kit Carson, forced the Navajo to surrender by destroying their winter food supplies and then shipped the survivors to an internment camp in New Mexico. Within 5 years they were returned to their land, though they were now forced to live on a reservation.

The Apache resisted white settlement 20 years longer than the Navajo did. Skillful guerrilla fighters, the Apache, under the leadership of Geronimo and Cochise, attacked settlers, forts, and towns despite the presence of U.S. Army troops sent to protect the white settlers. Geronimo and Cochise were the leaders of the last resistant bands of rebellious Apache. Cochise eventually died in his Chiricahua Mountains homeland, and Geronimo was finally forced to surrender in 1886. Geronimo and many of his followers were subsequently relocated to Florida by the U.S. government. Open conflicts between whites and Indians finally came to an end.

**TERRITORIAL DAYS** In 1846, the United States went to war with Mexico, which at the time extended all the way to northern California and included parts of Colorado, Wyoming, and New Mexico. When the war ended, the United States claimed almost all the land extending from Texas to northern California. This newly acquired land, called the New Mexico Territory, had its capital at Santa Fe. The land south of the Gila River, which included Tucson, was still part of Mexico, but when surveys determined that this land was the best route for a railroad from southern Mississippi to southern California, the U.S. government negotiated the Gadsden Purchase. In 1853, this land purchase established the current Arizona-Mexico border.

When the California Gold Rush began in 1849, many hopeful miners crossed Arizona en route to the goldfields, and some stayed to seek mineral riches in Arizona. Despite the ever-increasing numbers of settlers, the U.S. Congress refused to create a separate Arizona Territory. When the Civil War broke out, Arizonans, angered by Congress's inaction on their request to become a separate territory, sided with the Confederacy; in 1862, Arizona was proclaimed the Confederate Territory of Arizona. Although Union troops easily defeated the Confederate troops who had occupied Tucson, this dissension convinced Congress, in 1863, to create the Arizona Territory.

The capital of the new territory was temporarily established at Fort Whipple near Prescott, but later the same year the capital was moved to Prescott, and in 1867 to Tucson. Ten years later Prescott again became the capital, which it remained for another 12 years before the seat of government moved finally to Phoenix, which is today the Arizona state capital.

During this period mining flourished, and though small amounts of gold and silver were discovered, copper became the source of Arizona's economic wealth. With each mineral strike, a new mining town would boom, and when the ore ran out, the town would be abandoned. These towns were infamous for their gambling halls, bordellos, saloons, and shoot-outs in the street. Tombstone and Bisbee became the largest towns in the state and were known as the wildest towns between New Orleans and San Francisco.

In 1867, farmers in the newly founded town of Phoenix began irrigating their fields using canals that had been dug centuries earlier by the Hohokam. In the 1870s, ranching became another important source of revenue in the territory, particularly in the southeastern and northwestern parts of the state. In the 1880s, the railroads finally arrived, and life in Arizona began to change drastically. Suddenly the mineral resources and cattle of the region were accessible to the East.

**STATEHOOD & THE 20TH CENTURY** By the beginning of the 20th century, Arizonans were trying to convince Congress to make the territory a state. Congress balked at the requests, but finally, in 1910, allowed the territorial government to draw up a state constitution. Territorial legislators were progressive thinkers and the draft of Arizona's state constitution included clauses for the recall of elected officials. Pres. William Howard Taft vetoed the bill that would have made Arizona a state because he opposed the recall of judges. Arizona politicians removed the controversial clause, and on February 14, 1912, Arizona became the 48th state. One of the new state legislature's first acts was to reinstate the clause providing for the recall of judges.

Much of Washington's opposition to Arizona's statehood had been based on the belief that Arizona could never support economic development. This belief was changed in 1911 by one of the most important events in Arizona history—the completion of the Roosevelt Dam (later to be renamed the Theodore Roosevelt Dam) on the Salt River. The dam provided irrigation water to the Valley of the Sun and tamed the violent floods of the river. The introduction of water to the heart of Arizona's vast desert enabled large-scale agriculture and industry. Over the next decades more dams were built throughout Arizona. Completed in 1936, the Hoover Dam on the Colorado River became the largest concrete dam in the western hemisphere and formed the biggest man-made reservoir in North America. Arizona's dams would eventually provide not only water and electricity but recreation areas as well.

Despite labor problems, copper mining increased throughout the 1920s and 1930s, and with the onset of World War II the mines boomed as military munitions manufacturing increased the demand for copper. However, within a few years after the war, many mines were shut down. Arizona is still littered with old mining ghost towns that boomed and then went bust. A few towns,

Impressions

O yes, I have heard of that country—it is just like hell. All it lacks is water and good society.

—A 19th-century senator from Ohio

such as Jerome, Bisbee, and Chloride, managed to hang on after the mines shut down and were eventually rediscovered by artists, writers, and retirees. Bisbee and Jerome are now major tourist attractions known for their many art galleries.

World War II also created demand for beef, leather, and cotton (which became the state's most important crop). Clear desert skies were ideal for training pilots, and several military bases were established in the state. Phoenix's population doubled during the war years, and after the war many veterans returned with their families. However, it would take the invention of air-conditioning to truly open up the desert to major population growth.

During the postwar years, Arizona attracted a number of large manufacturing industries and slowly moved away from its agricultural economic base. Today, electronics manufacturing, aerospace engineering, and other high-tech industries provide employment for thousands of Arizonans. The largest segment of the economy, however, is now in the service industries, with tourism playing a crucial role.

Even by the 1920s, Arizona had become a winter destination for the wealthy, and the Grand Canyon, declared a national park in 1919, lured more and more visitors every year. The clear dry air attracted people suffering from allergies and lung ailments, and Arizona became known as a healthful place. Guest ranches of the 1930s eventually gave way to the resorts of the 1990s. Today Scottsdale and Phoenix together boast the greatest concentration of resorts in the United States. In addition, tens of thousands of retirees from as far north as Canada make Arizona their winter home and play a crucial role in Arizona's economy.

Continued population growth throughout the 20th century created an ever greater demand for water. However, despite the damming of virtually all of Arizona's rivers, the state still suffered from insufficient water supplies in the south-central population centers of Phoenix and Tucson. It would take the construction of the controversial and expensive Central Arizona Project (CAP) aqueduct to carry water from the Colorado River over mountains and deserts and deliver it where it was wanted. Construction on the CAP began in 1974, and in 1985 water from the project finally began irrigating fields near Phoenix. In 1992, the CAP finally reached Tucson. However, with the populations of Phoenix, Tucson, and Las Vegas skyrocketing, the future of Colorado River water usage may again become a question for hot debate.

By the 1960s, Arizona had become an urban state with all the problems confronting other areas around the nation. The once-healthful air of Phoenix now rivals that of Los Angeles for the thickness of its smog. Allergy sufferers are plagued by pollen from the nondesert plants that have been planted to make this desert region look more lush and inviting. Today, the state's economy is growing. High-tech companies continue to locate within the state, and the continued influx of both retirees and Californians fleeing earthquakes and urban problems is giving the state new energy and new ideas. The signing of the North American Free Trade Agreement (NAFTA) also gave the state an economic shot in the arm.

## 4 Southwestern Cuisine

In the past decade regional cuisines have become all the rage with chefs across the United States. Southwestern cuisine, whose hallmarks are the spices of Mexico (especially chile peppers), the unusual fruit-and-meat pairings of nouvelle cuisine, and flame broiling over mesquite, has won popularity across the country. The blue-corn industry has also been thriving as creative chefs in Arizona, New Mexico, and around the country try their hand at concocting new dishes with this colorful carbohydrate. Ingredients both familiar and foreign have found their way into this regional cuisine, much to the delight of daring diners.

Southwestern cuisine has become so much a part of the dining scene in Arizona that even in small-town restaurants you'll probably encounter dishes such as mesquite-grilled breast of chicken served with a fresh-fruit salsa. In the cities, meanwhile, chefs are still dreaming up new creations—say, pistachio-crusted breast of duckling with fig-and-orange chutney. Pacific salmon might be served with smoked yellow-pepper sauce and roasted black-bean and corn relish, while roast squab might be served with twice-cooked bacon and chipotle pepper and cider sauce. Other dishes could include marinated mahi mahi with avocado-papaya salsa and cilantro-scallion aioli, or Southwestern bouillabaisse with grilled nopal cactus. Even desserts get the desert treatment, as shown in such outlandish, though tasty, concoctions as chile-chocolate cake and raspberry-jalapeño ice cream.

With all those chile peppers, Southwestern isn't for everyone, and unfortunately, many of the restaurants that once served dishes such as those mentioned above are now joining a trend toward milder, more subtle flavors.

Arizona also offers some of the best Mexican food in the country. One specialty that you're likely to encounter at Arizona's Mexican restaurants, especially in Tucson, is *carne seca*, which is air-dried beef that's shredded and added to various sauces. It has a very distinctive texture and shouldn't be missed.

Although you won't find very much in the way of truly indigenous Native American food in Arizona, you will likely encounter the Indian taco, Navajo taco, or some variation of this standard reservation meal. These are basically just tacos made with fry bread (a thick, chewy slab of fried dough). The taco topping is usually just ground beef and lettuce with a bit of cheese thrown on top. Sound familiar? Indian tacos are basically fast food and usually have about as much flavor as any other fast food. On the Hopi Reservation, at the Hopi Cultural Center, you can try a couple of other simple dishes, including a stew made with hominy (corn). However, it is the Hopi piki bread, a paper-thin pancake made from blue cornmeal, that is the most authentic Native American food you're likely to encounter in Arizona (although you'll probably find piki only on the Hopi Reservation).

Also keep an eye out for anything made from prickly pear fruit. Though this fruit doesn't add much flavor to the ice cream, jams, and syrups it's used in, it does sometimes add a distinctive pink color. You'll probably encounter prickly pear cactus pads (*nopales*) served as a vegetable at Mexican restaurants in Arizona. And don't forget Cave Creek's famous chile beer; it really packs a burn.

## 5 A Look at Local Arts & Crafts

Though Santa Fe has for many years claimed the Southwest arts spotlight, Arizona, too, is a mecca for artists and art collectors. The Cowboy Artists of America, an organization of artists dedicated to capturing the lives and landscapes of the Old West, was formed in a tavern in Sedona in 1965 by Joe Beeler, George Phippen, Bob McLeod, Charlie Dye, John Hampton, and a few other local artists. Working primarily in oils and bronze, members of this organization depicted the lives of cowboys and Native Americans in their art, and today their work is sought after by collectors throughout the country.

As more and more artists and craftspeople headed for Arizona, the towns in which they congregated came to be known as artists' colonies, and galleries sprang up to serve a growing number of visitors. Although Sedona is probably the best known of these communities, others include the former mining towns of Jerome and Bisbee, and Tubac, the first Spanish settlement in Arizona. All three have numerous galleries and crafts shops. However, it is upscale Scottsdale that has the state's highest concentration of art galleries.

Red-rock canyons, pensive Indians, hardworking cowboys, desert wildflowers, majestic mesas, and stately saguaros have been the themes of this century's representational artists of Arizona. Although contemporary abstract art can be found in museums and galleries, the style pioneered by Frederic Remington and Charles M. Russell in the early 20th century still dominates the Arizona art scene. Remington, Russell, and those who followed in their footsteps romanticized the West, imbuing their depictions of cowboys, Indians, settlers, and soldiers with mythic proportions that would be taken up by Hollywood.

Further back, even before the first Spanish explorers arrived in Arizona, the ancient Anasazi were creating an artistic legacy in their intricately woven baskets, painted pottery, and cryptic petroglyphs and pictographs. In recent years both contemporary Native American and nonnative artists have been drawing on Anasazi designs for their works. Today's Hopi, Navajo, and Zuni artisans have become well known for their jewelry, which is made of silver and semiprecious stones, primarily turquoise. The Hopi now carve images of their traditional kachinas for commercial distribution, and the Navajo continue to weave traditional patterns in their rugs. The Zuni, noted for their skill in carving stone, have focused on their traditional animal fetishes. However, since the founding of the Santa Fe Indian School in 1932, and later the Institute of American Indian Art, Indian artists have also ventured into the realm of painting. Hopi artist Fred Kabotie and his son, Michael Kabotie, are among the best-known Native American painters.

Collectors, and those with a casual interest in Southwestern art, will find local arts and crafts available in every corner of the state. From exclusive Scottsdale galleries to roadside stands on the Navajo Reservation, Arizona arts and crafts are ubiquitous. The best places to look for Southwestern and cowboy (or Western) art are in Scottsdale, Tucson, Sedona, Tubac, and Jerome. Native American crafts can be found in these same towns, but it's somewhat more rewarding to visit trading posts and reservation studios and shops.

The best known of the trading posts are the Hubbell Trading Post in Ganado and the Cameron Trading Post in Cameron, but there are trading posts all over the state and many offer excellent selection and quality. Keep in mind that no matter where you shop for Native American arts and crafts, you'll find that prices are high.

The Indian tribes of Arizona tend to have one or two specialty crafts that they produce with consummate skill. Many of these crafts were disappearing when the first traders came to the reservations a century ago. Today most of the crafts are alive and well, but primarily as collectibles, not as items for everyday use. Prices are high because of the many hours that go into producing

these items—what you're buying is handmade by a method that goes back for generations.

these items—what you're buying is handmade by a method that goes back for generations.

You can avoid paying sales tax if you live outside Arizona and have your purchase shipped directly to your home.

You can avoid paying sales tax if you live outside Arizona and have your purchase shipped directly to your home. On a high-ticket item such as a Navajo rug, you could save quite a bit. Also keep in mind that it's a good idea to make your jewelry purchases from reputable stores rather than from roadside stalls, of which there are many in the Four Corners region of the state. Many of these stalls sell cheap imitation Indian jewelry.

For a discussion of individual native crafts, see "A Native American Crafts Primer" in chapter 7.

## 6 Desert Architecture: From Pueblos to Frank Lloyd Wright

Centuries before the first Europeans arrived in Arizona, the Anasazi people were building elaborate villages, which have come to be known by their Spanish name: pueblos. Many, but not all, of the Anasazi pueblos were built high on cliff walls in the rugged canyon lands of northern Arizona. Constructed of cut stones mortared together and roofed with logs and earth, the pueblo dwellings had thick walls that provided insulation from heat and cold. Pueblo architecture was characterized by small rooms with no windows, and it is believed that the buildings' flat roofs provided places to do chores. Some rooms were used for living, while others served as grain-storage rooms.

Earlier, the Anasazi developed a type of shelter known as a pit house, which was partially dug into the ground. Eventually these flat-roofed stone houses were adapted to apartment-style construction techniques when they moved up into the canyon walls. The pit-house style of architecture was retained in the form of the *kiva,* a round ceremonial room that's still used by the Hopi, Arizona's contemporary pueblo dwellers.

The Sinagua, a culture that developed at the same time as the Anasazi, built similar stone pueblos, but most Sinagua pueblos were on hills rather than in the canyons. At the Wupatki ruins, near Flagstaff, there are two unusual stone structures built by the Sinagua. One is a ball court similar in many ways to the ball courts of ancient Mexican and Central American cultures. The other unusual building is a low-walled round structure that may have been an amphitheater or large kiva.

Many Hopis still live in pueblos similar to those built by the Sinagua and Anasazi, with stone-walled rooms and round kivas that have ladders sticking through the roof (entrance to a kiva is prohibited to non-Hopis). The *hogan,* the traditional home of the Navajo people, displays a very different type of architecture. Usually built with six sides, hogans are constructed of logs and earth and resemble ancient dwellings of central Asia.

When the Spanish arrived in Arizona, they turned to sun-baked adobe bricks as their primary construction material. Because adobe walls must be made very thick, they provide excellent insulation. Very few adobe homes have survived from territorial days because, when not maintained, adobe quickly decays. The best place to see adobe homes is in Tucson, where many have been preserved in that city's downtown historic districts. However, when the railroads arrived in Arizona, many owners modified their adobe homes by adding slanted roofs, Victorian porches, and even siding. In the Barrio Histórico district of Tucson, town house architecture characteristic of Sonora, Mexico, has been preserved. These buildings have no front yards, just walls right at the sidewalk. This style of architecture was common during the Mexican and early territorial periods of Arizona history.

With only the two mission churches of San Xavier del Bac and Tumacacori, the Spanish did not leave as great an ecclesiastical architectural legacy in Arizona as they did elsewhere in the New World. However, mission-revival architecture has been popular for much of this century. A somewhat idealized concept of the style—with stucco walls, arches, and courtyards—has come to epitomize the ideal of Arizona living.

In the mid–20th century, architect Frank Lloyd Wright established his winter home and school, called Taliesin West, north of Scottsdale, and eventually designed several buildings around the Phoenix area. The architect of the Biltmore Hotel, one of the state's oldest resorts, relied on Wright for assistance in designing the hotel, and the hand of Wright is evident throughout. One of Wright's students, an Italian architect named Paolo Soleri, decided to settle in Arizona and has for many years pursued his dream of building an environmentally sensitive, ideal city in the desert north of Phoenix. He calls this city Arcosanti and has partially financed its construction by selling wind-bells at his Cosanti foundry in Paradise Valley. Arcosanti, the Cosanti foundry, and Taliesin West are all open to the public.

## 7 Recommended Books

**HISTORY**  Marshall Trimble's *Roadside History of Arizona* (Mountain Press Publishing, 1986), is an ideal book to take along on a driving tour of the state. The book goes road by road and discusses events that happened in the area. For a more thorough history of the state, pick up Thomas E. Sheridan's *Arizona: A History* (University of Arizona Press, 1995), which is an exploration of the state's past 11,000 years. *Arizona Memories* (University of Arizona, 1984), edited by Anne H. Morgan and Rennard Strickland, is an engaging collection of historical recollections by cowboys, miners, an Apache scout, a frontier doctor, a soldier's wife, and many other Arizonans.

**THE GRAND CANYON/COLORADO RIVER**  John Wesley Powell's diary produced the first published account (1869) of traveling through the Grand Canyon. Today, his writings still provide a fascinating glimpse into the canyon and the first trip through it. *The Exploration of the Colorado River and Its Canyons* (Penguin, 1997), with an introduction by Wallace Stegner, is a recent republishing of Powell's writings. Stegner, with Bernard Devoto, also writes about Powell in his *Beyond the Hundredth Meridian: John Wesley Powell and the Second Opening of the West* (Penguin USA, 1992). For an interesting account of the recent human history of the canyon, read Stephen J. Pyne's *How The Canyon Became Grand* (Viking Penguin, 1998), which focuses on the explorers, writers, and artists who have contributed to our current concept of the canyon. *The Man Who Walked Through Time* (Vintage Books, 1989), by Colin Fletcher, is a narrative of one man's hike through the rugged inner canyon.

Water rights and human impact on the deserts of the Southwest have raised many controversies this century, none more heated than those centering around the Colorado River. *Cadillac Desert: The American West and Its Disappearing Water* (Penguin, 1993), by Marc Reisner, focuses on the West's insatiable need for water. *A River No More: The Colorado River and the West* (University of California Press, 1996), by Philip L. Fradkin, addresses the fate of the river.

**NATURAL HISTORY/OUTDOORS** *Roadside Geology of Arizona* (Mountain Press Publishing, 1998) by Halka Chronic, is another handy book to keep in the car. If you're a hiker, you'll find Scott S. Warren's *100 Hikes in Arizona* (The Mountaineers, 1994) another invaluable traveling companion.

**FICTION** Tony Hillerman is perhaps the best-known contemporary author whose books rely on Arizona settings. Hillerman's murder mysteries are almost all set on the Navajo Reservation in the Four Corners area and include many references to actual locations that can be seen by visitors to the area. Among Hillerman's Navajo mysteries are *The First Eagle, Sacred Clowns, Coyote Waits, Thief of Time, The Blessing Way, Listening Woman, The Ghostway,* and *The Fallen Man.*

Barbara Kingsolver, a Tucson resident, biologist, and social activist, has set several of her novels either partly or entirely in Arizona. *The Bean Trees, Pigs in Heaven,* and *Animal Dreams* are peopled by Anglo, Indian, and Hispanic characters, allowing for quirky, humorous narratives with social and political overtones that provide insights into Arizona's cultural mélange. Kingsolver's nonfiction works include *High Tide in Tucson* (HarperPerennial, 1996) and *Holding the Line: Women in the Great Arizona Mine Strike of 1983* (Harper-Perennial, 1997). The former is a collection of essays, many of which focus on the author's life in Tucson, and the latter is an account of a copper-mine strike.

Edward Abbey's *The Monkey Wrench Gang* and *Hayduke Lives!* are tales of an unlikely gang of "ecoterrorists" determined to preserve the wildernesses of the Southwest, including parts of northern Arizona. The former book helped inspire the founding of the radical Earth First! movement.

Zane Grey spent many years living in north-central Arizona and based many of his Western novels on life in this region of the state. Among his books are *Riders of the Purple Sage, West of the Pecos, The Vanishing American, Call of the Canyon, The Arizona Clan,* and *To the Last Man.*

**TRAVEL** If you're particularly interested in Native American art and crafts, you may want to search out a copy of *Trading Post Guidebook* (Northland Publishing, 1995), by Patrick Eddington and Susan Makov, which is an invaluable guide to trading posts, artists' studios, galleries, and museums in the Four Corners region.

# Appendix B: Useful Toll-Free Numbers & Web Sites

## AIRLINES

**Air Canada**
☎ 800/776-3000
www.aircanada.ca

**Alaska Airlines**
☎ 800/426-0333
www.alaskaair.com

**America West Airlines**
☎ 800/235-9292
www.americawest.com

**American Airlines**
☎ 800/433-7300
www.americanair.com

**British Airways**
☎ 800/247-9297
☎ 0345/222-111 in Britain
www.british-airways.com

**Canadian Airlines International**
☎ 800/426-7000
www.cdnair.ca

**Continental Airlines**
☎ 800/525-0280
www.flycontinental.com

**Delta Air Lines**
☎ 800/221-1212
www.delta-air.com

**Frontier Airlines**
☎ 800/432-1359
www.frontierairlines.com

**Northwest Airlines**
☎ 800/225-2525
www.nwa.com

**Southwest Airlines**
☎ 800/435-9792
www.southwest.com

**Tower Air**
☎ 800/34-TOWER
☎ 800/348-6937 outside New York
☎ 718/553-8500 in New York
www.towerair.com

**Trans World Airlines (TWA)**
☎ 800/221-2000
www2.twa.com

**United Airlines**
☎ 800/241-6522
www.ual.com

**US Airways**
☎ 800/428-4322
www.usairways.com

**Virgin Atlantic Airways**
☎ 800/862-8621 in continental U.S.
☎ 0293/747-747 in Britain
www.fly.virgin.com

## MAJOR HOTEL & MOTEL CHAINS

**Best Western International**
☎ 800/528-1234
www.bestwestern.com

**Clarion Hotels**
☎ 800/CLARION
www.clarioninn.com

**Comfort Inns**
☎ 800/228-5150
www.comfortinn.com

**Courtyard by Marriott**
☎ 800/321-2211
www.courtyard.com

**Days Inn**
☎ 800/329-7466
www.daysinn.com

**Doubletree Hotels**
☎ 800/222-TREE
www.doubletreehotels.com

**Econo Lodges**
☎ 800/55-ECONO
www.econolodge.com

**Embassy Suites**
☎ 800/362-2779
www.embassy-suites.com

**Fairfield Inn by Marriott**
☎ 800/228-2800
www.fairfieldinn.com

**Hampton Inn**
☎ 800/HAMPTON
www.hampton-inn.com

**Hilton Hotels**
☎ 800/HILTONS
www.hilton.com

**Holiday Inn**
☎ 800/HOLIDAY
www.holiday-inn.com

**Howard Johnson**
☎ 800/654-2000
www.hojo.com

**Hyatt Hotels & Resorts**
☎ 800/228-9000
www.hyatt.com

**ITT Sheraton**
☎ 800/325-3535
www.sheraton.com

**La Quinta Motor Inns**
☎ 800/531-5900
www.laquinta.com

**Marriott Hotels**
☎ 800/228-9290
www.marriott.com

**Motel 6**
☎ 800/4-MOTEL6 (800/466-8356)

**Quality Inns**
☎ 800/228-5151
www.qualityinn.com

**Radisson Hotels International**
☎ 800/333-3333
www.radisson.com

**Ramada Inns**
☎ 800/2-RAMADA
www.ramada.com

**Red Carpet Inns**
☎ 800/251-1962
www.reservahost.com

**Red Lion Hotels & Inns**
☎ 800/547-8010
www.promus.com

**Red Roof Inns**
☎ 800/843-7663
www.redroof.com

**Residence Inn by Marriott**
☎ 800/331-3131
www.residenceinn.com

**Rodeway Inns**
☎ 800/228-2000
www.rodeway.com

**Super 8 Motels**
☎ 800/800-8000
www.super8.com

**Travelodge**
☎ 800/255-3050
www.travelodge.com

**Vagabond Inns**
☎ 800/522-1555
www.vagabondinns.com

**Wyndham Hotels and Resorts**
☎ 800/822-4200 in continental
U.S. and Canada
www.wyndham.com

Toll-Free Numbers & Web Sites

# Frommer's Online Directory

*by Michael Shapiro*

Michael Shapiro is the author of *Internet Travel Planning* (The Globe Pequot Press). The Arizona listings for this directory were compiled by Jason Turbow.

Frommer's Online Directory is a new feature designed to help you take advantage of the Internet to better plan your trip. Part 1 lists some general Internet resources that can make any trip easier, such as sites for booking airline tickets. Please keep in mind that this is not a comprehensive list, but rather a discriminating selection of useful sites to get you started. In section 2 you'll find some top on-line guides for Arizona.

## 1 The Top Travel-Planning Web Sites

Among the most popular sites are online travel agencies. The top agencies, including Expedia, Preview Travel, and Travelocity, offer an array of tools that are valuable even if you don't book online. You can check flight schedules, hotel availability, car rental prices, or even get paged if your flight is delayed.

While on-line agencies have come a long way over the past few years, they don't always yield the best price. Unlike a travel agent, they're unlikely to tell you, for example, that you can save money by flying a day earlier or a day later. On the other hand, if you're looking for a bargain fare, you might find something online that an agent wouldn't take the time to dig up. Because airline commissions have been cut, a travel agent may not find it worthwhile to spend half an hour trying to find you the best deal. On the Net, you can be your own agent and take all the time you want.

On-line booking sites aren't the only places to book airline tickets—all major airlines have their own Web sites and often offer incentives, such as bonus frequent flyer miles or Net-only discounts, for buying online. These incentives have helped airlines capture the majority of the online booking market. According to Jupiter Communications, online agencies such as Travelocity booked about 80 percent of tickets purchased online in 1996, but by 1999 airline sites were projected to own more than half of the online market, with online agencies' share of the pie dwindling each year.

### WHEN SHOULD YOU BOOK ON-LINE?

On-line booking is not for everyone. If you prefer to let others handle your travel arrangements, one call to an experienced travel agent should suffice. But if you want to know as much as possible about your options, the Net is a good place to start, especially for bargain hunters.

**Factoid**
See appendix B for toll-free numbers and Web addresses for airlines and hotels.

The most compelling reason to use on-line booking is to take advantage of last-minute specials, such as American Airlines' weekend deals or other Internet-only fares that must be purchased on-line. Another advantage is that you can cash in on incentives for booking online, such as rebates or bonus frequent flyer miles. On-line booking is certainly not for those with a complex itinerary. If you require follow-up services, such as itinerary changes, use a travel agent. Though Expedia and some other online agencies employ travel agents who are available by phone, these sites are geared primarily for self-service.

## LEADING BOOKING SITES

Below are listings for the top travel booking sites. The starred selections are the most useful and best designed sites.

**Cheap Tickets. www.cheaptickets.com**
*Essentials:* Discounted rates on domestic and international airline tickets and hotel rooms.

Sometimes discounters such as Cheap Tickets have exclusive deals that aren't available through more mainstream channels. Registration at Cheap Tickets requires inputting a credit card number before getting started, which is one reason many people elect to call the company's toll-free number rather than booking on-line. One of the most frustrating things about the Cheap Tickets site is that it will offer fare quotes for a route, then later show the fare as invalid for your dates of travel. Other Web sites, such as Preview Travel, consider your dates of travel before showing available fares. Despite its problems, Cheap Tickets can be worth the effort because its fares can be lower than those offered by its competitors.

**✪ Expedia. expedia.com**
*Essentials:* Domestic and international flight, hotel, and rental car booking; late-breaking travel news, destination features and commentary from travel experts; deals on cruises and vacation packages. Free registration is required for booking.

Expedia makes it easy to handle flight, hotel, and car booking on one itinerary, so it's a good place for one-stop shopping. Expedia's hotel search offers crisp, zoomable maps to pinpoint most properties; click on the camera icon to see images of the rooms and facilities. But like many on-line databases, Expedia focuses on the major chains, such as Hilton and Hyatt, so don't expect to find too many one-of-a-kind resorts or B&Bs here.

Once you're registered (it's only necessary to do this once from each computer you use), you can start booking with the Roundtrip Fare Finder box on the home page, which expedites the process. After selecting a flight, you can hold it until midnight the following day or purchase on-line. If you think you might do better through a travel agent, you'll have time to try to get a lower price. And you may do better with a travel agent because Expedia's computer reservation system does not include all airlines. Notably absent are some leading budget carriers, such as Southwest Airlines. (At press time, Travelocity was the only major booking service that included Southwest.)

Expedia's World Guide, offering destination information, is a glaring weakness—it takes a lot of page views to get very little information. However, Expedia compensates by linking to other Microsoft Network services, such as its Sidewalk city guides, which offer entertainment and dining advice for many of the cities it covers.

## Take a Look at Frommer's Site

We highly recommend Arthur Frommer's Budget Travel Online (**www.frommers. com**) as an excellent travel-planning resource. Of course, we're a little biased, but you will find indispensable travel tips, reviews, monthly vacation giveaways, and on-line booking on the site.

Subscribe to Arthur Frommer's Daily Newsletter (**www.frommers.com/ newsletters**) to receive the latest travel bargains and inside travel secrets in your mailbox every day. You'll read daily headlines and articles from the dean of travel himself, highlighting last-minute deals on airfares, accommodations, cruises, and package vacations. You'll also find great travel advice by checking our Tip of the Day or Hot Spot of the Month.

Search our Destinations archive (**www.frommers.com/destinations**) of more than 200 domestic and international destinations for great places to stay, tips for traveling there, and what to do while you're there. Once you've researched your trip, you might try our on-line reservation system (**www.frommers.com/ booktravelnow**) to book your dream vacation at affordable prices.

### Preview Travel. www.previewtravel.com

*Essentials:* Domestic and international flight, hotel, and rental car booking; Travel Newswire lists fare sales, deals on cruises, and vacation packages. Free (one-time) registration is required for booking. Preview offers express booking for members, but at press time this feature was buried below the fold on Preview's reservation page.

Preview features the most inviting interface for booking trips, though the wealth of graphics involved can make the site somewhat slow to load. Use Farefinder to quickly find the lowest current fares on flights to dozens of major cities. Carfinder offers a similar service for rental cars, but you can only search airport locations, not city pick-up sites. To see the lowest fare for your itinerary, input the dates and times for your route and see what Preview comes up with.

In recent years Preview and other leading booking services have added features such as Best Fare Finder, so after Preview searches for the best deal on your itinerary, it will check flights that are a bit later or earlier to see if it might be cheaper to fly at a different time. While these searches have become quite sophisticated, they still occasionally overlook deals that might be uncovered by a top-notch travel agent. If you have the time, see what you can find on-line and then call an agent to see if you can get a better price.

With Preview's Fare Alert feature, you can set fares for up to three routes and you'll receive E-mail notices when the fare drops below your target amount. For example, you could tell Preview to alert you when the fare from New York to Phoenix drops below $250. If it does, you'll get an e-mail telling you the current fare.

*Note to AOL Users:* You can book flights, hotels, rental cars, and cruises on AOL at keyword: Travel. The booking software is provided by Preview Travel and is similar to Preview on the Web. Use the AOL "Travelers Advantage" program to earn a 5% rebate on flights, hotel rooms, and car rentals.

### Priceline.com. www.priceline.com

Even people who aren't familiar with too many Web sites have heard about Priceline.com. Launched in 1998 with a $10 million ad campaign featuring William Shatner, Priceline lets you "name your price" for domestic and international airline tickets and hotel rooms. In other words, you select a route and dates, guarantee with a credit card, and make a bid for what you're willing to pay. If one of the airlines in

---

### A Worthy Stop

Far more people look on-line than book on-line, partly due to fear of putting their credit cards through on the Net. Though secure encryption has made this fear less justified, there's no reason why you can't find a flight on-line and then book it by calling a toll-free number or contacting your travel agent. To be sure you're in secure mode when you book on-line, look for a little key icon (in Netscape) or a padlock (Internet Explorer) at the bottom of your Web browser.

---

Priceline's database has a fare that's lower than your bid, your credit card will automatically be charged for a ticket.

You can't say what time you want to fly—you have to accept any flight leaving between 6am and 10pm on the dates you choose, and you may have to make one stopover. No frequent flyer miles are awarded, and tickets are non-refundable and can't be exchanged for another flight. So if your plans change, you're out of luck. Priceline can be good for travelers who have to take off on short notice (and who are thus unable to qualify for advance purchase discounts). But be sure to shop around first— if you overbid, you'll be required to purchase the ticket and Priceline will pocket the difference.

**Travelocity. www.travelocity.com**
*Essentials:* Domestic and international flight, hotel, and rental car booking; deals on cruises and vacation packages. Travel Headlines spotlights latest bargain airfares. Free (one-time) registration is required for booking.

Travelocity almost got it right. Its Express Booking feature enables travelers to complete the booking process more quickly than they could at Expedia or Preview, but Travelocity gums up the works with a page called "Featured Airlines." Big placards of several featured airlines compete for your attention—if you want to see the fares for all available airlines, click the much smaller box at the bottom of the page labeled "Book a Flight."

Some have worried that Travelocity, which is owned by American Airlines' parent company, AMR, directs bookings to American. This doesn't seem to be the case; I've booked there dozens of times and have always been directed to the cheapest listed flight. But the "Featured Airlines" page seems to be Travelocity's way of trying to cash in with ads and incentives for booking certain airlines. (It's hard to blame these booking services for trying to generate some revenue; many airlines have slashed commissions to $10 per domestic booking for on-line transactions, so these virtual agencies are struggling.) There are rewards for choosing one of the featured airlines. You'll get 1,500 bonus frequent flyer miles if you book through United's site, for example, but the site doesn't tell you about other airlines that might be cheaper. If the United flight costs $150 more than the best deal on another airline, it's not worth spending the extra money.

On the plus side, Travelocity has some leading-edge techie tools for modern travelers. Exhibit A is Fare Watcher E-mail, an "intelligent agent" that keeps you informed of the best fares offered for the city pairs (round-trips) of your choice. Whenever the fare changes by $25 or more, Fare Watcher will alert you by e-mail. Exhibit B is Flight Paging: If you own an alphanumeric pager with national access that can receive e-mail, Travelocity's paging system can alert you if your flight is delayed. Finally, though Travelocity doesn't include every budget airline, it does include Southwest, the leading U.S. budget carrier.

## FINDING LODGINGS ON-LINE

While the services above offer hotel booking, sites devoted primarily to lodging may include properties that aren't listed with more general on-line travel agencies. Some lodging sites specialize in a particular type of accommodation, such as bed-and-breakfast inns, which you won't find on the more mainstream booking services. Other services, such as TravelWeb, offer weekend deals on major chain properties, which cater to business travelers and have more empty rooms on weekends.

### All Hotels on the Web. www.all-hotels.com
Well, this site doesn't include all the hotels on the Web, but it does have tens of thousands of listings throughout the world. Bear in mind that each hotel listed has paid a small fee ($25 and up) for placement, so it's not an objective list, but more like a book of on-line brochures. Also see Hotels and Travel on the Net (**www.hotelstravel.com**), which claims to offer discount booking on more than 100,000 hotels and other lodgings in more than 120 countries.

### Go Camping America. www.gocampingamerica.com/main.html
An extensive listing of RV parks and campgrounds for the United States (and some Canadian provinces), organized by state. The listings include dates of operation, number of sites, hookup availability, tent sites, and modem access. Some campgrounds offer "on-line brochures" which, like printed brochures, put the best possible face on a place.

### Hotel Reservations Network (HRN). www.180096hotel.com
Bargain room rates at hotels in more than two dozen U.S. and international cities. HRN prebooks blocks of rooms in advance, so sometimes it has rooms—at discount rates—at hotels that are supposedly sold out. Select a city and input your dates, and you'll get a list of best prices for a selection of hotels. Descriptions include an image of the property and a locator map; to book on-line click the "Book Now" button. HRN is notable for some deep discounts, even in cities where hotel rooms are expensive. The toll-free number is printed all over this site; call it if you want more options than are listed on-line.

### InnSite. www.innsite.com
B&B listings for inns in all 50 U.S. states and dozens of countries around the globe.

Find an inn at your destination, have a look at images of the rooms, check prices and availability, and then send e-mail to the innkeeper if you have further questions. This is an extensive directory of bed-and-breakfast inns but only includes listings if the proprietor submitted one (note: it's free to get an inn listed). The descriptions are written by the innkeepers and many listings link to the inn's own Web sites, where you can find more information and images. Also see: Bed and Breakfast Channel (**bedandbreakfast.com**).

### Places to Stay. www.placestostay.com
Mostly one-of-a-kind places in the United States and abroad that you might not find in other directories, with a focus on resort accommodations. Again, listing is selective—this isn't a comprehensive directory, but it can give you a sense of what's available at different destinations.

### ✪ TravelWeb. www.travelweb.com
TravelWeb lists more than 16,000 hotels worldwide, focusing on chains such as Hyatt and Hilton, and you can book almost 90% of them on-line. TravelWeb's Click-It Weekends, updated each Monday, offers weekend deals at many leading hotel chains. TravelWeb is the on-line home for Pegasus Systems, which provides transaction processing systems for the hotel industry.

## LAST-MINUTE DEALS & OTHER ON-LINE BARGAINS
There's nothing airlines hate more than flying with lots of empty seats. The Net has enabled airlines to offer last-minute bargains to entice travelers to fill those seats. Most

## A Handy Tip

While most people learn about last-minute weekend deals from e-mail dispatches, you can get a jumpstart by finding out precisely when these deals become available and check airlines' Web sites at this time. Because these deals are limited, they can vanish within hours, sometimes even minutes, so it pays to log on as soon as they're available.

of these are announced on Tuesday or Wednesday and are valid for travel the following weekend, but some can be booked weeks or months in advance. You can sign up for weekly e-mail alerts at airlines' sites (see appendix B), or check with sites such as WebFlyer (see below) that compile lists of these bargains. To make it easier, visit a site such as Smarter Living (see below) that will round up all the deals and send them in one convenient weekly e-mail. But last-minute deals aren't the only on-line bargains—other sites can help you find value even if you can't wait until the eleventh hour.

✪ **1travel.com. www.1travel.com**
Deals on domestic and international flights, cruises, hotels, and all-inclusive resorts such as Club Med. 1travel.com's Saving Alert compiles last-minute air deals so you don't have to scroll through multiple e-mail alerts. A feature called "Drive a little using low-fare airlines" helps map out strategies for using alternate airports to find lower fares. And Farebeater searches a database that includes published fares, consolidator bargains, and special deals exclusive to 1travel.com. *Note:* The travel agencies listed by 1travel.com have paid for placement.

**BestFares. www.bestfares.com**
Bargain-seeker Tom Parsons lists some great offers on airfares, hotels, rental cars, and cruises, but the site is poorly organized. News Desk is a long list of hundreds of bargains, but they're not broken down into cities or even countries, so it's not easy to find what you're looking for. If you have time to wade through it, you might find a good deal. Some material is available only to paid subscribers.

**LastMinuteTravel.com. www.lastminutetravel.com**
Travel suppliers with excess inventory distribute unsold airline seats, hotel rooms, cruises, and vacation packages through this on-line agency.

**Moment's Notice. www.moments-notice.com**
As the name suggests, Moment's Notice specializes in last-minute vacation and cruise deals. You can browse for free, but if you want to purchase a trip you have to join Moment's Notice, which costs $25.

**Smarter Living. www.smarterliving.com**
Best known for its e-mail dispatch of weekend deals on 20 airlines, Smarter Living also keeps you posted about last-minute bargains on everything from Windjammer Cruises to flights to Iceland.

✪ **WebFlyer. www.webflyer.com**
WebFlyer is the ultimate on-line resource for frequent flyers and also has an excellent listing of last-minute air deals. Click on "Deal Watch" for a round-up of weekend deals on flights, hotels, and rental cars from domestic and international suppliers.

# TRAVELER'S TOOLKIT
Veteran travelers usually carry some essential items to make their trips easier. The following is a selection of on-line tools to smooth your journey.

✪ **CultureFinder.** www.culturefinder.com

Up-to-date listings for plays, opera, classical music, dance, film, and other cultural events in more than 1,300 U.S. cities. Enter the dates you'll be in a city and get a list of events happening then—you can also purchase tickets on-line. Also see Festival-Finder (www.festivalfinder.com) for the latest on more than 1,500 rock, folk, reggae, blues, and bluegrass festivals throughout North America.

**Intellicast.** www.intellicast.com

Weather forecasts for all 50 states and cities around the world.

✪ **MapQuest.** www.mapquest.com

Specializing in U.S. maps, MapQuest enables you to zoom in on a destination, calculate step-by-step driving directions between any two U.S. points, and locate restaurants, hotels, and other attractions on maps.

**Net Café Guide.** www.netcafeguide.com/mapindex.htm

Locate Internet cafes at hundreds of locations around the globe. Catch up on your e-mail, log onto the Web, and stay in touch with the home front, usually for just a few dollars per hour.

**Tourism Offices Worldwide Directory.** www.towd.com

An extensive listing of tourism offices, some with links to their Web sites.

**The Travelite FAQ.** www.travelite.org

Tips on packing light, choosing luggage, and selecting appropriate travel wear.

**Trip.com: Airport Maps and Flight Status.** www.trip.com

A business travel site where you can find out when an airborne flight is scheduled to arrive. Click on "Guides and Tools" to peruse airport maps for more than 40 domestic cities.

**Visa.** www.visa.com/pd/atm/
**MasterCard.** www.mastercard.com/atm

Find ATMs in hundreds of cities in the United States and around the world. Both sites include maps for some locations and list airport ATM locations, some with maps. Remarkably, MasterCard lists ATMs on all seven continents (there's one at Antarctica's

---

### Check Your E-mail at Internet Cafes

Until a few years ago, most travelers who checked their E-mail while traveling carried a laptop, but this posed some problems. Not only are laptops expensive, but they can be difficult to configure, incur expensive connection charges, and are attractive to thieves. Thankfully, Web-based free e-mail programs have made it much easier to check your mail.

Just open an account at a free-mail provider, such as Hotmail (www.hotmail.com) or Yahoo! Mail (www.mail.yahoo.com), and all you'll need to check your mail is a Web connection, easily available at Net cafes and copy shops around the world. After logging on, just point the browser to www.hotmail.com, enter your username and password, and you'll have access to your mail.

Internet cafes have become ubiquitous, so for a few dollars an hour you'll be able to check your mail and send messages back to colleagues, friends, and family. If you already have a primary e-mail account, you can set it to forward mail to your free-mail account while you're away. Free-mail programs have become enormously popular (Hotmail claims more than 10 million members), because they enable everyone, even those who don't own a computer, to have an e-mail address they can check wherever they log onto the Web.

McMurdo Station). *Tip:* You'll usually get a better exchange rate using ATMs than exchanging traveler's checks at banks.

# 2 The Top Web Sites for Arizona

## GENERAL SITES FOR ARIZONA

**Access Arizona. www.accessarizona.com**
An on-line news magazine devoted to the state, Access Arizona provides local news as well as a steady stream of entertainment, dining, and event listings.

✪ **Arizona Central. www.azcentral.com**
The on-line home of the *Arizona Republic,* this site isn't just a good on-line entertainment listing, it's a good on-line newspaper. It has music, movie, and restaurant reviews, as well as a complete rundown of local sports.

**Arizona History Traveler. www.azhistorytraveler.org**
A look at Arizona tourism from a historical perspective. The site offers summaries, by region, of about 15 monuments, museums, and landmarks that help define where the state has been in its 87-year history. It also includes contact information for nearly 100 historic parks, museums, and cultural centers around the state.

✪ **Arizona Guide. www.arizonaguide.com**
Produced by the Arizona Office of Tourism and Arizona Central (the on-line home of the *Arizona Republic* newspaper), Arizona Guide is a must-visit site for anyone planning a vacation here. The site offers weather reports from around the state, a trip planner, an events guide, city listings, and an extensive section on the Grand Canyon.

**Arizona Reporter. www.azreporter.com**
Provides a travel section with regular articles highlighting destinations around the state, as well as events calendars and entertainment listings.

**Arizona Tourist Bureau. www.arizonatourism.com/index.html**
This site offers information not only on tourist destinations, but on car rentals and RV parks. It lets you book hotel reservations on-line and take a photo tour.

**AZ US Web Works. azuswebworks.com/az/index.html**
US Web Works offers a virtually text-free breakdown of the entire state, offering extensive links to cities, monuments, colleges, and museums, as well as trails, maps, and travel information.

## PHOENIX
### ON-LINE GUIDES, NEWSPAPERS & ENTERTAINMENT SITES

✪ **CitySearch: Phoenix. www.phoenix.citysearch.com**
Movie, concert, and restaurant reviews, and a month-by-month list of recommended events make finding an evening's entertainment easier than ever. A visitors' guide breaks down the city's essentials, and links to maps and directions prove invaluable for those trying to find their way around town.

**Greater Phoenix Convention & Visitors Bureau. www.arizonaguide.com/cities/phoenix**
Everything the professional traveler to Phoenix needs, from accommodation information to meeting planners. And don't miss the golf course guide.

**Phoenix Area Guide. phoenix.areaguides.net**
This guide offers yellow pages, white pages, maps, classifieds, and more. A travel guide section includes things to see and do, as well as local history and a breakdown of cities in the area.

**Phoenix Downtown. www.downtownphx.org**
This site offers contact information for a huge number of downtown businesses, including events, restaurants, bars and clubs, and shopping.

## TOP ATTRACTIONS

**Arizona Diamondbacks (pro baseball team). www.azdiamondbacks.com**
The Diamondbacks were born in the latest round of major league expansion, and Phoenix is still giddy over its new team. Get the lowdown on the state-of-the-art Bank One Ballpark, with a massive air conditioning system and a hot tub in center field. The Web site offers team news and stats, as well as ticket ordering information.

**Arizona Opera. www.azopera.com**
Program listings, show reviews, composer biographies, opera trivia, and on-line ticket sales.

**Arizona Science Center. www.azscience.org**
A level-by-level exhibit map lets you plan out your visit in advance, and the planetarium section lists each show offered. For those wanting to teach their kids a thing or two, the Educators' Guide offers a breakdown of special presentations, center curriculums, and teacher study guides.

**Desert Botanical Garden. www.dbg.org**
A variety of group tours offer examinations of plants and people of the Southwest, or you can take a self-guided tour through the garden's mile-long winding stretch of paths. The Web site offers lists of special activities and events, as well as a useful page on desert gardening.

**Phoenix Golf Course Directory. golfsbestdeals.com/phoenix.htm**
A thorough list of links in and around a city known for its abundance of golf courses. Click the Home Page button to go to Golf's Best Deals, a rundown of golf bargains around the state.

**The Heard Museum. www.heard.org**
Numerous on-line exhibits, including an incredible collection of Hopi kachina dolls. Includes a Native American Fine Art Movement resource guide.

**Phoenix Art Museum. www.phxart.org**
You'll find extensive lists of galleries and exhibits, as well as links to classes, workshops, museum tours, and a virtual gift shop.

**Phoenix Coyotes (pro hockey team). www.nhlcoyotes.com/home.shtml**
The Coyotes moved to the desert from Winnipeg in 1995, making an instant impact on the Phoenix community. One of the NHL's better Web sites offers a vast array of information about the team, including schedule, ticket prices, and on-line ticket sales.

**Phoenix Mercury (pro women's basketball team). www.wnba.com/mercury**
News and feature articles update fans on players, while results and stats break down the action on the court. You'll also find ticket information for each of the Mercury's home games.

**Phoenix Suns (pro basketball team). www.nba.com/suns**
The Suns' Web site offers team stats, news, history, and schedule information, as well as ticket ordering info. And don't forget to check out virtual highlights from the team's most recent games.

**Phoenix Zoo. www.phoenixzoo.org**
The Zoo site will take you on one of four virtual adventures based on trails in the park—Africa, Arizona, the tropics, or the Discovery Trail. Each section offers maps and

tours, as well as narrative educational sections. You'll also find zoo news, hours of operation, and tour information.

# TUCSON

## ON-LINE GUIDES, NEWSPAPERS & ENTERTAINMENT SITES

✪ **Best of Tucson.** www.desert.net/tw/bot/index.htm
Produced by the *Tucson Weekly,* this is an essential site for visitors. Offering best-of lists for everything from fine dining to fried pickles, the site covers food, shopping, outdoors, bars, cafes, and city life.

**The Ultimate Arizona Vacation Guide.** www.webcreationsetc.com/Azguide/
   **Tucson**
Everything a visitor to Tucson could need, including maps, facts, attractions, and discounted hotel and car rentals. For those who want to explore, the guide covers not only Tucson, but all of Southern Arizona.

**Our Tucson: Guide to the Pueblo.** www.azstarnet.com/tucson_new
Created by the *Arizona Star,* Our Tucson provides a nice overview of the city, including restaurant reviews, a nightlife wrap-up, and a shopping guide. A historical perspective lets you explore the town's roots.

✪ **Tucson Area Guide.** tucson.areaguides.net
A well-rounded look at Tucson, offering advice on everything from food to lodging to weather reports. This site is very well organized, and is a great starting point for visitors who know little of the city.

**Tucson Citizen.** www.tucsoncitizen.com
The local newspaper offers current listings of arts, entertainment, and sports, as well as weather conditions and updated news reports.

## TOP ATTRACTIONS

✪ **Arizona Sonoran Desert Museum.** www.desertmuseum.org
Informative articles, interactive history maps, research programs, and an extensive events listing, this site doesn't quite eliminate the need to see the place in person, but it comes close.

✪ **Biosphere2.** www.bio2.edu
This Web site has all the basics: hours of operation, tour information, and special programs. But the heart of the site is the virtual tour, with 360° views from 13 locations around the facility.

**Colossal Cave Mountain Park.** www.colossalcave.com
Find out all about the cave and the surrounding nature on this Web site, then take an extensive virtual tour, with optional audio.

**Flandrau Science Center.** www.seds.org/flandrau
True to its name, the Science Center has one big animation program for its main interface (with a text-only option). It's really not all that spectacular, but very earnest in its execution. Make lights go from red to green as you find out about exhibits, museum hours, special events, and more.

**Old Tucson Studios.** www.emol.org/emol/tucson/oldtucson/otindex.html
A re-created Western movie studio brings you back to the Wild West through numerous live shows, gunfights, musicals, and wagon and train rides. The Web site is basic, but offers all the essentials: hours of operation, an events calendar, admission prices, and the studio's location.

**Southeastern Arizona Bird Observatory (SABO).** www.sabo.org
With a full calendar of activities and events, this site is all about birding. SABO offers articles and tips for birding travelers and guides to birding hot spots, as well as links to other bird-friendly sites on the Internet.

**Tucson Botanical Gardens.** www.azstarnet.com/~tbg/
The Botanical Gardens site provides a great on-line brochure, offering details on virtually any topic a visitor might need, including a rundown of the specialty gardens, garden events, and a mission and history page.

✪ **Tucson Hikes.** www.azstarnet.com/~aflach/index.htm
A thorough list of hikes in and around Tucson, cross-indexed by difficulty, season, and region. Each listing offers trail length, estimated time, difficulty, a description of the trail, and directions on how to get there. If you're a hiker, don't miss this site.

**Tucson Museum of Art.** www.tucsonarts.com
Find out about museum exhibits, programs, or the permanent collection.

# GRAND CANYON

✪ **National Park Service Site.** www.nps.gov/grca
A straightforward overview of the information visitors require: phone numbers, operating hours, transportation information, driving directions, fees, and recommended activities.

**Gateway to the Grand Canyon.** www.thegrandcanyon.com
Sponsored by the Williams–Grand Canyon Chamber of Commerce, Gateway offers nuts and bolts, including park information, attractions and tours, festivals and events, camping and lodging, and where to eat.

✪ **Grand Canyon Explorer.** www.kaibab.org
There are slicker sites on the Web, but the amount of information contained in the Grand Canyon Explorer is staggering. Dozens of articles offer news about what's going on, and links cover everything from how to get there to how the canyon got there, with maps, suggested hikes and trips, weather, and lodging. A virtual tour leads online visitors through the Canyon.

**Grand Canyon Information Site.** www.thecanyon.com
The information site of the National Park Service is just that—a place to find any and all information you need before you travel to the Canyon. Whether obtaining backcountry or river permits, looking for camping or lodging information, figuring out the logistics of your trip, or simply looking for news or a bit of history, this is a good place to start.

✪ **The American Experience: Lost in the Grand Canyon.** www.pbs.org/wgbh/pages/amex/canyon
If it's Grand Canyon history you're looking for, look no farther. This beautiful Web site accompanies PBS's documentary film about John Wesley Powell's 1869 expedition down the Colorado River into the last uncharted territory in the United States. Find your way around via timeline navigation, a People & Events section, or historical maps.

# OTHER ARIZONA PARKS & RECREATION AREAS

**Canyon Country.** www.canyon-country.com
Maps, tours, and lodging information for Lake Powell, Lake Mead, the Grand Canyon, and Monument Valley. Short articles and recommendations provide helpful information, but this site is best used for getting straight facts about Arizona's great outdoors.

**Ghost Town of the Month.** www.inficad.com/~ghosttown/ghost.html
A surprisingly deep list of the ghost towns of Arizona. Relive the wild, wild West through abandoned shacks in the middle of the desert.

**Glen Canyon.** www.nps.gov/glca/home.htm
The Glen Canyon site offers the straight facts: phone numbers, operating hours, transportation information, driving directions, fees, events, and recommended activities.

**Lake Mead National Recreation Area.** www.nps.gov/lame
Another in the National Park Service series, this site on Lake Mead offers the visitor all the essential information, including a sizable section on recommended activities.

**Monuments.** www.azuswebworks.com/az/monuments.html
Links to national monuments around the state, directing visitors to official government sites, unofficial sites put together by outdoor lovers, and quality commercial sites. If you're curious about a specific park, this is a great place to start.

**Petrified Forest National Park.** www.nps.gov/pefo
This National Park Service site provides all the basic information a visitor needs, including a list of program activities and camping facilities available in the park.

**Saguaro National Park.** www.saguaro.national-park.com
This independent site offers an array of informative links, including an activities calendar, camping, hiking and lodging guides, maps, weather forecasts, and even a chat room for nature lovers.

## GETTING AROUND

**Amtrak.** www.amtrak.com
Fares, schedules, and rail pass information for the U.S. train network (also includes some Canadian cities). Offers up-to-the-minute arrival time information for trains in progress.

**Arizona Department of Transportation Trailmaster.** www.azfms.com
All the information a traveler could need about road conditions, closures, and weather patterns. Nearly 50 freeway cameras help the prepared driver avoid congestion. You can even find parking information for locations around the state, as well as rules of the road to avoid being stopped by Arizona's finest.

**Arizona Rail Passenger Association.** www.psn.net/~azrail
This community organization promotes rail travel, featuring stories of interest on its site, as well as a deep array of information on train stations, schedules, rail maps, and background on the trains themselves.

**Phoenix Sky Harbor International Airport.** www.phxskyharbor.com
All the basics for Phoenix Sky Harbor Airport, including flight schedules and site map.

**Tucson International Airport.** www.tucsonairport.org
This site has plans to become a "time-saving tool for worldwide flight scheduling." Until this happens, however, about the only useful information you'll find here is directions to the airport.

**Sun Tran.** www.suntran.com
Tucson's public transportation system, Sun Tran, has a Web site that offers schedules, maps, and lists of services.

# Index

See also separate Accommodations and Golf Course indexes, below.
Page numbers in *italics* refer to maps.

## ACCOMMODATIONS

# FROMMER'S® COMPLETE TRAVEL GUIDES

## FROMMER'S® DOLLAR-A-DAY GUIDES

Australia from $50 a Day
California from $60 a Day
Caribbean from $70 a Day
England from $70 a Day
Europe from $60 a Day
Florida from $60 a Day

Hawaii from $70 a Day
Ireland from $50 a Day
Israel from $45 a Day
Italy from $70 a Day
London from $85 a Day
New York from $80 a Day

New Zealand from $50 a Day
Paris from $85 a Day
San Francisco from $60 a Day
Washington, D.C.,
   from $60 a Day

## FROMMER'S® PORTABLE GUIDES

Acapulco, Ixtapa &
   Zihuatanejo
Alaska Cruises & Ports of Call
Bahamas
Baja & Los Cabos
Berlin
California Wine Country
Charleston & Savannah
Chicago

Dublin
Hawaii: The Big Island
Las Vegas
London
Maine Coast
Maui
New Orleans
New York City
Paris

Puerto Vallarta, Manzanillo
   & Guadalajara
San Diego
San Francisco
Sydney
Tampa & St. Petersburg
Venice
Washington, D.C.

## FROMMER'S® NATIONAL PARK GUIDES

Family Vacations in the
   National Parks
Grand Canyon

National Parks of the
   American West
Rocky Mountain

Yellowstone & Grand Teton
Yosemite & Sequoia/
   Kings Canyon
Zion & Bryce Canyon

## FROMMER'S® GREAT OUTDOOR GUIDES

New England
Northern California

Southern California & Baja
Washington & Oregon

## FROMMER'S® MEMORABLE WALKS

Chicago
London

New York
Paris

San Francisco
Washington D.C.

## FROMMER'S® IRREVERENT GUIDES

Amsterdam
Boston
Chicago
Las Vegas

London
Los Angeles
Manhattan

New Orleans
Paris
San Francisco

Seattle & Portland
Vancouver
Walt Disney World
Washington, D.C.

## FROMMER'S® BEST-LOVED DRIVING TOURS

America
Britain
California

Florida
France
Germany

Ireland
Italy
New England

Scotland
Spain
Western Europe

## THE UNOFFICIAL GUIDES®

| | | | |
|---|---|---|---|
| Bed & Breakfast in New England | Cruises | London | Skiing in the West |
| | Disneyland | Miami & the Keys | Walt Disney World |
| Bed & Breakfast in the Northwest | Florida with Kids | Mini Las Vegas | Walt Disney World for Grown-ups |
| | The Great Smoky & Blue Ridge | Mini-Mickey | |
| Beyond Disney | | New Orleans | Walt Disney World for Kids |
| Branson, Missouri | Mountains | New York City | |
| California with Kids | Inside Disney | Paris | Washington, D.C. |
| Chicago | Las Vegas | San Francisco | |

## SPECIAL-INTEREST TITLES

Born to Shop: France
Born to Shop: Hong Kong
Born to Shop: Italy
Born to Shop: New York
Born to Shop: Paris
Frommer's Britain's Best Bike Rides
The Civil War Trust's Official Guide
   to the Civil War Discovery Trail
Frommer's Caribbean Hideaways
Frommer's Europe's Greatest Driving Tours
Frommer's Food Lover's Companion to France
Frommer's Food Lover's Companion to Italy
Frommer's Gay & Lesbian Europe
Israel Past & Present
Monks' Guide to California

Monks' Guide to New York City
The Moon
New York City with Kids
Unforgettable Weekends
Outside Magazine's Guide
   to Family Vacations
Places Rated Almanac
Retirement Places Rated
Road Atlas Britain
Road Atlas Europe
Washington, D.C., with Kids
Wonderful Weekends from Boston
Wonderful Weekends from New York City
Wonderful Weekends from San Francisco
Wonderful Weekends from Los Angeles

# WHEREVER YOU TRAVEL, *H*ELP IS NEVER FAR AWAY.

From planning your trip to providing travel assistance along the way, American Express® Travel Service Offices are always there to help you do more.

---

## *Arizona*

---

**PHOENIX**
American Express Travel Service
2508 E. Camelback Rd.
Biltmore Fashion Park
(602) 468-1199

**SCOTTSDALE**
American Express Travel Service
6900 E. Camelback Rd.
Scottsdale Fashion Sq.
(602) 949-7000

**Travel**

www.americanexpress.com/travel

American Express Travel Service Offices
are located throughout the United States.
For the office nearest you, call 1-800-AXP-3429.